C000093289

ISBN 978-0-260-70837-3
PIBN 10422736

FB &c Ltd, Dalton House, 60 Windsor Avenue, London, SW19 2RR.
Company number 08720141. Registered in England and Wales.

For support please visit www.forgottenbooks.com

THE

CENE AND APOSTLES' CREEDS.

THEIR LITERARY HISTORY;

TOGETHER WITH

AN ACCOUNT OF THE GROWTH AND RECEPTION OF THE SERMON ON THE FAITH,

COMMONLY CALLED

"THE CREED OF ST ATHANASIUS."

BY C. A. SWAINSON, D.D.

CANON OF CHICHESTER, NORRISIAN PROFESSOR OF DIVINITY AT CAMBRIDGE, AND EXAMINING CHAPLAIN TO THE BISHOP OF CHICHESTER; FORMERLY FELLOW AND TUTOR OF CHRIST'S COLLEGE, CAMBRIDGE.

London:

JOHN MURRAY, ALBEMARLE STREET.

1875

PREFACE.

THE following book originated in a proposal that was made to me some time ago by Professor Lightfoot, that I should prepare an Article on the History of the Creeds—apart from the History of Doctrine—for the *Dictionary of Christian Antiquities*, which is now being published by Mr Murray, under the Editorship of Dr W. Smith.

Upon entering on the work I was surprised to discover that the subject had hitherto attracted little attention, and that, with the exception of the books which I mention in my introductory Chapter, I could find little assistance in a collected form. The work has thus grown under my hand; whilst the attention that has been recently called to the subject of the Athanasian Creed has given additional interest to my researches. My readers have the result before them.

I have of course received great assistance from several friends. I have expressed in the body of the Book my obligations to many of them, but I would here particularly mention in addition Professor Wright, from whom I received introductions which were of the utmost value to me in journeys which I undertook to some of the Continental Libraries in 1872. Through the Dean of Westminster I obtained collations from Paris; and through the Rev. D. M. Clerk, photographs from Vienna and Milan. Mr Muller of Amsterdam was of the utmost service to me in a curious difficulty in which I found myself when I was prohibited from seeing the Utrecht Manuscript; and to him as well as to Dr Vermeulen I would here express my obligations. To Sir T. Duffus Hardy I am indebted not only for photographs of the Venice copies of the Athanasian Creed and of the two pages of the Colbertine Manuscript at Paris, but also for an introduction to Mr Rawdon Browne, who was of the utmost service to me in St Mark's Library. Of Signor Veludo's kindness I have spoken in my book.

To Professor Jones of St Beuno's College, St Asaph, the literary world is indebted for the first facsimile of the Utrecht Manuscript, a seed from which has grown the reproduction of the whole book by the autotype process. He has kindly obtained for me collations from Paris and from Rome. I am deeply indebted to Mr Bond and Mr Thompson of the British Museum, to Mr Coxe of the Bodleian, to Mr Bradshaw and Mr Bensly of the Cambridge Library. Archdeacon Groome supplied me with the interesting Volume of the early Beliefs of the German Church by Massmann, to which I have frequently referred. To these I must add Mr Lumby, Mr Skeat and Dr Bosworth, and Professors Max Müller and Westwood, to whom I feel under special obligations. The Master and Fellows of Magdalene College have allowed to me the almost uninterrupted use for some time, of Waterland's own copy of Tentzel's curious volume, and to them I must add my grateful acknowledgments. And I owe to Mr Ferrers the opportunity of examining and collating the interesting Greek translation of the Latin "Hours of the Virgin," printed in 1538 by Wechel.

CONTENTS.

CHAPTER VIII.

PAG

CHAPTER IX.

CHAPTER X.

CHAPTER XI.

LITURGICAL USE OF THE NICENE CREED.

CHAPTER XII.

THE HISTORY OF THE INTERPOLATIONS.

CHAPTER XIII.

EARLY HISTORY OF THE LATIN CREED.

CHAPTER XIV.

LATER HISTORY OF THE LATIN CREED.

PAGE

CHAPTER XV.

USE OF THE APOSTLES' CREED.

CHAPTER XVI.

THE ATHANASIAN CREED. INTRODUCTORY.

CHAPTER XVII.

INFLUENCE OF AUGUSTINE'S WRITINGS ON THE SUBJECT OF THE TRINITY.

CHAPTER XXI.

PROFESSIONS OFFERED AT CONSECRATION: AND NOTES FROM LATER SYNODS.

CHAPTER XXII.

CREEDS CONTAINED IN COLLECTIONS OF SERMONS AND BOOKS OF DEVOTION, &c.

CHAPTER XXIII.

GREEK AND LATIN PSALTERS WHICH DO NOT CONTAIN THE QUICUNQUE.

CHAPTER XXIV.

LATIN PSALTERS OF THE NINTH OR TENTH OR ELEVENTH CENTURY CONTAINING THE QUICUNQUE.

CHAPTER XXV.

CHARLEMAGNE AND PAULINUS.

CHAPTER XXVI.

WAS THE QUICUNQUE WRITTEN IN SPAIN?

CHAPTER XXVII.

WORKS OF ALCUIN.

CHAPTER XXVIII.

HINCMAR.

CHAPTER XXIX.

PAGE

THE EXPOSITION IN "JUNIUS 25."

CHAPTER XXX.

REVIEW OF EVIDENCE.

CHAPTER XXXI.

EXPOSITIONS OF THE QUICUNQUE.

CHAPTER XXXII.

GREEK VERSIONS OF THE QUICUNQUE.

CHAPTER XXXIII.

PAGE

GERMAN, FRENCH, AND ENGLISH VERSIONS.

CHAPTER XXXIV.

NOTES FROM THE YEAR 1200 TO THE REFORMATION.

CHAPTER XXXV.

ERA OF THE REFORMATION.

CHAPTER XXXVI.

RECENT NOTICES OF THE ATHANASIAN CREED.

THE CREEDS OF THE CHURCH.

INTRODUCTORY.

§ 1. Interest of the subject. § 2. Recent neglect. § 3. Obligations to Dr Heurtley. § 4. Dr Caspari and M. Nicolas.

§ 1. THERE are few subjects which deserve the careful and thoughtful consideration of the Christian student more than the origin and growth of the Creeds of the Christian Church; the history of their formation; the principles which shaped their development. These subjects are of course intimately connected with the history of those other confessions with which different parts of the Church have marked out some guiding lines for the teachers of their own communions; but (speaking generally) these latter confessions belong to recent periods of the Church's history, whilst, what we call the CREEDS OF THE CHURCH, belong to the earlier developments of the Church's teaching. Again: these Creeds of the Church may be regarded as having gained the adherence of Christians of almost all nations and all denominations —they are almost Catholic or universal in their character—whilst the other confessions to which I have referred, can be regarded only as national in their origin; indeed, in some instances, as limited in their reception. Thus the national or local Churches of England, of Scotland, and of Ireland, of Geneva and of Zurich, of the Palatinate and of Poland, of Augsburg and of Holland, have put forth at different but recent times each its Articles, its Confession, or its Catechism. So of the Church of Rome at the Council of Trent, and since; whilst no national Church has repudiated what we call the CREED OF THE APOSTLES; the NICENE or CONSTANTINOPOLITAN CREED is accepted, with two variations, over almost the whole of Christendom: and the teaching on the Trinity and the Incarnation contained and enforced in what is called the ATHANASIAN CREED is, with even less variation, maintained by the great body of Christians throughout the world.

§ 2. But the origin and growth of these documents, their relations to each other and to other formulæ,—which were originally of a similar character, but have given way to the predominating influence of these three,—have not met with the special attention of historians and students until comparatively recent times. If any one will take the trouble to look at the discourse of the learned Bishop Beveridge on the "Thirty-nine Articles of the Church of England," he will find that, although the great Bishop gives a short history of the growth of the so-called Nicene Creed, he gives no hint to his reader that the Creeds of the Apostles and of St Athanasius ever existed except in the forms which, to us, are so familiar. Dr Hey again is content with stating in regard to the Apostles' Creed that it is sometimes "called the *Roman* Creed because used in the Roman Church; yet several clauses have been added at unknown times, and by unknown persons. On these Bishop Pearson and Lord King may be consulted; and different forms may be seen in Bingham, and Usher, and Wall on Baptism." He adds that it is not credible that each Apostle contributed his clause, "seeing that the two passages 'the holy Catholic Church' and 'the Communion of Saints' were not in the Creed till some centuries after the age of the Apostles[1]." And here he leaves this subject. On the Nicene Creed he is content with repeating the usual account of its being "made" at Nicæa, whilst the latter clauses were added at Constantinople. He mentions however[2] Archbishop Usher's opinion (as he understood) "that the *whole* of our Nicene Creed was *known* at Nice in 325, although no more was *published* than what relates to *Arius*."—Coming down to later works, the Exposition of the 39 Articles by the present Bishop of Winchester (published originally about 1852) shews how little interest had been raised on the subject even at that time. Dr Harold Browne remarked that "many confessions of faith are to be found, nearly corresponding with the Creeds which we now possess, in the writings of the earliest Fathers," and referred in his notes to Wall and Bingham[3]. On a later page[4]

[1] Dr Hey, *Lectures*, Book IV. ch. viii. § 3.

[2] *Ibid.* § 5.

[3] 2nd edition, 1854, p. 212.

[4] p. 228.

the Bishop gave a translation of the Apostles' Creed in Greek, of the 15th century, as being the Creed in its "original language." Again, he thought[1] with Usher that possibly "shortly after the Council of Nice, the Nicene Fathers, or some of them, or others who had high authority, enlarged and amplified the Nicene symbol, and that this enlarged form obtained extensively in the Church"—a suggestion which, although not quite accurate (as we shall see), is well deserving of respectful consideration. Bishop Forbes, of Brechin, in his *Explanation of the Thirty-nine Articles*, published in 1867, remarks[2]: "As to the Eastern or Nicene Creed, we see how the faith against the perversions of heretics, flexibly adapting itself to meet the exigencies of the Church in maintenance of it, was expanded into that of Constantinople: the anathematisms having been dropped, and certain additions made, which by some were said to be due to St Gregory Nazianzen, by others to St Gregory of Nyssa, but which embodied in great measure expressions of ancient Creeds." On the growth of the Apostles' Creed Bishop Forbes is silent. Indeed so far as our modern theology goes, I believe that an obscure note appended to what is called the "Oxford Translation" of Tertullian furnished for many years the only results of English investigations on the subject. This note, published in 1842, was intended to shew[3] that "we know not in which form and precise words the Creed was verbally delivered by the Apostles; but the very variations, amid the general agreement, the more establish that the substance and general form and outline is Apostolic:" the writer assuming that the Apostles delivered "a large traditionary Creed which the Church had everywhere, but did not at once embody[4]:" "the Nicene Creed (he adds) itself closes with the words, 'I believe in the Holy Ghost,' not certainly as not having the other articles, but the fathers of the Nicene Council, having for their object to oppose heresy as to the Son only, stop short with the words which complete the confession of the Trinity[5]." On a later page[6] the direct assertion of St Jerome that "after the confession of the Trinity and the Unity of the Church, the whole mystery of Christian doctrine is concluded in the Resurrection of the Flesh"—an assertion which is most true of the Creed of Africa as repeatedly expounded by St Augus-

[1] p. 218.
[2] Vol. I. p. 126.
[3] Tertullian, *Oxford translation*, p. 480.
[4] *Ibid.* p. 481.
[5] *Ibid.*
[6] *Ibid.* p. 485.

tine,—and the direct statement of Ruffinus[1] that the article *He descended into hell* was "wanting in the Roman and Oriental Creeds," are supplemented by the remark that "the substance and order being, according to the statement of Ruffinus, arranged by the Apostles before their separation, the words would yet naturally be varied as they passed into different languages[2]."—This whole account is extremely unsatisfactory.

§ 3. Thus the first English divine, who of late years has grappled with the subject, is the Reverend Dr Heurtley, Margaret Professor of Divinity at Oxford and Canon of Christ Church. In the year 1858 he published, under the title of HARMONIA SYMBOLICA, a collection of the more important Creeds which have come down to us as belonging to branches of the ancient Western Church. The plan of Dr Heurtley's work was to exhibit these Creeds in chronological order, in such a manner as would shew most readily their variations from the now received form; and, simultaneously, to note the particular date at which any of the phrases, now well-known to us, appeared for the first time in any of these ancient documents. The work concluded with an historical review of the several articles of the Creed. As containing an accurate collection of evidence, such as may lead others to true conceptions of the subject, the work is of great value, and thus contrasts favourably with the obscure and elaborate attempt to defend an untenable position, which is the great characteristic of the note on Tertullian. The theory of the writer of that note was that the early or Apostolic Church received explicitly from the Apostles the full Rule of Faith as we find it current in later centuries, and that the object of the successive Councils was merely to renew and revive what was believed explicitly at the first but had from one cause or another been since overlooked: thus the writer taught that "The very silence about the Creed from which its non-existence has been inferred (Voss. *Dissert.* I. § 28), the rather proves that what did exist so early, always existed, and so

[1] *Ibid.* p. 487.

[2] Dr Pusey in the notes to his sermon preached at Oxford on Advent Sunday, 1872, stated that Eusebius suppressed for a time the word *ὁμοούσιον* from the Creed. This is a heavy charge; but, as we shall see, it is entirely without foundation. It is brought, I believe, in good faith: probably on the principle enunciated in p. 487 of this same note on Tertullian. "The doctrine, of course, was known to the Ancient Church, else it could not have been admitted at all into the Creed." But the admission is one thing: the suppression is another.

there was no occasion to notice what was known to all, as that confession, upon which themselves had been made members of Christ[1]." And this is supposed to be argument. With regard however to Dr Heurtley's work, it is satisfactory to notice that its value as furnishing authoritative documents has been recognised abroad as well as in England.

§ 4. The divine who, of late years, has paid most attention to the subject of Creeds on the Continent, is undoubtedly Dr C. P. Caspari, Professor of Theology in the University of Norway; in his "University Programmes" on the Baptismal Creed and the Rule of Faith[2], he frequently refers to the work of Dr Heurtley. M. Nicolas also, in his historical essay on the Apostles' Creed, published at Paris in 1867[3], has availed himself freely of Dr Heurtley's collections. No doubt the volume may be supplemented, ere long, by other series; for Dr Caspari has devoted many successive summers to research in the great libraries in England and throughout the Continent. In the mean time I gladly express my acknowledgments to Dr Heurtley's work, which supplied a great want and has awakened the desire for further research. It will be seen below that I have discovered a few additional memoranda on this subject. One object of the present volume is to attempt to perform for the Athanasian Creed a work similar to that which Dr Heurtley has accomplished for the Apostles' Creed. But it will be necessary for the fulfilment of my purpose to trace the history of earlier documents bearing on the subject before me; and, throughout, to give my readers the opportunity of testing any theories I may suggest, by the evidence which I shall adduce. I shall endeavour to be on my guard against representing in any degree unfairly or untruthfully the testimony which has come in my way:—attempts of this kind always recoil on the person or party that makes them:—and surely those can have learnt little from the history of the past who have not observed that "Lying even for God" meets with His strongest reprobation. The

[1] Tertullian, as above, p. 481.

[2] *Ungedruckte, unbeachtete und wenig beachtete Quellen zur Geschichte des Taufsymbols und der Glaubens-Regel*, herausgegeben und in Abhandlungen erläutert von Dr C. P. Caspari, &c., &c. Universitäts-Programm. Christiania, I. 1866, II. 1869.

[3] *Le Symbole des Apôtres, Essai historique par Michel Nicolas.* Paris, Michel Lévy, Frères, 1867. This was reviewed elaborately in the *Revue de Théologie*, Strasburg, vol. VI. June, 1868.

suppression of evidence, or still more, the falsification of evidence, on the part of upholders of any particular opinion or dogma, is one of the plainest proofs that the parties guilty of it have little faith in the truth of their opinion, little faith in the moral government of God. And such conduct always gives courage to the opposite side. I regret that I shall be compelled, in the course of this investigation, to draw attention to a few lamentable instances of such suppression and falsification in recent discussions or publications.

CHAPTER I.

DISTINCTION BETWEEN A CREED AND A RULE OF FAITH.

§ 1. Rules of Faith and Creeds. § 2. Nomenclature of Scientific Theology. § 3. Various names applied to compendia of the Faith. § 4. Distinction between a Creed and a Rule of Faith established from St Isidore.

§ 1. THE words which I quoted in my introductory chapter from the title page of Dr Caspari's "University Programmes" point to a distinction between Rules of Faith and Baptismal Creeds, which has not received among us the attention which it deserves. In the earliest study of any new Science the nomenclature is of necessity unfixed: the names employed are not at once appropriated for the purposes to which they are ultimately limited. Moreover, at early periods of investigation objects are frequently classified with an imperfect knowledge; so that further enquiry demonstrates that this suggested classification is erroneous. So has it been in the history of the Christian Church, and in the Science of Religion[1]. Words are imported into religious use without a distinct apprehension of the mode in which the use of these words ought to be limited: expressions, etymologically almost identical in meaning, are in process of time appropriated

[1] The fact that Religion is a Science is very often overlooked; and one consequence is that we hear far too frequently of the opposition between Science and Theology. But Theology is a Science: in the common consent of all intelligent believers, it has been made into one. Like Geology and Astronomy and History and Moral Philosophy (Mental Science) it has its peculiar region of facts and phenomena, its peculiar data, its own principles: but it is a serious mistake on the part of its advocates to conceive and represent that the laws which are to govern our investigations regarding it, are of a character totally different from those which govern our investigations into other sciences. It must be recognised that this is a mistake before we can hope to draw generally the intelligence of mankind or even devote ourselves in the spirit of St Paul to the study of Christianity. Of course I know that there is much of ψευδώνυμος γνῶσις in many of the so-called scientific men of the day—as there is in many of the so-called theologians: and I am not surprised that the chief attacks on the false knowledge of the one party proceed from those who pride themselves most on what is really a false knowledge in regard to the other series of subjects.

to distinct objects; and, if in future years these words and expressions are used or quoted without the history of their application being remembered, a great amount of confusion and misapprehension will be the necessary consequence.

§ 2. Instances of these alterations in the application of scientific terms will readily occur to every student. In the history of Christianity we have the well-known fact, that whereas in the New Testament the words *episcopi* and *presbyteri* are applied (the one primarily in Greek communions, the other, amongst converts from Judaism) to the second order of the Christian Ministry, before many years were over, it was found convenient to alter the usage, and appropriate the former to the members of the higher office, to those who fulfilled duties such as were assigned to Titus and Timotheus, and the latter to those over whom officers like Titus and Timotheus were directed to take charge. Thus, again, the classical word *Liturgia* was seized by the Alexandrian Jews; and, after being applied by Christian writers (as it had been in the Septuagint) to all portions of the Christian service, including herein even personal attendance on the Apostles (Philip. ii. 30), and the peculiar work of the Bishop (Eusebius, *History,* IV. 1)—its use was ultimately limited to the special service accompanying the celebration of the Eucharist. So the word *Deacons,* originally equivalent to *Servants,* became (almost like the Latin *Ministers*) appropriated to an order in the Church. And thus the various titles by which documents such as our CREEDS have been designated, have had their wider and their narrower applications; and it will be impossible to have a clear conception of the various modes in which these titles have been used, without devoting some little time to their history.

§ 3. If we look to the various names by which our Creeds have been designated[1], we shall find adduced from Greek writers the following expressions: *the rule of the old faith, the rule of the truth, the apostolic preaching, the evangelic and apostolic tradition, the faith, the holy and apostolic faith which has been delivered to us, the symbol, the instruction,* and so on. Many of these expressions occur also in their Latin equivalents. But the question occurs, Were all the documents to which the above titles were

[1] See Index to Hahn: or Mr Lumby, p. 2.

applied, of the same character? And if not, are we able to draw any distinction between these documents, so as to fix the meaning of the titles by which they were designated? Are we able to define them closer?

§ 4. On a subject of this kind, it is desirable to refer, where possible, to early sources of information, and, in the present instance, I shall appeal to a very interesting treatise written by Isidore, archbishop of Seville in the 7th century[1]. Among the genuine writings of this prelate are two books on the *Divine Offices,* which are usually printed in collections of treatises on the Liturgies; and in the 22nd and 23rd chapters of his second book we find the writer treating of the *Symbol* and of the *Rule of Faith.* On the *Symbol* Isidore gives the tradition current in his time, namely, that the Apostles, before they parted, threw together into one, each his own contribution; and this, their joint production, became in process of time a *symbolum* or watchword[2] by the use of which the faithful might be distinguished from the world at large: because this watchword was never made known in its entirety beyond the circle of the Church; "it was to be retained in the memory, and not to be committed to writing." It was short, "because the prophet had of old predicted, *a shortened word will the Lord make upon the earth.* But (St Isidore proceeds) this, after the symbol of the Apostles, is the most certain *faith,* which our teachers have handed down; that we profess that the Father and Son and Holy Spirit are of one essence... and that we hold such and such truths relating to the Incarnate Son of God, and that God is supremely and immutably good, whilst the creature is in an inferior degree and mutably good; that legitimate marriages are permissible in the Church, and baptism is not to be reiterated, and that we look to a future resurrection, and that Satan and his angels and followers shall suffer eternal condemnation, and shall not be restored (as some sacrilegiously have held) to their pristine, that is, the angelic condition. This (concludes the chapter of which I have given a very short account) is *the true entirety of the Catholic religion and faith,* of which, if one tittle is rejected, the whole belief of the faith is lost."

I shall have occasion to refer to this chapter again, but I have

[1] He died A.D. 636. [2] He recognises this meaning.

adduced it now to shew that early in the seventh century, a distinction was made between the *Symbol* and *a Rule of Faith.* If this distinction had been observed by the author of the note on Tertullian to which I have referred above, it would perhaps have helped him to attain clearer views of the Creeds of the early Church. With the assistance of the light which it pours forth, I will now pass on to the consideration of my subject.

CHAPTER II.

EARLIEST CREEDS.

§ 1. Difference between a Creed of the Church and a Baptismal Profession. § 2. The teaching of the Church essentially dogmatic. (Leibnitz.) § 3. The Faith once delivered to the Saints. § 4. Need of brief summaries: some of the earliest of such summaries. § 5. The sufficiency of Scripture.

§ 1. If I may make a further appeal to the customs of the Church of the West in the seventh and eighth centuries, I must add to the remarks of my previous chapter that these customs lead us to draw a further distinction between the faith as delivered to the candidate for baptism, *i.e.* the Creed of the Church, and the profession of faith made by the candidate before he was baptized. We have, at all events in Germany and France, during the earlier years of Charlemagne, distinct intimations that the candidate, in reply to the enquiry of the minister, did not recite the whole Creed, nor answer, as we do now in England, to a question comprehending the Creed in its entirety. Bearing this in mind, we may enter on the subject of Baptismal Confessions.

§ 2. Leibnitz, in the preface to his *Essais de Théodicée*, remarks with truth, that the nations which filled the earth before the establishment of Christianity had ceremonies of devotion, sacrifices, libations, and priesthood, but they had no articles of faith, no dogmatic theology. They were never taught whether the objects of their adoration were true personal beings, or merely personifications of the wondrous powers of nature: even their mysteries consisted only in the performance of certain rites and practices, and were not accompanied by the delivery and acceptance of any dogma. With the people of Israel it was different. They had a distinct creed, the fundamental articles of which were these: that JEHOVAH their GOD is one JEHOVAH;

that He it is who made heaven and earth and all things therein contained; that the laws which governed their nation came from Him; that He would protect the nation if it obeyed these laws, and would punish it if it neglected them. "From this clear and definite teaching as to the Being and Nature of God, the duty of serving Him and Him only with all their heart and mind, and in the way which He appointed, necessarily followed." "Christianity has inherited this peculiarity of the Jewish nation." It has a clear and definite teaching. More clearly than any of the Jewish Rabbis had done, more clearly than even Moses or David or any of the prophets, did Jesus our Saviour and our Teacher hold up to His followers our Father in heaven as our Example, our Guide and our Strength. In truth it may be said that He revealed God as our Father, so little had this truth been appreciated before. In addition to this fundamental doctrine, Jesus declared that He had Himself come down from heaven to fulfil His Father's will, to give His soul a ransom for many: and to those who believed on Him He repeatedly gave the promise that He would raise them up on the last day. He promised moreover that after He had left them He would send them another Comforter who should abide with them for ever; and, after He had gone, we read that this Comforter came, and that under His guidance and by His strength, the early disciples journeyed here and there, teaching men to turn from the vanities which they worshipped to serve the Living and True God: they spoke not only of the duties of temperance and righteousness and love to others and restraint of self, but they spoke also of a coming judgment: they insisted on the necessity of repentance towards God, and of faith towards our Lord Jesus Christ: they proclaimed that, in some mysterious way, Christ Jesus our Lord had died for our sins according to the Scriptures of old: they insisted in teaching that He had been raised again from the dead: they said that men must believe this and must confess it, if they would be saved, "for with the heart men believe unto righteousness, and with the tongue they confess unto salvation:" and what the Apostles taught they charged their followers to commit to faithful men, that they might be able to teach others also.

§ 3. Thus, undoubtedly, there was A FAITH ONCE DELIVERED TO THE SAINTS: and the substance of this faith, either as delivered *to* him or as passed on *by* him, St Paul calls a *deposit*[1], a "thing committed to him." Thus again he regarded his office as a *Stewardship*, describing himself as "a steward of God's mysteries[2]." So St Peter described the essence of his teaching as "the truth, the present truth," partly, no doubt, in contrast with the "cunningly devised myths[3]," by which it was surrounded. It is needless to accumulate passages wherein similar intimations are conveyed to us.

§ 4. But the teaching of the Apostles was so extensive and covered so large a space, containing not only what they themselves called "milk for the newly born babes in Christ," but also "meat" for those who had taken advantage of their early privileges and had grown on towards the Christian manhood, that at a very early period it was found necessary to collect together statements regarding some of the chief facts which were either revealed or substantiated by Christ, and to represent them as essential parts of the teaching of the Church, the fundamental doctrines of Christianity, "the things which are most surely believed among us." In our Saviour's life-time the Confession of Nathanael, "Thou art the Son of God, thou art the King of Israel," had drawn forth a commendation of his belief. When the Apostle Peter avowed, "Thou art the Christ, the Son of the living God," he was told that this inference, which he had drawn from all he had seen and heard, was in the highest degree a revelation, a drawing away of the veil, by the Father in heaven. A similar expression of belief was drawn out at another time, "Lord, to whom shall we go? Thou hast words of eternal life: and we have believed and known that Thou art the Holy One of God[4]." After the ascension, the chief doctrine taught to the Jews was, that "Jesus is the Christ:" and, although the account in Acts viii. 37, that the eunuch of Candace expressed, in answer to Philip's question, his belief that "Jesus Christ is the Son of God," is now considered to be an interpolation—though an interpolation of a very early date—there is nothing improbable in the conception that some such confession was made. When the gaoler

[1] παραθήκη or παρακαταθήκη. The MSS. vary. 1 Tim. vi. 20; 2 Tim. i. 12, 14.

[2] 1 Cor. ix. 17; Eph. iii. 2; 1 Cor. iv. 1; Titus i. 7.

[3] 2 Pet. i. 12.

[4] Such seems to be the true reading in John vi. 69.

at Philippi rushed in to St Paul with the cry, "What must I do that I may be saved?" the Apostle, carrying the man's desire for temporal safety upward into another and different sphere of life, replied, "Believe on the Lord Jesus, and thou shalt be saved, thou and thy house." These instances furnish short baptismal Creeds—for doubtless the belief was expressed before the baptism was administered.—I would refer again to Rom. x. 9: "If thou confess with thy mouth that Jesus is Lord, and believe in thine heart that God raised Him from the dead, thou shalt be saved."—And other summaries of Apostolic teaching have been observed elsewhere. Let us look to 1 Cor. xv., "I delivered unto you among the first things, that Christ died for our sins," &c.; to 1 Tim. iii. 16, "Great is the mystery of religion: who was manifested in the flesh," &c.; to 1 John iv. 2, "Every spirit that confesseth that Jesus has come in the flesh is of God." Whilst the distinction between the elements of Christian faith and the fulness of Christian knowledge is the foundation of the remark of the writer to the Hebrews, vi. 2[1]. Indeed it has been suggested with great probability[2] that the true meaning of the direction of St Paul to Timothy (2nd Ep. i. 13), is this, "Have a sketch or outline of the healing words which thou hast heard from me, in faith and love in Christ Jesus." Nor should we pass over, without a thought, the words addressed to the angel of the Church of Pergamos (Rev. ii. 13), "Thou didst not deny my faith;" words which clearly intimate that there was a Faith which might have been orally denied, to the dishonour of the Saviour and to the peril of men's souls.

§ 5. I shall not attempt to collect at present any of the contents of these more general teachings or outlines, as they are gradually disclosed to us in the remains of early Church writers. But I will anticipate what I may have to say hereafter by transferring bodily to my pages some important words uttered by one who, of all our English divines of the last half century, combined perhaps in the highest degree a knowledge of the past with a thoughtfulness for the present. In the first of his invaluable sermons on the "Temptation of Christ our Lord in the Wilderness," preached before the University of Cambridge in Lent 1844, the late

[1] "Leaving the word of the beginning of Christ let us pass on," &c.

[2] See Mr Wratislaw's valuable dissertation. Bell and Daldy, 1863.

Dr Mill declared as the result of his own convictions "that while it is certainly true that it was not by Scripture that these Christian truths"—relating to the mystery of the Incarnation, and the Holy Trinity—"were delivered to the Churches by the Apostles; nor are they ordinarily thus learnt, in the first instance, by any; yet in that sole inspired record, of which the Church was the early recipient and constant guardian, it is her belief and affirmation that the whole body of life-giving doctrines is essentially contained; that the Spirit of God has provided that no saving truth should be there wanting. And, however some important accessory facts may have been left to be proved altogether from minor ecclesiastical sources (such as the determination of the Canon of Scripture itself, the Apostolic observance of Sunday as the Lord's day, that of the Christian Pasch and Pentecost, &c.), yet with matters of doctrine properly so-called, this has never been the case: whatever, claiming to be such, an integral part of the faith once delivered to the saints, cannot be proved by sure warranty of the Christian Scriptures, is by that circumstance alone convicted of novelty and error[1]." We shall have the means of testing this dictum of Dr Mill's with reference to the contents of early rules of faith, as we proceed.

At present our concern is with the earliest forms of the baptismal confession, by which it will be seen that I mean distinctly *the confession made by the candidate before his baptism.*

[1] Page 17 of the edition of 1844: p. 16 of the recent reprint.

CHAPTER III.

BAPTISMAL PROFESSIONS.

§ 1. St Cyril of Jerusalem on the Creed of the Church and the Teaching of the Church. The latter resembles our Thirty-nine Articles. § 2. The Personal Profession much shorter than either. § 3. Thus there were three forms embodying the Faith. § 4. Other short personal Professions. § 5. The Baptismal Professions of Irenæus, Tertullian, Cyprian, Ambrose, &c. § 6. Old German Professions. § 7. That of the Gelasian Sacramentary. § 8. Before the Reformation the Apostles' Creed not used at full length at Baptism. § 9. Peculiar German usage of questions regarding the Trinity.

§ 1. THE fullest account which we have of the preparations made for Baptism in any Church during the first four centuries, is to be found in the Catechetical Lectures[1] of St Cyril of Jerusalem. These lectures are believed to have been delivered before Cyril was Bishop, and are assigned to the year 347 or 348. The Lectures, VI. to XVIII., contain an Exposition of the Faith, addressed to those who hoped to be baptized on the ensuing Easter Eve, the Faith thus expounded and explained having been recited in the course of Lecture V., with a strict injunction, however, that no one was to write it on paper; all ought to have it engraved by memory upon their hearts. Thus the Creed of the Church of Jerusalem is not given at length in the manuscripts, and it is only by a careful collection of the passages explained that we are able to put it together. The result will be found below. Of this faith the very phrases were to be learnt by heart—it was to be to the Christian layman an *ἐφόδιον*, a viaticum to accompany him on his journey through life; it was to serve him as a mean to test the teaching even of Cyril himself in future times, or of any other bishop that might follow

[1] A critical edition of these Lectures has been published at Munich. The first volume appeared in 1848 edited by Dr William Charles Reischl: the second in 1870 edited by Joseph Rupp. A translation from an older edition was made for the Oxford Library of the Fathers by Mr Church, the present Dean of St Paul's, and published in 1839 with a characteristic preface from the pen of Mr Newman.

him; for (as Cyril taught) it "enfolded in its bosom, in few words, all the knowledge of religion which was contained in the Old and New Testament:"—"the most seasonable things being collected together out of every Scripture complete in one the teaching of the Faith[1]." But over and above this Faith or Creed, Cyril gave his hearers in another and far more expanded form, a summary of necessary dogmas: delivering, under sixteen heads, first, truths relating to God, and Christ, and the Holy Spirit, the Soul and the Body of Man; and then, adding instruction as to chastity and marriage, as to meats and apparel, as to the Holy Laver and the Divine Scriptures, as to sorcery and Judaism. These instructions however were not to be committed to memory; but of course they who had heard them before, would be benefitted by hearing them again[2].

§ 2. But when we come to the profession of his own personal faith which was made at Jerusalem by the candidate for Baptism,

[1] I pick out these phrases from Lecture v. § xii.: it is not necessary to fill up the outline. *πίστιν δὲ ἐν μαθήσει καὶ ἀπαγγελίᾳ κτῆσαι καὶ τήρησον μόνην, τὴν ὑπὸ τῆς ἐκκλησίας νυνί σοι παραδιδομένην, τὴν ἐκ πάσης γραφῆς ὠχυρωμένην. ἐπειδὴ γὰρ οὐ πάντες δύνανται τὰς γραφὰς ἀναγινώσκειν......ὑπὲρ τοῦ μὴ τὴν ψυχὴν ἐξ ἀμαθίας ἀπολέσθαι, ἐν ὀλίγοις τοῖς στίχοις τὸ πᾶν δόγμα τῆς πίστεως περιλαμβάνομεν. ὅπερ καὶ ἐπ' αὐτῆς τῆς λέξεως μνημονεῦσαι ὑμᾶς βούλομαι......ἔχειν δὲ ταύτην ἐφόδιον ἐν παντὶ τῷ χρόνῳ τῆς ζωῆς καὶ παρὰ ταύτην ἄλλην μηκέτι δέξασθαι......καὶ τέως μὲν ἐπ' αὐτῆς τῆς λέξεως ἀκούων μνημόνευσον τῆς πίστεως, ἐκδέχου δὲ κατὰ τὸν δέοντα καιρὸν τὴν ἀπὸ τῶν θείων γραφῶν περὶ ἑκάστου τῶν ἐγκειμένων σύστασιν. Οὐ γὰρ ὡς ἔδοξεν ἀνθρώποις συνετέθη τὰ τῆς πίστεως· ἀλλ' ἐκ πάσης γραφῆς τὰ καιριώτατα συλλεχθέντα, μίαν ἀναπληροῖ τὴν τῆς πίστεως διδασκαλίαν. καὶ ὅνπερ τρόπον ὁ τοῦ σινάπεως σπόρος......οὕτω καὶ ἡ πίστις αὕτη ἐν ὀλίγοις ῥήμασι, πᾶσαν τὴν ἐν τῇ παλαιᾷ καὶ καινῇ τῆς εὐσεβείας γνῶσιν ἐγκεκόλπισται.*

In several clauses of this passage, I think I can trace marks of objections to the Faith as recently promulgated by the Council of Nicæa. Thus Cyril claims for the Faith which he delivers the characteristic of antiquity: it, at all events, was not put together according to the fancies of men, but "every word could be upheld by Scripture;" "his people were not to permit a phrase to be altered." Any one familiar with the Athanasian anxieties will notice allusions—they may be slight, they may be "innocent allusions"—to those anxieties. We may also remark that Cyril claims that every thing in the "Faith" was drawn from Scripture.

[2] Lecture iv. § iii. *πρὸ δὲ τῆς εἰς τὴν πίστιν παραδόσεως* (not, as the "Oxford translation," *Before making this tradition of the Faith:* for the words illustrate very beautifully Rom. vi. 17, *ὑπηκούσατε δὲ ἐκ καρδίας εἰς ὃν παρεδόθητε τύπον διδαχῆς*. The thought is that "they were delivered over *to* the Faith" rather than that "the Faith was delivered over to them." However before *this was done*) *καλῶς ἔχειν μοι δοκεῖ νῦν ἀνακεφαλαιώσει συντόμῳ χρήσασθαι τῶν ἀναγκαίων δογμάτων.. ...ἵνα νῦν κεφαλαιωδῶς ὑποσπείραντες μὴ ἐπιλαθώμεθα τῶν αὐτῶν πλατυτέρως γεωργουμένων ὕστερον.* And let those (he proceeds) who have their senses exercised to the discernment of good and evil bear with this: in order that they who are in want of instruction may receive benefit, and they who have the knowledge already may have their memory quickened as to that which they have known before. (This lecture is published in Dr Heurtley's little volume "*de fide et symbolo*.")

we find that this was far briefer not only than the collection of necessary things, but also than the Creed of the Church of Jerusalem. "After thou didst renounce Satan, thou wast with symbolic meaning turned from facing the West to the East—from the region of darkness to the countries of the light. Then it was commanded thee to say: I BELIEVE IN THE FATHER AND IN THE SON AND IN THE HOLY SPIRIT AND IN ONE BAPTISM OF REPENTANCE." The words are clear and definite[1]. In these words each answered the question of which we read elsewhere, "Did he believe in the name of the Father and the Son and the Holy Spirit?" In this his reply the candidate "confessed" what Cyril called "the saving confession[2]."

§ 3. We find therefore, in these lectures of St Cyril, three forms of Faith: *One*, a collection of necessary doctrines delivered in no fixed or unchangeable frame-work of words, covering ground far more extensive than any of our modern creeds, resembling in fact a series of articles as to the Church's teaching on many subjects. We find *another*, a precise and defined expression of belief, "We believe in one God the Father Almighty, Maker of heaven and earth, and of all things visible and invisible: and in one Lord Jesus Christ, the only begotten Son of God, who was begotten of the Father before all the worlds, very God, by whom all things were made: who coming in the flesh and made man[3], was crucified and was buried, who rose again on the third day, and ascended into the heavens, and sat on the right hand of the Father, and is coming in glory to judge quick and dead, of whose kingdom there shall be no end: and in one Holy Spirit, the Comforter, who spake in the prophets; [and in one baptism of repentance for the remission of sins] and in one holy Catholic Church, and in the resurrection of the flesh, and in life eternal." Of this all the phrases were fixed (although to us there is a little uncertainty in determining them): they were not to be made known even to the Catechumens until they were enlisted among the *φωτιζόμενοι*, the class who were "being illuminated." The *third* was the brief form in which the candidate for baptism was called upon to ex-

[1] Lect. XIX. (Mystic. I.) § 9, *τότε ἐλέγετο εἰπεῖν· πιστεύω εἰς τὸν πατέρα καὶ εἰς τὸν υἱὸν καὶ εἰς τὸ ἅγιον πνεῦμα καὶ εἰς ἓν βάπτισμα μετάνοιας.*

[2] Lect. XX. (Mystic. II.) § 4.

[3] *ἐν σαρκὶ παραγενόμενον καὶ ἐνανθρωπήσαντα.*

press his own personal belief: it was a still shorter, still more compact summary of the Faith: it was told thee to say, "I believe in the Father and in the Son, and in the Holy Spirit, and in one baptism of repentance:" the candidate was not required to assert with his own mouth that he believed all that was contained within the creed of the Church[1].

§ 4. I shall now exhibit a few additional instances of very short baptismal creeds, or brief personal confessions.

§ 5. That CREEDS as such—summaries which commence with the all-important words, *I believe*—took their origin in the administration of baptism, is a proposition which can scarcely be questioned. The words in which the holy Sacrament was administered were enjoined by our Lord Himself: "Go ye and make all the nations into disciples, baptizing them into the name of the Father and of the Son and of the Holy Ghost, teaching them to keep all things that I enjoined you." These solemn words of Baptism, we may well suppose, soon drew out from the new disciples corresponding expressions of their belief. I have not as yet referred to the words of St Paul to Timothy (1 Tim. vi. 12), "Fight the noble fight of the Faith; lay hold upon that eternal life to which thou wast called, and didst confess the good confession before many witnesses." This connecting of Timothy's *confession* with his *call* to life, has led many to think that it was at his baptism that the confession was made. At all events, the well-known passage in Justin Martyr's *Apology* shews, that in his day "they who were persuaded and believed that the things were

[1] See Hahn's *Bibliothek.* p. 51. The Oxford translation (p. xlvii.) after "who came in the flesh and was made man" inserts "of the Virgin Mary and the Holy Ghost." The editors must have read with Touttée ἐν σαρκὶ παραγενόμενον καὶ ἐνανθρωπήσαντα [ἐκ παρθένου καὶ πνεύματος ἁγίου] but they did not mention that Touttée was himself doubtful as to the words within the brackets. They added without any authority the *name* of Mary the Virgin. Dr Hahn (from whom I take the remark of Touttée) considered that the additional words represent fairly enough the belief of Cyril as opposed to the views of the Ebionites on the Incarnation, but that they did not form part of the Jerusalem Creed. They are not mentioned in the introductory title to chapter IV. nor in § 13 which professes to contain the words there to be explained. I have followed Abp. Usher (*de Symbolis*, p. 11). I find that Bishop Bull (*Judicium*, Oxford edition, Vol. VI. p. 134) inserts the words. (Dr Hahn here makes a slight mistake.) These two great divines of our Church considered that the Creed of the Church began with πιστεύω, I BELIEVE, but Hahn in support of πιστεύομεν refers to VII. § 3 &c., X. § 4, XI. §§ 1, 14. There is one other difference of importance: Bishop Bull reads καὶ εἰς τὸ ἅγιον πνεῦμα, but the title to Catechesis XVI. has ἓν ἅγ. πν., a reading which is supported by XVI. §§ 3 and 12, and XVII. § 3.

true which were taught by Christians, were led to some place where there was water, and were then passed through the laver in the name of the Father and Lord of all, and of our Saviour Jesus Christ, and of the Holy Spirit,"—words which imply that the persons mentioned must have given some expression, some outward assurance of their belief. I pass over as besides our present purpose, the passages where Irenæus writes of the "Canon of the truth" which every one received at his baptism: in these passages he says, "the Church believes" this and that; it is of the teaching of the Church that he is speaking: to it we must refer below. So of most of the passages quoted from Tertullian: but, in his treatise against Praxeas, we find a short description of the members of Christ's Body, which is immediately to our purpose: "the Holy Ghost (he says) is the Sanctifier of the faith of those who believe in the Father and the Son and the Holy Ghost," as if this were the accepted definition of the faithful Christians. In some parts of the Church the echo of such short baptismal confessions survived for many years. I may refer directly to a passage in the treatise *de Corona Militis*, § 3, where Tertullian says, that "in Baptism we were thrice immersed, answering something more than the Lord commanded in the Gospel." In the opinion of Bishop Bull[1] this answer contained mention of repentance and of remission of sins and of the Church (the reasons for this opinion I will give hereafter). The writings of St Cyprian distinctly tell us, that in his day the form of interrogation at baptism was fixed and definite. He speaks of the "usitata et legitima verba interrogationis"—and we know as distinctly that the interrogation included the words "Dost thou believe in God the Father, in [His] Son Christ, in the Holy Spirit? Dost thou

[1] See too Bull's *Judicium Eccl. Cath.* (Vol. VI. p. 139), on the passage in the Treatise *de Baptismo*, § 11. "Some would depreciate baptism, says Tertullian, because our Lord did not baptize. But His disciples baptized at His command. And whereunto should He have baptized? to Repentance? to what purpose His forerunner? To Remission of sins? He gave it by a word. Into Himself? He was concealing Himself in His humility. Into the Holy Ghost? He had not yet descended from the Father. Into the Church? which the Apostles had not founded!" Bishop Bull infers from this that mention was made of Repentance, of Remission of sins, and of the Church at the time of Baptism: but if so, they must have been spoken of by the Minister, not by the Catechumen, and therefore this Creed should fall under a later chapter. In § 6 of the same treatise Tertullian gives the reason why the Church is mentioned, "Where the Three are, the Father, the Son, the Holy Spirit, there is the Church, the Body of the Three." Under the Three are pledged the *testatio fidei et sponsio salutis*.

believe in remission of sins and eternal life through the Church?" The confession required may have also included the belief that God is the Creator, and possibly some mention of the Birth, Death, and Resurrection of the Saviour. Light upon it is undoubtedly cast by the Æthiopic version of the *Apostolic Constitutions*, as published by Archdeacon Tattam[1]: in this the candidate for baptism is represented as confessing "I believe in the only true God, the Father Almighty, and in His only begotten Son Jesus Christ our Lord and Saviour, and in the Holy Spirit the Giver of life." The next phrase as we there have it is, however, undoubtedly posterior to the Nicene Council: but of the remainder, some clauses may belong to the more ancient confessions: "one kingdom, one faith, one baptism in the Catholic Apostolic Church, and the life everlasting[2]." The echo, as it seems to me, is heard in the book *de Sacramentis*, falsely ascribed to St Ambrose: "Thou wast asked, Dost thou believe in God the Father Almighty? Thou didst answer, I believe; and thou wast baptized, *i.e.* thou wast buried. Again thou wast asked, Dost thou believe also in our Lord Jesus Christ and in His cross? Thou saidst, I believe; and thou wast baptized, *i.e.* together with Christ thou wast buried. Again thou wast asked, Dost thou believe also in the Holy Ghost? Thou saidst, I believe; and a third time thou wast immersed, that the triple confession should remove the

[1] *Constitutiones Copticæ*, ed. H. Tattam, 1848, § 46. The latter clauses "[I believe] the consubstantial Trinity, one Lordship, one kingdom, one faith, one Baptism, in the Catholic Apostolic Church, and in life everlasting" (as Dr Tattam reads them), must of course, if taken as a whole, date from a time when the word ὁμοούσιος was required as a test of orthodoxy: *i.e.* they must be later than the council of Nicæa. Bunsen however (*Analecta Ante-Nicæna*, Vol. III. p. 91) suggests that the latter words, "one Lordship, one kingdom, one faith, one baptism in the Catholic Apostolic Church (as he translates it), and in life everlasting," are of earlier date than the clause regarding the consubstantial Trinity.

Two short baptismal creeds are given in the notes to Daniel's *Codex Liturgicus*, IV. p. 497.

i. *The Copts and Æthiopians.* "Then shall the Deacon turn the Catechumen to the East ....and suggest to him the Faith in this manner, 'I believe in one God, the Father Almighty, and in His only begotten Son, Jesus Christ our Lord, and in the Holy Spirit, the Giver of Life, the Resurrection of the Flesh, and in one only Catholic Apostolic Holy Church which is His.'"

ii. *The Armenians.* The Catechumen says "I believe in the most Holy Trinity, in the Father, in the Son, and in the most Holy Spirit," and then they [all?] recite the Nicene Creed.

[2] A ray of light is thrown on this by the council of Carthage, A.D. 348 (Harduin, I. 685 c). The question was put, "ought a person—who, on his descent into the water, had been questioned in regard to the Trinity after the faith of the Gospels and the teaching of the Apostles, and had confessed a good confession towards God on the resurrection of Jesus Christ—again to be questioned in the same faith and be again baptized?" The answer was "absit, absit."

multiplied lapse of thy earlier life." We meet with it again in a passage to be found in the writings of Facundus of Hermiane (for which I am indebted to Dr Heurtley's work, page 53), in which, after speaking of the Creed at length, the writer refers to the profession made at baptism as a profession that "they believe in God the Father Almighty, and in Jesus Christ His Son, and in the Holy Spirit."

§ 6. This shortest of Creeds survived to the time of Charlemagne. The *Codex Palatinus* 577 of the Vatican Library, of the ninth and tenth centuries, contains a form of a renuntiation of the devil and a profession of belief, which have, ever since their discovery at the end of the seventeenth century, secured the attention of German philological and liturgical scholars: they are assigned in the manuscript to a council held at Liftenas or Listenas (supposed to be either Louvain or Lessines), in the year 743, under Boniface, the apostle of the Germans. The renuntiation is interesting. The faith professed must find a place in my text. The manuscript reads as follows:

gelobistu in got al^{a}mehtigan fadaer
    ec gelobo in got al^{a}mehtigan fadaer
gelobistu in crist godes suno
    ec gelobo in crist gotes suno·
gelobistu in halogan gast
    ec gelobo in halogan gasto·

Massmann considers this as a specimen of old Low German[1].

[1] A similar form but of an old High German character was copied from a MS., once in the Cathedral at Spire, apparently by one Jacob Camp, about the year 1607, into a book printed at Frankfort in 1606: (a facsimile of the writing is given by Professor Massmann in the work from which I have extracted the above: see p. 68 and the facsimile at the end). It runs thus: "Galaubistu heiligan geist. ih. g. Galaubistu heinan gott almachtigon in Thrinissi in din einnissi, ih. g. Galaubistu heiliga godes chirichon ih. g. Galaubistu thuruch taufȣnga suntheno farlaznissi. ih. g."

This form is clearly defective at the commencement: the questions as to the belief of the candidate in the Father, and in the Son, which invariably precede the expression of belief in the Holy Spirit, having disappeared from the manuscript when it was copied.

[I extract these and some other interesting passages from a work entitled "Die deutschen Abschwörungs-, Glaubens-, Beicht- und Betformeln vom achten bis zum Zwölften Jahrhundert. Nebst Anhängen und Schriftnachbildungen. Herausgegeben von H. F. Massmann. Quedlinburg und Leipzig, 1839." The form ordered by the council of Leftinas is well known; it is published by Migne, Vol. LXXXIX. p. 810, by Daniel, *Codex Liturgicus*, Vol. I. p. 186. I have seen a facsimile in Pertz, *Monumenta Ger.* Vol. III. pp. 18, 19. It is given in Mansi, XII. 369, and with the form of renunciation by Mr Lumby, p. 18.]

§ 7. Beyond the influence of the great Charles no profession appears to have been required regarding the Holy Trinity. The *Gelasian Sacramentary* describes the delivery of the Eastern Creed to the *competentes*, in terms which will soon engage our attention: but even in it the belief proclaimed at the time of

We have other similar short baptismal professions in the work from which I have extracted the above. I do not pretend to give them in exact chronological order, or to have discovered the exact periods during which they were respectively in use. My point is to exhibit the fact that some of these shortest of creeds have continually existed from the time of Tertullian until now[1]. The first is taken from a Manuscript at Vienna (122), and begins as follows: "I believe in one God the Father Almighty, the Creator of heaven and earth and of all created things. I believe in His only begotten Son our Lord Christ: and I believe in the Holy Ghost, and I believe that these Three named are one true Godhead." It then proceeds at great length. The second, from the library at St Gall, is shorter: the third is also from St Gall: the fourth from a MS. at Munich: they all contain a distinct expression of belief in the Unity in Trinity: a fifth of much greater length, given from a manuscript at Strasburg (now I fear destroyed), commences in similar fashion (p. 37): a sixth, entitled in the Manuscript *Fides Catholica* (p. 81), runs somewhat differently. After the renunciation it proceeds: "I believe in one God, the Father Almighty, who is the Creator of heaven and earth and all created things: I believe in His only begotten Son, our Lord Jesus Christ, born and murdered: I believe in the Holy Ghost. I believe that the three Names, the Father, the Son, and the Holy Ghost, are one true God, who ever was, and ever is, and ever shall be without end. I believe that the same Son of God was announced by the holy angel Saint Gabriel to our Lady Saint Mary, &c." Another (p. 82) is to a similar effect, though inasmuch as this and the next (p. 83) cannot be distinctly proved to be baptismal professions, I ought not without hesitation to quote them here. They may have been formed for the instruction of adults. But I may without blame refer to a series of questions, which I copied from a Manuscript at Vienna numbered 701, addressed to a *penitent* on Easter Eve, before his readmission to the Communion on the following day. "When all these things have been enquired into and the penitent is strengthened, let the priest ask him thus: Dost thou believe in God the Father, the Son and the Holy Spirit? Let the penitent answer, I believe." Then—the Manuscript proceeds—but on an erasure, signifying clearly that this is a later addition—"Dost thou believe that these three Persons, Father, Son and Holy Spirit, are one God?"

[The MS. is said to be of the twelfth century. The passage which I have paraphrased is this: [Post] "ista omnia scrutata et penitentem corroboratum, interroget eum sacerdos dicens: Credis in Deum Patrem et Filium et Spiritum Sanctum? Respondeat pœnitens Credo. *Item Credis quia istæ tres personæ Pater et Filius et Spiritus Sanctus unus Deus sit?*" The words in italics are on the erasure. Portions of a catechism from this manuscript I hope to give on a later page.]

Other short creeds at confession may be seen in Martene, Liber I. cap. VI. art. vii. ordo III. IV. VI. X.

The only baptismal profession of an analogous kind, which is given in the collection of Dr Heurtley, is extracted from the Gallican Missal published by Thomasius, *Codices Sacramentorum*, p. 475[2]. It runs as follows: "Dost thou believe that the Father, Son, and Holy Spirit are of one virtue? I believe. Dost thou believe that the Father, Son, and Holy Spirit are of the same power? I believe. Dost thou believe that the Father, Son, and Holy Spirit, of a triune unity, are perfect God, the substance remaining one? I believe." This creed given by Dr Heurtley, p. 111, is said by him on p. 69 to be "altogether *sui generis*" and is assigned to the eighth century. It has however an interesting resemblance to these German forms, although it is much shorter than most of them.

[1] The originals of these are in old German.
[2] This may be seen in Martene, Book I. Art. xviii. Ord. II.

baptism was short and resembled not the Nicene but our Apostles' Creed. The copy of this Sacramentary used by Thomasius was written apparently in the eighth century: it ran here as follows: "Dost thou believe in God the Father Almighty? I believe. Dost thou believe also in Jesus Christ, His only Son our Lord, born and suffered? I believe. And dost thou believe in the Holy Ghost, the Holy Church, Remission of Sins, the Resurrection of the Flesh? I believe[1]." Thus the words "Creator of heaven and earth," "conceived by the Holy Ghost, of the Virgin Mary," "under Pontius Pilate," and so to the end of the part relating to our Lord, were omitted, and so were the clauses or words "Catholic" "the Communion of Saints," "Life everlasting." Later baptismal creeds contain some of these words, but I believe none, before the Reformation, contains them all[2].

§ 8. Thus it would appear that, before the Reformation, the Apostles' Creed, as we have it now, was never used at baptism, either as a declaratory, or as an interrogatory creed. The clauses omitted were fewer at one time, more numerous at another: but I suppose that we may consider that the essential parts of the baptismal confession were deemed to be contained in that portion which is still retained in the service books of the Church of Rome.

§ 9. And another subject seems to be deserving of renewed attention: the introduction of questions relating to the Trinity was confined to a very small portion of the Christian Church and apparently the Creed so formed was used only during a limited period. We have noted it in the short creed in the Coptic manuscript of the *Apostolic Constitutions*, and in the German confessions

[1] Dr Heurtley notes that in three copies printed by Martene from MSS. written about 800 the clause "Life everlasting" is found; and that in a copy of the Gregorian Sacramentary, of the middle of the ninth century, the words "Creator of heaven and earth:" and "Catholic" are found.

[2] In the order as restored by Cardinal Casertanus (Daniel, I. p. 173), the catechumen is asked "Dost thou believe in God the Father Almighty, Maker of heaven and earth? I believe. Dost thou also believe in Jesus Christ His only Son? I believe. Dost thou also believe in the Holy Ghost, the Holy Catholic Church, the remission of sins, the resurrection of the flesh, and life everlasting? I believe." To this, the mediæval English service, as given by Mr Maskell, added the words "our Lord, born and suffered," as well as "the communion of saints" and the words "after death" to the clause "everlasting life." The modern Roman Ritual agrees with this older English use, except that the words "after death" are not inserted.

of the times of Charlemagne and his immediate successors. This fact may throw a little light on the vexed question of the history of the first formation of the so-called Athanasian Creed. Mr Massmann gives, p. 84, from another MS. at St Gall, an Anglo-Saxon Creed[1]. This follows the line of the Apostles' Creed, and so far strengthens me in my opinion that the effects of the Great Charles's action to which I have referred did not extend to England. "The Catholic Faith of the Holy Trinity" ordered at the Synod of Frankfort, and "the faith of the Holy Trinity, and Incarnation" enjoined at Aix, were probably substantially contained in one or other of these German documents which we have been now considering.

[1] In connection with this branch of my subject, viz. the short professions of belief which were used at baptism, I may add the following notices. The synodical letter given by Theodoret (*History*, v. 9) as addressed by "the bishops assembled at Constantinople [in 382] to the other holy bishops assembled at the great city of Rome" defends the adhesion of the writers to the Creed of Nicæa "in support of which they had suffered." They say this evangelical faith ought to please "you and us and all who do not pervert the word of the true faith, it is most ancient and *conformable to baptism* (ἀκόλουθον τῷ βαπτίσματι) *and teaches us to believe in the Name of the Father and of the Son and of the Holy Ghost*, that is to say, the deity and the power and the essence of the Father, of the Son and of the Holy Ghost being believed to be one in three perfect Hypostases or in three perfect Persons, &c." Thus apparently they viewed the Nicene Creed as an expansion of the baptismal profession. At a much later date we find from the Gallican missal (from which our form in note p. 23 is taken), that after the profession of belief "in the Father, the Son, and the Holy Spirit, as of one virtue, the same power, of triune unity" the priest used the words "I baptize thee believing in the name of the Father, and of the Son, and of the Holy Spirit, that thou mayest have eternal life for ever and ever." Baptizo te credentem in nomen Patris et Filii et Spiritus Sancti ut habeas vitam æternam in sæcula sæculorum. (Bishop Bull, Vol. VI. pp. 84, 86, and Episcopius agree that the first baptismal Creed was something like this. "I believe in God the Father, the Son and the Holy Spirit:" the latter regarding it as the germ of the larger creed: the former viewing it as an abbreviation of it.)

At the Laodicene council which was held sometime between 341 and 381, a code of canons was formed: No. 7 is to the effect that converted heretics were to learn the symbols of the faith and renounce their heresies: No. 46 was that the φωτιζόμενοι they who are in process of receiving light should learn the faith and repeat it to the Bishop or elders on the fifth day of "the week," *i.e.* on holy Thursday: No. 47 that they who receive τὸ φώτισμα in sickness must learn the creed after they recover.

CHAPTER IV.

RULES OF FAITH OF THE FIRST TWO AND A-HALF CENTURIES.

§ 1. Bingham's mistake. § 2. The original *doctrina tradita*. § 3. The letters to the Trallians and Smyrnæans. § 4. Irenæus, passages quoted. § 5. Inferences from these. § 6. Letter to Florinus. § 7. Hippolytus. § 8. Tertullian (difference between fixity of the faith and growth of ritual). § 9. Deductions from the above. § 10. Origen. § 11. Thoughts suggested. § 12. Cyprian. § 13. Council of Carthage. § 14. Novatian. § 15. Summary of the contents of all these Rules of Faith. § 16. Thoughts on the above. § 17. An anonymous writer against Artemon. § 18. Indications of an approaching change.

§ 1. THAT there was a marked distinction drawn in the time of St Isidore between the Rule of Faith and the Symbolum proper (*i. e.* between the teaching conveyed to the candidate for baptism and the formula recited or assented to by him at his baptism) has been exhibited on an earlier page. Our English divines, however, have generally followed the leading of Bingham (*Antiquities of the Christian Church*, Book x. ch. iii. § 2), and spoken of the terms "Rule of Faith" and "Creed" as being equivalent titles for the same thing; they have thus stated that "The Rule of Faith" is the common appellation for the "Creed" in Irenæus, Tertullian, Novatian, and Jerome. Whether they are herein correct, we may now proceed to examine.

§ 2. That there was a *doctrina tradita*, a traditionary teaching of the Church, delivered in the first instance *viva voce* and independently of the writings of the Apostles, no one can question. The Epistles of St Paul were clearly supplementary to his oral teaching. A careful student of his and the other Apostles' letters will notice that the chief facts of the Gospel narratives are assumed in these letters, as already known by those to whom they are addressed. The Epistles themselves are occupied in drawing out their theological import, or their practical application. Even in the Gospels themselves there are indications that they were written for persons who had had some prior though perhaps indefinite and inaccurate knowledge of details of our Lord's life and teaching.—If we would learn the contents of these traditional Expositions of the Faith, we must of course resort to the writings of the early Church; and we are referred by historians who have studied the subject, to those letters to the Trallians and to the Smyrnæans, which, although not accepted as the genuine writings of the great Bishop, whose name they bear, are yet believed, by our most careful critics, to have been composed or interpolated in the latter half of the second century. Thus they hold a place amongst the most important of early Christian documents.

§ 3. In the letter to the Trallians § 9, we find the writer urging his readers

"To stop their ears, if any would talk to them without reference to Jesus Christ, who was of the family of Mary, who was truly born, did eat and drink, was truly persecuted under Pontius Pilate, was truly crucified and died, whilst things in heaven, and things on earth, and things under the earth looked on; who also was truly raised from the dead, His Father raising Him, as after the same likeness His Father will raise up in Christ Jesus all of us who believe in Him—apart from Whom we have not that which is truly life[1]."

A passage of greater length may be seen in the commencement of the letter to the Christians at Smyrna, which I will also quote in full: I take it also from the shorter Greek recension, but this, as is known, cannot be identified as a genuine work of the Martyr:

"I glorify Jesus Christ the GOD who has thus far instructed you: for I understand that you are perfectly united in faith unmoved, as though you were nailed to the cross of the Lord Jesus Christ, both in flesh and spirit, and firmly established in love in the blood of Christ; fully believing in our Lord, as being truly of the family of David according to the flesh, Son of God according to the will and power of God, born truly of a virgin, baptized by John, in order that all righteousness should be fulfilled by Him, truly nailed [to the cross] for our sakes in the flesh under Pontius Pilate and Herod the tetrarch. From which fruit[2] are we from His most blessed suffering, in order that He might raise for ever through His resurrection a common standard for His holy

[1] *οὗ χῶρις τὸ ἀληθινὸν ζῆν οὐκ ἔχομεν.*
[2] Hanging upon the cross (?)

and faithful ones, whether among the Jews or Gentiles, in the one body of His Church. For He suffered all these things on our account, that we might be saved. And He truly suffered, as also He truly raised Himself; not, as some unbelievers say, that He suffered in appearance only,—they existing in appearance only, and, as they think, so shall it happen to them, seeing that they are bodiless and like demons. For *I* know (ἐγὼ οἶδα) that after His resurrection He was in the Flesh, and I believe that He still is. And when he came to Peter and his friends, He said, *Take, handle me, and see that I am not a bodiless demon.* And straightway they touched Him, and believed, being overcome by His Flesh and Spirit; and so they despised death, and were found superior to death. And after His resurrection He ate with them, and drank with them, as being Himself endued with flesh, although spiritually united (ἡνωμένος) with the Father."

I quote these passages at length, because, although they are not described as either Rules of Faith or Creeds, they are put forth as summaries of Christian teaching, and as containing in themselves an antidote to the poisonous heresies to which the readers of the letters were exposed. It must be noted in passing that they contain no statement regarding our Lord which is not plainly taught in Scripture.

§ 4. Our next authority shall be one who introduces the title *Canon of the Truth.* To the *Canon of the Truth* the sainted Irenæus appeals as being sufficient to cause the rejection of the more numerous heresies of his day. The passages are so well known, that it may seem at first sight superfluous in me to quote them: but still I shall adduce them all, in order that my readers may more easily compare together the various notices of the "canon" which Irenæus gives.

There are five passages at least in which the Bishop of Lyons may be said to quote or refer to the "Faith of the Church."

i. In the early portion of Book I. (iii. 6), he speaks of those who pervert the meaning and corrupt the exegesis of the evangelic and apostolic teaching: and thus by the cleverness of their inventions and the craftiness of their adaptations "lead away captive from the truth those who do not guard firmly the faith in one God the Father Almighty, and in one Lord Jesus Christ the Son of God." But it is a subsequent passage in the same book (I. x. 1) that contains the summary which is almost invariably quoted in this connection.

ii. Having shewn with a certain amount of humour the

absurdities of those heretics who heap together a number of names and phrases out of every book of Scripture, and then fancy that on a foundation such as this they may erect a superstructure of Christian teaching, Irenæus states that "any one who holds without wavering the CANON OF THE TRUTH which he received at his baptism," will know at once how these names and phrases are brought together, and will reject the teaching built upon them; and, accordingly, he takes the opportunity to exhibit this truth as it is proclaimed by the Church.

"For the Church (he proceeds), although now scattered over the face of the whole world, yet guards the faith which it received from the Apostles and their immediate disciples: the faith in one God the Father Almighty, who made the heaven and the earth and the sea and all things in them: and in one Jesus Christ, the Son of God, who was incarnate for our salvation: and in the Holy Spirit, who by the prophets had proclaimed the dispensations, and the advents, and the birth from the Virgin, and the suffering, and the resurrection from the dead, and the bodily assumption into the heavens of the beloved Christ Jesus our Lord, and His coming from the heavens in the glory of the Father, to gather again together all things, and to raise up all flesh of all humanity, in order that to Christ Jesus our Lord and God and Saviour and King, by the good pleasure of the Father invisible, every knee should bow, of things in heaven and on earth and under the earth, and every tongue confess to Him, and [He] do right judgment in all things: that He should send the spiritual powers of darkness and the angels who transgressed and remained in disobedience, and the impious of men, and the unjust and the lawless and blasphemers to the eternal fire; and to the just and holy, who keep His commandments and abide in His love, whether from the first or after repentance, should give life and then incorruptibility and eternal glory. This teaching and this faith the Church having so received, although now dispersed over the whole world, carefully guards, as if it still occupied one house: and in equal measure it believes these tenets, as having one soul and the same heart, and with one harmonious voice it proclaims and teaches, and hands them down as if it had one mouth. The dialects throughout the world may be dissimilar, but the force of the tradition is one and the same: and neither do the Churches settled in the Germanies believe differently or teach differently, nor in the Iberias, nor among the Celts, nor in the parts of the East, nor in Egypt, nor in Libya, nor those settled in the central parts of the inhabited world; but as the sun, the creation of God, is in the whole world one and the same, so too the preaching of the truth (τὸ κήρυγμα τῆς ἀληθείας) shines everywhere and enlightens all men who are willing to come to the knowledge of the truth; and neither will the most powerful of those who preside in the churches teach things alien from these (for no one is above his Master); nor will the weak in word diminish [shorten] the tradition. For, since there is one and the same faith, neither has he who has the power of saying much extended it; nor has he who can say only little diminished it."

So much for the first part of his work.

iii. The third book contains more that bears upon our subject. The bishop[1] speaks of the duty and privilege of contending for the truth: and he instructs his readers that if they will attend to him, they will be able with confidence and determination to resist these heretics in defence of the true and life-giving faith which the Church has received from the Apostles and distributed to her children.

"For (he says) it is only through those by whom the gospel has come to us that we have learnt the economy of our salvation—which gospel they preached, and which they through God's will delivered to us in the Scriptures; which gospel was to be the foundation and column of our faith."

iv. In another well-known passage[2] he speaks of the four Evangelists by name, and describes the qualifications each had for undertaking the work with which we connect his name.

"They all delivered to us the one God, Maker of heaven and earth, announced by the law and the prophets; and one Christ the Son of God; and if any one does not assent to this, he despises in fact the companions of the Lord; he despises Christ Himself the Lord, and he despises the Father also; and he becomes self-condemned, inasmuch as he resists and struggles against his own salvation—a thing which all heretics do. For (Irenæus proceeds) when they are convicted out of the Scriptures, they turn round to accuse the Scriptures themselves, as being incorrect, as having no authority, because, forsooth, they were uttered in divers ways, and because truth could not be learnt from them by those who know not tradition. For they say that what they teach was delivered them not by Scriptures, but by the living voice; for which cause Paul also said, *We speak wisdom among them that are perfect, but not a wisdom of this world:* and this wisdom every one claims as his own, as he may discover it out of himself—an utter fiction—so that, according to them, the truth is worthily to be found at one time in Valentinus, at another in Marcion, at another in Cerinthus, at a later date in Basilides, or else in some one who takes a part opposed to him; for each one of them, being thoroughly perverted, is not ashamed to deprave the rule of truth, and to preach himself. When we challenge them to refer to that tradition which is from the Apostles, and is guarded in the churches by the successions of presbyters, then they resist tradition, asserting that they, being wiser not only than all the presbyters, but also than the Apostles themselves, have discovered the pure and genuine truth: for

[1] III. Introduction and i. 1. [2] III. i. 1.

they say that the Apostles mixed up with the Saviour's words things which are merely legal; and not only the Apostles, but the Saviour Himself framed His discourses at one time from the Demiurge, at another time from the Intermediate[1], at another from the Height. But they say *they* know the hidden mystery without doubt and without contamination—an assertion which amounts indeed to a most shameless blasphemy of their Creator. Thus it comes to pass that they give their assent neither to Scripture, nor yet to tradition. You cannot argue with them: they struggle only to escape—slipping away like eels[2]."

And then Irenæus once more addresses himself to describe the true nature of apostolic tradition.

"In every Church, any one who wishes to know what is true, has it in his power to see the tradition of the Apostles as manifested in all the world. We have it in our power to count up those who were appointed by the Apostles to be Bishops in the Churches and their successors even to our own days—men who neither taught nor knew any such thing as is now dreamed by these people. For, if the Apostles had known these recondite mysteries which (it is said) they taught to the *perfect* privately and apart from others, they surely would have entrusted them to the men to whom they committed the Churches themselves. For these assuredly they must have wished to be *perfect* and unblameable in all things, seeing that they left them as their successors, devolving upon them their own place as masters: men from whom, if they did well, the utmost benefit would come upon the world: if they fell away, the utmost calamity."

Irenæus then enters on the question of the succession of bishops in the Churches, beginning from the Church of Rome, founded by the most glorious Apostles Peter and Paul, to which Church, "because of its more powerful lead[3]," it is necessary that every Church should recur[4], that is, the faithful from every quarter; "in which for those who come from every quarter the tradition which is from the Apostles is preserved," and he speaks of Linus and Anacletus and Clemens,

"Who himself saw the Apostles and held conference with them, keeping the preaching[5] of the Apostles ringing in his ears and their traditions before his eyes: and thus this Clemens in a most powerful letter to the Christians at Corinth, calling them together to peace and renewing the faith which he had received from the Apostles, announced to them One God Almighty, Maker of heaven and earth, former of man, who had brought in the deluge, and had called Abraham, and had led out the people from the land of Egypt, and had dispensed the law and

[1] "A medietate." The μεσότης of I. vi. 4 and vii. 1.

[2] III. ii.

[3] Propter potentiorem principalitatem.

[4] Convenire.

[5] τὸ κήρυγμα.

had sent prophets, and had prepared fire for the devil and his angels. And that He was declared by the Churches to be the Father of our Lord Jesus Christ, any who choose may learn from Scripture itself, and (so) understand the apostolic tradition of the Church; inasmuch as the letter from Clemens is of more ancient date than are the men who now teach falsely and pretend that there is another God besides the Demiurge, the Creator and Maker of all things."

Irenæus passes on to his contemporary Eleutherius[1], and says that through these twelve successors to the episcopate—by the same order and the same teaching—the tradition from the Apostles in the Church, and the preaching of the truth, have found their way to us.

And this lesson, which he had enforced by the history of the Church of Rome, he confirms, (why did it need confirmation?), by the instruction handed down in the Churches of Smyrna and Ephesus, of Asia and Philippi. St John himself, who lived to the time of Trajan, was a witness to the apostolic tradition. "Surely (he says, III. iv. 1)

"If there were any dispute on the most minute of questions we should have recourse to the most ancient Churches; churches in which Apostles lived—and we should learn from them the certainties about the points at issue. Supposing (even for an instant) that the Apostles had not delivered to us the Scriptures, should we not follow the order of the tradition which they delivered to those to whom they entrusted the Churches themselves?

"And to this many nations of barbarians assent, who believe in Christ, and have salvation written on their hearts by the Holy Spirit without paper or ink, and keep the old tradition; believing in one God the Maker of heaven and earth, and of all things in them by Jesus Christ: who because of His excellent love towards the creature underwent that birth which was by the Virgin, uniting by Himself man to God: who suffered under Pontius Pilate, and, rising again from the dead and received up into glory, will come again in glory as Saviour of those who are saved, and Judge of those who are judged; and sending to eternal fire those who corrupt the truth and despise the Father, and think little of His own future coming. They who believe the faith without letters are indeed barbarians so far as concerns their power of discourse with us: but so far as their opinions and their habits and their lives are concerned, they are, because of their faith, most wise, and they please God, living in all righteousness and chastity and wisdom. If any of these heretics were to come to them, and address them in their own tongue, they would instantly stop their ears and flee away, not enduring to hear such blaspheming talk. Thus by reason of that old tradition of the apostles, they do not even admit into their minds what are to them

[1] III. iii. 3.

mere prodigies of language: for with them there never was such a congregation formed, never such a doctrine taught...Since[1] the tradition which is from the Apostles is this and it remains with us, let us turn back to the Scriptural proofs coming from those Apostles who wrote the gospels, of whom some uttered this sentiment regarding God, that our Lord Jesus Christ is truth, and that there is no lie in Him."

And he traces this tradition to its origin.

v. In III. xii. 5, after quoting part of the account of the healing of the impotent man in Acts iv., Irenæus exclaims:

"These are the voices of that Church from which every Church has had its commencement: these are the voices of the metropolis of the citizens of the new covenant: these are the voices of the Apostles; these the voices of the disciples of the Lord, the truly *perfect*, perfected through the Spirit after the Ascension of our Lord, and invoking God as Him who had made heaven and earth and sea: as Him who had been announced of old by the prophets."

vi. Once more, in III. xvi. 6, he seems to teach us that the confession of belief in the one Christ Jesus was frequently *heard;* "the heretical (he says) hold themselves up to ridicule, believing one thing, saying another:" they believe that Christ is two, they say He is one:

"They believe that there is one Christ passible, another invisible and incomprehensible and impassible: not knowing that the Word, the only begotten of God, who always is present with the human race, being united and made one with His own creation, according to the pleasure of the Father, and made flesh, is Himself the Jesus Christ our Lord who suffered for us, and rose for us, and is coming again in the glory of the Father to raise all flesh, and to shew salvation and the rule of just judgment to all who have subjected themselves to Him. There is then one God the Father as we have shewn; and one Christ Jesus our Lord who came uniting together all things in Himself."

vii. In III. xxiv. 1, Irenæus appeals from the wicked opinions of the heretics

"Regarding our Maker and Creator, to the preaching of the Church, which is constant everywhere and equally persistent, receiving testimony from Apostles and Prophets and all the disciples; which, being received from the Church, we guard; and which, by the Spirit of God, as it were an ever juvenescent deposit in a precious vessel, makes that vessel juvenescent in which it is."

viii. In IV. xxxiii. 7, he writes that:

"The spiritual man will hereafter judge those who make schisms, men void of the love of God, looking out for their own advantage and

[1] III. v. 1.

not for the uniting[1] of the Church: who for the sake of trifling and incidental[2] reasons rend and divide the great and glorious Body of Christ—talking of peace and making war. He will judge too those who are outside the truth, that is, outside the Church, whilst he himself is judged of no man. For to his mind all things are consistent. He has a complete faith in one God Almighty, from whom are all things, and in the Son of God, Jesus Christ our Lord, by whom are all things, and in His dispensations by which the Son of God became a man[3]: and in the Spirit of God who reveals the dispensations of the Father and the Son to each generation of men, as the Father wills it."

ix. And lastly, in IV. xviii. 5, Irenæus seems to intimate that at the time of the offering in the Eucharistic service, mention was made of the Resurrection of the flesh and spirit[4].

§ 5. I have adduced these passages at length in order that my readers may have materials from which to form their judgment, (i.) whether the CANON OF THE TRUTH, of which Irenæus wrote, was as yet embodied in a fixed form, A CREED as we understand the word, and (ii.) whether this CANON contained any articles over and above what may be proved from Scripture. That Irenæus was ignorant of any hidden traditions, any *Disciplina Arcani,* is clear from a passage in III. xvii. 1:

"The Apostles at all events neither knew nor enunciated anything of the kind before us: for if they had known it, at all events they would have enunciated it."

§ 6. And to this, in conclusion, I will add a few lines from the fragment of a letter of this same great bishop to Florinus—preserved in Book V. ch. 20 of the *History of Eusebius.*

"These doctrines, Florinus, to speak even gently, contain no healthy sentiment. These doctrines are discordant with the Church. These doctrines not even the heretics who are without the Church ever ventured to disclose. These doctrines the presbyters who were before us, who companied even with the Apostles, did not deliver to thee...As to the miracles of our Lord and His teaching, as Polycarp received them from the eyewitnesses of the Word of Life, so he delivered them to us,—all things concordant with the Scriptures. These things I heard—committing them to writing not on paper but on my heart."

§ 7. And so Hippolytus (about 220), in that work against Noetus,—which was published by Fabricius and may be seen in

[1] τὴν ἕνωσιν.

[2] τυχούσας apparently.

[3] ἄνθρωπος ἐγένετο.

[4] This may have been in one of the prayers. See the Liturgies.

Dr Routh's collection[1]—after his reference to the writings of the New Testament, appeals to his readers thus:

"Let us believe, blessed brethren, in accordance with the tradition of the Apostles, that God the Word came down from heaven into the Holy Virgin Mary, in order that being of her incarnate and receiving too the human soul—I mean a reasonable soul—and becoming in all things as a man, sin only excepted, He might save him that had fallen, and give incorruptibility to those who believe on His name[2]."

A short account of his faith approaching to what we call a Creed, may be seen on an earlier page[3].

"We know one God truly: we know Christ: we know that the Son suffered as He suffered, died as He died, and rose again the third day, and is on the right hand of the Father, and is coming to judge quick and dead. And these things which we have learned we say[4]."

§ 8. And so we may pass from the Church at Lyons, and the Church at the Portus Romanus, to the Church of Carthage: from Irenæus and Hippolytus to the great Tertullian: and we find him too even with greater anxiety and greater vehemence appealing to THE RULE OF THE FAITH. And first as to its existence and character. For ordinary persons, he intimates, this should be sufficient. i. The Scriptures (he says, in his work on *Prescription*,) had been perverted; some heretics had mutilated them: to the ordinary mind, therefore, the appeal to Scripture might be dangerous in its consequences; but all are capable of understanding the appeal to the teaching of the Church: all could apply this test—

"From whom, and by whom (a quo et per quos), and when, and to whom was delivered the disciplina by which men are made Christians? For wheresoever it is clear that the truth of the Christian disciplina and the faith are, there will be also the truth both of the Scripture and of the explanations of Scripture, and all Christian tradition[5]."

[1] *Scriptorum Ecclesiasticorum Opuscula præcipua*, Vol. I. pp. 42, &c.

[2] § XVII. p. 75.

[3] § I. p. 50.

[4] This had reference to the appeal of Noetus to the Church belief in one God. "Why, what evil have I done? One God I glorify, one God I know (ἐπίσταμαι) and none other but Him, begotten, suffered, died." To this the fathers who met at Smyrna replied in language somewhat similar to that of Hippolytus: "We too glorify one God, but we know how to glorify Him rightly: and one Christ we have, but, as we know, one Christ the Son of God, suffered as He suffered, died as He died, rose again, ascended into heaven, is on the right hand of the Father, is coming to judge the quick and the dead. These things we say having learned them *from the divine Scriptures*." This is given by Epiphanius *Hær.* § 57 Migne (Greek) XLI. p. 995, or Dr Hahn's *Bibliothek*, p. 44.

[5] *De Præscriptionibus*, cap. 19. The so-called Oxford translation rendered by the same English word *Rule*, both *disciplina*, and *præscriptio*, and *regula*.

In chap. 26 of the book we find Tertullian repeating the statement of Irenæus, that the Apostles could not have had two sets of doctrines, one for their friends, another for the Church at large.

"It is not to be believed that they taught amongst their intimate acquaintance things which would superinduce another rule of faith, different from and contrary to that which they published universally (Catholice) to the world, so that they spoke of one God to the Church, another in the house; pointed to one substance of Christ openly, another secretly; preached one hope of the resurrection to all, another hope to the few."

So in § 32, he challenges the heretics to compare their doctrine with the doctrine of the Apostles. But perhaps the most interesting point for us to notice is that the Church of Africa is adduced amongst others as holding § 36—

"One God, the Creator of the universe, and Christ Jesus, Son of God the Creator, born of the Virgin Mary, and the resurrection of the flesh. She combines the law and the prophets with the evangelic and apostolic literature. Hence she drinks in the faith; she seals with water; she clothes with the Holy Spirit; she feeds with Eucharist; she exhorts to Martyrdom. Opposed to this teaching (institutio) she receives no one."

And once more in § 44 Tertullian introduces our Lord as saying ironically

"Once had I committed the Gospel and the teaching of the same rule to my Apostles; but, as you did not believe it, I thought it better to change it here and there. I had promised a resurrection even of the flesh, but I reconsidered it in fear that I should be unable to fulfil my promise. I had shewn that I was born of a Virgin, but, afterwards, that seemed too humiliating for me. I had called Him Father, who makes the sun and the rain, but another Father has adopted me and that is better. I had forbidden you to lend an ear to heretics, but I was wrong[1]."

ii. But we can find, from Tertullian's writings, other information as to the Rule of Faith. His treatise, "on the veiling of the Virgins," was written after he became a Montanist; but it is singularly interesting as exhibiting the growth of the ritual of the

[1] After referring to the dispute between Peter and Paul at Antioch, he says "utique conversationis fuit vitium, non prædicationis. Non enim ex hoc alius Deus quam Creator: alius Christus quam ex Maria: alia spes quam resurrectio adnuntiabatur." § 23.

Of the Valentinians and others "si alium Deum prædicant, quomodo ejus Dei rebus et literis et nominibus utuntur adversus quem prædicant? si ejusdem, quomodo aliter? Probent se novos apostolos esse: dicant Christum iterum descendisse, iterum ipsum docuisse, iterum crucifixum, iterum resuscitatum." § 30.

Of the Church of Rome "Unum Deum novit creatorem universitatis et Christum Jesum ex virgine Maria filium Dei creatoris et carnis resurrectionem." § 36.

third century, and the reasons urged by the promoters of that growth. Old customs were deemed insufficient: new customs were being enforced by arguments drawn from Scripture; when these failed, from nature; when these again failed, "Disciplina" furnished the argument. The law of Faith was constant; but the details of discipline and life admitted "a novelty of improvement, the grace of God working and advancing things even to the end." Of course this is not the time to examine whether in these latter words Tertullian lays down the principle of the Church, or merely the sentiment of the Montanist body which he had joined: perhaps we should not be far wrong if we regarded his eagerness to require all the unmarried women to be enveloped in the veil from the time they ceased to be children—because "truth required it irrespective of præscription, of authority, or of the custom of other countries"—to be an outcome of the spirit which dictated other novelties. That much that he enjoined on others, much that he illustrated by his own example, consisted of novelties, his very eagerness to enforce them shews; but he is perhaps, on this very account, the more trustworthy guide as to that which the Church's "Rule" contained.

"Customs (he says) grow out of ignorance or simplicity, and are then strengthened by repetition, and at last they are defended against the truth. But our Lord gave to Himself the Name not of Custom, but of Truth (Joh. xiv. 6). Let them look to it to whom a thing is new which to itself is old. Heresies are refuted not by (the test of) novelty, but by (that of) truth. But still the rule of the faith is absolutely one, alone immovable and unchangeable; the rule, that is, of believing in one God Almighty, Maker of the world, and in His Son Jesus Christ, born of the Virgin Mary, crucified under Pontius Pilate, on the third day raised from the dead, received in the heavens, who sitteth now at the right hand of the Father, will come to judge the quick and the dead[1]."

[1] *De virginibus velandis*, c. 1. The Latin may be also seen in Dr Hahn, p. 68, Dr Heurtley, p. 16. The passage is immediately followed by the sentence I have translated above: "Hac lege fidei manente, cætera jam disciplinæ et conversationis admittunt novitatem correctionis, operante scilicet et proficiente usque in finem gratia Dei." This was translated by E. B. P. in the Preface to the Oxford translation of Tertullian: "This law of faith remaining, all other matters of faith and conversation admit of the novelty of *correction*, the grace of God namely working and advancing even unto the end." That is, Dr Pusey here translated *disciplina* by the word *faith*. I have had frequent occasion to warn my readers against the inaccuracy of these Oxford Translations. They never can be depended upon. And yet how many of our clergy have been taught to trust them? Is there no one who has been emboldened by reading these words of Dr Pusey's to conceive that he has Tertullian's authority for the belief that the Church may alter and correct the early Faith of the Church "with the novelty of correction," trusting to God's grace "to operate and forward its work"?

iii. Tertullian's work against Praxeas was also written after he became a Montanist; but so far as concerns our enquiry, this, his error, does not diminish the value of his testimony. For Praxeas maintained the unity of God; and on the doctrine of the unity he framed his heresy. He said that the Father Himself descended into the Virgin, was born of her, and suffered; in short, that the Father was Jesus Christ. He therefore, of necessity though implicitly, denied the truthfulness of the gospel account of the Temptation. Praxeas was personally obnoxious to Tertullian, for he it was who roused the Bishop of Rome against the Montanists: "he drove away prophecy and brought in heresy: he put to flight the Paraclete, and crucified the Father." Thus (says Tertullian, c. 2):

"The Father being born after time began, and the Father having suffered, God Himself, the Lord Almighty, is preached to us as Jesus Christ. But we at all times—and more especially now that we are more instructed through the Paraclete who leads into all truth—believe indeed that there is only one God; but, under this dispensation, which we call the economy, we believe that of this one God there is a Son too, His Word, who proceedeth from Him, through whom all things are made, and without whom nothing is made: that He it was who was sent by the Father into the Virgin, and was born of her, Man and God, Son of Man and Son of God, and named Jesus Christ: that He it was who suffered, died, and was buried, according to the Scriptures, and was raised by the Father, and taken up into heaven, and sitteth at the right hand of the Father, and is coming to judge the quick and the dead: who, according to His promise, sent from the Father the Holy Spirit the Paraclete, the Sanctifier of the faith of those who believe in the Father and Son and Holy Spirit. And the truth that this rule has come down from the beginning of the Gospel, before even the earlier heretics existed (and of course before yesterday's Praxeas), is proved both by the lateness of all the heretics, and by the newness of this Praxeas." And he proceeds to argue on the opinion of his opponent, "as if there were no other way of holding the oneness of God, except by maintaining the identity of Father, Son, and Holy Spirit; as if all were not so One (unus), as all coming from One, by unity of substance; and still the sacrament of the economy is preserved which disposes the Unity into a Trinity, arranging the Three, Father and Son and Holy Spirit; but Three not in status but in degree; not in substance but in form; not in power but in appearance; yet of one substance and one status and one power, because God is One, from whom those degrees and forms and appearances are numbered in the one Name of Father and Son and Holy Spirit."

The position taken by Tertullian was really this: "the rule of faith is unalterable: the rule of discipline is capable of amendment;"—the very position which the Church of England occupies.

Discussions upon this fill up the treatise against Praxeas; but as our interest is rather with the Rule of Faith, I will collect only a few passages wherein it is appealed to. So we have c. 9: "Remember that this is the Rule professed by me, by which I hold that the Father and Son and Spirit are not separate from each other. I say that the Father is one, the Son another, the Spirit another," but distinction does not imply separation nor division. Tertullian appeals to Scripture for his proofs: he insists that there is no polytheism enjoined there:

"We who by the grace of God look into the times and causes of Scripture, disciples of the Paraclete, not of men, lay down that there are Two, the Father and the Son; yea, Three, with the Holy Spirit, according to the ratio of the economy, but never out of our mouths do we utter the words two Gods and two Lords" (ch. 13).

Further on we meet with the definition that "the Father is invisible, the Son rendered visible"—a conception that found its way into the Creed of the Church of Aquileia. In chapter 29 there are some indications that all agreed in *saying* that Christ was crucified: in ch. 30 an appeal is made to the "Christianum sacramentum" as contrasted with the "Judaic faith."

iv. From these Montanistic, but most deeply interesting writings, we may recur once more to the orthodox treatise on "Præscription." In chap. 13 we have a tolerably full account of "the Rule," to which, in the body of the book, Tertullian again and again refers. The woman who lost the piece of silver sought for it in her own house:

"Let us then seek in our own and from our own people and concerning our own, for that which—without damage to the rule of faith—may possibly come into question.

"But the rule of faith—that I may now put forth that which I am defending,—is that by which it is believed that there is one God, and none besides, the Creator of the world, who produced all things out of nothing, through His Word sent forth (emitted) first of all: that that Word, named His Son, was in the name of God, variously seen by Patriarchs, always heard in Prophets, afterwards sent down from the Spirit of God the Father and with power into the Virgin Mary, was made flesh in her womb, and was born of her, and appeared as Jesus Christ (egisse Jesum Christum); then preached a new law and a new promise of the kingdom of heaven, wrought miracles, was fixed to the cross, rose again the third day, was caught up to heaven, sitteth at the right hand of the Father, sent in His place the power of the Holy Spirit to move believers, will come again with majesty to receive the saints into the reward of the eternal life and the heavenly promises, and to condemn the impious to perpetual fire; the resurrection of each party having taken place with the restoration of the flesh. This rule (he proceeds) taught, as it will be proved, by Christ, has no questions stirred regarding it amongst us, save those which heresies introduce and which make heretics. Provided that this form remains in its order, you may seek and handle as much as you please, and apply the whole lust of curiosity, if there is anything [else] which seems to you to hang in doubt, or be shadowed in obscurity."

§ 9. I think few of my readers can hesitate to acknowledge that the variety of language with which Irenæus and Tertullian describe THE RULE OF FAITH and THE CANON OF THE TRUTH is such as to remove all doubt upon the question whether there was, in the time of either of them, a fixed and determined form of words which embraced the various subjects that they both have mentioned, a form (say) which was submitted to or uttered by the Candidate for Holy Baptism. If by a CREED we are to understand a series of Credenda, then, undoubtedly, the CREEDS of these two great writers, or rather of the Churches of Lyons and Africa at the time when they lived, were as extensive as were these Rules of Faith. But if we may limit (as I shall propose to do) the use of the word CREED to the form of words in which any Church or Council embodied its Faith, and which was used as a manifesto of that Faith,—either at baptism or elsewhere,—then, I say, we must maintain that the Creeds of Justin Martyr, Tertullian, and the rest were exceedingly limited, whilst the RULES OF FAITH, which guided the clergy and laity, were very extensive. In fact, if we refer to the fragment of the letter of Polycrates, Bishop of Ephesus, to Victor, Bishop of Rome, written towards the end of the second century, we find that the writer declared that he followed the CANON OF THE FAITH in keeping Easter on the fourteenth day of the month[1]. "The Canon of the Faith" in this case included a point of ceremonial.

§ 10. This result of our investigation receives additional support from the introduction to Origen's Work, *De Principiis*[2]. Of this introduction only a few words are preserved in Greek; for the rest we must trust to the translation of Ruffinus, who at all events

[1] The passage is preserved by Eusebius, *H. E.* v. 24, and may be seen in Routh, *Relliquiæ Sacræ*, Vol. II. p. 15.

[2] This introduction may be seen in Mr Harvey's *Ecclesiæ Anglicanæ Vindex Catholicus*, Vol. I. p. 526. The book is considered to have been written between 212 and 215.

is not likely to have seriously altered here the language of the great Alexandrian. Origen then drew marked lines in regard to the subjects which were settled "by the ecclesiastical preaching," which had been handed down by continuous succession from the Apostles and remained in the Churches until the present time: for that alone should be deemed to be the truth which differed in nothing from the ecclesiastical and apostolical tradition.

"For the Holy Apostles in preaching the Faith of Christ delivered openly to all whatever they deemed to be necessary even for those who seemed to be somewhat slow in searching out the divine science; whilst they left the reasons of things to be inquired into by those who might receive the excelling graces of the Spirit, and might have especially the gift of language, of wisdom, and of knowledge by the Spirit Himself; in the one case making statements regarding things that *they are:* leaving to others, the more studious of their posterity and the lovers of wisdom, to examine *how they are*, and *whence they are*[1]."

Amongst those things which were openly handed down by the apostolic preaching, Origen mentions[2]

"The creation of all things by the one God, and that this God in the last days had (as He had promised by His prophets) sent our Lord Jesus Christ to call first Israel, and then, after the unbelief of His people Israel, the Gentiles. This God is the God of the Apostles, the God both of the Old and New Testaments. Jesus Christ Himself, who came, was born of the Father before all creatures. He who had ministered to the Father in the creation of all things, had in the last days, emptying Himself, become Man Incarnate, even whilst He was God. He assumed a body like our body, except that it was born of a Virgin and the Holy Spirit. And inasmuch as this Jesus Christ was born and suffered in truth, so did He truly die; for He truly rose again from the dead, and, having after His resurrection conversed with His disciples, He was taken up. Then they delivered that the Holy Spirit was associated in honour and dignity with the Father and the Son. But whether the Holy Spirit was born or unborn (*natus an innatus*, later writers insisted that He was *nec genitus nec ingenitus*) was not part of the apostolic preaching, but was left for enquiry and investigation out of Scripture."

So it was part of the preaching that[3] "there should be a resurrection of the dead, and a future judgment, and that every rational soul possessed free will and choice, and that we have to pass through a struggle with the devil and his angels: but, as to the origin of the soul, and how the powers of the devil came to be what they are, the preaching of the Apostles does not with any clearness explain."

Once more[4]. "It is in the preaching of the Church that this world was made and began at a certain time, and is hereafter to be dissolved: but what there was before the world, and what will be after

[1] § 3.
[2] § 4 (abbreviated).
[3] § 5.
[4] § 7.

the world, is not known clearly to many; for as to these points no clear testimony is borne in the preaching of the Church."

Again[1]. "There is the fact that the Scriptures were written by (per) the Spirit of God, and have a meaning—not merely that which is apparent, but another which escapes the knowledge of many; and the opinion of the whole Church is that this second meaning is known only to those to whom the grace of the Holy Spirit is given in the word of wisdom and understanding."

And Origen passes on to a curious and apparently not very apposite discussion on the use of the word incorporeal (ἀσώματος) as applied to the Divine Beings: and he states that an object for the consideration of the thoughtful will be furnished by the nature of God and of Christ and of the Holy Spirit: and indeed by the nature of every soul and every rational being.

In conclusion:

"That there are angels of God and good powers ministering to Him for the benefit of mankind (he says) is clearly a part of the ecclesiastical preaching; but when they were created, and what their nature is, or how they are, is not enunciated with any clearness; and manifestly we have no tradition whether the sun and stars are animated or not. These are questions of science or knowledge."

§ 11. The subjects which this passage of Origen opens out are interesting in the highest degree; but we cannot of course now enter upon them at length. I will only say that, as the lines which I quoted a few pages back from Tertullian seem to account to us for the vast increase of ceremonial in the Church in the course of the third century, so does this passage assist us to understand the origin of our scientific theology. This theology was not part of the Primitive Tradition of the Church, but is the result of the long and painful exercise of thought on the original verbal and written Tradition. The "Ecclesiastical preaching" of Origen, like the Rules of Faith of Irenæus and Tertullian, contained *de facto* nothing which was not contained in Scripture. And so it is that on Scripture the spirits of devout men have ever been exercised during the more thoughtful ages and sections of the Church: the treatises of Augustine and Basil and others furnish adequate illustrations of the mode in which this exercise was carried on by them. And when we remember that the appeal to "Scripture only" for testimony in support of the doctrine of the Church on any particular difficult subject is the principle of the

[1] § 8.

Church of England as laid down by the great leaders of her Reformation,—we need not ask for better proofs that the same principle was the principle of Augustine and of Basil than are furnished by the Essays of the one on the Descent of our Lord into Hell, and of the other on the Holy Spirit.

§ 12. I do not remember that St Cyprian very frequently referred to the Rule of Faith; the few instances however in which he did so are important. Additional interest in his language arises from the circumstance that he is said to be the first person known who uses the word SYMBOL. In fact he uses three distinct terms, LEX, SYMBOLUM, INTERROGATIO BAPTISMI, and a fourth apparently combined of two of these, viz. LEX SYMBOLI. I conceive the first word "law" represents what Tertullian calls the *rule of faith:* the second, the "symbol," the gradually formed *Watchword of the Faith:* the third, the "*baptismal interrogation,*" was shorter than the symbol[1]: the fourth, "the law of the symbol" being the rule of faith,—regarded as that on which, or from which, the symbol was framed. Cyprian's language on this is well known, being quoted in all the books, but I will repeat it here, for it is instructive in many respects.

i. Novatian would be regarded at the present day not as a heretic but as a schismatic:

> So "if any one were to object that Novatian holds the same law which the Catholic church holds, baptizes with the same symbol that we do, knows the same God the Father, the same Son Christ, the same Holy Spirit, and therefore may usurp the power to baptize, because he seems in the interrogation of baptism not to differ from us, then let the objector know, first that we and the schismatics have not one law of symbol, nor yet the same interrogation. For when they ask; Dost thou believe in remission of sins and eternal life through the holy Church?—they speak falsely in the interrogation itself, seeing that they have not the Church. Then moreover they themselves confess with their own voice that remission of sins cannot be given except through the holy Church; and, as they have not the Church, they shew that with them sins are not remitted. Neither can it help them to have known the same God the Father that we know, the same Son Christ, the same Holy Spirit[2]."

[1] In the letter of Firmilian to Cyprian, No. 75, § 10, we read of the *usitata et legitima verba interrogationis* at baptism.

[2] Cyprianus Magno, *Epist.* LXIX. §§ 7, 8. I have followed the ordinary text, adding however with the MSS. *in* before *remissionem.* But I must note that according to Hartel, the *Codex Seguierianus* of Paris (it is of the sixth or seventh century, the earliest extant) omits *eundem Spiritum* in the earlier passage: and reads the whole passage "mentiuntur in

ii. A similar passage is found in the letter to the Bishops of Numidia (LXX. § 2), and this clearly shews that the form "credis in uitam æternam et remissionem peccatorum per sanctam ecclesiam[1]," was the form then used by all alike: for Cyprian calls upon the schismatics either to change the words of the interrogation, or to uphold their truth.

iii. But in this branch of our subject it will perhaps be of greater importance to draw attention to a few passages where the faith is mentioned, rather than the symbol. Thus to *Jubaianus*, Cyprian writes (Letter LXXIII. §§ 4, 5),

"If the faith is one with us and the heretics, then the grace may be one. If the same Father, the same Son, the same Holy Spirit, the same Church is confessed by us and by the Patripassiani, the Anthropiani, and so on, then the baptism may be one, if (as they allege) the faith is one."

As it is, their faith being different, their baptism is insufficient. Again, quoting the words in which our Saviour instituted the sacrament of baptism, Cyprian says:

Our Lord "here suggests (or implies) the Trinity in whose mystery (cujus sacramento) the nations were to be baptized. But does Marcion hold this Trinity? does he assert the same God, the Father, Creator, that we do? did he know the same Son, Christ, born of the Virgin Mary? which Word was made flesh, bore our sins, by dying overcame death, initiated the Resurrection of the flesh by Himself rising, and shewed to His disciples that in the same flesh He had risen? Far different is the faith with Marcion and the other heretics."

Thus, in § 20 of the same letter we read how we ought to hold firmly and to teach the faith and truth of the Catholic Church, and, by means of all the evangelic and apostolic precepts, to exhibit the reason of the divine dispensation (economy) and unity[2].

§ 13. As my object in this chapter is to note not merely the traces of the existence, but also the character of the "Rule of Faith"—not the growth of the symbol, nor the exact form of the baptismal interrogation—I shall refer my readers to the

interrogatione quando non habeant ecclesiam. tunc deinde uoce sua ipsi confitentur remissionem peccatorum." The subject is very difficult.

[1] I do not think the difference of the order of words is of any consequence.

[2] It is in the next section that we meet with the words *salus extra ecclesiam non est*. I would draw attention to the allusion to the *Creation* in the passage from the letter to Jubaianus.

collections of Dr Heurtley, of Dr Hahn, or of Mr Lumby on these latter subjects. I must notice, however, that in the account of the Council of Carthage given in the collection of Cyprian's works, Euchratius of Thenæ, § 29, appealed to the words of our Lord in Matt. xxviii. 18, as giving fully (*perimplevit* is the word used) "our Faith and the grace of baptism and the rule of the ecclesiastical law" (legis ecclesiasticæ regulam): and Vincentius of Thibaris, § 37, referred to our Saviour's words in Mark xvi. 18, as containing the "Rule of Truth" to be observed on the return of heretics. In its synodical letter (see Cyp. *Epist.* LXX.) the council claimed that it was merely carrying out the "truth and firmness of the Catholic Rule." And very interesting is it to find that some of the bishops during the council, and Cyprian himself after it was over, appealed to the Scriptures as the one authority when tradition failed. See, for example, Letter LXXIV. § 10:

"If a channel or conduit which had copiously and largely conveyed water from a fountain suddenly stops, do we not go to the fountain itself to know whether the springs themselves have failed, or whether the loss has arisen from defects in the channel which may be amended? And this the priests of God ought now to do, observing the divine precepts, so that if in anything the truth have wavered or tottered, we should revert to the divine original (originem dominicam) and to the evangelic and apostolic tradition; and thus the reason for our action should rise from that from which both its order and its origin burst forth[1]."

§ 14. But we find Novatian himself appealing to the "Rule

[1] Before we part with Cyprian I may remark that there are a few notes of his faith perceptible in his treatises *de Vanitate* (*Quod idola dii non sint*) § 11. The passage, written before the Nestorian controversy, has been much altered by copyists and editors as by the Oxford translators to make it orthodox. Thus *Deus cum homine miscetur* is there rendered "God is made one with man." *Carnem Spiritus Sanctus induitur* is altered in the editions, apparently without any authority, into *carnem Spiritu Sancto cooperante induitur*. Again *hominem induit* which might involve Nestorianism was translated correctly in the Oxford series "puts on man," but a note is added "i.e. human *nature*. Thus the orthodox doctrine differs from Nestorianism," &c. Of course it does, but what was Cyprian's view? The fact is that early writers frequently used language which was subsequently found to be capable of an heretical sense: and to evade this sense the words were often altered in olden time, as they are mistranslated in our own. In the *de Lapsis* § 2 we have "religiosa vox Christum locuta est in quem semel credidisse confessa est," i.e. the religious voice hath uttered the name of Christ in whom it once confessed that it believed. The Oxford translation renders it "which hath already made confession of His Creed." According to this, I cannot say I have believed in Christ, unless I repeat the Creed.

There is perhaps a more distinguishable reference to a Creed in the *de Mortalitate* § 21. *Qui autem in spe uiuimus et in Deum credimus* &c. "We who live in hope and believe in God, and trust that Christ has suffered for us and risen again, abiding in Christ, and ourselves rising again through Him and in Him—why are we unwilling ourselves to depart out of the world, or grieve over our friends that have departed as if they were lost?"

of the Truth." Fragments of his Belief have been collected out of his treatise *de Trinitate* by the care of Dr Heurtley, and in his pages the original may be seen. Novatian says, that the "Rule of Truth" requires, first of all, that you believe "in God the omnipotent Father and Lord, that is, the most perfect Creator of all things." This he discusses, §§ 1—8. The "same Rule of Truth" teaches us to believe, "after the Father, in the Son of God, Christ Jesus, our Lord God, but still Son of God." This subject occupies §§ 9—28. Then "the order of reason and the authority of the faith admonish us, having digested the words and letters of the Lord, to believe in the Holy Spirit," &c. Dr Heurtley considers that there can be no doubt that the *Regula Veritatis* of which Novatian speaks refers to the Creed: but I hope that the learned writer will, on reconsideration, agree with me, that the language adduced clearly shews that this Rule of Truth cannot be identical with the Baptismal Profession. It seems to me that Novatian informs us that the Baptismal Profession was required by the Rule of Truth, by the order of reason, and by the authority of the Faith, but was not identical with any of them[1].

§ 15. It may be useful now to arrange the subjects, which, according to the Fathers whom I have quoted, the RULE OF THE FAITH of the first three centuries contained. I need not specify the writers by whom the various items are mentioned: the comparison of the following account with the passages which I have cited from their works may be easily made by my readers.

We learn therefore the following: that this Rule of Faith required that all should believe "That there is one God, the Father Almighty, Who made heaven and earth, Who created all things out of nothing.

"And that they should believe in one Christ Jesus, the Son of God, the Word of God, our Lord God, Who was born of the Father before all creation, through whom God made all things, Who was seen by the Patriarchs, Who was heard in the Prophets, Who from (ex) the Spirit of God and with power was sent down

[1] Migne, Latin series III., pp. 886 &c. See Dr Heurtley p. 21, Hahn p. 74, Mr Lumby p. 29. In § 30, Novatian adds one word of interest: "*Nos scimus et legimus et credimus et tenemus unum esse Deum qui fecit cælum pariter et terram,*" the word *unum* forms a link of connection with the Eastern creeds.

into the Virgin Mary (in Virginem Mariam delatum): Who was for our salvation made flesh in her womb, uniting man to God: being Son of Man and Son of God: so that the Son of God became Man: He was born of her: He preached a new law, and gave new promises of the kingdom of heaven, and wrought miracles: He suffered under Pontius Pilate, was fixed to the cross (fixum cruci), died, was buried: rose again the third day from the dead: was taken up in the flesh into heaven; sat on the right hand of the Father and sent in His stead the power of the Holy Spirit to lead on believers: He will come again from heaven in the glory of the Father to collect all things together in Himself as Head (*ἀνακεφαλαιωσάσθαι τὰ πάντα*), to raise up all flesh of all humanity, and to judge the living and the dead, and receive the saints to Himself to life and incorruption, and condemn the wicked and the angels which sinned to everlasting fire.

"The belief must also be firm in the Holy Spirit; Who is associated in honour and dignity with the Father and the Son, who through the prophets proclaimed the dispensations, and the economies, and the birth from the Virgin, and the sufferings and the rising again."

And we learn from Cyprian that the candidate for baptism was required to express his belief "in Remission of Sins and Eternal Life through the Church[1]."

§ 16. My readers will be able to compare for themselves this series of *credenda* with the contents of our modern version of the Apostles' Creed: noting both the additions and the deficiencies. They will be able also to judge for themselves whether this Rule of Faith required a belief in anything which is not directly taught in Scripture. They will then understand why the earliest heretics felt themselves compelled to tamper with the books which we now reckon to be Canonical and Apostolical, before they could attempt to shew that their views were in accordance with the

[1] With this may be compared the Creed of Marcellus although it belongs to a later epoch. The original may be seen in Epiphanius *Hæres.* LXXII., Migne XLII. 385, Dr Heurtley p. 24, Mr Lumby p. 119, or Hahn p. 5. "I believe in God Almighty, and in Christ Jesus His only begotten Son, our Lord, who was born of the Holy Ghost and the Virgin Mary, who was crucified under Pontius Pilate, and was buried, and on the third day rose again from the dead, who ascended into heaven, and sitteth on the right hand of the Father, from whence He is coming to judge living and dead: and in the Holy Ghost, Holy Church, Remission of sins, Resurrection of the flesh, Life everlasting."

The last clause is found in the creed of the Church of Ravenna as given by Petrus Chrysologus, A.D. 445, but not in any intermediate creed.

written words of Christ's Apostles. We shall thus have an answer to the questions, "How far does early Church history enable us to form an estimate as to the contents of the Apostolical Tradition?" and "Did this Apostolical Tradition contain any thing of a doctrinal character for which we have not now ample warrant in the writings of the Evangelists and Apostles[1]?" The answer to this last question is, "Decidedly not."

[1] Before I pass on I may be allowed to draw attention to the appeals made by Mr Newman in 1844, to the Rule of Faith. The two volumes (or rather the two parts of the one volume) entitled "*Selected Treatises of S. Athanasius, Archbishop of Alexandria, in controversy with the Arians, translated with notes and Indices,*" (the advertisements to which are attested by the initials J. H. N.) appeared respectively in 1842 and 1844. On comparing the summary of chapter xi. of the first discourse against the Arians, as given in the table of contents p. vi. published in 1844, with the summary itself (p. 233) as published in 1842 a curious addition will be noted. The passage under discussion by Athanasius was Philippians ii. 9, 10. The special subject was whether the *exaltation* spoken of there shewed, as the Arian maintained, "the moral probation and advancement of the Saviour." This Arian opinion Athanasius resisted (according to Mr Newman), "First from the force of the word Son according to the Regula Fidei, which is inconsistent with such an interpretation." But this reference to the Regula Fidei was added in 1844; mention of it was not made in 1842. Athanasius however did not refer to the Rule of Faith at all, either directly or indirectly: the language which he used is this: "Such then I consider to be the meaning of the passage and this decidedly ecclesiastical." Again in the titles to Discourse II. p. vii. or 281 we have (on Hebrews iii. 2) "the *Regula Fidei* counter to an Arian sense of the text"; in those to chapter xv. (pp. vii. and 297) on Acts ii. 36 "The Regula Fidei must be observed"; in that to chapter xxii. on Proverbs viii. 22 (pp. ix. and 385) "It is right to interpret this passage by the Regula Fidei"; so chapter xxv. (pp. x. and 414) "The Arian explanation" of words in S. John's Gospel "is put aside by the *Regula Fidei*"; chapter xxvi. (pp. xi. and 436) "We must recur to the Regula Fidei"; chapter xxviii. (pp. xi. and 549) "Arian explanation of" Mark xiii. 32 "contradicts the Regula Fidei"; chapter xxix. (pp. xii. and 476) "Arian inferences" from Mat. xxvi. 39, &c. "are against the Regula Fidei" as before; chapter xxx. (pp. xii. and 484) "The Regula Fidei answers 'an objection' at once in the negative by contrary texts." I suppose that readers generally would consider that the *Regula Fidei* thus put prominently forward by so accomplished a theologian had, in every place cited, some counterpart in the writings of Athanasius, and that this counterpart corresponded to the Rule of Faith technically referred to by Tertullian. On examination however it appears that in many of the passages there is no reference in Athanasius to any Rule of Faith whatever: the conception is entirely imported into the text by the annotator. In some of them, as in III. 28, the appeal is made to the "σκόπος, the general tendency or aim of the faith of us Christians, which tendency or aim we should use *as* a rule in our attendance to the reading of inspired Scripture;" words which recall to my mind the wise instruction conveyed in Article XVII. and XX. of the Church of England, but have no reference to any traditional doctrine. In others the testimony of "the truth" is invoked. On these Mr Newman remarked that in some instances "the words ἀλήθεια λόγος (sic) &c., are almost synonymous with Regula Fidei," and he took as an example a passage in § 36, where Athanasius, after discouraging enquiries into such questions as "*How the Word is with God, How He is the brightness of God, How God begets,* and *What is the manner of such an action with Him,*"—adds, "but we must not, because of this, entertain conceptions against the truth, nor, if we are at a loss regarding these things, should we on this account disbelieve what is written." In III. § 29 (Migne XXVI. p. 385), Athanasius appeals to "the drift and character of Holy Scripture," Σκόπος τοίνυν οὗτος καὶ χαρακτὴρ τῆς ἁγίας γρα-

§ 17. One more reference to the Rule of Faith of the earliest centuries and to its relation with the written Scriptures must be permitted to me. Towards the middle or end of the second century, appeared one Artemon, who denied the Deity of our Lord; and, anticipating the heresy of Paul of Samosata, maintained that the Saviour had become a mere man (ψιλὸν ἄνθρωπον τὸν σωτῆρα γένεσθαι), and he claimed that this was the old opinion. A writer who had not attached his name to his essay, resisted this pretension. He wrote, says Eusebius[1], "These people say that all their predecessors and the apostles themselves received and taught what they now teach: and indeed that so it continued until the time of Victor, who was thirteenth in the succession from Peter at Rome: his successor, Zephyrinus[2], (they say) it was under whom the truth had been perverted." The argument of the anonymous writer will prove interesting to us: "they might have put their opinions in a persuasive form," he is reported to have said, "if the Holy Scriptures had not in the first instance stood in their way. But besides there are writings of some of the brethren, older than Victor, which they composed in behalf of the truth in reference to the Gentiles and to the then heresies:" and he specified Justin, and Miltiades, and Tatian, and Clemens and many others, by whom the Christ is spoken of as God (θεολογεῖται ὁ Χριστός). And he appealed to the works of Irenæus and Melito, and to the psalms and hymns (ᾠδαι) in which the same truth was assumed. "How then can these people affirm that theirs is the old doctrine, ours the new?" And the same writer complains:

"That these men had corrupted the Holy Scriptures, had put on one side the canon of the ancient faith, had ignored Christ, not asking, what did the divine Scriptures say? but, what was the kind of argument that might be found to prove the Deity? exercising their wits from mere love of labour! and then if any one puts before them a sentence of

φῆς, as teaching, as he had often said, both the Divinity and the Humanity of the Saviour: he states that if any one will after studying John i. 1—5, 14, and Philipp. ii. 6—8, with the same mind go through all the Scripture, he will see how at the beginning God said, *Let there be light* and *Let us make man*, and at the end of the ages sent the Saviour into the world to save the world; as it is written, *A virgin shall conceive, &c.* The fact is that the Rule of Faith as it was used by Tertullian failed to meet the heresies of the fourth century; and thus the appeal was made to the general scope and drift of Scripture, and special passages of Scripture were interpreted by the "Catholic Fathers" in harmony with that general drift.

[1] Eusebius, *H.E.*, Book v. last chapter, 28—32.

[2] Zephyrinus was Pope from 201—218.

Holy Scripture, they turn it over, this way and that way, to see whether by taking it with its context or without they may make it into a member of a syllogism. For they have given up the Holy Scriptures of God and study the measure of the earth[1], as being from the earth and speaking from the earth, and ignorant of Him that cometh from above." They take the measure of Euclid (proceeds our author) and admire Aristotle and Theophrastus and almost adore Galenus. "But surely I have no need to say that these fellows are far from the faith who use to the full the arts of the unbeliever in support of their heresy, and with the clever craft of the atheist adulterate the simple faith of the Holy Scriptures. Indeed they lay hands on the Scriptures themselves, and pretend that they have been rendering them correct."

I can scarcely resist a painful smile whilst I translate these words; a parallel in the modern interpretation of a few isolated passages of Scripture lies so close at hand, and the treatment of Scripture by modern divines seems to have been anticipated in the times of this anonymous writer.

"Asclepiodorus and Theodotus and Hermophilus and Apollonius have tried each his hand in correcting Scripture: how is it that the results of their operations differ so materially?"

§ 18. This passage gives additional signs of an approaching transition from the appeal to the traditional Rule of Faith to an appeal to Scripture—a transition of which I have already noted intimations. The fact was that the controversialists of the third century were compelled to enter on ground where the traditional Rule of Faith could not reach them: the Arian and the Catholic could each accept the whole of the contents of the canon as given by Irenæus or Tertullian. A new series of questions was now opening before the Church, and it required a new mode of treatment. On matters of discipline, Tertullian—almost, if not quite, a Montanist at the time—had appealed to the continuous action of the Holy Spirit in leading Christians into truth: the churchmen were compelled now to appeal to the same Spirit in matters of doctrine. They gradually came to recognise Christianity as a science: a science, the data of which were to be found in the contents of the Holy Volume; the power of reading which was sought for in the action of the life-giving Spirit. Two questions of deep interest to us had also now to find their answer: one was, What is Holy Scripture? what criteria are we to use in fixing its contents? the other was, Are we to allow the general

[1] They argue as they would of material objects.

scope of Scripture to be subordinated to what is the *prima facie* meaning of a few special texts? On the first of these questions I have written at length in my *Hulsean Lectures* of 1858: on the second in the series for 1857. I will not detain my readers to discuss the principles which guided the Church in making its arrangements. I shall be compelled, however, to give specimens of the mode in which these arrangements were carried out.

CHAPTER V.

RULES OF FAITH AFTER THE YEAR 250.

§ 1. Letter of synod of Antioch to Paul of Samosata, A D. 269. § 2. The exposition of Gregory of Neo-Cæsarea. § 3. Creed of Eusebius. § 4. Comparison of this with the Creeds of the Apostolic Constitutions and of Lucian the Martyr. § 5. Lucian's appeal to Scripture. § 6. Position now gained by the Church.

§ 1. IN my opinion the most important document of the third century that bears upon our present subject is the letter sent to Paul of Samosata by the orthodox bishops who met at Antioch in the year 269. It is true that the great synod held at Carthage on the subject of rebaptizing heretics had included some bishops who, when the choice had to be made between the suspension of an ecclesiastical custom and the infraction of God's law, maintained that custom must give way to Scripture; but as upholding the corresponding canon in doctrinal matters, this Council of Antioch has for us a deeper interest. This letter was first printed (we are told) in its original form in Rome in the year 1608, and thence it has found its way into the collections of the Councils[1]. It is to be seen also in Vol. III. of Dr Routh's collection of *Relliquiæ Sacræ*, and in Dr Hahn's volume, p. 91. The genuineness has been disputed, but I believe that all doubts regarding it are now considered to be at rest. The letter is said to have been composed by Malchion a presbyter of the Church of Antioch, and then to have been adopted by the bishops Hymenæus, Theophilus, and others who met in synod.

The Bishops, in addressing Paul, state that they had first compared together their own belief; and then, in order to render it more clear, they had resolved to put out in writing the faith which they had received from the beginning, which they held as it had been handed down and as it was kept in the Catholic and Holy Church even to the present day, being proclaimed by continuous succession from those blessed Apostles, who had been eyewitnesses and ministers of the Word, from

[1] Labbe, I. 843, Mansi, I. 1033.

the Law, from the Prophets, and from the New Testament. Their Faith was that God is unbegotten, one, without beginning, unseen, unchangeable, Whom no man hath seen or can see: Whose glory or majesty worthily to conceive or worthily to enunciate is beyond the reach of human nature; yea, to have even any, the poorest, conception of Him, is impossible for us if unassisted. His beloved Son alone reveals Him, as He saith, *No one knoweth the Father, save the Son and he to whom the Son may reveal Him.* And this Son we confess and believe (having known it both in the Old and New Testament) to be Begotten, Only-begotten, Image of the unseen God, First-born of all creation, Wisdom and Word and Power of God, Being before the worlds—not in foreknowledge but in essence and substance—God, and Son of God. And whoso shall contend against this, saying, that we ought not to believe and confess that the Son of God is God before the foundation of the world, but shall maintain that two Gods are preached if the Son of God is preached as God, him we consider to be alien to the ecclesiastical Canon. And all the Catholic Churches agree with us. For concerning Him it has been written, *Thy Throne, O God,* &c.—and they quote Ps. xlv. 6, 7, and Isaiah xxxv. 4, 5 *Our God repayeth judgment—He will come* (αὐτὸς ἥξει) *and save us,* &c., and Isaiah xlv. 14 *In Thee shall they pray; because God is in Thee and there is no God beside Thee,* &c., and Rom. ix. 5 *From whom is Christ after the flesh who is over all,* &c., where *Who is over all,* and *Beside Thee* must be conceived to embrace all created things[1]. And again Hosea xi. 9 *I am God and not man,* &c. And all the God-inspired Scriptures signify that the Son of God is God;—to put all these forward one by one we must defer for the present[2].

"Him we believe, ever being with the Father, to have fulfilled the Father's will with reference to the Creation of all things: for *He* (αὐτὸς) *spake and they were made; He commanded and they were created.* For he that commands commands some one; and who is commanded here save God, the Only-begotten Son of God, to Whom the words were spoken, *Let us make man,* &c.?" and the bishops quote John i. 3, *All things were made through Him,* and Col. i. 16, *In Him all things were created.* Then they proceed—"and thus He truly is, and He worketh at once as Word and as God: and by Him the Father hath made all things, yet not as by a material instrument or by an impersonal knowledge: but, the Father having begotten the Son, as a living and personal energy, working all in all: the Son not merely looking on, nor being merely present, but also working for the creation of the Universe, as it is written (Prov. viii. 30) *I was with Him, fitting all things for Him.* We say that it was He who came down and was seen by Abraham at the oak of Mamre, One of the mysterious Three: it was written of Him, *The LORD rained down fire from the LORD.* We say it was He who, in fulfilment of the Father's will, appeared to the Patriarchs, now as Angel, now as Lord, now testified to as God. He was *the Angel of the great Covenant* (Isaiah ix. 6). He was seen by Abraham as LORD (Gen. xxii. 12, 14), and as God by Jacob (xxxi. 11, xxxii. 30). The Man who is mentioned at first as appearing, we say, is the Son of God, and Him the

[1] πάντων γεννητῶν. Query γενητῶν?
[2] Routh suggests τὸ νῦν for τὸν υἱὸν here.

Scripture itself has signified to be God. So too we say that the Law was given to Moses through the ministering of the Son of God, as the Apostle teacheth (Gal. iii. 19), *ordained by angels, &c.* We know of no other Mediator between God and Man but Him, and we are taught this by Moses," and they refer to Exodus iii. 2, 4, 16, iv. 1; all of which are quoted in succession, as are Deut. xxxiii. 16; Exod. xxxiii. 17—19; xxxiv. 5, 6, and the passages are compared with our Lord's words in John vi. 46, v. 37, and St John's words in his Gospel i. 18, and St Paul's in 1 Tim. i. 17:—

the letter proceeds:

"And we confess and proclaim that the Son, being with the Father, God and Lord of all created things, and being sent by the Father from heaven, and incarnate, has assumed man (ἐνηνθρωπηκέναι): wherefore the Body, taken from the Virgin, containing all the fulness of the Godhead bodily, has been, without capability of change (ἀτρέπτως), united with the Godhead, and has been deified (τεθεοποίηται). And for the sake of this incarnation, the same God and Man, Jesus Christ, was prophesied in the Law and Prophets, and has been believed on in the whole Church which is under heaven; being, on the one hand, God, divesting Himself[1] of being equal with God, and, on the other, Man and of the seed of David according to the flesh: the signs and wonders which are described in the gospels, it was the God who wrought; but by participation of flesh and blood He was in all points tempted like as we are, without sin. And thus before the Incarnation the Christ was named in the divine Scriptures as One. In Jeremiah (Lament. iv. 20) *the Spirit of our countenance, the Christ:* and *the Spirit is the Lord* according to the Apostle (2 Cor. iii. 17). And the same Apostle says *They drank of the spiritual Rock and the Rock was the Christ,* and again *Let us not tempt the Lord,* &c., and of Moses *He considered the* (ὀνειδισμὸς) *bearing the reproach of the Christ as greater riches,* &c.: and Peter, *Of which salvation,* &c. And if *Christ, the power of God and the wisdom of God,* is before the ages, so also and so far is Christ one and the same Thing in essence even though He is regarded under many figures.

"Having signified these few things out of very many, we wish to know whether thou believest and teachest the same things that we do, and beg thee to inform us whether thou art satisfied with what we have written or not."

Several questions of great interest are opened out by this passage.

It will be seen, as I have said already, i. that the Rule of Faith, as we have collected its details from Tertullian and others, and, as we have found it embodied in the later personal belief of Marcellus, was not sufficient to meet the errors of Paul of Samosata; a new country was opening out, over which the early traditional instructions furnished no special maps to guide the tra-

[1] κενώσας, the word of Phil. ii. 7, "made himself of no reputation."

veller. On the *character* and work of the Christ, in His pre-existent state, the "Rule" was nearly silent: as to the mode of His Incarnation it gave no information. The orthodox writers of the latter half of the third century might address this Paul and his followers and accuse them of deserting the Canon, but they produced no proofs that the Canon contained clearly and explicitly a denial of his errors: the teaching of these men was novel certainly, but was it opposed directly to the earlier teaching of the Church? The Fathers at Antioch pointed to the pride and self-assumption of these new doctors: they accused them of petulance: they complained that they had forbidden the use of psalms which had been commonly sung in honour of our Lord Jesus Christ, on the pretence that these psalms were new and compositions of recent men; and they had really denied that God, the Son of God, had "come down from heaven,"—but the old Rule of Faith had not asserted this; and what were the orthodox to do?

ii. Thus the Antiochene bishops acted with reference to this new doctrine as the Fathers at Carthage had acted in their difficulty respecting the acknowledgment of heretical baptism: they appealed to Scripture: by the test of Scripture they tried and confirmed their own faith, that faith which had not yet been embodied in language. As years roll on, we shall find their newer rules of faith, supplemented out of the Scripture, crystallising as it were, more and more, round the thread which the early Canon enabled them to apply.

iii. And we must notice a third thing. We shall have ere long to discuss the words of Athanasius, that "the Son, in the fulness of time came down from the bosom of the Father, and from the undefiled Virgin Mary took our man Christ Jesus," and shall then draw attention to the fact that these words bear, *prima facie* at all events, a Nestorian meaning. So the words of Malchion will be found to be consistent with opinions which the Church afterwards rejected. "The Father commanded the Son;" "the Body from the Virgin was united to the Deity, and was deified." "He divested Himself of His equality." "He was one Thing in essence." And it may be noticed, that the unity of the Godhead is nowhere insisted on: the truth pressed is this, that in essence and in substance Christ was God before the Incarnation, *οὐσίᾳ καὶ ὑποστάσει Θεόν*. The confession is so imperfect that it is reconcileable in one part with Arian, in another with Nestorian, in another with Eutychian error.

But all this notwithstanding, it is most valuable. It furnishes the most important proof that in doctrinal matters, as in ceremonial, the Church was looking to the promise of the ever renewed guidance of the Holy Spirit of God. Tertullian had not lived in vain. The Church had rejected the personal pretensions of Montanus, but had learnt to see the truth which rendered even for a moment the pretensions of the Montanists tolerable. A guide was wanted to lead the followers of Jesus into the truth, and the words of the Saviour were remembered that the Spirit was to be their guide. The mode of His guidance had been proclaimed: He would bring to men's memory the words which the Redeemer had uttered and enable them to see the truths which underlie His words. The teaching of these men was imperfect: in part it was, if not erroneous, at least capable of an erroneous interpretation: the imperfections were to be filled up as years rolled on, the errors were to be corrected, the language was to be amended. Who will dare to say that the outline is even now filled up completely? May it not become necessary in formulæ handed down to us, to correct a shadow here, to erase a line there, to bring out a feature more prominently in another place, even as Augustine corrected Athanasius, and the aged Augustine corrected the young Augustine's writings?

§ 2. With this should be compared the ἔκθεσις πίστεως, "the setting forth of the Faith," which, according to the legend, was revealed to Gregory of Neo-Cæsarea, by the Apostle S. John; it may possibly be contemporaneous with the above[1]. Here the words approach in parts nearer to the words of our Nicene Creed, but the critical conception of the unity of the Divine Essence is not developed[2].

§ 3. More important, historically and permanently, is the Creed which Eusebius of Cæsarea produced at the Council of Nicæa in 325. He says that he had received it in substance during his period of instruction as a catechumen, and again when

[1] This Gregory is supposed to have died about 270.

[2] It may be seen in Hahn, p. 97, Harvey, *Vindex*, I. 532, Lumby 34, or in Mansi, I. 1030, or Migne, III. 983.

he was baptized. Thus, as he was born about the year 264, and, apparently, was brought up in the Christian faith from his earliest years, we may consider the document he adduces as the Creed of Cæsarea about the period at which we have now arrived[1]. Its antiquity is not affected by the statement that Eusebius was convinced of the truth of it "from the divine Scriptures," and had believed and taught it during the whole of his ministerial life—formerly when he was a presbyter, now when he was a bishop. It is so important that I will give it at length.

"We believe in one God the Father Almighty, Maker of all things visible and invisible: and in one Lord Jesus Christ the Word of God, God of (ἐκ) God, Light of Light, Life of Life, only begotten Son, First begotten of every creature, begotten of God the Father before all ages, by Whom too all things were made: who, for our salvation was made flesh (σαρκωθέντα), and lived among men, and suffered, and rose again the third day, and ascended to the Father, and will come again in glory to judge the quick and dead. We believe too in one Holy Ghost:" and Eusebius proceeds with a kind of supplement which requires our careful attention. "We believe that Each One is and subsists, Father truly Father, and Son truly Son, and Holy Spirit truly Holy Spirit: even as our Lord in sending out His disciples for their preaching bade them, *Go and make disciples of all nations, baptizing them in the Name of the Father, and of the Son and of the Holy Spirit.*"

§ 4. We should compare with this the Creed of the seventh book of the Apostolic Constitutions, which in its Greek form is deemed by competent critics to represent the customs of the Church of Antioch, at least as early as the year 280[2]; and the Creed given by Sozomen, *H. E.* III. 5, and Socrates, *H. E.* II. 10, and ascribed by them to Lucian the martyr, who had died in 311 or 312.

On making this comparison we may notice that the Creed of the Apostolic Constitutions introduces the thought of St Paul (1 Cor. viii. 6) *Of whom are all things,* regarding the Father: *By whom are all things,* relating to the Son. (We may notice this hereafter in some of the Western documents.) The other two expand into greater fulness the conception "God of God," the Creed of Lucian proceeding thus:

[1] Unless we accept the unsupported charge of suppression brought by Dr Pusey.

[2] The Creed of Eusebius is given by Hahn, p. 46, that of the Apostolic Constitutions, p. 40, that of Lucian, p. 100. They are printed by Mr Harvey, ut sup. pp. 533—540: and the first and third by Mr Lumby, pp. 48, and 36 respectively. Mr Caspari considers that the Creed of the Apostolical Constitutions was originally a Creed of the Syrian Church and of the fourth century, i. e. he puts it about fifty or sixty years later. See notes of an essay in his first *program.* p. vi.

"God of (ἐκ) God, Whole of Whole, Only of Only, Perfect of Perfect, King of King, Lord of Lord, Living Word, Living Wisdom, True Light, Way, Truth, Resurrection, Shepherd, Door, Incapable of mutation or of interchange, Unalterable, Image of the Godhead, both of the Essence and Will and Power of the Father, the First-begotten of all creation." It states that He "came down from above" as the Creed of the Constitutions says "He came down from heaven": and adds ἄνθρωπον γενόμενον He was made man[1]. The Creed of the Constitutions uses the words σάρκα ἀναλαβόντα He took flesh; the Creed of Cæsarea reading σαρκωθέντα was made flesh. Both the last-named Creeds agree in using the word πολιτευσάμενον, "made His home on earth," the former adding that He "lived holily after the laws of His God and Father": the latter merely stating that He "lived amongst men." But very noticeable are the additions in the former; i. of the clause "of whose Kingdom there shall be no end," and ii. of the words with which the Creed is summed up: "I am baptized too into the Holy Spirit, that is the Comforter, who wrought in all the Saints since the world began, and was afterwards sent to the Apostles also from the Father, according to the promise of our Saviour, the Lord Jesus Christ, and, after the Apostles, to all who believe within the Holy Catholic Church (ἐν—ἐκκλησίᾳ): I am baptized into the resurrection of the flesh and into remission of sins, into the kingdom of heaven and the life of the world to come."

The conclusion and indeed the entire framework of the Creed of Lucian[2] are more elaborate. As I have already said, I do not intend to transfer it as a whole to my pages, although I am tempted to do so because of the continual reference to Scripture. It commences:

"We believe, in accordance with the evangelic and apostolic tradition." Points not previously laid down in baptismal creeds are confirmed by quotations, as from S. John i. 1, 3 "the Word was God, and all things were made through Him." Christ is "the Mediator between God and Man; He is the Apostle of our Faith, the Prince of Life, as He says, I have come down from heaven." Like Eusebius, Lucian quotes S. Matt. xxviii. 19, and speaks of the Father being truly Father, &c.: the Names not being used simply or needlessly, but each accurately signifying the several proper Hypostasis and Order and Glory of each Being named, as being in hypostasis—(*substantia* as Hilary in both places translates it[3])—three (τρία): in agreement and harmony one (ἕν). "This faith we hold, and from the beginning to the end we hold it, and in the sight of God and Christ we anathematize every heretical false doctrine, and if any one teaches besides (παρὰ) the sound correct faith of the Scriptures, saying, that there is or has been time or season or age before the generation of the Son, let him be anathema. And, if any one says

[1] The thought does not occur in the Eusebian Creed.

[2] It is to be seen in Athanasius *de Synodis*, § 23 (Migne xxvi. p. 725), but Athanasius does not give its origin. It was produced he says at the synod of Antioch (A.D. 341). It is also in Socrates, *H. E.* II. 10. It was translated by Hilary of Poictiers: Hahn gives the translation.

[3] "Per substantiam tria, per consonantiam unum."

that the Son is a creature (κτίσμα) as one of the creatures, or a thing produced (γέννημα) as one of the things produced, or a thing made (ποίημα) as one of the things made, and not as the divine Scriptures have delivered each detail of the above[1], or if any one teaches anything different (ἄλλο), or preaches any other gospel than that we received (Gal. i. 9); let him be anathema. For *we* truly and reverently both believe and follow all that has been delivered to us out of the Holy Scriptures both by the Prophets and Apostles."

§ 5. The above recital is of service to us in two ways. It shews distinctly that Lucian was preparing for the Arian heresy, and as distinctly how he deemed that heresy was to be met. He appeals to Scripture: and he declares that all that he does believe, whatever was its origin, he believes because it is also delivered in Scripture. The three documents furnish to us a valuable and an interesting introduction to the Creeds as affected by the Arian controversy[2].

We may say that the Church had now attained to the belief in the equality of the three Persons of the Blessed Trinity, but the Unity of the Godhead was not brought out. We owe the distinct appreciation and enunciation of this to the next epoch in the Church's history.

[1] I follow Socrates' reading here.

[2] Of course Athanasius objected to this Creed *after* the Nicene was promulgated.

CHAPTER VI.

THE FAITH OF THE NICENE COUNCIL.

§ 1. Letters of Alexander of Alexandria. § 2. Arius' account of his own belief. § 3. Alexander's notice of it. § 4. Eusebius' account of the Council of Nicæa. § 5. Comparison of the Creeds of Cæsarea and Nicæa. § 6. What was the object of the framers of the Nicene Creed? § 7. Athanasius gives the answer. § 8. Thus the Nicene Creed was intended to be not a Symbol but a Rule of Faith. § 9. Explanation of some words in it. § 10. Athanasius satisfied with the document. § 11. The Baptismal Creed still short.

§ 1. It is not my object to write a history of the Arian controversy, but the two letters of Alexander, bishop of Alexandria—the one to his namesake at Constantinople, preserved by Theodoret, *H. E.* I. 4; the other to his honoured fellow-ministers everywhere, given by Socrates, *H. E.* I. 6—are too interesting to be passed over. Both letters describe the heresy of Arius in almost similar terms; and we learn from them what was believed to be its character. It was, or was suspected to be, an avowal, in the name of Christianity, of opinions regarding the Saviour which even a Jew or a Greek might hold: and possibly the secret of the long-continued struggle between the Arian and the Athanasian parties lay in this: the former were abetted by the secret followers of the older superstition, by men and women who, not daring to avow openly their hatred of Christianity, shrunk behind the shield of Arianism. The time had come, says Dorner, when the Church could not stand still: it must choose one of two courses: either take a step in advance and define the indefinite, or go backwards into heathenism or into Judaism.

But, as I have stated, my object is not to trace the history of the Arian controversy: it is to enquire into the growth of the Creeds and later Rules of Faith, as well as into the principles by which that growth was directed.

§ 2. Arius' own statement of the reasons why he was persecuted by Alexander was this:

We do not agree with Alexander in publicly stating "God is Ever, the Son Ever: together Father, together Son: the Son ever subsists with God, in an unbegotten mode (συνυπάρχει ἀγεννήτως ὁ Υἱὸς τῷ Θεῷ): He is begotten from eternity[1]: neither in conception nor by any atom of time does God precede the Son: ever God, ever Son: from God Himself is the Son."

And Arius complained to his old friend and fellow-pupil Eusebius of Nicomedia that his

"Brother Eusebius of Cæsarea and Theodotus and others were excommunicated (ἀνάθεμα ἐγένοντο) because they say that God being without beginning precedes the Son[2]. We however hold (he proceeds) and have taught and teach that the Son is not Unbegotten, nor yet in any way a part of the Unbegotten; nor yet is He from any presupposed thing; but that in will and counsel He subsisted before times and ages, perfect God, only begotten, immutable; and, before He was begotten or created or defined or founded[3] He was not: for He was not unbegotten. And we are persecuted because we say, The Son hath a beginning, but God hath no beginning. Because of this we are persecuted, and because we say, He is from things which are not; for so we say, because He is not a part of God, nor yet from any presupposed thing."

The meaning of this is very difficult to transfer to our language: but I think, on full consideration, the following will be found to be a tolerably correct representation of Arius' avowed opinion. He believed that the Son of God subsisted (ὑπέστη) essentially in the counsel and will of God before all ages: but that hypostatically, He was not before He was created or begotten. Thus He had a beginning. And, simultaneously, Arius maintained that the Son was created, as it were at once, as the universe was created out of nothing (ἐξ οὐκ ὄντων, but not ἐκ τῆς οὐσίας τοῦ Θεοῦ), so that on the one hand He was not what Arius called a part or division of God, nor yet on the other was He formed out of *previously created* matter.

§ 3. Thus we have Arius' account of his own views: now let us turn to the letter of Alexander to his namesake and see how

[1] Theodoret, *H. E.* I. 5. The words are very difficult. ἀειγενής (or ἀγεννής) ἐστιν, ἀγεννητογενής ἐστιν, "came into being without being begotten." This misrepresented the orthodox view.

[2] i.e. that God who is ἄναρχος precedes the Son.

[3] Most of these words come from Proverbs vii. 22, Κύριος ἔκτισέ με ἀρχὴν ὁδῶν αὐτοῦ εἰς ἔργα αὐτοῦ, πρὸ τοῦ αἰῶνος ἐθεμελίωσέ με, &c.

he represented these views and resisted them. He says (p. 10[1]) that

Arius and his friends did in fact deny the deity (τὴν θεότητα) of the Saviour, and preached that He was merely equal to any one else; they collected out of Scripture all the passages which speak of His incarnation and humiliation, and turned away from those which tell of His Godhead from the beginning, and of His unceasing glory with the Father. "We have therefore driven them out of the Church which adores the Deity of Christ. They are now wandering about, concealing their true sentiments and inducing other bishops to subscribe to their statements, and to receive them into the Church (p. 11)—which these bishops ought not to do, opposed as such action is to the Apostolic Canon. It is therefore my duty at once to inform you of the character of their unbelief, for they say there was a time[2] when the Son of God was not, and He who at first did not subsist afterwards came into being, becoming, when at last He came into being, such as every man is by nature. For (they say) God made all things out of things which are not, and they include even the Son of God within the creation of 'all things reasonable and unreasonable.' And, following out this, they say that He is of a nature mutable, being capable both of virtue and of vice; and then, on this hypothesis of theirs, they sweep away all those Scriptures which speak of Him as ever being and teach the unchangeable character of the Word and the Godhead of the Wisdom of the Word, which is the Christ; and these braggarts say that we too have the power to become Sons of God, even as He. For it is written, *I have begotten and brought up Sons*, and when we allege against them the rest of the verse *and they have despised me* (which is not suited to the nature of the Saviour), they reply that God, foreseeing and foreknowing that *He* will not despise Him, chose Him to Himself out of all. For they say He chose Him, not as being by nature and specially different from others (for they say no one by nature is a Son of God), nor yet as having any peculiar characteristic of His own; but as being indeed of a nature capable of change, yet by the carefulness of his habits and self-discipline never changing to the worse. Thus they act insolently towards the Scriptures, quoting the Psalm, *Thou hast loved righteousness, &c., therefore God anointed Thee with the oil of gladness above Thy fellows.*"

And now Alexander proceeds to shew how irreconcileable the views of these men are with Scripture. He quotes (p. 12) the words

"*The only-begotten Son who is in the bosom of the Father*, to shew that the Father and Son cannot be separated. Inconsistent with this verse is the conception that there was a time when He was not, and that He had been made of things which are not. Again the same John says *all things were made through Him*: to shew the peculiarity of His hypostasis, he says, *In the beginning was the Word and the Word was with God, and the Word was God. All things were made through Him, and without Him*

[1] I make my abstract from the copy in Theodoret. The references are to Reading's edition of Valèsius, as given by Dr Gaisford.

[2] I am obliged so to represent ἦν ποτὲ ὅτε οὐκ ἦν ὁ υἱὸς τοῦ Θεοῦ.

was made no single thing[1]. For if all things were made by Him, how could there be a time when He who gave to all things their being, Himself was not?" And he proceeds to argue that "the Word made all things out of things which are not; and *that which is*, τὸ ὄν, is essentially opposed to *things which are not*, τὰ οὐκ ὄντα. For there is no interval (διάστημα) between the Father and the Son, and the creation of the universe out of things which are not was by the Father through the Son. And thus, seeing how entirely above all human conception is the 'was' (τὸ ἦν) of the Son, S. John, in the depth of his reverence, shrank from speaking both of his Genesis and Making[2], not venturing to describe the Maker in the same terms as the things which are created—not because the Word is Unbegotten, for the Father is the only Being Unbegotten—but because the inexplicable Hypostasis of the only-begotten God exceeds the comprehension of the evangelists and perhaps the angels also. Let us remember, *Do not seek things too hard for thee, and things too high for thee do not investigate.*" And he quotes the words of S. Paul, 1 Cor. ii. 9, *things which eye hath not seen*, &c.; and Gen. xv. 5, *Canst thou count the stars?* and Ecclus. i. 2, *Who can number the sands of the sea?* and then, as it were *a fortiori*, the well-known words of Isaiah, *His generation who can declare?* and once more, *No one knoweth who the Son is but the Father, and who the Father is but the Son;* and the curious version of Isai. xxiv. 16, *My mystery is for me and mine.* Alexander proceeds (p. 13, l. 25) "If then all things were made through Him, then must all age and time and intervals, and the time or 'once,' in which 'was not' is found[3], have been made through Him. Yea (p. 14), according to them the Scripture speaks falsely, which describes Him as *the first-born of every creature*[4]. Consentient with this is Paul again when he says, *Whom He appointed heir of all things, by whom also He made the ages:* and again, *In Him all things were created, things in heaven and things on earth......and He is before all things.* It follows of necessity that the Father was always Father. For He is Father, seeing that the Son is always present, because of whom He is called Father. He is perfect Father: we can conceive of no time or interval when He is not Father; nor yet was it out of things which are not that He begat the Son." And so Alexander proceeds: "If the express Image of God was not ever, then He was not ever of Whom Christ is the express Image." Again (p. 15) "Christ is God's own Son. The Father said, *This is my beloved Son: the* LORD *said to me, Thou art my Son.* Once more: *From the womb before the day star I begat thee*[5]. And (p. 16) what can we say of the Saviour's words, *I and the Father are one.* He speaks this, not calling Himself Father, nor yet signifying that the natures are one, which in the Hypostases are two, but because the Son of the Father preserves accurately the likeness of the Father; so much so, that when Philip was anxious to see the Father, the Saviour said, *He that hath seen Me hath seen the Father*, the Father being seen, as it were, through

1. None of the manuscripts adds ὃ γέγονεν.

2 i.e. as I understand ποίησις, His making of the world.

3 διαστήματα καὶ τὸ πότε ἐν οἷς τὸ οὐκ ἦν εὑρίσκεται: i.e. all the things which correspond to the Arian phrases were made by Him.

4 Clearly the bishop understood this as we do, "Born before all creation."

5 Psalm cx. = cix. 3 according to the Septuagint.

an unstained spotless mirror, through a living divine image. Thus *he that honoureth the Son, honoureth the Father also.*"

And at last (p. 17) he comes to the question of antiquity:

"Are they not put to shame by the clear meaning of Holy Scripture? Is not their boldness against Christ reduced to nought by the consentient piety of their fellow-ministers? They say that we, when we refuse to accept their impious and unwritten blasphemy of the 'things which are not,' maintain that there are two unbegotten principles, putting the alternative thus,—either Christ is of things which are not, or there are two Beings unbegotten—ignorant how vast is the distance between the unbegotten Father and the things, reasonable and unreasonable, which were created by Him out of things which are not, and how, mediating between these, the only-begotten Nature—through which the Father of God the Word made all things out of things which are not—has been begotten from the Father Himself ὁ ὤν WHO IS."

And then (p. 18) the Bishop comes to the Creed, the authorized symbol (apparently) of his Church, which he explains with a running commentary, sufficient to shew how far the theological questions of the day had outrun the traditional form. I will content myself now with a brief analysis of this comment:

"We believe (he says, p. 18), as the Apostolic Church teaches, in one unbegotten Father, having no cause of His Being, ever the same, admitting neither of augmentation nor of diminution...and in one Lord Jesus Christ, the only-begotten Son of God; begotten, not of anything which is not, but of the Father WHO IS, in a way, which is beyond our power to conceive or describe: His hypostasis cannot be searched out, any more than can that of the Father, because the nature of reasonable creatures cannot embrace the knowledge of the Father's Theogony. He is in all points like the Father except in this point of His generation... And (p. 19, l. 33) in addition to this pious belief concerning the Father and the Son, we confess, as the Holy Scriptures teach us, one Holy Spirit who moved both the holy men of the Old Testament, and the divine teachers of what is called the New: one only Catholic—I mean, the Apostolic—Church, which cannot be overthrown even if the whole world should agree to fight against it. After this we know the resurrection from the dead, of which our Lord Jesus Christ has been the first fruits, having a body truly and not in appearance from Mary, the Mother of God; who in the consummation of the ages came to the race of men to put away sin; who died and was crucified—not because of this becoming less in His deity—who rose from the dead, was taken up into heaven, was seated at the right hand of majesty...These things we teach; these things we preach; these, the apostolic dogmas of the Church, and for these we are prepared to die. And it was because Arius and the rest opposed them that they were anathematised, according to the words of S. Paul *If any one teach any other gospel than that which ye have received let him be anathema, even if he pretend to be an angel from heaven.*"

And in conclusion Alexander gives the names of the nine deacons who were anathematised with the presbyter Arius[1].

§ 4. The account given by Eusebius of the proceedings of the Council of Nicæa in this respect is well known. This account was considered to be so important, that not only did the historians Socrates and Theodoret embody it in their works, but Athanasius himself deemed it desirable to place on record the words with which the panegyrist of Constantine had signified his assent to the declaration of the Council. He appended it to his Letter on the Decrees of the Nicene Council[2]. Eusebius described the willingness of Constantine to accept the Creed which he had adduced, *i.e.* the Creed of Cæsarea, the Creed (as Dean Stanley reminds us) of the Church of Palestine: but the majority were determined to introduce the word *ὁμοούσιος*, and under this pretext (he says) they framed the writing.

§ 5. A letter of Athanasius, written forty-four years after the Council, furnishes some details as to the discussion, which call for some consideration from us. But I must interrupt the narrative for the purpose of exhibiting together the Creed of Cæsarea and the Creed of the Council, the parts common to the two will go across the page, subordinate alterations will be found in the notes:

πιστεύομεν εἰς ἕνα θεὸν πατέρα παντοκράτορα
τὸν τῶν ἁπάντων | πάντων
ὁρατῶν τε καὶ ἀοράτων ποιητήν.
καὶ εἰς ἕνα Κύριον Ἰησοῦν Χριστὸν

[1] Dr Hahn, who gives only the portions of this letter which contain the Creed, notes that the characteristic form of the Oriental symbols is manifested here, for Alexander brings out only the essential ingredients of the Baptismal confession (compare above, p. 21) which, as we have seen, was in Jerusalem and elsewhere much briefer than the Creed at large. He compares it with the Carthaginian form as given in Tertullian, with the Rule of Faith as found in Origen, and with an interesting passage in Clemens Alex. *Strom.* VII. p. 764 on the unity of the Church. To me this Creed is of further interest: it seems to have a resemblance to the Coptic form as given above: for it commences with brief notes on the three Persons of the Trinity, and, after speaking of the Church and the Resurrection, it concludes with articles relating to our Lord: as if these had been an after thought. (We shall find hereafter Rules of Faith of similar character.) It has also an interesting resemblance to one of the Rules given by Irenæus.

[2] Migne, XXV. pp. 415—477, who however does not print it there. It may be seen in Mr Harvey's *Ecclesiæ Anglicanæ Vindex Catholicus*, Vol. I. p. 539, and is translated in the "Oxford translation" of Athanasius' works.

<table>
<tr><td>τὸν τοῦ Θεοῦ λόγον</td><td>τὸν υἱὸν τοῦ Θεοῦ γεννηθέντα ἐκ τοῦ Πατρὸς μονογενῆ τουτέστιν ἐκ τῆς οὐσίας τοῦ πατρός,</td></tr>
<tr><td colspan="2">Θεὸν ἐκ Θεοῦ, φῶς ἐκ φωτός,</td></tr>
<tr><td></td><td>Θεὸν ἀληθινὸν ἐκ Θεοῦ ἀληθινοῦ,
γεννηθέντα οὐ ποιηθέντα, ὁμοούσιον τῷ πατρί,</td></tr>
<tr><td>ζωὴν ἐκ ζωῆς,
υἱὸν μονογενῆ,
πρωτότοκον πάσης κτίσεως,
πρὸ πάντων τῶν αἰώνων ἐκ τοῦ Πατρὸς γεγεννημένον,</td><td></td></tr>
<tr><td colspan="2">δι' οὗ καὶ[1] ἐγένετο τὰ πάντα</td></tr>
<tr><td></td><td>τά τε ἐν τῷ οὐρανῷ καὶ τὰ ἐπὶ τῆς γῆς,</td></tr>
<tr><td colspan="2">τὸν</td></tr>
<tr><td></td><td>δι' ἡμᾶς ἀνθρώπους καὶ</td></tr>
<tr><td colspan="2">διὰ τὴν ἡμετέραν σωτηρίαν</td></tr>
<tr><td></td><td>κατελθόντα καὶ</td></tr>
<tr><td colspan="2">σαρκωθέντα καὶ</td></tr>
<tr><td>ἐν ἀνθρώποις πολιτευσάμενον καὶ</td><td>ἐνανθρωπήσαντα</td></tr>
<tr><td colspan="2">παθόντα· καὶ ἀναστάντα τῇ τρίτῃ ἡμέρᾳ καὶ ἀνελθόντα</td></tr>
<tr><td>πρὸς τὸν πατέρα καὶ ἥξοντα πάλιν ἐν δόξῃ</td><td>εἰς τοὺς οὐράνους καὶ ἐρχόμενον</td></tr>
<tr><td colspan="2">κρῖναι ζῶντας καὶ νεκρούς·</td></tr>
<tr><td>πιστεύομεν καὶ εἰς ἓν πνεῦμα ἅγιον.</td><td>καὶ εἰς τὸ ἅγιον πνεῦμα.</td></tr>
</table>

The anathematism follows in the Nicene formula:

τοὺς δὲ λέγοντας ὅτι ἦν ποτε ὅτε οὐκ ἦν, καὶ πρὶν γεννηθῆναι οὐκ ἦν, καὶ ὅτι ἐξ οὐκ ὄντων ἐγένετο, ἢ ἐξ ἑτέρας ὑποστάσεως ἢ οὐσίας φάσκοντας εἶναι, ἢ κτιστόν, τρεπτὸν ἢ ἀλλοιωτὸν τὸν υἱὸν τοῦ Θεοῦ, ἀναθεματίζει ἡ καθολικὴ [καὶ ἀποστολικὴ] ἐκκλησία[2].

[1] The Nicene Creed omits *καὶ* and reads *τὰ πάντα ἐγένετο*.

[2] The Nicene Creed is found (1) in Eusebius' letter to the Church of Cæsa-

§ 6. What was the object of the framers of the Nicene Creed? It was never quoted, so far as I know, at least for centuries, without the anathematism. Yet with the anathematism it is clearly unfitted for liturgical use; unfitted, it would seem, even for use at baptism. What was the object of it?

§ 7. Athanasius in his letter to the African bishops, to which I have already referred, gives us a plain answer to the question. It was prepared to be subscribed at the council, being so worded that none of the followers of Arius could subscribe it. It was intended to be made a declaration of the faith of the Church with reference to the points then in controversy; and the conversation and countenances of the Arian bishops were carefully watched, as every proposal was made, to see whether they were satisfied or dissatisfied with that proposal. If they were satisfied, the proposal was further altered: if they were dissatisfied, it was retained.

The account is curious; so curious, that part of it was extracted by Theodoret from the letter to the Africans and embodied in his *Ecclesiastical History*. I will transfer the chief portions to my pages.

The object of Athanasius when he wrote this letter (it is supposed to have been written about the year 369, only four years before his death) was to induce the African bishops to contend still for the words of the Creed, not for the sake of the words alone, but for the sake of the meaning which those words conveyed. The Arians were indeed the cause for the introduction of the words. And he would give an account of them that all might know the principles which had guided the Synod. "First they were determined to put out of the way those impious phrases

rea, (2) in Athanasius' letter to Jovianus, (3) in S. Basil, letter cxxv., (4) in Cyril of Alexandria, letter to Anastasius, (5) Eutyches quoted it (Council of Chalcedon), (6) in Theodotus of Ancyra against Nestorius, (7) in the Codex Canonum of the African Church, (8) again and again in later councils. I have never seen it without the anathematism. Sozomen (*H. E.* I. 20) writing about the year 440 has an interesting account: "At one time I thought it desirable with a view to the manifestation of the truth to append the writing itself—in order that the symbol of the Faith which then met with universal approbation (τὸ σύμβολον τῆς τότε συναρεσάσης πίστεως) might be made firm and plain for all future people. But since some friends of piety, acquainted with such things as (they suggested) ought to be spoken and heard only by the initiated and by those who act as initiators, advised me to withhold the symbol, I have followed their advice. For it is not improbable that even some of the uninitiated may meet with this book."

The notice is interesting. It is the earliest passage that I know in which the Faith of Nicæa is called the Symbol of the Faith; and here it is connected with the conception of initiation and mystery. The friends of Sozomen forgot for the moment that an unbaptized emperor had assisted at the framing of the symbol.

which the Arians had introduced: such as the words 'of things which are not,' saying that the Son was a Thing created or made, and that there was a time when He was not and that He is of a changed nature. This they did by the anathematism at the end. Then there came under discussion the phrase 'Of God, only begotten' which was adopted. The Eusebians assented. But they talked to each other: 'Let us agree to this, for *we* are of God, for there is one God *of whom are all things*.' So the bishops seeing their craftiness stated more plainly what they meant by the words 'Of God,' and wrote that the Son was *of* (ἐκ) *the essence or substance of the Father*, to exclude this explanation of the Arians: for this latter phrase can hold only of the True and Only-begotten Word." Such was the reason for the introduction of the words *of the substance*[1]. "Again, when the bishops asked the minority whether they would say that the Son was not a creature, but the power, the only wisdom of the Father, His eternal image, unchangeable in every respect like the Father and very God, the Eusebians were detected making signs to each other that this too is true of us, for we too are called the image and glory of God, and of us it is said *We who are alive are always*[2] and there are many 'powers:' nay, we hold ourselves to be the 'own[3]' of God, not absolutely, but because He calls us brethren. And if they call the Son *true God* or *very God* it does not hurt us: for whatever He is, that He is 'very' and true.

"The bishops discovered their scheme, and so they considered together passages of Scripture, and finally wrote more clearly and concisely that the Son is ὁμοούσιος with the Father. And when the complaint was made that this word was not a scriptural word, they replied that neither were the Arian phrases scriptural. At all events (says Athanasius) for a hundred and thirty years bishops both of old Rome and our own city have used the word, finding fault with any who maintained that the Son was a creature and not *homöusios* with the Father, and something like this Eusebius admitted in his letter to the people of Cæsarea."

§ 8. We have thus traced the Nicene Creed to its completion: and it must, I think, be acknowledged that the whole history shews that it was intended at first to be a Rule of Faith, not a Symbol to be used by the newly baptized or to be proposed to them. A few remarks on the phrases contained in it, as they were explained by Athanasius himself, may conclude this chapter.

§ 9. (1) The words *He is immutable* have the following meaning, "Men are called upon to *become* perfect, to *become* merciful; the Son of God *is* so. He does not become in this

[1] These words are now excluded from the Creed.

[2] ἀεὶ γὰρ ἡμεῖς οἱ ζῶντες, 2 Cor. iv. 11 (!)

[3] Of course referring to "His own Son."

respect different from what He is: with Him, as with the Father, there is no variableness nor shadow of turning."

(2) "God says in Exodus, I am ὁ ὤν. Now hypostasis is the same as οὐσία, and means nothing else than τὸ ὄν, THE EXISTENT. Thus the terms ἐκ τῆς οὐσίας αὐτοῦ mean 'of God's essence' and are contrasted with the Arian statement that the Son came into being out of things which had no existence—ἐξ οὐκ ὄντων."

(3) The word ὁμοούσιος is justified by the words of Scripture, "I and the Father are one:" "He that hath seen Me hath seen the Father."

(4) The above statements carry with them the condemnation of all who affirm that the Son is ἐξ ἑτέρας οὐσίας ἢ ὑποστάσεως, "of an essence or hypostasis different from the Father's."

(5) Athanasius concludes by saying that the words "We believe in the Holy Ghost," are alone sufficient to overthrow all who blaspheme against the Holy Spirit: they shew that "the Nicene Fathers confessed fully and completely the Faith in the Holy Trinity, and thus manifested both the character of the Christian faith and the teaching of the Catholic Church in this behalf. For it is clear that we cannot have faith in a creature, but only in one God the Father Almighty, Maker of all things, visible and invisible; and in one Lord Jesus Christ His only-begotten Son; and in one Holy Spirit: (that is) one God known in the holy and perfect Trinity: into this faith being baptized, and in it united to the Godhead, we believe that we shall also inherit the kingdom of heaven in Christ Jesus our Lord, through whom be ascribed to the Father all glory and might, for ever and ever, Amen[1]."

[1] The brief baptismal faith should be noticed.

With the words relating to the Holy Spirit, which I have quoted from Athanasius' letter to the African bishops, may be compared the following concluding words of his letter to Jovianus. "In this faith, Augustus, as being divine and apostolic, it is necessary that all should abide, and that no one should disturb it by persuasive arguments and logomachies, the very thing that the Arians have done......Because of their assertions the Synod held at Nicæa anathematised heresy like theirs, and confessed the Faith of the Truth. For it did not say that the Son was merely similar to the Father, its object being that He should be believed to be not merely similar to God, but very God of God: but it described Him as Homöusios, which is the property of the own and very Son, of the true and natural Father. Nor yet did it treat the Holy Spirit as alien from the Father and the Son, but rather it glorified Him with the Father and the Son in the one Faith of the Holy Trinity, because there is one Godhead in the Holy Trinity." So the faith of the Nicene Confession, as distinct from its anathema, is called thus early THE FAITH OF THE HOLY TRINITY.

§ 10. It must be remembered that the date assigned to this remarkable letter is 369, *i.e.* forty-four years after the assembly had separated whose proceedings Athanasius here records; four years, as I have said, before his own death. We have, therefore, here a distinct proof of the great bishop's own satisfaction with the Faith of the Council; enunciated as distinctly as we find it in his letter to the Emperor Jovianus, written six years earlier[1]. With this the suggestion of our great divine, Archbishop Usher, seems to be inconsistent, viz. that the fathers who met at Nicæa had, before they separated, modified the Creed, making it resemble the document which we are in the habit of attributing to the Council of Constantinople; equally inconsistent with it is the tradition that Athanasius wrote the Athanasian Creed. The piety of Jovianus led him to enquire what was the Faith of the Catholic Church. Athanasius replied that the Churches of Spain and Britain and Gaul, of all Italy, Dalmatia and Dacia, Mysia, Macedonia, Greece and all Africa, Sardinia, Cyprus, Crete, Pamphylia, Lycia, and Isauria, and the Churches of Egypt and the Libyas, of Pontus and Cappadocia, and the Churches of the East, except a few which held Arian views, all accepted the Faith which was confessed at Nicæa. And he once more transcribed the Creed.

It will be noticed that the Church of Jerusalem is not mentioned[2].

§ 11. One point more is worthy of attention. We know from the lectures of St Cyril of Jerusalem that the true baptismal confession in that city was this: "I believe in the name of the Father, and of the Son, and of the Holy Spirit." The concluding words which I have quoted from the letter of Athanasius to the African bishops seem to me to point to the same interpretation. This confirms the opinion I have already expressed, that the Nicene Confession was intended for theologians not for neophytes: for the guidance of the bishops and the clergy, not for the instruction of children. Much as we may respect the learning of those times, and high opinion as we may have of the intellectual

[1] The letter is well known. See Migne, XXVI. p. 813. It is contained in Theodoret, *H. E.* IV. c. 3.

[2] There was an Arianizing synod held at Jerusalem about the year 335 on the occasion of the dedication of the Church of the Martyrdom.

education given in the Alexandrian and other schools, we can scarcely conceive that they were preparing the members of the flock at large to understand the mysteries of words which, years afterwards, Athanasius felt himself compelled to explain to the bishops of Africa.

There is no proof that this Nicene Faith was ever used in what we should call public worship. The Church of Armenia, however, uses a Creed resembling it; the anathematism at the end including those who profane the Holy Spirit[1]. But of this below.

[1] See Mr Malan's *Divine Liturgy of the Armenian Church*, David Nutt, p. 32.

CHAPTER VII.

OTHER CREEDS OF THE FOURTH CENTURY.

§ 1. Frequency and nature of these. § 2. The exposition of his faith attributed to Athanasius. Routh *Opus*. Vol. II. § 3. Intense interest of this. § 4. Examination of it. § 5. Fresh examination of the Nicene Faith. § 6. Defects subsequently remedied. § 7. Comparison with Creed of St Cyril. § 8. The Ecthesis Macrostichus. § 9. Synod of Sardica.

§ 1. THE fourth century was a century for creeds; but these creeds, in their history, resemble rather the confessions of the Reformation period than symbola for the baptized. They were the Faiths of the respective synods or councils. Athanasius amuses us with this: he says that the bishops who met at the synods at Ariminum and Seleucia and elsewhere, did not say, "thus we believe;" but "the Catholic faith was set forth" on such a year and month and day, "thus proving, without gainsaying, that they began to believe thus on the day and year named." For example: "the Catholic faith was set forth in the presence of our lord the most pious and victorious Constantine Augustus, in the consulate of Flavius, Eusebius, and Hypatius; in Sirmium, on the eleventh of the Calends of June." The great bishop gives eleven forms of Arian creeds[1]. Of course I need not delay my readers over them. There is no pretence that they ever gained any general circulation; but the struggle which they had for existence, and the effort which was used to displace by one or other of them the Nicene formula, enables us to learn more clearly

[1] In the treatise *de Synodis* Dr Hahn reckons up four Antiochene forms, pp. 148—157 (the last being the "Ecthesis Macrostichus"), one adopted at a Synod at Philippopolis A.D. 347, p. 158 (given by Hilary of Poictiers): three Sirmian pp. 160—169. The third is interesting as enunciating for the first time in a Creed that our Lord went down to hell, εἰς τὰ καταχθόνια κατελθόντα. On p. 169 Hahn gives the formula of the Synod at Nicé in Thrace, A.D. 359 (from Theodoret): p. 171 that of Seleucia in Isauria of the same year: p. 173 that of Constantinople in 360 (it is to this that Ulphilas subscribed).

what the true object of the Nicene Confession was: it was to be used as a test, to be subscribed by bishops in proof of their orthodoxy. Some of these documents have laboured appendages, written apparently to shew an approach, as near as possible, to the Nicene Creed, without adopting the test words ἐκ τῆς οὐσίας and ὁμοούσιος. One of them has twenty-seven anathemas.

§ 2. More interesting to us, perhaps, is the fact, that Athanasius himself is considered to have set forth an "exposition of his faith," which is accepted as a genuine work by the Benedictine editors (Migne, Vol. xxv. p. 197); and their acceptance is quoted unhesitatingly by the learned Dr Routh,—who deemed the document so important that he printed it at length in the second volume of the *Scriptorum Ecclesiasticorum Opuscula præcipua quædam*. I can scarcely believe it to be authentic, although it is possible that Athanasius may have adopted the work of another. Facundus of Hermiane, who lived about the year 547—two hundred years later than the Nicene Council—called the document "an exposition of the symbol[1]."

My collection of orthodox rules of faith would be incomplete without it, and I will therefore give a translation of it: especially since an imperfect and misleading version has been recently printed[2].

I may notice in passing that the Church has never assigned any authority to this exposition, although it is believed to be a work of Athanasius. Perhaps we may be able to give some good reasons for this neglect. It begins:

"i. We believe in one God unbegotten, Father Almighty, Maker of all things both visible and invisible, who has His Being from Himself: and in one only-begotten Word, Wisdom, Son, having been begotten from the Father without beginning and eternally: Word[3]—not as uttered language not yet as internal Reason, not an effluence of the Perfect One, not a division of the impassible nature, nor a projection, but Son, self-

[1] In Suicer's *Thesaurus* the word ἔκθεσις is interpreted by *Formula doctrinæ* and some have thought that the word is equivalent to a Creed. This is not accurately true. Only very careless writers would use ἡ πίστις and ἡ ἔκθεσις τῆς πίστεως as equivalent terms. The latter is the setting out of the Faith in words few or many: and the mode in which the Faith is thus set out will in each case exhibit whether the *exposition* is an explanation or not. I suppose when Facundus called this document an *expositio symboli* he conceived that it was an exposition of the Creed in the modern sense of the word exposition. And so it is.

[2] In a book entitled "Athanasius contra Mundum" by William J. Irons, D.D. Prebendary of St Paul's.

[3] λόγον οὐ προφορικόν, οὐκ ἐνδιάθετον.

perfect, living and working, the very image of the Father, equal in honour, equal in glory[1], for *this* (He says) *is the will of the Father, that as they honour the Father, so should they honour the Son also.* Very God of very God, as John says in the Catholic epistles, *We are in the very* [True] One *in His Son Jesus Christ: This is the very God and eternal life.* Almighty of Almighty, for over all things over which the Father has rule and might, the Son also has rule and might: complete of complete; being like the Father, as the Lord saith, *He that hath seen Me hath seen the Father.* But He was begotten in a way beyond expression and beyond conception, for *His generation who shall declare?* This means that no one can. Who in the consummation of the ages[2], coming down from the bosom of the Father, did, of the undefiled Virgin Mary, take on Himself our Man, Christ Jesus, whom, for our sakes, He delivered[3] up to suffer, of His own free will, as saith the Lord, *No one taketh My Life from Me: I have power to lay it down and I have power to take it again:* in which Man[3], being crucified, and having died for us, He rose from the dead, and was taken up into heaven: being *created for us the beginning of* (God's) *ways*[4]: being on earth He shewed us darkness from light, salvation from error, life from death, entrance into the paradise from which Adam was cast out, into which he (Adam or man?) again entered by means of the thief, as saith the Lord, *To-day thou shalt be with me in Paradise:* into which Paul too entered. He shewed us also His ascent into heaven where the forerunner entered for us, the Lordly Man[5], in whom He is coming to judge quick and dead.

"ii. We believe likewise in the Holy Spirit who searcheth all things, even the deep things of God, anathematising the dogmas which are opposed to this: for we neither conceive a Son-Father as the Sabellians, who say that He is (*μονοούσιον οὐχ ὁμοούσιον*) of one only essence not coessential[6] and thus deprive Him of His Sonship. Neither do we assign to the Father the passible body which He bare for the salvation of the whole world; nor are we to conceive three Hypostases separated from each other[7] as is the case with bodily natures among men—in order that we may not introduce polytheism as the heathen do: but as a river, although begotten from a fountain, is not separated from it, though there chance to be two forms[8] and two names. For neither is the Father Son, nor is the Son Father. For the Father is Father of the Son, and the Son is Son of the Father. For as the fountain is not the river, nor the river the fountain, but both are one and the same water which is derived from the fountain into the river, so is the Godhead from the Father to the Son derived, though without flux and without separation. For the Lord saith: *I came from the Father and am come.* But He is ever with the Father who is *in the bosom of the Father:* for never was the bosom of the Father rendered empty of the Godhead of the Son: for he saith *I have been with Him as harmonizing with Him.* But we do not conceive Him to be a thing created or made, or to be out of things which are not—

[1] *ἰσότιμον καὶ ἰσόδοξον.*

[2] The words of Hebrews ix. 26.

[3] Note this.

[4] Prov. viii. 22.

[5] Or the Man of the Lord; the Lord's Man: *i.e.* the Man whom the Lord associated with Him.

[6] Note this. Whoever wrote this could not have attained the more recent conception of *ὁμοούσιος*.

[7] *μεμερισμένας καθ' ἑαυτάς.*

[8] *σχήματα* (not *μορφαί*).

Who is the Creator of the Universe; God the Son of God; who is from Him that is, the only from the only, for whom[1] from everlasting was there from the Father equal glory and power engendered with Him: for *he that hath seen the Son hath seen the Father.* For, as we all know, *all things were created through the Son:* and He is not Himself a created thing, for Paul says concerning the Lord: *In Him were all things created, and He is before all things.* He does not say that He was created before all things, but that *He is before all things:* the conception of *created* attaches to *all things*, but that of *is before all things* belongs to the Son alone.

"iii. He is therefore an offspring (γέννημα), naturally Perfect from the Perfect, begotten *before all the hills* (Prov. viii. 25 or 26), that is, before every reasonable and intelligent nature, as in another place he says *The First-born of every creature.* When he calls Him *First-born* he signifies that He is not a thing created, but is offspring of God: for to be called a thing created is strange with reference to His Deity. For *all things were created by the Father through the Son*, but the Son alone was begotten from the Father in eternity: wherefore God the Word is *first-born of every creature*, unchangeable from the unchangeable. But the body which He bare for our sakes is a thing created: concerning it Jeremiah[2] speaks thus, according to the translation of the Septuagint, *the Lord created for us for a planting a new salvation, in which salvation men will go about.* But, according to Aquila, the passage means *the Lord created a new thing in the woman.* Now that salvation, which was created for us for a *planting*, being new and not old, *for us* and not *before us*, is Jesus, who, with reference to the Saviour, became a man (Ἰησοῦς ἐστιν ὁ κατὰ τὸν Σωτῆρα γενόμενος ἄνθρωπος)[3], which word, *Jesus*, is interpreted in one place *Salvation*, in another *Saviour:* and salvation is from the Saviour, just as enlightening comes from the light. That Salvation from the Saviour being created new *did*, as Jeremiah says, *create for us a new salvation*, and as Aquila says *the Lord created a new thing in the woman*, i. e. in the Virgin Mary. For nothing was created new in the woman, except the Lordly body[4] which was born of the Virgin Mary without intercourse with man: as in the book of Proverbs also in the person of Jesus, it says *the Lord created me the beginning of His ways, for His works.* It does not say, *Before His works He created me*, lest any should refer the word *created* to the Deity of the Son.

"iv. Both passages therefore which speak of a thing created, were written with reference to Jesus, bodily: for the Lordly Man was created *the beginning of God's ways*, which Man He manifested for our salvation. *Through Him we have our access to the Father.* For He is *the way* which leadeth us to the Father. But a way is a kind of material visible thing (σωματικόν τι θέαμα), and such a way is the Lordly Man. At all events the Word of God created all things, not as being Himself a thing created, but as being offspring of God. For no created thing created anything equal to or like unto itself: but to the Father

[1] This ᾧ is a conjecture of the Benedictines for ὡς and is approved by Routh. But ὡς seems to make sense here, and I must say I prefer it.

[2] Jerem. xxxviii. 22 = xxxi. 22.

[3] Such, as I learn from Dr Routh, was the interpretation of Facundus: the words are capable of another meaning.

[4] τὸ κυριακὸν σῶμα.

belongs τὸ γεννᾶν the producing as offspring; to the Maker, the creating. At all events that Body which was borne for our sakes by the Lord is a thing made and created, which body *was begotten*[1] *for us* (as says Paul) *of God wisdom and sanctification and righteousness and redemption:* even though, before us and every creature, the Word was and is the *Wisdom of God.* But the Holy Spirit being a Thing Proceeding of the Father (ἐκπόρευμα ὂν τοῦ πατρός) is always in the hands of the Father who sends Him, and of the Son who conveys Him, through whom *He filled all things.* The Father containing from Himself His Being, begat the Son—as we have said, but did not create Him—as a river is from the fountain, a bud from the root, and as a brightness from the light,—things which nature knows to be unseparated from their source; through whom be glory, might, majesty to the Father, from all ages to all ages, and ever and ever."

§ 3. That this document is of deep interest in the history of theological science no one will hesitate to allow who will examine it carefully. It has been said, indeed, by a recent writer, that "it would almost seem as though this Ecthesis were, together with the Nicene Creed, a study—*the foundation of the entire Quicunque vult,* the doctrine being the same throughout, and the special terms of the theology sometimes almost identical." I am not yet intending to treat of the Quicunque: let us however examine the statements of the Ecthesis in the light of history.

§ 4. "The Word of God was begotten of the Father before all ages, and He is ὁμοούσιος with the Father." This is Catholic.

"The Body which He bare was *created* in the womb of the Virgin." This is now deemed erroneous.

"The Word took our Man of the undefiled Virgin, even Christ Jesus." This may be Nestorian.

"This man, Christ Jesus, the Word delivered up to suffer and be crucified." Thus the Word did not suffer.

"In this man being crucified and having died, He rose again."

"In this man," the Dominicus homo, of Augustine[2], the κυρίακος ἄνθρωπος, the Lordly Man, or the Lord's Man, "He is coming to judge." Surely two Personalities are taught here.

[1] ὃ ἐγεννήθη—as is requisite for the argument. But all the MSS. of 1 Cor. i. 30 have ὃς ἐγενήθη (see note 3, p. 78).

[2] Augustine used the words "Dominicus homo" (*de Sermone Domini in Monte*, Vol. III. part ii. p. 207): "No one will be ignorant of the kingdom of GOD, when His only-begotten Son, visible not only to the eye of the mind but also to the eye of the body, shall come from heaven, *in homine Dominico*, in the Lordly Man, to judge the quick and dead." But although the words were (he said) sanctioned by Catholic writers, he wished he had not used them (*Retract.* I. c. xix. 8, Vol. I. p. 30), "I have seen that they ought not to be used, although they may be defended with some reason."

"He bare a passible body for the salvation of the world."

"He was not created, but His Body was a thing created."

"The Lord's Body was created in the Virgin:" this is the interpretation of Prov. viii. 22: κύριος ἔκτισέ με ἀρχὴν ὁδῶν αὐτοῦ, and of Jeremiah xxxviii. (= xxxi.) 22.

The teaching regarding the Holy Spirit is very defective[1].

The Benedictine editors, and Dr Routh, defend the expression ὁ κυριακὸς ἄνθρωπος, on the ground that it is used also by Epiphanius and Cassian, and the corresponding *Dominicus homo* by Augustine. These writers wished it to be understood that Athanasius by ἄνθρωπος understood ἀνθρωπότης.

We must however remember first that Augustine, Athanasius, Epiphanius, and Cassian, all lived and wrote before the Council of Ephesus, A.D. 431. And secondly, that to Athanasius, at least in his later days (see his treatise *de Incarnatione*, written about 364), the word ἀνθρωπότης, manhood, was familiar. What can we say, therefore, of the use here of ἄνθρωπος, "the Man"? I can only answer that if, when he used the word *man*, the writer of this Exposition meant *manhood*, he was very careless and very misleading. As the document comes to us, it may be quoted in support of Apollinarianism, but its statements are scarcely consistent with our belief that the Son of God "was made Man:" it may be quoted in support of Nestorianism, because it almost openly teaches that the union of the Divine nature with the man Christ Jesus took place after the birth from Mary.

§ 5. We may now go back to the true Nicene Creed, and examine the clauses in it which bear upon these points.

Τὸν δι' ἡμᾶς τοὺς ἀνθρώπους καὶ διὰ τὴν ἡμέτεραν σωτηρίαν κατελθόντα καὶ σαρκωθέντα καὶ ἐνανθρωπήσαντα: "Who for us men, and for our salvation, came down, and was incarnate, and entered on man."

Is there anything here inconsistent and irreconcileable with the erroneous views with which the words of the Ecthesis may be charged?

I see none. Ἐνανθρωπήσαντα certainly is not inconsistent with Nestorianism, nor is σαρκωθέντα. The author of that

[1] See below, section 8, the ἔκθεσις μακρόστιχος.

wonderfully learned book, of which I give the title in my note[1], quotes "Joan. Garsias Loaisa" as remarking that before the condemnation of Eutyches and Nestorius, the ordinary use of the Fathers, Augustine, Ambrose, Origen, Jerome, Gregory of Nyssa, Hilary (we find it even in the sixth Council of Toledo), was to say that our Lord *suscepit hominem* when He became Incarnate. After the controversies of the fifth century commenced, the words were "suscepit humanitatem," which are the only words acknowledged by the Scholastic Theology. Thus the word of the Creed is scarcely ambiguous. Ἐνανθρώπησεν = He entered into a man, or He assumed the man. It is defective.

§ 6. This defect was remedied afterwards by the addition of the well-known words, "was incarnate *of the Holy Ghost and the Virgin Mary*," and to them we shall soon come. At present the stage in doctrine which we find the Church had reached is this: The Word of God or Son of God is ὁμοούσιος with the Father, perfect God. When He came down He entered into a man or entered into man[2].

Thus there was room for error, and error came[3].

§ 7. I have already drawn attention to the Creed of Cyril of Jerusalem: to its imperfections in the Athanasian point of view,

[1] *Judicia Eruditorum de symbolo Athanasiano, studiose collecta et inter se collata a Wilhelmo Ernesto Tentzelio. Francofurtæ et Lipsiæ, sumptibus Augusti Boeth. Gothæ. Typis Christophori Reyheri, Anno* MDCLXXXVIII. p. 46.

(J. C. Suicer in his book on the Nicene Creed, p. 213, speaks of the difficulty regarding the meaning of ἐνανθρώπησις.)

[2] Gregory of Nazianzus noted the ambiguity. He interpreted it that the Word of God was in a Man whom He affixed to Himself. The Apollinarians took it as meaning merely that He lived among men. Compare the Eusebian Creed. Gregory's words will be found below.

[3] Before we leave this part of our subject I think that attention should be drawn to the misquotation by "Athanasius" of St Paul's words ὃ ἐγεννήθη for ὃς ἐγενήθη. The argument of the writer required this reading, and he so read it. But not a single manuscript or quotation is referred to by Tischendorf as upholding such a reading. Was it a careless blunder or a wilful misrepresentation?

I allude to it because we know that about this time Scripture was perverted for polemical purposes. The direct evidence for the Catholic verities was weak, and the education of the great theologians was not such as to enable them to appreciate and exhibit the enormous force of the Inductive Proofs of these verities. Thus in minor details, copyists altered Mark i. 1 and Luke ii. 43 to suit orthodox views.

And the process extended to matters affecting the Christian life. It is well known how Montanus, and after him Tertullian, enforced an austerity of life which was not heard of in the second century. Scriptural authority was needed for this teaching, and as it was not at hand, some was invented. In the passage 1 Cor. vii. 5 *that ye may give yourselves unto prayer*, the text was altered to ἵνα σχολάζητε τῇ νηστείᾳ καὶ τῇ προσευχῇ, *that ye may give yourselves to fasting and prayer*. In Mark ix. 29, *This kind can come forth by nothing but by prayer*, εἰ μὴ ἐν προσευχῇ, the words καὶ νηστείᾳ were boldly added, *by prayer and fasting*. The verse (perhaps for another reason) was then interpolated into St Matthew.

to the anxiety of the Bishop that his catechumens should content themselves with it, and not allow the slightest deviation from it. Possibly Athanasius would have called it Arian, although the Son of God is described in it as Very God; but on this we need not delay. The words *σαρκωθέντα καὶ ἐνανθρωπήσαντα* are found in it, but no reference whatever is made to the birth from the Virgin. On another Creed or interpretation of the Creed assigned to Athanasius, I shall be compelled to touch below.

§ 8. I must not however leave this period without drawing attention to the Antiochene Ecthesis (called the *ἔκθεσις μακρόστιχος*) which was framed in the year 345, and sent to the West in anticipation of the Council which afterwards met at Sardica in 347[1]. It commences with a Creed affirming the eternal generation of the Son, and that He is God of God; it speaks of Him as *ἐνανθρωπήσαντα καὶ γεννηθέντα* of the Holy Virgin, and that His kingdom continues unceasing to unlimited ages. The exposition concludes: "We believe too in the Holy Ghost, that is, the Comforter, Whom, after His ascent to heaven, according to His promise to His Apostles, He sent to teach them and to bring everything to their remembrance; through Whom the souls of those who have truly believed in Him shall be sanctified." The anathema of the Nicene Faith, altered by the omission of the word *οὐσία* and in other respects, follows. And the teaching is repudiated of those who say there are three Gods, or that the Father, the Son, and the Holy Spirit are the same. The reason assigned for such repudiation is, that the doctrines rejected are not found in the inspired Scriptures. "We know (they say) only one unbegotten, the Father of Christ. Nor yet, when we acknowledge three Things and three Persons (*τρία πράγματα καὶ τρία πρόσωπα*) of the Father and of the Son and of the Holy Spirit according to the Scriptures, do we because of this make three Gods, since we know the Self-perfect and Unbegotten, Unoriginated and Invisible to be one God only; nor, when we say that there is one God only, do we deny that Christ too is God from eternity...We detest the opinion of all those who say that He is the mere word of God, and has no hypostasis—some describing Him as the word uttered and spoken, others as the word conceived and unspoken." And they speak of

[1] It is given by Athanasius *de Synodis* § 26, and by Socrates, *H. E.* IX. 11, and may be seen in Mansi II. 1361, and Hahn, p. 151.

Him as having "assumed our flesh from the Virgin about 400 years ago." Reference is then made to the opinion avowed by the Marcellians and Photinians, on the pretext of upholding the Monarchia, viz. that His kingdom will come to an end. The Sabellian or Patripassian heresy is repudiated by name. An orthodox interpretation is claimed for the words of Proverbs, *the Lord created me,* &c., the bishops saying that it is "impious and alien to the ecclesiastical faith to compare the Creator with the things created through Him." And the last division is occupied with an attempt to guard the faith from the imputation of teaching that the Father and the Son are ever dissociated or severed, either in space or time. "And when we believe in the all-perfect and most holy Trinity, that is, in the Father and in the Son and in the Holy Spirit; and when we say that the Father is God, and the Son also God, we acknowledge, not two Gods, but one majesty of the Godhead, and one perfect harmony of the kingdom: the Father ruling entirely over all things, even over the Son Himself, and the Son subjected to the Father, but, excepting Him, ruling over all things with Him, and bestowing at the Father's will, ungrudgingly, on the saints, the gift of the Holy Spirit. For thus have the sacred oracles delivered to us that the character of the Monarchia in regard to Christ consists."

This exposition of the Faith was not accepted at Sardica; nor can it be regarded as Catholic in any detail save where it repeats the language of the orthodox Creed. But I would notice that the Deity of the Holy Spirit is touched on very lightly, and that the document declares that there are not three Gods, but "one Godhead." The truth regarding the Holy Trinity was not yet worked out.

§ 9. The Council of Sardica accepted the Nicene Faith, thus giving it the seal of the Bishops of the West, three hundred of whom assembled at this Illyrian city. It also composed "another formula of faith, which was more copious than that of Nicæa, the intention being to convey the same signification in more perspicuous language[1]." The document appears to be lost.

[1] (Sozomen, *H. E.* III. 12). The synodical letter given by Theodoret *H. E.* II. 8 does not answer to this description, but it need not on that account be rejected as spurious, as is done by Baronius. The question is worthy of consideration whether the first form given by Epiphanius may not be "the other writing of the faith" referred to here.

CHAPTER VIII.

THE APOLLINARIAN CONTROVERSY AND COUNCILS OF CONSTANTINOPLE.

§ 1. The two Apollinarii. § 2. Gregory Nazianzene's account of the opinions of the younger Apollinarius. § 3. Principle involved in it. § 4. Epiphanius of Constantia. His Ancoratus. His Creed. § 5. Difficulty of this. § 6. Comparison with the Nicene Faith. § 7. The second exposition of Epiphanius. § 8. Examination of this. § 9. This latter exposition almost identical with one ascribed to Athanasius. § 10. This not noticed by Montfaucon. § 11. So far probably spurious. § 12. Synod of Constantinople, A.D. 381. § 13. Letter of the Bishops to Theodosius, and their canons. § 14. Council of Constantinople, A.D. 382. § 15. What is the *Tome* to which it referred? § 16. Letter of Damasus to Paulinus. § 17. The so-called Creed of Constantinople. § 18. Question of its authenticity. § 19. Comparison with the Creed of Epiphanius. § 20. Why were the alterations made?

§ 1. THERE were at Laodicea, towards the latter half of the fourth century, two distinguished men of the name of Apollinaris, or Apollinarius, father and son. The elder of the two was a great admirer and friend of Athanasius. When the great martyr was on his way back to Egypt from his banishment by Constantine, he passed through Laodicea, and there he made the acquaintance of Apollinaris, an acquaintance which ripened into a warm friendship. Because of this, Apollinaris was ejected from the Church by George its Arian bishop[1]. Meditating (as no doubt he did) on his undeserved excommunication, Apollinaris would be subjected to one of two temptations; either to abjure his Athanasian Creed, or to carry it to extremes. He gave way before the latter; and, deeply impressed with the conviction of the perfect Deity of our Blessed Lord, he was led to deny His true Humanity. The Ecthesis which I have quoted is entirely consistent with these earlier

[1] Sozomen, *H. E.* VI. 25, who attributes the erroneous teaching of Apollinaris (or Apollinarius, the name is spelt both ways) to μικροψυχία, "littleness of soul."

views of Apollinaris: he believed that the Divine Nature in Christ supplied all that was wanted to animate His flesh: he observed that it was not said in Scripture that He became man, but that He was made flesh: and he could not see how, if our Lord was not capable of change, He could share in the true characteristics of the human soul. At a later period father and son gave up the point so far as relates to the *animating* Soul, the ψυχή, by the possession of which man is a living animal[1], (for unless Christ had this Soul, how could *He* have *given His Soul a ransom for many?*) and confined their objection to a more limited point: they held that the Saviour had not, when Incarnate, the *Reasonable* Soul. Thus they held that He was *made flesh,* and took up His abode with men; but they denied that He was entirely or perfectly Man. Then they went further: they maintained that the Flesh which the Redeemer took was from heaven, and therefore free, on this account, from the imperfections of our fleshly nature. As this particular point (to which indeed we owe an important addition to the Nicene Faith, and perhaps an important omission from it,) is not touched upon in those famous chapters of Hooker's *Ecclesiastical Polity,* from which most of us have received our earliest philosophical impressions as to the Incarnation of our Redeemer, I will give a short account of the tenets of the younger Apollinaris as they were understood by the great Gregory of Nazianzus. Whether the account gives an adequate and true résumé of the opinions of the man has been questioned; but there is no reason to doubt that it gives a true representation of Gregory's view of them.

§ 2. In his letter to Nectarius, written about the year 387[2], Gregory complains first of the heresies of Arius and Eunomius, and then of that of Apollinaris.

He says that the book of the last-named contains things which exceed all heretical pravity. For "he affirms that the Flesh of our Lord was not acquired in the economy (*i. e.* the Incarnation) by the only-begotten Son, but that from the beginning that carnal nature *was* the Son. He misinterprets John iii. 13, *No one has ascended up into heaven, but He that came down from heaven, the Son of man, Who is in heaven:* as if He was the Son of Man before He came down from heaven, and came down

[1] "The first man Adam was made a living animal, the last Adam a lifegiving spirit."

[2] (Migne, *Greek Series,* Vol. XXXVII. col. 329).

bringing with Him His own flesh which He had had in heaven, being, as it were, itself eternal and made coessential with Him (*προαιώνιον* and *συνουσιωμένην*).

"Thus too he explains 1 Cor. xv. 47, *the second man from heaven*, tearing it away from its context. And thus Apollinaris makes out that the Man who *came down from heaven* had not the human intelligence, the *νοῦς*, but that the Deity of the only-Begotten supplied the place of this *νοῦς*: He had the Soul and Body, but the Logos replaced the human intelligence. But this is not all: he actually teaches that He, the only-begotten Son, the Judge of all, the Prince of Life, the Destroyer of death, was mortal: that in his own Deity He underwent suffering, and in that three days' submission to the death (*νέκρωσις*) of the Body, the Deity also died, and so was raised by the Father from death."

From the letters of Gregory to Cledonius[1], written in 382, we receive further information of importance. He there complains[2]

that the followers of Apollinaris assert that *ὁ κυριακὸς*, the Lordly One, (*or* the Lord's Man) as they call Him, "They ought to call Him Lord and God," was without the human intelligence (*ἄνους*). And then (clearly referring to their teaching as to the Body of our Lord), Gregory says, that "we hold that our Lord was from eternity not man, but God and Son, unmixed with Body or Bodily attributes: but that, at the end, the man was assumed for our salvation: thus He was passible in the flesh, impassible in the Spirit; circumscribed in the Body, uncircumscribed in the Spirit; so that by Him, entirely Man and God, the whole man should be formed again, since he has fallen under sin. If, therefore, any one considers that Mary was not Mother of God, he is severed from the Godhead: if any one says that He ran through the Virgin as through a canal, and was not formed in her in a divine as well as human fashion—divine as being without a human father, human as being by the law of fetal growth,—he is equally godless. If any one says that the man was first formed, and that then God assumed the man, he is condemned. If any one brings in two Sons, the one of God the Father, the second of the Mother, and not one and the same Son, may he fall away from the adoption of sons, which is promised to those who rightly believe. For there are two natures, God and Man, but not two Sons nor two Gods. We speak of one thing and another thing, but not of one Person and another Person (of *ἄλλο* and *ἄλλο*, but not of *ἄλλος* and *ἄλλος*). Thus two things took place in the blending together (*ἐν τῇ συγκράσει*); God entered on man, and man was made God. In the Trinity we speak of one Person and another (*ἄλλος* and *ἄλλος*), that we may not confuse the Hypostases, but not of one thing and another (*ἄλλο* and *ἄλλο*), for the three (*τὰ τριά*) are one and the same (*ἓν καὶ τὸ αὐτό*) in the Deity."

After a while he proceeds:

"If anyone says that the flesh has now been laid aside, and that the Godhead is deprived of the Body, and is not now with it, and will not

[1] Migne, *ut sup.* col. 175—202. [2] Col. 178.

come with it, associated with it, may he not see the glory of His coming." ...The passages quoted above from 1 Cor. xv., and St John iii., are true, because of the heavenly union. Gregory taught that the sanctification of each element in us is to be connected with the truth that that element was present in our Saviour, and in Him was holy. He charged against his opponents that they were deceived by the letter of Scripture, and were ignorant of the custom, the *con*suetudo (τὴν συνήθειαν) of the Scriptures; they interpreted too narrowly single passages such as this, *Unto Thee shall all flesh come.* And then they have gone entirely wrong in regard to the Trinity. "Apollinaris indeed gave the name of Deity to the Holy Spirit, but the full truth of His Deity he did not maintain." He thought that there was a Great and a Greater and a Greatest; the Holy Spirit, the Son, the Father; as it were the Splendour, the Ray, the Sun: whilst we acknowledge that the Names are not mere phrases, marking inequalities of dignities and power, but, as there is one and the same title, so is there one and the same Nature, and Essence, and Power.

In his second letter Gregory takes up the subject of the Faith. Many had come to Cledonius seeking further assurance regarding it, and therefore Cledonius had begged from his friend a short definition and canon of his own sentiments.

"We (he replies) have never preferred, and are now unable to prefer, anything to the faith settled at Nicæa by the holy Fathers who then met to put down the Arian heresy: to that faith we belong and will belong, even whilst we add some articles, in explanation of that which was stated there concerning the Holy Spirit, somewhat defectively (προσδιαρθροῦντες τὸ ἐλλιπῶς εἰρημένον ἐκείνης περὶ τοῦ ἁγίου πνεύματος)—because the question had not then been stirred." We add "that we ought to know that the Father and the Son and the Holy Spirit are of one Godhead, and that the Spirit is God. I beg you, therefore, regard those who so hold and teach as in communion with you: those who teach differently regard as aliens both from God and the Catholic Church." Gregory subjoins a few remarks on the divine "entering on man or incarnation" (ἐνανθρωπήσεως ἤτοι σαρκώσεως), and says, "If a man does not agree with us here, he shall have to give an account of it in the day of judgment." He complains again of the partial manner in which the Apollinarians understand Scripture: "Their idea of a perfect man (he says) is not of one who in every point has been tempted like us, yet without sin: but its subject is the mixture of God and flesh. They are mistaken again on the word ἐνανθρώπησις: they maintain, *not* that the Word was in the man whom He attached to Himself, *but* only that He mixed with men and conversed with men—taking refuge in the words (of Baruch iii. 37), *After this He was seen on the earth and conversed with man*...Again, they appeal to the words of the apostle—which they do not explain in the apostle's sense—that our Lord was *in the likeness of men, and was found in fashion as a man:* they say these words mean that the likeness was only apparent and put on to deceive. Damasus therefore reasonably rejected these, and returned their miserable description of their faith with an anathematism:—and they, instead of being put to shame, harass us with falsehoods." "Let them remove from the vestibules of their churches (Gregory cries) the sentence that we are to *worship not the god-bearing Man, but the flesh-bearing God.* What folly! what madness is this! and yet it has all arisen only within the last thirty years, whilst nearly four hundred years have passed since Christ was manifested!"

§ 3. No apology is required for my introduction of this passage, exhibiting (as it does) the clear conception which Gregory had of the true mode of overcoming heresies—not merely that of the Apollinarians, but all others as they might arise. I have introduced it too for the purpose of exhibiting the need of some further explanation of the Nicene Faith, a need which was ere long supplied.

§ 4. Epiphanius, Bishop of Constantia in Cyprus, was "a well-read man, but of narrow mind and obstinate." Among his works that have come down to us is one entitled *The Anchored One*, an exposition of the faith of the Trinity. It was composed at the request of some presbyters in Pamphylia, and apparently in the year 374. Towards the close of the work[1] he writes as follows:

The children of the Church have received from the holy fathers, that is from the holy Apostles, the faith to keep, and to hand down, and to teach their children. To these children you belong, and I beg you to receive it and pass it on. And whilst you teach your children these things and such as these from the holy Scriptures, cease not to confirm and strengthen them, and indeed all who hear you: telling them that this is the holy faith of the Holy Catholic Church, as the one holy Virgin of God received it from the holy Apostles of the Lord to keep: and thus every person who is in preparation for the holy laver of baptism must learn it: they must learn it themselves, and teach it expressly, as the one Mother of all, of you and of us, proclaims it, saying—"We believe in one God the Father Almighty, maker of heaven and earth, and of all things visible and invisible: and in one Lord Jesus Christ, the only begotten Son of God, begotten of the Father before all the ages, that is of the substance of the Father, Light of Light, very God of very God, begotten not made, consubstantial with the Father: by whom all things were made, both in heaven and earth: who for us men and for our salvation came down from heaven, and was incarnate of the Holy Ghost and the Virgin Mary, and was made man (ἐνανθρωπήσαντα), was crucified also for us under Pontius Pilate, and suffered, and was buried, and on the third day He rose again according to the Scriptures, and ascended into heaven, and sitteth on the right hand of the Father, and thence is

[1] ὁ ἀγκύρωτος, Migne, 43, p. 231.

coming with glory to judge the quick and the dead, of whose kingdom there shall be no end. And in the Holy Ghost, the Lord and Giver of life, who proceedeth from the Father; who, with the Father and the Son is worshipped and glorified, who spake by the prophets: in one holy Catholic and Apostolic Church. We acknowledge one baptism for the remission of sins; we look for the resurrection of the dead, and the life of the world to come. And those who say that there was a time when the Son of God was not, and before He was begotten He was not, or that He was of things which are not, or that He is of a different hypostasis or substance, or pretend that He is effluent or changeable, these the Catholic and Apostolic Church anathematizes. And this faith was delivered from the Holy Apostles and in the Church, the Holy City, from all the Holy Bishops together more than three hundred and ten in number."

§ 5. As this last sentence is incorrect, if it is to be understood of the Council of Nicæa, the question arises whether it was meant to refer to the Council of Sardica, which, according to Sozomen, collected some three hundred bishops from the West and seventy from the East: two hundred and fifty according to Theodoret. I throw it out as a suggestion. For this is not the Nicene Faith.

§ 6. Let us, however, compare it with the Nicene Faith.

The words *of heaven and earth* are added;

The order of the phrases *only begotten Son, begotten of the Father* is altered;

That He was begotten *before all worlds* is added;

The words of the Nicene Creed, *God of God,* are omitted;

The thought that He came down *from heaven* is more fully expressed;

The words *of the Holy Ghost and the Virgin Mary* are introduced;

That He was *crucified for us under Pontius Pilate,* and that *He was buried,* is added;

So too that His Resurrection was *according to the Scriptures;*

That *He is seated on the right hand of God;*

That His coming will be *with glory;*

And that *of His kingdom there shall be no end.*

This last may have been suggested by the Ecthesis Macrostichus.

The great addition, however, was in the words which follow *I believe in the Holy Ghost.*

In the anathematism, κτιστόν and τρεπτόν were altered to ῥευστόν. Apollinaris had never maintained that our Lord was *created:* we may possibly say that he held that He flowed through the Virgin without partaking of her substance.

§ 7. But, incomplete as this account of Epiphanius is, and incorrect, if he intended to refer us to the Faith of Nicæa, the puzzle is increased by a statement which immediately follows. He tells

"How in our own generation, that is in the times of Valentinus and Valens, and the ninetieth year from the succession of Diocletian the tyrant (*i. e.* in the year 374, seven years before the Synod of Constantinople), you and we and all the orthodox bishops of the whole Catholic Church together, make this address to those who come to baptism, in order that they may proclaim and say as follows"—

The words may be seen in Migne, Vol. XLIII. p. 233, and Hahn, p. 58.—This faith contains many interesting passages. It is almost identical with the true Nicene Creed until we come to the words "came down from heaven, and was incarnate;" here is added the sentence, "that is, was perfectly born of the Holy Mary, the ever Virgin, through the Holy Spirit." It then proceeds as follows:

"ἐνανθρωπήσαντα, that is He took a perfect man, soul, and body, and intelligence, and everything that man is, without sin; not from the seed of a man (ἀνδρὸς), nor yet in a man (ἐν ἀνθρώπῳ), but forming for Himself (εἰς ἑαυτὸν) flesh into one holy unity: not, as in the prophets, where He breathed and spoke and wrought, but [here] He became perfectly man (τελείως ἐνανθρωπήσαντα), for the *Word was made flesh,* not sustaining any change nor converting His Godhead into Manhood—[but] uniting into His own one holy perfection and Godhead—for there is one Lord Jesus Christ and not two, the same God, the same Lord, the same King—the same suffered in the flesh and rose again, and went up to heaven in the same body, sat down gloriously at the right hand of the Father, and is coming in the same body in glory to judge the quick and the dead; of whose kingdom there shall be no end. And we believe the Holy Spirit who spake in the law, and preached in the prophets, and came down at the Jordan, who speaks in Apostles, and dwells in saints; and thus we believe in Him; that there is a Holy Spirit, a Spirit of God, a perfect Spirit, a Comforter Spirit, uncreated, proceeding from the Father, received from the Son, and believed. We believe in one Catholic and Apostolic Church, and in one baptism of repentance and in a resurrection of the dead, and in the righteous judgment of souls and bodies, and in the kingdom of heaven and eternal life." And it concludes with the Nicene anathematism, extending, however, the statements regarding the Son to the Holy Spirit, "and again we anathematize those who will not confess a resurrection of the dead, and all the heresies which are not of this, the right faith."

§ 8. It will be seen that the explanations are confined to the subject of the Incarnation of our Lord: *i.e.* the Nicene Faith, where it treats of His Prior Existence, was left unaltered and without exposition. And these explanations insist upon His perfect humanity. The document must, therefore, have been drawn up in distinct reference to the Apollinarian controversy. But still the writers were not express believers in the Deity of the Holy Spirit: they explain the Nicene, "We believe in the Holy Spirit," in a way which is very different from the explanation of Athanasius in his letter to the African Bishops[1]. Nor is this weakness of the statement in the body of the document removed entirely by the anathema at the end[2].

§ 9. But in the Vatican Library there is a manuscript of "the best character and of great antiquity," which contains some works of Cyril. Amongst them is a tract headed: "Athanasius, archbishop of Alexandria: his interpretation of the Symbol[3]." This interpretation commences like the Nicene Creed and Epiphanius' Faith, but it omits the words "only begotten, that is of the substance of the Father," words which Epiphanius' second formula retained: it adds, with Epiphanius, "both which are in heaven and which are in earth." Like this same formula it omits the words "from heaven:" after the *ἐνανθρωπήσαντα* it proceeds almost exactly the same, "that is, was conceived (*γεννηθέντα*) perfectly of the Virgin Mary through the Holy Spirit, having taken body and soul and mind and everything that belongs to man, without sin, truly and not in appearance:" then it omits the clauses in Epiphanius, "not of the seed of a man," &c. down to "the same Lord, the same King:" it proceeds, "suffered, that is, was crucified and buried:" it adds, "the third day," to Epiphanius. The rest relating to our Saviour's session and future coming are identical in both. It concludes:

[1] Chapter VI. §§ 7, 10, above.

[2] It is interesting to notice that our English version *and was incarnate by the Holy Ghost of the Virgin Mary* comes from this, and not from what is called the "faith of Constantinople."

[3] *ἀθανασίου ἀρχιεπισκόπου ἀλεξάνδρειας ἑρμήνεια εἰς τὸ σύμβολον.* The great Montfaucon, the Benedictine editor, considered it to be genuine.

"And we believe in the Holy Spirit who is not alien from the Father and the Son, but consubstantial with the Father and the Son, who is uncreated, perfect, the Comforter, who spake in the Law and in the Prophets and in the Gospels, who came down on the Jordan, preached to the Apostles, dwells in the Saints. And we believe in this one only Catholic and Apostolic Church: in one baptism of repentance and of remission of sins, in the resurrection of the dead, in the eternal judging of souls and bodies, in the kingdom of heaven and eternal life. And those who say there was a time when the Son was not, or there was a time when the Holy Spirit was not, or that He was made of things which are not; or who say that the Son of God or the Holy Spirit is of a different hypostasis or essence—being capable of change—these we anathematize, because our mother the Catholic and Apostolic Church anathematizes them. And we anathematize all who will not confess that there is a resurrection of the flesh, as well as every heresy—that is, all those who are not of this faith of the holy and alone Catholic Church[1]."

§ 10. The great Benedictine editor did not notice the marked similarity between this "interpretation of the Creed," attributed in his manuscript to Athanasius, and the second formula of Epiphanius: nor I believe has any one else. What judgment it may produce ultimately as to the origin of the document, I am not prepared to say. My own impression is that future editors will place this "interpretation" among the spurious works with which the later of "Athanasius'" volumes are filled up. For Epiphanius' document is declared by him to have been composed in the year 374, and Athanasius ended his eventful life in 373.

§ 11. But we must not dismiss the subject without the further remark that this "interpretation" ascribed to Athanasius omits very important words, contained in the other, "that is from the substance of the Father." The improbability is very great, that the renowned Bishop of Alexandria, having struggled for those words all his life, should have resigned them needlessly within a few years of his death, whilst Epiphanius retained them. Thus we have, as it seems to me, no choice in this investigation. For the present we must conclude that the writer of the Vatican manuscript was led into an error: and that Athanasius was not the author of the "Interpretation." Leaving then this interesting enquiry, we fall back on the earlier document pub-

[1] Migne, Vol. XXVI. p. 1252.

lished by Epiphanius, and must note what an important place it seems to have occupied in the Church.

§ 12. A small synod, of 150 bishops, met at Constantinople in the year 381, seven years after the date which Epiphanius so carefully assigns to this second Creed, and of this synod we have brief accounts in most of the Church histories[1]. We have, indeed, no lengthened record of its proceedings; its "acts" have perished. But we have a copy of the letter which the assembled Bishops addressed to the emperor Theodosius; and two sets of canons, one longer than the other, but both sets containing one canon, with which we are now deeply interested.

§ 13. The Bishops informed Theodosius that they had renewed assurances of unity among themselves, and had then briefly laid down definitions or canons which confirmed the faith of the fathers who had met at Nicæa, and anathematized every heresy. In proof of this they referred to the document which accompanied the letter. The first canon was to the effect that

> "The faith of the 318 fathers who had met at Nicæa in Bithynia was not to be rejected, but that it remained confirmed, and every heresy was anathematized: and especially that of the Eunomians or Anomœans, that of the Arians or Eudoxians, that of the Semiarians or Pneumatomachi, that of the Sabellians, and that of the Marcellians; that of the Photinians, and that of the Apollinarians."

The fifth canon was this: "Concerning the Tome of the Occidentals: we receive those in Antioch also who confess one Godhead of the Father and the Son and the Holy Spirit." What is meant by the Tome of the Occidentals? no satisfactory answer is given, so far as I am aware. It can scarcely refer to the letter of Damasus to Paulinus, which Theodoret gives after the meeting of the Bishops at Constantinople of the succeeding year. And equal uncertainty exists as to the document referred to in the letter to Theodosius, unless the first canon of the Council answers the requirements of the problem. All that we hear from Theodoret as having happened at the time, is this: that after they had made some canons to regulate the good order of the Church, and ordained that the Faith of Nicæa should remain established, the Bishops departed to their own homes.

[1] Sozomen, *H. E.* VII. 7, Socrates V. 8.

§ 14. In the next year, 382, there was another gathering at Constantinople, arising from an invitation to a very great synod to be held at Rome. Instead, however, of taking the journey to Rome, the bishops sent a letter[1] to Damasus and Ambrose and the others. In this letter they speak of the persecutions they had undergone for the sake of the evangelical faith which had been confirmed at Nicæa in Bithynia by the 318 fathers:

This faith (they said) ought to satisfy all who cared only for the word of truth: it was ancient, and it was accordant with baptism, and it taught us to believe in the Name of the Father, and the Son, and the Holy Spirit, as being of one Godhead, and power, and substance: of a dignity equally precious, of a kingdom coeternal, of three perfect Hypostases or three perfect Persons, rejecting those, who, like Sabellius and others, either confused the Hypostases, or divided the essence, or nature, or godhead; or introduced into the uncreated and consubstantial Trinity any conception of a Nature later in time, or created, or different in essence. "We maintain also (they proceed) the statement of the unperverted Incarnation of the Lord, refusing to regard Him as being without soul or without intelligence, or to think that the economy of His flesh is imperfect, knowing that He was entirely perfect: God the Word before all ages, and that He became perfect man in these last days for our salvation. Such (they proceed) is the summary regarding the faith which is constantly preached amongst us:" and then they refer their western friends, in addition, to the Tome which had been made at Antioch by the synod that met there, and to that which was put out at Constantinople last year, by the œcumenical synod that met there, in which they confessed the faith at greater length, and have framed in writing an anathematism of the heresies which have been recently innovated[2].

§ 15. The question again arises, what was this Tome in which the 150 who met at Constantinople in 381 put forth at greater length the faith, and prepared an anathematism of the recent heresies? Was it the second formula of Epiphanius or the "Interpretation of Athanasius"? or was it the document which we now regard as the Creed of Constantinople? The so-called Creed of Constantinople can scarcely be regarded as containing all that the meeting of 382 declared that the Tome did contain, and it has no anathema. The question is puzzling. And the puzzling character is not diminished by the fact that we cannot find that any writer prior to the summons to the Council of Chalcedon, *i.e.* during the next seventy years, ever refer to the "faith" of this

[1] I have referred to this letter already note p. 25, for another purpose.

[2] Theodoret, *H. E.* v. 9. The letter is in Harduin I. 823, and I presume in other editions of the Councils.

Council. Indeed the number of those who met here was so small that it is only by the subsequent reception of its supposed Creed that it has attained the dignity of an œcumenical council at all. Its greatness was thrust upon it.

§ 16. But we must here draw attention for a brief space to the letter of Damasus to Paulinus of Antioch, which, from the account of Theodoret (*H. E.*, v. 10, 11), followed on this Synod at Rome, to which the orthodox Bishops of the East had been invited in 382. The letter is very celebrated: it is contained with variations in many collections of Canons, and the Brothers Ballerini copy with annotations Quesnel's learned note upon it[1]. The letter has a distinct reference to the heresy of Apollinaris, and states that the Catholic Church anathematizes those who hold that in the Saviour the Word took the place of the human intelligence. Damasus calls on all to subscribe his letter. He gives the true Nicene Creed, of course in Latin, adding however to the words "and in the Holy Spirit" the following, "neither made nor created, but of the substance of the Deity[2]." The Nicene anathematism follows, and then this interesting memorandum;—"After this Nicene Council, a council which was assembled at Rome of Catholic Bishops made additions relative to the Holy Spirit"—I presume, by inserting the words specified. Then there follows a series of anathematisms referring to errors regarding the Holy Spirit and the Incarnation and the Trinity.

§ 17. I may anticipate here what I must repeat hereafter, viz. that the only evidence *prima manu* in favour of the received account of the origin of the "Creed of Constantinople" is the unsupported statement of the deacon Aëtius at the Council of Chalcedon in the year 451. This will come under review ere long. When I reach that date, I will give further details regarding it: I will now merely transcribe the document, and at a later page draw attention to the chief points in which it differs from the Nicene, and from the earlier faith in the Ancorate of Epiphanius. I will content myself with a translation[3].

"We believe in one God, the Father Almighty, Maker of heaven and earth, and of all things visible and invisible: and in one Lord, Jesus

[1] Works of Leo the Great. Ballerini III. 399 (Migne, Vol. LVI. p. 686).

[2] Neque facturam neque creaturam sed de substantia deitatis.

[3] The original is in every collection.

Christ, the only-begotten Son of God, begotten of the Father before all worlds, Light of Light, Very God of Very God, Begotten not made, Being of one substance with the Father, by Whom all things were made; Who, for us men and for our salvation, came down from heaven, and was incarnate of the Holy Ghost and the Virgin Mary, and was made man (ἐνανθρωπήσαντα), and was crucified for us under Pontius Pilate, and suffered, and was buried; and on the third day He rose again according to the Scriptures, and ascended into the heaven, and sitteth on the right hand of the Father, and shall come again with glory to judge the quick and the dead: of Whose kingdom there shall be no end. And in the Holy Ghost, the Lord, the Giver of life, Who proceedeth from the Father, Who with the Father and the Son together is worshipped and glorified, Who spake by the prophets: In one holy Catholic and Apostolic Church. We acknowledge one baptism for the remission of sins; we look for the Resurrection of the dead and the life of the world to come. Amen."

§ 18. It has been almost universally assumed until lately that the account of this Creed given by Aëtius is correct, that it really did receive the sanction of the Council of Constantinople in 381. I cannot say that I believe it: and I must give my reasons.

i. The Council of 382 states (as we have seen) that the bishops assembled in the previous year had expressed their entire satisfaction with the Creed of Nicæa, and we know, from their undoubted canon and from their letter to Theodosius, they had confirmed that Creed. On looking at this new Creed, however, we find that it omits one very important clause of the faith of Nicæa: a clause for which (as I have said before) Athanasius appears to have fought continuously throughout his long and arduous life; a clause which, as he informs his friends in Africa and elsewhere, was inserted especially to annoy and exclude the Arians. The clause I refer to is that which follows, γεννηθέντα ἐκ τοῦ πατρὸς μονογενῆ, viz. τουτέστιν ἐκ τῆς οὐσίας τοῦ πατρός: "begotten of the Father, only begotten, *that is, of the substance of the Father.*" That clause was inserted, we may remember, because the Arians had whispered, "we can allow that the Son of God is of God, of the Father, because we are all of God: *of Him are all things.*" I can scarcely think it probable that the Bishops could have omitted the clause "in their explanation of the Nicene Faith" within eight years of the death of Athanasius, and at a time when they declared their resolve to maintain his Faith[1].

[1] Etherius and Beatus called the Creed the Creed of the Council of Ephesus. (Hahn, p. 112.)

ii. Again, the Tome put forth at Constantinople in 381 is described as "confessing the faith at greater length." It is true that the additions of the words "heaven and earth" in the first clause; further on, of the words "before all worlds" (omitting the clause "God of God"); "from heaven;" "of the Holy Ghost and the Virgin Mary;" "and was crucified for us under Pontius Pilate;" "and was buried;" "sitteth on the right hand of the Father;" "of whose Kingdom there shall be no end;" together with the whole of the clauses following on "And the Holy Ghost"—appear at first sight to satisfy some of the conditions of the problem. But where is "the anathematism of the recently invented heresies" which the Tome contained?

§ 19. And now let us compare the Creed put forth by Aëtius in 451 as "the faith of the 150 fathers who met at Constantinople" with the *first* faith in the Ancorate of Epiphanius. We find that they agree to a remarkable extent; but the Creed of Epiphanius retains the clause "that is of the substance of the Father," which is rejected in the Creed of Aëtius: it retains also the words "which are in heaven and earth" relating to the "things created through the Saviour." It has the anathematism of the Nicene formula, which is omitted by Aëtius. Thus the Creed attributed by Aëtius to the Synod of Constantinople was taken from the Creed of Epiphanius, by omitting the clauses mentioned above.

§ 20. Let us still enquire—*First:* Why were the *additions* to the Nicene faith made by the authors of the faith of Epiphanius? I can only answer, "they were felt to be needed:" and I presume chiefly in consequence of the errors of the Apollinarians. These held that our Lord brought His flesh down from heaven. The new Creed asserts that *He came down from heaven,* but added that *He was incarnate of the Holy Ghost and of the Virgin Mary.*

The part relating to the Holy Spirit was inserted to pronounce the faith of the Church at the time regarding Him; against both the Apollinarians and the Macedonians.

Secondly: But why were the *omissions* made? I can only again guess at the reason; but it may have been thought that after all the expression "of the substance of the Father" was too bold in face of the Apollinarian heretics: it may have been thought that the phrase gave them support for their opinion, that the Son of man, as regards both His Spirit and His Flesh, was "from the Substance or Essence of the Father." Again; I can well conceive that the words, "by whom all things were made, *both which are in heaven and which are in earth*," were found too extensive: they might be quoted to shew that the Church held that the Holy Spirit was "made" through the Son. Thus they were omitted. And, once more, the anathematism referred only to the Son of God, and not to the Spirit of God. An attempt was made (as we see in Epiphanius' second formula) to extend the anathematism so as to embrace the heresies regarding the Spirit, but this was so palpably an addition that any one could point to it and say, "You are altering the faith of the Church: you are modifying the anathema of Nicæa." So, in the exercise of a wise prudence, even though the anathematism was true in fact, it was allowed to drop out of sight: the Church still held as aliens and as excommunicate all who made the statements regarding the Son which were condemned; but as it was undesirable to draw attention to the difference of language used at Nicæa regarding the Son of God and the Holy Spirit of God, the anathematism was allowed to disappear. There is no evidence that the anathematism was removed at Constantinople in 381. In point of fact, the number of Bishops assembled there was too small to have ventured to make such an innovation. The Synod seems to have attracted little general attention. It is not mentioned (so far as I can discover) by S. Augustine. At the Council of Chalcedon the Egyptian bishops repudiated it (or at all events this action of it) entirely. Indeed it seems to have been due to the statement that this Creed proceeded from the Council of Constantinople, that the Council itself was elevated into the position which now it occupies[1].

[1] Amongst the numerous references to the Nicene faith, and to proposals to change it, the following seem worthy of especial notice.

In A.D. 362 the Council of Alexandria asks that all may confess the faith which had been confessed by the Holy Fathers at Nicæa: some persons had made additions to the Nicene Faith, but the council of Sardica had declared that a second faith ought not to be set forth, for this was perfect. And this, although people had declared that the Holy Spirit was a Creature, and thus tended to divide the Trinity.

In the year 366 at Rome it was ordered that it should be kept *ἀκεραία καὶ ἀσαλευτός*. The number of bishops met at Nicæa was noted as equal to the number of Abraham's servants. (In Athanasius' early writings he said the number was nearly 300, which the "Oxford translation" represents to English readers as "over 300.") It is called the Catholic and Apostolic faith. In the synodical letter they said that all who pretended to profess the Creed of Nicæa, and yet ventured to blaspheme against the Holy Ghost (by saying that He is a creature and by dividing Him from the substance of the Christ), do little else than this: they deny the Arian heresy in words, but they maintain it in their minds. They wished (vain thought!) to restrain further enquiry, resolved themselves to seek for nothing further than the Nicene confession. The latter is very important and should be compared with Socrates, *H. E.* III. 7, who informs us that there was much deliberation here on the words *οὐσία* and *ὑπόστασις*, and that the Synod of which Athanasius was president agreed that neither word *ought* to be used of God, for the word *οὐσία* never occurred in Scripture, and the word *ὑπόστασις* was used improperly there by the Apostle, under the necessity of dogma: but they were compelled by the exigency of the matter to retain both words.

In A.D. 374 the Council of Illyricum accepts the Nicene Faith as against the Pneumatomachi who would separate the Holy Spirit from the essence of the Father and the Son. The Bishops maintained that the Trinity is consubstantial—acccording to the Faith long ago put out at Nicæa.

In 377 the Council of Iconium accepts the Nicene Faith, but regrets that, in consequence of the difficulties since raised, it is necessary to go to the Fountain of the Faith. They taught that as we believe in the Father and the Son, so should we believe in the Spirit. But we must go beyond this Faith now, and appeal to the Tradition of the Lord. His words were *Go, baptize all nations, &c.* Thus it is necessary that we baptize as we were taught, and believe as we were baptized, and glorify as we have believed.

At the sixth session of the orthodox bishops at Ephesus in 431, both parties appealed to it with equal zest. It was again recited, and they said "It is fitting that all should agree to this holy Faith: for it is pious and sufficient for the good of the whole Church under heaven." (Could they have known of any Creed of Constantinople?) They wished however to adduce testimonies from the fathers to uphold and explain the Faith against Nestorius.

Then there came the decree against the putting out of any other Creed, of which more below. (Again I ask, Did they know of the Creed of Constantinople?) Turning to the rival Council, we find that they upheld the Nicene Faith, and complained that Cyril had corrupted it. (Harduin, p. 1531 D; 1535 B, E; 1537 A, B, C; 1574 A; 1575 B.) They certainly did not know of the addition "of the Virgin Mary," which so far savours of being a fifth century addition, 1594 E.

At the seventh action we have an interesting letter of Cyril, who declares that he would not have a single word altered in the Nicene Faith, for the Spirit of God spake by the Fathers there.

In A.D. 435 Theodosius refers to the Faith put out at Nicæa and Ephesus twice over. (Nothing of Constantinople.)

The circumstances of the recital of the Nicene Faith by Eutyches at the Robber Synod and of its use at Chalcedon will be given at greater length below. I must notice however here that after Aëtius had brought out his version of the Creed of Constantinople in the second session, Marcion addressed at the sixth session the assembly in Latin, and spoke of the deference due to the Nicene synod and the Nicene Faith; he said nothing of the Constantinopolitan Creed.

Passing on, I have memoranda that at the fifth general council (the second of Constantinople, A.D. 553) Eutychius Bishop of Constantinople speaks of the holy symbol, or rather instruction, *τὸ ἅγιον σύμβολον ἤτοι μάθημα* made at Nicæa, and says that the 100 fathers who met at Constantinople made the same holy Instruction clearer and explained the part relating to the Holy Spirit *τὸ αὐτὸ ἅγιον μάθημα ἐσαφήνισαν καὶ τὰ περὶ τῆς θεότητος τοῦ ἁγίου πνεύματος ἐτράνωσαν.* The fathers at Ephesus in all points followed the same holy symbol or instruction, and those at Chalcedon in all points assented to the aforenamed holy synods, and followed the aforenamed holy symbol or instruction which had been put forth by the 318 holy Fathers and explained by the 150 holy Fathers.

The two faiths were quoted at the sixth general Council held at Constantinople in 680.

At the second Council of Nicæa, 757, the Creed of Nicæa was again referred to, and the confessions of the Holy Faith of the six synods.

(At the seventh action the Creed of Constantinople was quoted with sundry additions.)

The true Nicene Creed with its anathemas was quoted as the "fides sanctæ Trinitatis et Incarnationis" at the Council of Aix, 788.

When Nicephorus bishop of Constantinople sent his confession to Leo III. about 806, he referred to the Creed of Nicæa and the fathers at Constantinople who explained it. Labbe and Cossart, VII. 1215.

CHAPTER IX.

THE NESTORIAN CONTROVERSY.

§ 1. Theodosius Emperor: his laws and fines. § 2. Nestorius Archbishop of Constantinople. § 3. Sermon of Anastasius. § 4. Judgment of Socrates on Nestorius. § 5. Argument of Cyril of Alexandria. § 6. A new mode of treatment necessary. Theology became Inductive. § 7. Cyril's argument not received at Ephesus. § 8. Appeal to the Nicene Creed. § 9. Creed of Charisius. § 10. Ecthesis of Theodore of Mopsuestia. § 11. Meaning (i) of the word Anathema, and (ii) of "Another faith." § 12. Cyril's exposition of the Nicene Creed. § 13. General acceptance of Cyril's results. § 14. Exposition of John of Antioch. § 15. Cyril satisfied with this.

§ 1. Confining our attention still to the subject of the Nature of our Incarnate Lord and Saviour Jesus Christ, we must note that although the arguments of Athanasius and his great band of followers cannot be said to have crushed the Arians, yet the active measures of the orthodox Emperors, of whom we may put Theodosius in the foreground, were successful in silencing them so far as the influence of these Emperors could spread. Public assemblies of heretics were first prohibited, and then the Catholics were empowered to interfere and disperse them even if they met privately. Apollinarians, Arians and Macedonians, alike fell under the ban of the Emperor. They were not permitted to keep up their succession of Bishops: the houses were to be confiscated where they assembled. Fleury thinks that these laws—enacted about the year 383—were not rigorously enforced; that they were intended to deter rather than to punish. Another law, however, was enacted which imposed a fine of ten pounds of gold upon every heretic. This law too may at first have been permitted to lie dormant, but attention was drawn to it at a

Council of Carthage in 404, with the view of applying it to the Donatists[1].

Beyond the range of the Empire Arianism continued to exist, and especially amongst the Goths.

§ 2. We thus pass somewhat easily from the Councils of Constantinople of 381, 382 and 383, to the election of Nestorius to the chair of the imperial city in the year 428. He was a native of Syria, and had been educated and baptized at Antioch. He is described as having been noted for his zeal against the Arians, and Apollinarians, and Origenists; and in his first sermon after his consecration in the presence of the Emperor, he addressed him thus: "Give me, O Emperor, the earth purged from heretics, and I will pay you with heaven. Destroy the heretics with me, and I will destroy the Persian with you[2]." Six weeks afterwards, his hearer, the younger Theodosius, passed an edict[3] which enjoined all heretics to restore to the Catholics the churches they had taken from them: and forbad them to ordain any fresh clergy under the old penalty, the fine of ten pounds of gold. The Arians, Apollinarians and Macedonians were prohibited from having any Church at all in any of the cities: whilst permission to assemble for the purpose of prayer was forbidden throughout the Roman Empire to the Eunomians, Valentinians, and fifteen other denominations of heretics, of whom the last-named are the Manichees. The Pelagians are not mentioned.

§ 3. Before the year had come to an end, Nestorius was involved in a controversy. His friend and confidant, Anastasius[4], whilst preaching in the Church of Constantinople, used the words: "Let no one call Mary Mother of God: for she was a woman; and it is impossible that God should be born of a human creature." Clergy and laity were disturbed by this. For they had been taught of old to speak of Christ as God (*θεολογεῖν τὸν Χριστὸν*), and on no account to separate Him as Man in the Incarnation from the Godhead, being persuaded to this by the Apostle's words, "Even if we have known Christ according to the flesh,

[1] Fleury, XXI. 53, refers to August. *Epis.* 186=50 *ad Bonif.* c. VII. § 23, and *Epis.* 93=48 *ad Vincent.* c. V. § 17.

[2] Socrates, *H. E.* VII. 29.

[3] Codex Theodos. 16, Tit. 5 *de Hær.* 65 (from Fleury, XXIV. 55).

[4] Socrates, VII. 32, from whom chiefly the following account is taken.

yet now know we Him so no more:" and "Wherefore leaving the discussions concerning Christ, let us be borne along towards perfection." Nestorius rushed to the support of Anastasius: he did not wish a friend of his to be convicted of blaspheming: and constantly did he teach in the Church, and, with continually increasing eagerness, until at last he was accused of maintaining with Paul of Samosata that Christ was a mere man.

§ 4. Socrates the historian considers that this was a false accusation: he thinks that Nestorius dreaded the word "Theotocos" like a "bugbear:" he describes him as a man of little learning, but of some fluency and great vanity; who did not care to read the books of his predecessors, thinking himself cleverer than them all. It is clear that neither Nestorius nor his opponents took time to comprehend each other's meaning; it is equally clear that Nestorius had some authority in antiquity for his opinions. True that Gregory of Nazianzus, and, before him, the Empress Helena, had described the Virgin as *Theotocos;* but the idea involved in that word was scarcely consistent with the words which had contented Augustine in his younger days, and which we find unhesitatingly attributed to Athanasius; I mean, that the Son "descending from the bosom of the Father has from the undefiled Virgin Mary assumed our Man, Christ Jesus, whom He delivered to suffer for us." Nestorius again and again expressed his assent to the faith of Nicæa—he believed on the Son of God κατελθόντα καὶ σαρκωθέντα καὶ ἐνανθρωπήσαντα. The question had not yet been settled by a council as to the moment when this Descent and Incarnation took place. Socrates declares very seriously that he examined the writings of Nestorius; and, whilst he blames him for his ignorance of the use of the term Theotocos and his consequent objection to it, he maintains that Nestorius never denied the Hypostasis of the Word, but ever confessed that the Word is Personal and Subsisting (ἐνυπόστατον καὶ ἐνούσιον). The mischief that followed was due to the exaggeration (ψυχρολογία) of Nestorius.

§ 5. In the present day we can well understand that it was absolutely necessary that this difficulty should be faced and fought out. And the very words which Socrates uses regarding it shew that a further difficulty lurked behind.

"Nestorius (he says) was ignorant that it is written in the Catholic letter of St John, according to old copies, *Every spirit that divides Jesus is not of God.* This sense of the passage those have endeavoured to remove who wish to separate the Godhead from the Man of the Incarnation. Wherefore the old interpreters have signified that there have been some who have tampered with the Epistle, wishing to divide the Man from the God. But the Manhood has been taken up together with the Godhead, and they are no more two, but one Thing; and, because of this, people of old did not shrink from calling Mary Theotocos."

Socrates would have been called an Eutychian[1] if he had written this twenty years later.

Happily after the instructive discourse of our own Hooker I need not pause to discuss the mistake of Nestorius or to examine the masterly way in which the difficulty was explained, and the truth exhibited by the acute Cyril of Alexandria. The genius and ability which he has exhibited here have gained for him the title of Saint,—a title of which his personal character where known has done much to exhibit him as unworthy. But we may look at the subject, free from the violent personalities with which it was then connected: and may feel deep sorrow that the vanity of Nestorius prevented him from acquiescing in the truth that the Virgin bare Him who is God and Man, though she was the Mother of the Saviour in regard to His Humanity alone. Seeing that in the earlier period of his episcopacy, Nestorius was so anxious to evince his orthodoxy by persecuting the Apollinarians who denied the true humanity of the Saviour, our knowledge of human nature would only lead us to expect that in his later years his zeal might drive him to the other extreme, and lay him open to the charge that he maintained the mere humanity. As we have seen, however, this charge was false though it was brought against him.

[1] And so perhaps would Cyril, for in the beginning of the controversy he used the words, "We do not say that the nature of the Word was changed and became flesh, nor that it was converted into the whole man, compounded of soul and body: but rather that the Word having united to Himself, in His Hypostasis, flesh rendered living by the reasonable soul, has become Man (*γέγονεν ἄνθρωπος*) in an ineffable and incomprehensible manner: and was called Son of Man, not merely out of condescension and favour, nor yet as if by the assumption of the Person (*πρόσωπον*, Persona) alone: but because the two different natures were united in true unity (*πρὸς ἑνότητα τὴν ἀληθινὴν συναχθεῖσαι*), and of both there was one Christ and Son: nor yet because the characteristics of the natures were removed because of the union, but rather because the Godhead and the Manhood formed for us the one Lord and Son, Jesus Christ, through this ineffable and inexplicable concurrence into a unity."

After the Eutychian controversy, the language would have been, not *πρὸς ἑνότητα, in a unity,* but *εἰς ἕνα, into one Being.*

§ 6. It is of more moment to us in our present enquiry, to ask how and on what grounds Nestorius was condemned.

Before this time the bishops at large had found that their education was not such as to enable them διακρίνειν τὰ διαφέροντα—to discern and distinguish the points of difference in the doctrinal questions that were rising. These questions had long overpassed the boundaries which the traditional RULE OF FAITH had mapped out: the country to which it furnished a chart had long been left behind. The Scriptures had next been appealed to, and almost direct deductions from Scripture were sufficient for the Arian and Apollinarian controversies: Jesus Christ must have had a soul, if *His soul was exceeding sorrowful:* He must have had an intelligent soul, if *He increased in wisdom and in stature.* But the subjects now broached were not such as could be settled by appeals to single texts: they required a more comprehensive treatment: they needed what I have called above a scientific investigation, built on a wide induction: and what we call induction had not been reduced to a science. Still the same Spirit who had been working hitherto in the Church was working still; and even in the din of Alexandrian violence and the mists of Constantinopolitan vanity, His voice was heard. And Cyril was the spokesman. We have his letters and they are wonderfully able and convincing.

§ 7. Yet when Cyril's letters were brought into the synod of Ephesus, the Fathers were not satisfied: they deemed it necessary to collect authorities from earlier writers to uphold the teaching of Cyril. If we are rightly informed, Sisinnius, who was reader to Nectarius and afterwards his successor in the chair of Constantinople, had been the first to advise this latter plan. This was at a synod held some fifty years before[1]. "He was a man of great practical experience: he knew both the interpretations of the Holy Scriptures and philosophical dogmas, and he had learnt that discussions of a dialectical character never heal divisions: on the contrary, they rather make the heresies more obstinate than they were before. His advice had been to call on the partisans of either side to bring forward the publications of older writers, and so exhibit which of the two had the greater authorities in their favour." And this course was adopted at the Council of Ephesus;

[1] About 383. Socrates v. 10.

and long quotations were made from Peter of Alexandria, Athanasius[1], Julius, Felix, Theophilus, Cyprian, Ambrose, Gregory of Nazianzus, Basil, Gregory of Nyssa, Atticus, Amphilochius, in support of the judgment of Cyril and of the views of the Council. The Nestorian formula was, that "Mary did not give birth to the Divinity:" the opinion of the bishops was, that "this dogma was not in accordance with the pious Faith which had been put forward by the holy Fathers who met at Nicæa, and we anathematize those who uphold it." And they anathematized Nestorius by acclamation[2].

§ 8. I have already mentioned that both parties appealed to the Nicene Faith. It is really wearisome to count up the number of times this Faith is recited in documents published in the *Concilia*, and connected with the meetings at Ephesus.—We never hear of the Creed of Constantinople. I notice, however, that in the letter of Nestorius to Celestine the Pope of Rome (Mansi, IV. 1309, B) the writer says that his opponents are not afraid to call the Virgin Theotocos, although those holy Fathers who are above all praise, that met at Nicæa, are said to have spoken only thus of the Virgin, viz. "that our Lord Jesus Christ was incarnate of the Holy Ghost and the Virgin Mary"—words which do not occur in the Nicene Creed[3]. They were in the Roman Creed, and in the first Creed of Epiphanius.

The most important documents connected with this controversy are printed in Dr Routh's *Opuscula*, Vol. II., and to them I must be content to refer the student. He will find among them the original synodical letter of Cyril: to it are appended the twelve anathemas which are as famous as they are important. In regard to the Canons we have the following:

"The exposition of the 318 holy Fathers who met at Nicæa having been read, and the impious symbol which had been concocted by

[1] The passages quoted from Athanasius are to be found in the third oration against the Arians, § 33 (Migne, Vol. XXVI. p. 393), and in the letter to Epictetus, § 2 and § 7 (Ibid. pp. 1053 and 1061).

[2] See the charge brought against him in the collections of Councils (Harduin, I. p. 1271). Paul of Samosata had said that "Mary did not give birth to the Word;" Nestorius, that "she did not give birth to the Deity." Paul said, "Mary brought forth a man similar to us." Nestorius spoke of "the man born of the Virgin." Nestorius' accusers called these equivalent expressions.

[3] In the *contestatio* these words are quoted as from the μάθημα of the Church of Antioch. Thus neither Nestorius (Bishop of Constantinople) nor his accusers knew of them as being in the Faith of Constantinople.

Theodore of Mopsuestia and exhibited by Charisius, presbyter of Philadelphia, to the holy Synod; the holy Synod decided (ὥρισεν) that no one should be allowed either to produce or write or compose another faith besides the one which had been agreed upon by the holy Fathers who had met at Nicæa with the Holy Spirit.

"And those who should dare either to compose another faith, or to offer, or to produce one to such as were willing to turn to the knowledge of the truth, whether from Hellenism, or Judaism, or any heresy whatever, were, if bishops, to be put out of their bishoprics; if clerics, out of their clerus; if laymen, they were to be anathematized: and, in the same way, if anyone were detected as either holding or teaching what was contained in the exposition which had been adduced by the presbyter Charisius relative to the becoming man of the only-begotten Son of God, or the bitter and perverse dogmas of Nestorius, he must be subjected to the sentence of the holy œcumenical Synod: i. e. if a bishop, he must be deprived of his bishopric and deposed; if a cleric he must be removed from his clerus; if a layman, he must be anathematized, as has been said[1]."

This was at the sixth session.—It would be of interest to exhibit the process by which this result of the Council was arrived at, but this is not the place to give a history of the Councils. The two rival gatherings under Cyril and under John of Antioch were conducted with almost equal violence; each party claimed that it alone stood by the Nicene Faith: the Nestorian body excommunicating Cyril and Memnon and the rest, until recognising their offence they should repent and receive the faith of the holy Fathers who had met at Nicæa, without any new or strange additions: whilst the other, under Cyril, maintained that his letter was consentient with the Holy Scriptures, and with the faith that had been handed down by tradition and set forth in the great Synod of Nicæa[2].

§ 9. Reference has been made in the canon of the Council to the "impious symbol which had been concocted by Theodore of Mopsuestia, and exhibited to the Council by Charisius, presbyter of Philadelphia."

This incident had occurred at the sixth session. Charisius complained that he had met with erroneous teaching among the Lydians, coming, as he alleged, from friends of Nestorius, who had reduced their sentiments to the form of an exposition of belief or rather of unbelief, and had then required their adherents to

[1] Routh, *Opusc.* II. pp. 8, 9. Harduin, I. 1526, et sqq.

[2] The account in Mosheim's notes is very saddening and well illustrates our Article XXI.

subscribe to it. By way, I suppose, of exhibiting his own orthodoxy, Charisius recited his faith: it differs seriously from the Faith of Nicæa, and therefore shews that this Faith had not even in 431 superseded, among the orthodox of the East, the Creeds that were in existence before it was framed[1]. It may be seen in the collections of Councils and elsewhere.

§ 10. This was followed by the reading of the Exposition of the concocted symbol, *i. e.* undoubtedly the symbol of Theodore of Mopsuestia.

To me this is interesting as giving another crucial instance of the difference of meaning between a Symbol and an Exposition of a Symbol: between a Creed and the Setting of a Creed[2].

It commences as follows:

"All who are now learning, for the first time, the accurate meaning of the dogmas of the Church, or who wish to turn from any heretical error to the truth[3], ought to be taught and confess that we believe in one God, the Father eternal, not at any late period beginning to be, but Who was from the first eternal God; nor yet at any time becoming Father, for He always was God and Father; and we believe in one only-begotten Son of God, being of the paternal substance, truly Son, and of the same substance as He of whom He is and is believed to be Son: and in the Holy Spirit, being of the substance of God, being not Son, but God in the substance, as being of that same substance of which is God the Father, from Whom substantially He is." And 1 Cor. ii. 12 is quoted in proof.

I cannot transcribe the whole. The writers maintained that the Three are not different Substances, but One in the oneness of the Godhead.

"And in regard to the Economy (Incarnation) which in our Lord Christ the Lord God wrought perfectly for our salvation, it is necessary

[1] Mansi, IV. 1347; Labbe and Cossart, III. 676, IV. 293; Harduin, I. 1515. (Fleury calls this the Nicene Creed, xxv. ch. 56.) It is printed in Hahn, p. 191. On comparing it with the Nicene Creed I find that it reads *κτίστην ἁπάντων, ὁρατῶν τε καὶ ἀοράτων ποιητὴν, τὸν υἱὸν τοῦ Θεοῦ μονογενῆ*, omitting *γεννηθέντα ἐκ τοῦ Θεοῦ μονογενῆ, τουτέστιν ἐκ τῆς οὐσίας τοῦ πατρός*: it omits too *γεννηθέντα οὐ ποιηθέντα, δι' οὗ τὰ πάντα ἐγένετο τά τε ἐν τῷ οὐρανῷ καὶ τὰ ἐπὶ τῆς γῆς*. It reads *δι' ἡμᾶς*, omitting *τοὺς ἀνθρώπους*; adds *ἐκ τῶν οὐρανῶν*, adds *γεννηθέντα ἐκ τῆς ἁγίας παρθένου*, adds *σταυρωθέντα ὑπὲρ ἡμῶν*; for *παθόντα* it has *ἀποθανόντα*. The conclusion is *καὶ εἰς τὸ πνεῦμα τῆς ἀληθείας, τὸ παράκλητον, ὁμοούσιον πατρὶ καὶ υἱῷ, καὶ εἰς ἁγίαν καθολικὴν ἐκκλησίαν, εἰς ἀνάστασιν νεκρῶν, εἰς ζωὴν αἰώνιον.*

The Creed is personal: *πιστεύω, I believe*, not synodal, *πιστεύομεν, we believe;* and of course there is no anathema.

[2] See the Councils, Mansi, IV. 1347; Harduin, I. 1515. It is printed by Hahn, p. 202.

[3] Compare "Whosoever wishes to be saved, &c."

that we should know that the Lord God, the Word, has taken a perfect Man, of the seed of Abraham and David, according to the plain meaning of Holy Scripture, being in nature exactly what they were of whose seed He was, perfect Man in nature, of a reasonable soul and human flesh subsisting; which Man, being like us in nature, formed by the power of the Holy Spirit in the womb of the Virgin—*made by* (ὑπὸ) *a woman, made under the law*—He in an ineffable way united to Himself. We deny that there are two Sons or two Lords (their reasons being given at length): we say that there is only one Son and Lord Jesus Christ; but, in our minds, we associate with Him (συνεπινοοῦντες) that which was taken up, Jesus of Nazareth, Whom God anointed with spirit and with power, as sharing in the Sonship and Lordship by the union with God the Word, and thus He became the second Adam." In conclusion, after quoting Acts xvii. 30, *the times of this ignorance... raising Him from the dead*, they proceed, "This is the teaching of the dogmas of the Church, and let every one who thinks contrary to them be anathema[1]. Let every one be anathema who will not receive the saving repentance. Let every one be anathema who will not observe the day of the holy Paschal feast according to the law of the holy and Catholic Church."

The last two anathemas are omitted in the early translation of Marius Mercator.

Thus so far as the framework or setting of our Athanasian Creed is concerned, we meet with it first in the Ecthesis of the heretic Theodore of Mopsuestia. This Ecthesis had been subscribed by about twenty bishops. (The subscriptions are not given by Hahn.)

§ 11. Two further subjects may be considered here, i. the meaning of the word *anathema*.

It must have been observed that the anathematizing of a layman was, at the Council of Ephesus, considered to be a punishment of the same class as the deposition of a bishop or clerk. It can scarcely be conceived therefore that, at this time, *i. e.* A. D. 431, the penalty of anathema was considered to involve eternal consequences. On the contrary the rules of the Bishops were very precise: a heretic might be admitted to communion on his death-bed. Thus it seems clear that, at this period of Church history, "we anathematize" meant merely this, "we refuse to hold communion with them." So St Augustine: "When a Christian is convicted of a crime deserving the censure of anathema, he is

[1] Compare "This is the Catholic Faith, which except a man believe faithfully and firmly, he cannot be saved."

separated from the Church for his amendment; and if he does not repent, it is by himself that he is cut off from the Church[1]." When we come to the fifth general Council we shall find that, at the date of it, the meaning of "Anathema" was much extended.

ii. The second subject to which I must devote a few lines is the meaning of the words "another faith," ἑτέρα πίστις, in the definition of Ephesus and in the canon of Chalcedon.

"The Council forbade any other profession of faith to be written or propounded than that of Nice, and ordained that they who should propose any other to people desirous of being converted from paganism, Judaism, or any heresy whatsoever, if bishops or clerks, should be deposed; if laymen, anathematized."

To this translation of a passage in Fleury (xxv. ch. 56, page 111), Mr Newman, in 1844, appended a note commencing thus:—

"This rule must evidently be interpreted by the occasion which called it forth; otherwise it might seem to be opposed to the practice of requiring the Athanasian Creed or other dogmatic formulæ of later times from heretics[2]."

A truer mode of solving the difficulty would be to exhibit this definition of Ephesus as relating to the discipline rather than to the doctrine of the Church; and no Church, I believe, considers itself bound by the disciplinary canons of the first four Councils[3].

[1] *Against Parmenianus*, Lib. III. c. ii. § 13 (Tom. IX. p. 131, ed. Gaume. I owe the reference to Fleury, XX. 46, p. 357 E). Thus the enunciation of the Athanasian Creed that "except a man believe this faithfully he cannot be saved" belongs to a date lower than the Council of Ephesus or (as we shall see) of Chalcedon.

[2] That is: if the later practice of the Church breaks a canon of an œcumenical Council we must find some way of "interpreting" the canon.

[3] I am compelled to give up the hope of escaping the difficulty by supposing that ἑτέρα πίστις meant a *differing faith.* Of course propounders of new faiths would say that their new faith did not differ from the Nicene. But the Greek fathers, at the time of this Council, did not acknowledge any such distinction between ἄλλος and ἕτερος. They used the two words indiscriminately. Indeed the context of the words shews that the Fathers at Ephesus would admit of no other faith save the Nicene. They dreaded the change of a single word: and if they had admitted any change whatever they would have exposed themselves to the attacks of the Nestorians. At a later period the objection of Eutyches to the alteration at Chalcedon and the attempted answer to it by Dioscorus shew that in their opinion the Creed of Constantinople was ἑτέρα πίστις in regard to that of Nicæa. L. and C. IV. 136 A.

[To an Englishman who accepts the XXXIIIrd Article of the English Church, the very modern usage relating to the Quicunque will not as such cause the slightest distress.]

We have in Socrates, *H. E.* II. 39, 18, the Acacians τὴν ἐν Νικαίᾳ πίστιν φανερῶς ἠθέτησαν ἀλλήν τε πίστιν ὑπαγορεύειν ἠνίττοντο.

In II. 12, we have in the title ἑτέραν ἔκθεσιν τῆς πίστεως.

II. 18, ἑτέραν ἔκθεσιν in the title, ἄλλην ἔκθεσιν in the body of the chapter.

II. 37, at Ariminum ἀναγινώσκεσθαι πεποιήκασιν ἄλλην ἔκθεσιν πίστεως.

II. 40, βουλόμενος ἑτέραν ἔκθεσιν πίστεως ἀντεισενεγκεῖν.

§ 12. The Council of Chalcedon invests the letters of Cyril with synodical authority. I will extract from one of them his exposition of the Nicene Faith. It is found in the letter addressed in the name of the Synod of Alexandria to Nestorius[1]. I will treat it as Cyril's composition. He begins with an appeal to the words of the Saviour,

"He that loveth son or daughter more than me"—and on these words he founds the duty of every one to maintain the faith. This faith had been dishonoured by Nestorius, and the upholders of it had been banished from his communion; hence the necessity of Cyril's interference. He was acting with the concurrence of his brother and fellow-minister, Celestinus of Rome.

"It[2] is not enough for Nestorius to confess with us the symbol of the faith which was put out at Nicæa; for whilst he accepts the words of it, he perverts its meaning. He must also anathematize his past impious errors." And Cyril[3] gives the Nicene Creed at length (anathematism of course included), and then expounds it. "We believe and say that the only-begotten Word of God, who was begotten of the very essence of the Father, very God of very God, came down for our salvation, and having reduced himself to a condition of humility (εἰς κένωσιν), became flesh, that is, He took flesh from the Holy Virgin, and made that flesh His own from the womb. He submitted to a birth like ours, and came forth, man from woman, without casting away what He was before....His flesh was not changed into the nature of Godhead, nor yet did the ineffable nature of the Word of God pass into the nature of flesh. Even whilst He lay as an infant on the bosom of his mother, He as God filled all creation, assessor to Him who begat Him. Thus[4] we say that the Word became hypostatically united to flesh, and so we worship one Son and Lord Jesus Christ. Nor do we say that the Word from God dwelt, as in an ordinary man, in Him that was born of the Virgin,—lest Christ should be conceived as a Godbearing man. Then[5] again we confess that He, the Son, the only-begotten God, although impassible in His own nature, has in the flesh suffered for us, according to the Scriptures, and in the crucified body claimed as His own (οἰκειούμενος) impassibly the sufferings of His own flesh; for by the grace of God *He tasted death for every man:* that so having trampled on death, He might, as it were, in His own flesh leading the way, become *the first-begotten from the dead and the first-fruits of them that slept*, and pave the ascent to incorruptibility for the nature of man. Thus He spoiled Hades.

"And this too we must add of necessity (proceeds Cyril)[6]. When we are proclaiming[7] the Death in the flesh of the only-begotten Son of God, and are confessing His Restoration to life from the dead, and His Ascent into heaven, we perform the bloodless sacrifice in our churches,

[1] Routh, II. 17.
[2] § 2.
[3] § 3.
[4] § 4.
[5] § 6.
[6] § 7.
[7] καταγγέλλοντες, cf. 1 Cor. xi. 26. Thus some Creed was used in Cyril's time in the Eucharistic office.

for so we draw near to the mystic blessings and are sanctified, being made partakers both of the holy Flesh and the precious Blood of Christ, the Saviour of us all. But not receiving it as common flesh, God forbid! nor yet as of a man who had been sanctified and was united to the Word by the unity of merit, that is to say as having a divine indwelling, but as flesh truly life-giving and belonging to the Word Himself.

"Nor do we divide[1] the words in the gospels of our Saviour between two Hypostases or Persons."..."The Lord Jesus Christ is one according to the Scriptures."

"And[2] if He is called *the Apostle and High Priest of our confession*, because as Priest He ministers (ὡς ἱερουργῶν) to God the Father *the confession* of the Faith, addressed by us to Him, and through Him to God the Father[3], we still say that He is by nature the only-begotten Son of God, and we do not assign to a man different from Him the name of the priesthood, or indeed the thing itself; for He has become Mediator between God and man....For He has offered as a sweet-smelling savour His own Body for us, not for Himself."

A few words are found relating to the Holy Spirit[4], and in the last section[5] Cyril states that "the Holy Virgin bare, according to the flesh, God united hypostatically to the flesh." This part of the letter concludes:—

"These things we have been taught from the holy Evangelists and Apostles and the whole God-inspired Scripture, and from the true confession of the blessed Fathers. To these things your piety ought to assent without any prevarication; and we have appended to the epistle the things which it is necessary for your piety to anathematize[6]."

The twelve anathemas are appended, but for these I must refer my readers to Dr Routh or the *Concilia*.

§ 13. The general acceptance of the results of Cyril's thought, at least in the west of Europe, has put that stamp of approval on them which all inductive proofs require. They are found by consent to satisfy the conditions of the problem. The key has been discovered which turns in the lock of Scripture. For few Christians could accept his dicta merely on the ground that they were sanctioned by a general Council. If ever there was a body of men of whom it must be said that they "were not all governed with the Spirit and Word of God[7]," that body was the Council—the Œcumenical Council (as it is called) of Ephesus. It is gratifying to learn that the great Roman Divines do not

[1] § 8.
[2] § 9.
[3] Note this.
[4] § 10.
[5] § 11.
[6] The series may be examined as above.
[7] Our Article (XXI) "Of the authority of general councils."

consider that any Council commands adherence and obedience *à priori:* these theologians maintain that it is the subsequent consent of Christendom that elevates a Synod into the region of authority. This merely means that the decisions are good when we have accepted them. The manifesto of the Church of England requires similar assent, only it states on what that assent must be founded. "Things ordained by Councils as necessary to salvation have neither strength nor authority unless it may be declared that they be taken out of Holy Scripture." We do not say that Cyril or the Council of Ephesus erred: we do say that we receive their definition (that is, here the canon of Chalcedon on Cyril's letter), because we think that it can be shewn to have been "taken from Scripture." For this is the meaning of our somewhat clumsy Article XXI., "quæ ab illis constituuntur ut ad salutem necessaria neque robur habent neque autoritatem nisi ostendi possint e sacris literis esse desumpta."

Many congregations in the East are not thus satisfied as to the anathemas of Cyril: and Churches of Chaldaic Christians, or Christians of St Thomas, as they are called, remain to the present day.

§ 14. After the two Councils of Ephesus had separated, John, Bishop of Antioch, wrote in the interests of peace a letter to Cyril, which may be seen in the Councils[1]. It contained a copy of an Exposition concerning the Incarnation, which had been agreed upon by the bishops of his party. It ought to be noticed:—

"Concerning the Theotocos, the Virgin Mary, and the mode of the Incarnation of the only-begotten Son of God, we will give our opinions not by way of addition (to the faith), but rather by way of filling it up, even as we have received them from the Holy Scriptures and from the tradition of the holy Fathers; certainly not adding anything to the Faith which was set out by the holy Fathers at Nicæa; for that (as we have said) is sufficient for the full knowledge of our religion, and for the rejection of all heretical false doctrines. So we will speak, not venturing on the unattainable, but by the confession of our own infirmity shutting the door against those who would attack us because of subjects which are beyond human ken.

"We confess therefore the Lord Jesus Christ, the only-begotten Son

[1] Harduin, I. 1692.

of God, to be perfect God and perfect Man, of a reasonable soul and a body, begotten of the Father before all the worlds as to His Godhead, and the same in these last days for our salvation [born] of the Virgin Mary as to His Manhood, the Same being consubstantial with the Father as to the Godhead, consubstantial with us as to the Manhood. For there has been an uniting (ἕνωσις) of two natures: hence we confess one Christ, one Son, one Lord: and in accordance with this idea of the uniting without confusion, we confess the Holy Virgin to be Theotocos, because God the Word was incarnate and made Man (ἐνανθρωπῆσαι), and from (the time of) that same conception united to Himself the temple which He took from her. But as to the evangelical and apostolical words relating to the Lord we know good theologians who understand some together as of one Person (προσώπου), and distinguish others as of two natures, and refer those of a divine character to the Godhead of the Christ, those of a humbler nature to His Manhood."

§ 15. Cyril wrote a reply embodying this document, and expressing his satisfaction with it. (Harduin, I. 1702, &c.) He expressed also his hope that John would join with him in "repressing the use of such language as this: that there is a mixing or confusion of the Word in the flesh, or *a shadow of a turning* as to the nature of the Word. For that remains ever what it is, nor was it changed, nor can it be changed." At the end of this reply he remarks that some had issued in a corrupt form the letter from Athanasius to Epictetus (from which one of the quotations at the Council had been taken), which letter was in itself entirely orthodox, as he could shew by ancient manuscripts which were in his possession. A copy of the letter he sent to John. John had promised that he and his friends would communicate with all ὅσοι τὴν ὀρθὴν καὶ ἀμώμητον πίστιν ἔχουσί τε καὶ κηρύττουσι, "rectam inculpatamque fidem habentibus et retinentibus" according to the old Latin; "who hold and preach the correct and blameless faith" according to the Greek[1].

[1] 1694 B. These words are coming into use. Compare Cyril's expression 1701 C. Of those "who keep secure and unshaken the right faith in their hearts" ἀσφαλῆ καὶ ἀκατάσειστον τὴν ὀρθὴν ἐν ἰδίαις ψυχαῖς φυλάττουσι πίστιν.

CHAPTER X.

THE EUTYCHIAN CONTROVERSY.

§ 1. Early history of Eutyches. § 2. Synod of Constantinople, 448. § 3. Eutyches' expression of his own opinions. § 4. Condemnation of Eutyches. § 5. Eutyches appealed to a larger council. § 6. Leo's first letter to Flavian, and Flavian's Exposition of his faith. § 7. Synod of Ephesus, 449. Eutyches upheld: Flavian killed. § 8. Struggle between the Churches of Alexandria and Constantinople. § 9. Preparation for the council of Chalcedon. § 10. Aetius. § 11. Council meets. First time we hear of the exposition of Constantinople. § 12. Second session. The exposition produced. § 13. Resistance of the Egyptian bishops. § 14. A new definition produced and withdrawn. § 15. The history of the received definition of Chalcedon. § 16. Thoughts upon the council. § 17. Early forgeries. § 18. The Letter of Leo to Flavian. § 19. Thoughts suggested by it. § 20. Protestant character of Leo's reasoning. § 21. No reference to the Athanasian Creed. § 22. The definition of Chalcedon.

§ 1. Amongst the strongest supporters of Cyril during his controversy with the Nestorians was Eutyches of Constantinople. He was employed or entreated by Cyril to intercede for him with the Emperor in the year 433[1]. He is mentioned again as instigating Uranius in the year 448 to the prosecution of Ibas, the bishop of Edessa, on the ground that he was a Nestorian[2]. No doubt therefore his enemies were on the alert to discover where he was slipping, and he soon gave them an opportunity. In this very year 448 we are informed that Leo the great, Pope of Rome, sent a letter to him commending his zeal in opposition to the Nestorians[3]. Eusebius, Bishop of Dorylæum, had, at first, supported him in his efforts; but, finding that Eutyches was going a little too far in his arguments, he turned against him; and within five

[1] See extract from the letter in Fleury, xxvi. 20: it is quoted from the Synodicon (Baluzius, p. 907), c. 202.

[2] Harduin, ii. 502, Labbe, iv. p. 627 d.

[3] Fleury, xxvii. 23, says that the Nestorians in question were in fact Catholics. The letter is no. xx. in the collection of the Ballerini. (Migne, liv. p. 713.)

months after the reception of the letter of St Leo he denounced him at a synod held at Constantinople in November, 448.

§ 2. The accounts of the proceedings at this synod were read at Ephesus in the succeeding year, and interrupted in the reading by the remarks of the bishops assembled there. The joint account was read at Chalcedon in 451, with similar interruptions, and we have to pick our way carefully amidst the Acts of Chalcedon to elicit what really occurred at each of the previous two meetings. Happily I am able to compare with my own memoranda the narrative as it has been drawn out by Fleury[1].

As we have seen, Cyril was content with the expressions of John of Antioch[2], "that the Lord Jesus was perfect God and perfect Man, of a reasonable soul and a body:—consubstantial with the Father as to the Godhead, consubstantial with us as to the Manhood. For there had been an uniting (ἕνωσις) of the two natures." And this was "an unconfused uniting." Flavian, Bishop of Constantinople, in expressing his belief, used the earlier part of these words; but instead of the last clause he affirmed that "He was consubstantial with his Father as to the Godhead and consubstantial with his Mother as to the Manhood: and we confess that the Christ is of (ἐκ) the two natures after His incarnation: in one Hypostasis and one Person, we confess one Christ, one Son, one Lord[3]."

At length we come to Eutyches' own account of his opinions. On Monday the fifteenth of November, John, the presbyter, who had been sent to Eutyches with a citation summoning him to the Synod, produced his answer[4]. I must not give it at length but content myself with stating that Eutyches declared his readiness to express his agreement with the "Expositions" of the holy Fathers who had met at Nicæa and Ephesus, and to subscribe to their interpretations:

"But if it should happen that any slip or mistake has been made by them in any phrase they have used, he will not find fault with them. He searched the Holy Scriptures only as being more secure than the Expositions of the Fathers; but after the Incarnation of the Son of God, i.e. after the conception (μετὰ τὴν γέννησιν) of our Lord Jesus Christ, he

[1] History, XXVII. chapters 24, &c. See Harduin, II. 110, where the proceedings at Constantinople commence.

[2] His letter was read at Constantinople and so at Ephesus, &c. Harduin, II. 119.

[3] Ibid. 127.

[4] See Fleury, XXVII. 25, or Harduin, II. 142. Mansi, V. 699, 715. L. and C. IV. 191, 208.

worshipped one nature and this the nature of God Incarnate. And he produced a little book out of which he read a complaint that he had been falsely charged with saying that God the Word had received Flesh from heaven. But (he added) that our Lord Jesus Christ was made of two natures hypostatically united, he had not[1] learned from the Expositions of the Holy Fathers, nor did he receive it, even though some one Father had said so, because, as he said, the Holy Scriptures were better than the teaching of the Fathers. And, when he said this, he confessed that He who was born of the Virgin Mary was perfect God and perfect Man, but had not flesh consubstantial with ours."

In the course of the day the bishops listened to "Expositions of the Holy Fathers concerning the faith[2];" to which they wished to compel Eutyches to assent, and then they would pardon him[3]. Flavian was kindly disposed to the Archimandrite, and at the end of the fourth session when they had risen from their seats to separate he uttered these remarkable words.

"Ye know the zeal of the accuser. Fire itself is cold compared with his zeal for piety. God knows I have entreated him, and have urged him not to proceed. But, when he insisted, what could I do? Do I wish you all to be scattered? No! I would rather collect you together. Enemies scatter: Fathers collect."

§ 3. Once more Eutyches sent to express his assent to everything that had been uttered by the Synods of Nicæa and Ephesus, and by the holy Cyril. But this was not enough. Eusebius must have a retractation of the past, as well as a promise for the future. At last, at the seventh session, Eutyches appeared. After he came, the Emperor expressed his desire that Florentius, a layman, and patrician of Rome—he had been proconsul—should be present. He came. Eusebius asked whether Eutyches believed that there was a union of two natures in one Person? Flavian altered the question; Did he confess a union out of two natures? He acknowledged this, but Eusebius was not content: he required a confession that the two natures remained after the Incarnation, and that the flesh of Jesus was consubstantial with ours.

When the Synod of Ephesus of the succeeding year heard this, they cried out, "Burn Eusebius. Burn him alive. As he divides Christ, may he be divided himself." At Chalcedon the Egyptians acknowledged that they had said this, and would say it again.

[1] So the Latin, and Fleury. The negative seems to have been dropped out in the Greek.

[2] Harduin, II. 143.

[3] 150 D.

Eutyches was more gentle. He had said before that he could not speculate on the Nature of his God: "he could not physiologize his God;" and he adduced his confession: "Thus I believe. I worship the Father with the Son and the Son with the Father: and the Holy Ghost with the Father and the Son. I confess that the Incarnate Presence has been made from flesh of the Holy Virgin, and that He *ἐνανθρωπῆσαι τελείως* became perfectly man[1] for our salvation. This I confess in the presence of the Father, and of the Son, and of the Holy Spirit, and of your holiness."

§ 4. The contest is very painful. It is well narrated by Fleury. At last Eutyches cried out: "I confess that our Lord was of (*ἐκ*) two natures before the union; but after the union I confess one nature[2]." The synod were not content: he must anathematize every thing opposed to the dogmas now read. "I have said to your holinesses what I never said before: because your holinesses teach it me. But the fathers have not all said this. And if I should pronounce the anathema—woe is me—I anathematize my fathers." The council stood to their feet and cried "Anathema to him." Flavian, Seleucus, and Florentius intervened. Eutyches, in his despair, appealed to the writings of Athanasius and Cyril: "they maintained that there was one nature after the union:" but for this the bishops did not care. They agreed that he was deposed from the priestly order, from communion with them, and from his position in the monastery: and all who held intercourse with him were liable to the penalty of excommunication (*ὑπεύθυνοι τῷ τῆς ἀκοινωνησίας ἐπιτιμίῳ*).

The judgment was subscribed (according to the Latin copies) by thirty-two bishops and twenty-three archimandrites.

§ 5. I have described this at length, partly, in order that my readers may have the opportunity of asking themselves the question whether, in the absence of all reference to it, it seems likely that the clause of the Quicunque, "God, of the substance of the Father, begotten before the worlds: Man, of the substance of His Mother, born in the world," could have been known as the work of Athanasius and enforced with the penalties of the Athanasian Creed before this discussion took place at Constantinople. And I would also ask them to contrast the sentences passed on Eutyches with

[1] Or "perfectly entered on man," p. 163.

[2] p. 165 B.

the condemnations of the Quicunque—"he cannot be saved:" "without doubt he shall perish everlastingly." It will be noticed that the Fathers did not ultimately proceed to the anathema which they had threatened. Possibly they were deterred by the bold appeal of Eutyches, in his despair, to the writings of Athanasius and Cyril.

I would also mention that although there are constant appeals here to the Councils of Nicæa and of Ephesus, I have not found a single reference to the Synod of Constantinople in 381, or to the document which we are told came from it[1]. The words "incarnate *of the Holy Ghost and the Virgin Mary*" would have been considered fatal to Eutyches, as was recognised at the Council of Chalcedon[2].

At the end of the gathering, when they were reading his condemnation, Eutyches appealed to the holy synod of the Bishops of Rome, and Alexandria, and Jerusalem, and Thessalonica. This appeal was not inserted in the minutes[3], but Florentius stated that he heard it, and informed Flavian.

§ 6. Of course a question like this could not be decided by a synod of 32 bishops, even though it was presided over by the Metropolitan of Constantinople. And perhaps Leo was not entirely unwilling to have the opportunity of revising an act of his brother of the Eastern Rome. He wrote to Flavian[4] expressing his surprise that he had received no information from him on the subject, and stating his opinion that Eutyches had been unjustly excommunicated. It is out of our way to give at length the history of the next troubled years. Suffice it to say that Leo approved of the action of Theodosius in convening a synod at Ephesus in August, 449, and sent letters to Flavian regarding it. Flavian too at the requisition of the Emperor furnished him with a kind of exposition or explanation of his faith, and I meet here with the first notice that I have found which places the Council of Constantinople on a par with those of Nicæa and Ephesus[5]. Flavian declares that "he has always followed the Holy Scriptures

[1] So in Leo's letter to Anatolius, p. 33, he refers to the Apollinarians, but makes no reference to the Council of Constantinople or to its Creed. He speaks of the Council of Nicæa as inspired. (Ep. 106, ed. Ballerini, § 2, Vol. I. p. 1165. Migne, Vol. LIV.)

[2] See below.

[3] See Harduin, II. 207 D.

[4] Ep. 23, Migne, ut sup., p. 731.

[5] The letter is in the "Councils," as Harduin, II. 7, Labbe IV. It will be remembered that Flavian was bishop of Constantinople.

and the expositions of the holy Fathers who had met at Nicæa and at Constantinople, and of those who had met at Ephesus under Cyril of holy memory, and we preach thus." He speaks of no other subject but the Incarnation, and follows at first the words which were laid down by John in that letter to Cyril, which was welcomed by the great champion of orthodoxy. He uses the phrase "consubstantial with His Mother according to His Manhood," and then proceeds,

"Thus when we confess that the Christ is, after His incarnation from the holy Virgin, in two natures, we still confess one Christ, one Son, one Lord in one Hypostasis and one Person; and we refuse to say one nature of God the Word incarnate and made man, because from the two natures there is the one and the same our Lord Jesus Christ. Still those who say two Sons or two Hypostases or two Persons, and not one and the same Lord Jesus Christ, the Son of God, we anathematize."

Flavian must have been retreating from his position in 448.

§ 7. This Council of Ephesus met on Aug. 1, 449. One hundred and thirty bishops were present from Egypt and the East, from Asia and Pontus and Thrace. Dioscorus of Alexandria, the successor of Cyril, presided by virtue of a direction from the Emperor. Eutyches read his faith[1]. It is identical with the Faith of Nicæa, save that he begins "I believe," instead of "we believe;" that is, he used the faith of the council as his own personal belief. He said he had received it from his ancestors; he had believed it, and believed it still; in that faith he was born, and in it was dedicated to God. Being baptized in that faith he had been sealed; in it he had lived, and in it he prayed to be perfected. He added that the great Cyril had given him documents to shew that the synod which met here, in Ephesus, in 431, had decreed that any one who made additions to it or alterations in it, should be subjected to the penalties therein prescribed.

The bishops unanimously upheld the Councils of Nicæa and Ephesus. On this Dioscorus claimed that they were bound to depose Flavian and Eusebius. Flavian disclaimed their authority. The Roman legate cried out in Latin, "We oppose it." Dioscorus persisted. Onesiphorus, bishop of Iconium, fell before his knees, and, clasping them, entreated him to desist. Dioscorus gave a signal, and the room was invaded by soldiers, bringing clubs and

[1] Harduin, II. 96.

chains. The signatures of the bishops were forced from them. Flavian and Eusebius were thrown into prison, and Flavian was banished. Before he reached his destination he died in consequence of the kicks he had received from the Syrian monks. The Emperor Theodosius issued an edict, upholding the authority of the "second Council of Ephesus."

It has received in ecclesiastical history the title of the "Robber Synod."

§ 8. It is necessary to read this painful narrative to appreciate the excitement under which the general Council of Chalcedon assembled two years later. Nor can the historian of the Creeds be far wrong if he draws attention in passing to the struggle that was now going on between the Churches of Constantinople and Alexandria. At Ephesus, in 431, the patriarch of Alexandria deposed the patriarch of Constantinople. The time was now come for the clergy of Constantinople to endeavour to crush the Egyptian bishops. Cyril had driven Nestorius into exile. Flavian in his death destroyed the prestige of the chair of Athanasius and Cyril.

§ 9. Theodosius died in July, 450. He was succeeded in August by Marcian, a distinguished soldier, who at once declared against Eutyches. He ordered that the body of Flavian should be brought to Constantinople and interred where the earlier bishops reposed. The change was as complete as when Elizabeth succeeded Mary.

We find now, seventy years after it had been held, the Council of Constantinople of the year 381, so long overlooked and neglected, starting into prominence. Leo wrote to Pulcheria, the sister of Theodosius, the virgin wife of Marcian, mentioning among other things that Eusebius of Dorylæum, the accuser of Eutyches, had declared his reception of the decrees of the three general councils of Nicæa, Constantinople, and Ephesus[1]. Marcian urged the desirability of holding another council, even though Leo was anxious that there should be no further examination into the mystery of the Faith. Marcian prevailed, and at length the bishops were summoned to meet at Nicæa on the first

[1] Ep. 59. Fleury, XXVII. 49.

day of September, 451. They met; but, before they proceeded to business, the seat was removed to Chalcedon, in order that the Emperor might the more easily take part in its proceedings. The first session was held on October 8. Nineteen laymen, chiefly officers of the Emperor, were present and took part in the business of the council; three hundred and sixty bishops of the East appear to be mentioned in the acts of the assembly.

Once more I must say that it is not my intention to give an account of the proceedings of the councils. But as there is one person in whose conduct we are deeply interested, I must make a few observations regarding him.

§ 10. Aëtius, now Archdeacon of Constantinople, had been present as Deacon and Notary at the synod held there in 448. He had prepared the acts of the synod. These acts were read, as we have seen, at Ephesus in the succeeding year, but not without a remonstrance on the part of Aëtius. "The production of the acts, in order that their accuracy might be attested, would give the impression that the notaries were deemed unworthy of confidence." He was compelled, however, to produce his copy; it was compared with notes which had been taken by the friends of Eutyches. It was found that opinions of single bishops were represented as being the judgment of the council. The appeal of Eutyches to the judgment of a synod to be held at Rome or Alexandria, or Jerusalem, had been omitted. Nevertheless Aëtius now appeared as the "promoter" at the Council of Chalcedon.

§ 11. The acts of Ephesus, which had been prepared by this advocate, were read at length at the first gathering of the council. The interruptions were numerous and disorderly; the magistrates had occasion again and again to interfere. "These tumultuous acclamations do not become bishops, nor will they assist the parties: let the reading proceed."

That which, from our point of view, was the most important interruption, was this. The minutes of the Robber Synod were being read, and the reader came to the recitation of the faith of Eutyches. He had proclaimed his belief in the words of the genuine Nicene Faith, and had declared that in it he had been baptized, and in it he hoped to be perfected, and then reminded the synod of the definition of the council of the year 431, which prohibited either additions to, or diminutions from, that Faith[1]. Here was a difficulty. But Diogenes, bishop of Cyzicus, was equal to the emergency. He cried out,

> "Eutyches adduced the synod falsely: it received an addition from the holy Fathers because of the perversities of Apollinarius and Valentinius and Macedonius and men like them; and there have been added to the Symbol of the Fathers the words *who came down and was incarnate of the Holy Ghost and of the Virgin Mary*[2]. This (he proceeded) Eutyches has passed over, for he is an Apollinarian; even Apollinarius received the Nicene Synod, understanding the letter of the Creed in accordance with his own perversity. The holy Fathers at Nicæa had only the words *He was incarnate*, but those that followed explained it by saying *of the Holy Ghost and the Virgin Mary.*"

This statement was immediately contradicted by the Egyptian bishops; they cried out, "No one admits of addition; no one admits of diminution: let the decree of Nicæa stand good. The orthodox Emperor has commanded it[3]."

The first day's session was of prolonged duration. It seems incredible that the council could have listened to all that is said to have taken place. The fact that they went through so much is itself a proof of the excitement they were under. They went on until it was dark, and then wax candles were lighted. Still they proceeded, cries being heard again for the condemnation of Dioscorus. At length the reading ceased, and the magistrates addressed the assembly[4]. They said that it appeared that Flaviau and Eusebius had been condemned unjustly. The bishop of Alexandria and others ought now to suffer. The Eastern bishops cried out their Trisagion, ἅγιος ὁ θεὸς, ἅγιος ἰσχυρὸς, ἅγιος ἀθάνατος, ἐλέησον ἡμᾶς. The magistrates proceeded to urge that each bishop present should, without delay, expound his own faith in writing, without fear of any one, "knowing that the Emperor accepted the exposition of the 318 fathers who had met at Nicæa, and the exposition of the 150 who had met at a later time, and the canonical epistles and expositions of the holy fathers, Gregory, and Athanasius, and Basil, and Hilary, and Ambrose, and the two

[1] Mansi, VI. 631, 632. Harduin, II. 98.

[2] δολερῶς προσέταξε τὴν ἐν Νικαίᾳ τῶν ἁγίων πατέρων σύνοδον· ἐδέξατο δὲ προσθήκην παρὰ τῶν ἁγίων πατέρων διὰ τὴν ἔννοιαν τὴν κακὴν Ἀπολιναρίου καὶ Βαλεντίνου καὶ Μακεδονίου—καὶ προστεθεῖται τῷ συμβόλῳ τῶν ἁγίων πατέρων "τὸν κατελθόντα καὶ σαρκωθέντα ἐκ πνεύματος ἁγίου καὶ Μαρίας τῆς παρθένου." Mansi, VI. 632.

[3] Mansi, VI. 632, Labbe and Coss. IV. 134, 5. Harduin, II. 99.

[4] Harduin, p. 271.

canonical epistles of Cyril, which had been published and confirmed at Ephesus." And they referred to the letter of Leo to Flavian.

Thus we hear now for the first time of an Exposition of the 150 fathers who had met subsequently to the Synod of Nicæa.

§ 12. The bishops and magistrates needed some rest on the day following this prolonged and excited meeting. They did not meet on that day, but assembled on the tenth of October. The magistrates again addressed the bishops in the same strain as that with which they had dismissed the previous meeting—expressing their anxiety for the removal of doubts regarding the truth, and urging all without fear or favour, love or hatred, to expound or set forth the faith in its purity. "The bishops were to remember that the magistrates as well as the Emperor guarded the Exposition[1] which had been handed down by the 318, and by the 150, and moreover by the other holy and venerable fathers."

The bishops cried out, "No one maketh another Exposition[2], nor do we undertake or venture to send one out: the fathers taught us: what was put out by them is preserved in writing: we cannot say more." The magistrates pressed their demand. The reply was, "We cannot make for ourselves a written Expositiou. There is a canon which directs us to be content with what is already expounded. The canon directs that there shall be no other Exposition made." Cecropius of Sebastopolis said: "The faith has been well distinguished by the 318 fathers, and confirmed by the holy fathers Athanasius, Cyril, Celestinus, Hilary, Basil, Gregory, and now by the most holy Leo: and we request that what was done by the 318 fathers and by Leo may be read."

Eunomius bishop of Nicomedia read: "The Exposition of the Synod held at Nicæa"—the Nicene Faith, of course with its anathemas.

The bishops cried out: "This is the faith of the orthodox; into this we were baptized; into this we baptize; Cyril believed thus; Leo has interpreted thus."

[1] Note the one exposition, τὴν ἔκθεσιν.

[2] ἔκθεσιν ἄλλην, Harduin, II. 285, A, B, C, i. e. three times. This is an almost contemporaneous explanation of the Canon of Ephesus.

The magistrates ordered—"Let the things set out[1] by the 150 holy fathers be also read."

Aëtius, the deacon of Constantinople, read thus: "The holy faith which the 150 fathers set out, agreeing with the holy and grand Synod in Nicæa."

And at length we have what is called the Creed of Constantinople.

The bishops cried out: "This is the faith of all the orthodox. This we all believe[2]."

Aëtius passed on at once to read two of Cyril's letters—the second being his reply accepting the proposals of the Synod of Antioch. And Veronicianus, as Secretary of the Consistory[3], then read the synodical letter of Leo to Flaviau—of which I must give an account hereafter[4].

Passages of the letter were called in question by the bishops of Illyricum and Palestine, but Aëtius, in each instance, produced testimony from Cyril in support of the language impugned.

The magistrates again insisted on having an Explanation of the Faith: the bishops still resisted.

At the next session, held three days afterwards, the trial of Dioscorus commenced in the proper form. Aëtius acted as prosecutor.

Thus was the "faith of Constantinople" launched upon the world. It was launched—certainly not without circumstances calculated to rouse our suspicions. The synod of the year 381 was not such as to attract attention at the time: this act of the synod—if performed—had been long buried in oblivion. We know that the 150 had confirmed the Faith of Nicæa: but that they had put forth a faith of their own, different in words, though agreeing in general sentiment, rests primarily on the statement of the magistrates in the first session of the Council of 451. The character of that faith rests on the unsupported testimony of the partisan Aëtius.

§ 13. It is needless to describe at length the scenes which now occurred: Dioscorus was deposed. And after his deposition

[1] τὰ ἐκτεθέντα, Harduin, II. 288, L. and C. 342, Mansi, VI. 957.

[2] Mansi, VI. 957, L. and C. IV. 342.

[3] σηκρητάριος τοῦ θειοῦ κονσιστωρίου (!).

[4] The Collections add here testimonies in support of Leo's teaching, from Hilary, Gregory and others. The Athanasian Creed is not quoted.

the Egyptian bishops were without a head and in a minority of ten in a body of 600; and the violence of the heterodox synod of 449 furnished some pretext to the orthodox council now. These orthodox bishops without exception gave in their adherence to the letter of Leo, and stated that it agreed with the faith of the 318 and the 150[1]. The ten Egyptian bishops presented a petition to the Emperor in which they assured him of their adherence to the faith of Nicæa, of Athanasius, and of Cyril. At the council they declared that they were ready to anathematize Eutyches. But even this was not enough. They must also subscribe to the letter of Leo. They replied that they durst not do this without the consent of the Archbishop of Alexandria: and there was no Archbishop now. "They must give bail then not to leave the city until a new Archbishop was appointed."

Another scene occurred on the same day with the Syrian archimandrites. They were urged to acquiesce in the condemnation of Dioscorus. But Barsumas was one of those who had taken part in the assault on Flavian. "The most reverend bishops cried out, Drive out the murderer Barsumas: the murderer to the arena! anathema to Barsumas! Barsumas to exile[2]!" He was allowed to speak: "I believe as the three hundred and eighteen fathers; and so was I baptized into the Name of the Father, and of the Son, and of the Holy Ghost, even as the Lord taught the Apostles themselves[3]." Others also stood to the Nicene Faith. Aëtius went up to them and said, "This holy and grand synod believes that the 318 fathers collected at Nicæa expounded the faith: and their symbol they keep and teach to all that come to them. But, inasmuch as in the meantime questions have been raised by some persons, and, in opposing them, the holy fathers Cyril, and Celestinus, and now the most holy Pope Leo, have issued letters interpreting the symbol but not putting forth (*ἐκτιθέμενοι*) any faith or dogma, and these letters the whole œcumenical synod accepts and assents to, and their interpretation it delivers to all who are anxious to learn:—does your love assent to this opinion of the whole synod? and does it anathematize Nestorius and Eutyches or not?"

The Egyptians adhered to the Nicene Faith.

[1] Harduin, II. 386. [2] 424 E. [3] 428 C.

§ 14. It will be remembered that at the end of the first session the magistrates expressed their desire that every one present should write down his faith, to meet the new difficulties of the day. One such definition (ὅρος) was produced at the fifth session, but the notary was instructed not to enter it on the minutes[1]. Yet with the exception of the Roman and some Eastern bishops, this definition pleased the synod. The majority said: "Let it be set down in the Symbol that the holy Mary is Mother of God." The Roman bishops, however, were firm, and the magistrates sent their secretary to the Emperor to report the difficulty.

§ 15. The Emperor ordered that six bishops of the East and three from each of the provinces of Pontus, Asia, Thrace and Illyricum should meet the Archbishop Anatolius and the Roman legate, and in consultation put into a proper shape a declaration on the points in dispute regarding the faith[2]. With a little modification the proposal was accepted, and to this committee we owe "The Definition of Chalcedon." It was adopted by the synod: and then, in the presence of Marcian[3], the bishops again expressed their adherence to it—and the Definition being thus read and subscribed, became the "Definition of the Church."

We need not push further our investigations as to the council: we must turn to the Definition itself.

§ 16. On reviewing the actions of the council, we must confess that they are clouded with difficulties: and when the veil is lifted, we find how true the words of our Reformers are that "A general council is an assembly of men, of whom all are not moved by the Spirit and Word of God."

There is little in its proceedings to command our respect apart from the conduct of the laymen who interfered from time to time, although even they occasionally acted as partisans. Among the bishops there was no commanding spirit present. From the heathenish cry proceeding from the orthodox, "Barsumas to the arena"—meaning (as Fleury quietly suggests), "cast him to the lions of the amphitheatre"—down to the

[1] Harduin, II. 448 A.

[2] τὰ περὶ τῆς πίστεως ὀρθῶς καὶ ἀνεπιλήπτως τυπῶσαι, p. 450 C.

[3] He spoke of the Council of Nicæa but not of Constantinople, Harduin, II. 576 C.

abject terror of the Egyptian bishops who rolled themselves upon the pavement asking fruitlessly for compassion on their gray hairs, we see that there was no room for debate, no opportunity for discussion. It was useless to cry, "The letter of Leo is new: let us consult our friends at home." The answer was, "Let them assent to the epistle at once or receive condemnation."

It was in the midst of an assembly such as this, that Aëtius produced what he called "the Holy Faith which the Holy Fathers in number one hundred and fifty put forth, agreeing with the holy and great Synod of Nicæa." Can the assent of the bishops to the document be deemed an intelligent approval of the statement of Aëtius? Let those judge who read the account. And who was Aëtius[1]?

§ 17. Greater men than he had been guilty of what we should call the crime of forging testimony. In the year 419, at a Council of Carthage a canon was quoted allowing a bishop who was deposed by the provincial council to appeal to the Pope. Such a canon had been passed at the western Synod of Sardica: but it was quoted at Carthage as having been passed at the great Council of Nicæa. A wonderful difference! The mistake was detected on the spot: and is explained by Gieseler. But the falsehood was repeated by no less a man than Leo in 449. To a letter addressed to Theodosius the great Pope annexed what he called the Canons of Nicæa: they contained this very Canon of Sardica. By the bishops at the Council of Carthage the mistake was detected: would the layman Theodosius be equally able to detect it? Would he suspect a fraud?—But what was the motive of Aëtius? The circumstances were these. The magistrates had demanded a new exposition of the faith of the bishops to meet

[1] Fleury, XXVII. 43, p. 313.

Usher in his famous treatise *de symbolo Romano* quotes Photius of Tyre as saying that the Bishops at Constantinople confirmed the orthodox faith, and proclaimed the Holy Spirit also as Very God and Consubstantial with the Father, and added to the symbol of the faith which had been put out at Nicæa, these words: "And in the Holy Ghost, the Lord and Giver of Life......Life of the world to come. Amen." And thus having filled up the entire symbol of the orthodox faith, they have delivered it to the Church.

This Photius was appointed Bishop of Tyre in 448, therefore even if the work is genuine, the evidence is scarcely corroborative: and the writer of his life in the *Dictionary of Biography* seems to question its genuineness. I believe the work has never been printed. The statement of Nicephorus Callistus that the additions were due to the influence of Gregory of Nyssa does not seem to be of much value, seeing that Nicephorus was living in 1400.

the difficulties of the day. They were unwilling to compromise themselves: unwilling, it may be, to confess that the Faith of Nicæa was insufficient. But Epiphanius had published a Creed which contained additions "very useful for these times." It is sufficiently clear that that Creed of Epiphanius was the foundation for this exposition adduced by Aëtius.—And here the veil comes down upon us, never perhaps to be removed.

§ 18. I have already shewn[1] the differences between this Creed of Aëtius and the other two with which it is allied. So my next step will be to exhibit THE LETTER OF LEO TO FLAVIAN to which the majority at Chalcedon demanded the subscription of the minority. The letter in the original is contained not only in the collections of Leo's works[2] and of the councils, but also in Mr Harvey's *Ecclesiæ Anglicanæ Vindex Catholicus,* and in Dr Heurtley's volume *De Fide et Symbolo.* It was written when Leo's opinion of Eutyches had changed. He complains now of his imprudence and want of skill.

People fall into this condition of folly "who, when they are hindered by any obscurity from obtaining knowledge of the truth, refer not to the words of the Prophets, not to the letters of the Apostles, not to the authority of the Gospels, but to themselves." "What knowledge can a man have of the pages of the Old and New Testament who does not even comprehend the first lessons of the Symbol?" And Leo quotes the Roman symbol (of which we have yet to treat) "in which the whole Body of the Faithful profess that they believe *in God the Father Almighty, and in Jesus Christ His only Son our Lord, who was born by the Holy Ghost of the Virgin Mary.* In these three sentences almost all the machinery of the heretics is destroyed. For where God is believed to be Omnipotent and Eternal Father, the Son is shewn to be coeternal with Him, in nothing differing from the Father. He is begotten, God of God, Omnipotent of Omnipotent, Eternal of Eternal; not later in time, not inferior in power, not dissimilar in glory, not divided in essence. He being the Eternal, Only-begotten of the Eternal Father, was born by the Holy Ghost of the Virgin Mary. And this birth in time took nothing from, added nothing to, that divine and eternal nativity, but devoted itself entirely to the restoration of man who had been deceived, so that He should both overcome death and also destroy the devil *who had the power of death.* For we should not be able to overcome the author of sin and death, if He had not undertaken our nature and made it His own; He, Whom neither sin could contaminate nor death destroy. For He was conceived of the Holy Ghost in the womb of the Virgin Mary, who brought Him forth, as she conceived Him,

[1] Above, p. 94.

[2] Migne, Vol. LIV. Ep. 38, p. 757.

without losing her virginity. If Eutyches could not have learnt thus much from this pure fountain of the Christian faith (*i.e.* the Creed) he might at all events have submitted himself to the teaching of the Gospels." And Leo quotes Matthew i. 1, and for Apostolic doctrine Romans i. 1, 2; and then Genesis xxxii. 18, for the prophetic announcement. And Gal. iii. 16, and Isaiah vii. 14, and Luke i. 34, and John i. 14 furnish proofs or illustrations. The last text "*The Word was made flesh, and dwelt in us*," he explains "dwelt, that is, in that flesh which He took from man, and which He animated by the spirit of the rational life (*vitæ rationalis* = τῆς λογικῆς ψυχῆς).

"Thus were the peculiarities of each nature preserved; they met in one Person, and humility was assumed by majesty, weakness by power, mortality by eternity; and, in order to enable Him to pay the debt of our condition, the inviolable nature was united to a passible nature. Thus there was one Mediator, and He could die in respect of the one, Who could not die in respect of the other. Yet He was free from sin. He augmented the human properties, He did not diminish the divine. This *making Himself of no reputation* was the assumption of misery, not the defection of power. He, Who remaining in the form of God made man, in the form of a servant was made man. Each nature retains its properties without defect. Born by a new nativity, as the inviolate virginity knew not concupiscence, so He ministers the material flesh. Thus from the Mother of the Lord our nature was assumed, but not our fault. Because the nativity was miraculous, we must not view the nature as dissimilar from ours. He that is true God is true Man. Each form (μορφή clearly) does what is proper to itself in communion with the other; the Word doing that which belongs to the Word; the Flesh that which belongs to the Flesh. To hunger, to thirst, to be weary and to sleep are evidently human: to feed five thousand with five loaves; to bestow on the Samaritan woman the living water, the draught of which would grant to her that she should thirst no more; to walk over the sea with footsteps that sank not in it, and to calm down the rising waves in the storm, are undoubtedly divine. As therefore it is not of the same nature to weep in tender affection over the friend that was dead, and to call that friend again to life when he had been dead four days; to hang upon the cross, and, turning light into darkness, to make all the elements tremble; to be pierced with nails, and to open the gates of paradise to the faith of the robber: so it is not of the same nature to say *I and the Father are one*, and to say *The Father is greater than I.* From us, His is a humanity less than the Father; from the Father, His is a divinity equal with the Father.

"Because of this unity of Person, understood in either nature, the Son of Man is said to have descended from heaven, whilst the Son of God assumed the flesh from the Virgin from whom He was born. Again the Son of God is said to have been crucified and buried, although He suffered this, not in the divinity wherein He is coeternal and consubstantial with the Father, but in the weakness of the human nature. Thus we acknowledge in the symbol that the only-begotten Son of God was *crucified and buried*[1]. The confession of Peter recognised as *Son*

[1] The Roman Creed again.

of the living God, Him Whom he saw *in the form of a servant*, and in the truth of the flesh[1]. And why, after the resurrection of His very Body, did He continue with His disciples those forty days, except to clear from every stain the integrity of our faith? Conversing with His disciples, living with them, allowing Himself to be handled by them, He came to His disciples *when the doors were shut*, and with His breathing gave them the Holy Spirit, and awakened their understandings to understand the Scriptures. And, once more, He gave them permission to handle Him and see, that so it might be recognised that the properties of the human and of the divine nature remained in Him unsevered."

He shews how Eutyches feared not to contravene 1 John iv. 2, according to his reading of it.

"For what is it *to solve Jesus* but to separate from Him the human nature, and render void that Sacrament of the Faith[2] through which alone we are saved?" and Leo shews that this error affects the whole doctrine regarding the death of Christ. He speaks of the blood and water flowing from His side as emblems that the Church should be bedewed with the laver and the chalice; and *the spirit and the water and the blood* of 1 John v. 4, he explains of "the Spirit of Sanctification, and the blood of Redemption, and the water of Baptism, which three are one and remain inseparable. None of them is parted from its connection with the others. The Catholic Church lives in this faith; so that in Christ Jesus neither is the humanity to be believed without the true divinity, nor yet the divinity without the true humanity."

§ 19. Such is the substance of this important letter, for which we have to thank, not the Council of Chalcedon, but the good Spirit of God guiding Leo into the truth. We cannot feel surprised that the council accepted its statements and gave it synodical authority; and it has remained a landmark for theologians from that day to this. In England only, during the last few years, has there arisen a school of clergy who have dared to contravene its teaching. In their anxiety to inculcate an objective presence of the Body and Blood of our Lord in the Consecrated Elements, some have adopted the conception that the Nature of our Lord's Body and Blood is changed, a conception which was condemned at Chalcedon. One indeed has denied the true human character of His Body during His earthly lifetime[3].

[1] I do not delay to give the passage on the primacy of Peter, which it must be remembered comes from a Bishop of Rome.

[2] Does this mean the Creed or the Incarnation? I presume the latter.

[3] And this person is claimed as a champion of orthodoxy. See my *Plea for Time in dealing with the Athanasian Creed*, 1873, p. 94.

§ 20. Two things remain to be noticed. One is what I may call the Protestant character of Leo's argument. The only authority he recognises is the authority of Scripture. With the assistance of this he explains, fills up, enlarges the simple scriptural statement of the early Symbol. There is no reference to other writers; no appeal to the Rule of Faith as enforcing that which he is pressing. Calm, reasoning, argumentative, majestic in his style, he shews an entire confidence that he will convince others as he is convinced himself. He had fought his way to his belief, and was now assured that others would follow him.

§ 21. The other is the entire absence of the phraseology of the Athanasian Creed, even where we should most expect it. The conceptions overlap at times, but the language is different. In the Quicunque we have *nihil majus aut minus; nihil prius aut posterius.* Leo speaks of the Son not being *minor* or *posterior.* The Quicunque says that the Son is *æqualis Patri secundum divinitatem, minor Patre secundum humanitatem.* Leo's words are *Illi minor Patre humanitas, æqualis cum Patre divinitas.* Hilary of Arles was well known to Leo; indeed there had been some clashing of opinions between them. Hilary had died in 449. If the Quicunque had been written by Hilary, it was either unknown to Leo, or if known disregarded by him. He did not think it of any great authority. The supposition recently revived that it was of Athanasian origin is utterly irreconcileable with the conduct of the Egyptian bishops at the Council of Chalcedon.

§ 22. We may now turn to the DEFINITION of the Council of Chalcedon[1]. But a few words of prelude may be excused as to the Canons of the council. By the first the bishops decided that all the Canons put forth by the several earlier synods remained in force. It would seem, therefore, that such Canons were deemed to lapse when the next council sat; a thing worthy of remembrance. The twenty-six which followed relate to the discipline and morals of the clergy, monks, nuns. Three others are found in the collection of Justellus (not however in the old translation of Dionysius Exiguus), the first of which confirmed and enlarged the canon of the year 381, regarding the privileges of the Church of

[1] It is entitled "expositio fidei" in one of the Vatican MSS. Rifferscheid in *Wiener Sitzungsberichte*, tom. LVI. p. 579, &c.

Constantinople, "the New Rome." The last had reference to the refusal of the bishops of Egypt to subscribe to the Epistle of Leo, unless they had the assent of the Bishop of Alexandria. They were directed to remain in the imperial city until an Archbishop should be appointed.

THE DEFINITION OF THE COUNCIL began as follows[1]:

"Our Lord and Saviour Jesus Christ, in confirming to His disciples the knowledge of the Faith, said, *My peace I leave unto you, My peace I give unto you;* so that no one should disagree with his neighbour in the dogmas of godliness, but the preaching of the truth be made alike to all. But inasmuch as the evil one never ceases to sow his tares among the seeds of godliness, ever finding out something new against the truth, therefore the Master, providing, as is His wont, for the human race, has raised up for us this pious and zealously faithful king, and has called together the leaders of the priesthood from every quarter, so that by the working of the grace of Christ (who is Master of us all) every pestilential falsehood may be removed from Christ's flock, and it may drink in freely from the fountain of truth. And this we have done, having by a common vote driven away the dogmas of error and renewed the unerring faith of the Fathers, proclaiming to all the Symbol of the 318, and adducing in support of it the Fathers who have accepted this composition (σύνθεμα) of godliness. Such are the one hundred and fifty who met in the great city of Constantine, who themselves also subscribed that Faith. Observing therefore the precedents regarding the Faith (some of us having been present at the holy synod held at Ephesus, in which Celestinus of Rome and Cyril of Alexandria were leaders), we define that predominant over all stands out the Exposition of the holy and undefiled Faith of the three hundred and eighteen Fathers who were collected at Nicæa in the time of Constantine of pious memory; and then that there remain in force the things defined by the 150 Fathers who met at Constantinople for the uprooting of such heresies as had then grown up, and for the confirmation of the same Catholic and Apostolic Faith."

Here is inserted "the Symbol of the 318 Fathers who met at Nicæa," not accurately, however, for (i.) the words *both which are in heaven and which are in earth* are omitted from the clause, *By whom all things were made;* (ii.) *from heaven* was added after *descended;* (iii.) *of the Holy Ghost and the Virgin Mary* was added after *was incarnate;* (iv.) *was buried* was inserted; (v.) *according to the Scriptures* was added; (vi.) *sitteth on the right hand of God the Father* was added; (vii.) *of whose kingdom there shall be no end* was added; (viii.) after *and the Holy Ghost* was added *the*

[1] This will be found in the acts of the fourth session. It is reprinted by Routh, *Reliquiæ*, Vol. II.

Lord and Giver of life; and (ix.) out of the anathematism the word *created* was omitted. Thus there were eight alterations introduced into the Confession or Creed. In eight places did this version differ from the text read by Eunomius a few days previously. Such was the Chalcedon notion of accuracy of quotation[1].

Then follow the words "The Symbol of the one hundred and fifty Fathers collected at Constantinople," and the symbol itself.

In consequence of the alterations introduced into the copy of the Nicene Creed, the differences between it and the symbol of the 150 as exhibited here are reduced to the following:—The Constantinopolitan Creed (i.) adds *of heaven and earth;* (ii.) instead of *Son of God, who was begotten of the Father, only-begotten, that is, from the substance of the Father,* it reads *the only-begotten Son of God, begotten of the Father before all worlds;* (iii.) it omits *God of God.* In regard to the Incarnation, Sufferings, &c. of our Lord, the Nicene Creed had been altered to suit this Creed of Constantinople. (iv.) After the words *Lord and Giver of life,* the words *who proceedeth from the Father* and all that follow were added. The anathematism is omitted.

The Definition proceeds as follows:

"This wise and saving symbol of God's grace was sufficient for the full knowledge and strengthening of godliness, for it plainly teaches the perfection of the Father and of the Son and of the Holy Ghost, and explains the Incarnation of the Lord to those who receive it faithfully. But, inasmuch as those who are endeavouring to put on one side the teaching of the truth, have by their heresies obtruded vain words—some attempting to corrupt the mystery of the Dispensation which the Lord underwent on our account, and denying the use of the word Theotocos of the Virgin; others introducing a confusion and a mixture [of natures], and supposing in their folly that there is one nature of the Flesh and the Godhead, and teaching the prodigious tenet that the Divine Nature was by this confusion capable of suffering—for this cause, this holy, vast, and œcumenical synod, being anxious to exclude all these machinations against the truth, and teaching openly what has been unshaken from the very first, DEFINES, first of all, that the Faith of the 318 Fathers remains untouched[2]. And, on the one hand, it confirms the teaching delivered by the 150 concerning the Essence of the Holy Spirit, a teaching which they made known to all not as introducing anything wanting in the earlier accounts, but as explaining by written testimonies their meaning in opposition to those who are eager to detract from the Majesty of the Holy Spirit. And, on the other hand, because of those who attempt to corrupt the mystery of the Dispensa-

[1] Neither Fleury nor Dr Routh notice these very important differences.
[2] After they had altered it!

tion, shamelessly fabling that He who was born of the Holy Virgin was a mere man, it has accepted the synodical letters written by Cyril to Nestorius and his supporters, to exhibit their folly, and to explain the meaning of the Symbol to such as in pious zeal desire it. And to these letters the synod has reasonably added that of Leo to Flavian, now among the saints, as consentient with the confession of the great Peter (Matt. xvi. 16), and as furnishing a boundary or limit marking off those who teach erroneously.

"Following therefore the holy Fathers, we confess One and the same Son, our Lord Jesus Christ; and we all together in harmony proclaim with one voice that the Same is perfect in Deity, the Same perfect in humanity, truly God, truly Man, the Same of a reasonable soul and body, consubstantial with the Father according to the Deity, the Same consubstantial with us according to the Humanity; in all points like us, sin excepted; begotten of the Father before all worlds according to the Deity, but the Same, in these last days, for us and for our salvation [born] of the Virgin Mary, the Mother of God, according to the Humanity; one and the same Christ, Son, Lord, only-begotten, acknowledged in two natures, without confusion, without change, indivisibly, inseparably; the difference of natures being in no way extinguished because of the union, but the properties of each nature being preserved, and meeting together in one Person and one Hypostasis; not, as it were, parted or divided into two Persons, but One and the same Son, only-begotten, God, the Word, the Lord Jesus Christ; as from the first the prophets [spake] of Him; as the Lord Jesus Christ Himself plainly taught us; and as the Symbol of the Fathers has delivered it to us.

"This therefore being laid down with all accuracy in every part, the holy and œcumenical synod decrees that no one shall be allowed to put forth or to compose a different Faith, or to conceive or teach differently. And it decrees that those who shall venture either to compose a different Faith, or to submit or teach or deliver a different Symbol to such as desire to turn to the knowledge of the truth from Hellenism, or from Judaism, or from any heresy whatever, shall, if they are bishops or clerks, be deposed from their episcopate or clerus; if they are monks or laymen, be anathematized."

"After the reading of the Definition, all the most pious bishops cried out, This is the faith of the Fathers; let the Metropolitans subscribe at once." And the thing was done.

Four hundred and seventy bishops subscribed. The Legates of the Pope, according to the Greek text, said, "I have subscribed." According to the Latin, Paschasius stated, "I have decreed, have consented, and have subscribed." The difference is instructive.

CHAPTER XI.

LITURGICAL USE OF THE NICENE CREED.

§ 1. The Nicene and Constantinopolitan Creeds as given in the Definition of Chalcedon. § 2. The latter introduced generally into the Liturgy about A. D. 568. § 3. Reverence paid to the four great Councils. Council under Menna, 536. § 4. Edict of Justinian. § 5. Received at Toledo in 589. § 6. When introduced into the Roman Church? § 7. Use of Nicene Creed at Baptism in Greek. § 8. It was recited in Greek also at the Eucharist in Germany. § 9. Used at Visitation of the Sick and Extreme Unction. § 10. True Nicene Creed used at Synods. § 11. Creed of Constantinople in the Eastern Churches. § 12. Used as an Episcopal profession. § 13. Creed of the Armenian Liturgy continues the anathematism.

WE have now reached such a stage in our work that it will be convenient to continue the histories of the Nicene and Constantinopolitan Creeds, leaving for the present all considerations as to the growth of precision of language on the Trinity, and all notes of the still ever-changing Rules or Definitions of the Faith. The history of the Roman Creed, thanks to the labours of Dr Heurtley, need not delay us long.

§ 1. It will be well to recite the Nicene Creed as given in the Definition of Chalcedon: in my notes will be found the deviations of the Creed of Constantinople as it is there delivered:

"We believe in one God, the Father Almighty, Maker[1] of all things visible and invisible: and in one Lord Jesus Christ[2], Son of God, who was begotten of the Father, only-begotten, that is from the substance of the Father, God of God, Light of Light, Very God of Very God, begotten not made, consubstantial with the Father, by whom all things were made: who for us men, and for our salvation came down from heaven, and was incarnate of the Holy Ghost and the Virgin Mary, and

[1] C. adds "of heaven and earth and."

[2] C. reads "the only-begotten Son of God, begotten of the Father before all worlds," and omits "God of God."

was made man, and was crucified also for us under Pontius Pilate, suffered and was buried: and on the third day He rose again according to the Scriptures, and ascended into heaven, and sitteth on the right hand of the Father, and shall come again with glory to judge the quick and the dead: of whose kingdom there shall be no end: and in the Holy Ghost, the Lord and Giver of life."

The Symbol of the 318 in Nicæa, as it is called in its title, concludes with the anathematism of the Council: the Symbol of the 150 Fathers who met at Constantinople continues thus: "Who proceedeth from the Father, who with the Father and the Son is worshipped and glorified," and so on to the concluding "Amen."

Thus was the document adapted for Liturgical use, like to the Creed of Cyril of Jerusalem, and the original Creed of Eusebius of Cæsarea. For such use the Symbol of Nicæa was not adapted. It was a declaration of the faith and act of the Council.

§ 2. Let us now pass on with their history. Timotheus, bishop of Constantinople in 511, is stated by Theodorus Lector, in his *History of the Church*[1], to have ordered that the Creed "should be recited at every congregation; whereas, before, it had been used only on the Thursday before Easter, when the bishop catechized the candidates for baptism." The language is curious: it may imply that this Creed had, prior to the date mentioned, been delivered privately to the candidates. A similar direction is said to have been given at Antioch at an earlier period: *i.e.* by Peter the Fuller, who had been patriarch there from 450 to 488. The learned Zaccaria[2] thought that these orders of heretical men could not have been obeyed to any extent. His opinion was that the Emperor Justin A.D. 568 was the first who directed that the Creed should be generally used in Service-time. Justin's direction was that, in every Catholic Church, the Creed of Constantinople should be sung by the people before the Lord's Prayer. It became however the custom to sing it before the Consecration. These facts are interesting because they enable us to correct some misstatements which have been made as to the date and character of what are called the Primitive Greek Liturgies[3].

[1] p. 563. See Usher ut sup. p. 16.

[2] *Bibliotheca Ritualis*, Rome 1776, Tom. II. p. civ. See too Nicolas, *Le Symbole des Apôtres*, pp. 52, 58.

[3] Thus Dr R. F. Littledale in the Preface to the second edition of the Liturgies of St Mark, St James, St Clement, &c. (London, Hayes, 1868): "The

§ 3. Passing onwards I must remark that we now find that these four great Councils are beginning to be grouped together as of co-ordinate authority. In the beginning of the sixth century, the Acephali, a kind of semi-Eutychians, attracted attention, and in 536 a council was held at Constantinople with reference to them. It is called the "Council under Menna," who was Archbishop and Patriarch of the imperial city. At the fourth session of this council, Anthimus was condemned, although he had "pretended" that he accepted the holy synods: he was put out of the priesthood of Trapezus, and deprived of all other (πάσης ἑτερας) priestly designation and honour, and of the privilege of being numbered among the orthodox[1]. In the fifth session a kind of Rule of Faith was read, as addressed to the Emperor Justinian, which is interesting as covering in part the same ground as our Athanasian Creed, yet with no verbal similarity with it[2]. But the great interest of the Synod arises from the "Professions of Faith" which were poured into it, of different dates and from many sides. Such professions we have from Dalmatia[3]; from Syria[4]; from Antioch[5] (this recognises only one Symbol, that of the 318); from

present edition of the Primitive Greek Liturgies is practically a reimpression of the former one......The great impetus which has been given to Liturgical studies by causes which lie deeper than the mere passing controversies of the day, is a sufficient warrant for bringing these priceless reliques of early Christian times once more before the public; and even in reference to those controversies it is impossible to overrate the clearness or importance of their testimony to the cardinal dogmas of the Real Objective Presence, and the Propitiatory Sacrifice of the Eucharist for the living and the dead." The fact is that these Liturgies as reprinted by Dr Littledale never speak of the Real Presence at all, nor have I found any allusion to the doctrine of a Propitiatory Sacrifice in the Eucharist. And yet the majority of the Liturgies, as they stand in Dr Littledale's reprint, must be of a date below 500. For the "Liturgy of St Mark," pp. 14, 15, directs that the priest, ὁ ἱερεύς, shall say the "I believe in one God." So the Liturgy of St James, p. 49. Of course the Creed is not in the Liturgy of St Clement, which is taken from "the Apostolic Constitutions," but we find it in the very modern Liturgy of St Chrysostom, p. 131. Thus all of the three Liturgies which are said to have been in use in the Churches of Alexandria, of Jerusalem, and of Constantinople, "in early Christian times," contain internal proof that they were reduced to their present form after the beginning or middle of the sixth century. Again, in these three Liturgies the Creed precedes the Lord's Prayer, by a considerable interval. Apparently Justin's direction was that it should immediately precede it. If so, we must come down to a date later than 568, and considerably later, because the Liturgies grew by accretions, and time was necessary for this growth. The date assigned by Dr Neale to the earliest MS. of which he speaks is the tenth century. Such is the conception of a "primitive Liturgy."

[1] Harduin, II. p. 1261 B. I must ask my readers to contrast the condemnations of the Quicunque.

[2] Harduin, II. p. 1272 B.C.

[3] p. 1284.

[4] p. 1306. The condemnation, p. 1315, is this: "If any one wander away from the path, he surrounds himself with a cloud of error."

[5] p. 1318.

Constantinople of the year 518 (which states that the Council of the 150 confirmed the Symbol of the 318[1]); from some Archimandrites, who used a phrase which has been rendered familiar to us by the Justinian Codex, "the Nicene Synod uttered the holy Symbol in which we were baptized and baptize; the Constantinopolitan Synod confirmed it; that of Ephesus established it; that of Chalcedon set its seal upon it[2]." The Council under Menna followed on this line. We again hear that the Creed of the 318 was that into which all were baptized[3]. And language, more or less resembling this, came from Jerusalem[4], from Tyre[5], and finally from the Emperor Justinian himself[6]; but I must confess that I do not recognise anywhere the language either of the Athanasian Faith or of its condemnations. The sentence pronounced on the heretics is still excommunication: it drives some away as wolves from the flock; it wounds others with the like anathema[7].

§ 4. But, perhaps, I ought to quote here from that long Confession or EDICT OF JUSTINIAN, which is inserted in the Acts of the Fifth General Council—the Council of Constantinople, held in the year 553. This edict contains thirteen anathemas: but, before they are enuntiated, we find the following[8]:

"There is one definition of the faith, to confess and rightly glorify the Father, and Christ the Son of God, and the Holy Spirit. This confession we keep into which we were baptized; it was given indeed by our great God and Saviour Jesus Christ to His holy Apostles and disciples, and by them it was preached in all the world. And the 318 holy Fathers who met at Nicæa against Arius have handed down the same confession or symbol and teaching of the faith to the holy Church of God: and after them the 150 holy Fathers who met at Constantinople against Macedonius and Magnus, following in every thing the same holy Symbol which was delivered by the 318, explained the words concerning the Godhead of the Holy Spirit: and then those who met at Ephesus against Nestorius, and those who met at Chalcedon against Eutyches, following in every respect the same holy symbol or teaching of the faith, condemned these heretics and all who thought or think like them. And moreover they anathematized all who would deliver to such as draw nigh to holy baptism, or turn from any heresy whatever, another definition of faith or symbol or teaching besides that which was delivered by the 318 and explained by the 150 holy Fathers."

1 p. 1321.

2 p. 1327. Note that the use of the Creed at Baptism is mentioned, not any use at the Eucharist.

3 Harduin, ut sup. p. 1335 C.

4 p. 1343 C.

5 p. 1351.

6 p. 1406 B.

7 p. 1398 E.

8 Harduin, III. p. 287.

Thus Justinian clearly distinguishes between the Nicene considered as a baptismal Creed, and the fulness of his own Rule of the Faith.

§ 5. Towards the end of the sixth century, however, the Creed must have come into general use in the Churches of the East. For King Reccared, at the Council of Toledo in 589, directed that the Creed of the 150 should be recited in the Liturgy before the Lord's Prayer, throughout all the Churches of Spain and Gallicia, according to the form of the Oriental Churches. The exact place may be seen by any one who will look to the Mozarabic Liturgy, as printed by Daniel, or elsewhere—and the reader will thus be able better to appreciate the amount of modification which the Greek Liturgies have undergone since the date before us. And it will be noted that the Creed spoken of by Reccared is distinctly called the "Creed of the 150."

§ 6. As for the time of its introduction into the Roman Liturgy, the authorities vary in opinion. Maldonatus says that Honorius of Autun (about the year 1130) is authority enough that Pope Damasus gave the order. Zaccaria asks, "Who can trust a writer that lived eight hundred years after the event which he records? All antiquity is silent on the subject." Yet Durandus repeated the statement, and possibly might be cited as an independent witness[1]. The fact is, that from Spain the custom of using the Nicene Creed (as I shall call it henceforth) at the Mass spread into France: and Martene brings a passage from Cæsarius of Arles that speaks of the *Credo in unum Deum* being then used. If this be genuine, we must fix the date of the custom in the diocese of Arles, or at all events amongst the Benedictines in that diocese, before the year 542. But this seems too early. For the book of St Germain on the Gallican Mass is entirely silent as to such a custom in his time, and he died about 575. But we do know that in the time of Charles the Great, the Nicene Creed was sung in the Royal Chapel, and after the Spanish type[2]. From the con-

[1] *De Divinis Officiis*, lib. IV. c. 25. I take it from Voss. Waterland quotes the context of the passage (leaving out this part), amongst his authorities as to the Athanasian Creed!

[2] Some consider that the order was given at the Council of Frankfort, A.D. 794. For example Zaccaria refers to Aimoin, *de gestis Francorum*, IV. c. 85, and Aemilius, lib. V. § 9. Æneas, bishop of Paris, 868, speaks of "the Catholic Faith which is chanted on the Lord's

versation of Leo III. with Charles' emissaries (of which below) it seems clear that the Nicene Creed was not used at Rome, in his time, during the Mass. Binterim[1] appears to agree with Martene in the opinion that it was not adopted there until the year 1014. At that time the Emperor Henry urged on Benedict VIII. the use of the Creed—possibly in its interpolated form. Benedict resisted, alleging that the Roman Church did not require it: "it had never been stained with heresy: from the first it had continued unshaken in the firmness of the Catholic Faith, according to the teaching of St Peter: it needed not therefore to chant the Creed as frequently as those Churches where heresy had appeared[2]." But Benedict yielded.

Up to this time, if we might trust some Liturgiologists, the Roman Church had used the Roman or Apostles' Creed at the Mass: but for their opinion there seems to be no support in history[3]. From the time of Benedict, however, the Nicene Creed has been used in the Eucharistic Service throughout the Churches of Western Europe. It was *sung*, however, only on great festivals, and then by the communicants, not by the priest. Innocent III., indeed (*de mysterio Missae*, II. c. 52; IV. c. 31), says that it was sung by the subdeacons; but Maldonatus explains this by saying that the subdeacons acted as precentors, leading the people[4].

§ 7. Before we consider the history of the later change of language in the Creed of Constantinople, we may devote a few

day at the Mass by the whole Church of Gaul:" he quotes the Nicene Creed. (Note the title, *The Catholic Faith.*) Caspari, p. 218, from D'Achery, *Spicilegium*, T. I. p. 131.

[1] *Denkwürdigkeiten*, Vol. IV. part iii. p. 356.

[2] See Berno Augiensis *de rebus ad missam pertin.* c. 2. (Migne, Vol. CXLII. p. 1061, cf. 1058, the passage is given by Daniel, *Codex Liturgicus*, I. 126.)

[3] The subject is discussed by Daniel, l.c.

[4] There is a passage in the works of Walfrid Strabo which seems at first sight to be opposed to this conclusion. He, writing in the ninth century on the Nicene Creed (*De Rebus Eccles.*, c. 22, Migne, Vol. CXIV. p. 947) says that from the Bishops of the East the use of the Nicene Creed is believed to have come to the Romans. As Abbot of Reichenau he probably drew his evidence from the Churches north of the Alps, not from the Churches of Italy proper. In the same passage Walfrid notices that after the deposition of the heretic Felix (about the year 800) the Creed began to be used generally more frequently in the mass. But this again must have been in Gallican and German Churches. For Walter, Bishop of Orleans, in the middle of the century, passed a canon directing that the *Gloria Patri et Filio et Spiritui Sancto*, and the *Credo in unum Deum*, should be sung by all at the same service. (Martene, Lib. I. IV., Art. vi. §§ 10, 11, and Migne, Vol. CXIX. p. 727.)

pages to the use of the Creed in the Baptismal Services of the West[1].

We learn from the Gelasian Sacramentary, as well as from the *Ordo Romanus*, and from the interesting Gellone Manuscript and other Manuscripts at St Gall and Vienna[2], that the Constantinopolitan Creed was thus used. Following the Ritual as restored by Casertanus and printed by Daniel[3], we learn that at the first scrutiny (which was held on the Wednesday of the third week in Lent), the catechumen was interrogated, amongst other things, in the brief Roman Creed that we have already noticed. "Dost thou believe in God the Father Almighty, Maker of heaven and earth? I believe. And dost thou believe in Jesus Christ, His only Son? I believe. And dost thou believe in the Holy Ghost, the holy Catholic Church, the Forgiveness of sins, the Resurrection of the flesh and Eternal Life? I believe." These questions were repeated on the second and third scrutiny—the latter being held on the Wednesday after the fourth Sunday in Lent. On this day the deacon brought in the four Gospels, the catechumens were told of the names of the writers and of their types in Ezekiel: and a few early verses from each were read[4]. Then the Presbyter (he is always called the Presbyter) addressed them:

"Beloved, now that ye are going to receive the Sacraments of Baptism, and to be made new creatures of the Holy Spirit, receive with all your heart the faith in the belief of which ye are to be justified. And with your feelings changed by a true conversion[5] come to God Who is the Illuminator of your minds; accepting the Sacrament of the Evangelical Symbol, inspired by the Lord, appointed by His Apostles—the words of which indeed are few, but the mysteries are great. For the Holy Spirit, who dictated it[6] to the Masters of the Church, framed the health-giving Faith with such openness and such brevity that that which is to be believed by you and always to be professed[7], can neither escape your intelligence nor weary your memory. Fix your minds therefore and learn the Symbol. And that which we deliver to you as we

[1] On this Dr Caspari has a learned discussion in his earlier *Program.* 1866, p. 213, &c.

[2] On this Gellone MS., see below, and the *Nouveau Traité de Diplomatique*, III. 221. The other MSS. are described by Caspari.

[3] *Codex Liturgicus*, Vol. I. p. 171, &c.

[4] Can this account for the manuscripts we have that contain a few verses from the beginning of each Gospel?

[5] *Conversatione* for *conversione* (as in some copies of the Athanasian Creed).

[6] Muratori's copy reads *ita:* Hittorp's Ordo Romanus *ista.*

[7] Mur. *providendum:* Hittorp *profitendum.*

have received it, do ye write not on any material which can be corrupted, but on the pages of your heart."

The Presbyter asks the Acolyth, "In what language do they confess our Lord Jesus Christ?" The answer is, "In Greek." The Presbyter proceeds, "Announce therefore the Faith as they believe." The Acolyth recites the Nicene Creed in Greek. He is then asked to recite it in Latin, and this he does also.

A short Exposition (so entitled) of the Symbol follows; and on the same day the Lord's Prayer was given to the Catechumens; this too had its Exposition. And the Catechumens departed, and the "Missa in traditione Symboli" followed. A fourth, fifth, sixth, seventh scrutiny was held on as many different days: on the last, which was held on Easter Eve, the Catechumens recited from memory the Symbol and the Lord's Prayer in Latin or Greek as they had professed it before. Yet, after all, they were not interrogated at the Font in the words of this Creed: the Roman Symbol furnished the few words which were there required.

The ceremony is given differently in Muratori's *Liturgia Romana Vetus*. There the Acolyth answers, "In Greek," if he holds a boy in his arm: "In Latin" if he holds a girl[1]. In the *Ordo Romanus* the question and answer are put in Greek. The three copies undoubtedly give three phases of an interesting relic, possibly the last surviving relic, of the Greek origin of the Western Churches[2].

§ 8. In the *Ordo Romanus* the Creed is given in Greek letters. But in the Gelasian Sacramentary, as well as in a MS. at St Gall, of the tenth century, described by Dr Caspari[3]; in another at Vienna of the tenth century[4], and in an early printed book (Venice, 1476)[5], the Greek Creed is given in Latin letters. In the tenth century the knowledge of Greek must have been low. These are so curious that I will give the beginning of the Symbol as it is found in the Gelasian Sacramentary and the two MSS.[6]

Gelasian:

Pisteuo . hisena . theon . pathera . pantocrat .
oran . pyetin . uranu . kaegis . oraton .

[1] See it in Dr Heurtley's *Harmonia Symbolica*, p. 157.

[2] Dr Caspari, l.c., p. 234, notes that in all these copies we have *I believe*, instead of the *We believe* of the Faith of the 150.

[3] p. 237. [4] p. 246. [5] p. 242.

[6] From Dr Caspari.

kaepanton . kaeauraton . kaehisena . kyrion .
Ihm . Xpm .

St Gall, 338:

Symbolum Apostolorum Graece.
Pisteuuo isena theon Pa
tira pantocratora piitin uranu kegis
oraton te panton ke aoraton keisena ky
rion ysun christon tonion tu theu ton mo
nogeni

Vienna, 830:

Credo in unum
Piste ugo isena theon panto
crathora pythin uranu keys ora
thonte panthon keaoraton keisena
kyrion ysun criston tonyon tuthe
u ton monogenin.

Of these all three omit with the Constantinopolitan Creed Θεὸν ἐκ Θεοῦ, *God of God:* the second and third read *who proceedeth from the Father:* the first *who proceedeth from the Father and the Son.* I must add, however, that in the two Manuscripts there is nothing to connect the Creed either with the Baptismal Service proper or with the preparation of the Catechumens. These copies must therefore have been prepared for some other purpose.

As to this purpose we may learn something from the Essay of the great Photius of Constantinople on the Procession of the Holy Spirit, against the Latins. He says that Leo and Benedict "the great High-Priests" directed that the Creed should be recited in Greek in Churches of the Roman obedience (if the account of Photius is correct it seems to refer only to Churches north of the Alps, where the Creed was already in use), *ἵνα μὴ τὸ στενὸν τῆς διαλέκτου βλασφημίας παρασχῇ πρόφασιν*, "lest the narrow character of the Latin dialect should afford pretext for irreverent expression." Binterim[1] assures us that in the ninth century the Germans sang the Creed both in Greek and Latin; and Daniel[2] states that it is known that at great festivals it was recited in Greek. It seems, therefore, that the MS. at St Gall was prepared for such occasions. It is described as richly illuminated: it contains, among other things, "the Angelic Hymn in Greek and Latin," and a Greek transla-

[1] *Denkwürdigkeiten*, p. 363. [2] p. 128.

tion of the Apostles' Creed[1]. The Nicene Creed is also called the Apostles' Creed: and under that title it is found both in Greek and Latin. It is accompanied with musical notes. In the Vienna MS. again the Greek Creed appears, with musical notation, between the Greek *Hymnus Angelicus* and the Greek *Trishagion* and *Agnus Dei*—all, like it, in Latin letters.

§ 9. But the Nicene Creed in Latin was used at other times and for other purposes. Thus from an old MS. of the eleventh century, mentioned by Martene[2] (it was a Pontifical belonging to the Church of Narbonne), we know that in the Office of Extreme Unction in that Church, the *Credo in unum Deum* was chanted. So in the Visitation Service of a MS. from Fleury of the thirteenth century[3]; and again at the end of the Office of Extreme Unction. This apparently was intended for use in a Benedictine Monastery. This usage was continued even to the sixteenth century at Chalons[4].

§ 10. I must add that Honorius of Autun, writing about the year 1130, speaks of[5] four Creeds. The second is the Faith *Credo in Deum Patrem* (sic), "which is read in Synods, which the Nicene Synod put forth." The third is the *Credo in unum Deum*, which was chanted at the Mass—having been put forth by the Council of Constantinople. I have not found any allusion to this use at Synods in any of the "orders" given by Martene for Provincial Gatherings in France. The Constantinopolitan Creed, as it is received in the Roman Church, was put prominently and specially forward at the first meeting for business of the Council of Trent.

§ 11. The true Creed of Constantinople is found in all the Liturgies of the Greek Maronites, and other Oriental Churches[6], and it is used in the Hour Services of the modern Horologion. In fact, it is the only Symbol of the Eastern Orthodox Church. It is employed, of course, in the Baptismal Service. On being made a Catechumen the candidate (or his sponsor) renounces

[1] This has not (I believe) been printed. It must be one of the earliest extant.

[2] *De antiquis Ecclesiæ ritibus*, l. VII. iv., ordo XIII.

[3] *Ibid.* ordo XXIV.

[4] No. XXIX.

[5] *Gemma Animæ*, Lib. II. cap. V.

[6] Bona, *Rerum Liturgicarum* Lib. II. pp. 384, 385, 388.

Satan, and ranges himself with Christ. He is asked, "Dost thou believe in Him?" He answers, "I believe Him as King and God;" and recites the *I believe in one God* three times. On being called to worship Christ, he replies, "I worship Father, Son, and Holy Ghost, consubstantial and indivisible Trinity[1]."

§ 12. One use more remains to be noticed. Down to the time of Sergius, Archbishop of Constantinople, each newly-elected bishop of Rome used to send to his brother at Constantinople, letters announcing his election, including a copy of the Creed which he professed—the Eastern Creed without alteration[2]. The Archbishops and Patriarchs of the Greek Churches confessed the Creed when they attained their dignity[3].

§ 13. In "the Divine Liturgy of the Armenian Church of St Gregory the Illuminator," as printed at Constantinople in 1823, and translated by Mr S. C. Malan, the learned vicar of Broad-

[1] Daniel, *Codex Liturg.*, IV. p. 496, &c. Daniel quotes a passage from Dr Neale's *History of the Eastern Church*, Introduction, p. 968, which shews that that great authority on Oriental Liturgies was not always on his guard against making somewhat rash statements regarding the Creeds of the West. The words are "It is an old subject of complaint by the Greek against the Latin Church that the latter employs [at baptism] the Apostles' instead of the Nicene Creed. And a late writer so far sympathizes with them as to propose, in the event of negociation for our union with the Oriental Church, that we should substitute that Creed for it. Such an inversion of order would seem not only unnecessary but objectionable. The Roman Church retained the Apostles' Creed, when the Eastern thought fit to substitute for it that of Nicæa. It is true that the Gelasian Sacramentary gives the latter in Roman letters," as above, p. 139. "But this seems never to have been extensively used even at Rome. And the Gallican Ritual never employed the Nicene Creed: indeed some Rituals are of that great age as to omit the clause *He descended into hell.* From Gaul we received an old Baptismal Canon, and this must have been used in England long before the Council of Nicæa. It is too much therefore to ask us to surrender an older for a more modern tradition." Perhaps it would have been wiser to say, that it is too much to ask us to surrender a rite of the National Church of England, because that rite does not prevail elsewhere.

Now as for the mistakes contained in this note of Dr Neale's:

(1) The Latin Church does not employ the Apostles' Creed as the Creed of the baptized, in the way in which the Greek Church employs the Nicene Creed.

(2) The Apostles' Creed, as we have it, is of far more recent date than is the Creed used in the East.

(3) The Manuscripts which have been brought recently to light, shew that the Gallican Ritual did employ the Nicene Creed.

We must remember that the Nicene Creed is called the Apostles' Creed in the St Gall manuscript. (See too Usher, p. 16, "Finito symbolo apostolorum dicat sacerdos, Dominus vobiscum.")

[2] There is some allusion to this custom in an epistle of Photius, in Labbe IX. p. 235. He congratulated himself that the Pope, John VIII., had not in his letter introduced the words *et filio* into the Creed. Binius' note on the subject (Labbe IX. p. 324) is curious. Compare Voss, XXXVI., and Mr Ffoulkes' *Christendom's Divisions*, Vol. II. p. 20.

[3] Voss, *On the Nicene Creed*, III.

windsor, we read, that after the Gospel follows the direction, "then shall the Nicene Creed be said in full." The Creed is not the Nicene nor yet the Constantinopolitan Faith, but bears a very marked resemblance to the second Creed of Epiphanius, with which it must have some connection. It will be remembered that we have met with a version of this Creed assigned to Athanasius. In the Armenian Liturgy it concludes with the anathematism. I have not met with any other instance where this anathematism is retained in the service. But even more interesting than this is the connection established between the Creed of the Armenians and the Creed of Epiphanius.

CHAPTER XII.

THE HISTORY OF THE INTERPOLATIONS.

§ 1. THERE are two important additions to the Western version of the Creed of Constantinople to which we must now devote some attention. At some time or other, the words *God of God* have been added in the early part, at another period the words *and of the Son* have been introduced into the clause regarding the Procession of the Holy Spirit. The former was probably added in error, the accuracy of the scribe having been affected by his memory of the Nicene Creed: with the latter a longer history is connected, of which however I need give here only the leading features.

§ 2. In regard to the first phrase, I may content myself with copying a note from Dr Routh's *Scriptorum Ecclesiasticorum Opuscula*, I. p. 426. That learned writer informs us that the words *God of God* are not found in any Greek copy of the Creed of Constantinople nor in the old Latin translations of the Acts of Chalcedon, nor in the *Prisca Canonum translatio* (Mansi, VI. 1125): nor in the translation by Dionysius Exiguus (which also omits *Light of Light*), nor in the Gelasian Sacramentary. It is found in the collections of Isidorus Mercator, in the Council of Toledo (of which we must speak ere long), and in the Creed which Etherius and Beatus quoted in their work against Elipandus (of which also

I must speak below). These data seem to warrant the conjecture that the words proceeded from a Spanish source[1].

§ 3. In the year 589[2], a synod was held at Toledo; it is called the third Council of Toledo. It was attended by 68 Spanish Bishops. (This was shortly before Gregory the Great became Pope.) The synod was convened by Reccared, the king of the Goths, who addressed the assembly in a speech preserved in the "Concilia." In this address—to which we must recur again—Reccared introduced the latter part of the "Definition of Chalcedon," commencing from the Creed of Nicæa and concluding with the condemnation of those who should introduce another symbol or another faith (aliud symbolum, aliam fidem). He then subscribed the address, "I king Reccared have subscribed this holy faith and this true confession which alone the Catholic Church through the whole globe professes." His wife followed, and ten Bishops uttered their acclamations and thanks in the way to which we have become accustomed. They then in synod framed twenty-three anathemas, of which the third was this: "Whosoever does not believe or has not believed that the Holy Spirit proceeds from the Father and the Son, and does not say that He is coequal and coeternal with the Father and the Son, let him be anathema." These were followed by the Creeds, to which eight bishops and a few laymen subscribed: and some Canons were subsequently enacted. The Nicene Creed which they followed was the true Creed, not the copy in the Definition of Chalcedon: and, as the translation is not identical with that of Hilary of Poictiers or any other of those given by Dr Hahn, it seems that it must have been a local or independent rendering from the Greek. This throws more interest on the fact that in the Creed of Constantinople we find that the words *Deum ex Deo* and *et Filio* were introduced; were they introduced intentionally or in error?

We have seen that the Council of Chalcedon set the example of misrepresenting the Nicene Creed. Looking at this fact and at the fact that this Synod of Toledo pronounced the anathema to which I have drawn attention, I have no hesitation in coming to

[1] Dr Routh says that they are found in the translation of the Creed by Hilary of Poictiers, *de Synodis*, § 84. But that Creed is the Nicene proper; and not to the point.

[2] Mansi, IX. 977. Harduin, III. 467. See Hefele, III. 46.

the opinion that the words were added intentionally. The circumstances are certainly not such as to warrant the conception that they were added merely by mistake.

§ 4. But however doubtful the origin of these interpolations may appear to be, the reason for their continuance is obvious. The same national synod at which this Definition was read and subscribed, passed the canon to which attention was drawn in my last chapter: viz.

"For the reverence of the Faith and to strengthen the minds of men, it is ordered by the synod, at the advice of Reccared, that in all the Churches of Spain and Gallicia, following the form of the Oriental Churches, the Symbol of the Faith of the Council of Constantinople, that is of the one hundred and fifty bishops, shall be recited; so that before the Lord's Prayer is said the Creed shall be chanted with a clear voice by the people; that testimony may thus be borne to the true faith, and that the hearts of the people may come purified by the faith to taste the Body and Blood of Christ[1]."

Thus the Spanish version of the "Nicene Creed" became the property of the laity: and the natural consequence followed, that when their attention was drawn to the difference between the Spanish and Italian versions, these Spanish laymen were unwilling to conform to the Roman rite[2].

[1] Hence it comes that in the Mozarabic Liturgy, the priest recited the Creed after the prayer of consecration, whilst he held the consecrated Host in his hand that it might be seen by the people (Daniel, I. p. 89). The text in the Liturgy differs from the text in the "Concilia" in the following particulars. The Liturgy reads *Dominum nostrum*, the Council omitting *nostrum:* the Council omitted *de cœlis* which the Liturgy inserts: both add *quæ in cœlo et quæ in terra*, words which are not in the true "Creed of Constantinople:" both read *de Spiritu sancto ex Maria Virgine:* the Council read *ad dexteram Patris*, the Liturgy *ad dexteram dei Patris omnipotentis:* the Council omitted *est* in *inde venturus est*, which the Liturgy inserts: the Liturgy adds *sanctam* as a property of the Church, and *futuri* before *sæculi*. It has *credimus* at the beginning: but *confiteor*, *expectans* at the end. It is clear therefore that the Creed of the Liturgy has suffered in the course of transmission. The Greek word *homoousion* is retained, and explained as *ejusdem cum Patre substantiæ: crucified* is not introduced, nor the thought *for us:* the words *according to the Scriptures* do not occur in many of the Latin translations, nor here. Lastly the Liturgy omits *in gloria*.

[2] In the Paris Library, 12047, is a very interesting MS., "The Gellone Sacramentary and Martyrology." It is considered to be of the 8th century, *i.e.* almost within a hundred years of the Council of Toledo. Its readings have not been noticed by Hahn: I learn them from the *Nouveau Traité de Diplomatique*, III. p. 82, note 1. They are "ascendit ad celos, sedit (*not* sedet) ad dexteram Patris, et iterum uenturus iudicare uiuos & mortuos, & spiritum sanctum dominum & uiuificantem ex patre procedentem qui cum patre et filio simul adunatum (*for* adoratum) & conglorificatum." The ordinary but less correct Latin is *adorandum et conglorificandum.* Thus, when the Gellone Sacramentary was prepared, the interpolation "and

§ 5. There were other Councils of Toledo in 653 and 681 at which the Creed was again recited, with the additions, "as we have received it and as we proclaim it openly in the solemnities of our mass[1]." From this I presume that at the latter dates the Spanish version had begun to be questioned.

§ 6. From Spain the interpolated Creed spread, and it seems to have reached England in the year 680. For in that year there was a synod at Heathfield (see Usher *de Symbolis* p. 24), and the words "from the Father and the Son" are pressed in one of the canons of this synod[2]. We thus pass on until we come to the time of Charlemagne, who urged both Hadrian II. and Leo III. to accept the change. The genuine Creed had been recited and renewed at what are called the fifth and sixth general councils which were held at Constantinople in the years 553 and 681, but now we come to the seventh council, *i.e.* the second Council of Nicæa, held in the year 787. At this gathering Tarasius, Patriarch of Constantinople, had delivered a long exposition in which he professed that he "believed in the Holy Spirit who proceedeth from the Father by the Son[3];" the papal legates accepted the words[4], but Charlemagne, the then "Defender of the Faith," was not satisfied with them. He wrote to Hadrian to the effect that Tarasius was wrong, in that whilst reciting his belief he had professed not that the "Holy Spirit proceedeth from the Father and the Son" according to the faith of the Nicene Symbol, but that "He proceedeth from the Father by the Son[5]." Hadrian did not object to the belief of Charles, nor did he write to inform him that in the true version of the Creed neither phrase, "and the Son," nor "by the Son," occurred: he contented himself with quoting Athanasius, Hilary, and others to prove that the belief of Tarasius was not heretical[6]. Neither of them referred to the Creed of Athanasius.

§ 7. The motive for Charles's remonstrance may be learnt

the Son" had not found its way into France. Neither had it when the Gelasian Sacramentary was written out for French use.

[1] Harduin, III. p. 956 and 1718.

[2] I suppose that the MS. has not been tampered with.

[3] Mansi, XII. 1121. Harduin, IV. 131.

[4] *Ibid.* p. 1145. Harduin, IV. 135.

[5] Mansi, XIII. 760.

[6] In the Latin version of the Creed, given by Mansi, XIII. 729, as having been recited at the seventh council, the added words are found. Of course this is an interpolation: but the fact shakes our confidence in these "Concilia."

from the very brief records that have survived of the Council of Gentilly, A.D. 767[1]. At this synod, as we learn from Ado of Vienne, our only authority, there was "a question between the Greeks and the Romans regarding the Trinity, and Whether the Spirit as He proceeds from the Father, so proceeds from the Son: as also regarding the figures of the Saints, Whether they are to be fixed or painted in the churches?" So the great warrior statesman and theologian had already been excited on the subject, and he now called for a council at Frankfort, to consider the papal answer. The council met in the year 794, and drew together (it is said) 300 bishops of Charles's dominions, Spaniards, French, and Germans: some came even from Britain. They declared their belief that the Holy Spirit proceeds from the Father and the Son[2].

Of more importance, in the literary point of view, is the Council of Friuli (Forum Julii), which met under Paulinus, Patriarch of Aquileia, in the year 796[3]. The subject of the Creed came again under discussion, and the interpolated form was adopted without much hesitation in the province of Aquileia.

Paulinus gives an account of the addition:

"Just as (he writes) the one hundred and fifty Fathers who met at Constantinople did, by way of exposition, supplement the meaning of the three hundred and eighteen, and confess that they *believed in the Holy Spirit the Lord and Giver of life*, so afterwards, because of those heretics who whispered about that the *Holy Spirit is of the Father alone*, the words were added *Who proceedeth from the Father and the Son.* Yet they are not to be blamed who effected this, as if they had added or diminished aught in the Creed of the 318—for they held no opinions different from theirs—they sought only to fill up the meaning which in other respects they left untouched[4]."

§ 8. At this council the Creed of Toledo was adopted[5], and then other complications followed. Some monks of a Frank convent on Mount Olivet complained to Leo III. (who succeeded Hadrian, December 795) that they had been accused of heresy and partially excluded from the Church of the Nativity on Christmas Day, because they held that the Holy Spirit proceedeth from the Father and the Son. Nay, they were accused that in reciting the

[1] Mansi, XII. 677. Harduin, III. 2011.

[2] Mansi, XIII. 905.

[3] Mansi, XIII. 827, gives the date 791, but it seems to be now generally thought it was held five years later.

[4] Mansi, XIII. 856. It seems hard to be called upon to believe that the Quicunque was regarded as authoritative at this time. Harduin, IV. 850.

[5] Mansi, XIII. 842.

Symbol they said more than the Romans did: they said *Who proceedeth from the Father and the Son.* But yet one of their number had so heard it sung in the West, in the chapel of the Emperor. What were they to do[1]?

A translation of this letter—sufficiently accurate for ordinary purposes, although not satisfactory to the theologian—is given in Dr Neale's *Introduction to the History of the Eastern Church*[2]. Other questions were involved besides the interpolation of the Creed. The Greeks were jealous of the growing power of Rome; the previous century had been that of its greatest early encroachments; and the monks of Olivet soon recognised that this attack by the Greeks upon them covered an attack upon the Pope. The letter also shews that some interesting points of difference had been noticed between the Greek and Latin Rituals. In the *Gloria in Excelsis* the Greeks did not say "Thou only art most High." They said the *Pater Noster* in a different way—adding the doxology. In the *Gloria Patri* they omitted "as it was in the beginning." Further interest in the letter is excited by this, viz. that the Latin monks averred that "the Faith of Athanasius" spake in the same manner as their version of the Symbol of the Faith. The monks begged the Holy Father to enquire, as well in Greek as in Latin, concerning the Fathers who composed the Symbol, as to the clause where it is said *Who proceedeth from the Father and the Son:* for in Greek they said not this, but they said *Who proceedeth from the Father.* They urged that the clause is weighty, and added, "Vouchsafe to send word to the Lord Charles that we have heard as we have said in his chapel."

§ 9. Leo had adopted the belief of the West, but he objected to the alteration in the Symbol. Notwithstanding his obligations to Charles, he was firm here. The question was becoming important: and Charles summoned his bishops to meet him at Aix-la-Chapelle[3] in 809, and from this synod two prelates were

[1] The letter was brought to light by Baluzius, and was published by him in his *Miscellanea*, Lib. VII. p. 14 (or Vol. II. p. 84 of Mansi's edition). It is quoted by Binterim, p. 358, and by Mr Ffoulkes, *Christendom's Divisions*, II. 71, and *On the Athanasian Creed*, p. 154. Binterim, who seems to have been anxious to pass over the difficulty as to the *Filioque*, considered that the passage shewed that the Roman Church still used the *Nicene* Creed proper. It leaves me with the impression that the Roman Church only used the Roman Symbol.

[2] Pages 1155—1158.

[3] Eginhard in Migne, CIV. p. 472.

despatched to Rome to discuss the subject with the Pope. The one was Bernhard, Bishop of Worms: the other Adelard, Abbot of Corbey. An account of the interview is given in the Councils, drawn up, it is said, by Smaragdus, Abbot of St Michael in Lorraine—and the account was deservedly regarded by Dr Neale as one of the most curious documents of mediæval history. It occupies about four columns in the folios: a brief summary is given by Dr Neale[1]. So far as we are at present concerned, I must be content with stating that the Pope recommended that the singing of the Creed should be abolished in Germany, as it was not sung at Rome; for thus the objectionable addition would drop out of knowledge, and the illicit custom of singing it would be abolished.

Martene[2] and Binterim[3] consider that the Pope wished that the Creed should be said—not sung—and without the words; but to me it seems that such a direction would not produce the effect desired. This could be gained only by the omission of the Creed entirely from the Mass. And I am strengthened in my opinion that this was the object of the Pope, by the evidence that the more frequent use of the Creed in the Churches of Germany had been only of recent introduction: it was due, as we have seen, to the energy of the Emperor after the deposition of Felix and Elipandus.

The message of the Pope was followed by a council held at Rome in the year 810, which protested against the addition[4].

§ 10. But neither the advice of Leo nor the protest of the council produced the desired effect on Charles. Neither Pope nor Emperor would give way. The latter died in 814, the Creed as he desired it being still sung in his chapel, and, no doubt, recited in the churches of his dominions. The former suspended in the Basilica of St Peter two silver shields or tablets, "each weighing one hundred pounds;" on these was engraved in Greek and in Latin, in its genuine form, the "Creed of the Council of Constantinople." The shields were subsequently moved to the shrine of St Paul, and were seen there by Damianus in the eleventh century[5]. The successors of Charlemagne were as obsti-

[1] Ut supra, p. 1163. Harduin, IV. 969.
[2] Ut supra, p. 138.
[3] Do. p. 357.
[4] Hefele, *Concilien-Geschichte*, III. 702.
[5] Damianus, XXXVIII., *de Process. S. S.*

nate as their ancestor, whilst in the Church of Rome, Leo IV. and Benedict III. (both between 847 and 858) directed that the Creed should be recited in Greek, to maintain its genuine character[1]. But the Spanish form was still spreading. It was of no avail that John VIII. condemned the addition in 879[2]: or that in the spring of the succeeding year his legate approved the act of the Synod of Constantinople, which reaffirmed the Creeds of the 318 and the 150, and rejected all interpolations[3]. For already in 868 we find from Æneas of. Paris[4] that the "whole Gallican Church chanted the Creed at the Mass every Sunday," of course with the interpolations. And Walfrid Strabo has told us that the same custom had spread wider and wider in the Churches of Germany[5]. At length the Teutonic Churches overcame the Church of Rome, and, as we have seen, the Emperor Henry persuaded Benedict VIII. to use the Creed at the Mass, and he must have used it in the Spanish or German form. For about the same year, 1014, the oath taken by the Pope upon his election appears to have been altered[6]. Up to that time each Pope had sworn to preserve unmutilated the decrees of the first five Councils, and the sixth as well: but in the eleventh century the oath was altered, and thus, in all the Churches of the West, the addition was accepted[7].

§ 11. I cannot follow out the later history of the *Credo in*

(from Mr Ffoulkes, *Athanasian Creed*, p. 161).

[1] Photius, *de Spiritus mystagog.* Migne, *Greek series*, 102, p. 395 (see above, p. 140).

[2] Labbe, IX. 235 (as above). Ffoulkes, *Christend. Divis.* II. 74, 399, 413.

[3] Mosheim, I. 150 (ed. Stubbs).

[4] Apud Dacher. *Spicil.* Tom. I. cap. xciii. p. 113.

[5] *De Rebus Eccles.*, cap. xxii. (Martene, p. 138, Binterim, IV. p. 3, § 9).

[6] See Mr Ffoulkes, *Church's Creed*, &c., pp. 5, 6.

[7] The following passage from Berno of Reichenau, which gives the account of the change of ritual at Rome, is interesting (*De quibusdam rebus ad Missam spectantibus*, c. 2): "If we are forbidden to sing the angelic hymn (*Gloria in Excelsis*) on festivals on the ground that the presbyters of the Romans are unaccustomed to sing it, we may just as well cease to repeat the Symbol after the gospel on the ground that the Romans never sang it even up to the present times, of the Emperor Henry. When they were asked by him Why they did so, I heard them (I was standing by) return answer to this effect: viz. that the Roman Church had never been infected even with the dregs of any heresy, but after the teaching of St Peter had remained unshaken in the firmness of the Catholic faith, and therefore it was more necessary that that Symbol should be frequently chanted by those who might possibly become stained with heresy. But the lord Emperor did not cease to press until, with the consent of all, he obtained that they should chant it at the public mass. But whether they keep up the custom now, we cannot say, because we have no certain information."

It would appear from this that all the early psalters which contain the *Gloria in Excelsis* must have been prepared north of the Alps.

unum Deum, because it would involve the history of the controversy on the Double Procession. Suffice it to say that when Eugene IV. in 1438 had opened the Council of Ferrara and excommunicated the Fathers assembled at Basle, the first subject that came before him was the projected union between the Greeks and the Latins. The Greeks, reduced to extremities by the Turks, were in hopes that the causes of their dissensions with the West might be removed, and that they might gain assistance in their distress. The council was removed to Florence in 1439, and to this, no doubt, we owe the fact that many of the documents to which I shall refer are found in the libraries of that city. Bessarion was gained over to the Latin side, and exerted his influence to induce his brethren to acknowledge, amongst other things, that the Holy Spirit proceedeth from the Father and the Son. But Mark of Ephesus was not to be won, either by entreaties, or bribes, or threats. The project resulted in greater anger, and a greater severance. The Latins allowed the second Rome, the city of that Constantine from whom they claim to have received the great Donation, to fall into the hands of the Turks. The city was taken and the Greek empire overthrown in 1453[1].

§ 12. It was, probably, with an eye to this difference with the Greek Church, that at the opening session for business of the Council of Trent, held on Feb. 4, 1546, the Latin Bishops there assembled put forth in the forefront of their dogmatic statements, not the Roman Creed, nor the *Quicunque Vult*, nor any of the other numerous Rules of Faith with which we have, or shall, become acquainted—but the SYMBOL OF CONSTANTINOPLE in its interpolated form. Having resolved to enunciate dogmas which would anathematize the Lutherans, their first act was to exclude the Greeks:

> "Following the example of the Fathers in the early councils, the œcumenical and general synod resolves that the Symbol of the Faith which the Holy Roman Church employs shall be expressed in the words in which it is recited in all the Churches: I BELIEVE IN ONE GOD, &c."

[1] This is little more than an abbreviation of Mosheim's short narrative.

CHAPTER XIII.

EARLY HISTORY OF THE LATIN CREED.

§ 1. Difference between the histories of the Greek and Latin Creeds. The latter not known at all in the East. The Greek translations modern. § 2. Name "Apostles' Creed." § 3. Tertullian, Cyprian, Novatian. § 4. Marcellus of Ancyra. § 5. Thoughts on his Creed. § 6. Probable origin.

§ 1. We may now turn to the consideration of the further development of the Roman Creed, "that which is commonly called the Apostles' Creed." (Article VIII.) The history of this Symbol differs essentially from the history of the Creed of Nicæa: of that document we can trace historically the successive steps, from the copy put out by Eusebius at the Council of the 318, past the modifications which that copy then underwent; then to the altered document promulgated at Chalcedon, and, finally, to the version now received, which was adopted by Reccared in 589. The successive steps of its growth may thus be recognised. Of all the symbols, this approaches nearest to the character of a "Catholic Creed:" but, as we have seen, no one form of it is universally received. The Greek Churches refuse to accept the words *God of God* and the words *And from the Son*, which the Latin Church has made part of its Symbol.

But the so-called Apostles' Creed has grown to its present dimensions almost without observation and in the dark. The persons or authorities by whom the several additions were inserted are unknown to us: the document was never discussed by a general council; in its complete form it has been sanctioned by national councils only in comparatively recent times: its use is confined to Churches now or formerly in communion with the great Church of olden Rome. We are told that at the Council of Florence, Mark of Ephesus, one of the legates of the Eastern Churches, declared that this Creed was not used in their services; indeed they had it not nor had they seen it before[1]. The Greek forms which are found occasionally in print are comparatively modern translations from the Latin and have no independent authority. The version published by Usher from a manuscript in the Library of Corpus Christi College, Cambridge, and referred to as of value by Bishop Pearson in his remarks on the word *Almighty*, is now considered to be of the fifteenth century—possibly contemporaneous with the Council of Florence. The Greek copy in the MS. *Galba* A. XVIII. at the British Museum, which was printed also by Usher, is indeed of the ninth century—but it is incomplete[2].

Dr Caspari speaks of two other Greek translations[3].

It must be noted too that both the Cambridge manuscript and the *Galba* A. XVIII. contain these Greek Creeds in Latin letters. Thus they cannot have been intended for the use of Greek-speaking Christians.

§ 2. In regard to the name *Apostles' Creed* we may note that it is only of late years that the title has been confined, even in the West, to the Symbol now before us. And it seems that no one gave the title to the Western germ of the document, before the beginning of the fifth century. Before that time this designation *Apostolic* was more freely used. Thus the canon of Irenæus was called Apostolic: the Constitutions are Apostolic, and speak of the Explanation of the Apostolic preaching: Lucian mentions the Evangelical and Apostolical Tradition: Cyprian, the "Prædicatio Apostolica."

Usher adduces proofs that the Nicene Creed was, at times, designated as the Apostolic Creed: and I have mentioned already that in one of the manuscripts at St Gall referred to by Dr Caspari both the Nicene and the Roman Creeds are designated as "Symbolum Apostolorum[4]." Thus when we meet with this title in the first ten centuries, we must be cautious not to assume that the Symbol meant is that to which we now confine the name.

[1] *ἡμεῖς οὔτε ἔχομεν οὔτε εἴδομεν τὸ σύμβολον τῶν ἀποστόλων. Vera historia unionis non veræ inter Græcos et Latinos per Sylvestrem Guropulum* (or *Sgyropulum*), sec. VI. cap. vi. p. 150. The passage is quoted by Waterland, *On the Athanasian Creed*, chap. vi. near the end: and by Nicolas, *Le Symbole des Apôtres*, p. 270.

[2] See Dr Heurtley, *Harmonia Symbolica*, pp. 74—80. The C. C. C. Creed is given pp. 81—83. This latter copy is found in what is called "Pope Gregory's Psalter:" a title which, whatever its origin, has proved to be very misleading.

[3] See *Ungedruckte Quellen*, I. p. viii. and 237.

[4] The "Symbolum Apostolorum" of Ambrose is undoubtedly the old Roman form, as the context shews. See below.

I shall refer freely to Dr Heurtley's and Dr Hahn's collections of Creeds, as diminishing the necessity for any lengthened dissertation on my part. The former is particularly valuable. It has been supplemented by the series of essays published by Dr C. P. Caspari, Professor of Theology in the Norwegian University, to which I have already referred[1].

§ 3. Dr Heurtley traces the growth of the Western Creed through Tertullian and Cyprian to Novatian, *i. e.* to the year 260[2]. Then we have to leap over about eighty years, and we meet with a curious and puzzling narrative.

§ 4. Marcellus, Bishop of Ancyra in Galatia, had been present at the Council of Nicæa, and claimed for himself the credit of there procuring the condemnation of some who had wandered from the true faith. Of these some in return accused him of error, retaliating his charge on them. They accused him of Sabellianism: and it would seem that whatever were his own views, "which (says Epiphanius) were known to God alone," a few at least of his disciples denied the three Hypostases, as being irreconcilable with the truth of the One Deity, one Doxology. Epiphanius, who seems to think that Marcellus was innocent of the charges brought against him, inserts in his account[3] a letter which Marcellus wrote to "his fellow minister Julius," to whom he had come in his distress and before whom he laid his views. Whether the letter was written in Latin or Greek we are not informed; of course the version that remains of it in the work of Epiphanius is Greek.

He had stayed (he says) at Rome for a year and a quarter, hoping that his accusers would have the courage to meet him there: he was now leaving, and before he left he was anxious to deliver in writing, penned with his own hand, and with all truth, his faith which he had learned and had been taught from the Holy Scriptures. From it Julius might discover with what artifices his opponents strove to conceal and pervert the truth. He hurls on his accusers the charge of Arianism: he avers that they deny that the Word of God is truly His Word: he declares that they come within the anathematism of the Nicene Faith: they use language which renders them, as he has believed, alien from

[1] Page 5, where I have mentioned that Dr Caspari (to whom I had the honour of being introduced at the Ambrosian Library in 1872) is now engaged in making further collections.

[2] See Chapter IV. above.

[3] Epiphanius, *Against Heresies*, § 52 (otherwise § 72).

the Catholic Church. But, following the Holy Scriptures, he believes that there is one God; and that His only-begotten Son, the Word, is always consubsisting with the Father, having had no beginning of being, but truly being of the Father, not created, not made, but ever being, ever reigning with God the Father, of Whose kingdom according to the testimony of the Apostle there shall be no end..........It is He Who in these last days came down for our salvation, and being born of the Virgin Mary, *τὸν ἄνθρωπον ἔλαβε*, took man.

"I believe therefore in God Almighty and in Christ Jesus, His only begotten Son our Lord, Who was born of the Holy Ghost and the Virgin Mary, was crucified under Pontius Pilate, and was buried; and on the third day He rose again from the dead, ascended into the heavens, and sitteth on the right hand of the Father, from whence He is coming to judge the quick and the dead. And in the Holy Ghost, the Holy Church, Forgiveness of sins, Resurrection of the flesh, Eternal life. We have learned from the Holy Scriptures that the Godhead of the Father and the Son is indivisible. For if anyone separates the Son, that is the Word of Almighty God, it is necessary that he must either conceive that there are two Gods—which is alien from the divine teaching—or must confess that the Word is not God—which also appears to be alien from the right faith, inasmuch as the evangelist says *the Word was God.* But I have learned accurately that the power of God the Son is inseparable and indivisible [from God]. For the Saviour, the Lord Jesus Christ, Himself says *The Father is in Me and I in the Father:* and *I and the Father are one,* and *He that hath seen Me hath seen the Father.* This faith then, having received from the Holy Scriptures and having been taught it by my predecessors in God, I both preach in the Church of God and now have sent in writing to you, retaining the copy of it by me. And I beg you to insert a copy of it in your letter to the Bishops, in order that of those who do not know me well, none may be deceived by listening to that which has been written against me. Farewell."

§ 5. I have given at length the contents of this remarkable letter—remarkable as containing a copy of the Creed which with two exceptions—the omission of the word *Father* at the commencement, and the addition of the clause *Life eternal* at the end—is identical with that which Ruffinus fifty years later described as the Symbol of the Roman Church. Yet Marcellus does not so describe it. Whence did he receive it? How did he elaborate it?

Dr Heurtley thinks that this was, at the time, the Creed of the Church of Rome: Mr Ffoulkes seems to consider that it may have been picked up from the Church of Aquileia, when Marcellus passed through that city. Neither suggestion seems to me to satisfy the requirements of the problem: the words *Life eternal* were neither in the Creed of Aquileia nor in the Creed of Rome in 390. In the Creeds north of the Alps, years, indeed centuries, elapsed before these two words gained admission.

And the circumstances of this document shew that it was composed before the Council of Sardica:—*i.e.* before the Creed of Nicæa was received in the West.

On comparing this Creed of Marcellus with the fullest of the earlier known Western Symbola (as distinct from Irenæus' Rule of Faith) we note only the following additions:

The epithet *Only-begotten;*

The *Conception and birth of the Spirit and the Virgin.*

The substance of all the other clauses, apart from their grouping, is contained in the Rules of Tertullian or of Cyprian. These two additions bear an Eastern aspect; the one being in the Eusebian and Nicene Creeds, the other in the Creed of Epiphanius.

§ 6. Looking at all these circumstances, I am led to the conclusion that this document is really a composition (I use the word carefully, σύνθεμα) by Marcellus: that he brought his oriental knowledge to bear on the Western modes of thought, and arranged the floating beliefs of the West, the chief contents of their various Rules of Faith, after the fashion of the Nicene Creed; and perhaps the distinct mention of the relations which our Lord bears to the Father and to the Holy Spirit was introduced to repudiate the charge of Sabellianism brought against him. The fact that we find the profession of Marcellus adopted into the Creeds of Aquileia and Rome in the time of Ruffinus (391) and into the Creeds of Hippo in the time of Augustine (400), and of Ravenna in the time of Peter Chrysologus (445), and of Turin in the time of Maximus (460), causes me no surprise. Intercourse was very rapid in those days, and Churchmen were as ready, then as now, to avail themselves of that which seemed best adapted to supply a void. The great merits of the profession found in this letter of Marcellus are evinced by the fact that it has survived in the usage of the present day.

There is however one hypothesis which seems to me to be worthy of great consideration: and, although it is inconsistent with the opinion which I have been led to adopt, I am of course bound to mention it. It is this: that the document which Marcellus incorporated into his letter was the Symbol of the Roman

Church, but he abstained from describing it as such, for, if he had done so, it would have ceased to be a Watch-Word. The suggestion is somewhat refined, but it deserves consideration. The secresy which prevailed in the fourth and fifth centuries regarding the Creed is well known; the lectures of Cyril of Jerusalem contain an instructive memorandum, that no one is to permit a copy of the lectures to become public property. Augustine says, again and again, that his hearers, the *competentes*, are to write what they receive from him on the tables of the heart, not with ink on paper or on parchment. Hence small variations in different Churches were unavoidable. "Ruffinus" states that the reasons why, in the Roman Creed, nothing had been added to the words "I believe in God the Father Almighty" were these: i. No heresy had arisen at Rome: ii. The custom was there retained, that they who were to receive the grace of baptism recited the Symbol in the hearing of the faithful, and thus the difficulty was great of making additions to the older form. But the problem in regard to this letter from Marcellus is a curious one, and ought not to be slurred over. I think Marcellus was its author.

CHAPTER XIV.

LATER HISTORY OF THE LATIN CREED.

§ 1. Commentary of "Ruffinus." § 2. Standard Creed of the Roman Church at the time of "Ruffinus." § 3. Comparison of various Creeds. i. Augustine's African. ii. Rome, Ravenna, Turin. iii. English. iv. Aquileian. v. Pseudo-Augustine. vi. Facundus of Hermiane. vii. Poictiers. viii. Verona. ix. Faustus of Riez in the province of Arles. x. Spanish Creed. xi. Mozarabic Liturgy. xii. Gallican Sacramentary (Symbolum Traditum and commentary). xiii. Book of Deer. xiv. Creed of Pirminius. xv. Amalarius and Alcuin. xvi. Antiphonary of Bangor. § 4. Origin of the various clauses. § 5. General result, that the completed Creed is Gallican.

§ 1. In the first volume of Mr W. W. Harvey's *Ecclesiæ Anglicanæ Vindex Catholicus*, as well as in Dr Heurtley's volume *De Fide et Symbolo*, appears a treatise well worthy of study, containing a very early and succinct comment on the Creed. It is more systematic than any of the Tracts or Sermons of St Augustine, and was clearly intended for the instruction of full believers; not merely for the preparation of *competentes* for the Holy Ordinance of Baptism. It has been often printed, and Mr Ffoulkes, to whose unwearied researches I am here as well as elsewhere deeply indebted, informs me that in 1468 it was edited at Oxford as "the Exposition of St Jerome on the Apostles' Creed, addressed to Pope Laurentius:" so again at Oxford in 1493. At Rome in 1470 and 1576 it appeared with the letters of Jerome as an Exposition on the Creed: at Basil in 1519 among the works of Cyprian: at Paris in 1570 without an author's name. Mr Ffoulkes says that few tracts have been attributed to so many different authors; and on the title, which is prefixed to the exposition in one, and only one, ancient manuscript—"Incipit Expositio Symboli sancti Rufini"—he remarks that Ruffinus was never deemed to be a saint. The general acceptance of its present name seems to be due to the great divines, Bishop Fell and Bishop Pearson, who, in the Oxford edition of Cyprian, 1682, altered the title from *Expositio Hieronymi* to *Expositio Ruffini*. It seems, however, certain, that the Exposition in its present form was "composed"—put together—at Aquileia. Still we have the difficulty of finding two other Creeds ascribed to the Church of Aquileia; these are placed by Dr Heurtley under Nos. XII. and XIII.

§ 2. It will be convenient to give here, as a kind of standard document, THE CREED OF ROME, as it is said by this author to have been received there at the time he wrote. It will furnish a means for comparison. I purposely omit all punctuation.

CREDO IN DEUM PATREM OMNIPOTENTEM
ET IN JESUM CHRISTUM FILIUM EJUS UNICUM[1]
DOMINUM NOSTRUM
QUI NATUS EST DE SPIRITU SANCTO
EX MARIA VIRGINE
CRUCIFIXUS SUB PONTIO PILATO
ET SEPULTUS
TERTIA DIE RESURREXIT A MORTUIS
ASCENDIT IN COELOS
SEDET AD DEXTERAM PATRIS
INDE VENTURUS EST JUDICARE VIVOS ET MORTUOS
ET IN SPIRITUM SANCTUM
SANCTAM ECCLESIAM
REMISSIONEM PECCATORUM
CARNIS RESURRECTIONEM

§ 3. Starting from this as a standard, we may compare with it the various documents which have come down to us, until we arrive at the present completed form. I shall not notice the more minute deviations.

i. The basis of the Creed of St Augustine was undoubtedly the same as this. The great African bishop treated on the Symbol in several parts of his works and at several periods of his life. Thus we have it commented upon in the tracts *De Fide et Symbolo* (vol. 6), *De Genesi ad Literam* (vol. 2), the *Enchiridion* (vol. 6), the Sermon *Ad Catechumenos* (vol. 6), his sermons CCXII.

[1] Ruffinus gives *unicum Filium ejus*. I have altered it, because I believe that the words never occur again in that order.

and CCXIV. (vol. 5). Unfortunately we are troubled with other sermons attributed with some uncertainty to the great writer; such as CCXIII. and CCXV. There are other three which are certainly spurious. The last five I shall pass over for the present.

In framing St Augustine's Symbol out of these materials we have this difficulty. He never gives it at length; he objected to write it out. Thus we have to separate the text from the comment, and this it is not always easy to do[1].

Comparing then his copies with the copy of Ruffinus I note that in two of the earlier tracts we have *unigenitum* for *unicum*. In one copy we have *natus est per Spiritum sanctum ex Virgine Maria*. In five we have *natus est de S. S. et V. M.* In three we have *passus sub P. P. crucifixus et sepultus*.

On these I shall speak hereafter (note p. 168).

ii. We may next take the Creeds of the Churches of Ravenna, of Turin, and of Rome under Leo the Great. They are all in the fifth century.

Ravenna has added *vitam eternam*, the other two agree with the Roman Creed as I have given it above.

iii. With this agrees very closely a Creed which has escaped Dr Heurtley's notice, my introduction to which I owe to Casley's account of the Royal Library[2]. I mean "British Museum, 2 A. XX."

It reads *qui natus est de S. S. et M. V.*, and has *ad dexteram dei patris*, but *dei* is marked as a mistake. It adds *Catholicam* to the article on the Church. I am informed by Mr E. Maund Thompson that it is of the eighth century. I shall give some account of the MS. below[3]. With our standard Creed agree very nearly the Creed of the

[1] In his treatise addressed to Pammachius (Vol. II. p. 435) Jerome uses the following language, "In symbolo fidei et spei nostræ, quod ab Apostolis traditum non scribitur in charta et atramento sed in tabulis cordis carnalibus, post confessionem Trinitatis et unitatem ecclesiæ omne Christiani dogmatis sacramentum carnis resurrectione concluditur."

[2] Or rather to the *Nouveau Traité*, where Casley is quoted.

[3] The volume ROYAL 2 A. XX contains some sections from the Gospels, the Lord's Prayer with a Saxon version, the Apostles' Creed, the Letter to Abgarus, the Fides Catholica (see below). The Apostles' Creed runs thus:

"Credo in dm̄ patrem
omnipotentem et in ihm xpm filium
eius unicum dnm nrm . qui natus
est de spu sco et maria uirgine .
qui sub pontio pilato crucifixus est
et sepultus . tertia die resurrexit
a mortuis . ascendit in coelos
sedit ad dexteram di̤ patris .
inde uenturus est iudicare uiuos
ac mortuos . et in spm scm scām
ecclesiam catholicam remissionē
peccatorum carnis resurrecti
onem : amen.
in nomine patris et filii et spūs sci."
(folio 12.)

The title *symbol. apōs* has been inserted apparently in two different hands,

Codex Laudianus of Oxford (Gr. 35. Laud) of the seventh century (it omits the *Catholicam*), and the Greek creed of the *Athelstane Psalter*, *Galba* A. XVIII. of the British Museum. (This, but apparently by an error of the scribe, omits notice of the Church.)

We have thus considered XI. XIV. XV. XIX. XX. XXI. XXVI. XXXIII. of Dr Heurtley's collection, and that of the Royal MS. 2 A. XX.

iv. Of the two Creeds of Aquileia of uncertain date,

(Heurtley, XII. XIII.) No. XII. agrees with our standard text: XIII. reads *resurrexit vivens a mortuis*, *Catholicam* and *et vitam eternam*.

v. Turning now to the Creeds questionably or falsely attributed to St Augustine, we have

(in Heurtley, XVI. *sermo* CCXIII. or *de tempore* 119 tom. 5) the full modern phrase *conceptus est de Spiritu Sancto, natus ex Virgine Maria.* Otherwise it agrees with our standard.

Dr Heurtley's XVII. (Augustine, sermon CCXV), if we put aside all dubious readings, agrees with our standard, except that it closes thus: *Vitam æternam per sanctam ecclesiam.* To this must be added Dr Heurtley XVIII., from three sermons, all of which place the *Church* last. These have *assumptus in cælos* or *cælum:* they seem to belong to another class, *assumptus* corresponding to ἀναληφθείς.

vi. Very distinct, in two respects, is the Creed of Facundus of Hermiane in Africa (A.D. 547). It reads

and in the margin the articles have been partly assigned to the various Apostles. Thus *petrus cred.* | *cred. iohannes* | *cred. philippus* | and so on. The Canticles *Magnificat*, *Benedictus*, *Benedictus es*, *Benedicite* follow. Then the hymn *Rivos cruoris.* Then prayers to the Trinity from which (as they are clearly indications of the spiritual character which was given by some to the results of the controversies of the period) I will transcribe *literatim* some extracts.

"In primis obsecro supplex obnixis prescibus summam et gloriosam majestatem dī atque inclytam scæ individuæque trinitatis almitatem ut me miserum indignumque homunculum exaudire dignetur."

Then a kind of Litany including prayer to *God the Father: Son of God, God omnipotent: Holy Spirit, Comforter, God omnipotent.* Then on fol. 18:

"Scam ergo unitatem Trinitatis iterum atque iterum frequenter flagitans suffragare. patrem et filium et spm scm cui est una natura et una substantia una majestas atque eadem gloria sine fine manens."

Then petitions to the Angels and Saints, *Rogo Michaelem* (before the Virgin): the hosts are saying

SCS SCS SCS ds Sabaoth
pleni sunt coeli ac terrae gloriae tuae
osanna in excelsis. Benedictus qui venit in nomine dn̄i. osanna in excelsis.

The invocations are numerous, that of Saint Mary follows those of the Apostles.

On folio 68*, we have some Greek in Saxon letters, eulogumen patera caevo caeigion pneuma.

On folio 69, is a prayer of (=to) Mary the mother of our Lord.

On folio 28, we have the following (it has been referred to above):

+ Fides Catholica.
credimus in unum dm̄ patrem
omnipotentem et in unum dnm̄
nrm̄ ihm̄ xpm̄ filium dī et in
spm̄ scm̄ dm̄ n̄ tres deos.
Sed patrem et filium et spm̄ scm̄. unum
dm̄ colimus et confitemur.

Credimus in unum deum P. O. et in unum Dominum J. C. Filium ejus.

As Dr Heurtley has noticed, the addition of the *unum* in the two clauses points to an Eastern influence. (This is No. XXII. in his collection[1].)

vii. The Creed of Poictiers, as we learn it from the genuine Venantius Fortunatus, is curious:

It omits *dominum nostrum* and *sepultus*, but has (possibly by way of substitution) *descendit ad infernum*: and for *venturus judicare* it reads *judicaturus*. (Heurtley, XXIII.)

viii. No. XXIV. of Dr Heurtley is taken from the Veronese manuscript, of which a copy was printed by Blanchini in 1732. It is taken from an explanation of the Creed, entitled in the manuscript, "Incipit Sancti Athanasii de Symbolo." I had the pleasure of seeing the printed volume at Venice in 1872.

Two pages of the MS. are lost. My memoranda differ from the account given by Walch as cited by Dr Heurtley thus: I read *descendit ad inferna*, and *die tertia resurrexit a mortuis*. Thus the difference between this and our standard Creed would consist in the addition of the clause on the descent into hell, and of the words *de vivis et mortuis* and *sanctam matrem ecclesiam*.

ix. Dr Heurtley, XXV. On this Creed, attributed by Dr Heurtley to Eusebius Gallus, Dr Caspari has a learned and interesting dissertation. He accepts Oudin's conclusion that the author of the sermons from which the Creed is extracted (which sermons he prints) was Faustus of Reji or Riez, in the province of Arles, about 490.

This Creed adopts the Augustinian or pseudo-Augustinian phrase now usual, *conceptus de S. S. natus ex M. V.*, it omits *sub Pontio Pilato*: (Dr H. seems to be in error when he represents it as containing *mortuus*): it omits *a mortuis*: it reads *Dei patris omnipotentis*: it adds *sanctorum communionem*, and reads *vitam eternam*. Thus it makes the greatest step yet observed, since Marcellus, towards our present text.

x. I now come to the Spanish Symbol. I find it first in the Creed of Hildefonsus, Archbishop of Toledo, who died in 669[2]. He has a Sermon or Tract, *De Symbolo*, in which he makes the usual distinction between the Faith and the Symbol: "the

[1] See Mr Ffoulkes, p. 141. The not infrequent punctuation of the MSS. *Filium ejus, unicum dominum nostrum* seems also to be an echo of the same Eastern Creed.

[2] Migne, XCVI. p. 126, &c.

Catholic Faith is in the Symbol." The Creed is certainly worthy of being given at length, especially as it has escaped the notice of Dr Heurtley and Dr Hahn.

Credimus in Deum Patrem Omnipotentem.
Credimus et in Jesum Christum Filium Dei
unicum deum et dominum nostrum
qui natus est de Spiritu Sancto et Maria Virgine
passus sub Pontio Pilato
crucifixus et sepultus
descendit ad inferna
tertia die resurrexit vivus a mortuis
ascendit in coelum
sedet ad dexteram Dei patris omnipotentis
inde venturus judicare vivos et mortuos.
credo in Spiritum Sanctum
sanctam ecclesiam Catholicam
remissionem peccatorum
carnis resurrectionem
et vitam eternam.

On comparing this with the Creed of Etherius and Beatus (given in Heurtley XXXII.) in their treatise against Elipandus[1] (A. D. 785) it will be seen that they correspond exactly, except that in the latter we read *omnium peccatorum.* This shews that the Creed of Etherius was not a private document but the Symbol of the Spanish Church, at least that of the province of Toledo. So now turning to the Symbol *at the end* of the Gallican Sacramentary (Mabillon, *Museum Italicum* I., part 2, p. 396[2], Heurtley, XXVII.) we must I think ascribe that Creed also to a Spanish origin. Its title there is "Symbolum apostolorum cum magna cautela collectum et credentibus adsignatum." We have the same *Deum et dominum nostrum.* The varieties *natum de M. V. per S. S.:* the omission of *a mortuis;* the phrases *credo in ecclesiam sanctam* (without *Catholicam*)*; per baptismum sanctum remissionem peccatorum; carnis resurrectionem in vitam eternam* indicate other influences. The words *deum et dominum nostrum* are found again in Beatus and Etherius, on pp. 358, 362, 392. On the last-named page the passage runs thus: *credere in Deum P. O. et in Ihm Xpm Filium ejus unicum deum et dominum nostrum qui natus est de S. S. ex M. V. et in Spiritum sanctum, in qua fide baptizati sunt.* On the whole we see that the words *Dei patris omnipotentis* and *ecclesiam Catholicam* and the last clause were spreading in quarters which had not as yet accepted the phraseology *conceptus de Spiritu Sancto, natus ex Maria Virgine.*

xi. The Creed of the Mozarabic Liturgy (Migne, LXXXV. p. 385)

[1] This treatise is in the *Bibliotheca Patrum,* Lugdun. Tom. XIII. p. 360.

[2] Mabillon's tract is republished in Migne, LXXII. p. 447, see p. 579.

is curious, and has escaped notice. It is found in the service for Palm Sunday:

Credo in deum Patrem omnipotentem: et in Jesum Christum filium ejus unicum dominum nostrum: natum de Spiritu sancto ex utero Marie Virginis: passus sub P. P. crucifixus et sepultus: tertia die resurrexit vivus a mortuis: ascendit in celum: sedet ad dexteram dei Patris omnipotentis: inde venturus judicaturus vivos et mortuos: credo in Sanctum Spiritum: sanctam ecclesiam Catholicam: sanctorum communionem: remissionem omnium peccatorum: carnis hujus resurrectionem et vitam eternam. Amen.

It is impossible to say how far this represents the symbol of the date of Isidore to whom the Missal is attributed. Comparing it with the Creed of Etherius and Beatus I note that, like it, it omits *creatorem cœli et terræ*: but it omits also *deum et:* for *et Maria Virgine* it reads *ex utero M. V:* and it omits *descendit ad inferna*, words which occur both in Hildefonsus and Etherius: it has *vivus a mortuis*, as they both have: but it adds *sanctorum communionem:* again like the creed of Etherius it has *omnium peccatorum:* and like the Aquileian Creed of Ruffinus and the Creed in the appendix to Augustine's works (v. Ser. CCXLII. p. 2978) it has *carnis hujus.* On the words *ex utero* compare Council of Seville, A.D. 613 (Harduin III. 563). The use there made of the words increases the value of this copy. (See note on p. 168 below.)

xii. We have as yet met with no instance in which the clause *creatorem cœli et terræ* appears. It is found first in the Creed delivered to the candidates for baptism in the Gallican Sacramentary (Heurtley, XXVIII)[1].

The same Creed has *Filium ejus unigenitum sempiternum* but omits *Dominum nostrum:* it has *conceptum de S. S., passum, mortuum:* following to the close our present version. So runs the Creed. But it is followed by a commentary clearly of an earlier date: here the words *creatorem cœli et terræ, dei, sanctorum communionem* are omitted.

The words *unigenitum, sempiternum* are found also in the first creed of the Gallican Missal (Heurtley, XXIX.[2]), *dominum nostrum* being omitted in the text: the comment omits also to notice *creatorem cœli et terræ*, and *descendit ad inferna.* The second Creed[3] omits the descent into hell, and reads "He went up *Victor* into heaven." Otherwise it resembles the Creed of the present day. The greater part of the comment is lost.

xiii. We have approached very nearly to the Creed of modern times. I must, however, mention that the BOOK OF DEER, a Scotch book of the ninth century, omits *mortuus*, and reads *carnis resurrectionis vitam eternam.* Of this below[4].

[1] Migne, LXXII. p. 489.
[2] Migne, ut sup. p. 349.
[3] *Ibid.* p. 356.

[4] The "BOOK OF DEER" (Cambridge University Library, Ii. 6. 32: see facsimile reprint in the SPALDING CLUB

xiv. We have come at last to the first dated instance of a Creed complete as in the present day. It occurs in a treatise by one Pirminius, a Benedictine, who laboured much in France and Germany, in the eighth century, dying about the year 758[1]. The next instance of a completed Creed that I know of is in the interesting Gellone Codex of the Paris Library (see Martene, Vol. I. p. 37 of the edition of 1783, Lib. I. cap. i. Art. xii. ordo ii). Dr Heurtley has noticed an identity also in the interrogative Creed of the same Codex[2] (Martene, Vol. I. p. 67, Lib. I. cap. i. Art. xviii. ordo vi). This manuscript is assigned to the very end of the eighth century, say 790. Older versions of the Symbol were still retained, as we see by the Latin of the Book of Deer, and the Greek of *Galba* A. XVIII., but the spread in the ninth century of Psalters, from the writing schools of Charlemagne, speedily carried this Gallican version of the Creed throughout the world.

It is interesting to notice that we have now connected this completed version with a French or German original.

xv. Yet still the completed copy was not accepted even throughout France in the early part of the ninth century. We have an exposition of the Symbol by Amalarius, in reply to Charlemagne, from which we infer that the clauses *Conceptum de Spiritu Sancto,* and *Vitam eternam* were not in his copy of the Creed[3]. And Alcuin had read *De Spiritu Sancto et de M. V.*, as we learn from his work on the Trinity[4].

collections, A.D. 1869) has a copy of the Creed on the last folio 85, after the end of the Gospel of St. John. It reads thus:

Credo in dm̄ patrem omnipoten
tem . creatorem celi et terre
Et in ihm xpm filium ejus . unicū
dnm̄ nrm̄ . qui conceptus ÷ de spū scō..
Natus ex maria uirgine . passus
sub pontio pylato . crucifixus
et sepultus . discendit ad inferna.
Tertia die resurrexit a mortuis.
ascendit in celum . sedit ad dexte
ram di patris omnipotentis...
Inde uenturus ÷ iudicare uiuos et
mortuos . credo et in spm̄ scm̄ scāmq;
æclisiam catholicam . scorum com
munionem . remissionem peccator.
Carnis resurrectionis uitam eter
nam amen...

Two points are especially interesting: the punctuation connects *unicum* with the following words *dominum nostrum* as they are connected in some of Augustine's (or others') sermons. (Dr Heurtley unfortunately has not attended to the old punctuation.) The other is the reading in the last line, *carnis resurrectionis vitam eternam.* I have only found one MS. with this reading: that is the Codex Laudianus Gr. 35 of the Bodleian, where the folio ends *carnis resurrectionis*, as will be seen in Dr Heurtley's facsimile, and not *carnis resurrectione* as in Dr Heurtley's text (p. 63, compare p. 64). The fact that two MSS. present this curious reading must be remembered.

1 Heurtley, XXXI. 2 *Ibid.* LVI. note.

3 Migne, XCIX. p. 896.

4 Migne, CI. p. 58.

xvi. One nation remains. In the celebrated "Antiphonary of Bangor" (Bangor in the province of Ulster), which is one of the treasures of the Library at Milan, we have on folio 19 the following[1]:

Incipit symmulum. Credo in deum Patrem omnipotentem invisibilem omnium creaturarum visibilium et invisibilium conditorem. Credo et in Jesum Christum Filium eius unicum dominum nostrum deum omnipotentem conceptum de Spiritu sancto, natum de Maria Virgine passum sub Pontio Pylato qui crucifixus et sepultus descendit ad inferos tertia die resurrexit a mortuis ascendit in coelis seditque ad dexteram Dei patris omnipotentis exinde venturum judicare vivos et mortuos. credo et in spiritum sanctum deum omnipotentem unam habentem substantiam cum patre et filio sanctam esse ecclesiam catholicam abremissa peccatorum sanctorum communionem carnis resurrectionem credo vitam post mortem et vitam aeternam in gloriam Christi. haec omnia credo in deum. amen.

The MS. is most deeply interesting and I believe has been entirely transcribed for "the Irish Archæological and Celtic Society," amongst whose publications and under the care of the learned Dr Reeves it is to be shortly produced. Dr Caspari has devoted an essay to this copy of the creed in the second part of his work, but he seems to have followed the ever untrustworthy accounts of Muratori. I must confess however that my own collation was taken somewhat hastily. [*Remissa peccatorum* occurs in Tertullian against Marcion IV. 18 and Cyprian, Ep. 59, 70, 73. Cyprian again is quoted in Augustine *de Baptismo* IV. 18 tom. IX. c. 233. *Abremissa* or *abremissam* may be an intensification of the similar word. See below. Perhaps *in gloriam Christi* is a mistake of Muratori's for *in gloria Christi.*]

This early Irish Creed has interesting points of resemblance with the Nicene and African and Antiochene formulæ. I will recapitulate these points, and leave the further consideration to my readers.

invisibilem, as in the Aquileian creed of Ruffinus:

omnium creaturarum visibilium et invisibilium conditorem, as in the Nicene Creed, and Cassian's Creed of Antioch.

Deum omnipotentem of the Saviour is unique.

conceptum de S. S. natum ex M. V., with the Augustinian (?) sermon CCXIII. and Faustus of Riez.

mortuus is omitted.

descendit ad inferos, not *ad inferna* (see below).

We have *Dei Patris Omnipotentis*, and *sanctorum communionem*, as in Faustus.

Deum omnipotentem of the Holy Spirit is also unique, as is *the unam habentem substantiam cum Patre et Filio.*

The phrase *abremissa peccatorum* is peculiar both in language and position.

[1] I have expanded all the contractions. A copy is in Migne, LXXII. p. 597.

The Creed has another interest, as throwing some additional light on the origin of the Church in Ireland.

§ 4. Turning now to the various important readings in succession, we can have no doubt, I think, that the words *Creator of heaven and earth* came into the Western Creed from the Nicene Symbol, through the Creeds of the Gallican Sacramentary and the Gallican Missal (Heurtley, XXVIII. XXIX. XXX). The phrase was not in the Spanish Creeds, even in the time of Charlemagne, though it was of course in the Frank Creed of Pirminius.

The accepted words *our Lord,* instead of the words *our God and Lord,* carry us away also from the Spanish Creeds.

The exact phrase, *conceived of the Holy Ghost, born of the Virgin Mary,* appears first in the Creed assigned to Augustine (Heurtley, XVI.): then in that of Faustus of Riez: (it is not in the Spanish Creeds): then in the Creeds of the Gallican Sacramentary and Missal: then in Pirminius[1].

[1] The oscillation between these different modes of representing this part of the Creed is to be attributed to two causes:

i. The difficulty of representing in Latin the Greek word γεννηθέντα. The verb is used in St Luke i. 13, *Elizabeth thy wife shall bear thee a son.* It is also the verb used throughout the early part of the first chapter of St Matthew. Thus the *natus de S.S.* was insufficient: indeed the phrase might be deemed in a moderate degree Nestorian: and so the words *conceptus de S.S. natus ex M.V.* bore a character about them which ensured for them the final victory.

ii. Another cause is suggested by M. Nicolas. He says truly that before the time of Saint Augustine the phrase now received was unknown: it was adopted by his imitators, to whom we owe the Sermons 115, 131, and 195 *de tempore.* The older words might be quoted as suggesting that the Holy Spirit was the Father of the Saviour, as the Virgin was His mother: Augustine saw the difficulty and endeavoured to avoid it. "If we use the words born of the Holy Ghost and the Virgin Mary (he said *Enchiridion,* § 12, Vol. VI. col. 367) it is difficult to explain how He is the Son of the Virgin Mary and not the Son of the Holy Spirit." Thus the first alteration was from *Natus de Spiritu Sancto et Maria Virgine,* to *Natus de Spiritu Sancto ex Maria Virgine.* But this was insufficient. *Natus per S.S. ex M.V.* was better. Then another difficulty arose. The Manicheans mocked the expression. Augustine was driven to put more prominently forward the part of the Holy Spirit in the conception, and to make the part of the Virgin more passive: hence the phrase *conceptus de,* conceived of the Holy Ghost, *natus ex,* born from the Virgin Mary. At the Synod of Seville, A.D. 613 (Harduin, Vol. III. p. 563), there was a long *actio* on the two natures of Christ in the one Person, against those who confuse the natures, and hold that in Him the Deity was passible. The bishops referred to Scripture largely, and then say "Again in the very beginning of the apostolic symbol the distinction of the natures in one and the same Christ is thus shewn: *of the Deity from the Father* when it says, I believe in God the Father Almighty, and in Jesus Christ His only Son our Lord: *of the Humanity from the Mother* when it says, born of the Holy Spirit from the womb of the Virgin Mary." After a while the bishops quote the Fathers largely: St Hilary, St Ambrose, St Athanasius "in the tract which he wrote on the Nativity of Christ...The same in his Exposition of the Faith," but this is not the *Quicunque,* of the existence of which there is not a hint given. Yet it would have

Mortuum occurs for the first time, undoubtedly, in the Gallican books. It is not in the Spanish, English, Scotch, or Irish Creeds.

He descended into hell (*descendit ad inferna*) was in the Aquileian Creed of Ruffinus, but not in the other Aquileian Creeds: then it appeared in the French Creed of Venantius Fortunatus (*ad infernum*): in the Veronese explanation of the Pseudo-Athanasius (*in inferna*): but not in Faustus nor in the English Creeds: it was in the Spanish Creeds and then in the Gallican books[1].

furnished, if it had been known to the Spanish bishops, very valuable corroboration. The words so far as they are quoted agree entirely with the Creed of the Mozarabic Liturgy. (The Greek did not present the same difficulty: the phrase *γεννηθέντα ἐκ πνεύματος ἁγίου* is taken from St Matt. i. 20, and there is a difference between *πνεῦμα ἅγιον* and *τὸ ἅγιον πνεῦμα* or *τὸ πνεῦμα τὸ ἅγιον*. The latter expression must refer to the Holy Spirit personally: the former not necessarily: it *may* refer to His effusion, His operation, His work, thus *πνεῦμα ἅγιον ἐπελεύσεται ἐπὶ σέ*: *πνεῦμα ἅγιον ἦν ἐπ' αὐτόν*: *οὔπω ἦν πνεῦμα ἅγιον*: *ἀλλ' οὐδὲ εἰ πνεῦμα ἅγιόν ἐστιν ἠκούσαμεν*. So *λάβετε πνεῦμα ἅγιον*. On this see Hooker, *E. P.*, v. lxxvii. 5. The distinction is difficult to convey into other languages without a periphrasis. I have drawn attention to the mode in which the Chalcedon or Constantinopolitan words are here altered in our "Nicene Creed.")

[1] We cannot enter into the meaning of these different expressions without looking to the earlier and later conceptions of the meaning of Psalm xxx. 3 (xxix. 4). The account of the words given by Ruffinus is this: "The same meaning seems to be contained in the word *sepultus*."—"But that He descended into *infernum* is evidently taught in the Psalms when we read, *Thou hast brought me into the dust of death*, and again, *What profit is in my blood when I shall descend to corruption?* And again, *I descended into the mud of the deep and there is no substance.* But John too says, *Art thou he that is to come* (into *infernum* no doubt) *or do we expect another?* Whence also Peter says, *Because Christ, being mortified in the flesh, vivified in the Spirit which dwells in Him, descended to preach to those spirits which are detained in prison, which were unbelieving in the days of Noah:* a passage in which it is also declared what work He performed there. Yea the Lord Himself speaks by the prophet as of something future, *Thou wilt not leave my soul in inferno nor wilt thou give thy Holy One to see corruption.* And again, the prophet exhibits this as completed when he says, *Lord, thou hast brought out my soul from infernum, thou hast saved me from them that go down to the pit.*" Every one remembers the expression of St Augustine in his tract on this subject.

Let us now look to the change of language. *In infernum* clearly means *into infernum*, just as *ad inferna* or *ad infernum* means *to*, i.e. to the gates of *infernum*. Thus at first it was regarded that the sentence of the Aquileian Creed meant *He was buried:* for Sheol = the grave. *He descended into the grave.* But in time (as we see in Ruffinus) the words of the Psalmist were more carefully examined, and it was felt that it was improper to speak of Christ's soul going into the grave: and then they thought that *infernum* or *inferna* must mean something else. It was the place of misery. But Christ could not have been in misery during the hours of the great Sabbath; on the contrary He went to Paradise: so when His soul descended—as it must have done—to *inferna* He must have gone there not to stay there, but to burst the door and set the captives free. Thus at last *ad inferos* was seen to be safer language than even *ad inferna:* we have it in one Creed of the Saxon Church: we have it in every copy that I know of the *completed* Quicunque. (In the *incomplete* copy commented upon in the Oxford MS., Junius 25, it is *ad inferna*, as well as in the early form remaining in the Codex Colbertinus. But of this below.)

This mediæval difference between *infernum* and *inferi* may be noted by comparing two passages in the letter of St Boniface to Ethelbald king of Mercia

The right hand of God the Father Almighty. First in Faustus, then in the Gallican and Spanish Creeds, but not in the English. (In the Royal MS. 2 A. xx. di is marked as a mistake[1].)

The epithet *Catholic* appeared for the first time, undoubtedly, in Faustus: then in the Gallican books and the Spanish Creeds of Hildefonsus, Etherius, and the Mozarabic Liturgy.

The *Communion of Saints* for the first time in Faustus, then in the Gallican Sacramentary and Missal. Not in the genuine Spanish nor English books.

Life eternal was received in the same way.

§ 5. The general result of this is unquestionable. The complete copy of the Apostles' Creed, as it exists in the present day, was Frank: the separate articles which distinguish it from the old Roman, Aquileian, African, Spanish, English, Scotch, and Irish types are all of Gallican origin. They came through, or from, Faustus of Riez and the old Gallican Service-books to Pirminius, the Frank missionary of the middle of the eighth century: and the completed Creed gradually spread from that time.

The progress of this spreading movement is not noted, I think, either by Dr Caspari or Dr Hahn. But the vehicle by which it was circulated far and wide was furnished by the Psalters which were written in abundance in and after the time of Charlemagne. It will be necessary for me, ere long, to devote a few pages to the description of these Psalters; one of the earliest known is attributed to Charles himself, and is supposed (rightly or wrongly, as we shall see hereafter) to have been offered or sent by him to his friend Hadrian II. It contains a completed copy of the Apostles' Creed. The Psalters of the next century, almost invariably, contain the Creed. Thus the text was considered to be settled, so far as the new Holy Roman Empire was concerned. And if for a time some older form lingered in

(Haddan and Stubbs, III. pp. 354, 355), "The harlots whether nuns or seculars often slew the infants they had conceived in their sins, filling not the churches of Christ with adopted children, but the graves with corpses and *inferi* with miserable souls:" whilst undoubtedly, *sine dubio*, "Ethelbald's predecessor Ceolred who had died in his sins had passed from this world to the torments of *infernum*."

[1] Here again we are brought into contact with the *Quicunque.* Claudius C. VII. and all the psalters have *ad dexteram Dei patris omnipotentis:* the Ambrosian Codex and the codices of Junius' commentary, read *ad dexteram patris.* The Codex of St Germains (now lost) is said by Montfaucon to have had *ad dexteram patris omnipotentis:* the Colber. *ad dexteram dei patris.*

England, or Scotland, or Ireland, beyond the direct influence of the Emperor, such form could not have lasted long. We have a manuscript of the ninth century at Lambeth (No. 427), which contains the Creed, reading, however, *ad inferos;* and one in the Library of Trinity College, Cambridge, of the twelfth century (which belonged at one time to the Church of Canterbury), in which the Creed is exactly the same as in Pirminius[1].

[1] On page 126 Dr Heurtley has the following passage and note: "By the end of the eighth century the formula now in use may be considered as on the whole established. And this date as it coincides with the time at which the Bishops of Rome were strenuously engaged in endeavouring to conform the Liturgies of the other churches to the Roman order, so it suggests what is in all probability the true account of the eventual prevalence of one and the same type of the Creed throughout Western Christendom." I may have misunderstood this passage, but the impression it conveys to my mind is certainly incorrect in fact. There is no proof whatever that the Creed which thus ultimately prevailed came from Rome in its complete form. The last hint of a Roman Creed that we have, is in the imperfect account of Leo the Great, and the words there are distinct, "*Natus de Spiritu Sancto ex* (or *et*) *Maria Virgine.*" There is no proof that the Roman Church had altered this in the time of Hadrian. And if the *Romanus ordo* as to Baptism was introduced into Gaul in the middle or end of the eighth century, it must have brought in the use of the Nicene Creed, not the Apostles' Creed. I am thus confirmed in the opinion I have mentioned in the text, that this copy of the Apostles' Creed is really of Gallican origin. The anxiety of Charles to conform to the Church of Rome must not be put too high. We know that he refused to accept the Roman version of the Creed of Constantinople: we know that two hundred years later the Church of Rome accepted his version of that Creed. We know that the Gallican use of the *Gloria in Excelsis* spread to Rome: and we know that the Gallican Psalter displaced the so-called Roman Psalter. There is nothing, therefore, *à priori* improbable in the supposition—which we see has in its favour whatever little historical evidence is forthcoming—that as Pirminius' version of the Apostles' Creed spread speedily over Germany and France, so it spread ultimately to Italy and Rome.

CHAPTER XV.

USE OF THE APOSTLES' CREED.

§ 1. The title *symbolum*, "signum" or "collatio." Account by "Ruffinus." § 2. The introduction of the conception of a "mystery." § 3. Cyprian, Ambrose, Augustine, &c. § 4. The *traditio symboli*. § 5. The use in the Hour services in the time of Amalarius and Rabanus Maurus. § 6. Augustine's and Aquinas' account of its origin from Scripture. § 7. Importance attached to the Creed. i. Chrodegang. ii. Ordo Romanus, &c. iii. The Capitulars of Pepin; Charlemagne, Louis. iv. Canons of Aix, 789. v. Synod of Frankfort, 794. vi. Theodulf. vii. Synod of Aix, 801. viii. "Visitation Articles" of Charlemagne and the replies. § 8. Death of Charlemagne. § 9. Further growing importance of the Creed. Hatto. Hincmar. § 10. Influence on the Psalter. § 11. Later use at the Hour services. § 12. Old English versions. APPENDIX.—Additional illustrations of the value set in England and Germany on the Creed as containing the Catholic Faith.

§ 1. THE earliest use of the Latin Creed was in the preparation for baptism. "The Novatians baptize with the Symbol which we employ," are the well-known words of St. Cyprian: and the name or title, Symbol, suggests the object which it was deemed to serve. As early as the time when the commentary ascribed to Ruffinus was composed, doubts had arisen amongst Latin writers as to the origin of this designation: confusion had arisen between *σύμβολον*, a mark or sign, and *συμβολή*, a collation or joint contribution: or rather, attempts were made to ascribe to *σύμβολον* the signification of *συμβολή*.

"Our fathers tell us (says Ruffinus) that after the Ascension of our Lord, at the time when the tongues of fire sat upon each of the Apostles through the coming of the Holy Spirit, command was given to them by God to go and preach the word to every nation. When they were about to part from each other, they agreed upon a rule to guide their future preaching: lest by any means when they were separated, one in one place, another in another, they should expound the faith differently to such as were invited to believe in Christ. Thus, being present all together and all filled with the Holy Spirit, they composed this short index of their future preaching, bringing together what each thought, and then they agreed that this should be given as a rule to believers. And so, for reasons good and sound, they wished that it should be called a SYMBOL. For the word SYMBOL in Greek means both a sign and a collation—a collation being the result when many bring together into one common store. And it is called a Sign or Index or Watchword, because at that time (as Paul the Apostle tells us) there were many Jews who pretended to be Apostles of Christ, and wandered about for the sake of gain, naming indeed the name of Christ, but not preaching Him according to the lines of the old tradition. Thus the Apostles fixed upon this index by which might be recognised the man who preached according to the Apostolic rules. Just as in civil war, where men wear the same dress and speak the same language, watchwords are given to the soldiery to distinguish friend from foe; so is it amongst us. And thus they handed it down that their watchword should not be written on paper or parchment, but be retained in the hearts of the believers, so that there could be no doubt that, if any one knew it, he must have received it from the Apostles by tradition, and not by reading it in a book; for a book perchance might fall into the hands of unbelievers."

We need not delay to speak of the futility of this explanation: Ruffinus forgot that followers of the Apostolic tradition might become schismatics or even heretical as to points not distinctly enuntiated in this document, and then carry away their watchword into the enemies' camp: "the Novatians use the same Symbol that we do." Nestorians and Eutychians were as earnest as were the followers of Cyril and Flavian in standing by the Faith of the Nicene Council.

§ 2. We must look out for another explanation: and we have it in the circumstances of the third century, when the precept of the Saviour, that the Gospel should be preached to every creature, became checked by the prevalent persecutions; and the example set by St Paul, when he stood before Agrippa, was, from the same causes, deprived of its force. Driven unwillingly to secresy, the Christians, with a not unusual aptitude, began to represent to themselves and others that their secresy had its advantages; in point of fact it was in itself desirable. For did not St Paul speak of Christian rites as a mystery? and if so, was it not necessary that the faith should be treated as such? Was it not a mistake of the early ages, of Justin Martyr and the Apologists, to exhibit to the heathen Emperors and to the heathen world the character of the initiatory rite? the character of the mystic feast?

And thus, as it seems to me, the conception spread most rapidly, by which the candidates for baptism were styled "those who are being enlightened," and the baptized were "the initiated," and the Services of the Church were designated as "the mystic rites," and doctrines were reserved to be the *disciplina arcani*, and the formula of initiation was the Symbol[1]. But the fact is undoubted that in the Eastern Church the unbaptized Constantine took part in framing the Faith of Nicæa; the shorter password into the Church being still taught only to the candidate for baptism, as we learn from the Lectures of St Cyril of Jerusalem. In the Western Church the longer password was kept equally sacred. It was kept secret—unwritten—long after the dates of Ruffinus, and Ambrose, and Hilary, and Augustine.

§ 3. The first intimation I have met with as to the sacredness of the Symbol, is found in the *Testimonies* of Cyprian: "That the sacrament of the faith is not to be profaned, we are taught by Solomon in the Proverbs (xxiii. 9), *Speak not in the ear of an imprudent man, lest when he has heard he may ridicule the wisdom of thy words:* and by the Gospel according to Matthew, *Give not that which is holy, &c.*[2]" And St Ambrose says[3], "Be cautious, lest thou divulge the mysteries of the Symbol and of the Lord's Prayer." So Peter Chrysologus[4] frequently. In point of fact, it was only at a late period of their preparation that the candidates for baptism received the Symbol in this age of the Church. "It was on the Lord's day, when, after the Lessons and the Sermon *and the Catechumens had been dismissed*, I was delivering the Symbol to the Competentes in the Baptistery," that, as Ambrose tells us, he was called upon to rescue an Arian[5]. We have frequent allusions to this secresy in the

[1] For further illustrations, see King's *History of the Creed*, p. 20.

[2] *Testim.* III. no. 50.

[3] *De Cain et Abel*, Lib. I. c. ix.

[4] *Sermones* 58, 59, 60.

[5] Lib. v. ep. 35. In the second programme of Dr Caspari, pp. 50, 51, are printed two copies of an exposition on the Creed, attributed to St Ambrose. The writer accepts the interpretation of *symbolum* as = *collatio*, and calls the Creed a *breviarium fidei*, made by the Apostles themselves: he knows that "in the parts of the east" they have added to the Creed, and says that possibly they have added too much: he says that the words *invisibilem et impassibilem* (of the Aquileian Creed?) were thus added to exclude the Patripassian error, but such additions are not required by us: we cannot be charged with maintaining the error, because *symbolum Romanæ ecclesiæ nos tenemus*. On page 57, we have the Creed complete. Comparing it with the Roman Creed as learnt from Ruffinus, I remark that it contains the words *qui conceptus est de S. S., natus de Maria Virgine passus sub P. P. crucifixus*,

writings of St Augustine. Indeed, the great bishop says, that "the Creed is called the Symbol, because by the confession of it, as it were by a signal, the faithful Christian is recognised[1]." So again St Leo the Great, and Maximus of Turin.

§ 4. At a later period the order was this. The Creed was delivered to the Competentes eight days before Easter Eve[2]: it was delivered with short expositions of the several clauses, of which expositions we have many instances in the genuine writings of St Augustine, and others amongst the spurious sermons attributed to the great bishop; others again in the older Liturgies. This ceremony was called the TRADITIO SYMBOLI[3]. The candi-

mortuus et sepultus: it has *Dei Patris:* and *sanctorum communionem*, and it concludes with *vitam æternam.* And so the writer counts up *duodecim sententiæ* corresponding to the twelve Apostles. He distinctly says that the Creed ought not to be written, but "retained in the memory, it will prove of more use there." There certainly may be some hesitation in accepting this as an entirely correct representation of the Milanese and Roman Creed of the date of St Ambrose. But the same indefatigable investigator has printed (p. 134) another Creed from an "exhortation of St Ambrose," found in a MS. at Vienna, which has the clause "natus de S. S. et ex Maria Virgine," but, omitting "sanctorum communionem," ends (as Jerome says all Creeds end) with "carnis resurrectionem." On p. 204, he prints a more correct copy (as would seem) of the Creed which Dr Heurtley ascribes to Eusebius Gallus, but Dr Caspari to Faustus of Riez; this contains the clauses "qui conceptus est de S. S. natus ex M. V." and "sanctorum communionem." There is much other information, which must be seen in the "Programme" itself.

[1] *Sermon.* 214 § 12, Tom. v. col. 1379 (Gaume).

[2] In the Churches of Spain, 20 days.

[3] I will give a specimen from the Mozarabic Liturgy (Martene, IV. cap. XX. ordo VIII., or Migne, LXXXV. p. 394).

In the course of the service on Palm Sunday, we have the following. It is corrupt at parts.

"Hic fiat sermo ad populum.

Symboli traditio in dominica palmarum.

Carissimi accipite regulam fidei quod symbolum dicitur: et, cum acceperitis, in corde scribite et quotidie apud vosmet ipsos dicite; antequam dormiatis, antequam procedatis, vestro symbolo vos munite. Symbolum nemo scribit ut legi possit; sed ad recensendum ne forte deleat oblivio quod non tradidit lectio, sit vobis quod ex vestra memoria, quod audituri estis, hoc credituri: et quod credituri, hoc etiam lingua reddituri: ait enim apostolus, *Corde creditur ad justitiam, oris confessio fit ad salutem.* Hoc enim symbolum quod retenturi estis et credituri. Signate vos, respondete.

Fides."

The Creed follows of which I have already given a description, Chap. XIV. p. 165. Then we have the following.

Submissa voce. Ut facilius memoriæ vestræ possint inhærere quæ dicta sunt, textum symboli ordinemque repetamus. CREDO IN D. P. O.

Submissa voce. Tertio quoque textum symboli recenseamus, ut quia fidem divinæ Trinitatis symbolum in se continet, ipse numerus repetitionis cum sacramento conveniat Trinitatis. CREDO IN DEUM PATREM O.

Submissa voce. Hanc sanctæ fidei regulam quam vobis nunc tradidit sancta mater ecclesia, firmissima mentis vestræ retinete sententia: ne aliquando dubitationis scrupulum in corde vestro oriatur: quia si, quod absit, in hoc vel tenuiter dubitatur, omne fidei fundamentum subruitur et animæ periculum generatur. Et ideo, si aliquem vestrum inde quidpiam movet, reputet quia hoc intelligere non possit, vera tamen esse credat omnia quæ audivit.

&c. &c.

dates then learnt it by heart: and immediately before their baptism it was recited either by them or by the bishop in their hearing. A similar course of proceeding took place before Whitsuntide: for on Whitsun Eve as on Easter Eve the sacrament of baptism was administered. The custom at Rome was to recite the "Creed from a position of some eminence in the sight of the faithful people," as we learn from St Augustine[1]. And to this fact Ruffinus distinctly (and perhaps the pseudo-Ambrose by implication) points as being the means by which the Church of Rome retained uninjured and unaltered the "Symbol of the Apostles." Its copy must have been very different from our modern version.

§ 5. The first intimation that we have of the use of the Apostles' Creed in the Hour Services is to be found in the fourth book of the work *De Ecclesiasticis Officiis*, which used to be attributed to Amalarius Fortunatus, Archbishop of Treves, who died in 819, but is now assigned to Symphronius Amalarius, a presbyter of Metz, who survived his namesake by about fifteen years[2]. We have records of the Hour Services in use in Spain,

Then came the *missa*, in which the following address was made:

"Catholicam fidem, fratres charissimi, cordis integritate servantes, Deum Patrem, Deum Filium, Deum fateamur et Spiritum Sanctum, nec tamen Deos plures adfirmare gentiliter audeamus, sed in tribus unum Deum fiducialiter adoremus. Una quippe est Trinitatis essentia, nec est altera creatrix et æterna substantia..........Nullus impares gradus, ubi summa æqualitas reperitur, interserat: non est Pater Filio, quia generavit, antiquior: neque Filius est gignente posterior......Istam proinde fidem delectemur, usque ad sanguinem, vindicare, si volumus Dei Patris hæredes existere, ut hac fidei firmitate muniti ad cœleste regnum perveniamus inlæsi.
R. Amen."

The prayers *Inlatio*, &c., all bear on the Trinity, but I cannot recognise any verbal identity with the Athanasian Creed.

In the *Inlatio* come the words "Spiritus Sanctus qui procedens de utroque non est genitus aut creatus sed creator Universitatis Dominus."

The whole ought to be studied. And the notes on the Lord's Prayer, and the Benedictio are especially interesting.

[1] *Confessions*, VIII. c. 2, Tom. I. p. 253. The custom may have extended further. At all events in the sixth century Ferrandus, a deacon of Carthage, wrote thus to Fulgentius of Ruspe: "Universa quoque religionis catholicæ veneranda mysteria cognoscens atque percipiens celebrato solemniter scrutinio per exorcismum contra diabolum vindicatur (catechumenus), cui se renunciare constanter *sicut hic consuetudo poscebat*, auditurus symbolum profitetur. Ipse insuper sancti symboli verba memoriter in conspectu fidelis populi *clara voce* pronuntians, piam regulam dominicæ orationis accepit." So too apparently in the Churches of Spain, Concil. Braccar. (I take these from Massmann: p. 12, note.)

[2] Bede however reminded Egbert that Ambrose urged all the faithful to recite or chant the words of the Symbol at the matin hours: it would serve as an antidote against the poison of the devil by night and by day. His language shews that this was not ordinarily done in England, though custom did enjoin the frequent use of the Lord's Prayer with

in the time of St Isidore of Seville (who died in 636), but there is no mention there of the Apostles' Creed: on the contrary, the language which the Archbishop uses of the Creed of the 318 seems to decide against there being any contemporaneous use, in any service, of the Apostolic Symbol. St Isidore says[1]:

"The Symbol which at the time of the sacrifice is proclaimed to the people was put forth at the Synod of Nicæa by the collation of three hundred and eighteen holy Fathers, and the rule of this faith is so excellent relating the mysteries of Christian doctrine, that it speaks of every part of the faith, and there is scarcely any heresy for which an answer is not found here in some one word or phrase. For it tramples down every impious error, every misbelieving blasphemy; and on this account it is proclaimed by the people in all the churches with one and a like profession[2]."

The Prime office is so far different from the modern usage that I may be allowed to give Amalarius' description of it[3]:

It began with the *Deus in adjutorium meum: Domine ad adjuvandum.* The *Gloria Patri* followed, or the *Alleluia* at certain seasons. The Psalm followed "which David sang when the Ziphites wished to seize him and deliver him into the hands of Saul" (i.e. our Psalm liv.), and then, apparently, two portions of Psalm cxix (verses 5 and 18) and the verse *Arise, help us and deliver us for thy name's sake.* After this the pieces *Kyrie eleeson: Christe eleeson: Kyrie eleeson,* which Amalarius explains as appealing to Christ, (1) as it were before His Incarnation, (2) as incarnate, (3) as glorified. Then followed the Lord's Prayer, and after that the Apostles' Creed. Of this I will give his own description. "After the Lord's Prayer follows our Belief (nostra credulitas) which the Holy Apostles framed concerning the Faith of the Holy Trinity and the economy of the Incarnation of the Lord and the state of our Church[4]."

This is, as Mr Ffoulkes describes[5], the first indication known of the use of the Apostles' Creed at the Canonical Hours. It follows, as will be observed, on the reforms of Charlemagne and Alcuin.

Rabanus Maurus[6], who died in 855, wrote three books *De Institutione Clericorum.* He speaks of the use of the "Symbol of the Apostolic Faith" in the preparation of the catechumens for

bended knee. Haddan and Stubbs, III. p. 316.

[1] S. Isidori *de Ecclesiæ Officiis* Lib. I. cap. 16. Migne, Vol. LXXXIII. p. 815.

[2] St Isidore speaks of the services of the third, sixth and ninth hours, of vespers and compline, vigils and matins: but no mention is made of the Apostles' Creed.

[3] Book IV. chap. 2. Migne, CV. col. 1165.

[4] Migne, CV. c. 1168.

[5] *Athanasian Creed*, p. 186.

[6] Migne, CVII. c. 311, 327.

baptism (Apostolicæ fidei ostenditur ei symbolum): and he has a few words on the Offices for the Hours. Nothing, however, can be learnt from these last, as bearing on the point before us. Walfrid Strabo, who died in 849, is more profuse than Rabanus on the Hour Services, and yet his chief value to us arises from the intimation which he gives that these services were receiving frequent alterations. He maintained that new matter "ought not to be rejected if it did not disagree with the Faith of Truth." Thus, "Paulinus of Forisjulii, the Patriarch, had introduced into private masses the use of hymns composed either by himself or others[1]." He refers to a dispute between the Greeks and the Latins on the precise form of the *Gloria Patri* (no doubt the same difference that had attracted the attention of the monks of the convent at Bethlehem), and he mentions that some of his contemporaries believed that this last short hymn had been put forth by the Council of Nicæa, "in order that, mingling with all the offices and all the prayers, it should enforce the Faith of the Coeternal Trinity."

§ 6. It is impossible to overrate the importance attached to the Latin Symbol now that it had assumed its present and completed form. It was believed, and therefore taught, that it had proceeded in that form from the gathering of the twelve on the day of Pentecost. I have a photograph from a manuscript at Venice where it is entitled SYMBOLUM APOSTOLORUM IN PENTECOSTEN (*sic*). The ingenuity of the age soon discovered which article was contributed by each of the twelve. It is true that these accounts varied—but the variation was of little moment. Then Sermons were attributed to St Augustine, and thus his name was used as giving authority to the statement. But these writers were not over anxious to make their oracle consistent with himself. Two Sermons (Vol. v., Appendix, CCXL. and CCXLI., columns 2970 and 2972) distribute the articles differently. The former sermon adds brief explanations, as from the Apostles, of the clauses which they severally added. It terminates with enforcing the duty of "our holding faithfully and firmly the faith and gospel of the Apostles handed on to us by their successors, and guarding inviolate the pact made by us in baptism with the

[1] Migne, CXIV. c. 952, 954.

Lord." Still the nobler spirits rejected the tradition. As Eucherius, Bishop of Lyons in the fifth century, had taught that the Creed was collected out of Scripture, its existence being due to the anxiety of the Fathers of the Churches regarding the salvation of their flocks, so did Thomas of Aquino in the thirteenth teach:

"Only a few have the opportunity of learning from Scripture what is necessary to be believed, therefore a summary was collected out of the sacred writings; and this summary must be regarded not as added to Scripture, but as extracted from it."

Such too had been the opinion of the great Augustine[1].

§ 7. The opinion which I have adduced that the Lord's Prayer contained all that was necessary to be asked from God, and the Apostles' Creed all that was necessary to be believed of God, was constantly put forward in the age of Charlemagne. I must add further proofs of its acceptance, but I will not attempt to arrange them in precisely chronological order. I shall not shrink, however, from mixing with them proofs of the prevalence of other and shorter Creeds, such as I have already noted as being used at the time of Baptism, reserving for a later chapter Creeds or Professions of another character.

i. In the rule of Crodegang, Bishop of Metz[2], we have an

[1] "In sanctis scripturis et in sermonibus ecclesiasticis ea (the contents of the symbol) multis modis posita soletis audire. Sed collecta breviter et in ordinem certum redacta atque constructa tradenda sunt vobis ut fides vestra ædificetur, et confessio præparetur, et memoria non gravetur." S. August. Opera, v. col. 1371. *Serm.* CCXIV. *In traditione symboli*, III.

So *Eucherius:*

"Ecclesiarum patres de populorum salute solliciti ex diversis voluminibus scripturarum collegerunt testimonia divinis gravida sacramentis. Disponentes itaque ad animarum pastum salubre convivium collegerunt verba brevia et certa expedita sententiis sed diffusa mysteriis et hoc Symbolum nominaverunt. De canonicis itaque lectionibus facta est in unum pretiosa collatio, angusta sermonibus sed divisa sensibus et de utroque testamento totius corporis virtus in paucas est diffusa sententias." *Homilia* I. *de symbolo.* (It will be noticed that Eucherius adopted the conception that symbolum = collatio: but the persons who made the *collatio* were the bishops of the churches, not the Apostles.)

The following is the passage from Aquinas:

"Veritas fidei in sacra scriptura diffusa continetur et variis modis, et quibusdam obscure; ita quod ad eliciendam fidei veritatem ex sacra scriptura requiritur longum studium et exercitium, ad quod non possunt pervenire omnes illi quibus necessarium est cognoscere fidei veritatem, quorum plerique aliis negotiis occupati studio vacare non possunt. Et ideo fuit necessarium ut ex sententiis sacræ scripturæ aliquid manifestum summarie colligeretur quod proponeretur omnibus ad credendum: quod quidem non est additum sacræ scripturæ, sed potius ex sacra scriptura sumptum." *Summa*, pars II. quæst. 1, articul. 9. (I have taken these passages from *Nicolas*, pp. 38, 39.)

[2] Migne, LXXXIX. p. 1073.

account of the Faith on which the monks or priests of his order were to be interrogated at the time of Confession. The Confessor asked the servant of God:

"Dost thou believe in God the Father Almighty, Maker of heaven and earth? Dost thou believe in the Father, the Son, and the Holy Spirit? Dost thou believe that these three Persons, as we have said, Father, Son, and Holy Spirit, are three Persons and one God? Dost thou believe that in the Flesh in which thou now art, thou shalt receive (recipere habes) what thou hast done and what thou shalt do, whether it be good or bad? Dost thou believe that there will be a resurrection to eternal life after death?" To each of these questions the penitent replied "I believe," and then the question was put "Art thou willing to forgive?"

ii. The Confession in the *Ordo Romanus*[1] was almost identical, and we meet with numerous similar questions in the "Orders" printed by Martene out of several ancient manuscripts[2]. Thus we are introduced to the mode in which the enquiries enjoined by Charlemagne as to the belief of his people in the Holy Trinity were practically enforced: but we should err if we thought that the full teaching of the Church on this grand subject was pressed either at that time, or for many subsequent generations, on all alike. It was a direction of Chrodegang, that in teaching dogma great discretion must be used; "One and the same doctrine must not be taught to all indiscriminately, for things which are closed must not be opened to all alike[3]."

iii. We may now turn to the Capitulars, which I shall quote from the grand edition published by Baluzius, at Paris, in the year 1677.

I have, I think, already referred to the direction of the Synod under Pepin, in the year 744, that "the Catholic Faith, as given by the Bishops in the Nicene Synod, should be taught; that so the law of God and the Ecclesiastical Rule should be recovered where it had been lost sight of under earlier princes[4]." Allied to

[1] Hiltorp, p. 18*.

[2] e. g. out of the MS. of St Gatien of Tours, I. VI. VII. ordo iii. iv. Gellone, VI. Noyeau, X.

[3] Migne, vol. LXXXIX. p. 1094. St Boniface, about A.D. 745, directed that the presbyters should enjoin all the faithful subject to them to commit to memory the Symbol and the Lord's Prayer, that by faith and prayer under the illumination of the Holy Spirit they might be saved. And no one was to "take up a child from the font" unless he knew by memory the Symbol and the Lord's Prayer. Cf. Rules, XXV. XXVI.

[4] This seems to me to be worthy of being borne in mind in questions as to the dates of manuscripts.

this is a direction of which we find a note in Pertz[1], that every presbyter was to give an account "de fide catholica," to his bishop each Lent. Very interesting is it to notice the determination of these grim old kings to maintain their Church, not only pure in the faith but also national: and this determination is particularly to be noted in the reign and acts of Charlemagne. Scarcely had he entered on his work when we find a decree repeating the order which I have just quoted from Pertz[2]: it was enjoined that

> "Every presbyter residing in any diocese should be subject to the Bishop in whose diocese he is, and that he should each Lent submit to the Bishop a report of his ministry with reference to Baptism, to the Catholic Faith, to the Prayers and Order of the Mass."

The zeal of this great king increased as time rolled on. In the year 782[3] we have his famous order about the improvement of service-books, an order which was repeated in 787 or 788[4]. He speaks of the study of letters as having almost perished; he states that the books of the Old and New Testament had been depraved by want of skill in the copyists: he mentions his appointment of a suitable officer to investigate carefully the books which remained, and out of them, as out of a choice garden, to cull the flowers, and place them, as it were, in a border. Two volumes were to be prepared of treatises and sermons of the Catholic Fathers, suited for each festival, and these were to be handed to the clergy for them to learn[5].

iv. In 789 was held the famous Synod of Aix, at which a very important and voluminous collection of Canons was prepared, compiled from earlier Councils. It was then published. In the preface Charles compared himself to King Josiah[6], who had in his day endeavoured to recall his people to the worship of the true God, going about his dominions, correcting and admonishing. We find that he insisted that the faith and the life of each

[1] *Monumenta Germaniæ historiæ.* Legum, Tom. I. p. 17. This is under the year 742.

[2] Baluzius, p. 192, or Pertz under the year 771. Such was the ignorance of some of the clergy that a question arose in 754 concerning a presbyter who had baptized, but did not know either the Symbol or the Lord's Prayer: nor did he remember the Psalms, or know whether a bishop had blessed him. Labbe, VI. p. 1652.

[3] Pertz, ut sup. p. 44.

[4] *Ibid.* 52. Baluzius, p. 203.

[5] This certainly gave the opportunity for compiling the numerous collections which now appeared. The collectors were not scrupulous as to the authors to whom they assigned the documents they copied, an over regard for accuracy not being a fault of the times.

[6] Baluzius, p. 209.

person who applied for ordination should be examined into by the Bishop[1]. We find the Psalms limited to 150[2]: we find (no. 31 or 32[3]) the order which directs that "the Faith of the Holy Trinity and the Incarnation of Christ, His Passion, His Resurrection, His Ascension should be proclaimed to all." For this is quoted the authority of a Council of Carthage; it can refer only to the true Nicene Creed, and so it is understood by both Baluzius and Labbe[4]. In a later Canon (59 or 60[5]) we find that "the Catholic Faith shall be diligently read and taught by Bishops and Presbyters to all the people, because this is the first Commandment: *Hear, O Israel, the* LORD *our God is one God.*" In a later Canon (68 or 69 or 70[6]) we meet with an order which I must exhibit at greater length. It is this:

"The Bishops must enquire diligently through their dioceses from the Presbyters, as to their Faith, their Baptism, and celebration of Masses; whether they hold the right Faith and observe the Catholic Baptism, and well understand the Prayers of the Mass; whether the Psalms are properly modulated according to the divisions into verses[7]; whether they themselves understand the Lord's Prayer, and teach it so as to be understood by others, that each may know what he is asking from God; whether the *Gloria Patri* is sung by all with all honour; whether the Priest himself with the holy Angels and with the people of God sings as with one voice the HOLY, HOLY, HOLY." Not boys but men were to be employed to copy the Evangel, the Psalter, and the Missal (No. 70 or 72)[8]. All doubtful narratives against the Catholic Faith were to be suppressed (No. 77 or 78)[9], whilst in the last canon the subjects for the sermons of the clergy were laid down. The Presbyters whom the Bishops send forth are to proclaim to all alike that "they must believe that the Father and the Son and the Holy Spirit are one God, omnipotent, eternal, invisible; Who created heaven and earth, the sea and all things that are therein; and that there is one Deity, Substance, and Majesty in the three Persons of the Father, of the Son, and of the Holy Spirit. They must preach next how the Son of God was incarnate of the Holy Ghost and of Mary ever Virgin, for the salvation and reparation of the human race; how He suffered, was buried, and rose again the third day, and ascended into heaven, and will come again to judge all men according to their merits; how the impious because of their crimes shall be sent with the Devil into eternal fire, but the just with Christ and His holy Angels shall go into life everlasting. Then they must preach diligently concerning the resurrection of the dead, that

1 Baluzius, p. 214.

2 An additional hint as to the dates of the various Psalters.

3 Pertz, ut sup. Baluzius, p. 223. Labbe, VII. 977.

4 Baluzius, p. 225. Waterland does not notice this.

5 Baluzius, p. 233, or Labbe, or Pertz.

6 Labbe, VII. 985. Baluzius, p. 236.

7 It was now that the Roman chant was enforced.

8 Baluzius, p. 237.

9 Labbe, VII. 986.

people may know and believe that in the same bodies they shall receive the reward of their deeds: and lastly they are to preach what those sins are for which men shall be condemned with the Devil to eternal punishment (they are the sins mentioned by St Paul in the letter to the Galatians): each of these the great preacher of the Church of God mentioned one by one, and it is for us to remember how terrible are the words which he added, that *they who do such things shall not inherit the Kingdom of God*[1]."

v. But I have been led insensibly away from the distinct subject of this chapter, which is the use of the Apostles' Creed, and of forms cognate to it[2]. We must pass then to the Synod of Frankfort held in the year 794, from the 18th Canon of which we learn that the King and Synod directed that it could not be permitted that a Bishop should be ignorant of "the Canons and the Rule," and in the 31st (or 33rd) we read that the Catholic Faith of the Sacred Trinity, and the Lord's Prayer, and the Symbol should be delivered to all[3].

vi. In the Capitular of Theodulf, No. XXII.[4] enquiries were enjoined:

Whether all the faithful learn the Lord's Prayer and the Symbol, because they are sufficient. "They are to be told that in these two documents all the foundation of the Christian faith reposes, and unless a man has in his memory these two, and believes with all his heart, and

[1] Baluzius, p. 240.

[2] Yet in the previous extract we see the Apostles' Creed used as a sermon.

[3] Labbe, VII. p. 1061. Baluzius, p. 267. Pertz (who puts the Synod under the year 791), p. 72. Waterland both in Chap. II. and in Chap. VI. (under "Germany") refers to this canon. In the latter chapter he says, "What passed in the Council of Frankfort (if I mistake not in my construction of it) may warrant the carrying the Athanasian Creed up as high as 794." In the earlier passage he explains his view: "Besides that *Fides Catholica*, &c. has been more peculiarly the *title* of the Athanasian Creed: and it was no uncommon thing either before or after this time to recommend it in this manner together with the Lord's Prayer and Apostles' Creed just as we find here." On this I merely remark that there is no evidence that the title *Fides Catholica Sanctæ Trinitatis* (which, as it seems, Waterland meant by his words *Fides Catholica*, &c.) was ever given by any person whatever to the Athanasian Creed: and no evidence is adduced or adducible that it was the custom at any time, either after or before the year 794, to recommend that this Creed should be proclaimed to all (omnibus prædicetur et tradatur), together with the Lord's Prayer, and Apostles' Symbol. Indeed, we learn from the canon of 789, that the people were instructed in the Faith of the Trinity, and we learn too how they were instructed in it. And both Baluzius (p. 267) and Pertz refer to that canon, as illustrating the one which is now before us. The two series of canons of 789 and 794 run to a considerable length parallel to each other. The *Fides Catholica Sanctæ Trinitatis* of the one, must mean the same thing as the *Fides Sanctæ Trinitatis* of the other.

Charles wrote about this time to Offa king of the Mercians to express his satisfaction that the latter held the Catholic Faith. Baluzius, p. 273.

[4] Labbe, VII. 1141. Baluzius, p. 413. Migne, CV. p. 198.

is most frequent in prayer, he cannot be a Catholic. And so it is appointed that no one receive the chrism, or be baptized, or receive another from the font, or present another to the bishop to be confirmed, if he do not hold in his memory the Symbol and the Lord's Prayer, except those whose age has not permitted them as yet to speak[1]."

vii. In the Council of Aix, 801, the order was repeated that every priest should preach the Gospel every Sunday and teach the Lord's Prayer and the Symbol to the people[2]. The same injunction appears to have been delivered the next year[3]. In 804 the words were altered:

God's priests were "to be learned in the Divine Scriptures and believe rightly the Faith of the Trinity and teach it to others; to know the whole Psalter by memory, the mode of baptism, the penitential, the *cantus* and the *compotus* (the Calendar), and not to baptize except at Easter and Pentecost[4]."

This was the capitular of Salz. In the same year Charles wrote to the bishop, Garibaldus[5], urging him to take care that

"Every one of you shall preach and teach according to the canons; first of all, of the Catholic Faith, that those who can do no more shall at least hold and recite from memory the Lord's Prayer and the Symbol of the Catholic Faith as the Apostles taught it."

Then follows in Pertz the Encyclic of Garibaldus to his clergy, bidding them that every one must, according to his ability, obey these directions, and learn the Lord's Prayer, *i.e. Pater Noster qui es in cœlis,* and the Symbol. This was pressed under pains and penalties: "If a man did not know them, he was to be put on bread and water: and the women to be flogged or starved[6]."

At Aix, in 809, it was directed that the Lord's Prayer, *i.e. Pater Noster,* and the *Credo in Deum* were to be taught to men and women as well as children[7].

[1] These capitulars are in the MS. 914, at Vienna, which I shall quote below. They are there introduced thus, "Haec et quae sequuntur capitula Theotolfus epus edidit." The MS. is said to be of the tenth century.

[2] Pertz, p. 87.

[3] Labbe, VII. 1179.

[4] Labbe, VII. 1183. Pertz, p. 124. Baluzius, p. 417.

[5] Pertz, p. 128.

[6] Pertz, p. 130, Et si quis ea nunc non teneat, aut vapulet aut jejunet de omni potu excepta aqua usque dum hæc pleniter valeat. Et qui ista consentire noluerit, ad nostram præsentiam dirigatur. Feminæ vero aut flagellis aut jejuniis constringantur. Quod missi nostri cum episcopis prævideant, ut ita perficiatur; et comites similiter adjuvent episcopis, si gratiam nostram velint habere, ad hoc constringere populum ut ista discant.

[7] Pertz, p. 160. The Council was summoned to consider the question of the double procession. Ado of Vienne remarks, "that the rule and ecclesiastical faith establishes that the Holy Spirit proceeds from the Father and the Son,

viii. And now we come to one of the most interesting acts of Charlemagne's later years: the enquiry which he issued to the metropolitans of his dominions as to the life and teaching of their suffragans.

In the year 811 the Emperor issued this Encyclic[1]:

He pressed the archbishops once more to watch those entrusted to them; to urge them more and more "to labour in holy preaching and salutary doctrine, that so through their devoted attention the word of eternal life might grow and run, and the number of Christian people be multiplied. We wish therefore (he proceeded) to know, either by writing or by personal intercourse, how you and your suffragans instruct the priests of God and the people committed to you on the subject of baptism; that is, how at first an infant is made a catechumen; what a catechumen is; and then, in order, every thing that is done. Of the scrutiny, what the scrutiny is; of the Symbol, and what is its meaning in Latin; of the Creed (de credulitate), how we are to believe in God the Father Almighty, and in Jesus Christ His Son, and in the Holy Spirit, the Holy Catholic Church, and the other things which follow in the same Symbol; of the renouncing of Satan and all his works, and what renouncing is, and what are the works of the devil and his pomps. Why the child is breathed upon; why he is exorcised; why salt is used, and oil, and the white vestments, and the sacred chrism, and the mystic veil; and why he is confirmed with the Body and Blood of the Lord." These are the questions for which he desires to have answers. He bids them farewell and begs their prayers.

These questions are the more important, because we have, scattered in various works, four series of answers. Pertz (p. 170) gives the replies of Odilbert of Milan: Migne (LXXXIX. p. 896) the answers of Amalarius of Treves: Martene (I. i. XVII.) those of Magnus of Sens: Mabillon (*Anecdota*, III. or IV.) those of Leidrad of Lyons. They are all interesting, all instructive: and they are the more valuable because they are all dated documents.

We learn from these replies that the Creed of Amalarius did not as yet contain the clauses *unicum dominum nostrum, conceptum de Spiritu sancto;* it omitted *Patris* and *Vitam eternam.* The Archbishop gives his belief on the Trinity, but nothing in any way bearing on our controversies regarding the Athanasian Creed. The Emperor was satisfied with his reply, and deemed it Catholic. In the answer of Odilbert no passage occurs in any degree reminding us of the *Quicunque vult.* The answer of Magnus is interesting. It describes how his clergy teach the catechumen,

and is not created nor begotten, but co-eternal and consubstantial with the Father and the Son." Labbe, VII. 1194.

[1] Baluzius, pp. 479, 483. Pertz, p. 170.

that he must hear and learn the mystic sacraments of the Christian religion, and then learn the Faith of the Holy Trinity and the Symbol, and the other things which the Christian law advises. As to the enquiry on the Symbol, the Archbishop of Sens states:

"How they who are to be baptized profess to believe in God the Father Almighty and in His Son Jesus Christ (the phrase *unicum dominum nostrum* was again either missing or passed over), and in the Holy Spirit and the rest—although little children are not able to make their profession by themselves, still by the hearts and mouths of those that hold them (their sponsors), the Catholic Faith is professed, i.e. the Father, Son and Holy Spirit, of one essence, one power and eternity, without beginning and without end; one God invisible; so that the properties of each Person being maintained in each, the Trinity may not be divided in Substance or confounded in Person: that the Father is unbegotten; the Son is begotten, and, being born of the Virgin Mary and crucified and dead, hath both risen again and ascended into the heavens, and is sitting on the right hand of the Father, and thence will come in the same flesh to judge the quick and the dead; and the Holy Spirit is neither begotten nor unbegotten, but proceeding from the Father and the Son. And moreover they confess one Catholic Church and Communion of Saints, i.e. the congregation of all faithful men in Christ, and they believe the remission of sins and resurrection of the flesh and life after death, and that they will reign with Christ for ever and ever. Amen."

Thus after the renunciation of Satan, "The confession of the Holy Trinity rightly followed, in order that where sin abounded, grace might much more abound."

We have learnt from other sources that the ordinary confession at this time in Germany resembled the following: "Dost thou believe in God the Father Almighty? Dost thou believe in Christ, God's Son? Dost thou believe in the Holy Ghost? Dost thou believe one God Almighty in three Persons? Dost thou believe in God's Holy Church[1]?" This, therefore, or something resembling it, must have been regarded as containing the "Confession of the Holy Trinity[2]."

Passing onwards, I notice that we have a repetition of the order that the priests should teach the Catholic Faith and the Lord's Prayer, in the 45th Canon of the Council of Mayence, held in the year 813[3]: and, in a council at Rheims, of the same date,

1 See note, p. 23.
2 See too above, p. 180.
3 Labbe, VII. 1251. Parents were to instruct their children in the faith. Baluzius, p. 503. Of course, in the vernacular, Massmann, p. 10.

all were enjoined to learn, and in their own language, *de Fidei ratione*, as well as the Lord's Prayer[1].

§ 8. In the succeeding year, 814, Charles died. He left a mark behind him which has never been and can never be obliterated. I must confess, that on my mind the impression is made that no man has ever occupied such a prominent position, who was of a grander character, of a mind of so many sides, of a will so determined, but yet of views and objects so self-denying and so pure. The effect which he produced on the Church, on the Church's literature, and on the Church's usefulness, is beyond our measure now. But I cannot pass on without drawing attention once more to his anxiety for purity of doctrine, at a time when the bishops of the great Western metropolis, the old Rome, seem to have been mainly anxious for the aggrandisement of the see which they held and for the consolidation of its power. If, as St Ambrose says, "Rome kept ever uninjured the Symbol of the Apostles," we must say that with the exception of a few Popes, men like St Leo the Great and St Gregory the Great, her retention of that Creed was rather passive than active. She left to others the duty of contending for the Faith. When her bishops ceased to be Greeks and became uniformly Latins, the Roman lust of power and the Roman instinct for consolidation predominated over the general Christian anxiety for purity and truth. Leo III., who crowned Charles Emperor, was careful to quarrel neither with him nor with the East in the matter of the Creed of Constantinople. Neither at that time nor in subsequent ages, did the Pope of Rome often aim to direct public thought on matters of doctrine: the policy of his court has been to wait until opinions have been formed elsewhere and opposition apparently dropped, and then to pronounce that to be Catholic, on which the Churches in communion with her have agreed. In one point only has she taken the lead, and that point has been the subject of her own prerogative, her own possessions, her own claim for power. And here too Charlemagne's conduct is instructive. His view of the Catholic Church was, that it is a body made up of many members and that all the members have not the same office. The Church of his dominion was, in his idea, a national Church; and

1 Labbe, VII. 1256.

it was his interest, as he felt it to be his duty, to keep that Church faithful to its work and pure in its teaching. He held that its Archbishops, its Bishops, its Clergy, were responsible to him for the way in which they fulfilled their duties. And he would see that they were so. The Royal Supremacy was claimed by him: and no Pope attempted to deprive him of it. He would not say, without consultation, what was heresy: but he insisted that his clergy should not adopt views which he deemed after consultation to be heretical. He would not say what the duties of the clergy were in detail: councils and synods must declare that: but he insisted that the clergy should fulfil their duties or answer to him for their omission. In matters of ritual he claimed independence of Rome.

§ 9. I shall reserve other remarks for a later page. I must, however, briefly note some other proofs of the growing importance attached in this century to the Apostles' Creed and the Lord's Prayer. In the Capitularies of Hatto or Ahyto, Bishop of Basle, about the year 820[1], it was ordered:

> I. That the faith of the priests should be enquired into; how they believed, how they taught others to believe. II. It must be ordered that the Lord's Prayer, in which every thing necessary to the life of man is comprehended, and the Symbol of the Apostles in which the Catholic Faith is entirely comprehended, should be learnt by all, both in Latin and in the vulgar tongue, so that what they profess by the mouth may be believed by the heart and understood[2].

The effect of Charlemagne's energy still continued. Thus, I notice that in a synod held at Aix, in the year 836, it was ordered that every Bishop should know the sincere faith: and inquiries should be made how each held and believed the Faith

[1] Pertz, III. 439, puts them down to the year 856.

[2] Mansi, XIV. 395. Labbe, VII. 1522. The fourth rule is that which relates to "the Faith of St Athanasius" mentioned in Waterland, Chapter II. under the year 820. There is a copy of these regulations in the MS. 914, of the Library at Vienna, fol. 23. It is introduced thus: "Haec capitula que secuntur arto basiliensis ecclesie antistes et abbas cenobii qd augia dicitur presbyteris si *diocesian* (*sic*, on an erasure) eos ordinavit quibus monerentur qualiter se ipsos ac plebem sibi commissam caste et juste regere atque in religione divina confirmare deberent" As the manuscript is of the tenth century, it must be regarded as conclusive as to the identity of the author of these Constitutions. They are twenty-five in number: at the close we read, "Finiunt capitula eitoni epī." The second begins thus: "Secundo jubendum ut oratio dominica in qua omnia necessaria humanae vitæ comprehenduntur et simbolum apostolorum in quo fides catholica ex integro comprehenditur ab omnibus discatur tam latine quam barbarice." (Note the *fides catholica.*)

and Creed of the Holy Trinity[1]. Again, all were to learn the Apostles' Symbol and the Lord's Prayer[2]. Again, at the Council of Mayence, 847, all were to be taught regarding the Catholic Faith, as they were able to receive it; of the perpetual retribution of the good, the eternal damnation of the bad, of the future resurrection, of the final judgment[3]. The injunctions of Hatto were repeated by Louis II., in the year 856[4]. In the instructions of Hincmar to his presbyters, we read that Christ Jesus, in the words recorded by St Matthew (chap. xxviii.), bade His Apostles first of all to teach the Catholic Faith, and when the Faith was received, to baptize in the name of the Holy Trinity[5]. And he describes how the Faith of the Apostolic Symbol is delivered, and the Lord's Prayer. The Apostles made the Symbol: the clergy are to have expositions of it: the baptized person professes that he believes in the Father, and the Son, and the Holy Spirit[6]. In the capitula of Herard, Bishop of Tours, 858, it was ordered that the Faith should be preached to all the faithful by the presbyters in their own language: the Incarnation, Passion, Resurrection, and Ascension: the giving of the Holy Spirit, the Remission of Sins. Again, by Canon XVI., all should know by memory the Lord's Prayer and Symbol: and the Gloria Patri, and Sanctus, and Creed (credulitas), and the Kyrie Eleeson should be sung by all reverently, and the Psalms by the clerks[7]; and no one was to receive a child at the font who did not know the Symbol and the Pater Noster. And here I might pause, thankful that we have attained some degree of proof that the Credulitas, or Creed, of which we have been anxious to have a hint, was the so-called Nicene Creed that was sung at the Mass. But one more set of orders must be mentioned: those of Walter of Orleans, about the year 866. The Archdeacons were to examine their clergy's Faith, Baptism, Celebration of Mass. Did they understand the Lord's Prayer, with the Symbol, and the Catholic Faith, the Gloria Patri, the Credo in Unum Deum, the Sanctus Sanctus.

1 Labbe, VII. 1707.

2 *Ibid.* VIII. 37.

3 *Ibid.* VIII. 42.

4 Pertz, ut supra, p. 439.

5 Labbe, VIII. 593. Other injunctions of Hincmar will engage us afterwards. Somewhat earlier than this we have an injunction (Baluzius, p. 531, no. III.) that the clergy should teach the Lord's Prayer, i.e. the Pater Noster, and the Credo in Deum, to all who were placed under their charge, and see that as well men and women as children should repeat them to them.

6 Labbe, VIII. 595—598.

7 *Ibid.* VIII. 628—631. Massmann, p. 10. The *Kyrie eleeson* is the early Litany.

I was tempted to believe that the "Catholic Faith" here must signify the *Quicunque*, but I was shaken in my opinion by the words that follow in the second Canon. Here the enquiry is put: "How is every person fitted to teach his brethren in the Faith of the Sacred Trinity? that they should believe that the Father, Son, and Holy Spirit are one God, omnipotent, eternal? and that there is one Deity and Substance and Majesty[1]?"

§ 10. I have been at considerable pains to collect these intimations of the use and importance of the Apostles' Creed in this century, because we find here both the object and the result of its being inserted in all the copies of the Psalter which now come into notice. The schools of Charlemagne and Alcuin had wrought a revolution in the literary no less than in the theological world: and it is gratifying to find surviving to the present day so many exquisite specimens of calligraphy, assigned by experts to the period of, or immediately succeeding to, the lifetime of Charlemagne. This Emperor had ordered that only men should be employed in copying the sacred books. Walter, of Orleans, in synod directed that each of his clergy should have a Missal, a Psalter, and so on, and amend his copies by comparing them with well-corrected manuscripts.

§ 11. Thus the APOSTLES' CREED found its way into the Matins Service of the Gallican Church. How soon it was recited under breath I know not: I only know that this was the custom in the time of Durandus, who gives his explanation of the custom[2]. I understand from Mr Freeman's valuable work, that in the English Church the Creed and Lord's Prayer always followed the Psalms in the nocturnal office or Matins, which was said, of course, only by the choir and privately. The two were used also, almost daily, in the body of the English services at Prime. Hence it passed at the revision of 1549 into our Reformed Service-Book: being then "said by the Minister, with a loud voice, all devoutly kneeling." The modern order that the Creed "should be said by the Minister and people, standing," dates from 1552: the direc-

[1] Labbe, VIII. 637, 638.

[2] "The Creed is said in a low voice, but the conclusion aloud: to signify that with the heart man believeth unto righteousness, but with the mouth confession is made unto salvation." Durandus, *ad Prin.* (Freeman, I. 98.)

tion that it should be omitted when "the Creed of St Athanasius is appointed to be said," from 1662.

§ 12. Several early Saxon and English versions of the Creed from Manuscripts supposed to be of the ninth and later centuries may be seen in the pages of Dr Heurtley's and Mr Maskell's volumes. There is another in the Royal Library, 8 A. XV. (see Casley). The full Creed is given in the Saxon *Ordo ad faciendum Catechumenum* (Maskell, I. p. 12): and the godfathers and godmothers were enjoined to see that the child was taught the "Credo" (p. 14). A shortened Creed was asked at Baptism (p. 23). At the visitation of a sick person, if he was well instructed, his examination on his belief was framed on the Articles of Faith put forth by John Peckham, Archbishop of Canterbury, 1278—1292: if he was a layman, or simply literate, he was examined on a kind of Exposition of the Apostles' Creed[1]; of this I must speak again hereafter. The traces of these directions in our present Prayer-Book are perceptible to all. But the Church of England interrogates the catechumen, not on portions of the Apostles' Creed, but on it as a whole: in her Catechism she describes it as containing "all the Articles of the Christian Faith," in her Visitation Service as containing "the Articles of our Faith, so that hence we may all know whether we believe as Christian men should believe or not." It forms the basis of the instruction conveyed according to the Catechism of the Council of Trent, where it is stated to have been composed by the Apostles themselves. It is adopted by all the Reformed Churches, except the Presbyterian. Allowing for this exception, and also regarding the omission by the Episcopal Church of America of the words "He descended into hell" as justifiable, on the ground that the meaning of the words is much disputed among those who retain the clause, we must regard this Symbol as the SYMBOL OF THE GREAT WESTERN BODY OF CHRISTIANS. We have here the ONE FAITH taught indeed throughout the world: taught by us and by the Roman Church as necessary and sufficient for the salvation of those with whom we have to do.

[1] At confessions in Germany, at one time the Nicene Creed was used. Massmann, pp. 122, 150. Very interesting is it to notice that in a form of confession (from a Dusseldorf MS. of the middle of the ninth century) special mention is made of this: "I have not taught my children or my god-children as I should." Massmann, p. 137. After confession they used to repeat the Apostles' Creed with the priest (clearly not as a penance). *Ibid.* p. 149, cf. 46.

APPENDIX TO CHAPTER XV.

To prevent my work from becoming too cumbersome I will add here some further illustrations of the use and importance of the Symbol in the 150 years between 720 and 870.

The references to the FIDES CATHOLICA in the third volume of Haddan and Stubbs' *Councils and Ecclesiastical Documents* are very numerous. The key-note to the meaning of the phrase is given in a passage from a letter from Bede to Egbert, Bishop of York (p. 316), which the learned editors have taken as the motto for their volumes (p. 6). "In qua prædicatione hoc præ ceteris omni constantia procurandum arbitror, ut fidem catholicam quæ Apostolorum symbolo continetur et Dominicam orationem quam sancti evangelii nos scriptura edocet, omnium qui ad tuum regimen pertinent memoriæ radicitus infigere cures." They who knew not Latin were to learn the two in their own tongue. Thus the Catholic Faith was contained in the Apostles' Creed, and was not identified with it, still less was it independent of it. After this caution I will refer to some other passages which I have noted in this volume. Thus p. 52 (A.D. 604): pp. 111, 112 (A.D. 667). See too the prayer of Oswy that all his subjects might be converted to the Catholic and Apostolic Faith (pp. 116, 133); and Agatho's anxiety as to the testing of the faith of the English Bishops (p. 140). Bishop Wilfrid of York confessed the true and Catholic Faith, and attested it with his signature. So, at the Council of Hatfield, Theodore, Archbishop of Canterbury, and his suffragans put forth the right and orthodox faith: "sicut dominus noster Jesus Christus incarnatus tradidit discipulis suis qui præsentialiter viderunt et audierunt sermones ejus, atque sanctorum patrum tradidit symbolum......Hos itaque sequentes, nos pie et orthodoxe, juxta divinitus inspiratam doctrinam eorum professi, credimus consonanter, et confitemur, secundum sanctos patres, proprie et veraciter, Patrem et Filium et Spiritum Sanctum Trinitatem in Unitate consubstantialem et Unitatem in Trinitate; hoc est unum deum in tribus subsistentiis vel personis consubstantialibus æqualis gloriæ et honoris." At the end they added "glorificamur...Deum Patrem sine initio, et Filium ejus unigenitum ex Patre generatum ante sæcula, et Spiritum Sanctum procedentem ex Patre et Filio inenarrabiliter...Et nos omnes subscripsimus qui cum Theodoro Archiepiscopo fidem Catholicam exposuimus." This was in the year 680.

We find that so far as the British bishops were concerned "inventa est in omnibus fides inviolata catholica" (p. 144). This phrase is interesting (p. 185); "de presbitero pagano, qui se baptizatum estimat, fidem Catholicam operibus tenens," he must be baptized and ordained. Compare pp. 270, 313, 336, 359. On page 385 we have the canons from the capitulary of Carloman. On p. 443 Simon of Durham speaks of the legates of Hadrian (A.D. 786) renewing the old friendship which existed between the Roman and the English Churches as well as the

Catholic Faith which St Gregory the Pope taught by the blessed Augustine.

Thus it is clear that the Catholic Faith was considered to be contained in the orthodox creeds, and was not identified with any of them.

Bede (p. 59) speaks of Sigberct, king of the East Angles (about the year 636), as having been *fidei sacramentis imbutus* in Gaul, during an exile. When he became king he made all his province partakers of the same.

On page 341, under the Council of Cloveshoo (A. D. 742), there is an interesting statement that under the presidency of Athelstan, king of the Mercians, the bishops diligently examined "circa necessaria totius religionis, et de symbolo ex antiquis sanctorum patrum institutionibus tradito." No results are given. William of Malmesbury states that at the Council of Cloveshoo orders were given that the presbyters should learn and teach the Lord's Prayer and the Symbol in English (p. 361).

The Acts of the Council, as published by Spelman (H. and S. p. 366), call the Creed "symbolum fidei," and direct that the presbyters shall explain in English the sacred words used in the celebration of the Mass and at Baptism. The clergy are to have right views "de fide sacræ Trinitatis."

At the legatine synod of 787 the legates of Hadrian I. directed that the presbyters should be yearly examined as to their knowledge of the Nicene faith, which they were to hold "faithfully and firmly;" everyone in general was to learn the Lord's Prayer and the Symbol, so that when Sponsors had to answer for infants "ob renuntiationem Satanæ seu fidei credulitatem," they should know what they were undertaking (p. 448).

On pages 511, 526, 543, 580, 615, 623 we have mention of the Catholic Faith. On 580 this mention is found in the first canon of the Council of Celchyth, A. D. 816, where the Bishops say "Primo in loco exposuimus fidem catholicam."

There are several confessions in the volume, as made by several bishops on their consecration. They lead me to believe that the Apostles' Creed, as we have it now, was not yet fully accepted in England.

I find from Labbe, IX. 683, that in the year 967 King Edgar ordered that every person should imbue his children with the Christian Faith and teach them the Pater Noster and the Credo, that is, the Lord's Prayer and the Apostolic Symbol; and no one was to be buried in consecrated ground unless he had known them.

In the laws of Canute (XXII) we read: "We exhort that every Christian shall know at least the sincere faith and learn thoroughly the Lord's Prayer and the Apostles' Creed." (Labbe IX. 919.) "If a person will not learn them let him be deprived of the Eucharist." (*Ibid.*)

Of the Canons of Ælfric (1049), No. XXIII. enjoined that on Sundays and missal days "the presbyter was to teach the people the meaning of the Gospel in English, and to use for their instruction the Pater Noster and the Credo, so that they might know by memory the Symbol of the faith." (Labbe IX. 1006.) And on a later page (1014) we read that "all, from the least to the greatest, were to learn the Symbol and the Lord's Prayer, and unless a person knew these by memory and believed them with his whole heart, and was very frequent in prayer, he could not be a Catholic." (We have had something resembling this before.)

To the German instances which I have quoted from Baluzius and Pertz and Labbe, I may add the following (Massmann, ut supra, p. 6): In the Wolfenbuttel MS. of the "Catechesis Theotisca" it was directed that "every presbyter should admonish his people that all males and females should know by memory the Lord's Prayer and the Symbol, *i.e.* the Credo in Deum."

Massmann draws great attention to the anxiety of Charlemagne and his successors to present the teaching of the Church to the people in their own language, whether it was *rustica romana* or *theotisca.* (p. 10.)

A similar order was given by an unknown bishop, whose directions may be seen in Martene and Durand's *Amplissima collectio,* VII. 4: he added that every clergyman "was to have by him an exposition of the Symbol and the Lord's Prayer, and be able to explain the Epistle and Gospel *juxta litteram.*"

From the same volume, p. 16, I learn of a MS. "about 800 years old," *i.e.* about the date 900, in which Gerhard, Bishop of Liege, described the Apostles' Creed as containing the "*fides recta et catholica:*" and all sponsors were to know it. He gives a continuous exhortation.

The fact is that Paulinus, the Patriarch of Aquileia, represented the unanimous sentiment of antiquity on that subject. "The common people were to learn the Symbolum and the Lord's Prayer. Any one who observed these and kept himself from wicked works would be safe (salvus) in the present world, and rejoice together with the angels in the world to come." The Clergy were to know and believe more (Migne, XCIX. p. 295).

CHAPTER XVI.

THE ATHANASIAN CREED. INTRODUCTORY.

§ 1. Introductory. § 2. General belief from A.D. 1200 to 1500 as to the origin of the Creed. Jewel. § 3. Voss. § 4. Usher. § 5. Utrecht Psalter. § 6. Athelstan's Psalter. § 7. Vienna Psalter. § 8. General result. § 9. Comparison with Athanasius' writings. i. In regard to the damnatory clauses. ii. In regard to the Holy Spirit. iii. In regard to the Incarnation. § 10. Result.

§ 1. WE now come to investigate one of the most intricate of literary questions, the date of the Athanasian Creed. Perhaps it will be best that I should at once state the opinion to which I have been led, which is this: that the Creed was not known in its present form before the latter years of the eighth century. This I conceive to be capable of proof. But I will simply lay down now some facts which may help to guide others to form their own decision. Whether that decision agrees with my opinion on the subject, may be deemed a matter of little importance; and it is of little importance, so far as I am concerned. For every investigator must be content in his search after truth to find himself committing many mistakes; he must make many guesses which he will have to throw aside before he suggests the hypothesis which ultimately satisfies the requirements of the case. Very probably the true solution of the difficulty will come from another quarter. But if I produce my evidence fairly, and uphold my opinion calmly, I trust that I shall not be excluded from the honourable class of Scientific Investigators.

§ 2. For two or three centuries before the Reformation, it was regarded as almost unquestionable, that the *Quicunque vult* was written by St Athanasius. When Bishop Jewel, however, published his answer to Harding (it was dated December, 1569), this opinion seems to have been shaken. For in the beginning of the Second Part of the *Defence of the Apology*, the Bishop speaks "of the Creed called *Quicunque vult*, written as some think by Athanasius; as some others by Eusebius Vercellensis[1]." The notion seems to have been that Athanasius wrote it in Greek, and Eusebius transferred it into Latin. I have not seen the work of Pithæus, to which Voss refers with great respect in the book to which I must next refer. Pithæus seems to have adduced strong arguments against the received opinion, and prepared the next generation for a more determined onslaught on that opinion.

§ 3. The ablest investigators into the history of our Creeds, which the seventeenth century produced, were, undoubtedly, G. J. Voss and Archbishop Usher. The former, in a work, *De tribus Symbolis*, published in the year 1642, exhibited the results of considerable research as to the Athanasian Creed. He was led to believe that it was first put forth in the beginning of the ninth century. The great Roman annalist, Baronius, had adopted the opinion that it had been produced at Rome by Athanasius himself during his exile, and had remained long unnoticed among the archives of the great metropolis. This was mere surmise. Voss rejected the opinion, and attempted to arrive at a conclusion supported by some historical evidence.

§ 4. Five years later, *i.e.* in the year 1647, the learned Usher printed his famous treatise, *De Symbolo Romano*, now found in volume VII. of his collected works. In it he addressed a kind of dedicatory letter to Voss, in which he gently remonstrated against the conclusion at which his friend had arrived. Usher's evidence seemed very strong. He had found amongst the manuscripts of the Cotton Library two, which he deemed to be of greater antiquity than the date to which Voss assigned the Creed.

[1] Parker Society's edition, p. 254. The passage is curious, and as it was known to Voss is worthy to be produced here. Harding had ridiculed the formulæ of Protestants, representing that of old there was only one Creed—the Apostles' Creed. Jewel replies: "Yet being learned and having travailed through the ancient writers, you must needs have seen the Apostles' Creed, the Nicene Creed, St Basil's Creed, Damasus' Creed, St Hierome's Creed, St Cyprian's or Rufine's Creed, Gregorius' Creed, the Creed called Quicunque vult, written as some think by Athanasius, as some others by Eusebius Vercellensis, the Creed contained in the hymn called Te Deum, whether it were written by St Augustine or St Ambrose; every of these under several and sundry forms."

They both contained the Athanasian and Apostles' Creeds, and the Te Deum. The former MS. he judged from the character of the pictures and of the writing to be of a date not later than Gregory I.: the latter bore the name of Athelstan, but from the Calendar prefixed (he said) it must have been written about the year 703. Thus, if he was correct as to either Manuscript, the arguments of Voss would be superseded by this additional evidence of antiquity.

§ 5. From the time of Usher until the autumn of 1871, the former Manuscript was lost to England and to English writers. In 1871, with a view to the controversy which was impending in regard to the Quicunque, I was preparing materials for an edition of Waterland's celebrated treatise upon it, and endeavouring to identify the Manuscripts which Waterland refers to. In the course of my enquiries I met with great attention and kindness from Mr Henry Bradshaw, the distinguished Librarian of the University of Cambridge. He mentioned to me, one day in the month of November, that he had discovered a notice of the Athanasian Creed of the seventh or eighth century. He led me to Professor Westwood's magnificent work on *The Miniatures and Ornaments of Anglo-Saxon and Irish Manuscripts*, and shewed me a drawing from a Utrecht Psalter, and the accompanying letterpress. I examined the latter with avidity. I felt confident that Professor Westwood had discovered the long missing Manuscript, by which Usher had overthrown (as was thought) the theory of Voss; but I wished to see once more what Usher had said before I gave vent to my delight. A few minutes were sufficient: and Mr Bradshaw also was convinced. I mentioned the discovery in a little pamphlet which I put out on Nov. 30 of that year. The circumstance attracted attention. Through the liberality of Professor Jones, S. J., of St Beuno's College, St Asaph, and the exertions of Professor Arntz of the Seminary at Cuilemberg, near to Utrecht, a few coloured lithographs of the pages containing the Athanasian Creed were received in England in May, 1872; one of which I was able to deposit in the Library of the University of Cambridge. They were followed by others of a slightly different impression, late in June or early in July. These attracted greater attention, for one was transmitted to the Record Office and placed in the hands of Sir Thomas Duffus Hardy, the distinguished Deputy

Keeper of the Public Rolls, who rapidly formed an opinion on the lithograph, similar to that of Archbishop Usher. A few days later, this copy was produced in the Upper House of Convocation, where it received great attention. At a later period of the year, the authorities of the University of Utrecht transmitted three photographs of the pages in question; of which I had the honour of receiving one. Increased attention was drawn to the Manuscript by Sir Duffus Hardy in a Report which he submitted to Lord Romilly, the Master of the Rolls. It was with great regret that I found that the learned writer upheld his earlier opinion by arguments of a literary character, which I knew were untenable; and I waited with some anxiety the judgment of Palæographers, whose experience had been gained rather amongst books than amongst charters. The interest in the subject waxed greater: reference was made to this Report at an excited meeting held in the spring of 1873, and at last, through the intervention of the Foreign Office, the Trustees of the British Museum obtained temporary possession of the precious volume. It was then examined by some of the most experienced librarians and palæographers in England. The result is, so far as I am aware, that Sir Duffus Hardy stands alone of living authorities in his opinion. I believe that every other authority who has examined the volume simply on artistic and palæographical principles, has come to an opinion similar to that which I have been compelled to form from the general contents of the volume. The Manuscript is said by these gentlemen to be not earlier than the school of Charlemagne. The Canons and Capitulars of that monarch, to which I have already drawn attention[1], throw great interest upon the manuscripts of the period, and help to set the question at rest.

The Cottonian press-mark for the Psalter was *Claudius* C. VII.: and by this title I shall generally refer to it. I shall have to discuss some points regarding it hereafter.

§ 6. Of the other Manuscript mentioned by Archbishop Usher, a clear and interesting account may be seen in Dr Heurtley's volume on the Creed[2]. The Manuscript, as it exists at present, consists of three parts, written at three different periods. And the part which contains the Athanasian Creed

[1] Chapter XV. pp. 181, 182, 190. [2] *Harmonia Symbolica*, pp. 74—80.

is acknowledged by all modern authorities to belong to the ninth or tenth, or even the eleventh century. The press-mark is *Galba* A. XVIII.

Thus the two documents on which Usher's objections to the theory of his friend were founded, are too frail to build a decided opinion upon: and the literary arguments of the learned Voss again assume an important character.

§ 7. Another disturbing element, affecting the arguments of more recent enquirers, was furnished by a third volume, to which I must briefly refer. It is the beautiful Psalter in the Library at Vienna, which Lambecius, the librarian in the seventeenth century, described at length, and which he regarded, without any hesitation, as having been prepared by the orders of Charlemagne as a present for the Pope, Hadrian I. If so, it must belong to some year between 772 and 795. The precise date of this Manuscript is, at the present stage of our enquiry, comparatively unimportant. I must, however, add, that more recent palæographers have been led to question the account, on arguments purely scientific: and that the librarians at Vienna (who, of course, can take little interest in our English questionings as such) consider that the Charles from whom it was a present, was Charles the Bald, and the Hadrian, to whom it was offered, was Hadrian II. To use the words of one of them, they consider that the account of its being of Charlemagne's time is "a myth, and not true[1]."

§ 8. I do not know that the controversy has been much affected by the mistake of Usher as to the date of "Athelstan's Psalter." But the very interesting account given by Tentzel—(in the little volume from which Waterland drew most of his information as to the opinions of foreign divines)—of the grounds on which Leo Allatius, and Ruelius, and Quesnel, and Sandius, and Gundling, and Cabassutius, formed their respective opinions, shews the great importance which these learned men attached to the judgments of Usher and Lambecius respectively as to the dates of the other two famous Psalters. We need not, therefore, now enquire into the respective claims of Vigilius of Tapsus, or Athanasius of Spire, or Vincentius of Lerins, or Venantius Fortunatus, or Hilary of Arles,—although, perhaps, some reference is due to a

[1] Private letter.

work, which created a little sensation when it appeared in the course of 1872, entitled *The Athanasian Origin of the Athanasian Creed.* To this book I shall devote the remainder of this chapter.

§ 9. Of the work to which I have now referred, the following is stated to have been the object of the writer: "To shew the harmony of the Athanasian Creed with the teaching of St Athanasius."

As the Church of England has on no occasion identified herself with the teaching of Athanasius—which we have seen to have been, according to all accounts, very imperfect—we are concerned with the proofs of this proposition in their literary and historical bearings only. The interesting question is simply this: "Are the sentiments throughout identical with the sentiments of the great Patriarch of Alexandria?" I have in an earlier chapter adduced a work of the Bishop, which is generally considered to be genuine, that shews a marked divergence in thought from the document before us: it contains an expression, which to our more accurate knowledge is decidedly imperfect, if it is not heretical; an expression which Augustine used in his earlier days, and regretted in his later years that he had ever adopted. No one amongst us charges the teaching of the Quicunque, in its Theological or Christological statements, as being so far erroneous: the great objections to it are, (i) that it presses on our people distinctions which only an educated mind can appreciate: and (ii) that it enforces the reception of these distinctions, in language which has recently called forth a Synodical Declaration to explain. Thus it is regarded as unintelligible to the ordinary churchman in its language: and unintelligible to him in its sanctions.

i. However, I turn to the volume the title of which I have given above, and I find an attempt made to exhibit clause by clause words of Athanasius, similar in their purport to words of the Quicunque. And what is the result? In the statement of the first two clauses: "Whosoever will be saved, before all things it is necessary that he hold the Catholic Faith; which faith, except every one do keep whole and undefiled, without doubt he shall perish everlastingly," the penalty of the non-retention of the Faith of the Church is represented as being everlasting death. Nothing is adduced from Athanasius in proof that he held such an opinion. It seems that he held and taught something, which, though in direct antagonism to the words of our Saviour, still ought not to have been adduced, as it is, in proof that he would have accepted the sentiment of these clauses. The Saviour had said (Matt. xii. 32), "Whosoever shall speak a word against the Son of Man, it shall be forgiven him:" but Athanasius is quoted (p. 20 of this book) as stating: "Whosoever blasphemes (speaks against) any one Person (ὑποστάσεων) in the Trinity, has no forgiveness, neither in this world nor yet in the world to come: but God can open his eyes," &c. But, putting on one side this strange perversion of the words of our Saviour, I contend that the non-acceptance or the non-retention of scientific truth relating to the Holy Trinity, is not a sin to be compared with the blaspheming of One of the Three Divine Persons. Athanasius condemned positive and active blasphemy: this Creed condemns the want of a correct or Catholic Belief. Elsewhere (p. 31) language of Athanasius regarding the Son as self-complete, living and energising, the true Image of the Father, equal in honour, equal in glory, is referred to (it is not quoted) as in strict accordance with "the Athanasian and Nicene Creeds," "Who with the Father and the Son is magnified (*sic*) and glorified"—words of which of course the Holy Spirit is the subject, and which, by the way, are not found in either the Athanasian or Nicene Creed proper. Again, the words "all things were created through the Son, but He Himself is not a thing created," are quoted (p. 33), as throwing the sanction of Athanasius over the clause, "the Son uncreate, the Holy Ghost uncreate."

ii. The fact, however, is that the statements of the Quicunque relating to the HOLY SPIRIT are historically of a date later than the active period of the life of Athanasius. The work of his age and the work of his life was to exhibit the truth that the SON OF GOD is of the Substance of the Father, illimitable, eternal, co-essential. He was unwilling to modify the Nicene Creed, so as to introduce in it even similar language regarding the Holy Spirit. His letter to Jovianus proves this. The Arian heresy was reviving, he says (§ 1), and the heretics represented that the Holy Spirit κτίσμα εἶναι καὶ ποίημα διὰ τοῦ υἱοῦ γεγενῆσθαι, is "a thing created, and had been made through the Son: *therefore* he will enuntiate once more the Faith of the Nicene Council, accepted, as it is, throughout almost all Christendom." The contrasts in this respect between the Creed of Nicæa and the second Creed of Epiphanius, and again between the writings of Athanasius and the *Panarion* of the latter writer, are most instructive. I shall refer to the latter in a succeeding chapter[1].

iii. When we come to the clauses relating to the Incarnation, we may notice an increased difficulty in finding parallel expressions

[1] Chap. XVII. The book which exists only in Latin "de Trinitate et de Spiritu Sancto," was long considered to be spurious. The Benedictine editors, however, have placed it among the genuine works. Before I pass on, I am compelled to remonstrate against a practice that has come into vogue in late years, of interpreting clauses of the Creeds not by the original Greek or Latin, but by the English, even where the meaning of the original is definite and the meaning of the English is ambiguous. Thus the English expression, "The Holy Ghost is of the Father and of the Son," might mean that "He is the Spirit of the Father and the Spirit of the Son." It is assumed that this is the meaning, and then in proof of the agreement of the clause with the opinions of St Athanasius, the following words of the latter (I. 552, Epist. III. *ad Serap.* II. 626 of Migne) are referred to and partly quoted. "As the Son saith, *All things that the Father hath are mine*, so shall we find that these *all* are through the Son and in the Spirit. And as the Father pointed out the Son, saying, *This is my Beloved Son in Whom I am well pleased*, so too is the Spirit the Spirit of the Son (οὕτως τοῦ υἱοῦ ἐστι τὸ πνεῦμα), for the Apostle saith, *He sent forth the Spirit of His Son into your hearts, crying, Abba, Father?* And the paradox is, that as the Son saith, *All mine are the Father's*, so the Holy Spirit is the Father's also, even when He is called the Son's"......"So throughout the Holy Scripture you will find that the Holy Spirit Which is said to be the Son's is also said to be the Father's." These are the words of Athanasius. The following are the words of his commentator (p. 47): "Now it is worth observing that the expression, 'is *of* the Father and *of* the Son,' is a close imitation of the words of Athanasius (τοῦ υἱοῦ, τοῦ πατρός), and scarcely amounts to the strict terminology by which the Greek heresy was afterwards met, 'proceeding from the Father and the Son.'" But to make the parallel with the words of Athanasius in any degree applicable, the Latin of our Creed ought to be, "Spiritus Sanctus Patris est et Filii, non factus, nec creatus, nec genitus, sed procedens." Yet every tiro in this matter knows that the words are "Spiritus Sanctus a Patre et Filio." Thus the quotation from Athanasius is entirely out of place. And yet the same writer in 1871 adduced in favour of a Greek original of the Creed, the facts that "John Plusiadenus" read the words, τὸ πνεῦμα τὸ ἅγιον ἀπὸ τοῦ πατρὸς καὶ τοῦ υἱοῦ οὐ ποιητὸν, οὐ κτιστὸν, οὐδὲ γεννητὸν, ἀλλ' ἐκπορευτόν; and John Veccius or Becchius, τὸ πνεῦμα τὸ ἅγιον ἐκ τοῦ πατρὸς καὶ ἐκ τοῦ υἱοῦ, κ.τ.λ. The Greek manuscript in Venice, for a photograph of which we are indebted to the energy of Sir Duffus Hardy, reads, τὸ πνεῦμα τὸ ἅγιον ἀπὸ τοῦ πατρός. The copy in the modern Greek *Horologium* reads the same.

Again, a notice was given in the Lower House of the Convocation of the Province of Canterbury, on May 6, 1873, of a proposal to the following effect: "That in the words 'of the Son' in the Athanasian Confession of Faith, and in the words 'and the Son' in the Niceno-Constantinopolitan Creed, we profess and teach that the Holy Ghost Who ineffably and from all eternity proceedeth from the Father is ineffably and from all eternity the Spirit of the Father and of the Son, &c.;" that is to say, it was proposed that the Clergy of the Convocation of Canterbury should avow that when we recite "the Holy Spirit is of the Father and of the Son," we mean that He is the Spirit of the Father and the Son. Somehow the words of the motion were altered after the notice was given: and the new motion was withdrawn entirely on May 8. Convocation was thus preserved from the temptation of putting on the words of a translation, a signification which the words of the original do not and cannot bear: and this with the hope of removing what was called "a condemnation of the Eastern Church."

amongst the writings of Athanasius. The perfect Deity of the Saviour was taught by him, as well as His perfect Humanity; but on the Union of the two Natures in the one Person Athanasius is not explicit. Nothing is adduced to shew that he held that the Saviour was Man of the Substance of His Mother. I think he would have shrunk from such words: to his acute mind they would have seemed (as they do to others) to introduce a materialistic conception of the words "of the Substance of the Father" in the original Nicene Creed. Nor, again, is there a single passage adduced to illustrate the antithesis, "Equal to the Father as touching His Godhead, and inferior to the Father as touching His Manhood." So, again, the words "by the taking of the Manhood into God" (or "in God"), belong to a date later than Athanasius; and the phrases "not by confusion of Substance, but by unity of Person," are due to the controversies of the next generation. To illustrate the connection of Athanasius with clause 37, "As the reasonable soul," &c., a passage is taken from a Greek monk, who was living in the year 1118, more than seven hundred years after the death of Athanasius.

§ 10. We are thus enabled to judge how far the conclusion of this writer can be maintained, "That these proofs are sufficient to convince all men of ordinary candour that the similarity between the teaching of St Athanasius and the Athanasian Creed, is sufficiently close to justify the Church of England in retaining that Creed unimpaired and unaltered as a Confession of our Christian Faith." I have before stated that we have what is considered to be a genuine confession of the Faith of Athanasius, which we entirely neglect: and again, that the Church of England does not as yet accept as Scriptural any dogma because it has been enuntiated by any number of Fathers. This work, therefore, elaborate though it may be considered to be, is, in its aim, so far as we are concerned, completely beside the mark. But when we notice that the extracts adduced fail to prove that Athanasius sympathized in any degree with those clauses against which the continuous opposition of members of the English Church has been raised; yea, moreover, that so far as we can judge, Athanasius did not hold, as assuredly he did not express, the opinion, that the Arian Emperors who persecuted him from city to city were beyond the pale of Salvation, the contrast becomes more striking. Henceforth we may point to the pages of this little volume as proving that, even by a zealous and earnest advocate, no adequate support for these clauses could be found in the writings of Athanasius.

As it will be necessary to refer from time to time to the clauses of the Athanasian Creed by number, I will here print the received text of the Creed as it is found in the Roman Breviary, adopting however our English division of the clauses.

Symbolum Athanasii.

1 Quicunque vult salvus esse : ante omnia opus est ut teneat Catholicam fidem.

2 Quam nisi quisque integram inviolatamque servaverit : absque dubio in æternum peribit.

3 Fides autem Catholica hæc est : ut unum Deum in Trinitate, et Trinitatem in Unitate veneremur.

4 Neque confundentes personas : neque substantiam separantes.

5 Alia est enim persona Patris, alia Filii : alia Spiritus Sancti.

6 Sed Patris et Filii et Spiritus Sancti una est Divinitas : æqualis gloria, coæterna majestas.

7 Qualis Pater, talis Filius : talis Spiritus Sanctus.

8 Increatus Pater, increatus Filius : increatus Spiritus Sanctus.

9 Immensus Pater, immensus Filius : immensus Spiritus Sanctus.

10 Æternus Pater, æternus Filius : æternus Spiritus Sanctus.

11 Et tamen non tres æterni : sed unus æternus.

12 Sicut non tres increati nec tres immensi : sed unus increatus et unus immensus.

13 Similiter omnipotens Pater, omnipotens Filius : omnipotens Spiritus Sanctus.

14 Et tamen non tres omnipotentes : sed unus omnipotens.

15 Ita Deus Pater, Deus Filius : Deus Spiritus Sanctus.

16 Et tamen non tres Dii : sed unus est Deus.

17 Ita Dominus Pater, Dominus Filius : Dominus Spiritus Sanctus.

18 Et tamen non tres Domini : sed unus est Dominus.

19 Quia sicut singillatim unamquamque Personam Deum et Dominum confiteri : Christiana veritate compellimur;

20 Ita tres Deos aut Dominos dicere : Catholica religione prohibemur.

21 Pater a nullo est factus : nec creatus nec genitus.

22 Filius a Patre solo est : non factus nec creatus sed genitus.

23 Spiritus Sanctus a Patre et Filio : non factus nec creatus nec genitus sed procedens.

24 Unus ergo Pater, non tres Patres : unus Filius, non tres Filii : unus Spiritus Sanctus, non tres Spiritus Sancti.

25 Et in hac Trinitate nihil prius aut posterius : nihil majus aut minus.

26 Sed totæ tres Personæ : coæternæ sibi sunt et coæquales.

27 Ita ut per omnia (sicut jam supra dictum est) et Unitas in Trinitate : et Trinitas in Unitate veneranda sit.

28 Qui vult ergo salvus esse : ita de Trinitate sentiat.

29 Sed necessarium est ad æternam salutem : ut incarnationem quoque Domini nostri Jesu Christi fideliter credat.

30 Est ergo fides recta ut credamus et confiteamur : quia Dominus noster Jesus Christus, Dei Filius, Deus et homo est.

31 Deus est ex substantia Patris ante sæcula genitus : et homo est ex substantia matris in sæculo natus.

32 Perfectus Deus, perfectus homo : ex anima rationali et humana carne subsistens.

33 Æqualis Patri secundum Divinitatem : minor Patre secundum humanitatem.

34 Qui licet Deus sit et homo : non duo tamen sed unus est Christus.

35 Unus autem non conversione Divinitatis in carnem : sed assumptione humanitatis in Deum.

36 Unus omnino, non confusione substantiæ : sed unitate Personæ.

37 Nam sicut anima rationalis et caro unus est homo : ita Deus et homo unus est Christus.

38 Qui passus est pro salute nostra, descendit ad inferos : tertia die resurrexit a mortuis.

39 Ascendit ad cælos, sedet ad dexteram Dei Patris Omnipotentis : inde venturus est judicare vivos et mortuos,

40 Ad cujus adventum omnes homines resurgere habent cum corporibus suis : et reddituri sunt de factis propriis rationem.

41 Et qui bona egerunt, ibunt in vitam æternam : qui vero mala, in ignem æternum.

42 Hæc est fides Catholica, quam nisi quisque fideliter firmiterque crediderit : salvus esse non poterit.

CHAPTER XVII.

INFLUENCE OF AUGUSTINE'S WRITINGS ON THE SUBJECT OF THE TRINITY.

§ 1. Review. We must look to the West for further developments. § 2. The Quicunque does not use the language of the Definition of Chalcedon. § 3. We go back to the times and writings of St Augustine. § 4. Still earlier to Philastrius. § 5. Augustine's commendation of the truth. § 6. Influence of Epiphanius on Augustine. § 7. St Augustine *de Trinitate.* § 8. The work used by Alcuin. § 9. Augustine's conference with Maximinus. § 10. His Sermons. § 11. Results. § 12. Augustine's Prayer.

THE discoveries of the last few years have thus left, as it were, a *tabula rasa,* for future investigators on the history of the so-called Athanasian Creed. We have, in fact, to do everything over again. And first we have to collect our evidence.

§ 1. We must then notice first, that, so far as the Eastern Churches and the Eastern Councils spoke, they considered that the Ecthesis of the 318 at Nicæa and the Definition of the 150 at Constantinople ought to have been enough to proclaim the perfect faith of the Church concerning the Father and the Son and the Holy Spirit. Further investigations regarding the Holy Trinity were almost inconsistent with this Decision of Chalcedon. I am almost inclined to suppose that these words were used with reference to the great work of St Augustine, Bishop of Hippo.

§ 2. But looking at the language of the Council of Chalcedon concerning the Incarnation, and comparing it with the corresponding phrases in the latter part of the Athanasian Creed, we cannot but observe, I conceive, a refinement of phraseology in the latter which indicates that it was prepared at a later period than the Definition of the Council: in other words, the languag of the Council led up to the language of the Creed. The clauses are more compact: the subjects better arranged: the "antithetical swing of the sentences, forcing and exulting in forcing a mystery on recalcitrant minds," is surely due to long years of meditation over the truths established at the fourth great Council. In lieu of the words *reasonable soul and body,* we have in the Creed *reasonable soul and human flesh:* in lieu of *in these last days,* we have *in sæculo, in the world,* so as to balance the *ante sæcula, before the worlds.* And we must notice that the latter portion of the Creed follows the lines of the Western Symbol. The phrase *descendit ad inferos, He descended into hell,* shews this.

§ 3. But the perusal of the great work of Augustine on the Trinity sufficiently exhibits that it is to him that we owe, directly or indirectly, the substance and the language of the earlier part of the Creed—the part relating to the Trinity. He had been asked by a friend ("Quod-vult-deus"), a deacon of Carthage, to give an account of all the heresies which had then appeared. At first he referred his friend to the work of Philastrius, Bishop of Brescia, and to the similar, though more learned, treatise written by Epiphanius. From Philastrius, probably, Augustine learnt some of the phrases which he adopted: he had met him, he says, during his visit to Milan (384 to 387), and there had probably learnt his character. And thus it is that we look to an Italian bishop for our first glimpse of expressions which have come to us, expressions which have gained their currency from the stamp that was given to them by the Bishop of Hippo.

§ 4. Thus we read in his fifty-first chapter that Philastrius mentions

Some who separated themselves from the Catholic Church, not understanding that *qualis immensus est Pater, talis est et Filius, talis est et Spiritus Sanctus,* "as the Father is unmeasured (*incomprehensible* is our English word here), so too is the Son, so too is the Holy Spirit: equal in all things, so that the Trinity is immovable, unmeasured, omnipotent, and eternal." In chapter LV. we read that *Seleucus* denied that the Saviour is seated in the flesh at the right hand of the Father: in LVI. the *Procliniatæ* denied that Christ had come in the flesh, or that there shall be a resurrection and a judgment: in LVII. the *Florians* denied also that Christ was born of a Virgin. *Paul of Samosata* (chap. LXIII.) denied that the Word of God, *i.e.* Christ, is God the Son, substantive, and personal, and eternal with the Father. The *Arians* are referred to in chap. LXVI.; and in chap. LXVII. we are told that the *Semi-Arians* hold right opinions of the Father and the Son, believing that there is only one Divinity, but teach that the Holy Spirit is not of the Divine substance, nor is He very God, but is made and created. The *Tropitæ* (ch. LXX.) say that the Word was converted into flesh. *Photinus* (XCI.) denied that Christ the Lord was with the Father *ante sæcula*, before all worlds. But chapter XCIII. is even more to our purpose: Philastrius was speaking of those who made "Triformem Deum." He enunciated the Catholic Faith on the subject thus: "There is a true Person of the Father which sent the Son: and there is a true Person of the Son which came from the Father: and there is a true Person of the Holy Spirit which was sent from the Father and the Son. Of these three Persons there is one truth, majesty, equality of substance, and eternal divinity. For as the Person of the Father is immeasurable and ineffable, such is the Person of the Son, such is the Person of the Holy Spirit. So that in the distinction of Names and of three Persons there is no diversity of nature. This Trinity therefore is immeasurable (immensibilis), invisible, and ineffable[1]."

§ 5. But although St Augustine owed some of the expressions which we shall find him using to his predecessor, Philaster or Philastrius, it is clear that he exercised his own maturer judgment upon them. He was not entirely satisfied with the work of Philaster. He speaks of its being prolix: and, whereas Philaster had used the term "equality of substance," Augustine very carefully avoided the words, and in his book, *De Hæresibus*[2], declares that "the Father, and Son, and Holy Spirit are of one and the same Nature and Substance, or (that it may be said more expressly) Essence; which in the Greek is called *οὐσία*." He mentions, too, that the Donatist Bishop, Majorinus, "had not Catholic views regarding the Trinity; for, although he held that They are of the same substance, he considered that the Son is less than (or inferior to, *minor*) the Father, and the Holy Spirit less than the Son[3]." The progress of thought on this subject is indicated, I conceive, by the entire omission in the Quicunque of the Nicene phrase *ὁμοούσιος*, of its Latinized form *homöusios*, or its Latin equivalent. From the words with which Augustine closes his tract, I quote the following: they will shew that, at all events, he is not responsible for the sentiment with which the Quicunque ends.

[1] Migne (Vol. XII.) reprints this work from the edition of Gallard, canon of Brescia, published in 1738. Thus perhaps it was not known to Waterland, whose first edition came out in 1723, and second in 1727.

[2] In Vol. VIII. of Gaume.

[3] Ch. LXIX.

"It is of great assistance to the faithful heart to know what ought not to be believed, even though he may not have the power of refuting such errors by disputation. Every Catholic Christian ought not to believe these things, but it does not follow that every one who does not believe them ought to call himself a Catholic Christian. There may be other heresies which are not spoken of in my work; and if a man holds any one of these he cannot be a Catholic Christian. Our duty is to avoid all heretical poisons, not only what we know but what we do not know; not only such as have arisen already, but such as may arise hereafter." Augustine does not intimate that every person who is not a Catholic Christian cannot be saved.

§ 6. The great work of Augustine on the subject before us is entitled from it *De Trinitate*. It was commenced (as he informs us, through his friend Aurelius, Bishop of Carthage) when he was a young man: it was published when he was old[1]. We must regard it, therefore, as embodying the result of much study and much thought. He was not a mere producer of other men's language.

And it is interesting to know that he was acquainted with the writings of Epiphanius, to whose work on the Heresies of his day we have already found references in the writings of the great African Bishop. Thus Augustine knew of the language which the Bishop of Constantia had used of the Incarnate Word; that "He had flesh and soul in truth, and all that belongs to man:" that "He was perfect God and perfect Man, without sin, having taken the body from Mary, and received soul and *νοῦς* and all that belongs to man:" that "He underwent no conversion, nor did He change His Deity into Humanity: that the Word was not turned into flesh; that the Godhead did not die, but Christ died in the flesh: the same, God; the same, Man; that empowering an earthly body with the Godhead, He united them in one Power, gathered them into one Godhead, being one Lord, one Christ, not two Christs nor two Gods: God and Man, not two but one; uniting but not confusing[2]." Nor was the language of Epiphanius concerning the Trinity of less assistance to him. "There was never a time when the Son was not: never a time when the Holy

[1] About the year 416.

[2] Most of these expressions on the Incarnation will be found in the long chapter of Epiphanius' "Panarion" against the *Dimoerites*, who denied the perfect Incarnation of the Christ (*Heresy*, LXXVII. or LVII.). The chapter is long, because it contains not only the whole of the letter of Athanasius to Epictetus, but also an account of a disputation which Epiphanius held with the Apollinarian bishop Vitalis. (Epiphanius described Apollinaris as *εὐλαβέστατος*.)

Spirit was not:" "the Father ever, the Son ever, the Holy Spirit ever:" "the Holy Spirit ever; not begotten, not created, but of the same substance with the Father and the Son:" "proceeding from the Father, receiving from the Son[1]."

§ 7. Such was the language with which Augustine's mind had been familiarized—and with this brief account before me, I would adduce some of the many passages from this great WORK ON THE TRINITY, which seem to have given rise to expressions in our so-called Athanasian Creed. I have endeavoured to find something corroborative of every clause of the Creed. When I am silent, it must be assumed that I have been unsuccessful. I will arrange his words in the order of the verses of the Creed.

Of the Catholic Faith he uses words which might well be the motto of my present volume: "Let not my reader love me more than the Catholic Faith: let him not love himself more than the Catholic Truth" (III. 2, p. 1214).

"Let there be no confusion of Persons, nor such a distinction as to represent One as unequal to Another" (VII. 12, p. 1320). "The Trinity is inseparable" (I. 7, p. 1159). The question is put "If we say Three Persons, why not Three Gods? Surely as the Father is a Person, the Son a Person, the Holy Spirit a Person, they are Three Persons; if then the Father is God, the Son God, the Holy Spirit God, are they not three Gods?" The answer is "In saying three Gods we contradict Scripture; in saying three Persons we do not" (VII. 8, p. 1312). The words "equal and coeternal" are found together in III. 27 (p. 1240). In

[1] No. LXXIV. (or LIV.) of the *Panarion* is directed against the *Pneumatomachi;* and in connection with them the controversies of Augustine's time regarding the terms to be used of the Holy Trinity arose. Epiphanius held (cap. IV.) *τρία ἅγια, τρία συνάγια, τρία ἐνύπαρκτα, τρία συνύπαρκτα...τρία ἐνυπόστατα, τρία συνυπόστατα. τρίας αὕτη ἁγία καλεῖται, τρία ὄντα, μία συμφωνία, μία θεότης τῆς αὐτῆς δυνάμεως, τῆς αὐτῆς ὑποστάσεως.* (cap. XI.) *ὁ μονογενὴς υἱὸς ἀκατάληπτος, τὸ δὲ πνεῦμα ἀκατάληπτον.* (cap. XII.) *τέλειος ὁ πατὴρ, τέλειος ὁ υἱὸς, τέλειον τὸ ἅγιον πνεῦμα... ἦν ἀεὶ πατὴρ καὶ υἱὸς καὶ ἅγιον πνεῦμα... πατὴρ οὖν ἀεὶ ἀγέννητος καὶ ἄκτιστος καὶ ἀκατάληπτος· υἱὸς δὲ γέννητος ἀλλ' ἄκτιστος καὶ ἀκατάληπτος· πνεῦμα ἅγιον ἀεὶ οὐ γεννητὸν, οὐ κτιστὸν, οὐ προπατόρον, οὐκ ἔγγονον ἀλλ' ἐκ τῆς οὐσίας πατρὸς καὶ υἱοῦ.*

Hagenbach in his *History of Doctrines* § 94, note 2 (Clark's Translation, I. p. 262), adduces these passages. Epiphanius, *Ancorat.* § 9, after having proved the Divinity of the Spirit, *e.g.* from Acts v. 3, says *ἄρα Θεὸς ἐκ πατρὸς καὶ υἱοῦ τὸ πνεῦμα*, without expressly stating that He *ἐκπορεύεται ἐκ τοῦ υἱοῦ.* Compare *Ancor.* § 8, *πνεῦμα γὰρ Θεοῦ καὶ πνεῦμα τοῦ πατρὸς καὶ πνεῦμα υἱοῦ οὐ κατά τινα σύνθεσιν, καθάπερ ἐν ἡμῖν ψυχὴ καὶ σῶμα, ἀλλ' ἐν μέσῳ πατρὸς καὶ υἱοῦ, ἐκ τοῦ πατρὸς καὶ τοῦ υἱοῦ, τρίτον τῇ ὀνομασίᾳ.*

If we are to look for a Greek author of the Athanasian Creed, we must prefer Epiphanius to Athanasius.

The *Panarion* was written in or after the 92nd year of "Diocletian," *i.e.* in or after the year 376. Thus the language of Epiphanius in it may be deemed more careful than in the *Ancorate*, §§ 8, 9.

v. 9 (p. 1280) we have St Augustine insisting that it is improper not only to say Three Gods, but also to say Three Great Ones (tres magnos). Thus again, "the Father is good, the Son is good, the Holy Spirit is good; not Three Good but One Good, of whom it is written *There is none good but one, that is God.*" "The Father is Almighty, the Son Almighty, the Holy Ghost Almighty; yet not three Almighties but one Almighty." The words "The Father is God, the Son God, the Holy Ghost God; yet not three Gods but one God" occur almost in the same connection in I. 7 (p. 1159), I. 8 (p. 1160), and elsewhere. The word *singillatim*, the meaning of which is (unhappily) inadequately represented in our English translation of clause 19, occurs again and again in Augustine: but, in a passage which resembles that clause (v. 9, p. 1281), we find *singulariter* used in preference. "Quicquid ergo ad seipsum dicitur, et de singulis Personis similariter dicitur, id est de Patre et Filio et Spiritu Sancto, et simul de ipsa Trinitate, non pluraliter sed singulariter dicitur." The true meaning of the clause is given in the following passage (v. 14, p. 1285). "If we are asked separately of the Holy Spirit, (*sigillatim si interrogemur de Spiritu sancto, respondemus,*) we answer most surely that He is God, and with the Father and the Son together one God." In the last book, which was written latest, he maintains that "*As the Father hath life in Himself and hath given to the Son to have life in Himself*, so from the Father proceedeth the Holy Spirit; and the Father hath given to the Son that the Holy Spirit proceed from Him, and both without time" (xv. 47, p. 1511). Our clause 24 "So there is one Father not three Fathers" is explained in VII. 27 (p. 1311). "The name of Father is not common to Them, as if They were Fathers reciprocally to each other; as friends, when spoken of relatively to each other, may be described as three friends. Not so here. For only is the Father Father, and still not the Father of the other Two, but Father of the Son alone: nor are there three Sons; for the Father is not Son, nor is the Holy Spirit Son: nor are there three Holy Spirits; because the Holy Spirit also, in His proper signification, when spoken of as the gift of God, is neither Father nor Son." The conception of priority in any One, or of greater power in any One, is repudiated again and again.

On the Incarnation of our Lord and Saviour, Augustine was clear and precise: but this work on the Trinity does not furnish many passages on this subject. The heresies of Nestorius and Eutyches attracted attention after his day. And although he wrote after the Council of Constantinople, I have not found any reference to that so-called œcumenical assembly. But Augustine was aware of and rejected the heresy of Apollinarius:

Thus he speaks of the reasonable Soul of Christ in III. 8, p. 1222, and elsewhere; and in I. 3, p. 1156, appear the words *divina virtus in qua æqualis est Patri.* The expression that "in the form of God He is equal to the Father, in the form of the servant less" (which are not the words of the Quicunque), occurs again and again. In one place it is modified thus: *natura æqualis, habitu minor*, "equal in nature, in fashion less." The time had not come for the necessity of insisting much on the union of the two natures, but we have in I. 14, p. 1166, "Neither was the Divinity changed into creature so that it ceased to be Divinity; nor was the creature changed into the Divinity so that it ceased to be creature." And we find that "the Unity of Person" is spoken of in II. 12, p. 1198, and IV. 31, p. 1272.

But in vain have I searched throughout these books for anything resembling the clauses with which, in the Quicunque, the *Catholica fides* is enforced. I find however this passage early in the first book: "This is my Faith, because this is the Catholic Faith." The spirit of the whole work is exhibited in the passage with which the whole work concludes. That passage I will translate below.

§ 8. These books of Augustine's are also historically of great moment: for out of them Alcuin, the great friend of Charlemagne, collected and compiled, for his imperial patron, a treatise on the Trinity. To this borrowed work our attention must be turned ere long.

§ 9. But there are other works of the great African Doctor, which, though not of the same historic importance, are of equal value in admitting us to an insight of the latest workings of his great mind on this grand and difficult subject. His conference with Maximinus, and two books which he wrote when that conference was over, belong to a date twelve years[1] after his work on the Trinity was completed. The conference arose from questions started in his greater volume.

Maximinus attacked the opinion of Augustine and of the Church in its most tender part.

"You acknowledge that there are Three Equals: prove this from Scripture: prove that there are Three Equals, Three Omnipotents, Three Unrevealed, Three Invisibles, Three Incomprehensibles (tres incapabiles)." Augustine replied, as we should expect; "We do not say there are Three Omnipotents, inasmuch as we do not say there are Three Gods. If we are asked Is the Father God? we answer Yes: Is the Son God? we answer Yes: Is the Holy Spirit God? we answer Yes: Are there three Gods? we answer No: for the Scripture teaches *Hear O Israel, the Lord thy God is one Lord*, and in this divine præscription we learn that the Holy Trinity is one God." So of the Omnipotent: so of the Invisible[2].

[1] About the year 427 or 428.

[2] Of the anathematisms of which Damasus is considered to be the author (Hahn, p. 183, Harduin, 803, under the date 379) no. XXI. was this:

"Si quis non dixerit tres Personas

The conference proceeds, and I think that every one who will read it carefully will rise with clearer views of the Arian difficulties than he had before; he will know, too, what meanings were attached to the words *omnipotens, immensus, incapabilis.* Maximinus contended that we have no right to argue from Scripture: we must look to direct testimony only; we have no right, he says or seems to say, to ask what was the thought in the minds of the writers when they used such and such language, and then apply our inference to the case in hand.

This is not the place to discuss this principle: I have treated the subject elsewhere[1], and maintain that it is simply impossible to cramp men's minds within the narrow limits within which Maximinus would have confined them. The surest proof of the weakness of the Arians was this: They did not ask, and would not ask, What was, what must have been, the Nature of our Lord, to justify Him in using the language which He did? Mr F. W. Newman, I believe, held at one time that He was not authorized in uttering the reproaches found in Mat. xxiii., and so as a man was justly condemned. There is no resting-ground between this view and the Catholic doctrine of the perfect Deity and perfect Humanity of our Lord and Saviour Jesus Christ.

The conference, I say, is interesting: it was conducted on the whole with moderation on both sides, and certainly there was no expression on the part of St Augustine of what is now called "the true charity" of informing Maximinus that he was in danger of perishing everlastingly, since he did not hold the Catholic Faith.

The conference was, however, so important, that Maximinus put in writing his objections to the opinions of Augustine, and Augustine promised him a written reply. And thus they parted; Maximinus stating that he would acknowledge himself worthy of blame if he did not in turn reply to Augustine's proofs.

veras Patris et Filii et Spiritus Sancti æquales, semper viventes, omnia continentes visibilia et invisibilia, omnia potentes, omnia vivificantes, omnia facientes, omnia quæ sunt salvanda salvantes; anathema sit."

I cannot see how it is possible to avoid the conclusion that Damasus taught under the pain of anathema that there were three Eternals, three Incomprehensibles, three Omnipotents.

Theodoret, *H. E.* v. 11, gives a Greek translation of this series, entitling it, *ὁμολογία τῆς καθολικῆς πίστεως ἣν ὁ πάπας Δάμασος ἀπέστειλε πρὸς Παυλῖνον ἐν τῇ Μακεδονίᾳ.*

The author most certainly denied (no. XIV.) that "God, the Son of God, suffered on the cross:" he held that it was the flesh with the soul that suffered. I suppose therefore that, according to the Quicunque, this Pope is doubly condemned.

[1] My *Hulsean Lectures.*

I need not give an abstract of Augustine's books against Maximinus. They were written with the same courtesy that characterised the interview. The nearest approach to his opinion on Maximinus' spiritual state is given in Book II. chap. V. (Tom. VIII. p. 1067):

> "If you place such idols in your heart, as to make two Gods, one greater, *i.e.* the Father, the other less, *i.e.* the Son; and pretend that the Holy Spirit is so far least of all that you will not deign even to call Him God:—this is not our Faith, for it is not the Christian Faith, and so it is not the Faith at all."

The "Right Faith" is spoken of in Book II. ch. XII. 2, p. 1076. In ch. XIV. p. 1079, we may note further progress in Augustine's thoughts: "The Son is of (*de*) the Father: the Holy Spirit is of (*de*) the Father: but the One Begotten, the Other Proceeding: the One is the Son of the Father from whom He is begotten: the Other is the Spirit of Both, because He proceeds from Both." In § 3, p. 1082, he appeals to the Scriptures as authority to which both Maximinus and he would bow; the opinions of councils were insufficient: in XVIII. p. 1099, he uses the Pauline expression, *fulness of time,* where the Quicunque has *in sæculo.* But it is from chapter XXII. onwards that our interest augments. And I cannot but note the increase of precision in the language used regarding the Persons of the Trinity: a precision for which few seem to know that they are indebted to the Doctor of the West.

He insists that the Father and the Son are *unum, non unus,* but not absolutely so; They are *unum,* because They are of one substance; but yet we affirm, that as *He who cleaveth to the Lord is one Spirit, unus Spiritus* (of course Augustine follows the Latin), so we may say, that the Father and Son are *unus,* provided always that we add something to this *unus,* as *unus Deus, unus Dominus, unus Omnipotens.* He quotes 1 John v. 8: *There are three witnesses, the spirit and the water and the blood, and three are one, tres unum sunt;* these witnesses being *sacramenta,* as to which we must enquire, not what they are, but what they indicate; they are signs of something higher; being one thing, signifying another. They signify—the spirit, God the Father—the blood, the Son—the water, the Holy Spirit. These are the three witnesses to the Saviour, and *Three are One,* because They are of one substance.

Thus these signs, as proceeding from the Body of the Saviour, figured the Church preaching one and the same nature of the Trinity; for the Church is the Body of Christ. And thus from the Body of Christ proceeded the words, *Go, baptize all nations in the name of the Father and the Son and the Holy Spirit.* He said, *In the Name,* not *In the Names,* for *These Three are one, unum sunt,* and these Three is One God, *Hi tres unus est Deus.* "But," he proceeds, "if the depth of the Sacrament in the letter of St John can be expounded in any other way—according to the Catholic Faith, which neither confounds nor yet separates the Trinity, which neither denies the Three Persons, nor yet believes that they are different substances—on no account let such explanation be rejected."

After this it becomes of less moment to observe that in XXIII. § 2, pp. 1115, 1116, we have, "*Hear, O Israel, the Lord thy God is one Lord,* because the Father, the Son, and the Holy Ghost is (*est*) not three Gods but one God, not three Lords but one Lord[1]. So if you ask me Which is Lord? I answer Each One: but at the same time I say, Not three Lord Gods, but one Lord God (p. 1117). This is my Faith, because it is the right Faith, because it is the Catholic Faith."

It is not necessary that I should multiply quotations in which the same thoughts, and almost the same words, are repeated again and again. But there is one sentence which seems to be specially worthy of remark: for it is just possible that to an earlier expression of the sentiment therein conveyed we owe one word of the Quicunque. "You (says Augustine to Maximinus) have spoken with incredible temerity of the Son of God—as good *according to the measure of faith* (XXIII. § 7, pp. 1121, 1122). You cannot, with sound faith, say even that the Father is without measure, *immensus.* You assert that the Son is not equally *immensus:* you regard Him as limited by measure (*mensura terminatum*). Keep your measure to yourself, because you are measuring (*metiaris*) your own false lord, but of the true God you are telling falsehoods (*mentiaris*)." In XXVI. § 13, p. 1136, he sums up the subject and adduces the passage from Baruch (iii. 25), whence the word must have come originally. Augustine applies

[1] Of course Augustine did not know that *Lord* is here the proper name, JEHOVAH. He puts 1 Cor. viii. 6 in connection with it.

the whole to the Saviour, *He is great and hath no end: high and unmeasurable,* "excelsus et immensus."

The commendatory words with which Augustine closes this discussion are these: "If you peacefully acquiesce in these testimonies and others like them"—I have not space to put them all together—"you will become what you say you desire to be, a disciple of the Holy Scriptures. Then I shall rejoice in your brotherhood." May I refer once more to his appeal to Scripture?

§ 10. Of course in other works of St Augustine we shall find the same thoughts reproduced: in some, we shall find additional clauses illustrated. Thus, Sermon CV. (Vol. V. p. 777), *On the Three Loaves*, furnishes the following language: "Panis est, et Panis est, et Panis est. The Father God, the Son God, the Holy Spirit God. The Father eternal, the Son co-eternal, the Holy Spirit co-eternal. The Father immutable (*incommutabilis*), the Son immutable, the Holy Spirit immutable. The Father, and Son, and Holy Spirit, Creator. The Father, and Son, and Holy Spirit, the food and bread eternal. Learn and teach: live and feed." The following furnish specimens of his warnings: "This is the Faith: hold what you do not see. Necessary is it that you should continue to believe in that which you do not see, that so you be not ashamed when you do see Him" (CXIX. p. 853). "Hold this firm and fixed, if you would remain Catholics: that God the Father begat the Son without time, and made Him of the Virgin in time" (CXL. p. 981). "The impious say this: thus do the heretics blaspheme the Son: but what says the Catholic Faith? God the Son is from God the Father, but God the Father is not from God the Son[1]."

§ 11. Thus, if we have been led to state that Epiphanius furnished to Augustine some conceptions now embodied in the

[1] The Sermons *On the Nativity* may also be consulted, especially CLXXXVI. and CLXXXVII.; so Sermon CCXIV. (III. *On the Tradition of the Creed*), CCLXIV. (*On the Ascension*). Out of the *Enchiridion* (Vol. VI. p. 364, ch. XXXV.) the following words have been quoted, "Proinde Christus Iesus Dei Filius est et Deus et Homo, Deus ante omnia sæcula, Homo in nostro sæculo." The words "nec tamen tria hæc tres Christi sed unus Christus," occur in *Tract.* XLVII. *on S. John*, § 12, and in the same section, "Quomodo est unus homo anima et corpus, sic unus Christus Verbum et Homo" (Vol. III. p. 2153): compare "sicut unus est homo anima rationalis et caro, sic unus est Christus Deus et Homo." (*Ibid.* p. 2285.)

St Augustine's own Creed in the *de civitate Dei* (Book XI. chap. XXIV. Vol. VII. p. 466) has been neglected in these discussions.

Athanasian Creed, we must add to our statement that these conceptions took root and grew in Augustine's mind. With the exceptions of the commending clauses, of a few turns of the language, and of a few phrases which savour of the fifth century, the document is made up, to a large extent, of Augustine's thoughts and Augustine's words. Yet, often as we meet with an identity of expression, no one has ever suggested that Augustine was the writer of the Quicunque, or that Augustine quoted from it.

1. Thus, when we meet hereafter with manifest coincidences of expression between the Quicunque and other documents, we must at least suspend our judgment before we say that to the writers of these documents the Quicunque was known in its present form. They may possibly have been quoting Augustine as using language which, having been used by Augustine, was now the property of the Church at large.

2. Again, if in this language Augustine did not quote the Quicunque, it follows that the expressions used were not formulated in his time. It becomes, therefore, a subject for further enquiry: When were the phrases formulated?

3. It is clear, moreover, that with St Augustine the *Catholica Fides* meant something, I will not say independent of the *Symbolum*, but additional to it. It went into subjects on which the Symbolum was silent; into subjects on which the Catholic Christian ought to hold definite opinions if he were capable of doing so, but which, at least in their fulness, were beyond the capacity of ordinary believers. I do not remember ever to have read in English an explanation of the differences between *unum* and *unus*, and between *unus* and *unus æternus*. Yet a knowledge of these differences is essential to the understanding of the meaning of the Quicunque.

§ 12. I need no apology for concluding my chapter with the following attempt to reproduce the closing words of St Augustine's treatise:

"O Lord our God, we believe in Thee, the Father, and the Son, and the Holy Spirit. For the Truth would not have said *Go, baptize all nations in the Name of the Father and of the Son and of the Holy Spirit*, if Thou wast not a Trinity. Nor wouldest Thou have commanded us, O Lord God, to be baptized in the name of One Who is not Lord God, nor would it have been said by the voice divine *Hear, O Israel, the Lord thy God is one God*, if Thou wast not so a Trinity as also to be One God. And if Thou, O God, wast Thyself the Father and Thyself the Son, Thy Word Jesus Christ, and Your gift the Holy Spirit, then we should not have read in the Creed of truth, *God sent His Son*, nor wouldest Thou, O Only-begotten One, have said of the Holy Spirit, *Whom the Father will send in My Name*, nor *Whom I will send from the Father*. By this rule of Faith have I directed the efforts of my mind, as much as I had the power, as much as Thou hast given me the power; and so have I sought Thee. I have longed with my intellect to see that which I have believed, and much have I disputed and much have I laboured. O Lord my God, my only hope, hear me I beseech Thee, that I may not through weariness cease to seek Thee. Let me rather seek Thy face, always, eagerly. Do Thou give me the power to seek Thee, Who hast created me to find Thee, and hast given me the hope of finding Thee more and more. Before Thee lie my strength and my weakness; preserve the former, heal the latter. Before Thee are my knowledge and my ignorance. Where Thou hast opened to me, receive me entering: where Thou hast closed to me, open to me knocking. May I remember Thee. May I understand Thee. May I love Thee.

"O Lord God, one God, God the Trinity: whatever of Thine I have said in these books, may Thy people also acknowledge; whatever of mine I have said, do Thou forgive—and they. Amen."

CHAPTER XVIII.

VINCENTIUS OF LERINS.

§ 1. The opinion of Antelmi that Vincentius was the author. § 2. Design of the *Commonitorium*. § 3. Résumé of the work, with notices of parallel passages. § 4. Summary of results. § 5. What do we learn from this? § 6. Clause 33 not in Vincentius. § 7. Still it seems that Augustine and Vincentius furnished most of the language. § 8. Exhibition of the result.

§ 1. I HAVE remarked on the influence of St Augustine's writings upon the earlier part of the Quicunque, and noted some expressions in the latter part as probably of Augustinian origin. But the verses which are directed against the views of the Nestorians and Eutychians meet with no parallel in the writings of the great Bishop. They must belong to a later epoch.

I believe it was Antelmi who first suggested that Vincentius of Lerins was the author of the Quicunque. Waterland refers to this opinion under the year 1693[1]. It does not appear that Waterland had seen Antelmi's work: I have been equally unsuccessful[2]. Antelmi's judgment was influenced (as I learn from the Benedictine edition of Athanasius, Vol. IV. 1578) by the interesting Colbertine Manuscript, to which I must, ere long, request the attention of my readers. Antelmi seems to have discovered the manuscript. He considered it to be, when he wrote, eleven hundred years old, *i.e.* to have been written about the year 590. Montfaucon regarded the manuscript to be of a much later age: no one to whom he had shewn it considered it to be older than the eighth century[3].

§ 2. That there is great verbal similarity between passages in the Creed and passages in the famous Commonitory of Vincent,

[1] In his first chapter.

[2] Mr King has been more successful.

[3] Montfaucon devotes much respectful attention to the surmise of Antelmi that Vincent was the author. He however rejects it.

is evident. Some of these passages Antelmi placed in corresponding columns, so as to exhibit the similarity more clearly. Before I had seen the Benedictine reproduction of these tables, I had made my own collation. And this I will place before my readers.

I must remind them however of the character of the *Commonitorium.* It was intended to shew to the young theologian how he should protect himself against errors of any kind that might grow up. And the famous, but practically useless, phrase is found herein: "In the Catholic Church we must especially take care that we hold *quod ubique, quod semper, quod ab omnibus creditum est,*" in other words, we must follow "universality, antiquity, consent." The pious author quotes Ambrose, and refers to Athanasius, Cyril, Basil, the Gregories; he appeals boldly and frequently to the words of St Paul to the Galatians (i. 8, 9), words which cut away—or ought to cut away—from the Faith of the Church all additions to *the Faith once delivered to the saints:* and, in one place where he quotes the words (ch. VIII.), he exhibits to us what was his conception of the anathema of the Apostle. It meant, not eternal death, but excommunication: "Let him be anathema, that is, separated, put apart, excluded; lest the dire contagion of one sheep should by a poisonous intermingling contaminate the innocent flock of Christ." Vincent was a contemporary of Nestorius and Eutyches, and his view of the anathema corresponded with those of the Fathers of the Council of Chalcedon. For he says (ch. XXIX.) that his work was written three years after the Council of Ephesus, *i.e.* in the year 434.

§ 3. There are two modes of exhibiting this similarity of thought and language: the one would be to set side by side the clauses wherein the likeness may be observed; the other to give a kind of résumé of Vincent's work, noticing more at length the passages where the similarity is most striking. I will adopt the latter.

The object then of Vincentius being to protect the young from the dangers of falling away from the truth of the Catholic Faith, especially at a time when the approach of the day of judgment required the study of religion to be increased, he lays down his grand principle that amidst the various teachings of Novatian and Photinus, Sabellius and Donatus, Arius, Eunomius and Macedonius, Apollinaris and Priscellianus, Jovinianus, Pelagius, Cœlestius, and lastly Nestorius, one point should be observed, viz. that we follow universality, antiquity, unanimity. He proceeds to apply this to the times of Donatus and the Donatists, when only those in Africa who preferred the consensus of the Church of Christ to the sacrilegious rashness of one man, could be safe within the sanctuary of the Catholic Faith. He applies the same principle to the times of the Arians, whilst of the Donatists he says, chap. VI., "Who is so mad as to doubt that that light of all Saints and Bishops and Martyrs, the blessed Cyprian, will with his colleagues reign for ever with Christ? or who so sacrilegious as to deny that the Donatists and other pests, who boast that on the authority of the Council of Carthage they re-baptize, will burn for ever with the devil?" He is severe on schismatics: he does not say this of heretics. In chap. VIII. he cuts away the ground on which, in modern days, the authority of the Church of Rome is built. "Even if Peter, even if Andrew, even if John, in short, even if the whole band of the Apostles bring you tidings besides that which we have brought, let him be anathema. Tremendous difficulty! for the sake of maintaining the hold of the first faith, Paul spared neither himself nor the rest of the Apostles!" "He cries out, and he repeats the cry: and for all persons, and for all times, and for all places, does he cry: he, the vessel of election; he, the teacher of the Gentiles; he, the trumpet of the Apostles; he, the herald of the earth; he, who was admitted into the secrets of heaven—he cries out, *If anyone shall teach a new dogma, let him be anathematized.*"

In chap. XI. Vincent refers to the teaching of Nestorius, of Photinus, of Apollinaris; and, in the next, he explains what their teaching was. "The sect of Photinus (he says) declares that God is single and solitary, and must be confessed after the manner of the Jews: it denies the fulness of the Trinity, nor thinks that there is any Person of the Word of God, or any of the Holy Spirit; it asserts that Christ is a mere solitary man, whose beginning is from Mary; and it declares that we ought to worship only the Person of God the Father, and only Christ the Man. Apollinaris boasts, as it were, that he agrees as to the Unity of the Trinity, but he openly blasphemes in regard to the Incarnation of our Lord: he says that in the flesh of our Saviour there was either absolutely no human soul, or, at all events, not a soul in which was mind and reason. The flesh of the Lord (he asserts) was not taken from the flesh of the Holy Virgin Mary, but descended from heaven into the Virgin. Unsteady and uncertain, he held, at one time, that it was coeternal with God the Word; at another, that it was made out of the Divinity of the Word. He would not acknowledge two substances in Christ, the one divine, the other human: the one from the Father, the other from the Mother: but held that the nature of the Word was itself divided into two; as if one part of it remained in God, another part was changed into flesh, so that, where the truth saith, that there is one Christ of two substances, he, in opposition to the truth, maintained that the two substances were both made. Nestorius again, in opposition to the pestilence of Apollinaris, suddenly introduces two Persons, and, with an unheard-of wickedness, would have two Sons of God; two Christs; the one God, the other Man; the one generated of the Father, the other from the Mother: and thus he asserts that the holy Mary is to be called not Theotokos but Christotokos; because from her was born not the Christ Who is God, but the Christ who is Man.

"But (ch. XIII.) the Catholic Church, having right views both of God and of our Saviour, blasphemes not against the mystery of the Trinity nor against the Incarnation of Christ, for it worships (veneratur) one Divinity in the fulness of the Trinity, and the equality of the Trinity in one and the same majesty: and it confesses one Christ Jesus, not two; and Him to be equally God and Man: one Person in them but two substances, two substances but one Person; two substances, because the Word of God is not mutable, so that it should be changed into flesh; one Person, lest by professing two Sons it should seem that we worshipped a Quaternity, not a Trinity." But the Church holds (ch. XIII.) "In God there is one Substance, but three Persons; in Christ two Substances, one Person. In the Trinity One and Another, but not one Thing and another Thing; in the Saviour one Thing and another Thing, not One and Another. But how is there in the Trinity One and Another, not one Thing and another Thing? because, indeed, there is one Person of the Father, another of the Son, another of the Holy Ghost; but still the nature of the Father and of the Son and of the Holy Ghost is not one and another, but one and the same." Again: "In the one and the same Christ there are two Substances; one divine, the other human; one from His Father, God, the other from His Mother, the Virgin; the one coeternal and equal with the Father, the other in time and less than the Father; the one consubstantial with the Father, the other consubstantial with the Mother, but still one and the same Christ in each substance. There is therefore, not one Christ, God, the other Man; one increate, the other create; one impassible, the other passible; one equal with the Father, the other less than the Father; one from the Father, the other from the Mother; but one and the same Christ, God and Man; the same increate and create; the same incommutable and impassible, and commuted and passible; the same equal to and less than the Father; the same begotten of the Father before all times (ante sæcula), and born of the Mother (in sæculo) in time; in the God supreme Divinity, in the man full humanity; full humanity, I say, because He possesses soul and flesh, but true flesh, our flesh, the maternal flesh; and a soul endowed with intellect, strong with mind and reason. There are therefore in Christ, the Word, the Soul, the Flesh; but these all form one Christ, one Son of God, one our Saviour and Redeemer; but one, not by any kind of corruptible confusion of Divinity and Humanity, but by a complete and singular unity of Person."

The work itself consists of thirty-three chapters, but I have extracted the passages which most nearly illustrate and contain our Creed. Of course there are some repetitions in it. I will content myself with two more quotations.

In chapter XXII. Vincent explains the words *guard the deposit* thus: "preserve inviolate and pure the talent of the Catholic Faith" (Catholicæ fidei talentum inviolatum illibatumque conserva).

Vincentius had correct views of the true growth of Christian dogma. He says (chap. XXIII.):

"Like as the human form becomes grander and larger, not by the addition of features but by the growth of those with which the infant is born; so does the dogma of the Christian religion follow the same law. It is consolidated with years, it unfolds with time, it is elevated with age, but it remains uncorrupt and uninjured, in all the measure of its various parts, in all its members and all its senses, admitting of no other permutation, no loss of its properties, no variation of its definition."

§ 4. Summing up now the passages in the Quicunque which meet here with illustration, I find that they include the following:

The phrases *Catholica fides* and *Salvus esse* of clause 1 are paralleled by the words of chap. IV., which I have quoted above; Soli ex illis omnibus *inter sacraria Catholicæ fidei salvi esse* potuerunt; and clauses 1 and 2 together by chap. V., Satis claruit eos *qui violaverunt fidem tutos esse non posse.* The duty of preserving the faith whole and undefiled, I have illustrated from chapters XXII. and XXIII. Clause 3 is very similar to a passage in XVI., and clause 5 is found *totidem verbis* in XIII., the passage proceeding *Sed Patris et Filii et Spiritus Sancti, non alia et alia, sed una eademque natura.* Sabellius was charged with daring *Trinitatem confundere* (in XXIV.), and the Catholic Church lauded in XVI., because it held the truth so that *Neither did the unity of the substance confound the properties of the Persons, nor did the distinction of the Trinity separate the Unity of the Deity.* Thus with the exception of the words *Absque dubio in æternum peribit, æqualis gloria, coeterna majestas,* we must consider that the language contained in the first six clauses is as old as the time of Vincentius. But we have, in Vincentius, nothing in any way bearing on the thoughts which follow, the thoughts of clauses 7—29 inclusive; the language of these, as we have seen, has been taken largely from Augustine.

Passing to the Incarnation of our Lord I note that the words of clause 30, as they are found in the Colbertine fragment and in some old MSS.[1], are similar to these words of chap. XIII., *Deum pariter atque hominem confitetur.* With clause 31 compare the words in the same chapter; *Idem ex Patre ante sæcula genitus; idem in sæculo ex matre generatus:* with clause 32, *perfectus Deus, perfectus homo.* The *anima rationalis* of the Creed is the same as the *anima ratione pollens* of chap. XIII. *Non duo, sed unus Christus,* may be seen in XII. Clauses 35, 36, 37 are also virtually contained in the Commonitory. Apollinaris is held up to reproach for holding *Quasi aliud ejus permaneret in Deo, aliud vero versum fuisset in carnem* (chap. XII.). We meet with the words *Non conversione naturæ, sed personæ ratione* in XVI.; and with *Unus non corruptibili nescio qua divinitatis et humanitatis confusione, sed integra et singulari quadam unitate personæ* in XIII.; whilst clause 37 had its parallel in a passage in the same chapter, of which I have given a translation above: *Sicut in homine aliud caro et aliud anima...... ita in uno eodemque Christo duæ substantiæ......una ex Patre Deo, altera ex matre Virgine.*

[1] For this see below.

The remaining clauses of the Quicunque have nothing specially resembling them in Vincentius.

§ 5. Now I think that no one can hesitate in coming to the conclusion that there must have been some connection between component parts of Vincent's *Commonitorium* and parts of the Quicunque. The resemblance extends even to the *sicut* of clause 37 of the latter. The question is, What is the character of this connection? Three answers occur to my mind. One is, that the writer or writers of the Quicunque had Vincentius' words before their eyes: another, that Vincentius had the Quicunque before his eyes: the third, that both the one and the other had, before them, the common Faith of the Church, the Catholic Faith—although, perhaps, not formulated as yet to the extent to which it has now attained—and that they both adopted phrases which were already in use.

To assist us to the true solution, it is worthy of notice: first, that there is no appearance in his work that Vincentius was quoting any particular document. Although, of course, the Quicunque may have been written then, there is nothing that appears to be a quotation from it or reference to it. The decrees of the Council of Ephesus are Vincent's great authorities: besides these, he refers only to the great Fathers who were present at the council or whose writings were quoted at it. Their names, as he gives them, are St Peter of Alexandria, a most excellent Doctor and blessed Martyr; St Athanasius, Bishop of the same city, a most faithful Master and eminent Confessor; Theophilus, Cyril, Gregory of Nazianzus, Basil, Gregory of Nyssa, and so on. We know from the Acts of the council what quotations were taken from these writers; and, surely, the inference is, that if there was any document known to Vincentius having the authority we now assign to the Quicunque, and from which Vincentius drew his language, that document would have been quoted by name. Another point is, that Vincentius never, I believe, refers to Augustine. The inference is, to my mind, clear and unquestionable; and it is this: The latter part of the Quicunque (like the Commonitory) embodies the teaching of the Council of Ephesus, and must (like the Commonitory) have been composed after that council.

§ 6. But there is one clause of the Quicunque which has no parallel in Vincentius. It is the clause *Æqualis Patri secundum Divinitatem: minor Patre secundum humanitatem.* Nor do I find the words *adsumptio humanitatis in Deo* or *Deum*, or anything equivalent to them. Of course I have a right to ask, What was there which rendered these words unnecessary in the time of Vincentius, but called them forth at another period? The answer must bring us into contact with the error of Eutyches. The former phrase exhibits, more clearly than do any words of Vincentius, the permanent distinction of the two Natures: the latter —especially in the old reading *in Deo*—suggests the mode in which this distinction was maintained. On earth the Son of God was "equal to the Father as to His Divinity; inferior to the Father as to His Humanity." "He took up the Humanity in God." Thus, as it seems to me, the writers of the Quicunque avoided an expression, which, as used in the second Creed of Epiphanius, is capable of an Eutychian interpretation: I mean the expression *συνενώσας*[1].

§ 7. Thus again, we find that the language of the Quicunque is drawn from a Latin channel. And it would seem to be almost demonstrated that the dogmatic parts of the Quicunque were "composed," made up, of thoughts and language drawn partly from Augustine, partly from Vincentius of Lerins; and that Vincentius was not acquainted with the writings of Augustine. Thus the hypothesis of Antelmi falls to the ground. It remains, therefore, for us to enquire when this composition can have been effected. Assuming the truth of Waterland's conclusion that the Quicunque is of Gallican origin, we must, in our investigations, be eagerly on the watch to note the epoch when the language of Augustine became familiar to the Gallican Church; and when the conception embodied in what we call the Damnatory Clauses appears either there or elsewhere. For, as Montfaucon truly remarks, all conceptions and language must have become familiar

[1] I must give the passage: *σαρκωθέντα, τούτεστι τέλειον ἄνθρωπον λαβόντα, ψυχὴν καὶ σῶμα καὶ νοῦν καὶ πάντα, εἴ τι ἐστὶν ἄνθρωπος, χωρὶς ἁμαρτίας, οὐκ ἀπὸ σπέρματος ἀνδρὸς οὐδὲ ἐν ἀνθρώπῳ, ἀλλὰ εἰς ἑαυτὸν σάρκα ἀναπλάσαντα εἰς μίαν ἁγίαν ἑνότητα... τελείως ἐνανθρωπήσαντα· (ὁ γὰρ λόγος σὰρξ ἐγένετο οὐ τροπὴν ὑποστὰς οὐδὲ μεταβαλὼν τὴν ἑαυτοῦ θεότητα εἰς ἀνθρωπότητα) εἰς μίαν συνενώσαντα ἑαυτοῦ ἁγίαν τελειότητά τε καὶ θεότητα.* The *τελειότητα* at the end of the quotation refers (I presume) to the "perfection of the humanity."

to the religious mind before they were adopted into a Creed of the Church.

§ 8. I think we may now sum up the passages or clauses of the document which we find nearly in the same words in Augustine or Vincentius. Thus,

Clauses 1, 2. The conception of being *salvus, safe, tutus,* within the bounds of the Catholic Faith, belongs to Vincentius, who also speaks of the duty of preserving inviolate the faith; *inviolatam illibatamque conserva. Integrum* occurs in the same connection in chap. vi.

Clauses 3, 4, 5 and the first half of 6, are found scattered over the Commonitory.

Of clauses 7 to 26 we find the substance and, one might almost say, the words in Augustine, but not in Vincentius.

The commending or damnatory clauses (as Waterland calls them) 27, 28, 29 are found neither in Augustine nor Vincentius.

The substance of 30 is of course in both.

Clause. 31, *Deus est ex substantia Patris,* &c., is found in part in Vincentius, who however never uses the words *ex substantia matris.*

Clause 32 may be from Vincentius.

Clause 33 in its essence is from Augustine.

Clauses 34—37, except for the word "assumption," might be from Vincentius.

For 37 we have found authority in Augustine.

Clauses 38—41 are taken, with interesting variations, from the Apostles' Creed.

For the final clause, 42, we have no support either in the Commonitory or in Augustine.

CHAPTER XIX.

RULES OF FAITH FOUND IN COUNCILS AND SYNODS BETWEEN 451 AND 700.

§ 1. Language of St Augustine unnoticed except by Sophronius. § 2. Profession submitted to Hunneric, A.D. 484. § 3. Conference of Constantinople, A.D. 533. § 4. The Fifth General Council of Constantinople, A.D. 553. Justinian's Ecthesis. § 5. Third Synod of Toledo, A.D. 589. § 6. Fourth Synod of Toledo, A.D. 633. § 7. Synod of Seville, A.D. 619. § 8. Isidore's Rule of Faith. § 9. Council of Toledo, A.D. 638. § 10. Lateran Council, A.D. 649. § 11. Chalons, A.D. 650. § 12. Toledo, A.D. 653. § 13. Merida, A.D. 666. § 14. Autun, A.D. 670 (?). § 15. Toledo, A.D. 675. § 16. Other Spanish Councils. § 17. Summary of Spanish testimony. § 18. Council of Constantinople, A.D. 680. § 19. Summary of evidence up to this time.

§ 1. IT would be wearisome to accumulate testimony to shew how little the expressions of St Augustine affected the theology or theological language of the generations which immediately succeeded him. He was one of those wonderful men who are so far in advance of their contemporaries as to foresee and provide for difficulties which are unperceived by others, not only in their own time, but in times directly following. His writings are of the class which affects later ages: he himself, one of those few great men, who, like great mountains, impress the beholder more as he recedes from them. Thus, with the exception of some passages in Sophronius, who was made Patriarch of Jerusalem in 634, I do not remember any instance at this time, of writings through which the same lines of thought in regard to the Unity in Trinity and Trinity in Unity, that we have noticed above, appear to run.

§ 2. Thus if we look to the long Profession of Faith, which Eugenius, Bishop of Carthage, in connection with the Catholic Bishops of Africa, Mauritania, Sardinia and Corsica, delivered in

484 to the Arian Huneric, king of the Vandals, we find much regarding each Person of the Holy Trinity, but little of their relations to each other in the Unity. The Profession is deeply interesting, and exhibits the truth in a form which even now cannot be regarded as out of date: it includes the great scriptural proofs which we still adduce to shew that the Son of God is God of the substance of the Father; it contains much which enables us to see that these bishops professed "the Father, the Son, the Holy Spirit in the Unity of the Deity; so that the Father subsists in the Person of singularity, the Son exists in His proper Person, the Holy Spirit retains the propriety of His Person." The Confession occupies more than ten closely printed columns in the folio of Labbe and Cossart, yet we meet with very little of the language in which the Quicunque coincides with the language of St Augustine, and nothing approaching to the Augustinian formula, *non tres immensi, sed unus immensus.* It is true that this Confession was called out by an appeal from an Arian king, and so it may be said that there was no room for the antitheses in which the Quicunque has been said to glory. This, I say, is true: but the same prevalence of Arianism might be adduced with equal fairness to prove that as long as Arianism existed, so long were the times unsuited for the composition of the Quicunque in the form in which we have it[1].

The paper concludes thus: "This is our Faith, established by the traditions of the Gospels and Apostles, and by the society of all the Catholic Churches of the world: and in this we trust and hope to continue, by the grace of the omnipotent God, to the end of our life."

§ 3. I have already mentioned that the Church of Rome seems to have become so involved in a constant effort to assert

[1] Labbe, IV. 1132. Harduin, II. 858. I extract a few phrases which have struck me:

"Ingenitus pater: genitus filius: spiritus procedens." "Gratias agamus domino nostro Jesu Christo qui propter nos et propter nostram salutem de cœlo descendit, sua passione nos redemit, sua morte nos vivificavit, sua ascensione glorificavit. Qui sedens ad dexteram Patris venturus est judicare vivos et mortuos, justis æternæ vitæ præmium largiturus: impiis atque incredulis merita supplicia redditurus." I also catch the words "detestamur Sabellianam hæresim, quæ Trinitatem confundit.—Hæc fides plena, hæc nostra credulitas est...In hac Trinitate unitatem substantiæ fatemur."—The words *Tres sunt qui testimonium dant in cælo, Pater, Verbum et Spiritus Sanctus et hi tres unum sunt*, are quoted here as words of John the Evangelist. (I do not find the fact mentioned by Tischendorf.)

its own supremacy, that we look in vain to it, during this period, for efforts to promote the purity of the faith. But at Constantinople, under the year 533[1] we find that there was a conference on the Eutychian controversy; which I notice the more readily, because Cyril, Athanasius, Flavian, the Gregories, and Ambrose were quoted, with more or less profuseness, but I have not found the name of Augustine. Amongst other quotations I find a passage from the letter of Cyril to John of Antioch; it is really from the Creed of the latter; a passage which I have given above[2].

§ 4. A few years passed, and in 553, what is called the fifth general Council, the second of Constantinople, was held. The Pope of Rome, Vigilius, was present at Constantinople, but he did not attend the council. The council was directed against writings of Theodore of Mopsuestia, Theodoret of Cyrus, and Ibas: but the interesting point to us is, that it was addressed by the Emperor Justinian, now in his sixty-second year, on the subject of these writings. Justinian had circulated in 544 a long Ecthesis or Confession of his Faith, addressed to the "fulness" of the Catholic and Apostolic Church; it occupies twenty-one columns in Labbe's edition of the Councils[3], and includes thirteen Anathemas against those who held as many heresies. I have read this Ecthesis carefully through, and once more I note that there is nothing in it in any way reflecting the words or thoughts of Augustine on the Trinity. Justinian quotes Cyril and the Gregories; he refers to Athanasius; he cites St Augustine's letter to Boniface on the treatment of Cœlestinus, but that is all: his books on the Trinity were unknown or disregarded. We have expressions bearing on the old questions which occupied the minds of earlier generations:

"We do not confuse the persons or subsistences in the Trinity. We worship the Unity in Trinity and the Trinity in Unity:" but the main subject of the letter is the Incarnate Word of God. The Emperor adopted phrases with which we are already familiar. "He is God, of the Father, born before the ages, and in the last days born of His Mother. He is consubstantial with the Father in His Deity, with His Mother in His Humanity: He is perfect God and perfect Man: He is one Christ: the divine nature was not transmuted into the human,

[1] Labbe, IV. 1764. Harduin, II. 1159.
[2] pp. 109, 110.
[3] Nineteen in Harduin, II. 287, &c.

nor was the human converted into the divine: Christ was not formed (ἐδημιουργήθη) from the first of Deity and Humanity, as man is of soul and body, but in these last days He became man." Justinian refers to the earlier usage of the thought that "as man is one, though consisting of soul and body, so is Christ one, though composed (συντεθεὶς) of Deity and Humanity." The terms in which he enforces this confession are these: "This *good deposit* which we have received from the holy Fathers we keep; in it we live, and it we would take as our companion out of this life, our confession in the Father, and in Christ the Son of the living God, and in the Holy Spirit." Or again, where he introduces the anathemas, "These things being confessed by the Catholic Church of God, we desire all Christians to know, that as we have one God and Lord, so we may have one Faith. For there is one definition of the Faith, to confess and rightly glorify the Father and Christ the Son of God and the Holy Spirit. This confession we keep; into it we were baptized." He refers to the Confession or Symbol or Instruction in the Faith composed at Nicæa, and to the Explanation of the part relating to the Holy Spirit given by the Fathers at Constantinople (ἐτράνωσαν τὰ περὶ τῆς θεότητος τοῦ ἁγίου πνεύματος[1]).

But the most important part of this edict in my opinion is this; when it was resolved to anathematize those who defended Theodorus, it became necessary in all consistency to anathematize Theodorus himself; but he had died in the year 429, and so the meaning of the word 'anathema' had to be extended:

"Every heretic persisting in his error to the end of his life is with justice subjected to a continuous anathematism even after death." "Theodorus was accused in his lifetime, anathematized after his death." The narrative was wrong, but the object is manifest. Thus "Anathema means nothing else than separation from God; as, both in the Old and New Testaments, the sentence of anathema exhibits[2]."

Thus the meaning of the word was altered: and, so far, we approach nearer to the signification of the first and last clauses of the Quicunque.

The Emperor and the obsequious council condemned the books of Theodorus, though they had passed uncondemned at the Council of Chalcedon. The imperial edict usurped the form of a Confession of Faith, and trespassed on the exclusive right of the clergy to anathematize those who hold erroneous doctrine. "Great part of the submissive or consentient East received the dictates of the imperial theologian: the West as generally refused compliance."

[1] Words which I have quoted already, p. 135.

[2] Harduin, III. 314.

§ 5. We now come to a series of provincial or national synods which have a peculiar interest. Their history is tolerably continuous, and we can trace in it the effects of an intense and honest anxiety to be correct in the Faith. They are interesting also as exhibiting to us the working of a National Church, long before National Churches were crushed under the domineering influence of later Rome: and they exhibit the effect which one such National Church acquired in influencing the action, in theological matters, of Rome itself.

I refer to the series of synods held at Toledo, stretching, so far as we are concerned, from the year 589 to the year 683. To us they are of the greater importance, because in his sixth chapter Waterland has assumed, after Baronius, that the Fourth Council of Toledo, held in the year 633, cited a considerable part of the Quicunque, "adopting it into its own Confession."

The first of the series was the famous one in which King Reccared produced the Creed of Constantinople, with the clause *Deum de Deo* and the words *et ex Filio*. The converted Arian king recited, as we have noticed[1], the Creeds of Nicæa and Constantinople and the tract of the Council of Chalcedon; and avowed that his object was to bring his people back "to the knowledge of the Faith and the fellowship of the Catholic Church." The Synod in its eleventh, and again in its nineteenth and following canons, had maintained the value of the four great Councils (it passed over the fifth), and in its twenty-third declared that there was nothing "more lucid for the knowledge of the truth than the statements of these four Councils. With reference to the Trinity and Unity of the Father, the Son, and the Holy Spirit, nothing more true, nothing more clear could be exhibited either then or at any future time. As to the mystery of the Incarnation also, sufficient had been set forward in these councils, and what was set forward they believed."

Let us notice, however, the phrases which are found in the records of this council analogous in any way to the phrases of our "Creed." We shall be better able then to form an opinion whether the Creed was composed after the Council, or the declaration of the council was prepared posterior to the Creed.

[1] Chapter XI. p. 136. See Harduin, III. p. 467.

The canons speak of Christ Jesus "being begotten of the substance of the Father, without beginning, and equal to the Father;" they speak of "the Holy Spirit as proceeding from the Father and the Son, co-equal and co-eternal;" they require us to "distinguish the Persons," and to "acknowledge the unity of substance." We must not hold that "either the Holy Spirit or the Son of God is less than the Father:" we must believe "that the Father, the Son, the Holy Spirit are of one substance, omnipotence, eternity." I notice the word *separate* in canon XII.; and, in the preliminary speech of Reccared, that it is a mark of true salvation to "think (of) the Trinity in Unity and Unity in Trinity." The words "perfect in Deity, perfect in Humanity, true God, true Man, of reasonable soul and body: in His Divinity of one nature with the Father; in His Humanity of one nature with us; in all things like us, yet without sin; born of the Father before all worlds in regard to His Divinity, but in these last days for us and for our salvation made Man of the Virgin Mary, Mother of God," are quoted from the decree of the Council of Chalcedon; and in Reccared's opening speech he uses words with which we find analogies in the Quicunque. "The Father from Whom is the Son, but He Himself of no one else; the Son Who has a Father, but subsists without beginning and without diminution in that Divinity in which He is coeternal and coequal with the Father. The Holy Spirit is equally to be confessed by us, and to be proclaimed as proceeding from the Father and the Son, and of one substance with the Father and the Son, but the third Person in the Trinity. He has common essence of Divinity with the Father and the Son; for this Trinity is one God." Thoughts like these lie scattered, as we have seen, over the pages of Augustine; but I think this is the first time that they are brought together. Yet Reccared repudiates all authority, save the authority of the four great councils[1].

§ 6. This was in the year 589. Baronius and Waterland omit to notice this similarity; they reserve their strength for the fourth Council of Toledo, held in 633. The former says that the words used by this council are taken from the Creed: the latter that the council cites a considerable part of it, adopting it into its own Confession. "We may be confident," he proceeds, "that the Creed did not borrow the expressions from them, but they from the Creed; since we are certain that this Creed was made

[1] Before we leave this synod, I must note some of the clauses with which the faith of the councils is pressed on attention. We may remark some progress. Thus Canon XVIII. "Hæc est vera fides quam omnis ecclesia Dei per totum mundum tenet: catholica esse creditur et probatur. Cui hæc fides non placet aut non placuerit, sit anathema, maranata, in adventum Domini nostri Jesu Christi." Once more, in Canon XXIII. "Quicunque hanc fidem sanctam depravare, corrumpere, mutare tentaverint, aut ab eadem fide vel communione catholica, quam nuper sumus Deo miserante adepti, egredi, separari vel dissociari voluerint, sint Deo et universo mundo crimine infidelitatis in æternum obnoxii." The parties who are anathematized are those who reject or corrupt the faith.

long before the year 633." This statement is utterly worthless, as we shall see. "Baronius is positive that the council took their expressions from it. Calvisius dates the *publication* of the Creed from that council: so also Alstedius," and so on. Yet the Creed resembles the Commonitory of Vincentius far more than either resembles the Declaration of Faith of this Synod of Toledo. The only phrase to be found in identically the same language in the two documents now before us, is our clause 33. Moreover, if the Spanish bishops had our Creed before them, one thing of importance becomes apparent. They must have deliberately rejected its first and last clauses, and as deliberately adopted language less severe. The circumstances were these. Sixty-two bishops met and were presided over by St Isidore, the Archbishop of Seville. They passed seventy-five Canons, but first of all they must lay the foundation of Faith in God. And thus their first Canon commenced:

> "In accordance with the divine Scriptures and the teaching which we have received from the holy Fathers, we confess that the Father and the Son and the Holy Spirit are of one Deity and Substance; in the divinity of Persons believing a Trinity, we neither confound the Persons nor divide the Substance."

They have also language similar to the language of portions of our clauses 21, 22, 23, 31, 33, but with this the similarity ends. They have nothing corresponding to clauses 1, 2, 5—20, 24—28, 35—37 of the Quicunque. I notice too that the words are, Our Saviour when incarnate "received a perfect man without sin" (*perfectum sine peccato hominem suscipiens*), whereas the Creed adopts a later phrase: it speaks of the "assumption of humanity," or "the taking of the manhood." The concluding words of the council are: "This is the Faith of the Catholic Church. This Confession we keep and hold. And whosoever shall guard it most firmly shall inherit eternal salvation." The declaration of the Faith of this Council of Toledo was adopted *in toto* by a synod held at Arles in 813, in preference to the Athanasian Creed. I give the document in my note[1]. With all deference to the

[1] Council of Toledo, iv. a.d. 633.
Canon I.
Secundum divinas scripturas doctrinam quam a sanctis Patribus accepimus Patrem et Filium et Spiritum Sanctum unius deitatis atque substantiæ confitemur in personarum diversitate Trinitatem credentes, in divinitate unitatem prædicantes, nec personas confundimus nec substantiam separamus. Patrem a nullo factum vel genitum dicimus: Filium a Patre non factum sed genitum

opinions of Baronius, Calvisius, Alstedius, Gavantus and Waterland, I throw myself unhesitatingly on the side of the Ballerini and Muratori, whose opinion was, that the Fathers of the Council did not take their language from our Creed.

§ 7. Isidore, Archbishop of Seville, was, as I have mentioned, president at this council. We meet with him on two other occasions parallel to this. He had presided at a smaller assembly held at Seville in the year 619, and in the proceedings of the thirteenth day of their assembly we find recorded a long declaration of their Faith with reference to the Incarnate Word of God, illustrated and supported by scriptural proofs. There is not much here relating to the Trinity, but with reference to the two natures of the One Person of our Blessed Lord the exposition is profuse. The document may be seen in all Collections of the Councils, and in it, as I may repeat in passing, the Apostles' Creed is quoted without the words "Maker of heaven and earth[1]." Instead of the words *in sæculo* of the Athanasian Creed of the time of the Incarnation, we still read *in these last days;* but more interesting to us in our present investigation is it to remark that passages are introduced from the writings of Ambrose, Athanasius, Gregory of Nazianzus, Basil, Cyril, Augustine, Leo, and Fulgentius; those from Athanasius are taken from the tract which he wrote on *The Nativity of our Lord,* and from his *Exposition of Faith;* the phrases professing to come from the latter may be

asserimus; Spiritum vero Sanctum nec creatum nec genitum sed procedentem ex Patre et Filio profitemur. Ipsum autem Dominum nostrum Jesum Christum Dei Filium et Creatorem omnium, ex substantia Patris ante sæcula genitum, descendisse ultimo tempore pro redemptione mundi a Patre, qui nunquam desiit esse cum Patre. Incarnatus est enim ex Spiritu Sancto et sancta gloriosa Dei genitrice Virgine Maria, et natus ex ipsa, solus autem Dominus Jesus Christus; unus de Sancta Trinitate, anima et carne perfectum, sine peccato, suscipiens hominem, manens quod erat, assumens quod non erat: æqualis Patri secundum divinitatem, minor Patre secundum humanitatem; habens in una Persona duarum naturarum proprietatem; naturæ enim in illo duæ, Deus et homo, non autem duo Filii et Dei duo, sed idem una persona in utraque natura, perferens passionem et mortem pro nostra salute: non in virtute divinitatis sed infirmitate humanitatis. Descendit ad inferos, ut sanctos qui ibi tenebantur erueret: devictoque mortis imperio, resurrexit, assumptus deinde in cœlum, venturus est in futurum ad judicium vivorum et mortuorum: cujus nos morte et sanguine mundati remissionem peccatorum consecuti sumus, resuscitandi ab eo in die novissimo, in ea qua nunc vivimus carne, et in ea qua resurrexit idem Dominus forma, percepturi ab ipso, alii pro justitiæ meritis vitam æternam, alii pro peccatis supplicii æterni sententiam.

Hæc est catholicæ ecclesiæ fides: hanc confessionem conservamus atque tenemus: quam quisquis firmissime custodierit perpetuam salutem habebit.

[1] Labbe, v. 1669—1672. Harduin, III. 562—568.

said, with some degree of laxity, to be contained in the *Ecthesis*, but they are not taken from our Athanasian Creed.

§ 8. But Isidore adduces further testimony. I have mentioned already his work *On the Offices of the Church*, and illustrated from it the difference between a Creed and a Rule of Faith. To the Archbishop's *Rule of Faith* I must now draw more attention.

The chapter entitled "De Regula Fidei" is numbered twenty-three and commences thus:

"This, after the Apostles' Creed, is the most certain faith, which our doctors have handed down to us, that we should profess that the Father and the Son and the Holy Spirit are of one essence and of the same power and eternity, one God invisible; so that, the properties of each Person being preserved, neither should the Trinity be divided in its substance nor confused in its Persons. We should confess the Father as unbegotten, the Son as begotten, the Holy Spirit as neither begotten nor unbegotten, but proceeding from the Father and the Son." It states that the Son took perfect man of the Virgin without sin; it speaks of His crucifixion, His resurrection, His ascension in the flesh; it declares that in that flesh He will come to judge the quick and the dead.

The document is so important that I have given large extracts from it in my note[1]. Its existence shews that the example set by

[1] This Rule is of the greater interest, because it was adopted almost verbatim by Rabanus Maurus in the ninth century. The varieties of reading are very minute and not worthy of notice.

S. Isidori *De Ecclesiasticis Officiis*, Lib. II. cap. 23, *De Regula Fidei*. (Migne, LXXXIII. p. 817.)

"Hæc est autem post apostolorum symbolum certissima fides quam doctores nostri tradiderunt ut profiteamur Patrem et Filium et Spiritum Sanctum unius esse essentiæ ejusdemque potestatis et sempiternitatis, unum Deum invisibilem, ita ut singulis Personarum proprietate servata, nec substantialiter Trinitas dividi, nec personaliter debeat omnino confundi. Patrem quoque confiteri ingenitum, Filium genitum, Spiritum autem Sanctum nec genitum nec ingenitum sed ex Patre et Filio procedentem: Filium autem ex Patre nascendo procedere, Spiritum vero Sanctum procedendo non nasci. Ipsum quoque Filium perfectum ex Virgine hominem sine peccato suscepisse ut quem sola bonitate creaverat, sponte lapsum misericorditer repararet. Quem veraciter crucifixum, et tertia die resurrexisse et cum eadem ipsa carne glorificata adscendisse in cœlum, in qua et ad judicium vivorum et mortuorum expectatur venturus. Et quod divinam humanamque naturam, in utroque perfectus, una Christus persona gestaverit: quia nec geminavit utriusque substantiæ integritas personam, nec confudit geminam unitas personæ substantiam. Altero quippe neutrum exclusit, quia utrumque unus intemerato jure servavit. Quod novi et veteris testamenti salubri commendatur auctoritate, illa per prophetiam, ista per historiam, veraciter persoluta: quod neque de Deo neque de creatura veraciter sit cum paganis aut hereticis aliquid sentiendum in his quibus a veritate dissentiunt, sed quod in utroque testamento divina protestantur eloquia, hoc tantummodo sentiendum." The Rule proceeds by stating that God created the worlds under no necessity compelling Him to do so: that God is supremely and immutably good, the creature in an inferior sense and muta-

the Council of Chalcedon in issuing, after the Symbol, a much longer exposition or declaration of the Faith, was not forgotten: the Symbol being intended for the baptized; the Rule of Faith for the clergy. It shews too that the Quicunque could not have come under the ban of the Councils of Ephesus and Chalcedon until it was allowed, as in our Services, to supersede the Apostles' Creed.

It concludes, "This is the true fulness of the Catholic tradition and faith: out of which, if one point alone is rejected, the whole belief of the faith is lost."

Many subjects of interest arise from the study of this document. We see that it was framed after the questions regarding the Person of the Incarnate Son of God were settled: again, that it must have succeeded the fifth Council, wherein the opinions of Origen were condemned. The words regarding the Procession of the Holy Spirit shew that it was composed after the tenet had been received in Spain, *i.e.* after the council at which Reccared presided in 589. It is equally clear that the Quicunque was not known to Isidore, or, if known, it had no authority: for this Rule of Faith, however it may resemble the Quicunque in the conceptions of its first part, has in its final words no verbal similarity with it. The mixed resemblances and disagreements in the clauses "Patrem ingenitum," &c. prove its independent origin.

But there is another point of detail to be considered before we come to the grand fact demonstrated by the existence of this

bly good: that the origin of the soul is uncertain, but it was created, yet is not corporeal: that it was created after the image of God in a moral probity, without which the faith of the divine worship would be torpid, but with which the integrity of the divine worship is perfected; so that whosoever loveth God, and his neighbour in God, may stretch forward even to the love of his enemies, and by stretching forward may obtain it. One man cannot be polluted by another's sin, unless there is a consent of the will thereto. The Rule proceeds to the defence of lawful marriage, even though from it an offspring is produced tainted with original sin, and a virgin life is to be preferred. Baptism is not to be repeated, for the blessing thereof comes not from the minister but from God alone. Repentance (penitence, penance) is needed and must not be rejected. It proceeds with speaking sensibly enough of worldly goods, that it is not by the possession of them, but by the use we make of them, that we shall be judged. It concludes with speaking of our resurrection and of the eternal punishment of Satan with his angels and worshippers, "Nor, as some persons sacrilegiously dispute, is he to be restored to his former, that is, his angelic condition." It concludes:

"Hæc est catholicæ traditionis et fidei vera integritas, de qua, si unum quodlibet respuatur, tota fidei credulitas amittetur."

It must be remembered that Rabanus Maurus must have adopted this in preference to the Athanasian Creed if he knew the latter.

document. The Faith of the Trinity, though put most clearly in the opening of this Rule, as we find it in that of others, is exhibited in a comparatively simple form, without that "glorying in subtle antitheses," which proceeded from the labours of Augustine. In this respect it resembles the version of the Catholic Faith contained in the Profession of Denebert, the clauses quoted in the treatise of Hincmar, and the Faith as given in the Vienna Manuscript, all of which I shall adduce below. Once more: the reference we find here to questions relating to the origin of the soul and the ultimate salvation of Satan—things omitted in our Athanasian formula—shews that the points put forward in these Rules of Faith varied according to the exigencies of the times.

But the grand fact which these documents exhibit is this: that in the seventh and later centuries there was, in addition to the Symbolum or Creed, a series of wider and more expansive documents, which went into details, expounding and enforcing the Faith of the Symbolum—the very thing which the "Fides Athanasii" is evidently, from its construction, intended to do. The "Creed of Saint Athanasius" begins *Fides autem Catholica hæc est:* the one before us commences *Hæc est autem post Apostolicum symbolum certissima fides.* Our version of the Faith is commended by the words *Hæc est fides Catholica, quam nisi quisque fideliter firmiterque crediderit, salvus esse non poterit:* that of St Isidore is similarly, though more mildly enforced, *Hæc est Catholica traditionis et fidei vera integritas, de qua si unum quodlibet respuatur, tota fidei credulitas amittetur*[1]. Our question is, Which is the more ancient?

§ 9. There was another Council at Toledo in 636, and another in 638. The latter again put forth a profession of its belief. The leader of the Church had changed. St Isidore was dead: and possibly the later bishops thought that they might improve on the work which their predecessor had accomplished. Again I think an extract from the Canon or Chapter worthy of being

[1] I may mention that Canon XIII. of this council defends the use of hymns in the Church. The same canon is frequently referred to as noting that, in the *Gloria in Excelsis*, the ecclesiastical doctors composed all that followed on the angelic words. The direction that "This is not to be sung in the Church in consequence" appears to be ironical. Canon XIV. directs that the "Hymn of the three Children," which had been sung on Sundays and the Festivals of the Martyrs only, should throughout Spain and "Gaul" be chanted in the pulpit at every mass.

reprinted[1]: the progress of thought is thus more easily perceived. On comparing this and the last together, we find the conception that "God is solitary" expressly excluded from the Faith: other phrases draw nearer to our Creed:

"The Father unbegotten, uncreated, the fount and origin of all divinity; the Son from the Father without time and before all creation, without beginning; begotten, not created...in all things coequal with the Father, very God of very God; the Holy Spirit neither begotten nor created, but proceeding from the Father and the Son, is the Spirit of

[1] TOLEDO, VI. A.D. 638.
From Canon I. (Harduin, III. 601.)
Credimus et profitemur sacratissimam et omnipotentissimam Trinitatem Patrem et F. et S. S. unum Deum, solum non solitarium; unius essentiæ, virtutis, potestatis, uniusque naturæ: discretam inseparabiliter personis: indiscretam essentialiter substantiam deitatis: creatricem omnium creaturarum. Patrem ingenitum, increatum, fontem et originem totius divinitatis: Filium a Patre intemporaliter et ante omnem creaturam sine initio genitum non creatum: nam nec Pater usquam sine Filio nec Filius extitit sine Patre: sed tamen Filius Deus de Patre Deo non Pater Deus de Filio Deo: ille autem Filius Patris et Deus de Patre per omnia coæqualis Patri: Deus verus de Deo vero: Spiritum vero Sanctum, neque genitum, neque creatum, sed de Patre Filioque procedentem utriusque esse Spiritum: ac per hoc substantialiter unum sunt, quia et unus ab utroque procedit. In hac autem Trinitate tanta est unitas substantiæ, ut pluralitate careat et æqualitatem teneat: nec minor in singulis quam in omnibus nec major in omnibus quam in singulis maneat Personis. Ex his igitur tribus divinitatis Personis solum Filium fatemur ad Redemptionem humani generis propter culparum debita, quæ per inobedientiam Adæ originaliter et nostro libero arbitrio contraxeramus, resolvenda a secreto Patris et arcano prodiisse et hominem sine peccato de sancta semper Virgine Maria assumpsisse, ut idem Filius Dei Patris esset Filius hominis: Deus perfectus et Homo perfectus, ut Homo Deus esset unus Christus naturis in duabus, in persona unus; ne quaternitas Trinitati accederet si in Christo Persona geminata esset. Ergo a Patre et Spiritu Sancto inseparabiliter discretus est persona; ab homine autem assumpto, natura. Item, cum eodem homine unus extat persona, cum Patre et Spiritu Sancto natura: ac, sicut diximus, ex duabus naturis et una persona unus est dominus noster Jesus Christus in forma divinitatis æqualis Patri, in forma servi minor Patre: hinc enim est vox ejus in Psalmo: *de ventre matris meæ Deus meus es tu.* Natus itaque a Deo sine matre, natus a virgine sine patre: solum *Verbum caro factum est et habitavit in nobis:* et cum tota cooperata sit Trinitas formationem suscepti hominis (quoniam inseparabilia sunt opera Trinitatis), solus tamen accepit hominem in singularitate personæ, non in unitate divinæ naturæ, in id quod est proprium Filii non quod commune Trinitatis. Nam si naturam hominis Deique alteram (? omit) confudisset, tota Trinitas corpus adsumsisset: quoniam constat naturam Trinitatis esse unam, non tamen personam. Hic igitur dominus Jesus Christus missus a Patre suscipiens quod non erat nec amittens quod erat, inviolabilis de suo, mortalis de nostro, venit in hunc mundum, peccatores salvos facere et credentes justificare, faciensque mirabilia, traditus est propter delicta nostra, mortuus est propter expiationem nostram, resurrexit propter justificationem nostram, cujus livore sanati, cujus morte Deo Patri reconciliati, cujus resurrectione sumus resuscitati. Quem etiam venturum in fine expectamus sæculorum et cum resurrectione omnium æquissimo suo judicio redditurum justis præmia et impiis pœnas. Ecclesiam quoque catholicam credimus sine macula in opere et sine ruga in fide corpus ejus esse, regnumque habiturum cum capite suo omnipotente Christo Jesu, postquam *hoc corruptibile induerit incorruptionem et mortale immortalitatem, ut sit Deus omnia in omnibus.* Hac fide corda purificantur, hac hæreses extirpantur; in hac omnis ecclesia collocata jam in regno cœlesti et degens in sæculo præsenti gloriatur: et non est in alia fide salus *nec enim nomen aliud est sub cœlo datum hominibus in quo oporteat nos salvos fieri.*

Both, and by Him They are substantially One (unum) because the One (unus) proceedeth from Both; and this Trinity is not less in any than in all, nor greater in all than it remains in the several Persons." And then avoiding once more the subject of clauses 5—20 of the Quicunque, the Profession passes on to the subject of Christ's Humanity. Once more we read of Him assuming man. We have the words "Perfect God, perfect Man, the Man-God one Christ, in the form of divinity equal to the Father, in the form of servant less than the Father." And it proceeds with the history of the Redeemer's work. After speaking of His return to judgment, it adds a few words on the Catholic Church, and of that glorious time when *God shall be all in all;* and concludes "with this faith hearts are purified; with this heresies are extirpated; every Church grounded in this already glories in the kingdom of heaven; there is no salvation in any other, *For there is none other Name given under heaven whereby we can be saved.*"

The persistency of the mention of the Holy Trinity in these formulæ was probably due to the sect which had grown up at the end of the sixth century under Philoponus of Alexandria, a sect which held a modified tritheism: whilst ere long the monothelistic disputations made the latter of the Toletan Canons important. The introduction of the words *non solitarius* may be due to the influence of Vincentius as against the Photinians. Perhaps it is worthy of notice that we see a glimmer of the language of St Augustine appearing in the latter part of the Canon. The phrase "In the form of God, Christ Jesus is equal to the Father, in the form of the servant, less," I have quoted from the great Bishop's work. We shall see further proofs of his influence hereafter.

§ 10. We find the Lateran Council of 649[1] insisting on the expression of belief in the Trinity and the Incarnation. The form should be observed: "If any one does not confess" this or that "may he be condemned." The great object of the synod was to discuss, and its great result was to condemn, the opinions of the Monothelites, and the Canons were framed accordingly. But I remark no progress in regard to the subject of the Trinity[2]. I notice, however, what is to me most interesting, that Augustine's works were frequently quoted in the discussions of the council, and those of Athanasius also. I cannot, in all fairness, build anything on the fact that the Quicunque is not quoted: because the

[1] Labbe, VI. p. 350. Harduin, III. 687.

[2] *Incomprehensibilis* is used where we now have *immensus*.

Quicunque contains nothing which bears particularly on the question in dispute[1].

§ 11. In the Council of Chalons, in the year 650, attended by about forty bishops from Lyons and the neighbourhood, the "Fidei norma" of the first four Councils was alone confirmed.

§ 12. The eighth Council of Toledo contented themselves with reciting the Creed "as they say it at the mass" and passed on to other business. This was in 653. They urged, however, the bishops to clear up anything that was obscure in the doctrine of the Trinity, even whilst they were content with the interpolated Constantinopolitan Creed.

§ 13. The Council of *Emerita* (Merida), in the year 666, recited the Spanish version of the Creed of Constantinople, and added:

> "This is our faith; this our belief; whosoever holds this worthily shall, at the day of judgment, receive a worthy remuneration; whosoever shall have departed from it, or shall be unwilling to be in the faith, shall with the devil suffer eternal punishment...If any one will not believe or confess that the Father, Son, and Holy Spirit are One in the Trinity, let him be anathema."

The next Canon gives directions for the observance of vespers.

§ 14. We now come to a Council of Autun, supposed to have been held in the year 670: at which it is said that a Canon was passed to the effect that

> "If any presbyter, deacon, subdeacon, or clerk shall not learn, without fail or fault, the Symbol which under the inspiration of the Holy Spirit the Apostles handed down, and the Faith of the holy bishop Athanasius, let him be condemned by the Bishop."

As this Canon does not give the text of the "Faith of Athanasius," it will not assist us at present to any great extent. All discussion regarding it may, therefore, be delayed until we come

[1] We have *Trinitas in unitate et unitas in Trinitate* (Canon I.); *tribus subsistentiis* not *personis: crucifixum carne* (the descent into hell is not mentioned): *resurrexisse tertia die, sedentem in dextra Patris* (Canon II.): *a Deo Patre ante omnia sæcula natus, in ultimis sæculorum de sancta Virgine* (Canons III. and IV.): *consubstantialem Deo et Patri secundum divinitatem, consubstantialem homini et matri secundum humanitatem* (*Ibid.*). The preface is taken largely from the Chalcedon definition; "pariter" occurs in Canon XIV. (Harduin, II. 822.)

to the consideration of the disciplinary canons of a similar character. It will be remembered that we have already met with three documents, three expositions of the faith which have been attributed to Athanasius: to two others, besides the Quicunque, I must draw attention ere long.

§ 15. In the year 675 was held what is called the eleventh Synod of Toledo. It was attended by seventeen bishops.

Their first object (they said) was to confer on the "sacred purity of the faith; for, seeing that to men who have to be initiated into the life of blessedness, this is the first step of salvation, they ought to point out the road both in action and in precept." They agreed, therefore, to discuss the subject among themselves, taking their start from the first four councils, and then to reduce to writing the results of their deliberations, in order that the clergy "might thus have in an expanded form what otherwise might be perplexing from its brevity." Their declaration took the form of a Creed, "We confess and believe;" an expansion of the Eastern Creed, occupying more than four columns of Labbe's folios[1].

Comparing the language of this Confession with that of our Quicunque, as already illustrated from the earlier councils held in this city, I notice that the substance of our clauses (21, 22, 23) appears once more, with language approaching nearer to our own. It is expanded and explained at length. I will take the words or thoughts as they occur, begging the reader to remember that he may have to supply many words in the intervals which I have marked. "We profess that the Father indeed is not begotten nor created, but unbegotten. We confess that the Son is of the substance of the Father born (natum) without beginning before the ages, but not made. The Father therefore is eternal, and the Son eternal...but this Son of God is Son by nature, not by adoption; and we believe that the Holy Spirit, Who is the third Person in the Trinity is God, one and equal with the Father and the Son, but not begotten nor created, but proceeding from both. This Holy Spirit is believed to be neither begotten nor unbegotten. Nor though we speak of three Persons, do we speak of three Substances, but one Substance, three Persons. For, if we are asked of the Persons severally (de singulis Personis) we confess of necessity that each is God. The Father is said to be God, the Son God, the Holy Ghost God, one by one (singulariter); yet not three Gods, but one God. The Father is said to be Almighty, the Son Almighty, the Holy Ghost Almighty, one by one; yet not three Almighties, but one Almighty." For other expressions I must refer to the note[2], adding, however, that the phrase

[1] Four in Harduin, III. 1020.

[2] "Patrem quidem non genitum, non creatum, sed ingenitum profitemur... Filium vero de substantia Patris sine initio ante sæcula natum nec tamen factum esse fatemur...sempiternus ergo Pater, sempiternus et Filius:...hic enim Filius Dei natura est Filius, non adoptione...Spiritum quoque Sanctum qui est tertia in Trinitate Persona unum atque æqualem cum Patre et Filio credimus esse Deum—...non tamen genitum vel creatum sed ab utrisque procedentem...Hic Spiritus Sanctus nec ingenitus nec genitus creditur (which they explain). Hæc est Sanctæ Trinitatis re-

employed is still that the Son of God *assumed man;* not, as it is in the Quicunque, that He became man by the *assumption of humanity*, or, as our version reads it, *by the taking of the manhood into God.*

The last words are: "This is the Faith of our Confession, exhibited and explained;" or, "This Faith of our Confession is exhibited and set forth: by which the teaching of all heretics is destroyed, the hearts of the faithful are cleansed, and we draw nigh to God in glory."

It seems to me that we may note here further progress towards the language of the Quicunque: but the differences are still such that I cannot reconcile them on the supposition that the Quicunque, if known, was regarded as of any authority by the Spanish Bishops in the year 675. And in their long account we find nothing in any way approaching to the meaning of the first or last clauses of the Athanasian Creed.

§ 16. I will now finish with the Spanish Councils. The bishops who met at Bracara, in the same year, were content with quoting "the Rule of Faith as settled at Nicæa," when they were

lata narratio: quæ non triplex sed Trinitas et dici et credi debet. Nec recte dici potest ut in uno Deo sit Trinitas, sed unus Deus Trinitas...Nec sicut tres Personas, ita tres Substantias prædicamus, sed unam Substantiam, tres autem Personas...Nam si de singulis Personis interrogemur (it will be remembered that these are the words of St Augustine; although Augustine's name is not mentioned we shall hear of him a few years later, in this neighbourhood), Deum necesse esse fateamur. Deus ergo Pater, Deus Filius, Deus Spiritus Sanctus, singulariter dicitur: nec tamen tres Dii, sed unus est Deus. Ita Pater omnipotens, et Filius omnipotens, et Spiritus Sanctus omnipotens, singulariter dicitur, nec tamen tres omnipotentes sed unus omnipotens: sicut et unum lumen unumque principium prædicatur ...Una est majestas sive potestas, nec minoratur in singulis nec augetur in tribus:...Personas distinguimus, non deitatem separamus." Passing on to speak of the Incarnation, the Confession (as I have remarked above) still retains the phrase, "verum hominem sine peccato credimus assumpsisse." After a while we read "Nec tamen Verbum ipsum ita in carne conversum atque mutatum ut desisteret Deus esse, qui homo esse voluisset: sed ita *Verbum caro factum est*, ut non tantum ibi sit Verbum Dei et hominis caro, sed etiam rationalis hominis anima. Unde perfectus Deus, perfectus et Homo in unitate Personæ unius est Christus...Deus Verbum non accepit Personam hominis, sed naturam; et in æternam Personam divinitatis temporalem accepit substantiam carnis." Thus they had the conception of the *humanitas*, although they did not catch the word. Lower down, I find the phrase "in fine sæculorum" (not *in sæculo*), replacing the *novissimis diebus* of the earlier councils, but the words *forma Dei, forma servi*, are still retained. As we approach the end of the document, we find the identity of the Resurrection-body with our present frame insisted upon with greater clearness than as yet I have been able to notice: "Nec in aerea nec qualibet alia carne, ut quidam delirant, surrecturos nos credimus, sed in ista qua vivimus consistimus et movemur." The hope of a future resurrection to eternal life is gently expressed, and the document concludes "Hæc est confessionis nostræ fides exposita, per quam omnium hæreticorum dogma perimitur, fidelium corda mundantur: per quam etiam ad Deum gloriose acceditur."

really taking up the Spanish version of the so-called Creed of Constantinople. At Toledo, in 681, the bishops were more cautious: they recited the interpolated Creed as "the Sacramentum handed down to them, and used in the solemn service of the Mass." This they thought would render unnecessary any longer exposition on the subject of the Trinity. The same was done at the thirteenth Council in 683. At the fourteenth Council in 684 the Fathers expressed at length in their Canon VIII. the orthodox view of the union of the two natures in our Lord; from it they deduced the twofold will and the double operation. And they declared anathema to those who subtracted aught from the orthodox faith. Four years later and they met in larger numbers, sixty-one in all, to consider the decrees of the sixth general Council, which had been held in 680. They commenced once more with reciting the Creed of Constantinople as they received it, and then, in considering the question of the will, they quoted at some length passages, spurious and genuine, from Athanasius, Cyril, Ambrose, Fulgentius; from Augustine's "Book of Questions against the Apollinarians[1]," from the *Enchiridion*, from the *Liber Trinitatis Dei* (they quote book XV.); from one of the "Tracts on the Symbol;" and from the *De Fide ad Petrum* (which is now considered to be a work of Fulgentius).

They brought out, once more, the Definition of Chalcedon, and upheld the truth of the two wills in our Redeemer by the analogy of man's nature, "who consists not only of soul but of body, not only of body but of soul." I do not find anything analogous to the final clause of the Quicunque. The following passage will scarcely be deemed so: "If any one shall willingly act against these definitions, he shall be fined in one-tenth of his property, and moreover be smitten with the sentence of excommunication."

One more of these Spanish Synods and we must dismiss them. It was held in 692 or 693; and the decrees were signed by fifty-seven bishops, five abbots, three vicars of bishops, fourteen counts, and two other laymen. It was opened (as were many of the others) with the reading of a letter from the king, informing them of the subjects which he was anxious that they should discuss. They received the letter with thankfulness—the more

[1] Is this the *liber quæstionum*, § LXXX. Tom. VI.? (p. 129, of Gaume.)

fervent souls with hymns of praise. Then they recited their Creed—"We believe and confess"—different from any that I have noticed elsewhere, but still the Trinity and the Incarnation occupy the whole of its length. In addition to the clauses which I have already illustrated, I cannot find any on which light is thrown from this document, unless, perhaps, the subject of clauses 13, 14, 15, 16 is brought out still more clearly (not three Omnipotents but one Omnipotent)[1].

The Confession towards its close speaks of our Resurrection, of the future Judgment, and of the reign of the Church with Christ. And at length we have a phrase which covers the ground which our final clause may be said to occupy: "And all who do not stand by this in every, even the least degree, or who have receded from it, or shall recede from it...or do not believe without the slightest shadow of doubt," what the four general and other Councils have ordained, "shall be punished with the sentence of eternal damnation, and in the end of the world shall burn with the devil and his angels in devouring flames[2]."

In 694 there was another synod, at which the bishops were contented with repeating the interpolated Nicene Creed.

We have thus traced to the Spanish Bishops, and to the year 693, the first appearance in any council of the thought of the final clause of the Quicunque[3].

§ 17. We must notice one or two points by way of summary.

One is the gradual way in which the enuntiation of what I must call the great verities of our Faith was unfolded. The substance of clauses 4 and 5 of the Quicunque is met with in the year 589; it is met with again in 693. But we have found as yet nothing analogous to clauses 6, 7, 8, 9. Clause 13 is found in the year 589; clauses 14, 15, 16 in 675 and 693 contem-

[1] I read "Pater a nullo originem sumpsit: Filius Patre generante existit. Spiritus quoque Sanctus ex Patris Filiique unione consistit." I read too "Nihil in eadem Trinitate anterius posteriusve credendum est......Nihil in eadem sancta Trinitate majus aut minus credere oportet." This is a marked advance. I find too the quotation from Hosea xiii. 14, "O mors, ero mors tua," "O inferne, ero morsus tuus," which I have noticed in one of the Pseudo-Augustine Sermons (Vol. VI. 1740), and which will be found in the Exposition of Fortunatus.

[2] Perpetua damnationis sententia ulciscetur, atque in fine sæculi cum diabolo ejusque sociis ignivomis rogis cremabitur. (Harduin, IV. 1793.)

[3] And even this was limited to the subjects laid down in the four great Councils.

poraneously, as it will be observed, with an increased knowledge of the writings of St Augustine. To clauses 17 and 18 we have no parallel. The true meaning of our clause 19 is given by the Council in the year 675; clauses 21, 22, 23 were substantially (not verbally) contained in the Confessions of 633 and later years, though the words *nec creatus* of 21, 22, and *non factus* of 23 nowhere appear. The antithetical language

Pater a nullo	est	factus nec creatus nec genitus
Filius a Patre solo	est	non factus nec creatus sed genitus
S. Sanctus a Patre et Filio		non factus nec creatus nec genitus sed procedens,

was a later refinement. For the sake of it the composers of the Quicunque avoided the cautious expression of earlier days that the Holy Spirit was *nec genitus nec ingenitus.* We find the explanation of 24 in more than one council, but not the language. The two clauses of 25 are not found until the year 693, and then at a somewhat wide interval apart. Clauses 28, 29, 30 nowhere appear. The words *in sæculo* are not to be found in the Spanish Councils; and for *genitus* the older word *natus* is invariably met with; of the next clauses we have had the substance again and again; of 31 and 32 in 633; of 33 in 589, and later years; but the words have always been *in forma servi, in forma Dei.* We have never met with the expression that our Lord *assumed humanity;* it always has been that He *assumed man.* The substance of the remaining clauses, *i.e.* 36 to 41, has been noted at various times. In regard to 42, however, although we have met with punishment of varied degrees of severity denounced against those who deny or reject the truth, we have found nothing directed against those who, *de facto,* do not believe. I have found nothing resembling clauses 1, 2, 3.

I have thus traced down to the year 693, the history of the Spanish Rules of Faith, including what I may call the warnings of orthodoxy, the monitory words by which the True Faith was commended to the attention of Spanish Christians. I have shewn, how, from being at first encouraging, the language of the Spanish Councils became minatory, and, finally, condemnatory; but it did not become condemnatory until more than three hundred years after the death of Athanasius or two hundred and sixty years after the death of Augustine; *i.e.* two hundred and forty years after the Council of Chalcedon, at which we may consider that the truths of our Quicunque relating to the Incarnate Word of God were worked out in the Church. Thus the framework of the Athanasian Creed is historically of later date than the Catholic Faith which it contains: the setting is of later date than the gems. But there is no proof that we have as yet reached the time when the framework was completed, or the setting assumed its present form.

§ 18. We must now turn back to ask the question, Was the Faith of the Quicunque as yet received in the Italian or Roman Churches? Before we can answer the enquiry, we must go to the documents which preceded, to the debates which accompanied, and to the definitions which resulted from the sixth general Council—*i.e.* the third of Constantinople—held in the years 680 and 681. At this council, in which the Emperor Constantinus Pogonatus took an active part, an Address from a Synod at Milan, enclosed in a letter from their Metropolitan Mansuetus, and containing an Exposition of their Faith, first calls for attention. We learn from the two documents that St Augustine's writings were now attracting attention: the synod referred to Gregory of Nazianzus, Basil, Cyril of Alexandria, Athanasius, John Chrysostom, Hilary of Poictiers, Augustine of Hippo, whom it described as *omni sapientia clarum*, Ambrose, and Jerome, "the most learned, and brilliant with every light." The exposition of their Faith[1] commences:

"We profess that we believe the Holy indivisible Trinity, that is, Father and Son and Holy Spirit, one God, yet so one as trine, so trine as one; Trinity in distinct Persons, that is the Father, of Whom are all things; the Son, by Whom are all things; the Holy Spirit, in Whom are all things; but yet of one divinity, one essence, and one substance." I must resist the temptation of reciting the whole; I will note only any words in which there is a close approximation to the language of the formula before us. I find these: "We confess the Holy Trinity in Unity and Unity in Trinity. When we call Him Holy Spirit we shew that He proceeds from the Person of the Eternal Father[2]. We believe that the Word of God was Incarnate and made Man within the Virgin's womb." He is "perfect God, perfect Man, in two natures, that is of the divinity and humanity; consubstantial with the Father in regard to His

[1] Harduin, III. 1053.
[2] The Church of Milan had not received as yet the double Procession.

divinity, consubstantial with us in regard to His humanity. He was born before the worlds (natus ante sæcula), but in the last days was incarnate of the Virgin." The synod then proceeded to speak of the two wills, the subject which was attracting so much attention at the time and was forgotten in the West so soon afterwards.

I notice one more resemblance to our Quicunque: the document ends with speaking of the Return of the Lord to judgment.

At the end of the first session, Constantine called for proofs "from universal Synods and from approved Fathers," bearing upon the subject before him. The reign of authority had commenced. The bishops could no longer do that which St Augustine and St Athanasius had done, and on the successful performance of which their value and their fame are built up. They had lost confidence in the promise of their Saviour that the Holy Spirit should lead His followers into all truth, and so they ceased to ask for wisdom direct from God: all that they could do was this, to trust to earlier writers for guidance, and appeal to that which they had deduced or inferred from Scripture.

And so it is, that now we have, I will not say the earliest, but one of the most noticeable attempts to forge documents where evidence was missing. Paul, "the magnificent secretary[1]" of the Emperor, produced a volume which was said to be the record of the fifth Synod. It began "The discourse of the Holy Menna, Archbishop of Constantinople, addressed to Vigilius, Pope of Rome, on the subject that there is only one will in Christ." The legates of the Apostolic see rose up and cried, "O pious Sir, the book is falsified: it is corrupted! Let it not be read!" The volume was examined, and it was found that "three quaternions (or quires) had been inserted at the beginning, not having the subscribed number[2], which is usually fixed upon the quire; on the contrary, the fourth quire was numbered one, and the fifth was numbered two, and so on:" thus the addition was detected. The part thus inserted into the volume was not read at the synod, but they began with the prooemium proper of the Council. This curious and instructive scene occurred at the third session[3].

At the next meeting a long letter from Agatho, the Pope of Rome, was read[4]. It occupies more than twenty columns both in Harduin and Labbe; and, although it contains quotations from Ambrose, Athanasius, Augustine against Maximinus and against

[1] Ὁ μεγαλοπρεπέστατος ἀσέγκρετις. This is the Greek of the synod!

[2] The "signature."

[3] Harduin, III. 1067.

[4] Harduin, III. 1073.

Julian, Gregory of Nazianzus, and others, and the Chalcedon Council, it contains, what is even more valuable, arguments from Scripture—opening them and alleging, that as there were two natures in the Incarnate Word, so of necessity were there two wills. The Pope begged for freedom of discussion, so that "no one speaking for the purity and integrity of the Catholic Faith, should be deterred or hindered." The letter is followed by a copy of the instructions given by the Pope to the Roman legates[1]: in the middle of which I find a passage which merits our attention[2]:

"This is our perfect knowledge—that we should preserve (tota mentis custodia conservemus) with the whole energy of our mind those limits of the Catholic and Apostolic faith, which up to the present time the Apostolic see with us both holds and passes on (tradit et tenet), believing in God the Father Almighty, Maker of heaven and earth, and of all things visible and invisible, and in His only-begotten Son, Who was born of Him before all worlds, very God of very God, Light of Light, born not made, consubstantial with the Father, that is of the same substance with the Father, through Whom all things were made, which are in heaven and which are in earth: and in the Holy Spirit, the Lord and Giver of life, proceeding from the Father, who with the Father and the Son is to be worshipped and glorified[3]: the Trinity in Unity and Unity in Trinity; a Unity of essence, but a Trinity of Persons or subsistences[4]: God the Father, God the Son, God the Holy Spirit; not three Gods but one God, Father, and Son, and Holy Spirit." And so it proceeds to the Incarnation, differing little from the Definition of Chalcedon, and thence deducing (as before) the necessity of the truth that there were two wills in the Saviour[5].

They use the phrase which is still of interest to us as coming from a Roman Pontiff: "the true faith cannot be altered; nor can it be preached, at one time in this way, at another in that[6]."

Reading onwards, I find a regret expressed that our Theodore, Bishop of Canterbury, was not able to join the bishops in their deliberations: but Agatho was thankful that amongst the Lombards and Sclaves and Franks and Goths and Britons were many who were watching with interest the course of the deliberations of the council. (It is curious that the Spaniards are not mentioned[7].) And towards the conclusion we find the following admonition:

[1] Harduin, l.c. p. 1115.

[2] *Ibid.* 1119.

[3] Coadorandum et conglorificandum.

[4] Personarum sive subsistentiarum. Harduin, p. 1119 B.

[5] See the clause "Hanc etiam meræ catholicæ confessionis regulam," p. 1122 B.

[6] p. 1122 D.

[7] I infer that the Spaniards alone held the double Procession at this time.

"Whatever priests are anxious to preach, with us, the things which are contained in this confession of our humility, we receive, as joining in our Apostolic faith. But those who may be unwilling to confess these things we regard to be liable to eternal condemnation, as being hostile to the Catholic and Apostolic confession[1]."

This document was signed by the Pope and about one hundred and twenty Italian bishops.

In the eighth Session of the council we find the Confession of Macarius[2], who was called upon to account for his opinions.

This confession also contains extracts from the Creed of Constantinople; it speaks of the Holy Spirit as proceeding from the Father, and manifested through the Son. It proceeds, of course, to the subject of the Incarnation, and asserts that we do not say "that the flesh passed into the nature of the Divinity; nor again that the ineffable nature of the Word of God was derived into the nature of the flesh[3]." Macarius makes some statements with regard to the Eucharist which are worthy of notice, and declares that he accepts the five great Councils.

This over, his cross-examination commenced, and the day passed. At the tenth Session, a book[4] was produced on parchment, bound in silver, from the Treasury of the great Church of Constantinople, having this superscription:

"The testimonies of holy and approved fathers, shewing that there are two Wills and two Operations in our Lord and God and Saviour, Jesus Christ."

From this volume were recited passages from Leo, Ambrose, Chrysostom, and others; from a book of Athanasius on the Trinity and Incarnation, which is clearly spurious[5], and from his genuine work against the Apollinarians. Augustine furnished another passage, and Gregory of Nyssa others, and Anastasius of Antioch[6] many more. Towards the end of the day another Creed was read, which had been offered by Peter, Bishop of Lycomedia, on the Trinity and the Incarnation[7], beginning with portions of the Creed of Constantinople; in other respects similar to, though not the same as many that we have seen before.

But in the next Session we find at length a tract which exercised important influence on the controversies between Hincmar and Godeschalk. It is a synodical letter of Sophronius, who had been Patriarch of Jerusalem in the early part of the century

1 Harduin, 1126 B.

2 *Ibid.* p. 1167.

3 Harduin, p. 1169 E, "Nec enim carnem dicimus in divinitatis transire naturam neque iterum in naturam carnis ineffabilem Dei Verbi derivari naturam, &c."

4 Harduin, p. 1201 D.

5 Harduin, p. 1207.

6 p. 1235.

7 p. 1250.

and died about the year 688. It occupies 21 columns in our folios[1] and is too long either to copy or to abbreviate. He says that

"He believes in One God the Father Almighty...and in One Jesus Christ, the only-begotten Son of God, and in One Holy Spirit, Who everlastingly proceedeth from God the Father, Who is Himself to be acknowledged as God, coeternal, consubstantial with the Father and the Son, of the same essence, nature and deity...We believe (he says) the Trinity in Unity, and glorify the Unity in Trinity. One God is believed by us; One Lord is proclaimed by us; One God, One Deity, not three Gods, three Deities. We maintain One first Principle: One Godhead, One kingdom." Once more[2], "The Father is perfect God, the Son perfect God, the Holy Ghost perfect God, but these three are one God; the Deity does not admit of division."

Sophronius shortly proceeds to speak of the Incarnation, making special mention of the errors of Nestorius, Apollinarius, and others[3]. On a later page[4] I notice that he held that men's souls have not a natural immortality; it is by the gift of God that they receive the grant of immortality and incorruptibility. Towards the end he gives a long list of errors and heresies which he anathematizes, but I see nothing that I can compare with the last clause of the Quicunque.

This being read, Constantine called upon the bishops to test the writings of Macarius by the documents which they had heard recited. Shortly afterwards the council proceeded to depose and banish him; he declaring that he would rather be torn limb from limb than renounce his opinions. I need not proceed with relating the further incidents of the council: its Definition was put forth in the eighteenth Session[5], and may be seen in the second volume of Dr Routh's *Opuscula*. The synod confirmed the actions of the previous five Councils; it received and confirmed the Symbolum which was put out by the 318 Fathers and confirmed by the 150. The two are recited at length (the former being the true Creed, of course with its anathema), and then the Holy Œcumenical Synod said:

"This pious and orthodox symbol at one time sufficed for the perfect knowledge and confirmation of the orthodox faith; but the worker of evil has always found organs to spread some poison, and now Theodore, Bishop of Pharan, and Sergius, and Pyrrhus, and Paul and Peter, who have been Bishops of this royal city of Constantinople, and Honorius, too, who has been Pope of the older Rome, and Cyrus of Alexandria,

[1] Harduin, III. 1258. Labbe, p. 852.
[2] Harduin, 1263 E, 1265 A. Labbe, 861 B.
[3] Harduin, 1265 E. Labbe, 864.
[4] Harduin, 1282 C. Labbe, 881 C.
[5] Labbe, 1019. Harduin, 1395.

and Macarius of Antioch have denied the perfection of the Incarnation of our one Lord Jesus Christ, by asserting that there was only one will and one energy in His two natures."

The Definition follows the course of the similar document which proceeded from Chalcedon, having, however, noteworthy additions here and there. Thus we find our Saviour spoken of twice as One of the Holy Consubstantial and life-giving Trinity[1]. In regard to our Lord's Incarnation, the words were added, "that He was born of the Holy Spirit and the Virgin Mary, who was truly and specially Mother of God." The older phrase was, "that He was born of the Virgin Mary, the Mother of God." Then comes a long insertion, called out by the question of the Will, in which the all-wise Athanasius[2] is quoted as speaking of the Will of Christ's flesh being subjected to His Divine Will. This Definition concludes, as does the other, with declaring that "those who should venture to compose a different faith should, if bishops or clergy, be deprived of their office; if monks or laymen, they should be anathematized," but the warning was extended to those who should introduce any new language or expressions[3], such as would tend to the subversion of what was now defined.

§ 19. I have gone into this at some length to shew that, up to this time, neither the Church of Milan nor that of Rome nor the Bishops assembled at Constantinople in 681, had deviated in any way from the statement of the Creed of Constantinople on the procession of the Holy Spirit; and that so it is inconceivable that what we call the Athanasian Creed could have been received or known as such by either Church. The Italian bishops insisted everywhere that "the Holy Spirit proceeds from the Father;" the Spanish Councils maintained that "He proceedeth from the Father and the Son." Even St Augustine's influence had produced no effect as yet, in this respect, on the theology of Italy: nor, as yet, had it produced effect on the theology of France. The Frank Churches were at one with the Roman Church. Whatever was meant by the Faith of Athanasius in the undated canon of Autun, we must hesitate before we affirm that the Quicunque, as we now have it, was signified by those

[1] Τὸν ἀληθινὸν Θεὸν ἡμῶν, τὸν ἕνα τῆς ἁγίας ὁμοουσίου καὶ ζωαρχικῆς τριαδός.

[2] Κατὰ τὸν πάνσοφον Ἀθανάσιον.

[3] Καινοφωνίαν ἤτοι λέξεως ἐφεύρεσιν.

momentous words; unless indeed we put the date of the synod at a much later period than 670. Anything framed at that time would have borne marks of the Monothelitic enquiries: the Quicunque has no such marks. It must have been composed either much earlier than 670, before the question was mooted; or later, when it had died away. Amidst the crowd of professed quotations, amidst the mass of testimonies adduced, amidst the accumulated and ever-varying Confessions that we have noted, there is not one professed quotation from "the Faith of Athanasius." What can our conclusion be, save that the *Quicunque vult* was not known in its present form? or, at least, that it was not known as the work of Athanasius or of any Father of the Church? Yet its substance was known. The Rule of Faith of Isidore, the Confession of Toledo, the Encyclic of Sophronius, the Address of the Milanese Bishops to the sixth general Council, the Letter of the Synod of Rome under Agatho, the Belief of Peter, Bishop of Lycomedia, the Confession of the heretical Macarius, are all framed on the same general lines as the Quicunque (omitting always the first two clauses) and they approach to it in general conception. Of these many are clumsy, verbose, wearisome. This is neat, concise, attractive; in every respect, save one, superior.

CHAPTER XX.

CREEDS AND RULES OF FAITH FOUND IN SYSTEMATIC COLLECTIONS OF CANONS AND CONSTITUTIONS.

§ 1. Quesnel's Collection and argument. § 2. The Exposition against the Arians. § 3. The Faith of Faustinus. § 4. "Fides Romanorum," attributed to Athanasius and to Augustine. § 5. "Augustini Libellus de Fide Catholica." § 6. The Creed of Jerome. § 7. Other attributed to Augustine. "Rogo et ammoneo. Quicunque vult, &c." § 8. St Blaise Collection. Account of the St Blaise manuscript. § 9. The other manuscripts. § 10. Paris, 3836. § 11. Consideration on the fragment. § 12. Comparison with our present text. § 13. Probable origin of the legend that Athanasius wrote the Quicunque. § 14. Bearing on the Canon of Autun, § 15. and on the Commonitory of Vincentius. § 16. Other collections containing the Quicunque. Vat. Pal. 574. § 17. Paris, 1451. § 18. Paris, 3848 B. § 19. Reflections. § 20. The "Hadriana." § 21. Vatican Collection. § 22. The Herovallian Collection and Canon of Autun. Appendix. Creeds of Faustinus, Pelagius, &c.

§ 1. Leaving for the present the history of Confessions of Faith put forth at any particular Council or Synod after the year 700, I would draw the attention of my readers to another source of information on which Waterland was silent. I refer to the old Collections of Canons and Constitutions, of which many contain documents of the nature of Creeds; some, as we shall see, contain copies of the Athanasian Creed. The Archdeacon was, however, aware of the nature of these collections, for in his first chapter, under the year 1675, we have the following:

"Our next man of eminent character is Paschasius Quesnel, a celebrated French Divine. In the year 1675 he published his famous edition of Pope Leo's works, with several very valuable dissertations of his own. His fourteenth contains, among other matters, a particular enquiry about the Author of this Creed. He ascribes it to Vigilius Tapsensis, the African, and so well defends his position that he has almost drawn the learned world after him. He is looked upon as the father of that opinion, because he has so learnedly and handsomely supported it; but he is not the first that espoused it."

The occasion on which Quesnel entered on the discussion was this:—

He had paid much attention to a Manuscript, which he considered to be of great antiquity, of "the Canons of the Church of Rome." He had received a transcript of this from Oxford, where the original was, and is, in the library of Oriel College. He considered it to be nearly 600 years old, *i.e.* of the eleventh century, but to have been a copy of a much earlier manuscript. Another manuscript of the same collection existed in the library of Augustus de Thou. This was of the ninth or tenth century[1].

The first-named manuscript contained some letters of Leo, and this fact furnished the motive for Quesnel's dissertations.

Of these the fourteenth is devoted to the consideration of various treatises or specimens of Creeds contained in this Oxford manuscript; and, in consequence, Quesnel entered on the question of the origin of the Athanasian Creed[2].

The manuscript contains canons of several early Councils, various edicts against Pelagianism, four decretals of Pope Innocent I. (402—417): Acts of the Council of Chalcedon: Constitutions of Valentinian and Marcian (about 450): some writings of Siricius, Zosimus, Boniface I., and Cœlestinus I. (432). Then come four formulæ of the Faith to which I must refer just now. And these are followed by letters written to or by Athanasius, Leo, and others; some genuine and others spurious.

Quesnel's surprise was excited by the fact that the Symbol of St Athanasius was not among these formulæ of the Faith, and he noted that in the famous letter of Pope Leo to the Emperor Leo (p. 134 or 166), where every one would expect mention to be made of the Creed of Athanasius if such a document had been known, the Pope was entirely silent regarding it. He remarked next that the Creed was never mentioned by any writer of the fifth century. But Quesnel believed that it must have existed in 670 "when it was mentioned by the Synod of

[1] Professor Maassen, in his *Geschichte der Quellen und der Literatur des canonischen Rechts im Abendlande*, Gratz, 1870, devotes a section to what, from Quesnel, he calls *die Quesnel'sche Sammlung*. He speaks of five other manuscripts as containing this collection. The oldest, Codex Lat. Paris, 3848 A, is of the end of the eighth or beginning of the ninth century: the Codex Einsidl. 191, is nearly of the same date. Another, Vienna, 2141, is of the ninth century, and a second at Paris, 1454, is of the ninth or tenth. And so is a second at Vienna, 2147, to which Professor Maassen devotes most attention (§ 618, pp. 486—500). The collection of Quesnel was republished by the brothers Ballerini in their beautiful edition of St Leo's works; and, from this, has been reprinted by Migne, Vol. LXVI. p. 339, &c.

[2] Migne, ut sup. 1041.

Autun;" nay, in 633, when portions of it seem to have been used by the Council of Toledo. Thus he was led to look out for some notable man before the earlier date, whom he might regard as likely to have composed it; and he fixed upon Vigilius of Tapsus, who was a warm defender of the Faith and living about the year 500; one of whose merits seems to have been, that things which he wrote under the pressure of persecution he put forth under the name of some more ancient Father or more celebrated Author.

Quesnel however felt some scruple in accepting the received date of this Council of Autun; and he says distinctly that he should not have ventured to do so if Sirmond, de la Lande, and Godfrey Hermant had not been positive on the subject. The MSS. of the Council do not help us to the date, nor have we any collateral information on the subject. "There is no more reason to fix this Synod of Autun to the time of St Ledger, than to that of any other bishop[1]."

I do not see that we have any reason to trouble ourselves with the conclusion to which Quesnel arrived. We have our own opportunities, greater than he had, of judging whether the Quicunque is older than 670 or 633. My object here is to draw attention to these older Formulæ of Faith which Quesnel's manuscript contained, and to others of a similar character; to discover the countries over which the knowledge of these formulæ extended; and then to search how far the *Quicunque* was embodied in other collections of a similar character.

I must mention that Professor Maassen arranges these collections of Canons under several heads: and I shall follow him in the names or titles by which he describes those which contain the documents to which I shall now refer.

§ 2. I shall pass over, of course, the Creeds of Nicæa and Constantinople. They are given, I believe, in every manuscript which contains the canons of the Councils of Nicæa and Chalcedon.

The first of the four Formulæ of Faith contained in this Quesnel collection (the four are numbered XXXVII., XXXVIII., XXXIX., XL.), is *An Exposition of the Catholic and Apostolic Faith against the Arian Heresy.* Some manuscripts entitle it simply *Expositio Fidei Catholicæ:* others simply *De Fide Catholica.* This is found not only in the Quesnel collection (Maassen, p. 394), but also in the collections i. of the MS. of Saint Blaise, which Prof. Maassen describes, p. 504: and ii. of the manuscript of Diessen, p. 624.

[1] Ballerini, III. p. 940. Migne, 1063.

Of the former, one manuscript is of the sixth century. Of course, therefore, the Creed is at least as old as the sixth century.

It is as follows[1]:

"We confess the Father, Son and Holy Spirit in a perfect Trinity, so that there shall be both a fulness of Divinity and a Unity of power. For he who separates the Godhead of the Trinity, speaks of Three Gods. The Father is God, the Son God, the Holy Ghost God, and the three are one (unum) in Christ Jesus. There are therefore three Persons but one Power. Diversity makes more than one, but unity of power excludes quantity of number, because unity is not a number. Therefore there is one God, one Faith, one Baptism. If any one has not this Faith he cannot be called a Catholic, because he does not hold the Catholic Faith. He is a liar, profane, and rebellious against the truth[2]."

§ 3. The next of the four is entitled, *The Faith of the Presbyter Faustinus, sent to Theodosius the Emperor.* It is contained only in this Quesnel collection[3]: and is from it copied into the edition of the Ballerini, III. p. 278; Walch, 202; Hahn, 190; and Migne, 582. I will give a copy of it below[4]. It was written to defend the opponents of Arius from the imputation of Sabellianism.

§ 4. The next formula was one of the greatest favourites of antiquity[5]. It is said by Maassen (p. 395) to be found in eight different series of collections: one manuscript is of the sixth century: two are of the eighth: thirteen of the eighth or ninth. It commences generally *Credimus in unum deum patrem omnipotentem et in unum unigenitum, &c.:* but sometimes we have *Credo* for *Credimus;* and *unum* is omitted. In the various collections noted by Maassen it is entitled, sometimes *Expositio fidei* and is attributed to Damasus (the second half is often separated and called *ejusdem sermo*), (pp. 507, 631); sometimes *alter libellus fidei* (p. 497); in a Vatican manuscript of the ninth or tenth century and elsewhere, it is called *fides catholice romane aecclesiae*[6] (pp. 460, 521); in another of the ninth, *fides romanorum* (pp. 606, 616). But a Creed so similar as to be ranked by the Ballerini with this (for it differs only in what we might call

[1] Ballerini, 277. Migne, 582. Maassen, 497.

[2] See the original in Appendix I.

[3] Maassen, § 353, p. 348.

[4] Appendix II.

[5] Ballerini, 279. Migne, 583.

[6] Did the Church of Rome refuse at first the Catholic faith of Athanasius?

various readings), is in two manuscripts described as Jerome's (it is printed in Jerome's works as *Damasi Symbolum*). An expanded form of it is printed by the Benedictines in the Appendix to Vol. v. of their edition of Augustine (Sermon CCXXXV. p. 2957, Gaume[1]). It was claimed by Chifflet as the work of Vigilius of Tapsus, but he speaks of it as being also assigned to Gregory of Nazianzus: Quesnel thinks it may have been written by Gregory "Bœticus," afterwards Bishop of Elvira. But one curious fact remains to be noticed. In several manuscripts it is ascribed to Athanasius, and placed at the end of the eight books on the Trinity, which are published in the Paris edition of Athanasius' works. In these MSS., the title generally runs thus: *Incipit libellus fidei Patris et Filii et Spiritus Sancti Athanasii episcopi.* It was so designated in *Sangerman.* 724, and I found it so in the *Arundel* manuscript, 241, of the British Museum. Migne reprints the work in his edition of Vigilius of Tapsus, and, therefore, omits it in his reprint of the Benedictine Athanasius. Montfaucon remarked that Hincmar quoted from the books as from a genuine work of Athanasius; and I have discovered that the Archbishop's famous quotation from what he calls the *Symbolum Athanasii* is taken from this *Libellus.* Usher too, who printed it (*De Symbolo Romano,* near the end), remarked that Ratram of Corbey quoted it as Athanasius'. This, therefore, was the belief regarding it in the ninth century, and as we know it was in existence in the sixth, the question arises whether it be not the "Faith of Athanasius" referred to in the Canon of Autun.

I print it in my Appendix III. in the form in which it is ascribed to Athanasius.

§ 5. The fourth of these Confessions which attracted the attention of Quesnel is known as *Augustini Libellus de Fide Catholica contra omnes Hæreses.* It used to be printed among St Augustine's works, being numbered *Sermo* 129 *de Tempore;* but we are told (Ballerini, p. 282) that it is not found in any manuscript of Augustine, and, therefore, it is now relegated to the Appendix of Vol. v. (No. 233 in the Benedictine edition, Gaume, v. p. 2950), except that the second series of anathemas there appended belong to a Faith different from this *Augustini*

[1] In the Cambridge Library there is a late manuscript in which it is called "Symbolum dictatum a beato Augustino."

Libellus, and are almost the same as are usually found amongst the anathemas of Damasus[1].

I print this also below, Appendix IV.

It is considered by some to be as old as the Council of Toledo in 400, where it is inserted in the Acts as *Regula Fidei*, and the Ballerini[2] have no hesitation in stating their opinion that it was known to Leo the Great in 447.

§ 6. I also print Appendix V., the so-called Creed of Jerome.

§ 7. But there were other expositions which found their way into these collections.

Thus an *expositio fidei* commencing *Profitemur nos credere*, published by Mai[3]: an *exemplar fidei Sancti Augustini*, which seems never to have been printed (it is found in a MS. of the IXth century). So a sermon falsely attributed to St Augustine[4]. *Sermo antequam symbolum tradatur*, commencing *Quæso vos fratres carissimi*, and ending, *vitam eternam: absque ulla dubitatione fatemur vos vitam eternam consecuturos si hæc quæ vobis exposuimus sacramenta fideliter teneatis et bonis actibus conservetis.* "Without any hesitation we confess that ye shall obtain eternal life if ye faithfully hold the mysteries we expound to you, and preserve them by a good life." This is found in two manuscripts of what is called the Herovallian collection. They are of the ninth century. The same manuscripts have another sermon which is sufficiently interesting for me to give an analysis of it[5]. I do not know the authority on which these two documents have found their way into the works of Augustine. In the two manuscripts in which Professor Maassen[6] found them they have no author's name assigned. The title of the one I have given above. The second is ushered in with the words *Item expositio fidei.* Gieseler considers that this sermon refers to the Athanasian Creed, and alludes to a belief of the Benedictine editors that its author was Cæsarius of Arles; but this (he adds) is mere conjecture[7].

This is a translation of the sermon: "I beseech and admonish you, dearest brethren, that whoever would be saved should learn the right and Catholic Faith, firmly hold it and preserve it inviolate. Thus then ought every one to observe, that he should believe that the Father is, believe that the Son is, believe that the Holy Spirit is. The

[1] Numbered 10—16, 18—24, in Hahn, pp. 181—183.

[2] Ballerini, p. 950. Maassen, 395.

[3] *Bibliotheca nova Patrum*, I. p. 463. (I take these references from Maassen, p. 349.)

[4] Augustin. v. Appendix CCXLII. (p. 2975).

[5] St Augustine's works, Vol. v. Appendix, *Sermo* CCXLIV. (Gaume, Vol. v. p. 2980.)

[6] Maassen, p. 396. See too his *Bibliotheca Latina juris Canonici manuscripta*. First part, II. pp. 214, 241. They are both Paris manuscripts numbered respectively 2123 and 3848 B, the latter contains the Athanasian Creed, of which below.

[7] Gieseler, *Third Period*, *Division* I. § 12, note 7. (Translation, Vol. II. p. 278.)

Father is God, the Son is God, and the Holy Ghost God; but yet not three Gods, but one God. Such as the Father is, such is the Son, and such is the Holy Ghost. And yet let every faithful one believe that the Son is equal to the Father as touching the Godhead, and is less than the Father as touching the manhood of the flesh, which He assumed of ours. And the Holy Ghost (is) proceeding from both. Believe, therefore, most beloved, in God the Father Almighty; believe too in Jesus Christ, His only Son, our Lord; believe that He was conceived of the Holy Ghost and born of the Virgin Mary, who was a virgin before His birth, and virgin ever after His birth, and continued without contagion or spot of sin. Believe that He for our sins suffered under Pontius Pilate; believe that He was crucified, dead and buried; believe that He descended into hell, that He bound the devil, and that He liberated the souls who were there detained in custody, and led them up, with Himself, to His heavenly country. Believe that He rose from the dead on the third day, and shewed to us an example of a Resurrection. Believe that He ascended to the heavens with the flesh which He assumed of ours (de nostro). Believe that He sitteth at the right hand of the Father; believe that He is coming to judge the quick and the dead. Believe in the Holy Spirit; believe that there is a Holy Catholic Church; believe that there is a Communion of Saints; believe that there is a Resurrection of the flesh; believe that there is a remission of sins; believe too that there is a life eternal.

"Therefore (it proceeds) if any one would be a disciple of Christ, let him keep His commandments; let him learn humility, as He Himself says, Learn of me, for I am meek and lowly of heart; let him pray God with his heart, because there are many who appear outwardly to humble themselves, but inwardly are full of the swellings of pride. But Christ humbled Himself for us. He took the form of a servant, being obedient to the Father, even to death and that the death of the cross. For us, brethren, in order that He might wipe away our sins, He assumed the human flesh; He was born of a virgin, laid in a manger, covered with swaddling clothes, by the Jews rejected, persecuted, apprehended, scourged, insulted with spittle, crowned with thorns, transfixed with nails, pierced with the lance, suspended on the cross, fed with vinegar mixed with gall, numbered with the transgressors. All these things, beloved, He underwent, that He might deliver us from the jaws of hell. Therefore, beloved, since the Lord sustained such things and so many things for us, we, if we would come to Him, ought to follow His steps and imitate the examples of His Saints. The Lord saith in the Gospel, If any one would come after Me, let him deny himself and take up his cross and follow Me. And elsewhere He says, Go, sell all that thou hast and come, follow Me. Holy martyrs, beloved, followed the steps of Christ, and drank of the cup of suffering which He drank. Peter the Apostle was crucified for the name of Christ; Paul beheaded; Stephen stoned; and others, very many, so suffered for His Name.

"Therefore, beloved, crucify and mortify your members which are upon the earth, that ye may be able to please Him Who created you. He that was proud, let him be humble; he that was unbelieving, let him be faithful; he that was luxurious, let him be chaste; let him who was a robber, become fit for duty; that was a drunkard, be sober; that was sleepy, be watchful; that was a miser, be bountiful; that was double-tongued, speak good things; that was a backbiter and envious, be pure and kind; let him who used to come late to Church, now hasten to it more frequently. Let every one redeem himself with an abundance of alms, because as water extinguisheth fire, so doth alms sin. Of all the fruit that ye collect, give a tenth each year to the churches and the poor. Love fasting; avoid gluttony and excess of wine. Feed the hungry, give drink to the thirsty, clothe the naked, seek out those that are in prison. Visit the weak, collect guests into your houses, wash their feet, wipe them with a towel, kiss them with your mouth, prepare their beds. Let no one commit murder, theft, adultery, perjury, or bear false witness. Let every one honour his father and mother, that he may live long on the earth. Let him love God more than himself; let him love his neighbour as himself. Whoever has committed any of the things that have been mentioned, let him speedily amend, let him give his confession; do true penitence, and his sins shall be remitted to him. If ye fulfil the commands which I have suggested, ye shall receive remission of sins and obtain eternal life from the hand of our Lord Jesus Christ, who liveth and reigneth for ever and ever. Amen."

The manuscript is of the ninth century; but the question is, What is the date of the document? The Apostle's Creed illustrated by it, omits *creatorem cœli et terræ;* it reads, *conceived of the Holy Ghost, &c.; the right hand of the Father.* This seems to be of the sixth or seventh century. Were the first words *Quicunque vult* taken from the Athanasian Creed? Or did they suggest the opening of the Athanasian Creed? These are questions which it is impossible to answer hastily. I must, however, notice that one manuscript which contains the document does not include the *Quicunque* in its contents (I refer to Paris, 2123): the other has it (do. 3848 B).

We may now enquire under what circumstances the Quicunque first appears in these collections.

§ 8. Amongst the series to the study of which Professor Maassen has devoted so many years of his life, is one which has the title *Collection of the Manuscripts of St Blaise,* from the character of the earliest copy of the Collection[1]. This is now, I understand, in the library of the monastery of St Paul in Kärnthen: it formerly belonged to the monastery of Augia, *i.e.* either Reichenau, or Rheinau, or Mehrerau. This manuscript is of the sixth century. The other manuscripts which contain the same collection are *Paris,* 3836 (*Colb.* 784) of the eighth century: one at

[1] Maassen, 504.

Cologne (*Darmst.* 2336) of the eighth: one at Lucca (490, formerly 89) of the time of Charlemagne: another at Paris (4279, *Colb.* 2489) of the ninth. Thus there are five in all. The learned Coustant has given an account of the Paris 3836 in the preface to his volume entitled *Epistolæ Romanorum Pontificum;* and Mansi an account of the Lucca manuscript, in a work entitled *D. Angelo Calogierà Raccolta d'Opusculi scientifici e filosofici*[1].

The St Blaise manuscript contains

1. The Nicene Canons of the Isidore version [2].
2. The Canons of Ancyra, Neocæsarea, and Gangra [7, &c.].
3. "Constituta quae aput Kartagine acta sunt" [15].
4. "Statuta quingentesimo anno sub imperatore piissimo Marciano constituta." (These are the Canons of Chalcedon, partly the old version, partly in that of Dionysius Exiguus.) [?].
5. Canons of Constantinople [?].
6. "Canones Serdicenses" [37].
7. "Constituta canonum Antiocensium" [43].
8. Five apocryphal pieces, viz.: Constitution of Sylvester, Acts of Liberius, Acts on the purgation of Sixtus, Acts regarding the accusation of Polychronius, and the Synod of Sinuessa [48, &c.].
9. Some writings of Siricius, Boniface I., Zosimus, Cœlestine I., Innocent I., Leo I. [62, &c.]. Then we have this:
10. "Incipit synodus episcopalis Calcedonensis habitus a quingentis viginti episcopis contra Euthicitem" [87]. This includes the Definition of Faith of the Council. At the end we read "Explicit synodum mundanum id est universalem apud Calcedona" [89].
11. "Incipit synodo Nicaeno scribta papae Damassi a Paulinum Antiocene urbis episcopum." Here follow the Nicene symbol, and the anathematisms of the synod of the year 378 under Damasus [89 verso].
12. "Incipit expositio fidei. *Credimus unum Deum*" [91].
13. "Incipit ejusdem sermo. *Credimus Jesum Christum*" [91].
14. The anti-Arian formula *Nos patrem* [91].

15, 16. Statutes and constitutions of Gelasius [93][2].

§ 9. The contents of the other four manuscripts are generally the same; and it seems pretty clear that this manuscript of St Blaise approaches nearest to the character of being the original collection. But when we go into details, we find that each of the five has peculiarities of its own: two contain documents which are absent from the others. Yet the "planless" though, generally

[1] I have seen Coustant's account and examined the Paris 3836 carefully. The information regarding the others I take from Maassen; but the number within brackets thus [7] represents the folio of 3836 on which the corresponding articles are found: these are from my own observation.

[2] According to Maassen in the Paris MS. there follows the letter of Innocent I. to Bishop Decentius of Gubbio.

speaking, uniform arrangement of the contents, shews, either that they are (with the exceptions named) copied one from another, or else that all are derived from some lost original.

§ 10. The Paris manuscript, 3836[1], alone contains a document which is to us of the deepest interest. Between the articles which I have numbered 10 and 11 of the St Blaise collection, *i.e.* after the words *explicit sinodum. mundanum. id est uniuersale. aput Calcedona.* which are in red; the writer proceeds in another line, still in red, *Hœc inuini treveris in uno libro scriptum. sic incipiente Domini nostri Ihesu Christi. et reliqua. Domini. nostri Ihesu Christi fideliter credat.* Then in black ink, *Est ergo fides recta.* The resemblance between this and the latter part of our Athanasian Creed has been marked from the time that the discovery was made, as I believe, by Antelmi. Montfaucon considered it to be "of an earlier date than Charlemagne, probably nine hundred years old," bringing it to the year 760: other skilled witnesses regarded it as of the time of Pepin: but I believe that the opinion is now nearly uniform that the manuscript was written about the year 730.

The manuscript proceeds as follows:

Est ergo fides recta
ut credamus et confitemur quia dominus ihesus christus dei filius. deus pariter et homo est. deus est
de substantia patris ante saecula genitus. et homo de substantia matris in saeculo natus. perfectus deus. per
fectus homo ex anima rationabili. et humana carne subsistens
aequalis patri saecundum diuinitatem minor patri. saecundum humanita
tem qui licet deus. sit homo non duo tamen sed unus est christus. Unus autem non ex eo
quod sit in carne. conuersa divinitas. sed quia est in deo adsumpta dignanter
humanitas. unus christus est non confusione substantiæ sed unitatem personæ
qui saecundum fidem nostram passus et mortuus ad inferna discendens. et die

[1] This manuscript has long attracted a great deal of attention from palæographers. It furnished many illustrations to the Benedictine editors of the *Nouveau Traité de Diplomatique*, see *Tab.* 36. III. 1. 1, 2, and IV. and VI. *Table* 49. II. V. 1, and 50. III. VI. and thence the INVINI TREVERIS found its way into Astley's History of Writing, and other books. Professor Westwood informs me that several pages are copied in Count Bastard's magnificent work. The two pages have been printed in facsimile (except the colours) for the members of the Palæographical Society.

tertia resurrexit adque ad celos ascendit. ad dexteram dei patris sedet sicut
uobis in simbulo tradutum est. Inde ad iudicandos uiuos et mortuos. credimus
et speramus eum esse uenturum. ad cujus aduentum erunt omnes homines. sine dubio
in suis corporibus resurrecturi et reddituri de factis propriis rationem ut qui bona
egerunt eant in uitam aeternam qui mala in ignem aeternum. Haec est fides sancta
et Catholica. quam omnes homo qui ad uitam aeternam peruenire desiderat scire integrae debet. et fideliter custodire.

It proceeds with the subject numbered above as 11 of St Blaise

INCIPIT DE SINODO NICAENO SCRIPTA PAPE
DAMASI AD PAULINUM ANTIOCHENAE URBIS EPISCOPUM.

The first line having yellow, green, and brown capitals: the second being chiefly in red uncials.

This fragment was, I believe, never printed consecutively until I published it in the autumn of 1871[1]. Montfaucon, and therefore, of course, Waterland, represented the manuscript as containing merely a copy of the Athanasian Creed, which might be compared with the received text in the ordinary way of exhibiting various readings. The brothers Ballerini[2] simply say that "it contains *Est ergo fides recta* &c. *usque ad finem.*" A very little consideration will shew that this gives a very imperfect, and, indeed, erroneous view of the subject.

For, first of all, the fragment, as it was found by the writer of this manuscript (Paris, 3836), was evidently part of an address of a preacher to his congregation. As to the purport of the preceding part of the address, we are left in the most complete ignorance; and, therefore, any amount of surmise is legitimate. We may, therefore, note that the sermon was found at the beginning of a book, *i.e.* it would appear that only a few leaves had been torn away. Again, it clearly had not been known previously to the copyist; for he was struck with its appropriateness as connected with and illustrative of the Definition of Faith of the fourth Council on the

1 "Further investigations as to the origin and object of the Athanasian Creed," by the present writer: my attention had been drawn to it by Professor Westcott.

2 Leo's works, III. p. 959. Migne, ut sup. 1075.

Incarnation. Again, although the writer was a travelled man, he had not met anywhere else with a complete copy of the address. The inference seems to be inevitable, as Professor Maassen suggests, that this was an entirely new discovery; and that the latter part of the Quicunque could not have been generally known at the time that the discovery was made. I gladly avail myself of an expression of opinion by the distinguished Professor Stubbs: "The Athanasian Creed could not have formed part of the education of the ordinary clerk at the beginning of the eighth century."

§ 11. I say then that this fragment, discovered at Treves, bears unquestionable marks that it was an address to persons under instruction, and that it was to a certain extent an Expositiou of the Apostles' Creed. The teacher refers to the Creed twice: *Who, according to our Faith, suffered; He sitteth at the right hand of God the Father, as is delivered to you in the Symbol.* It is thus analogous to those numerous Expositions of the Symbol which we find, among the writings, or in the Appendix to the writings, of St Augustine.

Looking at the photograph of the manuscript very carefully, any one may see that the line which begins *de substantia patris*, has been rewritten; and a very careful inspection will shew that it was rewritten on purpose to introduce the words *ante sæcula genitus*. At what period these words were inserted we cannot of course discover. I will merely mention now that the same words were not contained originally in the Ambrosian copy, to which I shall speedily call attention.

§ 12. On comparing this fragment with the present version of the Quicunque, we shall see, I think, that the "antithetical swing" of which we have heard so much, the parallelism which renders it so well adapted for chanting, was not developed in the early form to the extent in which it is developed now. From the fact that the words *Domini nostri Jesu Christi fideliter credat* were in red letters, not black, I conjecture that it was fully understood by the copyist that they were not part of the Credenda of the document, but were introductory to those Credenda; as if they were part of the framework or setting of the Creed. Thus comparing this version with our present text, I note the following differences:

In our clause 30, *noster* has been introduced, but *pariter* has been omitted:

in our clause 31, *ante sæcula genitus* has been introduced:

in 32 we read *rationali* where the manuscript had *rationabili:*

our clause 35 is read in an entirely different way, the rhythm being, comparatively speaking, very imperfect in the manuscript:

our clause 37 (which is really Augustinian) does not appear at all:

in our 38, *secundum fidem nostram* has disappeared, but *pro salute nostra* has been added:

mortuus has dropped out:

we have *descendit ad inferos* where the manuscript had *ad inferna descendens:*

we have introduced *a mortuis;*

in 39 we have introduced *omnipotentis;* and have left out all reference to the *simbulum:*

the alteration as to the judgment is immaterial, but we must notice the words *credimus et speramus:*

in 40, for *erunt...sine dubio in suis corporibus resurrecturi*, we have *resurgere habent cum corporibus suis*[1]:

in 41, for *et qui...ibunt,* the manuscript has *ut qui...eant.*

The summary is different. For our well-known words the manuscript reads: *Hæc est fides sancta et catholica quam omnis homo qui ad vitam eternam pervenire desiderat scire integre debet et fideliter custodire:* "This is the holy and Catholic Faith, which every one who desires to attain eternal life ought to know entirely and guard faithfully."

§ 13. I believe that every person who has devoted any attention to this most interesting document since Usher's Cottonian manuscript has been rediscovered, has come to the conclusion that this Treves fragment must have furnished the lines on which the latter part of the Quicunque was framed, as well as the occasion of ultimately referring the whole document to Athanasius. It was known that Athanasius had taken refuge at Treves,—what more satisfactory than to suggest that he was the writer of the paper[2]? Certainly those who have been satisfied for years with

[1] On this use of *habeo* see a note below.

[2] The Benedictines who prepared the *Nouveau Traité* seem to have considered

the arguments of Waterland to shew that Hilary of Arles compiled the Quicunque, have no reason to quarrel with such a conclusion, so easily taken up. There were other notable men besides Hilary in the fifth century; but there was no one more notable than Athanasius connected with Treves[1].

that this was the origin of the tradition. They must have thrown on one side all difficulty as to the Canon of Autun.

[1] I have not thought it necessary to refer to the *Sylloge dissertationum* of Galland, where (on pp. 35, &c., and 134, &c.) notes are given of this manuscript and of another at Paris numbered 3268 or 3368, which is said to contain a similar series of documents. I suppose that Professor Maassen's work has superseded all earlier dissertations. I would however ask attention to two illustrations which these pages offer of the change from the Latin of classical times to the French of the modern age.

(1) In regard to *unus*. *Hæc invini in uno libro* = dans un livre. On *unus* Ducange has the following: "UNUS pro *quidam:* quomodo dicimus *un.* Vetus Charta Hispanica apud Bivarium ad Chron. Maximi, p. 330, *Et unus discipulus proterva mente respondit.* Hispani dicerent, *Un disciputo respondio.* Vita S. Wunebaldi, cap. 30, *Evenit ut unus homo vinctus diceretur.* Adde Hodæporicum S. Willebaldi, n. 14, 15. Vorstium de Latinitate falso suspecta et Olaum Borrichium de variis linguæ Latinæ ætatibus, pag. 265."

(2) The *Resurrecturi erunt* of the Colbertine manuscript was altered to *Resurgere habent* = *ressusciter-ont.* On this I will again quote Ducange. "HABERE, velle, vel debere. Lib. I. Capitular. c. 61. *Qui in sanctis habet jurare, hoc jejunus faciat,* &c. Rupertus abb. in vita S. Heriberti Archiep. Colon. n. 23. *Currens affer illum ad me, ego enim eum habeo baptizare.* Num. 26. *Ipse enim, quia ægrotat, habeo eum visitare.* Fulbertus Carnot. Epist. 102. *Rex proximo rugitu, ut dicitur, venire habet in silvam Legium,* &c....Leges Luitprandi Regis Longob. tit. 108, § 1. *Veni et occide dominum tuum, et ego tibi facere habeo bonitatem quam volueris.* Mox: *Feri eum adhuc, nam si non feriveris, ego te ferire habeo.* Statuta ordinis S. Gilberti: *omnes Canonici, qui Sacerdotes non fuerint, omni die Dominica habent communicare,* id est tenentur. Occurrit ibi pluries: formula loquendi a veteribus etiam usitata. Vide Pœnitentiale Theodori, c. 3. Juretum ad Symmachum, Lib. I. Epist. 26, et Cerdam in Adven. Sacr. cap. 17, num. 3. Vide Glossar. med. Græcit. in ἔχειν."

Rönsch, "Itala und Vulgata," p. 447, gives additional instances of this use in the translation of Irenæus, in Tertullian, Cyprian, Ambrose, Lactantius. Thus *qui pro salute nostra pati habuit.* In Haddan and Stubbs, III. p. 96 (A. D. 653) I find *tu mori habes.* See too Sir G. Cornwall Lewis' well-known volume.

Before we leave this manuscript I would mention that it has for many years attracted a great amount of attention. The Benedictines who edited the wonderful *Nouveau Traité de Diplomatique,* remarked, Vol. III. p. 70, that we find in it notes full of solecisms; and they comment upon the barbarous Latin in which the additions made by the transcriber are composed, and, conceiving that it was written at Rome, make some contemptuous remarks on the state of scholarship at the Papal city at the time. (Professor Maassen however adduces evidence that the collection was probably made North of the Alps.) They remark (as others have done) on the spurious pieces contained in it: but we have seen that these are in the earliest "edition" of it, in that of the sixth century. They say that two whole quires are inserted in the manuscript, and that at the end of folio 47, and on folio 51, there are memoranda which shake the character of the document. Again, on folio 53, they say there is another forged piece for which Baronius "sweats blood and water" (!) to prove its genuineness. This is about Xystus. Another forgery Baronius abandons, although Pope Nicholas quotes it as genuine. Folio 67 contains the pretended Council of Sinuessa. All these (they say) are written in a hand different from that of the earlier pages. After a while the old hand appears again. They are inclined to suspect some fraud: the quires are in much disorder, some consist of six folios, some of twelve, others of four, others of three because one has been cut out, others of two be-

§ 14. This investigation seems to sweep away all thought that the Canon of Autun, if published before 730, could have reference to our Quicunque as it is. For Treves and Autun are not very far apart, although the latter was in the province of Lyons. At all events it is difficult to believe that the Quicunque was so well known at Autun in 670, that every priest and deacon was required to repeat it by heart, whilst fifty or sixty years later our "travelled man" was content with copying the fragment that he found at Treves. The *Faith of Athanasius* mentioned at Autun is more probably the same as the *Symbolum Athanasii* of Hincmar.

§ 15. There is, however, a connection between the Treves copy and the Commonitory of Vincentius. Words used by Vincentius, but unknown or unused in the versions of Chalcedon, appear once more here. The phrase *in sæculo natus* is one. Again, Vincent had nothing bearing on the comparison between the constitution of man, and the constitution of the Incarnate Son of God.—The clause is omitted here.

§ 16. Out of the large number of collections which Professor Maassen has examined by himself or friends, there are three others which contain the Athanasian Creed.

One manuscript is in the Vatican, having come thither from the Palatinate Library. Its origin was Lorsch.

The collection is different from others. The manuscript is of the ninth century according to Reifferscheid. In the catalogue it is numbered Vat. Pal. 574. It contains a series of synodical canons, the later ones entirely Gallican; almost all these are in chronological order. The latest is of the year 549. It has one sermon of St Augustine's. Towards the end of the book we have:

Incipit fides catholica atanasi episcopi Quicumque vult salvus esse[1].

cause two have been removed, either before or after the manuscript was bound. The quires have no signatures. Unluckily it was rebound by Colbert. "These new bindings are very injurious to old manuscripts."

They observe moreover (p. 67 note) that, after the letter of Innocent to Decentius, we may note the names of the Books of Scripture "which were read in the Church of St Peter." On this they conclude that the manuscript was written at Rome. If the note is not found in the other "editions" we may perhaps infer that the writer had at least extended his travels to Rome.

[1] Maassen, p. 590.

§ 17. Another is at Paris, 1451[1] (Colber. 1868). This contains, after folio 25, a long series of Canons, the later ones again of French Councils (including, however, the Canons of Toledo, "when Reccared was converted").

But on the first 24 folia is a series of papers of great interest to us. The first fixes the date as after March 25, 793. The second is *Incipit exemplar fidei sancti Athanasii Alexandriæ ecclesiae. Quicunque vult*, &c.[2] Then a copy of the faith of St Augustine. Then *Interrogationes de trinitate et unitate patris et filii et spiritus sancti. Interroget, Dic mihi*, &c. Then the "Creed of St Jerome," really the creed of Pelagius, to which I have drawn attention. After which, *Statuta antiqua ecclesiae*, and some apocryphal pieces attributed to Jerome and Damasus. After the Councils, we have the *Fides Romanorum*, of which I have already spoken. Then the Nicene Creed, and, after a while, again, *Adcansi* (i.e. Athanasii) *sanctissimi episcopi Alexandriae adversus Arrium*, the collection of quotations used in the Council of Ephesus.

§ 18. A third is 3848 B (*Bibliotheca*, II. p. 241), of the early ninth century. These three volumes in which the Quicunque appears are clearly of French origin. Their date is after the year 793 or 800[3].

§ 19. The force of this evidence can only be appreciated when we learn that the Canons of the Councils which are contained in these two manuscripts, Vat. Pal. 574, and Paris, 1451, are contained also, speaking generally, in ten or more other collections, including on the whole more than thirty manuscripts, but the Athanasian Creed is only in these two. Of the others some are of the sixth century, some of the seventh, some of the eighth. But not one of the early copies contains the Quicunque. Their history is this. When a Frank Synod met, it was the rule to read over Canons of earlier Synods, and to signify in what points the meeting was prepared to dissent from such earlier rules[4]. Thus the Canons gradually accumulated, and we now see the meaning of the fact to which I have invited attention. Although several of the earlier manuscripts contain the documents I print in my Appendix, and these documents were afterwards copied again and again, we come to the extreme

1 Maassen, p. 614.

2 M. Delisle gives it *fidei cht sci*, i.e. *catholicæ sancti?*

3 I am indebted through Professor Jones to Père Martinoff, the eminent Russian savant, for a collation of these Paris manuscripts.

4 See Maassen, p. 186.

end of the eighth century or to the beginning of the ninth before we find any trace in these collections of the *Quicunque vult salvus esse.*

§ 20. It is surely worthy of remark that the Quicunque is not contained in any manuscript of the collection called the "Hadriana," *i.e.* the collection which Hadrian transmitted to Charlemagne. Of this there is an enlarged edition containing some of the Confessions of Faith to which I have drawn attention[1]. The manuscripts of this series are more than seventy in number, and of these at least twenty-six are assigned to the eighth or ninth century.

§ 21. What is called the Collection of the Vatican Manuscript contains some of these Confessions but not the Quicunque[2].

§ 22. The famous Canon of Autun really comes before us in a systematized collection, and should therefore be treated of here rather than in the last chapter. It is thus found in a manuscript at Einsiedeln (205) of the ninth century.

"Can. gustodunens Neri. Si quis presbyter diaconus subdiaconus vel clericus symbolum quod inspirante Sancto Spiritu Apostoli tradiderunt et fidem sancti Athanasii præsulis irreprehensibiliter non recensuerit ab episcopo condemnetur[3]."

"If any presbyter, deacon, subdeacon or clerk, cannot repeat without fault the Symbol, which under the inspiration of the Holy Spirit, the Apostles have handed down, and the Faith of the prelate Saint Athanasius, let him be condemned by the bishop."

This Canon is found in manuscripts of two collections, called respectively the Herovallian and that of the manuscript of Anjou. Of the latter there are six manuscripts extant, one of the eighth or ninth, the rest of the ninth century: all contain Canons of various Councils and Synods (most of the later being Gallican), down to one at Autun under St Leodgar[4]. Of the other, there are four

[1] Maassen, p. 457, no. LXXXVI. and p. 460, nos. CXXII. CXXIII. CXXIV.

[2] *Ibid.* p. 517, no. XXXVI., and 521, no. XC.

[3] I will not answer for the spelling (except in the title) nor indeed for the exact text, for some of the manuscripts omit subdiaconus entirely. Tentzel, p. 58. The title is taken from a paper of Professor Maassen's in the *Sitzungsberichte der philos. hist. Cl. der kaiserli. Akademie der Wissenschaften*, 1867, p. 205.

[4] Maassen, p. 821, &c., §§ 859—865.

manuscripts of the ninth century, three of the tenth and eleventh[1]. The Herovallian bears strong marks that it is a kind of revision of the former. The Canons are generally arranged under subjects; and under Cap. XLV. of the Anjou, LI. of the Herovallian collection, we find some "de monachis et monasteriis[2]." And here we have inserted Canons I., V., VI., VIII., X., XV., of a series put forth by "St Leodgar, Bishop of Autun, with the consent of his brethren[3]." These may be seen in Mansi[4]. There is some doubt as to the year when they were promulgated, opinions differing whether they should be assigned to 663, or 666, or 670. In two manuscripts of the Anjou collection (Paris, 1603; Cologne, Darmstadt, 2179), at the very beginning, before the table of contents, is found this Canon of Autun[5] which is interesting us; and as I understand, it is also found under the first title in all the manuscripts of the collection of Herouvalle[6]. The learned Jesuit, Sirmond, was the first to discover this Canon in a manuscript belonging to the Church of Dijon, now, I am afraid, lost; and printed it in his magnificent *Concilia Antiqua Galliæ*, Vol. I. 507.

Sirmond "guessed" (*autumavit*) that the canon might be assigned to the Council of Autun under Leodgar, although in every manuscript where it is found it is dissociated from the Council. And the process by which his guess was upheld is rather amusing.

This NERI of the Einsiedeln Codex is given in the Paris manuscript as HIRA PRIMA[7]. It was assumed[8] that HIRA meant AERA, and that AERA I. was a mistake for AERAE DCCI. This would correspond to A.D. 663, when Leodgar was bishop.

"Therefore, &c. Q.E.D."

Tentzel asks, Why not read DCCCI or DCCCCI? *i.e.* A.D. 763 or 863? The evidence is just as satisfactory.

Thus we shall probably agree with Natalis Alexander and Tentzel, that the evidence afforded by this Canon as to the existence of the Quicunque in the year 663 is of a somewhat "slippery character[9]." And, perhaps, I may be excused if I

[1] Maassen, p. 828, &c., §§ 866—870.
[2] Maassen, 823, and 830 (misprinted 380).
[3] Maassen, 969, 971.
[4] *Concilia*, XI. 123.
[5] Maassen, p. 823.
[6] *Ibid.* p. 830.
[7] There is a facsimile in the *Nouveau Traité*, Vol. III., Plate 38.
[8] By Le Cointe. See Tentzel.
[9] Si omnia accuratius ponderaveris lubricam admodum deprehendes Canonis illius auctoritatem. Tentzel, p. 59.

express my regret and surprise that Waterland, acknowledging as he did in his Chapter II., that the evidence can amount to no more than probable presumption or conjecture, should yet insert the date 670 in his table at the end of the chapter without a note of hesitation or doubt, and subsequently appeal to this date as confirming his argument in regard to the supposed knowledge of the document by Venantius Fortunatus[1]. But an increased acquaintance with the technical knowledge of the old collections shews to us, that this Canon cannot have been put forth in the Council held under St Leodgar. For it is now known that the word *Hira* was used for *Canon*, and *Hira prima* meant *First Canon or Chapter*. The editors of the *Nouveau Traité* give another facsimile from the Paris Codex, 1603, "Canon Nicen. Hira X.," beginning *Quicunque de lapsis*. So we have in copies of this same collection[2] "Can. Sardicensis hera XIII.:" "In Synodo Tolitanæ urbis in Spaniis, hera XII.:" "Canon Cartagii, hera XXIII.:" "In ipso can. Cartagin. hera XXIIII." Thus "Canones Augustodunenses. hera prima," means "First Canon." But of the Synod held under St Leodgar we have a First Canon of a different character. So the rule before us cannot belong to the Synod held under him: and the words of the Vienna manuscript, 2171 (Maassen, p. 969), preclude us from supposing that he held a second. Thus the evidence that this canon belongs to the end of the seventh century completely breaks down[3]. And I am afraid that the troubles which St Leodgar had to meet were of such a kind as to preclude him from enforcing the knowledge of the Quicunque. The monks in those days were too riotous to listen to such a direction as this. Aigulf, Abbot of Lerins, who merely wished to keep order in his monastery, was abused, banished, and in 675 murdered. And St Leodgar himself was put to death by the Major domûs Ebrun in 678[4]. It is not unlikely that he was the

[1] Waterland, chap. VI.

[2] Maassen, p. 824, 825. This Codex met with much attention from the editors of the *Nouveau Traité*, III. They assigned it to the eighth century, Maassen to the ninth. See also their plates, 46. III. ii. iii.: 51. IV. i. v., and II. iv. 2, and 54. VIII. ii., as well as plates 38 and 39. On the word *æra*, see their Vol. III. p. 100.

[3] To me it is interesting to note that one of the Paris Codices which contains the Canon contains also the Quicunque. I refer to 3848 B, from which I shall print a collation. The connection will shew that the supposition of Papebrochius (over which Waterland spends some time) is untenable, viz.: that the Faith of Athanasius in the Canon meant the Nicene Creed. It may have been the title for the Creed of which I have spoken above, p. 257.

[4] Gieseler, *Translation*, Vol. II. p. 187, note 2.

author of another Canon attributed to him, to the effect that "no one filled with food, or elated with wine, should presume to touch the sacrifice or offer the mass[1]."

We must not, however, forget that the Canon is found in five manuscripts of the ninth century, and one of the eighth or ninth. It has, therefore, great antiquity; and our ultimate judgment of its purport will be formed, as on a question of probabilities. Which of the many documents that have been entitled *The Faith of Athanasius*, is it likely would be associated with the Apostles' Creed in the Rule before us?

[1] "Nullus presbyter confertus cibo aut crapulatus vino (cf. Ps. lxxvii. 65 vulg.) sacrificia contrectare aut missas facere præsumat: quod, si quis præsumpserit amittat honorem." Mansi, XI. 125. Does this throw any light upon the history of Fasting Communion?

There is an interesting account of St Leodgar in Duchesne (Vol. I. p. 600, Paris, 1696). Amongst other things it is mentioned that he instructed the clergy in the Divine Offices.

In the same volume there is a letter to Queen Chlodosainda from Archbishop Nicetus, who, I suppose, is the Nicetus to whom the TE DEUM has been ascribed. He urges the Queen to strive to bring her husband over to the Catholic Faith. He warns her against those who preach two gods: "Alium Deitate Patrem, alterum in Deitate sed pro creatura Filium" (p. 854 B). He draws near to the condemnation of our Quicunque when he says, "In the day of the Resurrection he will not be able to abide or to appear, who has not believed the Trinity in Unity." (In die resurrectionis nec manere nec apparere poterit, qui Trinitatem in Unitate non crediderit. Compare the Latin of our last clause, above p. 205). He says "Non tres sancti sed ter sanctum: dixit, Dominus Deus Zabaoth, Sanctus Pater, sanctus Filius, sanctus Spiritus: unus Sanctus, sicut unus Dominus." There is not a word regarding the Faith of St Athanasius.

I have adduced evidence enough to shew that the quotation adduced by the Ballerini (*Leonis Opera*, Vol. III. p. 954) of an old canon, in which "all priests, deacons and subdeacons were enjoined to know by memory the Catholic Faith, and if any one omitted to do so he was to abstain from wine for forty days," cannot be assumed to refer to the Quicunque. The manuscripts (*Barbarini* 2888 and *Vat.* 1342) are very old and must be very interesting, but this canon is of the same character as those which I have adduced from the Capitulars and elsewhere (pp. 181, 192).

APPENDIX I.

Expositio fidei catholicæ atque apostolicæ contra hæresim Arianam.

Nos Patrem, et Filium, et Spiritum sanctum confitemur, ita in Trinitate perfecta, ut et plenitudo sit Divinitatis, et unitas potestatis. Nam tres Deos dicit qui Divinitatem separat Trinitatis. Pater Deus, Filius Deus, Spiritus sanctus Deus, et tres unum sunt in Christo Jesu. Tres itaque Personæ, sed una potestas. Ergo diversitas plures facit; unitas vero potestatis excludit numeri quantitatem: quia unitas numerus non est. Itaque unus Deus, una Fides, unum Baptisma. Si quis vero hanc fidem non habet, catholicus non potest dici, quia catholicam non tenet fidem; alienus est, profanus est, et adversus veritatem rebellis.

APPENDIX II.

Faustini presbyteri fides missa Theodosio imperatori.

Sufficiebat fides conscripta apud Nicæam adversus hæresim Arianam. Sed quia pravo ingenio quidam sub illius fidei confessione impia verba commutant, nobis invidiam facientes, quod velut hæresim Sabellii tueamur, paucis et contra Sabellium primæ fidei confessione signamus et contra hos, qui sub nomine catholicæ fidei impia verba defendunt, dicentes tres esse substantias, cum semper catholica fides unam substantiam Patris, et Filii, et Spiritus sancti, confessa sit.

Nos Patrem credimus, qui non sit Filius, sed habeat Filium de se sine initio genitum, non factum; et Filium credimus, qui non sit Pater, sed habeat Patrem, de quo sit genitus, non factus; et Spiritum sanctum credimus, qui sit vere Spiritus Dei. Unde et divinæ Trinitatis unam substantiam confitemur: quia qualis est Pater secundum substantiam, talem genuit et Filium; et Spiritus sanctus non creatura existens, sed Spiritus Dei, non est alienus a substantia Patris et Filii, sed est ejusdem et ipse substantiæ cum Patre et Filio, sicut ejusdem Deitatis. Nam qui nos putant esse Apollinaristas, sciant quod non minus Apollinaris hæresim exsecramur quam Arianam. Miramur autem illos catholicos probari posse, qui Patris, et Filii, et Spiritus sancti, tres substantias confitentur. Sed et si dicunt non se credere Filium Dei aut Spiritum sanctum creaturam, tamen contra impiam fidem sentiunt cum dicunt tres esse substantias: consequens est enim ut tres Deos confiteantur, qui tres substantias confitentur. Quam vocem semper catholici exsecrati sunt.

APPENDIX III.

Alter libellus fidei.

Credimus unum Deum, Patrem omnipotentem, et unum unigenitum Filium ejus Deum et Dominum Salvatorem nostrum, et Spiritum sanctum

Deum: non tres deos Patrem, et Filium, et Spiritum sanctum, sed unum Deum esse confitemur. Non sic unum Deum, quasi solitarium; nec eumdem, qui ipse sibi Pater sit, ipse et Filius; sed Patrem verum, qui genuit Filium verum, ut est Deus de Deo, lumen de lumine, vita ex vita, perfectum de perfecto, totum a toto, plenum a pleno; non creatum, sed genitum; non ex nihilo, sed ex Patre, unius substantiæ cum Patre: Spiritum vero sanctum Deum, non ingenitum, neque genitum, non creatum, nec factum; sed Patris et Filii, semper in Patre et Filio coæternum. Veneramur tamen unum Deum; quia ex uno Patre totum quod Patris est, natus est, Filius Deus, et in Patre totum quod inest, totum genuit Filium. Pater Filium generans non minuit, nec amisit plenitudinis suæ deitatem, totum autem quod Deus Pater est, id esse et Filium ab eo natum, certissime tenentes. Cum Spiritu sancto unum Deum piissime confitemur Jesum Christum Dominum nostrum, Dei Filium, per quem omnia facta sunt quæ in cœlis et quæ in terra, visibilia et invisibilia: propter nostram salutem descendit de cœlo, qui nunquam desierit esse in cœlo natus de Spiritu sancto ex Virgine Maria. Verbum caro factum, non amisit quod fuerat, sed cœpit esse quod non erat. Non demutatum, sed permanentem, etiam hominem natum, non putative, sed vere; non aerium, sed corporeum; non phantasticum, sed carneum; ossa, sanguinem, sensum, et animam habentem, ita verum Deum et verum hominem intelligimus; ita verum hominem, verum Deum fuisse nullo modo ambigimus. Confitendum est hunc eumdem Dominum nostrum Jesum Christum adimplesse legem et prophetas, passum sub Pontio Pilato, crucifixum secundum Scripturas, mortuum et sepultum secundum Scripturas, tertia die a mortuis resurrexisse, assumptum in cœlos, sedere ad dexteram Patris, inde venturum judicare vivos et mortuos. Exspectamus in hujus morte et sanguine mundatos, remissionem peccatorum consecutos, resuscitandos nos ab eo in his corporibus et in eadem carne qua nunc sumus; sicut et ipse in eadem carne qua natus est, et passus, et mortuus, resurrexit; et animas cum hac carne vel corpora nostra ab eo, aut vitam æternam, præmium boni meriti, aut sententiam pro peccatis æterni supplicii recepturos.

APPENDIX IV.

Libellus Augustini de fide catholica contra omnes hæreses.

Credimus in unum verum Deum, Patrem, et Filium, et Spiritum sanctum, visibilium et invisibilium factorem, per quem creata sunt omnia in cœlo et in terra. Hunc unum Deum, et hanc unam divini nominis esse Trinitatem. Patrem non esse Filium, sed habere Filium, qui Pater non sit; Filium non esse Patrem, sed Filium Dei esse natura; Spiritum quoque Paraclitum esse, qui nec Pater sit ipse, nec Filius, sed a Patre procedat. Est ergo ingenitus Pater, genitus Filius, non genitus Paraclitus, sed a Patre procedens. Pater est cujus vox est hæc audita de cœlis: *Hic est Filius meus dilectus, in quo mihi bene complacui; ipsum audite:* Filius est qui ait: *Ego a Patre exivi, et a Deo veni in hunc mundum.* Paraclitus ipse est de quo Filius ait: *Nisi abiero ad Patrem*

Paraclitus non veniet ad vos. Hanc Trinitatem personis distinctam, substantiam unam, virtutem, potestatem, majestatem, indivisibilem, indifferentem. Præter illam nullam divinam esse naturam, vel angeli, vel spiritus, vel virtutis alicujus, quæ Deus esse credatur. Hunc igitur Filium Dei, Deum natum a Patre ante omne omnino principium, sanctificasse uterum Mariæ Virginis, atque ex ea verum hominem, sine viri generatum semine, suscepisse: id est, Dominum Jesum Christum, non imaginarium corpus, aut forma sola compositum, sed solidum; atque hunc et esurisse, et sitisse, et doluisse, et flevisse, et omnia corporis exitia sensisse; postremo crucifixum, mortuum et sepultum, tertia die resurrexisse; conversatum postmodum cum discipulis, misisse ipsis Paraclitum, dum ad cœlos ipse ascendisset. Hunc Filium hominis vocari veraciter credimus vel confitemur. Resurrectionem veram humanæ credimus carnis; animam autem hominis non divinam esse substantiam vel Dei partem, sed creaturam divina voluntate factam, non de cœlo lapsam.

Si quis ergo dixerit vel crediderit a Deo omnipotente mundum hunc factum non fuisse, atque ejus omnia instrumenta; anathema sit.

Si quis crediderit atque dixerit Deum Patrem eumdem Filium esse, vel Paraclitum; anathema sit.

Si quis dixerit atque crediderit Dominum Filium eumdem esse, vel Patrem, vel Paraclitum; anathema sit.

Si quis dixerit Paraclitum Spiritum eumdem esse vel Patrem, vel Filium; anathema sit.

Si quis dixerit atque crediderit hominem Jesum Christum a Filio Dei assumptum non fuisse; anathema sit.

Si quis dixerit atque crediderit Filium Dei Deum passum; anathema sit.

Si quis dixerit atque crediderit hominem Jesum Christum hominem impassibilem fuisse; anathema sit.

Si quis dixerit atque crediderit alterum Deum esse priscæ legis, alterum Evangeliorum; anathema sit.

Si quis dixerit atque crediderit ab altero Deo mundum fuisse factum quam ab illo de quo scriptum est: *In principio Deus fecit cœlum et terram:* qui solus Deus verus est; anathema sit.

Si quis dixerit atque crediderit corpora humana non resurrectura post mortem; anathema sit.

Si quis dixerit atque crediderit animam humanam Dei portionem vel Dei esse substantiam; anathema sit.

Si quis aliquas Scripturas præter eas quas catholica Ecclesia recipit, vel in auctoritatem habendas esse crediderit, vel fuerit veneratus; anathema sit.

APPENDIX V.

Hieronymi Fides.

Credimus in Deum, et Patrem omnipotentem, cunctorum visibilium et invisibilium conditorem. Credimus et in Dominum nostrum Jesum Christum, per quem creata sunt omnia, verum Deum, unigenitum et verum

Dei Filium, non factum aut adoptivum, sed genitum, et unius cum Patre substantiæ, quod Græci dicunt ὁμοούσιον: atque ita per omnia æqualem Deo Patri, ut nec tempore, nec gradu, nec potestate possit esse inferior, tantumque confitemur esse illum qui est genitus, quantus est ille, qui genuit. Non autem quia dicimus genitum a Patre Filium, divina et ineffabili generatione aliquod ei tempus adscribimus, sed nec Patrem aliquando cœpisse, nec Filium; ex Filio enim Pater dicitur, et qui semper Pater fuit, semper Filium habuit. Credimus et in Spiritum sanctum, verum Deum, ex Patre procedentem, æqualem per omnia Patri et Filio, voluntate, potestate, æternitate, substantia.

Nec est prorsus aliquis in Trinitate gradus, nihil quod inferius superiusve dici possit: sed tota deitas sua perfectione æqualis est; ut, exceptis vocabulis quæ proprietatem personarum indicant, quidquid de una persona dicitur, de tribus dignissime possit intelligi. Atque ut, confundentes Arium, unam eandemque dicimus Trinitatis esse substantiam, et unum in tribus personis fatemur Deum: ita impietatem Sabellii declinantes, tres personas expressas sub proprietate distinguimus, non ipsum sibi Patrem, ipsum sibi Filium, ipsum sibi Spiritum sanctum esse dicentes, sed aliam Patris, aliam Filii, aliam Spiritus sancti esse personam. Non enim nomina tantummodo, sed etiam nominum proprietates, id est, personas, vel, ut Græci exprimunt, hypostases, hoc est, subsistentias confitemur. Nec Pater Filii aut Spiritus sancti personam aliquando excludit, nec rursus Filius aut Spiritus sanctus Patris nomen personamque recipit, sed Pater semper Pater est, Filius semper Filius est, Spiritus sanctus semper Spiritus sanctus est. Itaque substantia unum sunt; personis ac nominibus distinguuntur.

Ipsum autem Dei Filium, qui absque initio æternitatem cum Patre et Spiritu sancto possidet, dicimus in fine sæculorum perfectum naturæ nostræ hominem suscepisse ex Maria semper virgine, et Verbum carnem esse factum, assumendo hominem, non permutando deitatem. Nec, ut quidam sceleratissime opinantur, Spiritum sanctum dicimus fuisse pro semine, sed potentia ac virtute Creatoris operatum. Sic autem confitemur, in Christo unam Filii esse personam, ut dicamus, duas perfectas atque integras esse substantias, id est, deitatis et humanitatis, quæ ex anima continetur et corpore. Atque ut condemnamus Photinum, qui solum et nudum in Christo hominem confitetur, ita anathematizamus Apollinarem et ejus similes, qui dicunt, Dei Filium minus aliquid de humana suscepisse natura, et vel in carne, vel in anima, vel in sensu assumptum hominem his, propter quos assumptus est, fuisse dissimilem, quem absque sola peccati macula (quæ naturalis non est) nobis confitemur conformem. Illorum quoque similiter exsecramur blasphemiam, qui novo sensu asserere conantur, a tempore susceptæ carnis, omnia, quæ erant deitatis, in hominem demigrasse; et rursum quæ erant humanitatis, in Deum esse transfusa: ut, quod nulla unquam hæresis dicere ausa est, videatur hac confusione utraque natura exinanita, substantia deitatis scilicet et humanitatis, et a proprio statu in aliud esse mutata: qui tam Deum imperfectum in Filio quam hominem confitentur, ut nec Deum verum nec hominem tenere credantur. Nos autem dicimus, susceptum ita a Filio Dei passibile nostrum, ut deitas impassibilis permaneret. Passus est enim Dei Filius non putative, sed vere, omnia, quæ Scriptura testatur, id est, esuriem, sitim, lassitudinem, dolorem, mortem et cætera hujusmodi: secundum illud passus est quod pati poterat, id est, non secundum illam substantiam, quæ assumpsit, sed secundum illam, quæ assumpta est. Ipse enim Dei Filius secundum suam deitatem impassibilis est ut Pater, incomprehensibilis ut Pater, invisibilis ut Pater, inconvertibilis ut Pater; et quamvis propria persona Filii, id est, Dei Verbum, suscepit passibilem hominem; ita tamen ejus habitatione secundum suam substantiam deitas Verbi nihil passa est, ut tota Trinitas, quam impassibilem confiteri necesse est. Mortuus est ergo Dei Filius secundum Scripturas juxta illud, quod mori poterat, resurrexit tertia die, ascendit in cœlum, sedet ad dexteram Dei Patris, manente ea natura carnis, in qua natus et passus est, in qua etiam resurrexit; non enim exinanita est humanitatis substantia, sed glorificata in æternum cum deitate mansura. Accepta ergo a Patre omnium potestate, quæ in cœlo sunt et in terra, venturus est ad judicium vivorum et mortuorum, ut et justos remuneret, et puniat peccatores. Resurrectionem etiam carnis credimus, ut dicamus, nos in eadem, in qua nunc sumus, veritate membrorum esse reparandos; qualesque semel post resurrectionem fuerimus effecti, in perpetuum permansuros. Unam esse vitam sanctorum omnium, sed præmia pro labore diversa; e contrario pro modo delictorum, peccatorum quoque esse supplicia. Baptisma unum tenemus, quod iisdem Sacramenti verbis in infantibus, quibus etiam in majoribus, asserimus esse celebrandum. Hominem, si post Baptismum lapsus fuerit, per pœnitentiam credimus posse salvari.

Novum et Vetus Testamentum recipimus in eo librorum numero, quem sanctæ Ecclesiæ catholicæ tradit auctoritas. Animas a Deo dari credimus, quas ab ipso factas dicimus; anathematizantes eos, qui animas quasi partem divinæ dicunt esse substantiæ. Eorum quoque condemnamus errorem, qui eas ante peccasse, vel in cœlis conversatas esse dicunt, quam in corpora mitterentur. Exsecramur etiam eorum blasphemiam qui dicunt, impossibile aliquid homini a Deo præceptum esse; et mandata Dei non a singulis, sed omnibus in commune posse servari: vel qui primas nuptias cum Manichæo, vel secundas cum Cataphrygis damnant. Anathematizamus etiam illos qui Dei Filium necessitate carnis mentitum esse dicunt, et eum propter assumptum hominem non omnia facere potuisse quæ voluit. Joviniani quoque damnamus hæresim, qui dicit nullam in futuro meritorum esse distantiam; nosque eas ibi habituros esse virtutes, quas hic habere neglexerimus. Liberum sic confitemur arbitrium, ut dicamus, nos semper Dei indigere auxilio, et tam illos errare, qui cum Manichæo dicunt hominem peccatum vitare non posse, quam illos, qui cum Joviniano asserunt hominem non posse peccare: uterque enim tollit arbitrii libertatem. Nos vero dicimus, hominem et peccare, et non peccare posse; ut semper nos liberi confiteamur esse arbitrii[1].

[1] This is really the Creed of Pelagius, but it was referred at one time to Jerome, at another to Augustine. It was adopted by Charlemagne, with a little change in the setting, as we shall see hereafter. I have omitted this "setting" here, nor have I attempted to give any of the various readings in which the various editions of the five documents abound.

CHAPTER XXI.

PROFESSIONS OFFERED AT CONSECRATION: AND NOTES FROM LATER SYNODS.

§ 1. Council of Carthage, A. D. 398. § 2. Profession of the Roman Pontiff from the *Liber Diurnus*. § 3. *Ordo Romanus*. § 4. English Professions, 796 to 857. § 5. Province of Aquileia, 801. § 6. Council of Aix, 802 (according to Pertz). § 7. Creed of Leo III. § 8. Theodulf. § 9. Unknown writer. § 10. Council of Arles, 813. § 11. Hatto of Basil, about 820. § 12. Agobard of Lyons, 820. § 13. Amalarius of Metz. § 14. The Bishop Amalarius. § 15. Collections of Ansegius and Benedictus Levita. § 16. Council of Worms, 829. § 17. Council of Paris, 829. § 18. Mayence, 847. § 19. Carisiacum, 849. § 20. Walfrid Strabo, 840. § 21. Rabanus Maurus, 855. § 22. Synod under Louis, 856. § 23. Synod of Tours, 858. § 24. Council of Rome, 862. § 25. Anschar, Archbishop of Bremen, 865. § 26. Walter, Bishop of Orleans, 866. § 27. Council of Worms, 868. § 28. Fourth Council of Constantinople, 869. § 29. Æneas of Paris, 868. § 30. Ratram of Corbey, 868. § 31. Pseudo-Alcuin. § 32. Adalbert of Morinum, 871. § 33. Willibert of Catalaunum, 871 (?). § 34. Other three. § 35. Hincmar's Capitular. § 36. Pope John VIII. (873—882). Letter to Photius. § 37. To Willibert of Cologne. § 38. To the Archbishop of Ravenna. § 39. Pope Marinus and Archbishop Fulco of Rheims. § 40. Riculfus of Soissons, 889. § 41. Regino of Prum, 900. § 42. Ratherius of Verona, 960 or 1009. § 43. Pilgrim of Lorsch, 975. § 44. Gerbert, 991. § 45. Abbo of Fleury, 1001. § 46. Gualdo of Corbey. § 47. Honorius of Autun. § 48. Quicunque in 1147 assigned to Athanasius while at Treves. § 49. First spoken of as *Symbolum Fidei* about 1171. Not recognized as such by Innocent III. § 50. Robertus Paululus, 1178. § 51. Usage from 922 onwards.

I WOULD pass now to another and very interesting kind of evidence: the character of the Confessions made by Bishops and Presbyters when they were consecrated or ordained.

§ 1. There is a Canon or Decree of the Council of Carthage of the year 398 on the subject, which seems to have remained *viridi observantia* even to the end of the ninth century, for it is quoted and adopted in the collection made by Regino, of which I shall speak just now. The directions were that when the necessity arose for a bishop to be ordained, examination was to be made whether he were by nature prudent, &c., and especially whether he could exhibit the teaching of the faith in simple words:

"Avowing, that is, that the Father, Son, and Holy Spirit are one God; and that the whole Deity in the Trinity is coessential, consubstantial, coeternal, and co-omnipotent: whether he taught that each Person in the Trinity is fully God, and the whole three Persons one God. Did he believe that the Incarnation took place, not in the Father nor in the Holy Spirit, but only in the Son? so that He, Who was in the Divinity Son of God the Father, Himself was made in man Son of a human Mother; very God of His Father, very Man of His Mother, having flesh from the bowels of His Mother, and a human rational soul; so that in Him there were together two natures, i.e. God and Man, one Person, one Son, one Christ, one Lord, Creator of all things which are, and, together with the Father and Holy Spirit, Author and Lord and Governor of all created things: Who suffered with a true suffering of the flesh, died with a true death of His Body, rose again with a true Resurrection of His flesh and a true resumption of His Soul, in which He will come to judge the quick and the dead. He must be asked also, Does he believe that of the Old and the New Testament, i.e. of the Law and the Prophets and Apostles, there is one and the same Author and God? is the devil wicked, not by his own nature, but of his own free will? Does he believe the resurrection of the flesh which we now bear with us, not of another flesh? Does he believe that there will be a judgment to come, and that all will severally receive, according as they have done in the flesh, either punishment or reward?" Intermediate details have curious and interesting relations to the moral troubles of the earlier time: "Does he object to second marriages? does he object to marriage entirely? will he communicate with penitents when reconciled?" and so on. The last enquiry is, "Does he believe that out of the Catholic Church no one can be saved?"

§ 2. The custom spread. And we owe to the learned Jesuit, Garner, a copy of the profession of the faith which, at one time, was made by the Roman Pontiff on his election to the Apostolic See. It was published at Paris in 1680, and has been republished in Vol. CV. of Migne's *Latin Series*[1]. As given by Migne, we have three professions, made at different periods of the ceremony. One must have been prepared shortly after the sixth general Council (Constantinople, A.D. 681), for it makes mention of it as having been recently held. There is much, in this, on the Trinity, but not a word that seems to me to connect it with the

[1] Usher on the Creed quotes Anastasius' *Life of Vitalian* to shew the existence of a custom on the part of the Pope of Rome to send a confession of his faith to Constantinople.

Quicunque. The second is more important for us: it is considered to have been composed between the years 685 and 715. The third is attributed to Leo II., about the year 682, and there we read

"We believe in one God, Father and Son and Holy Ghost, an inseparable Trinity." And words which we must remember are here introduced; "The Holy Spirit neither begotten nor unbegotten, but proceeding from the Father and the Son." (Spiritum Sanctum nec genitum nec ingenitum sed de Patre Filioque procedentem.)

To the second part of this document I must now refer[1]. It is too long to print at length. I must be content to give an abstract.

The bishop of the Holy Catholic and Apostolic Church of the city of Rome declares, for the satisfaction of the Church, that he will do everything necessary for the stability of the Christian Religion and for the rectitude of the Catholic Faith.

He begs therefore the Church to trust that he will preach, hold, and defend the Faith of Christ which the Apostles delivered, which the disciples of the Apostles taught, and which their successors, our Apostolic and most approved predecessors, have unchangeably preserved and defended.

Thus he will guard inviolably the Rule of the Apostolic Tradition, which the Fathers of the Council of Nicæa, guided by the revelation of God's grace, reduced to a Symbol, proclaiming that the Son is consubstantial with the Father: and by confirming the truth that our Lord Jesus Christ, the Word of God, is true God, drove out Arius and his fellows, and, with an eternal anathema, condemned them as being ministers of the devil.

Then the second Council, equally sacred, expounded (or set forth, *exposuit*) what was thought to be wanting in the Symbol, and, under the illumination of the Holy Spirit, added that the Holy Spirit is God to be worshipped with the Father and the Son, as consubstantial: and overthrew Macedonius and Apollinaris and their accomplices with the censure of perpetual anathema.

By means of these two sacred Councils (the document proceeds) we acknowledge the Holy and Inseparable Trinity, one God and one substance of the Trinity: we have learnt to proclaim the Trinity in Unity and Unity in Trinity, so that we confess one God, because of the unity of essence; and teach an inseparable Trinity, because of the difference of subsistences and persons: whilst the Son is born from all eternity of the Father, the Holy Spirit is confirmed to proceed from the Father: and the Son of God proclaims that the same Spirit receives of His, and manifests that in His Name the Holy Spirit is sent from the Father, and in breathing on the disciples, *Receive ye the Holy Spirit*, proclaims Him as proceeding from Himself.

[1] This was printed by Dr Routh in the second volume of his *Opuscula*.

Thus we are taught to proclaim one essence of Divinity; and, because of the unconfused properties of the Subsistences, a perfect Trinity. Of the Father, therefore, and the Son and the Holy Spirit, as there is one true Divinity, so is there one glory, empire, majesty, virtue, power, one natural will, one operation.

Thus the completed doctrine of the Trinity is represented as being enuntiated implicitly in the decisions of the two earliest Councils. The document proceeds to the subject of the Incarnation.

The Pope quotes the decision of the third Council, of Ephesus, in which the uniting (*unitio*) of the two Natures meeting in Christ, that is, the connexion of the Deity and Humanity in the same Subsistence, is proclaimed; and the profane man-worshipper (*hominicola*) Nestorius is cast down into a perpetual condemnation.

And the fourth Council is quoted which met at Chalcedon, at which, the grace of God opening the matter, the six hundred and thirty Fathers, supported by the tome of Pope Leo, promulged that out of the two and in the two natures or substances there is One and the Same Son of God: and that in no respect was the difference of natures destroyed, but, rather, the properties of each being preserved, each met together in one Subsistence or Person.

And the fifth is also appealed to, by whose salutary deliberations our Lord Jesus Christ was truly proclaimed to be one of the Holy Trinity, and Origen and Didymus and Evagrius were subjected to eternal condemnation; and Theodore of Mopsuestia and others, who refused to acknowledge that the Son of God, whilst He was God consubstantial and coeternal with the Father, did for us and for our salvation descend from heaven, and was incarnate of the Holy Spirit: that is, by the operation of the Holy Spirit the Virgin conceived the Son of God, the flesh having a rational and intellectual soul: in which flesh He was crucified and died, and on the third day, as He willed, He rose again from the dead, dissolving the dominion of our death: in which flesh, which He assumed from us but without sin, He is sitting at the right hand of the Father, to come in it to judge quick and dead: of Whose kingdom there shall be no end.

And then he appeals to the sixth Council, at which the assembled bishops declared that, like as we confess the two natures of our Lord Jesus Christ, Whose two Births we recognise, the one from the Father from eternity, the other from the Mother in time (ex tempore), so we confess the two Substances united in one Subsistence, from which and in which the same our Lord Jesus Christ is announced and believed; because complete God became complete Man: and thus it bound Sergius and Pyrrhus and Honorius with the bond of a perpetual anathema.

In all these anathemas the new Pope joined.

This document seems to me to possess peculiar interest. It so fully covers the ground occupied now by the Quicunque, that

I cannot believe that the Quicunque, as we have it, could have preceded the sixth Council (A.D. 681), as it is here epitomised. Neither can I believe that it was known to the Popes, for whom, or by whom, this profession was composed. In fact, whilst it embraces the subjects of the latter part of the Quicunque, it systematically avoids the technicalities of its language. Again, to the fulness of the language of the early part of the Quicunque, we have nothing similar here: we have no allusion to the assertion "not three Eternals, not three Almighties, not three Incomprehensibles, but One[1]."

§ 3. I give in the note[2] an account of the questions regard-

[1] In the résumé of Canons sent by Hadrian to Charles we have one directing "ut sancta Trinitas populo Dei prædicetur." Labbe, VI. 1812.

[2] The following is given by Hittorp (*Ordo Romanus*, p. 71) as the series of questions on his belief, which, according to Gallican use, were put to the Bishop elect, before the imposition of hands. (With this may be compared the Sarum rite immediately before the Reformation. Maskell, *Monum. Ritual.* III. p. 247. It seems that, with the exceptions mentioned below, these questions were retained until that period.) The Bishop had promised canonical obedience, kindness to the poor; then followed:

Interrogatio de credulitate. Credis secundum intelligentiam et capacitatem sensus tui sanctam Trinitatem, Patrem et Filium et Spiritum Sanctum unum [esse] Deum omnipotentem, totamque in Trinitate Deitatem coessentialem, et consubstantialem, coæternam, et coomnipotentem unius voluntatis potestatis et majestatis, creatorem omnium creaturarum, a quo omnia, per quem omnia, in quo omnia quæ sunt in cœlo et in terra, visibilia et invisibilia et spiritualia? R. Assentior et ita credo.

Credis singulam quamque in Trinitate Personam unum verum Deum plenum et perfectum? R. Credo. (This was subsequently omitted. In fact it savours of heresy.)

Credis ipsum Filium Dei Verbum Dei æternum natum de Patre, consubstantialem, coomnipotentem et æqualem per omnia Patri in divinitate, temporaliter natum de Spiritu Sancto ex Maria semper Virgine cum anima rationali, duas habentem nativitates, unam ex Patre æternam, alteram ex Matre temporalem, Deum verum et Hominem verum, proprium in utraque natura atque perfectum, non adoptivum neque phantasmaticum, unicum et unum filium Dei in duabus et ex duabus (the Salisbury Pontifical omits et ex duabus) naturis sed in unius singularitate personæ; impassibilem et immortalem divinitate, sed in humanitate pro nobis et pro salute nostra passum vera carnis passione, et sepultum et resurgentem a mortuis tertia die vera carnis resurrectione, die quadragesima post resurrectionem cum carne qua resurrexit et anima adscendisse in cœlum et sedere ad dexteram Patris, inde venturum judicare vivos et mortuos et redditurum unicuique secundum opera sua, sive bona fuerint sive mala? *Responsio ordinandi.* Assentior et per omnia credo.

Credis etiam Spiritum Sanctum plenum et perfectum verumque Deum a Patre Filioque procedentem, coæqualem et coessentialem, coomnipotentem et coæternum per omnia Patri et Filio? R. Credo.

Credis hanc Sanctam Trinitatem non tres deos sed unum Deum omnipotentem, æternum, invisibilem et incommutabilem? R. Credo.

Credis sanctam Catholicam et Apostolicam unam esse veram Ecclesiam, in qua unum datur baptisma et vera omnium remissio peccatorum? R. Credo. (Here in the Sarum and Winchester Pontificals are interpolated two questions as to the belief of the elected Bishop in the conversion of (1) the nature of the Bread into the nature of the Flesh of Christ as incarnate from the Virgin (2) of the mixed wine into the Blood which flowed from our Saviour's side.) Anathematizas etiam omnem hæresim extol-

ing his faith, which in the old *Ordo Romanus* were addressed to a newly elected bishop prior to his consecration: questions, which with slight modifications were continued in England through the time of the Conquest to the somewhat late copy of the *Sarum Pontifical,* from which Mr Maskell drew his text, and which indeed remain with small alterations to the present day. This form of enquiry I can have no doubt originated before the Quicunque was drawn up. I append also an abstract of an interesting sermon, addressed under the same circumstances and on the same occasion, to the bishop[1].

lentem se adversus hanc sanctam ecclesiam Catholicam? R. Facio vel anathematizo.

Credis etiam veram resurrectionem ejusdem carnis quam nunc gestas et vitam æternam? R. Credo.

Credis etiam novi et veteris testamenti, Legis et Prophetarum et Apostolorum unum esse Auctorem Deum et Dominum omnipotentem? R. Credo.

Et dicatur ei:

Hæc tibi fides augeatur a Domino ad veram et æternam beatitudinem, dilectissime frater in Christo.

Et respondeant omnes Amen.

I think that we should note that the words *non adoptivum* seem to give a date to these enquiries after 790, whilst the silence (or error?) on the more delicate questions mooted by Godeschalk would shew that the enquiries were composed before 860. At the same time the enquiries are, to a remarkable extent, independent of the language of the Athanasian Creed. And it was recognised that even a Bishop might not have the ability to enter into the difficulties of the language regarding the Trinity.

There were no such questions put to the candidates for priests' orders.

These questions (omitting, however, those in the Sarum book relating to transubstantiation) are still retained in the Roman Pontifical. See too Mabillon, *Analecta*, II. 469, as to the Rouen Pontifical.

The *Liber Diurnus* (Migne, CV. p. 65) contains also a series of promises made by an elected Bishop, apparently composed before the sixth general Council. There is no special Creed.

[1] The sermon on the Faith addressed to the newly elected bishop, according to the *Ordo Romanus* (Hittorp, p. 74; compare p. 70), was this: "Finally we desire to exhort your Love, to keep pure and undefiled the Faith which briefly and lucidly we have arranged:" It proceeds

"Credimus in unum Deum omnipotentem visibilium omnium et invisibilium factorem, et in unum dominum nostrum Jesum Christum Filium Dei vivi et Spiritum Sanctum Domini; non tres Deos sed Patrem et Filium et Spiritum Sanctum unum Deum colimus, confitemur et adoramus. Patrem credimus ingenitum, Filium genitum, Spiritum vero sanctum non genitum non creatum neque factum sed de Patre et Filio procedentem, Patri et Filio coæternum et coæqualem et cooperatorem. Et in hac Trinitate nihil est prius aut posterius, nihil est minus aut majus, sed coæterni sibi sunt et coæquales. Itaque Pater et Filius et Spiritus Sanctus, Hi tres unum sunt. Tres, non confusi nec divisi, sed distinctim conjuncti et conjunctim distincti, æquales divinitate, consimiles majestate, qui ita uniti sunt ut tres quoque non dubitemus: ita tres sunt, ut separari a se non posse fateamur. Dividitur, ut ita dicam, hæc sancta Trinitas indivisibiliter, et conjungitur divisibiliter, quemadmodum ipse Dei Filius Jesus Christus effatus est dicens *Ego et Pater unum sumus*. *Unum* quod dixit pluralitatem exclusit: *sumus* quod addidit personas manifeste ostendit. Credimus et in novissimis temporibus, propter nos homines et propter nostram salutem, Dei Filium descendisse de cœlis et adsumsisse humanam carnem ex Maria semper virgine, &c."

This Creed goes on at great length to enumerate facts relating to the life and sufferings and death of our Redeemer, His descent *ad inferos* whence He recalled to heaven such souls bound there

§ 4. And so we come to a series of English professions, which are found in one grand collection in the British Museum: the volume CLEOPATRA, E. 1.

In this manuscript there are copies of ninety-three professions, chiefly of bishops before their consecration, a few also of abbots and such high officers. Of these many were published by Hearne, the antiquarian, in his *Textus Roffensis* (Oxon. 1720). But I am indebted to Professor Stubbs for the copies of which I avail myself. The first volume of the Councils and Ecclesiastical documents edited by him and Mr Haddan contains one of these professions, the third volume contains about twenty-five. They range from the year 796 downwards. And they seem to exhibit that a new custom, the custom of bishops expressing in their own language their profession of faith and obedience to the archbishop, had commenced in England at the end of the eighth century.

Most of these professions contain an explicit declaration of faith in the Trinity. The first, for example, having begun by referring to the custom of making enquiry as to the faith and morals of the newly elected bishop, proceeds as follows:

"I am not fit, most loving father, to satisfy the requirements of these old traditions; but, as far as I have a knowledge of the true faith, I will endeavour quickly to explain it to you. I believe God the Father and Son and Holy Spirit, maintaining, that in the Trinity is perfect God, and that the whole three Persons are one God: I believe too that the Divine Incarnation took place not in the Father nor in the Holy Spirit but in the Son alone: so that He who was in the Divinity the Son of God the Father, became Himself in man the Son of Man His Mother: true God from the Father, true Man from the Mother: Who is one God, with the Father and Holy Spirit Creator of all things which are: Who suffered with a true suffering of the flesh, and was with a true resurrection of the flesh and rèsumption of the soul; in which He will come to judge the quick and the dead. This, without

as He chose: His resurrection, ascension, and future return to judgment. The Creed itself ends thus: "Credimus unum baptisma, credimus carnis resurrectionem, et *in triginta annorum ætate ad judicium venturos* (?): credimus sanctam ecclesiam catholicam, toto orbe diffusam, credimus remissionem omnium peccatorum, communionemque sanctorum, et vitam æternam. Amen."

The preacher proceeds with his address, which now bears on the teaching of the bishop and his government of the Church. It is very interesting.

This Creed is compounded of the Western and Eastern Symbols. It possesses, however, peculiarly interesting features. Thus, note the addition *omnium peccatorum* as in the Creeds of Spain. The position of the clause *sanctorum communionem* is also remarkable.

It does not enter on any of the questions of the fifth century relating to the Incarnation.

any doubt, I believe: this I praise; this I confess and desire to preach among my people."

The next is dated 798, and here Tidferth, Bishop of Dunwich, expresses his anxiety to give his experience of the Catholic Faith, and states that

As the universal Church teaches, "he will preach the Father the Son and the Holy Spirit to be one Deity, and each Person in the Trinity to be one God."

He, therefore, did not know of the Quicunque as authentic. We next come to the profession of Denebert, Bishop of Worcester, to which much attention has deservedly been called. He deserts phrases of his own and adopts language that he has been taught. I must give his own words:

"According to the rite of our sacred Canon, and according to the Ecclesiastical rule, as far as my strength permits, I promise that I, together with those who are with me in the Lord, will exhibit to thy pious commands all service of obedience with an entire devotion of heart: and, moreover, I will expound in a few words the orthodox Catholic and Apostolic Faith as I have learned it, because it is written: Whoever wishes to be saved, before all things it is necessary that he hold the Catholic Faith. Now the Catholic Faith is this, that we worship one God in Trinity and Trinity in Unity, neither confounding the Persons nor separating the Substance: for there is one Person of the Father, another of the Son, another of the Holy Ghost, but the Divinity of the Father and of the Son and of the Holy Ghost is one, the glory equal, the majesty coeternal. The Father is made of none, neither created nor begotten. The Son is of the Father alone, not made, nor created, but begotten. The Holy Spirit is of the Father and the Son, neither made, nor created, nor begotten, but proceeding. In this Trinity there is nothing before or after: there is nothing greater or less; but the whole three Persons are coeternal together and coequal; so that in all things, as has above been said, the Trinity in Unity, and the Unity in Trinity, is to be worshipped. Moreover, I receive the decrees of the Pontiffs; and the six catholic synods of old heroic men, and I keep the rule prefixed by them with a sincere devotion. This is our Faith, strengthened by the evangelical and apostolical traditions and authority, and settled by the society of all the Catholic Churches which are in the world: in which, by the grace of God Almighty, we hope and trust that we may remain even to the end of this life. Amen."

Other professions follow, but of these none given by Hearne, none published as yet by Professor Stubbs, repeat any words of the Quicunque. The Bishop of Rochester in 804, and the Bishop of Leicester in 814—816, refer, like Denebert, to the decrees of the Pontiffs. Another Bishop, of Lichfield, in 832—836, makes a Creed of his own out of the Nicene and Apostles' Creeds: he too speaks of the decrees of the Popes in the language of Denebert: and language, so far almost identical, is used by Behrtred, Bishop of Lindsey, in 839.

It is surely worthy of notice that the Creeds of four of these Bishops (Heabert in 822, Humbert in 828, Herefrith in 825, and Ceolrith in 839), as they are found in the manuscript, run as follows: *Credo in Deum, Patrem et Filium et Spiritum Sanctum natum et passum, &c.* "I believe in God, Father, Son, and Holy Spirit, born and suffered." They are Sabellian. One great point which the Quicunque aims to enforce, the distinction between the faith in the Trinity, and the faith in the Incarnation of the Son of God, is passed over. And it is worthy of notice also that Denebert, who is the only bishop that quotes the language which we now find in the Quicunque, is the first who acknowledges the decrees of the Pontiffs. Coupling this with the fact that of the later English Bishops whose professions have been published, not one repeats the language of the Quicunque—it was different, as we shall see, on the Continent—and with the peculiar phraseology which Denebert uses regarding himself, I feel compelled to yield to the suggestion of a friend, that to Denebert himself the language was comparatively new, whilst to Ethelbeard, his Archbishop, it had been unknown. Else why should the bishop have taken the trouble to copy it out at length, instead of referring to the Quicunque, as others had referred to the Councils and Synods of the Church[1]?

[1] The following extracts from some of these English professions seem to me to be especially worthy of attention. Herewin, Bishop of Lichfield, declares "Nunquam me declinare ad dexteram neque ad sinistram ab illa sede sancta Dorobernensis ecclesiæ quæ caput est totius gentis Angliorum (sic)." The Church of Canterbury was head of the English Church. Many of them say "illam sanctam apostolicam fidem...semper servare me velle." Eadulf, Bishop of York, promises to look to the seat of Augustine "et ad Dorobernensem ecclesiam unde nobis omnibus ecclesiasticæ dignitatis ordo, Beato Gregorio ordinante, ministratur." Wulfhard, Bishop of Hereford, speaks of his belief in the Trinity "trinum personis, unum subsistentia (1) qui est Pater et Filius et Spiritus Sanctus, Deus unus incomprehensibilis, inæstimabilis, ineffabilis, invisibilis, quia quod est et quod erit hoc semper fuit." Derwulf of London says "Ego confiteor Deum Patrem omnipotentem ante omnia sæcula consistentem et in sua divina potestate omnem creaturam creantem ac regentem; et Filium unigenitum ex Patre venientemque in mundum sicut per ora patriarcharum et prophetarum promissum est; et Spiritum Sanctum procedentem ex Patre et Filio......eundemque Filium pro salute mundi passum et sepultum." The following will conclude my series. "Insuper etiam et orthodoxam catholicam apostolicamque fidem, sicut ab illis (his venerable predecessors, of whom he

An examination of this and later professions of which I have given extracts in my notes, seems to prove convincingly that the language of the Quicunque had not taken root in England among the bishops in the middle of the ninth century.

§ 5. From the Sponsio of the Bishops of the Province of Aquileia, ascribed to the year 801, we learn that the bishop elect promised

> That he would both retain inviolably in his heart, and proclaim sincerely in his mouth, the rule of the Catholic Faith, according to the definition of the Nicene Council and as the volume of the blessed Pope Leo declared it, to the utmost strength of his intelligence and as far as with God's help he might have the power[1].

§ 6. We now come to a celebrated document which Pertz has edited from a manuscript once at St Emmeran's Church in Ratisbon, but now at Munich—and which Pertz assigns, apparently without any authority, to the year 802[2]. This document directs that enquiries shall be made

> How the clergy know the psalms: how they teach the faith to catechumens: how they teach the Lord's Prayer and the meaning of the Symbol: and it enjoins that all Christians shall know the Symbol and the Lord's Prayer. Then the presbyters are to be further asked how they hold the Catholic Faith or Symbol, and how they know and understand the Lord's Prayer: and then it proceeds "These are the things which all ecclesiastics are ordered to learn. (i) The Catholic Faith of Saint Athanasius and all other things relating to the Faith: (ii) the Apostles' Creed: (iii) the Lord's Prayer." Then reference is made to the book of Sacraments and Canon: the forms of exorcism and commending of the soul, and the Penitential: the Computus, the use of the Roman

particularly mentions Cudulf and Eadulf and Beonnan) paucis verbis exponam. In primis itaque credo in unum Deum Patrem omnipotentem, conditorem visibilium et invisibilium rerum. Credo et in Jesum Christum, filium ejus unicum dominum nostrum, conceptum de S. S. et natum ex M. V., Deum verum hominemque perfectum, sub Pontio Pilato passum, a Judæis crucifixum, et sepultum, ad inferos descendentem, die tertia resurgentem ex mortuis, ascendentem in cœlos, ubi numquam defuit, considentem in dextera Dei Patris, virtutem et Dei sapientiam, eundemque venturum post finem sæculi judicare vivos ac mortuos et sæculum per ignem. Credo et in Spiritum Sanctum, procedentem a Patre et Filio, vivificantem omnia quæ in cœlis sunt et in terris: et unam Sanctam Catholicam et Apostolicam Ecclesiam: confiteor unum Baptisma in remissionem peccatorum, et carnis resurrectionem, et vitam æternam futuri sæculi." This was the confession of Diorlaf, Bishop of Hereford, made between 857 and 866.

[1] Madrisius' Paulinus, p. 635. Migne, Vol. XCIX.

[2] The MS. itself is said to be of the ninth or tenth century.

chant at night: to the gospel and the lessons of the "liber comitis:" to homilies, to the Pastoral Book and book of Offices: and to the letter of Gelasius: and enquiries are made whether the clergy can write "letters." The document is of great interest independently of its bearing on this controversy[1].

§ 7. I have already mentioned[2] that the monks of Mount Olivet reminded Pope Leo that the doctrine of the procession of the Holy Spirit from the Son was taught in the faith of St Athanasius. I should, however, state here

That in the dialogue between Leo and the Envoys of Charles, Leo never alluded in any way to the Faith of Athanasius. The account of the message of the monks to the Pope was first published, I believe, by Baluzius in his *Collectio*[3] from a manuscript at Limoges. The Creed of Leo follows in the same manuscript; it may be seen in Lequien, as Waterland, states, or in Mansi, XIII. 978. Dr Neale gave a translation of a small portion in his history of the Holy Eastern Church[4]. It is introduced thus. "We send you this Symbol of the orthodox faith, that ye, as well as all the world, may hold the correct and inviolate faith, according to the Roman Holy Catholic and Apostolic Church. We believe the Holy Trinity, &c." It is a long Creed or Symbol: but in it there is no reference at all to the *Quicunque* even though to a certain extent it runs parallel to it. We have the words, "The Father from Himself, not from another: the Son begotten by the Father...the Holy Spirit proceeding equally from the Father and the Son:...but yet we do not speak of three Gods but of one God omnipotent, eternal, invisible, incommutable: these Three (hæc tria) are one God: the Father is one in Person: the Son

[1] A. It will be noticed that the words "Catholica fides seu simbolum" seem to represent the Catholic Faith and the Creed as identical, and they alone are sufficient to make us hesitate before we identify the former expression wherever we meet it, with the Quicunque. B. I conceive that *cætera quæcunque de fide* would embrace the shorter or longer confessions which I have noticed in chapter XX. C. The *computus* became in the ninth century a great subject of enquiry. In its shorter form it would correspond to our tables and rules for the moveable and immoveable feasts, and it might include the rules about the Epact. (Martene and Durand, *Ampl. Coll.*, VII. p. 4.) I find references to it in the directions of Riculfus A.D. 889. (The greater *computus* was a more elaborate calendar, answering to our table of feasts for so many years. One may be seen in the Salisbury Psalter.) D. On the *Liber Comitis;* we are told distinctly that Alcuin (*Frobenius' edition*, Vol. I. p. lxxx.) took in hand a book called the *Comes*, and reduced it to order, correcting it and taking care that it should be marked with stops for the sake of pronouncing it properly. "Nobis autem curæ fuit ita hunc emendate atque distincte transcribere sicut ab eodem magistro emendatus extat." The book was properly a table of lessons, but it seems to have sometimes included the lessons themselves. E. I am inclined to suppose that the letter of Gelasius was that on the canonical books. Some of my readers will probably agree with me in thinking that the order which I am now discussing must have followed, at all events, by some little interval, the labours of Alcuin on the *Comes*, and so questioning the date which Pertz assigns to the canon.

[2] Chapter XII. p. 148.

[3] VII. 14. or II. p. 12.

[4] General Introduction, p. 1162.

another in Person: the Holy Spirit another in Person:" and then it passes on to the subject of the Incarnation. "We believe that the same Son, Word of God, having been coeternally begotten from the Father, consubstantial with the Father, was, in time (temporaliter) born of the Holy Spirit and the Virgin Mary, having two nativities...We confess that He, very God, was conceived, and, very God, was born:—and that from hell (ab inferis) returning, the prince of all iniquity being condemned and spoiled, He rose on the third day from the dead..,and ascended into heaven." It concludes: "Him who does not believe (qui non crediderit) in accordance with this faith, the Holy Catholic and Apostolic Church condemns."

If this is genuine (and I know not why it should be questioned), we have here Leo III., not availing himself of the Quicunque, but composing and transmitting, as the Creed or Symbol of the Roman Church, an independent but yet equivalent document. Nor in his answer to Leo, does Charles quote the Athanasian Creed: he quotes Athanasius' work against Arius, although not quite to the point[1].

§ 8. But we have other authorities of the ninth century which I must briefly enumerate, although I can add little here to the accounts which Waterland has reproduced (without acknowledgment) from Tentzel, Montfaucon, Muratori or Beveridge.

Theodulf, Bishop of Orleans, had been brought by Charlemagne out of Italy[2]; he is mentioned by Alcuin in his fourth letter to the Emperor, in connection with the Patriarch Paulinus.

We have a series of *capitula* from him, amongst which he directs that all the faithful shall learn the Lord's Prayer and the Symbol, because on these two documents the whole foundation of the faith rests, and unless a person holds them in his memory, and believes them with his heart, and is very frequently engaged in prayer, he cannot be a Catholic. Every one should say the Creed or the Lord's Prayer, morning and evening; and should daily, or twice, thrice a day confess his sins to God, according to the words of the Psalmist: "I will acknowledge my sin unto thee[3]."

Baluzius found another series of orders, ascribed to Theodulf, in which we read

"Wherefore we admonish you, O priests of the Lord, that ye should hold in your memories and understand with your hearts the Catholic faith, i. e. the Credo and *Quicunque vult salvus esse ante omnia opus est ut teneat Catholicam fidem*[4]."

[1] Labbe, VII. 1199, 1201.

[2] This is, however, questioned by Fabricius (Migne, CV. p. 187). Yet Döllinger, p. 109, agrees with the older writers that Speria or Hesperia = Italy.

[3] Migne, CV. pp. 198, 200.

[4] *Ib.* p. 209 from Baluzius, *Miscell.* Tom. II. p. 99. = VII. p. 21. (From a manuscript at Limoges.)

This series must be spurious; because a suffragan bishop like Theodulf could not have issued directions how presbyters were to be treated. Indeed the directions go so far as to make provision for the case when a bishop is infirm and needs unction; and appoint that under certain circumstances the bishop must do penance for seven days[1]. The next paper is clearly Theodulf's answer to the enquiry which Charlemagne addressed to him through Magnus, Archbishop of Sens: it contains chapters on the Symbol and on the Credulitas[2]. Here we should expect a reference to the "Faith of Athanasius," but we find no such reference. The fourth work is that out of which the well-known quotation, given by Waterland, is taken. This is a work on the Holy Spirit, in support of the double Procession; it was addressed to Charles the Great, and contains a series of quotations: the first four profess to be taken from the books "which Athanasius wrote against the Arians," *i.e.* from the work now attributed to Vigilius of Tapsus; "all supposititious[3]," although Hincmar quoted them with equal zest, in his controversy with Godeschalk.

The last quotation of all consists of clauses 21—28 of the Quicunque. I must confess that I should like to know the date of the manuscripts which contain the passage[4]. The clauses are identically the same as those which were adduced by Æneas of Paris. In his exposition of the Credulitas mentioned above[5], Theodulf speaks of the

> "Word made flesh, by assuming the manhood not by changing the Godhead:" he insists that we shall rise again in the same flesh in which we now live "and that there are not in the Trinity any degrees by which Any might be said to be inferior or superior to Another."

Thus the document shews a familiarity with the thoughts of our Quicunque, even though the language is not quoted.

Once more: Baluzius extracted from a "vetus codex" in the Colbertine Library, and printed in his *Miscellanies* (I. 491),

> A catalogue of certain abbots of Fleury, in which it is said that this Theodulf was remarkable for his learning; amongst other things "he published an exposition of the Symbol of Saint Athanasius, which is

[1] Migne, ut supra, p. 220 A. B.
[2] pp. 226, 227.
[3] Note in Migne, p. 242.
[4] It professes to come from the *Symbolum* of Athanasius, but Sirmond questions the authenticity of the heading.
[5] Migne, ut supra, 227.

chanted by the monks daily at prime, after the three regular psalms. He wrote also of the Mass and of everything contained in the Service."

With Baluzius however, unhappily, *vetus codex* might mean a manuscript of the twelfth, or even of the fourteenth, century. Therefore, much confidence cannot be placed in the authority here.

This Explanation may therefore have been that of the Creed of which I have spoken already: or it may have been the Explanation published by Cardinal Mai in his *Scriptorum veterum nova collectio*, of which I must speak hereafter. But the title "Symbol of St Athanasius" carries us down to the twelfth century at least, as the date of the record[1].

In the appendix to Labbe and Cossart, vol. VII. (p. 1855), we have another addition to the *Capitula* of Theodulf. "Learn the Catholic Faith: preach most diligently: preach it to the people, everyone of you in his own Church[2]."

It is not unlikely that the copyists were correct who attributed to Theodulf the most recent edition of the *Speculum*[3], even though Mai assigns it to the seventh century. The Cardinal would not allow Dr Tregelles to examine the manuscript, (m of Tischendorf,) for more than a few seconds.

§ 9. I can of course add no more to the quotation from an "uncertain author," which Montfaucon, Tentzel, and Waterland have taken from Sirmond's note on Theodulf:

Sirmond found another collection of testimonies addressed to Charlemagne, adduced to prove that the Holy Spirit proceeds from the Father and the Son. This writer says: "The blessed Athanasius in the Exposition of the Catholic Faith, which the great writer himself composed and which the universal Church confesses....says *Pater a nullo est factus*, &c.[4]" Sirmond does not inform us where he saw the manuscript, nor how much of the Quicunque was quoted. It may be noticed that he calls it "an Exposition of the Catholic Faith."

§ 10. I have given on page 233 an account of the Rule of Faith put forth at Toledo in the year 633. I must repeat that it is very strange that exactly the same language was adopted, exactly the same form used, at a Council held at Arles in the year 813; and without acknowledgment. This fact seems, as I have said, to cast on one side the surmise that Hilary of Arles wrote the Quicunque. It shews too that the Quicunque was not

[1] This passage from Baluzius has attracted much attention. Amongst others Martene quotes it, Lib. IV. ch. viii. on the hour services.

[2] Migne, p. 206 c.

[3] Published amongst Augustine's works, VI. 1409.

[4] Migne, Vol. CV. p. 239, note 247. Is this author the pseudo-Alcuin mentioned below?

established as of any authority in the province of Arles even as late as the year which we have now reached. In this year 813 it had not superseded the Faith of the Spanish Council of the seventh century in the minds of the Bishops collected in council in the South of France.

§ 11. I cannot see any reason to reject the evidence of Hatto, which Waterland, after Tentzel, quotes under the year 820[1].

The name of the bishop comes to us spelled in a variety of fashions—Hayto, Ahyto, Aito, Hatto, Haido, Heito: but, notwithstanding this variety, he was a notable man in his day, and is mentioned honorably in the Reichenau annals of the time[2].

He had been abbot of Reichenau and was made Bishop of Basil in 806, holding apparently his abbacy "in commendam." In 811 he was sent by Charles on an embassy to Constantinople: in 822 he gave up the abbacy and in 836 he died[3]. We cannot specify the year in which these edicts were issued: the date may have been as early as 820 or as late as 834 or 835: but it can scarcely be questioned that this bishop was their author. They run as follows: "(1) First of all, enquiry must be made as regards the Faith of the Priests, how they believe, and how they teach others to believe. (2) Order must be given that the Lord's Prayer in which all things necessary to human life are contained, and the Apostles' Symbol in which the Catholic Faith is entirely comprehended, should be learnt by all, as well in Latin as in the vernacular, so that the professions made by the mouth may be by the heart believed and understood." (3) The third directed that every one should learn how to respond duly to the Priest in the Mass: (4) the fourth, as it is quoted by Waterland, was this: "That the Faith of Saint Athanasius should be learnt by the priests and recited by them by heart at prime on Sundays[4]."

Of course the question might be put, Which "Faith of Athanasius" is meant? but the order that it should be recited at the prime *seems* almost sufficient to identify the document. But see below under § 22.

[1] At one time I confess that I considered that the Hatto who is quoted at this point, was the bishop of Mayence to whom Regino of Prum addressed his collection of Canons. This Hatto died in 912. But the manuscripts are decisive. Thus at Vienna I saw one, No. 914, of the tenth century, containing (on folios 33—36) *Aito Haito seu Hatto Basileensis ecclesiæ antistes: capitula xxv: diœcesiani ordines.* The volume contains also works of Isidore of Seville and others, on the Ecclesiastical offices.

[2] Pertz, *Monumenta*, I.

[3] *Annalium Alamannicorum continuatio Augiensis*, apud Pertz, *Monumenta*, &c. I. 49.

[4] Waterland (apparently from Tentzel, p. 71 or Montfaucon's Diatribe). The originals may be seen in Harduin, IV. 1241 or Labbe, VII. 1523, Mansi, XIV. 395. The direction does not appear to have been known to Regino. It is said that the orders were first discovered by Johannes Bona in the Barbarini palace and published by D'Achery in his *Spicilegium*, Tom. VI. art. 4.

§ 12. Montfaucon, Muratori, Tentzel, and Waterland refer to another quotation from the *Quicunque*, found in the writings of Agobard, Archbishop of Lyons, about the year 820.

Mr Robertson informs us of the part which this bishop took in the degradation of Louis the Pious, but it was before this period that he wrote against Felix[1]. In this work he speaks of the revival of old heresies in his day: he says that although many who believe well perish by living ill, no one who believes ill is saved by living well. "What is the use of a golden key (he asks), if it cannot open what we want? or why object to a wooden key if it will do this, when we want nothing else?" He urges his reader not to neglect to purify his faith: because, as the blessed Athanasius says—"The Catholic Faith, which except a man keep whole and undefiled, without doubt he shall perish everlastingly." He refers to Nestorius and Eutyches: he says that the difficulty of Felix was that he maintained that it was wrong to say "God, the Son of God the Father, suffered and died": we should say that the Man who was assumed by Him so suffered and so died...Thus Felix had become in part a Nestorian. And he quotes the anathemas against Nestorius, but, even where, as in chapter XI, the opportunity comes to adduce the Athanasian Creed, Agobardus passes it over: it seems to have been scarcely familiar to him: he does quote Augustine, and Vigilius of Tapsus, and the letter of Symmachus to the Emperor Anastasius (not correctly), and Hilary of Arles: but nothing more from St Athanasius. In § xxxvi. the "Catholica fides" is the Apostles' Creed. The treatise finishes thus, "Wherefore He, after humanity was assumed, is one true God with the Father, not later nor less than the Father or the Holy Spirit, not differing in majesty, not unequal in power, not dissociated in operation. For this Holy Trinity, distinguished in Persons but not separable, is One Thing (unum est). It is not one Person (unus) in one essence; but it is one essence, one substance, one name, one nature, living and reigning without recording of the past, without expectation of the future."

§ 13. We have seen that about the year 820 Hatto of Basil is said to have given directions that the Faith of Athanasius should be recited at prime every Lord's day; and that Theodulf has been considered as the author of an equivalent direction.

Now there was no service for prime in the time of Isidore of Seville, whose date was of course before the date at which we have arrived.

But Symphrosius Amalarius, who was a presbyter of Metz, after the accession of Louis, wrote a long and interesting account of the Divine Offices; from which we gain much information. Judging from the subjects on which he comments, we should reasonably expect that he would have said something on the Quicunque, if he had known it or held it in any value: but he is silent. He has chapters on the lessons, on the

[1] Migne, Vol. CIV. pp. 30, &c. &c.

litanies, on the *Kyrie eleison*, on the *Gloria in excelsis*, on the *Ter Sanctus*, on the *Te igitur*, on the *Agnus Dei*, the Canticles, and so on; he speaks of the use of the Creed (Credulitas) on Easter Eve (1041). And in the beginning of the fourth book he describes at length the service of prime (p. 1165), the *Deus in adjutorium*, the Psalms, the *Kyrie eleison*, the Lord's Prayer. "After the Lord's Prayer follows our Belief which the Holy Apostles appointed on the Faith of the Holy Trinity and the Dispensation of the Incarnation of the Lord and the state of the Church." The Apostles' Creed was followed by versicles[1].

Thus in the time of Amalarius the Quicunque was not introduced into his neighbourhood, nor does he appear to have known it.

§ 14. A work on the Creeds, *De Symbolis*, is printed among the writings of the other Amalarius[2], but no mention is made there of the Quicunque.

§ 15. The collections of Ansegius, and Benedictus, the Levite or Deacon, made in the year 827[3], never mention the Quicunque: a fact which seems to me to throw some discredit on the date which Pertz assigns to the "Canons of 802," as well as on the full meaning which Waterland and Mansi give to the order of Hatto.

§ 16. Nor again is the Quicunque mentioned, as I think we should reasonably expect, at the Synod of Worms in 829[4].

§ 17. There was a Council of Paris in 829, in whose Capitula we meet the words *unusquisque fidelis si salvus esse vult.* We have here notes of numerous documents in which the Faith of Christ is delivered: but I find nothing else to remind me of the Athanasian Creed. The Faith of the Trinity is put in a very simple way[5].

§ 18. There was a Council at Mayence in 847, where, after speaking of the Catholic Faith, the Bishops insisted still more on the necessity of works. Again we read:

[1] Migne, Vol. cv.

[2] Migne, Vol. xcix. p. 919.

[3] These occupy 430 pages or columns in Baluzius' magnificent edition. Why was Waterland silent regarding this? Athanasius is quoted on another subject, column 994.

[4] Pertz, III. 332—342.

[5] Labbe, VII. 1598, 1599. "The foundation of the Christian religion is the Catholic Faith, that is to believe in the Father, the Son, and the Holy Spirit, one God and trine God, trine in Persons, one in substance."

"All are to be taught concerning the Catholic Faith as they are able to believe: of the perpetual retribution of the good and the eternal damnation of the bad; of the future resurrection and the final judgment." At this council it was decided that masses might be said for those who had been hung for their crimes[1].

§ 19. I have noted that at the Synod held in the year 849, at Carisiacum, in the province of Rheims, against Godeschalk, concerning his views on predestination, the words which at a later period were considered to be momentous, *Quicunque vult salvus esse,* "Whosoever wishes to be saved," were not quoted[2].

§ 20. I have before referred to Walfrid Strabo (who died in 849), as giving us some interesting information regarding the use of the Nicene or Constantinopolitan Creed.

He too (Book I. cap. 25) has a chapter on the canonical hours, but he too passes over the Quicunque. Yet he makes some remarks on the introduction of novelties into the service—a change to which he does not object. He mentions that Paulinus of Aquileia had introduced (more?) hymns. He has a very good passage on the varieties in different countries[3]. He says that the use of the *Credo in unum Deum* at the Mass was introduced from the Greeks: he speaks of the importance of the *Gloria Patri* as inculcating the Faith of the Trinity; but he has not a word about the Athanasian Creed[4].

Of course the Quicunque was in existence, at least in part, at this time: but it was systematically, and it would seem purposely, neglected by these learned men.

I do not intend to carry my readers below the year 900, unless for some special purpose: but there are a few quotations from our document, or references to it, which I wish to notice before we enquire into the relations borne to it by Paulinus and Alcuin and Hincmar.

§ 21. Rabanus Maurus, Archbishop of Mayence, was a little later: he is described by Dr Waddington[5] as the most profound theologian of the age.

[1] Labbe, VIII. 42—50.

[2] Labbe, VIII. 57. It may be interesting to note that Benedict III. acknowledged the right of laymen to be present at synods where the faith is treated, because that is the concern of all. Labbe, VIII. 310.

[3] Migne, CXIV. pp. 947, &c.

[4] He describes an organ in his note on Psalm CL.

[5] Mr Scrivener: *Codex Augiensis*, pp. xxiv. xxv.

He wrote a book *de Institutione clericorum*[1], and in it he describes the Apostles' Creed as the "Symbol of the Apostolic Faith." But he simply copies out the words of Isidore of Seville regarding both the Symbolum and the Rule of Faith[2]. Thus he preferred Isidore to the Quicunque, if he knew it. He has a few words on the prime service; too few for us to learn anything from, if it were not for his absolute silence elsewhere as to the Quicunque. He has a homily on the second Sunday in Lent "de fidei catholicæ veritate et bonorum operum concordia," where he says "ante omnia necessaria est nobis fides recta," and so he gives an exposition of the Symbol. "Doctrina symboli est...plenitudo credendi, quia quod in eo docetur et discitur et unitas est Trinitatis et Trinitas distincta in personis, et excellentia Creatoris et misericordia Redemptoris." It is all interesting[3]. We have another exposition of the Symbol in his fifth book *de universis*[4]: and another in his second book *de ecclesiastica disciplina*[5]. But he knew no Creed save the Apostles', and there is no allusion whatever to the Quicunque. He died in 855.

§ 22. But in the year 856, under Louis II., there seems to have been a synod: and to this, without any apparent hesitation, Pertz assigns the Canons which I have quoted above as those of Hatto. For the two series are identical in meaning and the variations in language are scarcely worthy of notice[6]. What are we to believe?

§ 23. At the Council of Tours, in the year 858, we meet with another order with which we are now familiar:

"The faith shall be preached to all the faithful by the presbyters; the Incarnation, Passion, Resurrection and Ascension, the giving of the Holy Spirit, the Remission of sins. And again with reference to the Lord's Prayer and Symbol all shall know them by memory: and the *Gloria Patri* and the *Sanctus* and the *Credulitas* and the *Kyrie eleison* shall be sung by all reverently: and the Psalms distinctly by the clerks; and the presbyters must not commence the *Secreta* before the *Sanctus* is finished."

These are orders put forth by Herard, Bishop of Tours. It will be noticed that no mention is made of the Quicunque: the *Credulitas* (if we may judge from its position in the canon) must be here the Nicene Creed[7].

§ 24. At Rome, in 862, we hear of the error of the Theopaschites: an error against which the latter half of the Quicunque

[1] Migne, CVII. p. 311.
[2] p. 368.
[3] Tom. CX. p. 27.
[4] Tom. CXI. p. 136.
[5] Tom. CXII. p. 1224.
[6] Pertz, III. 439.
[7] Labbe, VIII. No. ix. xvi. pp. 628, 629.

might have been directed. We may say that the rising again of such an error is inconsistent with the general use and acceptance of the Quicunque[1].

§ 25. I must reserve the testimony furnished by Hincmar to another chapter: but we have a curious instance of the use of the Quicunque from a death-bed scene. The dying Bishop Anscharius, Archbishop of Hamburg and Bremen[2], expressed his

"Desire that the brethren who were about him, when they offered the Litany and sung the psalms for his departure, should also sing the hymn composed in the praise of God, that is, the *Te Deum laudamus;* and also the Catholic Faith composed by the blessed Athanasius." Anscharius died in 865 and his successor and biographer St Rembert in 888[3].

§ 26. In or about 866, Walter, Bishop of Orleans, seems to have put out some instructions.

The Archdeacons were to examine as to the Faith of the clergy, their mode of administering baptism and of celebrating the mass. "Do they understand the Lord's Prayer *cum symbolo et fide catholica:* the *Gloria Patri, Credo in unum Deum, Sanctus, sanctus?*" The *Fides Catholica* may be the Quicunque or any other form in which the Faith was set. We find indeed a little later the enquiry "how each one is fitted to teach his brethren in the faith of the Holy Trinity, that they may believe that the Father, the Son and the Holy Spirit are one God, omnipotent, eternal...and that there is one Deity and substance and majesty...." This seems to weaken the evidence that *Fides Catholica* in the earlier chapter meant the Quicunque[4].

A further memorandum is interesting as throwing light upon the literary history of the church books. All the clergy were to have missal, psalter, &c., and correct them by good copies "per libros bene correctos emendent."

§ 27. There was an important gathering of Bishops at Worms in the year 868; so important that the assembled Fathers were

[1] Labbe, VIII. p. 738.

[2] He had been a monk of Corbey: thus again we note the connection with France and indeed with the province of Rheims. Waterland made a curious mistake. "Among his dying instructions (he says) to his clergy Anscharius left this for one, that they should be careful to recite the Catholic Faith composed by Athanasius." He quoted the words of Montfaucon as if they were the words of the biographer of Anschar, and misunderstood their meaning. My text represents the truth.

[3] I have referred of course to the original. It is (as Montfaucon describes it) in Anscharius' life in "*Pet. Lambecii in Appendice lib.* I. *Rerum Hamburg.* p. 237;" and I believe in Mabillon's *Acta Sanctorum*, VI. 78, and Migne.

[4] Labbe, VIII. pp. 637, 638.

disposed to claim for it the credit due to a general Council. On these grounds they deemed it necessary that

"Their first words should relate to God, that so the works which they might build upon the profession of their faith might be erected on this firm foundation." They began therefore with a long confession, which took the form of an enlargement of the Apostles' Creed. Thus we find them declaring[1], "We believe and confess that the Holy and ineffable Trinity, Father, Son, and Holy Spirit, are one God naturally, of one substance, one nature, one majesty and power, and we profess that the Father is not begotten nor made, but unbegotten. He is therefore the Fountain and Origin of the whole Trinity....We confess that the Son is of the substance of the Father, born without beginning before the ages, but not made....We believe that the Holy Spirit, Who is the Third Person of the Trinity is God, one and equal with the Father and the Son, of one substance, of one nature, but not begotten nor created, but proceeding from the Father and the Son is the Spirit of Both. For neither does He proceed from the Father upon the Son (in Filium); nor from the Son alone does He proceed to sanctify all creation: but He is shewn to proceed from Both because He is acknowledged to be the Love and Holiness of Both...and, although relatively they are called Three Persons, yet only one Nature or Substance must be believed: nor, as we speak of Three Persons, do we predicate three Substances, but Three Persons and One Substance. Thus while we maintain that the Father is not the same Person as the Son or the Holy Spirit, yet we hold that what the Father is, that is the Son, and that the Holy Spirit: we distinguish Three Persons, we do not separate the Nature of the Deity. As therefore we do not confound those Three Persons of the one inseparable Nature, so neither do we regard Them as in any way separable: inasmuch as no one Person is believed to have existed before Other or after Other or without Other; or to have wrought anything before or after or without Another. The Father has eternity without nativity; the Son eternity with nativity; the Holy Spirit eternity of procession from the Father and the Son, without nativity. But of these Three Persons, the Person of the Son alone for the redemption of the human race assumed true man without sin of the Virgin Mary, by a new nativity, a new order...The Son of God received not the person of a man, but the nature of a man. For He assumed our nature into the Unity of His Person; and therefore the Son of God and Son of Man is one Christ. In that He is Son of God, He is equal to the Father: in that He is Son of Man, He is less than the Father: Who, in that He was made man, endured sufferings for our sins and underwent the true death upon the cross. [The descent into Hell is not mentioned.] Raised on the third day by His own Power, He left the sepulchre. After the example of our Head, we believe that we shall rise again, in that flesh in which we live and move. The same Lord and Saviour having thus completed His triumph sought again His Paternal Seat from which, as concerns His Divinity, He was never absent. Coming thence at the end of the world, He will judge the quick and dead, and

[1] Labbe, VIII. p. 944. At a council held here in 786 the bishops had been content with reciting the Nicene Creed. Labbe, VI. 1863.

will render to every one according as he has done in the body whether good or bad. And the Catholic Church, Redeemed with His precious blood shall, we believe, reign with Him hereafter for ever. We believe and confess one Baptism for the Remission of all sins. We promise that we will retain this profession of our faith inviolate and will never deviate from it, and this whosoever desires to be saved let him study to retain without any ambiguity."

I have given these long extracts to enable my reader to form his own judgment on the evidence contained in this document as to the existence or authority or use of the Athanasian Creed amongst the Bishops assembled at Worms about the year 868[1]. I need not draw his attention to the facts that the style of thought is the same, and that the conclusion bears some similarity to the last verse of the Quicunque, even whilst, in addition to those which we have already noticed, it offers another mode of putting the statement contained in that verse. But it seems to me that, although we find here explanations of some of the clauses of the Quicunque, it is clear that the language before us is not drawn from that document: and this shews that that document, even if in existence in its completed form, had not as yet displaced other sermons, or professions, or treatises on the faith, which covered the same ground. I have appealed to the Profession of Arles of the year 813, as shewing that the Quicunque had no authority in that province at the beginning of the century: with equal boldness I appeal to the Profession of Worms, in the year 868, in proof that the Quicunque was not sanctioned there even after two-thirds of the century had gone by.

§ 28. The fourth Council of Constantinople — the eighth general Council as it is sometimes called—held in the year 869, instead of giving or repeating any Profession of Faith, stated its acceptance of the Roman Faith. What was meant by this?

§ 29. About the year 868 Æneas of Paris quoted some eighteen passages from "Athanasius" in proof of the double Procession: most, if not all, of them spurious. Of these Waterland took no notice. He only mentioned that Æneas quoted "the Athanasian Creed under the name of Fides Catholica, producing the same paragraph of it which Theodulphus had

[1] There is much more on the Trinity and Unity. Labbe, VIII. p. 947.

done sixty years before," *i.e.* clauses 21 to 28 inclusive. Can we consider this an independent testimony? The passage was adduced by Montfaucon and by Tentzel (p. 81). It was discovered by Usher in manuscript.

§ 30. "A.D. 868, about the same time, and in the same cause Ratram, or Bertram, monk of Corbey in France, makes a like use of this Creed, calling it a Treatise of the Faith." So Waterland. This too may be seen in Montfaucon's *Diatribe:* or in Tentzel, pp. 79, 80, who gives the credit of discovering the passage to Usher, to whom it is due. Ratram adduces only the clauses 21—23, and thus adds nothing to our knowledge of the details of the Creed as then received. He quotes them from the "libellus quem edidit [Athanasius] et omnibus Catholicis proposuit tenendum." But I think few people will commend Waterland for omitting to notice what he must, as a reader of Usher[1], have seen, that this same Ratram also brings "ex Athanasii libello fidei," a passage which is not found in the Quicunque, but is found in the document I have printed in the Appendix IV. to my last chapter. Thus we have additional proof that the Creed which I have there printed was known in France in the middle of the ninth century and attributed to Athanasius. In point of fact Ratram could not distinguish the sources from which he drew his quotations.

§ 31. Waterland has omitted to notice the work on the *Procession of the Holy Spirit,* which was attributed to Alcuin within forty years after his death, but the genuineness of which Sirmond very properly, in my opinion, hesitated to accept. This pseudo-Alcuin adduced clauses 21, 22, 23 in one part of the work[2], and 7, 25, 26, 27, 28 in another[3]. In the earlier passage these are his words "The blessed Athanasius in the Exposition of the Catholic Faith, which the admirable doctor himself composed, and which the universal Church confesses, declares the procession of the Holy Spirit from the Father and the Son, &c."

[1] *De Romano Symbolo.* Near the end (Vol. VII. p. 333 of the collected edition).

[2] Frobenius, II. p. 750. Migne, CI. p. 73.

[3] Ditto, p. 756. Migne, LXXXII. The Codex professes to have been given by Dido, bishop, to the Church of Laon. He died 891. But no one ever mentioned the work in the controversies which arose after Alcuin's death; and the style is not Alcuin's. Sirmond, Vol. II. p. 695, published it as the work of an uncertain author. See above p. 291, § 9.

It certainly was not true in the time of Alcuin that the Church universal acknowledged the Quicunque: it seems to have been unknown out of France. But this was a small matter. I would, however, draw attention to the description of the Quicunque, "the Exposition of the Catholic Faith." "Alcuin" quotes here also as genuine the *Altercation with Arius*[1].

§ 32. The profession of Adelbert when he was made Bishop of Morinum in 871, occupies an interesting position in our history. In some respects it resembles the professions of the English Bishops before their form became stereotyped; but we shall see that it has a character of its own[2].

He receives the six councils, the sixth being on "the two natures in the one Person of Christ:" and all who are condemned by the Fathers speaking in these Synods or afterwards by the Holy Spirit, he condemns. He promises to guard inviolably the epistle of Leo to Flavian, Bishop of Constantinople, and all his other epistles, "in which, amongst other things (as in the sermon of the blessed Athanasius which the Catholic Church is accustomed to use with veneration, and which begins, Whosoever would be saved before all things it is necessary that he hold the Catholic Faith)—after the proof by which we are taught how the Trinity of Persons in the Unity of Divinity and the Unity of Deity in the Trinity of Persons is to be worshipped—it is most plainly contained that alone of the same sacred Trinity our Lord and Saviour Jesus Christ, Son of God, and Son of Man, of two natures and in two natures, that is, divine and human, united in one Person, but remaining each in its properties and distinctiveness, is to be believed and preached: Who, according to the Apostolic Symbol being born according to the flesh of Mary, ever virgin, who is truly Mother of God, and having suffered and died, rose again and ascended into heaven, and sat at the right hand of God the Father Almighty, from whence He shall come to judge the quick and the dead: at Whose coming all men shall rise (*resurgent*) with their bodies, and shall give account of their own works, and shall receive, from the same just Judge, every one according as he has lived and persevered in his deeds, and shall go away for ever, the wicked into eternal fire, but the just into life eternal. I anathematize also all heresies, &c."

This profession is remarkable. Adelbert speaks of the *Sermon of Athanasius* as having been frequently used in the Church: but he does not say how it was used. The text of the Sermon is scarcely adequately represented, and the reference to the Apostles' Creed reminds us, in noteworthy fashion, of the document con-

[1] Frobenius, p. 755. Migne, p. 81. The writer adduces Jerome's *Symbolum* as authority that "in the Trinity there is nihil quod inferius superiusve dici possit." "The Creed of Jerome" does not contain any such passage.

[2] Labbe, VIII. 1883. Morinum = Taruenne in the province of Rheims, to the Church of which he promised canonical obedience. (Baluzius, *Capit.* II. p. 616.)

tained in the Treves manuscript. It should be noted also that the descent into hell is omitted: and that the bishop read *resurgent* where the Quicunque now has *resurgere habent:* the questions mooted by Godeschalk are entirely passed over[1].

§ 33. Almost contemporaneously with the last, we have an account of the Examination of Willibert, Bishop of Catalaunum (Chalons-sur-Marne), by Hincmar, before he would consecrate him. I cannot but connect with services like these the directions which Pertz so loosely assigned to the year 802. These directions tally closely with the forms now observed. The Profession of Faith is not given: but the newly-elected bishop read out one; and he bound himself to write out with his own hand the "Book of his Faith and Profession which he had now read over[2]."

§ 34. We have another confession at a later page[3], and a third against Pelagianism[4]. And once more, an order of consecration is described[5]—almost as in our Canterbury Registers—and we have reference again to a "libellus."

§ 35. There can be no doubt of the genuineness of the Capitulum of Hincmar, which I will cite next, although it refers to the examination of the clergy rather than to the professions of a bishop.

Hincmar required that each of his presbyters should learn, at fuller length than any had yet done, an Exposition of the Creed and of the Lord's Prayer, according to the tradition of the orthodox Fathers, and so diligently instruct the people committed to him. Then he is to learn the preface to the canon, and the canon of the mass itself, and the prayers of the mass; and be able to read the "Apostle" and Gospel, and know the words of the Psalms, and the pauses, by rule: and how to pronounce them from memory, and the usual Canticles. "And also let every one commit to memory the Sermon of Athanasius on the Faith, of which the commencement is *Quicunque vult salvus esse*—and let him comprehend its meaning, and be able to explain it in the vulgar tongue (communibus verbis enuntiare queat). He must also know the bap-

[1] This is the first profession in which I have found a promise to maintain the privileges of the metropolitan Roman Church.

[2] Labbe, VIII. 1881. The Archbishop promised obedience to the Blessed Peter and his vicar. See too Baluzius, *Capitularia*, Tom. II. p. 612.

[3] p. 1884.

[4] p. 1885.

[5] p. 1941.

tismal order, the exorcism of catechumens, and the reconciliation, and unction of the sick: the homilies of Gregory, and the computus, and the cantus, the matin office, and the hours[1].

§ 36. I may mention here that among the writings of John VIII., who was Pope from 873 to 882, is a letter which he is said to have written to Photius—it is of course disputed in recent times—in which he is reported to have stated

"We do not say *ex Filio* in the Symbol, and moreover we condemn those, who, at the beginning, dared in their madness to make this addition, as being transgressors of the divine law, as being subverters of the Theology of Christ our Lord and of the holy pontiffs and other holy fathers, who, being synodically assembled, delivered to us the holy Symbol." If this is genuine (and it does little more than repeat in stronger language the sentiments which Leo III. held at the beginning of the century) it is clear that the Athanasian Creed could not have been received at Rome at this period of the century[2].

§ 37. There is a curious letter from John to Willibert of Cologne, on the deficiency of his profession: "he had not mentioned the Universal Synods, nor the Decretals[3]."

§ 38. In 878 I find an order from John, addressed to the Archbishop of Ravenna; "all Metropolitans were to send an Exposition of their Faith to Rome, within three months after their consecration[4]."

§ 39. Marinus gave Fulco the pallium *post emissam orthodoxæ fidei professionem*[5]. As the Roman Church seems not to have adopted the Athanasian Creed for some years to come, it is improbable that this Profession could have embraced the Quicunque. One of our manuscripts seems to shew that Fulco must have known it[6].

§ 40. We owe to Waterland, not only the quotation of the profession of Adelbert, but also the charge of Riculfus of Soissons, in the year 889. "He calls it a Treatise or Discourse of the Catholic Faith, *Sermonem Fidei Catholicæ cujus initium est Quicunque vult salvus esse*, and places it between the Psalms and the Canon of the Mass, requiring all his clergy to know it by

1 Labbe, VIII. 569 and elsewhere.
2 The letter is in Labbe, IX. 235.
3 Labbe, ut supra, p. 238.
4 Ditto, p. 300.
5 p. 357.
6 C. C. C. Cambridge.

memory, truly and correctly." The order bears a strong resemblance to that of Hincmar, and indeed Soissons was in the province of Rheims. We learn thus that the direction of the Archbishop in 852 was supplemented by a suffragan, forty-seven years later. The Quicunque could scarcely have been introduced as yet into the regular daily service in the diocese of Soissons.

§ 41. Under the year 760 Waterland has the following:

"Regino, abbot of Prom in Germany, an author of the ninth and tenth century, has, among other collections, some Articles of Inquiry, supposed by Baluzius the editor to be as old, or very nearly, as the age of Boniface, Bishop of Mentz, who died in the year 754. In those Articles, there is one to this purpose: Whether the clergy have by heart Athanasius's Tract upon the Faith of the Trinity, beginning with *Whosoever will be saved*, &c. This testimony I may venture to place about 760, a little after the death of Boniface."

The note as to the supposition of Baluzius was probably taken (as was much of Waterland's information) from Tentzel's little volume, p. 69.

Regino had been Abbot of Prum, a monastery in the diocese of Treves, from the year 892 to the year 899. He was then deposed, and went to Treves, where he resided at the monastery of Maximinus. At the request of Ratbod, the Archbishop of Treves, Regino compiled a series of articles of inquiry, Visitation articles as we should call them, ninety-five in number, for the Archbishop to use in his visitations. To these he appended a series of authorities by which he justified his selection. I need not say that they are deeply interesting, giving, as they do, an insight into the manners and requirements of the age.

Some of the visitation inquiries refer to pagans, and to customs and superstitions handed down from pagan times; and, consequently, Baluzius says in his notes (p. 534), that he might think that the series was first formed in the age of Boniface, or certainly not much later, and was then gradually increased and amended according to the various wants and customs of the churches. But Baluzius never makes the broad statement which Waterland professes to extract from him. In fact the volume itself contains the refutation of Waterland's assertion.

Of the articles of inquiry the first sixteen relate to the Church and its furniture: the seventeenth and following questions regard the life of the presbyters. No. 55 enquires Whether he has taught the Lord's Prayer and the Symbolum to all his parishioners? No. 59, Does he invite to confession on the Wednesday before Lent all his parishioners, ascribing to each his due penance? No. 60, Do all communicate three times a year? No. 34, Does he celebrate at the appointed hour, *i.e.* at 9 o'clock, and then fast till noon, in order that he may sing mass for any stranger that may happen to come? No. 82, Has he, by him, an Exposition of the Symbol and the Lord's Prayer, written according to the tradition of the orthodox Fathers? does he understand it and diligently teach, out of it, the people committed to his charge? The next three enquire, Does he well understand the prayers of the mass? Can he read and expound the Epistle and the Gospel? Does he know how to pronounce, regularly, the words and pauses of the Psalms with the accustomed Canticles? Does he know the Sermon of Athanasius? Has he a computus? a martyrology? and so on. These articles of enquiry are followed up thus: "These things which we have laid down above under their several heads as to be enquired into, ought to be corroborated by Canonical authority."

When we pass on to examine these Canonical authorities, we find they are taken from all countries and from all ages. From the Apostolic Constitutions; from the Decretals; from writings of Leo, Augustine, Benedict; from Councils of Carthage, Neocæsarea, and Antioch. But they are taken, almost equally, from the Capitulars, from Synods of Rheims, Aix 805, 847, Salzburg 803, Worms 868, Mayence 888, Nantz 895, and the authorities are given by the collector. How Waterland could say that the enquiries belong to the time of Boniface, I cannot make out: the very chapter which directs that the trees and stones which had been dedicated to dæmons should be cut down and destroyed, dates from the Council of Nantz: our own records of English superstitions are such that we cannot agree with Baluzius that a canon of this kind must have belonged to the middle of the eighth century: in point of fact we see that it was extracted from a canon of the end of the ninth century.

Yet, amongst all them, the canon of Autun relating to the Faith of Athanasius is not quoted; nor the order of Hatto; nor the Capitula of Aix which Pertz assigns to the year 802. In fact there is no authority adduced for the enquiry regarding the "Sermon of Athanasius." Canons 204 and 205 of the first book are merely copies of the Capitula regarding the preaching of the presbyter: canon 275 is the ordinance of Rheims enforcing the knowledge of the Symbol and the Lord's Prayer[1]. Canon 453 gives directions as to the examination for orders. One of these directions shews clearly that the *fides catholica* did not mean the Quicunque. "Before all things, do they hold firmly the Catholic Faith? and are they able to teach it in simple language?" Thus I repeat that Regino, who found a superabundance of authorities for his other topics of enquiry, has adduced none to uphold the question regarding the Sermon of Athanasius. I can only conclude that he was either ignorant of the canon of Autun, or believed that it referred to something else, and

[1] Canon 304 contains the absolution after confession: "Deus omnipotens sit adjutor et protector tuus et præstet indulgentiam de peccatis tuis præteritis, præsentibus et futuris."

that the order of Hatto had escaped his notice. At all events the supposition that we may reasonably assign this canon to the time of Boniface falls to the ground. We cannot ascribe it to a higher date than the time of Regino himself.

§ 42. The Quicunque, however, spread into the North of Italy before the end of the tenth century. In the second volume of D'Achery's *Spicilegium* is a long address which is attributed to Ratherius of Verona, and which, I believe, is nearly the same as one found in the Vienna Manuscript, 1261, which contains the short copy of the Quicunque that I have printed elsewhere. This is an admonition by a bishop to his brethren, presbyters and ministers of the Lord.

"We are your shepherds (he says), as you are shepherds of souls." He urges them to a holy and chaste life, to rise for nocturns, to observe the celebration of masses, to wash the holy vessels with their own hands. He speaks of the lectionary, the antiphonary and the gradual[1]: every one should have his own. They should baptize only on the Eves of Easter and Pentecost except in case of danger: they were to teach their parishioners the Creed and Lord's Prayer: they were to urge all their parishioners to come three times a year to the Communion of the Body and Blood of Christ (*four times* in Labbe, *i. e.* Christmas, Thursday in Holy Week, Easter, and Pentecost). They were to observe Sunday. Godfathers were to teach their godchildren the Creed and the Lord's Prayer: and every one of the clergy was to have (if it can be done, says Labbe) in writing an Exposition of the Symbol and Lord's Prayer in accordance with the traditions of the orthodox Fathers, and understand it thoroughly, and from it, in his preaching, carefully instruct the people committed to his charge: "he must know the words and pauses of the Psalms, and hold in his memory the Sermon of the Bishop Athanasius on the Faith of the Holy Trinity which commences *Quicunque vult*, &c.[2], and understand its meaning and be able to explain it in the vulgar tongue."

Thus these directions, so far as the Quicunque is concerned, are merely a repetition of the orders of Hincmar, a circumstance which, for some reason or other, Waterland omits to notice in his quotation.

Waterland assigns the date of this to 960: Labbe, who ascribes it to two different authorities, gives the later date as 1009, the reign of Henry[3].

[1] In Labbe we have "missal, lectionary and antiphonary."

[2] There seems to be a slight play on the words "quæ ita incipit Quicunque vult salvus esse. Quicunque vult ergo sacerdos in nostra parochia esse."

[3] I have noticed the spread of the Creed into the diocese of Verona in the year 960, contemporaneously, as it seems, with the corrected, *i. e.* the Gallican psal-

§ 43. About 975, Pilgrim, Bishop of Laureacum (Lorsch, near Salzburg), sent his confession to the Pope and asked for the pallium. He describes it thus:

"The Venerable Symbol of that Catholic Faith which I hold and teach." It began "I confess and believe," following on the lines of many documents which we have seen before—and ending "This faith of my profession I promise to retain inviolate and never to deviate from it[1]." The Pope was satisfied and Pilgrim was made Archbishop; his province being taken out of Salzburg. All I need say here is this; Although the Symbol really contained nothing additional to the Quicunque, it was not it. I conjecture that the Quicunque was not as yet cared for—or, perhaps, known—in the province of Salzburg.

§ 44. There is a profession of Faith by Gerbert in the *Concilia* under the year 991[2].

§ 45. A passage in the Apology of Abbo of Fleury has deservedly attracted much attention. Baronius was the first, I believe, to adduce it under the year 1001, and it was noticed by Voss, Tentzel, Montfaucon, Muratori, and Beveridge, before it fell into the way of Waterland. It occurs in a somewhat curious letter which Abbo wrote to the Counts Hugh and Robert, a letter[3] which gives us some insight into the opinions of the times:

"First of all (he says) I wish to speak of my Faith, without which I shall not be able to be saved (salvus esse non potero), so that, by my examination, others may receive benefit, or by my remonstrances others may know if they have fallen into heresy. If they have so fallen, they must seek to be drawn out of it, as rapidly as possible, lest, if they remain in it until death, they become (stipula diaboli) chaff for the devil: for, whosoever, whether regarding God or religion or the common state of holy Church, believes differently from what Christ has taught, or under the holy Apostles the Catholic Church has held and handed down to the succession of the Apostles, is plainly not a Catholic, nor faithful, but a heretic.

ter. Ratherius directed that his clergy should lose no time in learning the faith or belief (credulitas) of God in its three forms: i. according to the Symbol or "collation" of the Apostles *as it is found in the corrected psalters;* ii. that which is sung at the mass; iii. that which begins *Quicunque vult.* This is not adduced by Montfaucon, Muratori, or Tentzel; they are content with quoting the enquiry; "Si sermonem... Athanasii episcopi de fide Trinitatis, cujus initium est Quicunque vult salvus esse, memoriter teneat." Sandius (says Tentzel) remarks that the admonition is generally attributed to Leo IV. (?), but Tentzel prudently declines to discuss the question.

[1] Labbe, IX. 716.

[2] p. 739.

[3] This is to be seen in Migne, CXXXIX. p. 462.

"Our fathers followed up all heresies, in order that no one should think contrary to the Apostles, and if any one did so think, he might be deprived of the Holy Communion and be shunned more than a serpent. Thus we are prohibited even from praying with such: and I hope that ye, Hugh and Robert, Kings of the Franks, will follow the example of earlier orthodox princes, if ye wish to be heirs and joint heirs of those who lived on earth for Christ: and will expel from your kingdom every heretical pravity, in order that God may guard you in eternal peace."

Then on pages 470, 471 we find the passage which Waterland and others quote.

"First I thought I ought to speak of the Faith, which I have heard varied, when sung with alternate choirs in France and in the Church of the English. Some say (according to Athanasius in my opinion) *the Holy Spirit is of the Father and the Son: not made nor created nor begotten but proceeding:* others *the Holy Spirit is of the Father and the Son, not made nor created but proceeding.* These when they withdraw the phrase *not begotten* think that they are following the Synodical letter of Pope Gregory where it is written, *the Holy Spirit is not unbegotten nor begotten, but only proceeding*[1]."

Of the many copies of the Creed which I have seen, I have only discovered one which does not contain the words "non genitus:" it is the copy in the great Venice Bible.

§ 46. The lines

Catholicamque fidem quam composuisse beatus
Fertur Athanasius,

which Waterland after Montfaucon and Tentzel (p. 87) quotes from Gualdo of Corbey, are not worthy of more than a passing notice.

§ 47. But the next authority, Honorius of Autun, whom Waterland seems to have been the first to adduce, is deserving of larger consideration.

His *Gemma Animæ*, a work on the sacred offices, is of great interest at a time like the present, when the usages of various Churches are attracting so much attention:

Thus we hear that the two candles which precede the gospel represent the law and the prophets: the two candle-bearers being Moses and Elias. We read of the people sacrificing some gold, some silver, others of their substance: the women "offer the victim of praise (hostiam laudis) to the Lord." In chapter xxix he says (truly enough) that the rite of the synagogue had passed over into the religion of the Church, and tells us, shortly afterwards, that tithes are the legal sacrifice, any-

[1] I take this from Migne, who differs from Waterland.

thing else being voluntary: "they offer for sin when they pay for the penance enjoined by the priest." The Sacrifice in the Eucharist seems in his opinion to have consisted of the bread and the wine and the water; the bread was in the form of the denarii, because Christ the Bread of Life was sold for so many denarii, and His image and superscription are put on each. The Mass is sung daily, because (i) as labourers in the vineyard, we need daily to be refreshed by Him: because (ii) we are daily incorporated with Him, in order that (iii) the memory of Christ's sufferings may be daily inculcated on the faithful.

There is much of interest in the symbolism of Honorius. The expanded arms of the priest signify Christ upon the cross: the deacons behind the Bishop signify the Apostles running away: the subdeacons behind the altar represent the women standing afar off. The priest inclines to the altar: the raising of the cup denotes the elevation of Christ upon the cross: the priest bows his head where Christ, bowing His head, gave up the ghost: the Deacon washes his hands, as Pilate did; the covering of the cup with the napkin represents Joseph wrapping the body in fine linen, the Chalice then signifying the sepulchre, and the Paten on the top of it, the stone. All received; First, the Bishop, as Christ did eat of the broiled fish and the honey-comb with the Apostles; then the ministers, as the Apostles did eat with their Lord at Tiberias; and then the people, because the Lord on the point of His Ascension did eat with the people. So Jesus, when He made His Body and Blood out of the Bread and Wine, directed His people to celebrate these things in memory of Him.

Honorius then describes how the additions were made in the mass service by different popes: Leo added the words *Holy sacrifice, spotless victim.* He delights in noting that the words, Alleluia, Osanna, Amen are Hebrew: Kyrie eleison ymas, are Greek: the rest is Latin. The Angelic Choir sang the *Gloria in excelsis* toward the eastern Bethlehem: so do we sing it toward the East. *Panis* is so important, because it is derived from *pan*, and *pan omne dicitur.* Mass was celebrated *hora tertia, hora sexta, hora nona.* The *Credo in unum Deum* was sung on all Sundays and feasts commemorative of events in the life of the Lord, feasts of the Virgin, birthdays of the Apostles, festivals of the Saints, and on the dedication of the Church. Pope Pelagius had introduced nine prefaces: Gregory, the tenth, *i. e.* for St Andrew's: and, lately, Urban the second (he was Pope from March 1088 to July 1099) the preface *de Sancta Maria.*

The *casula* represents charity covering the multitude of sins: the *cope* is the proper dress of the singers.

"We bow to the East and the West, shewing that we adore God as everywhere present."

And thus we come to the passage regarding the Creeds which Waterland quoted. "The Catholic Faith, as uttered or rather strengthened at four various times, the Catholic Church receives, and in the four quarters of the world observes and keeps inviolably. First, the Apostolic Symbol, the *Credo in Deum*, she lays down for herself as the Foundation of all: she sings it daily at the commencement of the day and at the commencement of the Hours, *i. e.* at Prime: and with it she completes her daily work when she recites it at Compline. Then the Faith *I believe in God the Father* is read in the Synods: this Creed the Nicene Synod put forth. Thirdly, the Faith *I believe in one God* she sings in the congregation of her people at mass: that I mean, which was promulgated by the means of the Council of Constantinople. Fourthly she repeats daily at prime the Faith *Quicunque vult,* which Athanasius, Bishop of Alexandria, at the request of the Emperor Theodosius put forth. During the other hours the Holy Trinity is worshipped."

On a later page I read "the faith *Quicunque* exhibits our course through life: for by faith we walk, in order that we may attain to sight."

In Book III. I find a chapter stating that over male children the Creed is recited in Greek, over female children in Latin. This must be the Nicene Creed. Section 166 describes how the Nativity of the Blessed Virgin was discovered. Book IV. § 41 speaks of Trinity Sunday as the Baptismal Sunday after Pentecost.

§ 48. It is unnecessary to follow out the notices of the Athanasian Creed further. We know that it was now used at prime generally, north of the Alps; and that it was sung with alternate choirs. I will only add that there is no memorial as yet that it was known in Greece. Three memoranda I will add however. One is from Otho of Frisingen (1147), whom Waterland, after Antelmi, adduces as the earliest authority for the statement that Athanasius wrote the Creed in Treves. Antelmi, I believe, considered that our "Colbertine Manuscript" was the authority for this. In time, as Dean Stanley has said, the very hole in the Abbey of St Maximin, near the Black Gate, was pointed out, where Athanasius wrote it in the concealment of his Western exile[1].

§ 49. Another is, that Arnoldus in his Chronicle, about the year 1171, quotes one Henry, Abbot of Brunswick, as adducing "Athanasium in Symbolo Fidei:" the first known instance where it is called a Symbol or Creed. This notwithstanding, Innocent III., who was Pope from 1198 to 1216, taught that there were only two Creeds, two Symbols, the Apostles' and Nicene.

[1] Dean of Westminster on the Athanasian Creed, p. 2.

The legends about Athanasius' doings at Treves grew up very rapidly in the tenth and eleventh centuries. Thus (Pertz, IX. p. 171) Henger, bishop of Liege (Leodiensium), made a great deal of Athanasius being received by Maximinus, Archbishop of Treves; he it is that said that the great patriarch was confined six years in a cistern and never saw the sun for the whole time; and, whilst in this confinement, composed the Quicunque. About the year 1019 (Pertz, XII. p. 605) we read that St Haimond was wont "accedente passione ymnum Athanasii Quicunque vult salvus esse—decantare." So in 1121 (Pertz, X. 201) Godfrey, Archbishop, referred to the Quicunque as the work of Athanasius. The passage from Arnold, which Waterland quotes, is in vol. XXI. (=Laws, vol. IV.) p. 127 of Pertz. (The name is spelt Athanasius, Atanasius, Anastasius.) We have superabundant evidence that the dispute of Athanasius with Arius was in the ninth century considered to be genuine (Pertz, I. 297).

§ 50. We have seen that in their Books on the Divine Offices, neither Isidore of Seville, nor Walfrid Strabo, nor Rabanus Maurus, nor Amalarius, makes any reference to the use of the Athanasian Creed in the Church. The order of Hatto does not carry conviction to me, except of a local use, because it is not mentioned in the Collection of Ansegius, nor in that of Benedict the "Levite," nor in that of Regino—who, as I have said, merely gives a recommendation without citing any older authority. The mistake of Waterland regarding Anscharius I have pointed out. Adelbert speaks of it as a *Sermo*, and, as I understand him, in frequent use: Abbo of Fleury as sung with alternating choirs. It is interesting, therefore, to add the following description of the Prime service from a book, *De Officiis Ecclesiasticis*, which used to be assigned to Hugo of St Victor, but is now generally attributed to one Robertus Paululus, who is supposed to have lived about the year 1178[1]. After speaking of the Psalms and stating how, to each repetition, the Gloria Patri is added, in order that we might not, in reciting parts of the Old Testament, forget our duty towards the New, he proceeds:

"To these the devotion of the faithful had added *Quicunque vult salvus esse* in order that at no hour of the day should we forget those articles of the faith which are necessary to salvation." The *Quicunque* was followed by a lesson from Isaiah, and, after a while, by the *Kyrie eleison* and the Lord's Prayer: but the Symbolum is not mentioned here.

In another work, attributed to the same writer, but which is spurious, we have another chapter on the Offices of the Canonical Hours[2]. On Prime the writer says:

"Since this hour is the beginning of the day, in it we praise God Who has granted us to pass the night in safety. Having invoked therefore the divine aid and glorified the Trinity of Persons, that is having uttered the words *Deus in adjutorium, Gloria Patri*—we sing the hymn *Jam lucis orto sidere.* Then at this first hour we daily sing five psalms, in order that our five senses may be protected from heaven during the day. To this we add the Exposition of the Catholic Faith, because *This is the victory that overcometh the world, even our faith:* and it is a strong shield against our ancient enemy; therefore Peter saith *Whom resist stedfast in the faith.* At this hour the Lord's Prayer is said, in which the seven petitions go up for the seven gifts of the Holy Spirit, through which we may receive the seven virtues, so that, delivered by them from

[1] *De Officiis Ecclesiasticis.* Lib. II. cap. 1, de hora prima. Migne, CLXXVII. p. 408.

[2] *Speculum de mysteriis ecclesiæ.* Migne, CLXXVII. p. 344.

the seven sins, we may attain to the seven beatitudes." Then by means of the Symbol of the Faith they are armed against all adversities, who are purified by the use of the Lord's Prayer.

We have this interesting corroboration of the statement of Abbo of Fleury: and now we have proof that the original order that the Quicunque should be sung on Sundays at Prime was extended, as in the Canons of Regino, to a daily usage. It will be noticed that it was distinguished, very clearly, from the Symbolum Fidei, the Apostles' Creed, which always followed it; and that it was still viewed as an Exposition of the Catholic Faith.

Hugo was a Canon of the Augustinian Church of St Victor at Paris, and died in the year 1140. We may fairly, I think, assume that when this work was assigned to him, the custom at Paris was to repeat the Quicunque daily.

§ 51. I have also quoted the curious passage which Baluzius printed[1] from the Catalogue of the Abbots of Fleury, where it is said that Theodulf gave an Explanation "of the Symbol of Athanasius which the monks chant daily at Prime after the regular psalms." Of course this evidence is comparatively late[2]. Martene, however, shews that at the Church of St Martins at Tours, it was directed to be sung daily at Prime, with the consent of all the Chapter, in the year 922. And he cites Udalric as stating (in Book I. *Of the Customs of the Cluniack Churches*), that whilst amongst other churches the Quicunque was chanted on Sundays only, in this order it was never omitted even on "private days." It was sung "with other Psalms." So, "ex Tullensi S. Afri Ordinario," it seems that on Sundays it was said after the *Domine exaudi*, on other days before the Antiphon. The Carthusians (as Waterland informs us) kept its use up daily. At the Church of Laon we learn that "after the *Symbol* Quicunque," there came Prayer and the Credo.

As for the neighbourhood of Rupert of Deutz, the Athanasian Creed was not introduced at Prime when he wrote his book, *De Canonum Observatione*[3].

I must reserve further remarks to a later page.

[1] *Miscellanea*, Tom. I.

[2] See Martene, Lib. IV. cap. 4, or prima (Vol. IV. p. 17).

[3] See Hittorp's Collection. It is not in Migne.

CHAPTER XXII.

CREEDS CONTAINED IN COLLECTIONS OF SERMONS AND BOOKS OF DEVOTION, &c.

§ 1. Muratori's Milan Manuscript. § 2. Anglo-Saxon Ritual. § 3. Book of Deer. § 4. Royal 2 A. xx. § 5. Vienna Manuscript, 1032. § 6. Vienna Manuscript, 1261. § 7. Vienna Manuscript, 2223. § 8. Bobio Manuscript, Milan, I. 101. sup. § 9. Bangor Antiphonary, Milan, C. 5. inf. § 10. St Germain des Près. § 11. Paris, National Library, 4908. § 12. Book of Cerne, Cambridge, Ll. 1. 10. § 13. Usher's Hymn Book. § 14. Hymn Book of Franciscan Convent, Dublin.

AMONG the most interesting documents which have come to us from the Church of the early middle ages, a prominent place must be given to the COLLECTIONS OF SERMONS and BOOKS OF DEVOTION. I do not know that any attempt has been made to form a series of these documents, and the volumes which I shall bring forward in the present chapter merely represent those which have fallen under my own notice in connection with our present subject. Yet knowing the excitement which was roused at the end of the seventeenth century on that subject, and which indeed has been sustained since, I feel confident that very few copies of the Quicunque have escaped attention in any of the libraries of Europe.

§ 1. The most celebrated of these collections that contain the Quicunque was discovered by Muratori in the Ambrosian Library. Of this he gave some account in the second volume of his famous *Anecdota*, and I think it will be a relief to my readers if I here insert an abstract of his important paper.

"Cardinal Vincentius Maria Ursini, archbishop of Benevento, in his dissertation claiming the relicks of St Bartholomew for Benevento, happens to speak of some of the faults to be found in the Roman Breviary. Among them he mentions that the Symbol, *Quicunque vult salvus esse*, is, in our modern Breviaries, ascribed to St Athanasius, a thing which the great majority of the most learned men consider to be not his, although they do not agree as to the true Author; and he refers to Quesnel." Muratori, in corroboration of this assertion, appeals to the writings of Voss, Godefridus Hermantius, Dupin, Natalis Alexander, Daniel Papebroche, Cabassutius, John Mabillon, William Cave, Casimer Oudin, and others. He himself considers that "there is in the Creed such a complete and direct repudiation of the errors of Nestorius and Eutyches, that it must have been written long after the times of both these heretics, and à fortiori long after the time of St Athanasius. Moreover, if Athanasius did write it, why was it never quoted in those later disputes, by men like Gregory Nazianzenus, Jerome, Augustine, Popes Cœlestinus and Leo the Great, Cyril of Alexandria, Cassian and others—to whom this testimony would have been of the greatest value, if known? Why was it overlooked in our later disputes—when the Photian schism was waxing hot? Surely, because Photius did not know it, and thus would not have acknowledged its authority, if it had been adduced. Once more: how, if Athanasius was the Author, is it conceivable that both word and sentiment of the ὁμοούσιος are absent? For years this was the one and only watchword of the Catholics. Fourthly: although there were many Professions of Faith in the fourth century, yet Athanasius attributed so much importance to the Nicene Symbol, that it was the only formula that he used in testimony of his own faith. See the commencement of his letter to the Emperor Jovinianus (Migne, XXVI. p. 814), and so again in his letter to the Antiochenes (*ibid.*, p. 800). Nor was there any occasion for Athanasius ever to compose it. Certainly the occasion which the great father of the Annals suggests, namely, the visit to the Pope Julius, is insufficient for the purpose. For of what heresy was this great Catholic Doctor ever suspected? The Arians had accused him not of heresy, but that he was addicted to magic, fond of money, and rebellious against the Emperor.

"But there are other arguments. I would not lay much stress on the fact, although fact it is, that the Creed seems to be of Latin and not of Greek origin; that the Latin text is almost uniform, the Greek texts vary largely; or that the Creed was early known to the Latins, and only in later times to the Greeks. But I do think much of this: that amongst the very numerous Greek manuscripts in which the Ambrosian Library abounds, I have never met with a single copy of the Creed in Greek; on the other hand, I have met with some in Latin, and these of very ancient date, as I shall shew below[1]. 'Still why should not Athanasius write in Latin?' This is not enough. Montfaucon in his edition of *Athanasius* published this year (1698) puts the Creed among the spurious works. And *Thomasius* in his Psalter published last year (which he quotes) takes the same view.

"In regard to the true Author, Peter Pithæus leans to a French writer, and Voss follows his opinion. Quesnel (whose argument he gives) leans to Vigilius of Tapsus; his date suits the circumstances, as being after the Chalcedon Council, and it was his fashion to father his

[1] Muratori adduces only one copy.

works on men of greater renown than himself. And one Manuscript is known, in which, immediately after a dialogue against the Arians, Sabellians and Photinians, written by Vigilius and assigned to Athanasius, follows this *Fides dicta a Sancto Athanasio Episcopo*[1]. I don't think much of this (says Muratori). Antelmi followed in the year 1693[2]; he first shewed that there was no resemblance between the Quicunque and the works of Vigilius. He said there was a likeness to Augustine's works; yet no one attributed it to St Augustine. Why then to Vigilius, even if the statements of Quesnel were well founded? Moreover, in the olden time, the name of Athanasius was not prefixed to the Quicunque. Antelmi was led to regard Vincentius of Lerins as the author, for he was born either in Treves or on the borders of Belgium, and thus was near enough to Gaul to satisfy the conditions of the problem. Antelmi shewed, by comparison, how close the resemblance is between some sentences of Vincent's and some passages of the Creed." Muratori thinks that Antelmi is nearest to the truth. Then he quotes Cardinal Bona, *de diversa Psalmodia*, cap. XVI. § 18 (the passage given by Waterland)[3], and speaks also of Anastasius of Sinai, and Athanasius of Spire. "To my mind, on the whole (he proceeds), these people have rather involved the subject in the clouds than freed it from them." And so he enters on the question, "What was the first date when it was assigned to Athanasius?" Muratori refers with contempt to the interpolation in Augustine's *Enarratio ad Psal.* CXX. p. 1970 (vol. IV.). "The first record is that which Sirmond *æterni nominis* found *in Divoniensi quodam codice*, and which he printed in his *Concil. Gall.* Tom. I. p. 507[4]. Both Sirmond and Labbe guessed that this might perhaps be referred to the Council of Autun held about the year 670 under S. Leodegard." "*Canonem hunc ad Synodum Augustodunensem, circiter annum Christi DC.LXX. sub Sancto Leodegardo celebratam, fortasse referendum tum ipsemet Sirmondus tum Labbeus autumarunt.*" Then comes the passage about Papebroche quoted by Waterland in his note[5], followed by a passage which Waterland does not quote, asserting Muratori's opinion that "the canon in question does not appear to belong to the council under Leodegard, but rather to some other, celebrated at another time doubtless in the same city[6]. Wherefore we cannot draw from this statement any good argument for the antiquity of the Creed. The verbal similarities with the fourth Synod of Toledo are not of such a character as to shew that the Fathers there knew the Creed. Indeed any one can see that the formula may have been drawn from the Synod and that the Creed may have been thus compounded[7]. Thus we come to the ninth century after Christ, before the first mention of the Athanasian Creed occurs. Theodulf bishop of Orleans in his book de Spiritu Sancto quotes the Creed and attributes it to Athanasius. So does Hincmar against Godeschalk: and there agree with them Agobard of

[1] I question whether this is the Quicunque. It must be that printed p. 273.

[2] Muratori only knew his work second-hand.

[3] Chapter II. note to the year 1337. It is the passage in which William of Baldensal is quoted as assigning the Latin translation to Eusebius of Vercelli.

[4] The Canon of Autun.

[5] Chapter II. second note.

[6] Why did Waterland omit this?

[7] This passage is quoted by Waterland in a note to Chapter VI.

Lyons, Frederick of Utrecht, Anschar of Hamburg, Ratram of Corbey, Æneas of Paris, Abbo of Fleury, Ratherius of Liege[1], and others, of whom you may find a catalogue in a dissertation, which I have not yet seen, written by Tentzel and published in the year 1687. So far then as we can gather from the literary history it began to be first known in the ninth century, and to be then pressed under the name of St Athanasius. Thus you may see how mistaken Voss was in attributing it, in the first instance, to the thirteenth century, although, afterwards, overcome by the arguments of learned men, he threw the date back to the thousandth year after Christ.

"The enquiry now comes, Can any vestiges of it be found prior to the ninth century? In answer to this, Usher of Armagh refers to a Gallican Psalter in the Cotton Library, which he considers to be as old as the time of Gregory the Great. And Antelmi in his disquisition declares that there is preserved in the Colbertine Collection a most ancient codex wherein the Creed is found, again without the name of Athanasius, which codex he considers to be older than the Cottonian. For my part (says Muratori) I could scarcely believe even a theologian of the high character of Antelmi, when he maintained that the manuscript had such antiquity, and I grieved beyond measure that I had not myself seen the Disquisition of this divine; when, behold, the renowned Bernard de Montfaucon himself relieved me of my anxiety. He visited me at Milan, and, during my intercourse with him, he affirmed that the two Manuscripts mentioned were written in the times of Charles the Great, and that the antiquity could not possibly be assigned to them, which Antelmi was disposed to give. But, in our Ambrosian Library, we have a Manuscript of no less excellence, brought to us from the celebrated Library of Bobio; and here too you may find the Creed, introduced however without any title. It is the same codex out of which I have extracted the Apology of Bachiarius (which he had printed on pages 9 to 26 of this second volume)—a codex clearly of a most ancient date, written a thousand years ago or more—as I have conjectured (conjeci) in the prolegomena to Bachiarius and on page 16 of my earlier tome. In the front of the book there is written, in another yet still ancient hand, *In this book the following things are contained: a Book of the dogma of faith: the Faith of Bachiarius: Sermon on the Ascension of the Lord: the Faith of Jerome: Confession of faith of Ambrose: Jerome's Rule of the Catholic faith: Book on the Trinity: Three books of Ambrose on the Trinity: the same Father's book of faith.* Yet, out of these nine books, the five last are not found, and as the codex has never been mutilated, they seem never to have been in it. The *Book of the Dogma* is *The Book on Ecclesiastical Dogmas* which was once attributed to Augustine but is now by all assigned to Gennadius of Marseilles. On this (says Muratori) the reader may expect some notes in a little tract I am about to commit to the press. After the *Faith of Bachiarius* and the Symbol Quicunque[2], follows (as the table of contents indicates) a sermon on the Ascension, with fragments on the Trinity; I know not who is the author. Then follows the Faith of Jerome—that which used

[1] He introduced the Creed at Verona after his return from Liege. See Waterland.

[2] The Symbol is not mentioned in the table of contents.

to be published among Jerome's works under the name of Pope Damasus." The rest are, as I have mentioned, missing. Muratori then says a few words on the Greek copies of the Creed, and prints the Quicunque as he found it in his codex—a corrected copy of this I will give ere long—and then he mentions that after the words *salvus esse non poterit* with which our Creed concludes, these words immediately follow in the same line: "Lacta, mater, eum qui fecit te, qui talem fecit te, ut ipse fieret in te. Lacta eum qui fructum fecunditatis tibi dedit conceptus, et decus virginitatis non abstulit natus."

Muratori regrets that he does not know the writer of the lines: if he did, "they might lead him to make conjectures as to the writer of the Creed."

On this codex Muratori takes his stand. He maintains that it must have been written before the time of Photius, and that the words *a Patre et Filio* are genuine; although both in the Book of Gennadius and the so-called Confession of Damasus, the Holy Spirit is spoken of as proceeding from the Father only.

Muratori has another essay on the Exposition of Fortunatus (of which below). He thought that Venantius Fortunatus was the author not only of the Comment but also of the Creed itself.

Thus, as will be seen, Muratori's supports for his opinion that the Creed (as he calls it) is earlier than the time of Charlemagne are (i) the character of the writing of this manuscript from Bobio, and (ii) his surmise that the Fortunatus whose name is introduced into the title of the Exposition was Venantius Fortunatus. This last is mere surmise. So we are reduced to the former; and as to it, Montfaucon's opinion is given in his Italian travels. He considered that it is a "Codex of the eighth century, Lombardic character: in it are the Book of Gennadius, the Faith of Bachiarius, the Creed of Athanasius, all in the same handwriting."

I saw the MS. at Milan in the month of August, 1872. Dr Ceriani, the well-known librarian, to whom I would here express my great obligations, assured me that he considered it to be of the eighth century. Through the kindness of the Rev. D. M. Clerke, Prebendary of Wells and Rector of Kingston Deverill, Wilts., I have since received a photograph of three pages containing the Quicunque[1], and from it and my notes I would supplement and correct the account given by Muratori. The manuscript is marked O. 212. sup. The Quicunque follows closely upon a kind of sermon, entitled by Muratori, *Fides Bachiarii*, which he printed at length[2]. This "Faith," properly speaking, commences on page 14 of Muratori's volume, and occupies about five pages. It seems to me to be on the whole consentient with the Athanasian Creed, except perhaps in regard to clauses 21, 22, 23, from which

[1] A facsimile of the first page is given below.
[2] *Anecdota*, II. p. 8.

it differs seriously[1]; thus it is clear that it was not taken from the Quicunque. The verbal similarities are very few[2]. This ends, according to Muratori, with some remarks on the Resurrection of the Dead, followed up by this:

"Hic est nostrae fidei thesaurus quem signatum Ecclesiastico Symbolo, quod in baptismo accepimus, custodimus. Sic coram Deo corde credimus: sic coram hominibus labiis confitemur, ut et hominibus cognitio sua fidem faciat, et Deo imago sua testimonium reddat."

Thus once more we come upon a document entitled "a Faith," which expands, expounds, and enforces the Baptismal Creed. According to the table of contents of this manuscript, as I have given it above from Muratori, a sermon on the Ascension of our Lord immediately follows on this Faith of Bachiarius. Thus the maker of the table of contents regarded the two documents which follow the Faith of Bachiarius, as part of that Faith itself. There is no mark of division or separation between them. The first appears to be a prayer founded upon the destruction of the Egyptians; it closes thus, "Suffragia orationum tuarum ad ihm Xpm. dnm. nostrum cui gloria in saecula saeculorum. finit. amen. do gratias." This fills up the line. The next line begins without further introduction,

Quicunque uult esse saluus ante omnia opus est ut
teneat Catholicam fidem quam nisi quisq; inti-
gram inuiolatamque seruauerit absque dubio
in aeternum peribit. Fides autem Catholica haec est
ut unum deum in trinitate et trinitatem in unitate
ueneremur neque confundentes personas neque substantiam separantes. alia est enim persona patris alia per-
sona filii alia persona spiritus sancti *sed patris et filii et spiritus sancti*[3] una est diuinitas aequalis gloria coaeterna majestas qualis pater talis
filius talis et spiritus sanctus increatus pater increatus filius
increatus spiritus sanctus inmensus pater inmensus filius inmensus spiritus sanctus aeternus pater aeternus filius aeternus spiritus sanctus et tamen non .III. aeterni sed unus aeter-

[1] Muratori, ut sup. pp. 16, 17.

[2] I have noted "Pater Deus, Filius Deus, Spiritus Sanctus Deus, unus Deus. Nec communicans major nec accipiens minor."

[3] The words "sed patris et filii et spiritus sancti," have been added by an interlineation.

nus sicut non tres increati nec tres inmensi sed unus increatus et unus inmensus similiter omnipotens pater
omnipotens filius omnipotens spiritus sanctus et non tres omnipotentes sed unus omnipotens ita deus pater
deus filius deus spiritus sanctus et tamen non .III. dii sed unus deus ita dominus pater
dominus filius dominus spiritus sanctus et tamen non .III. domini sed unus dominus quia sicut singillatim unamquamque personam et deum et dominum confiteri
christiana ueritate conpellimur ita tres deos aut dominos dicere
catholica religione prohibemur. pater a nullo est factus nec
creatus nec genitus filius a patre solo est non factus nec creatus sed genitus. spiritus sanctus a patre et filio non factus nec creatus
nec genitus sed procedens patri et filio coaeternus est.
unus ergo pater non .III. patres unus filius non .III. filii unus
spiritus sanctus non .III. spiritus sancti. et in hac trinitate nihil prius aut posterius nihil majus aut minus sed totae tres personae coaeter-
nae sibi sunt et coaequales ita ut per omnia sicut iam
supra dictum est et trinitas in unitate et unitas in trinitate ueneranda sit qui uult ergo saluus esse ita de trinitate
sentiat. sed necessarium est ad aeternam salutem ut
incarnationem quoque domini nostri ihesu christi fideliter credat est ergo
fides recta ut credamus et confiteamur quia dominus noster ihesus christus
dei filius et deus pariter et homo est deus est ex substantia patris *ante saecula genitus*[1] homo est ex substantia matris in saeculo natus perfectus deus perfectus homo ex anima rationabili et humana
carne subsistens aequalis patri secundum diuinitatem minor
patre secundum humanitatem qui licet deus sit et homo non
duo tamen sed unus est christus unus autem non conuersione diuinitatis in carne sed adsumptione humanitatis in deo unus omnino non confusione substantiae sed unitate personae nam

[1] The words "ante sæcula genitus," have been added more lately in the margin. It will be remembered that the line in the Colbertine manuscript was erased and rewritten to enable the same words to be introduced.

sicut anima rationabilis et caro unus est homo ita deus et homo unus est christus qui passus est pro salute nostra discendit ad inferos surrexit a mortuis ascendit ad caelos sedit ad dexteram dei patris inde uenturus judicare uiuos ac mortuos. ad cujus aduentum omnes homines resurgere habent cum corporibus suis et reddituri sunt de factis propriis rationem. Et qui bona egerunt ibuut in uitam aeternam qui mala in ignem aeternum. Haec est fides catholica quam nisi quisque fideliter firmiterque crediderit saluus esse non poterit. Lacta mater eum qui fecit te quia talem fecit te ut ipse fieret in te. Lacta eum qui fructum fecunditatis tibi dedit conceptus et decus uirginitatis non abstulit natus. incipit de ascensione dni nri ihu xpi sermo dicendus.

I must remark that in my photograph *sicut non tres increati*, &c. is scarcely legible; and I am uncertain whether *Dei* is to be read in our 39th clause.

In our clause 6, *Sed patris et filii et spiritus sancti* has been interlined with a different hand, and the words *ante sæcula genitus* have been added in the margin to clause 31. The word in clause 34 had been *conversatione*, but the letters *at* have been erased.

My notes taken at Milan indicated that in clause 12 the two phrases are inverted; thus *unus inmensus et unus increatus;* but my photograph is too obscure here to decide whether I was correct in this point.

THERE IS MUCH of curious interest in this copy of the Quicunque.

First: I must draw attention to its peculiar position. It is preceded by what may be, and probably is, a prayer to the Virgin, at the end of a sermon; and it is followed even in the same line by an undoubted apostrophe to the Virgin, and then by a sermon on the Ascension of our Lord. Thus it appears amongst a collection of sermons or discourses on the Faith.

Secondly: The Latin is accurate throughout. This seems to me to indicate that if the manuscript is of the eighth century, it was written after the revival of learning under Charles the Great.

Thirdly: Alcuin is known to have collected and reduced to order some two hundred homilies of Augustine, Chrysostom, Leo,

Bede and others, with the intention that these homilies, so arranged, should be read in the Churches. It is not improbable that we owe to him many of the sermons now in the appendix to Augustine's works: and it is known that a sermon composed by him on the Presentation in the Temple was, before many years had expired, ascribed to St Ambrose: and so it is entitled in "a very old manuscript" in the Colbertine Library[1].

Fourthly: And the following passage, occurring in a letter written by Alcuin, and printed by Baluzius, reminded me of the apostrophe, *Lacta Mater eum.* "If it were possible for the blessed Virgin to give birth to a Son of her own, which Son was from eternity the Son of God, how was it impossible for God the Father to have as His own Son a Man who was in time (*ex tempore*) born of the Virgin[2]?" I fancy I see here a fondness for antitheses, and, in the end of the letter, antitheses like this appear in greater numbers. Thus I am led to connect the Bobio manuscript before us with Alcuin. For

Fifthly: I am disposed to think that both here and in the Treves original of the Colbertine manuscript, the reading was distinctly this: *Deus est ex substantia Patris, homo est ex substantia Matris in sæculo natus,* "He is God of the substance of His Father, He is Man of the substance of His Mother, born in the world:" *i.e.* "He that is born in the world is God and Man." The addition, *ante sæcula genitus,* seems to have been made by some one who, in his love for antithesis, lost sight of the original meaning.

Lastly: I would draw attention to the fact that Montfaucon and Waterland have followed Muratori's reading *prohibemus* in clause 19; the word is, distinctly, *prohibemur.* Yet, as we shall see, some of the Greek copies have *κωλύομεν.* And the copy of the interpolated Greek Creed, printed by Usher from a manuscript which belonged to Patrick Junius, has *παντελῶς ἀπαγορεύομεν,* "we absolutely prohibit."

I will only add that we learn from Montfaucon's *Diarium Italicum,* p. 18, that the great Benedictine saw the manuscript on his way southwards, on July 3, 1698—the visit, no doubt, recorded by Muratori. He tells us that he was not disposed to assign to it a date so early as was the Milanese librarian. He put

[1] Baluzii *Miscellanea*, Preface.

[2] *Ibid.* Vol. I. pp. 377, &c.

it no higher than the eighth century[1]. The manuscript consists of only 18 folios. It measures ten inches by seven and a half. The parchment is thick and dark and the ink faint, and thus the photograph does not appear to be very successful. The manuscript concludes "Hieronymi incipit fides,"—the formula which I have printed above[2]. Unfortunately I did not note whether it reads *de Patre Filioque procedentem* with the ordinary copies, or *de Patre procedentem* as in the copy contained in the introduction to "Charlemagne's Psalter."

§ 2. Collections approaching more or less to the character of this manuscript at Milan are numerous, but I have heard only of one which contains the Quicunque, and that is of a late date. Thus the Surtees Society published in 1840 a transcript of *An Anglo-Saxon Ritual*. It contained (p. 166) an account of the "Capitula" read at prime; the *Pater noster;* the antiphon *Vivit anima mea et*, &c.; *Erravi sicut ovis quœ periit*, &c., and the *Credo;* concluding with the words *Carnis resurrectionem in vitam eternam.* But there is no Quicunque.

§ 3. *The Book of Deer* has attracted our attention already. Perhaps it is scarcely right to lay much stress upon this volume, because it contains very little of ritual. It has, however, a service for the Visitation of the Sick. But there is no Quicunque[3].

§ 4. I have described in Chapter XIV.[4] a very interesting manuscript in the British Museum, of the eighth century, 2 A. XX., and given a copy of the FIDES CATHOLICA therein contained. That version must have anticipated the "Fides Catholica" of the ninth century. There is no Quicunque in this volume.

§ 5. At Vienna there are several manuscripts which are of interest to us in this part of our investigation. I will take one numbered 1032. There is some account of it in Denis, I. CCLXIX. p. 964; and I am indebted to Dr Joseph Haupt for a transcript of several pages from it, the accuracy of which (if there were need for such corroboration) I could vouch for, from a personal comparison.

[1] Yet Waterland (Chapter IV.) "to make a round number" is "content to place it" in the year 700! Montfaucon repeats his opinion in his famous Diatribe.

[2] Appendix to Chapter XX.

[3] See above, p. 165. Professor Westwood gives some facsimiles. *Miniatures*, p. 91.

[4] p. 161.

There is a picture of St Isidore at the commencement of the book. The writing is in Caroline minuscules; the contents are divided into two books. The first piece professes to be a work on the Catholic Faith written by Isidore for Florentina, his sister. It consists of 62 chapters, of which the subjects of the first three are:

Quia Christus a Deo Patre genitus est;
Quia Christus ante saecula ineffabiliter a Patre genitus est;
Quia Christus Deus et Dominus est[1]*;*

the fifth is *De Trinitatis Significantia;* and so on.

Chapter LXI. is on the return of Christ to judgment. The Second Book consists of twenty-seven chapters. The object of Chap. I. is to shew that all nations are called to the worship of God; of Chap. V. that the Jews will believe in the end of the world; of Chap. XXIIIII. that through the sign of the Cross believers are saved. After a while *explicit feliciter. dō gratias. amen.* Then INCIPIT DEINDE CATHOLICA ATHANASI[2].

It proceeds (I copy the errors):

"Haec est fides cathólicam quam exposuerunt patres nostri, | Primum quidem aduersus arrium blasphemantem et dicentem. | creaturam esse filium dei, et aduersus omnem haeresim. Quicunque | exsurrexerit contra catholicam et apostolicam fidem quos etiam dam | nauerunt in ciuitatem nicea congregati episcopi CCC.X.VIII. Credi | mus in unum deo omnipotentem. omnium uisibilium et inuisibilium | factorem &c." The true Nicene Creed follows. Thus we have "et in spiritu sancto eos qui dicunt. Erat quando non erat, &c.," with the anathematism. Then in the same line with "apostolica ecclesia," nos pa | trem et filium et spiritum sanctum unum deum confitemur. Ita in trinitatem | perfecta et plenitudo diuinitatis sit et unitas potestatis nam tres | deos dicit. qui diuinitatem separat trinitas pater deus et filius deus | et spiritus sanctus deus et tres unum sunt. Tres itaque personae sed una potestas | Ergo diuersitas·pluris facit. unitas potestatis. Excludit numeri | quantitate. Quia unitas numerus non est. Sic itaque unus deus unum |. fides unum baptisma. Qui catholicam non tenit fidem alienus | est profanus·est aduersus ueritatem rebellus est. | Quicumque uult saluus esse ante omnia opus est &c.

The Athanasian Creed follows. The few mark-worthy readings I will note on a future page. This ends on folio 85 thus:

Haec est fides catholica | quam nisi quisque fideliter firmiterque crediderit saluus esse | non poterit. Quicunque uult saluus esse ante

[1] It will be remembered that we find *Deum et Dominum nostrum* in the Spanish Creeds.

[2] Denis and others suggest that *inde* is a mistake of the scribe for *fide*. It would thus run:

Incipit de fide catholica Athanasi.

I prefer to take it as we find it.

omnia opus est ut teneat catholicam fidem. | Fides dicitur credulitas ibi credentia catholicam | universalem quia catholicam universalis dicitur."

The beginning of the comment of "Fortunatus." Of this below. We should note, however, the use of the words in 1 John v., *tres unum sunt,* and compare the Faith on page 273.

The exposition of "Fortunatus" ends with "compellimur" on 86 a. Turning over the leaf we find that the subject is entirely changed: the volume commences to treat on the difference between the historic and spiritual interpretations of Scripture[1].

§ 6. From another manuscript at Vienna I have drawn some very interesting information, and to it I must now refer at length. It is numbered 1261, and is a Spanish manuscript of the twelfth century. It belonged once to Don Rodriguo,

"By the grace of God (King?) of Castille, Toledo, Leon, Galicia, Seville, Cordova, Murcia, &c." It is about eleven inches and a half long, by $7\frac{1}{8}$ broad, and contains only 24 folia. Its first article is entitled in a contemporaneous hand S. AUGUSTINI DE DECEM CHORDIS. (See Gaume's edition v. p. 18, and Denis I. ccxxvii. p. 719.) It is in two columns. On folio 16 verso col. b at the end of a passage said to be from Augustine's sermon "quales debent esse Christiani," ending thus "nobis concedat vobiscum implere quod prædicamus adjuvante domino nostro ihesu Christo cui est honor et imperium in sæcula sæculorum," there follows a title "*De eodem Augustino digna.* Rogo vos fratres charissimi ut adtentius cogitemus quare Christiani sumus et crucem Christi in fronte portamus. Scire enim debemus quia non nobis sufficiat quod nomen Christianum accepimus si opera Christi non fecerimus sicut ipse"—words which to some extent resemble a passage in the Appendix to Augustine's works (vol. v. cclxvi. p. 3050, 3051 of Gaume[2]). Then on fol. 17 recto col. a we have

"De fide catholica.

"Patres venerabiles cari fratres filii dei aliquid uobis uolumus memorare de his que nunquam uobis obliuisci oportet, uidelicet quomodo credere debeatis et uiuere et si quis peccat quomodo possit recuperare. Tria sunt hec. audite de primo. Fides catholica hec est ut unum deum in Trinitate et Trinitatem in unitate ueneremur.

"Multi sunt qui non possunt hoc intelligere nisi per quasdam quasi similitudines inducantur."

I will give this part in the appendix to this chapter.

[1] I will give the chapter from Isidore that explains the article on the descent into hell. "In infernum descendit. Sic idem dominus in ecclesiastico dicit Penetrabo omnes inferiores partes terræ et inspiciam omnes dormientes et inluminabo omnes sperantes in dominum. Item in psalmis Vita mea in inferno adpropiavit. Estimatus sum cum descendentibus in lacum. Factus sum sicut homo sine adjutorio inter mortuos liber. Descendit enim sicut homo in infernum sed solus inter mortuos liber fuit, quia mors illum tenere non potuit."

[2] These are clearly of the Charlemagne type.

Then, in the middle of the column b, we have

"De duodecim abusionibus.

"Duodecim abusiua sunt seculi. Hoc est sapiens sine operibus, senex sine religione, adolescens sine obedientia, diues sine eleemosyna, femina sine pudicitia, dominus sine ueritate et uirtute. Christianus contentiosus. Pauper superbus. Rex iniquus. Episcopus negligens. Plebs sine disciplina. Populus sine lege. Suffocator justitie. Haec sunt duodecim abusiua seculi per que seculi rota &c. &c.[1]."

Each of these is expanded. The tenth is "Decimus abusionis gradus est epūs negligens. qui gradus sui honorem inter homines requirit, sed ministerii sui dignitatem coram deo, pro quo legatione fungitur, non custodit. Epūs enim grecum est et latine speculator dicitur. Epūs sit sobrius prudens castus sapiens modestus hospitalis filios habens subditos cum omni castitate."

The whole concludes:

"Non faciamus ergo sine Christo quicquam in hoc tempore transitorio ne sine nobis Christus esse incipiat in futuro. (Then *immediately*)

"De Catholica fide.

"Quicunque uult saluus esse ante omnia opus est ut teneat catholicam fidem. Quam nisi quisque integram inuiolatamque seruauerit absque dubio in eternum peribit. Fides autem catholica hec est ut unum deum in trinitate et trinitatem in unitate ueneremur. neque confundantes personas neque substantiam separantes. alia est enim persona patris alia filii alia spiritus sancti. sed patris et filii et spiritus sancti una est diuinitas equalis gloria coeterna majestas. Qui in hac trinitate nichil prius aut posterius nichil maius aut minus sed tote tres persone coeterne sibi sunt et coequales. Quicunque ergo cupit saluus esse et catholicus hec teneat et credat et uita uiuet. Sed tamen post hec si ad celeste regnum desiderat peruenire et eterna bona concupiscere contra diaboli insidias quotidie necesse est certare, paullo apostolo dicente Per multas tribulationes et temptationes oportet nos intrare in regnum celorum.

"Quia non sunt condigne passiones huius temporis ad futuram gloriam quae reuelabitur in nobis. Quamdiu ergo fuerimus in hac uita fratres contra demonium aduersitates reluctandum est nobis.

"Tribulatio enim in hoc mundo parui temporis est ad comparationem celestium premiorum sine fine manentium. Curramus ergo dum tempus habemus operemur bonum ad omnes et bonum faciendo non deficiamus."

The remainder of the sermon is so interesting that I will give a translation of it in my Appendix.

The sermon ends on the first column of fol. 20 verso. On the second column begins "Augustinus de decimis servatoribus ecclesiæ reddendis." (On this I have a memorandum that Binius thought it was written by Udalric, who died A.D. 973.) Then fol. 21 verso, col. b, "ammonitio sacerdotum et conuentus," which I think is the document printed by Labbe, IX. 803. I have

[1] The completion of this sentence may be seen in Augustine or Cyprian, as given below.

spoken of this on an earlier page. It would certainly appear from this manuscript, that the Quicunque, whether in its complete or incomplete form, was regarded as a Sermon or Exposition rather than a Profession of Faith. I must resist, however, the temptation to discuss this at present.

But I must mention that a treatise *De Duodecim Abusionibus* was written by Hincmar, who, as we have seen[1], was Bishop of Rheims in the middle of the ninth century. We are expressly told this by his biographer Flodoard. Yet a tract under this title has come down to us, ascribed to St Augustine (see Vol. VI. Appendix, p. 1570, Gaume); and the same work is attributed in other manuscripts to Cyprian, and is published amongst the spurious writings by Hartel. A St Gall manuscript of the ninth century so assigns it. The surmise arises, whether Hincmar fathered this work of his on Augustine. The copy in Vienna, 1261, which we have been now discussing, is of a much briefer form than that printed among St Augustine's works.

§ 7. I do not know whether the Creed which I now produce has ever been printed. It follows on the second of the Creeds attributed to Damasus (Hahn, p. 188), in an early manuscript written in Anglo-Saxon letters. The manuscript is numbered 2223 of the Vienna library, folio 77. The manuscript is considered to be of the ninth or tenth century. I am indebted again for my copy to Dr Jos. Haupt.

Unus deus pater verbi uiuentis sapientiae subsis
tentis et uirtutis sue figure perfectus
perfecti genitor pater filii unigeniti unus dominus
solus ex solo deo figura et imago deitatis
uerbum perpetrans sapientia conprehendens
omnia et uirtus qua tota creatura fieri
potuit filius uerus ex ueri et inuisibilis ex in
uisibili et incorruptibilis ex incorruptibili
et inmortalis ex inmortali et sempiternus
ex sempiterno unus spiritus sanctus ex deo substantiam
habens et qui per filium aparuit imago filii perfecta
uiuentium causa sanctitas sanctificationis presta
trix per quem deus super omnia et in omnibus
cognoscitur et filius per omnis trinitas et per
facta maiestate et sempiternitate et regno

f. 77 verso,

minime diuidetur neque abalienatur neque factum
quid aut serui eis in trinitate neque super inductum

[1] Page 302.

tanquam ante ac quidem non subsistens postea
uero super ingressum neque itaque defuit
umquam filius patris neque filio spiritus sanctus sed in
conuertibilis et inmutabilis eadem trinitas
semper amen.

§ 8. Through the forethought and attention of Dr Ceriani I was permitted to see another manuscript at Milan, the interest of which was to me very great. The press mark is I. 101. sup. It also came from Bobio, and is of the seventh or eighth century. Its dimensions are 10¼ by 5⅞, and it contains 75 folios. The parchment is thick and coarse.

The early portion of this volume is said to contain writings of St Chrysostom (some say St Eucherius). The latter folia contain a series of Creeds.

Fol. 73 verso has on it

"Incipit Fides Sci. Ambrosii episcopi.
Nos Patrem et Filium et Sanctum Spiritum," &c.

about six lines in length. Probably the same that I have presented above, p. 273.

Fol. 74 recto has

"Fides Catholica
Credimus unum Deum," &c.

This (if my memoranda are correct) runs without any distinguishing mark into the same Faith which I have given, p. 273: for it closes on folio 75 recto "quia catholicam non tenet fidem alienus est adversus veritatem rebellis."

Then follows "Incipit fides Luciferi episcopi. Nos patrem credimus qui non sit filius sed..."

This occupies eleven lines. Then

"Incipit fides quæ ex Niceno concilio processit. Credimus unum deum."

The true Nicene Creed. Then, a fourth, or fifth, or sixth Faith, attributed to Athanasius.

"Incipit fides beati Athanasii.

Fides unius substantiae trinitatis patris et filii et spiritus
sancti sine inicio tempurum super sensum et sermonem
et spū. una virtus unus deus. trea uero uocabula
nascitur de uirgine maria accipiens corpus anima
le sed ipse sensum precellens dei verbum non com
prehensus a carne sermo sed in carne et super car
nem sic ut deus prescius. dei uirtus dei ueritas passus
autem humana sermo dei impassibilis est. In passione
quidem moritur ut uiuificaret protoplaustum

qui ceciderat per inobedientiam. O homo deitate
quærens uitupero te. si credis benefacis. si autem
dicis quomodo pater de lumine excidisti et si dixeris
quomodo filius similiter excidisti de lumine nemo
enim nouit patrem nisi filius neque filium nisi pater
qui trē uirtutes inducit tres deus confitetur
nos autem credimus tres personas unam uero uir
tutem unam deitatem quando autem nominaueris
patrem glorificas filium et quando nominaueris filium
adoras patrem. si terum una personam trinitatis
dicimus iudei nomen portamus qui iudei unam
personam dicunt et unum dominum confitentur. si
tres deos inducimus similes sumus gentibus sed
confitemur patrem in filio et filium in patre cum
spiritu sancto non separatur non diuiditur deitas deus
enim de deo uirtus de uirtute lumen de lumine ueritas
de ueritate testis non est non coelum non terra.

Here the book ends.

It will be noted that it does not contain the Quicunque.

§ 9. The Ambrosian Library possesses another most interesting volume: I mean the Bangor *Antiphonary* to which I have referred before. It was regarded by Muratori as 1000 years old; if so, it is nearly 1200 years old now. Towards the end we find in it "versiculi familiæ Benchuir," which give it its well-known title. Its class mark is C. 5. inf.

It consists, at present, of 36 leaves: and contains a collection of canticles, hymns and prayers[1].

[1] The first is the canticle, *Audite cœli quæ loquor* (Deut. xxxii.). Then come some hymns. "Hymnum sancti Hilarii de Christo. *Hymnum dicit turba fidelium.*"

Then according to Muratori, "Hymnum apostolorum." It begins:

"Precamur Patrem
Regem omnipotentem
Et Jesum Christum
Sanctum quoque Spiritum. Alleluia.
Deum in una
Perfectum substantia
Trinum......"

(The manuscript fails, but the hymn is again taken up.) On folio 6* (according to my notes) appears

"Canticum sancti Zachariæ.
"*Benedictus*, &c."

This is followed on folio 7 by the *Cantemus domino:* and on folio 8*, by the "Benedictio puerorum. *Benedicite omnia opera;*" and on folio 10 by "Ymnus in die dominico,

Laudate pueri dominum | laudate nomen | Domini. Te Deum laudamus" (a peculiar version of the Te Deum).

This is followed by a "Hymnum quando communicarent sacerdotes,

"Sancti venite
Christi corpus sumite
Sanctum bibentes
Quo redempti sanguinem."

Then "hymnum quando ceria benedicitur. *Ignis Creator igneus.*

"Hymnus mediæ noctis. *Mediæ noctis tempus est.*

"Hymnum in natali martyrum vel sabbato ad matutinam. *Sacratissimi martyres summi Dei.*

But, according to my memoranda, on fol. 35 there are these two prayers which, as they are not mentioned by Muratori, I will here transcribe.

"Te patrem adoramus eternum. te sempiternum filium inuocamus teque spiritum sanctum in una diuinitatis substantia manentem confitemur. tibi uni deo in trinitate debitas laudes et gratias referemus ut te incessabili uoce laudare mereamur per eterna secula seculorum."

On folio 35 verso the same invocation is repeated up to the word *confitemur*. It then proceeds,

"tibi trinitas laudes et gratias
referemus tibi uni deo
incessabilem dicimus
laudem te patrem
ingenitum te filium unigenitum
te spiritum sanctum a patre
procedentem corde credimus
tibi inestimabili incompre
hensibili omnipotens
deus qui regnas in eternum."

After the words *a patre*, but beyond the line, *et filio* has been subsequently added. *Sic:* te spm̄ sanctum a patre et filio
procedentem.

This antiphonary contains in all four canticles, a Creed, and these invocations to the Trinity. But it does not contain the Quicunque[1].

§ 10. One manuscript containing the Quicunque, which was collated by Montfaucon, appears to have been of a character that would assign it to this chapter: but it is unhappily lost at present, although it is possible that, like others of the treasures of the library of St Germain des Près at Paris, it may be found in the Imperial Library at St Petersburg. Montfaucon (*Diatribe*, p. 654; Migne, XXVIII. 1571) considered it at least of the age of the

"Hymnum ad matutinam in Dominica.

Spiritus divinæ	*Lumen de Lumine*
Lucis gloriæ	*Referemus Filium Patris*
Respice in me	*Sanctumque Spiritum in una substantia.*
Domine.	*Respice.*
* * *	

"Hymnum sancte Patricii magistri Scotorum."

This is a hymn of 24 stanzas, of eight lines each. They begin with the successive letters of the alphabet. (Muratori spoils this by writing *Christus* for *Xps*, and *Hymnos* for *Ymnos* in stanzas 22 and 23.)

This is followed by two other hymns in which an alphabetical arrangement is kept up: and then come some short collects (some of them rhythmical), for the various hours of the day. On folio 19 is the Creed which I have printed above, p. 167. Then the Lord's Prayer. Several interesting intercessory prayers follow, and seven or eight series of collects to be used after the various canticles, and, towards the end, a few short prayers on communicating. These look like fragments sewn together.

[1] It will be seen that I have supplemented Muratori's account by my own memoranda: see his *Anecdota*, Tom. IV. p. 127, or Migne, LXXII.

Colbertine, 784 (the Paris, 3836), *i.e.* a little earlier than the time of Charlemagne. It was called by Mabillon "Codex Corbeiensis," and three lines of it were given by him in facsimile in his great book, *De Re Diplomatica*, p. 351. We learn from Mabillon that this volume contained *Isidori de Officiis libros cum multis aliis*, and from his facsimile that the Quicunque was not divided into verses.

§ 11. Another copy, or rather a fragment of another copy, is yet to be seen at Paris at the end of a Latin translation of Eusebius' *Chronicon*. This is "Regius 4908" (now 4858) of Montfaucon, who considered it to be nearly 900 years old, *i.e.* to have been written about the year 800. The Quicunque has no title nor author's name. The Chronicon ends on the folio 108 verso, with Olympiad CCLXXXVIII., and these words, "Ambrosio episcopo constituto ad fidem rectam italia convertitur." Folio 109 commences with something relating to Aquileia—followed in the nineteenth line by "CCLXXXVIIII. Olympias." Then some reckoning up of dates, concluding with a memorandum that from the time of Adam to the thirteenth year of Valens were V̄.DLXXVIIII years. Then follows (the words are partly illegible),

> .... eisque hieronymus presbyter ordinum
> ...... tum decedit annorum
> Quicunque uult saluus esse an
> te omnia opus ē ut teneat catho
> licam fidem quam nisi quisque
> integram inuiolatamque seruauerit in ae
> ternum peribit. fides autem catholica
> &c. &c. &c.

The first two lines of the Quicunque are in large (rustic?) capitals; the second three in small uncials, the rest in Caroline minuscules, but the page ends with the words *non tres aeterni*— and the next page and the rest of the volume have been torn off. It was in the same condition in the time of Montfaucon.

We should note the omission of *sine dubio*. A collation of this manuscript was made by Mr A. A. Vansittart of Trinity College, Cambridge, who kindly placed his copy in my hands.

§ 12. I may mention that the curious manuscript Ll. I. 10 of the Cambridge University Library (an Anglo-Saxon book of the eighth century, containing several morning hymns and prayers, including the *Laudatio Dei; Te Deum Laudamus*)—does not include the Quicunque. This volume is known under the title "Book of Cerne" or "Book of Ethelwald." Amongst its contents is a curious dialogue between our Saviour and Adam and Eve.

§ 13. There are two other volumes resembling each other, though different from any I have yet touched upon, which I am anxious to bring before my readers. They are Irish collections of hymns. The one is well known as the Book of Hymns of the ancient Church of Ireland, which belonged once to the great Usher. It was being most carefully and most learnedly edited for the "Irish Archæological and Celtic Society," by the late Dr James Henthorn Todd, when that lamented divine was removed from his earthly labours. The other is a volume of a similar character, the curious history of which I will give below. Many of the contents of the two volumes are identically the same; and some of them are also found in the Bangor *Antiphonary*.

Of the Canticles, with which we shall soon have occasion to associate the Quicunque, both volumes contain the *Magnificat*, the *Benedictus*, and the *Te Deum* under the title *Laudate pueri Dominum*. They both contain the *Gloria in excelsis*, not in its ordinary Latin form, but as a translation of the Greek Morning Hymn[1]. The Usher manuscript does not contain either the *Benedicite* or the *Cantemus Domino* or the *Quicunque.*

§ 14. The other manuscript contains these two canticles and two other hymns, beginning *Christe qui lux es* and *Christe Patris in dextera;* and the *Quicunque* concludes the volume.

The theological world is indebted to the Rev. W. Reeves, D.D., of Armagh, for a most interesting account of this manuscript, which that learned scholar contributed as an appendix to a sermon on the Athanasian Creed, published in May, 1872, by Archdeacon William Lee, D.D., Archbishop King's Lecturer in Divinity at Trinity College, Dublin. The manuscript was referred to by Archbishop Usher in the momentous treatise on the Roman Symbol in which he spoke of the Cottonian Psalter; and, curiously enough, it, like the Cottonian Psalter, has been removed from the sight of British archæologists for many generations. It migrated

[1] This is worthy of remark with reference to the origin of the Irish Church.

from the old Franciscan convent of Donegal to Louvain, and from Louvain to the convent of St Isidore at Rome: in the spring of 1872 it was removed, with the other manuscripts belonging to that house, to the Franciscan Church on Merchants' Quay, Dublin. There Dr Reeves examined it, and thence he sent his memoranda to Archdeacon Lee. And he has most kindly made and forwarded to me a transcript of the Creed, which I shall use hereafter.

The manuscript is considered to be of a hand not later than the year 1100.

The interest of the copy of the Quicunque is, however, increased by the introduction, partly in Irish, partly in Latin, prefixed to it. This gives the opinion of the collector of the series as to the origin of the Quicunque. I append Dr Reeves' translation of this curious introduction, retaining the Latin.

"The Synod of Nece that made the Faith Catholic and three Bishops of them only that made it that is Eusebius and Dionysius and nomen tertii nescimus. But it is said that the whole Synod made it for it was it that published it. In Necea vero urbe it was made. And in Bithinia is that city that is a territory in Little Asia. Now to expel the error of Arius it was made for it was his belief that the Father is greater quam Filius and that the Filius is greater quam Spiritus Sanctus. The Synod therefore was assembled by Constantine at Necea, namely three hundred and eighteen bishops, and they were not able to overcome him because of his eloquence, but God overcame him."

And the tradition as to Arius' death is added.

I must hereafter return to this copy. I will merely now say that it furnishes an interesting conclusion to our chapter.

Our summary is this, that there are several collections of hymns and prayers and other formulæ earlier than the middle of the eighth century, but of these not one contains the Quicunque. That at some as yet undetermined period after the middle of that century, the Quicunque begins to appear, but in a form, which though slightly different from the received form, is yet sufficient to shew that it was not yet accepted for public service. And, when at last it appeared in Ireland, it appeared with the legend connected with it that it had been composed at the Council of Nicæa by Eusebius, Dionysius, and a third whose name was unknown.

The statement is interesting and important, and I do not think that it should be merely dismissed with this contemptuous language of Waterland, "the author of that book of hymns must have been very ignorant not to know Athanasius, who was undoubtedly the third man, and for whose sake the whole story seems to have been conceived." The legend belongs to some time and place at which the name of Athanasius was displaced from the Creed and an attempt made to represent the Nicene Council as responsible for its production; as we find it in the Great Bible at Venice, and in the illustration contained in the Utrecht Psalter.

Thus the Quicunque was not known in Ireland when Archbishop Usher's "Collection of Hymns" was made: it was known there, with this strange legend, when the Franciscan series was compiled.

APPENDIX.

The following passages from the Manuscript 1261 of the Imperial Library at Vienna have such a peculiar character about them, that I am sure they will prove interesting to many of my readers even where not directly relevant to the Athanasian Creed. I begin with the first column of folio 17 recto. I retain the paragraphs of the original.

"Of the Catholic Faith.

"Venerable Fathers, dear brothers, children of God, we wish to speak to you of things which ye ought never to forget, namely how ye ought to believe, and to live, and, if a man sins, how he may recover himself. These are three points, listen as to the first. The Catholic Faith is this, that we worship one God in Trinity and Trinity in Unity.

"There are many who cannot understand this unless they are led to it, as it were, by some similitudes; wherefore let us say something of this kind. In the Sun there are three things naturally; its sphere, its light, its heat. The sphere of the Sun is naturally brilliant and heating. The Supreme Father is naturally wise and loving. The sphere of the Sun and its splendour and its heat are not three Suns, but one Sun. The supreme Father, and His Wisdom and His Love, are not three Gods but one God. The Wisdom of God is the Son of God; the Holy Spirit is the Love of God.

"Thus the Father and the Son and the Holy Spirit is one God. This God before the ages, and now, and ever, has made all things, visible and invisible. But the question is put, Did God the Father wish His Son, that is, His Wisdom, to be made man? Let us answer as briefly as we can. This was done for the purpose of redeeming man, because by his own fault he had perished, and by himself he could not be recovered. For before man fell, he was prudent and immortal and free of will, but such was the subtlety of the devil as to seduce him and render him unwise, mortal and frail.

"How then could he, when rendered foolish and frail and mortal, overcome the devil and recover of himself what he had lost, and what, even when strong, he had not kept for himself? He could not in any way. Still it was impossible for that to remain unfulfilled which the Omnipotent desired."

Here there follows in the Manuscript the treatise on the twelve abuses of which I have spoken in my text. It occupies from the second column of folio 17 recto, to the second column of folio 19 recto. Then we have the following.

"On the Catholic Faith.

"Whosoever would be saved, before all things it is necessary that he hold the Catholic Faith, which Faith except a man keep whole and undefiled, without doubt he shall perish everlastingly. And the Catholic Faith is this, that we worship one God in Trinity and Trinity in Unity, neither confounding the Persons, nor dividing the substance.

"For there is one person of the Father, another of the Son, another of the Holy Ghost; but the Divinity of the Father and the Son and the Holy Ghost is one, the Glory equal, the Majesty co-eternal.

"Because in this Trinity there is nothing before or after, nothing greater or less, but the whole Three Persons are co-eternal together, and co-equal. Whosoever therefore desires (cupit) to be safe and to be catholic, let him hold and believe this and he shall live. Yet still, after this, if he desires to reach the kingdom of heaven and to attain eternal good, it is necessary that he should daily struggle against the snares of the devil; for Paul the Apostle said, We must through many tribulations and temptations enter into the kingdom of heaven.

"For the sufferings of this present time are not worthy to be compared to the glory that shall be revealed in us. Therefore, brethren, as long as we are in this life, we must strive against the attacks of the demons.

"For our tribulation in this world is but of a short time, when compared with the heavenly reward which shall endure for ever. Let us run then whilst we have time; let us do good to all; let us not fail in living well.

"Let us consider therefore in our minds, that even though death may not be at hand, old age is continually drawing nigh. Years slip by; time flows on; all we see is temporal and has an end. Wherefore, beloved, whether we wish it or not, we are hourly hastening on to the last day. Sinners therefore ought to consider what excuse they will be able to make when they stand, on the day of judgment, before the tribunal of the Lord, and He, seated on the throne of His Majesty, begins to call upon them to give an account of their lives.

"Then He shall begin to accuse the guilty, saying unto them; I formed and made thee with My own hands out of the clay of the earth.

"I vouchsafed to confer on thee Our own image and likeness.

"I placed thee amongst the delights of Paradise, but thou didst choose rather to despise My life-giving commands and follow another than the Lord. Yet still, in My mercy, I redeemed thee with My own blood; I drank vinegar with gall; I underwent My death upon the cross, in order that I might give thee celestial glory, and that thou mightest live for ever with Me. And thou, what hast thou done to this?

"Then shall they answer Him, saying; We do not know Thee, Lord; we have not seen the Prophets; Thou didst not send the Law into the world; Thou didst not give Patriarchs; we have not seen the examples of the holy Prophets; Peter was silent to us; Paul would not preach to us; the Evangelists did not teach us; there were no martyrs whose examples we should follow; Thy future judgments no one proclaimed to us; in our want of knowledge we have fallen, in our ignorance we have sinned.

"But then, out of the choir of those saints, just Noah will first say, They do not speak the truth, Lord; for I prophesied of the deluge which was to come in consequence of the sins of men; and after the deluge I furnished an example; in order that they might know amongst the nations What salvation was, and What was the penalty of sinners.

"After him Abraham will stand up, saying; I was chosen to be father to the Gentiles whose example they might follow; I hesitated not to offer to Thee my son Isaac for a victim,

"In order that they might learn that Thou givest all things freely.

Again after him Moses will rise up, saying; I said, Lord: Thou shalt do no murder, thou shalt not commit adultery, thou shalt not steal, thou shalt not bear false witness against thy neighbour, thou shalt not covet thy neighbour's goods, thou shalt not desire his wife, nor his man-servant, nor his maid-servant, nor anything that is his. I said this that no one should covet that which is not his own.

"I said, Honour thy Father and thy Mother, that thy days may be long on the earth. This signifies that the obedience of children to their parents extends their life on the earth. I proclaimed this and many things like this, in order that they might know what was about to come.

"After this, David will stand up, saying; I said, Blessed is the man who feareth the Lord, he hath great delight in His commandments. The Saints shall exult in glory, they shall rejoice in their beds.

"I, when I was endowed with royal power, mingled my bread with weeping, in order that I might afford them an example of penitence and humility. After him Isaiah comes, saying; I said, Woe to you who join house to house and couple field to field even to the boundaries of the place: never shall ye alone possess the earth. After these and many more, the Son of God shall say; I, when I was exalted on My throne on high, holding heaven and earth in My hand, vouchsafed to be born in the flesh, as touching the manhood receiving the form of a servant. I gave health to all the infirm; I cleansed lepers; I raised the dead; I gave feet to the lame: in order that by these heavenly signs ye might believe in Me and in the things which I proclaimed. How is it, that I do not find in you any good work? Why did not ye, unhappy men, repent of your wicked acts before the end of your lives? What profit is it that ye honoured Me with your lips, if in works and deeds ye denied Me? Where are now your riches? Where are your pleasures? Where are your ornaments? Behold! now ye have the judgment which I proclaimed before!

"Then these miserable sinners, proud men and heretics, fornicators and liars, treacherous and envious, returning evil for evil and causing injury to the poor, receiving bribes against the innocent, and mutually hating each other, shall weep and lament before the Lord, saying with one voice—

"Have mercy upon us, Omnipotent God, and pardon our sins! Then shall He answer them with great indignation, saying; Depart from Me, ye cursed, into fire eternal; ye did not act with mercy while ye were in the world, nor have I pity on you now. Then shall follow their miserable departure, and never will their names be mentioned again through all eternity. But then shall all the Saints, who have perfectly believed in the Trinity, and fulfilled the precepts of God in their works,

"Reign with Christ, shining as the Sun in the kingdom of their Father; and God shall lead them to their heavenly home and shall give them eternal life and fulness of joy with choirs of angels; things which eye never saw, nor has it entered into the heart of man how great and how glorious are the things which God hath prepared for them that love Him. All these things may the Saviour of the world vouchsafe to grant to us, Who with the Father and the Holy Ghost liveth."

Thus again a portion of our present Athanasian Creed appears embodied in a sermon.

CHAPTER XXIII.

GREEK AND LATIN PSALTERS WHICH DO NOT CONTAIN THE QUICUNQUE.

§ 1. WE now come to a series of authorities of a very interesting character, which have attracted much attention from the artist and palæographer; but very little, so far as I am aware, from the liturgical scholar. I refer to the Psalters.

It is well known that at one time the repetition of the Psalms was regarded as the great act of devotion, and the great medium of intercession. In the West, and during the Carlovingian era, the faithful were instructed not to offer masses for the success of an expedition, or for the removal of an evil, or for the repose of a soul, but they were bidden to repeat the Psalter so many times. Thus we have an order in the time of Pepin (A.D. 765) that a hundred Psalters should be sung for a bishop on his death[1]. In 779 bishops were enjoined to sing three Psalters, one for the king, one for his army, one for the present trouble. There was a great

[1] Pertz, *Monumenta Germaniæ historiæ*, Tom. III. = Legum Tom. I. p. 30.

famine[1]. In the dubious Canons assigned by Pertz to the year 802, the question was ordered to be put to the clergy, How do they know the Psalms[2]? Because of this, in A.D. 806, every presbyter, according to his ability, was bound to have a Psalter[3]. In 810 there was again a famine, and every presbyter was enjoined to sing fifty Psalms each day[4]. In the Psalter, Ff. I. 23 of the Cambridge University Library, we have an interesting prayer in behalf of those for whom the Psalter is said.

Thus we have a motive for the multiplication of manuscripts containing the Psalms in the times of Pepin and of Charlemagne.

§ 2. But let us look to the Greek Psalters first. The oldest Psalter of which I have heard is incorporated in the famous Alexandrine manuscript at the British Museum. For in this codex the Book of Psalms is not followed immediately by the Book of Proverbs, but by the Odes or Canticles from Exodus, Deuteronomy, and so on, and by the Morning Hymn of the Eastern Church[5]. The same order is observed in the very beautiful Zurich Psalter which Tischendorf has published in his *Anecdota Sacra;* the Alexandrine manuscript is considered to be of the fifth century; the Zurich manuscript of the seventh. And Zaccaria informs us that in the Greek Psalters the Psalms are invariably followed by the Odes[6]. They are α. the Song of Moses in Exodus; β. the Song of Moses in Deuteronomy; γ. the Prayer of Hannah; δ. the Prayer of Habakkuk (iii. 2—19); ε. the Prayer of Isaiah (xxvi. 9—20); ζ. the Prayer of Jonah; η. the Prayer of the Three Children, "Blessed art Thou, O Lord God of our Fathers;" θ. the Song of the Three Children, "All ye works of the Lord, &c.;" ι. the Song of the Virgin; κ. the Song of Zacharias[7]. To these sometimes were added λ. the Prayer of Hezekiah (Isai. xxxviii.); μ. the Prayer of Manasseh; ν. the Song of Simeon.

§ 3. These Greek Psalters are not confined to the East. They are found in curious connections in the West also, and they are of sufficient interest to call for further remark.

[1] Pertz, *Mon. Germ. hist.* p. 39.
[2] *Ibid.* p. 106.
[3] *Ibid.* p. 139.
[4] *Ibid.* p. 165.
[5] This morning hymn may be seen in the later editions of Dr Campion's *Interleaved Prayer-Book*, p. 321. See too Usher *de Symbolo*, or Bunsen's *Analecta ante-Nicena*.
[6] *Bibliotheca Ritualis*, Romæ, 1776, p. 80.
[7] See the *Dictionary of Christian Antiquities*. CANTICLES.

It appears from the *History of the Monastery of St Gall*, by Arx[1], that there were there in the ninth and tenth centuries some monks who studied Greek, and were designated in consequence as the "Fratres Ellinici" (sic). To them—as seems to be the opinion of Dr S. Schönfelder, the chaplain of St Martin's in Bamberg, the learned writer of the Article to which I have just referred—is due not only the transposition into Latin letters of the Greek Psalms of this Bamberg Psalter, but also a similar transposition of other documents. I have on an earlier page[2] spoken of the Greek Nicene Creed as being represented in Latin letters; and one copy at least of this is in the library of St Gall. Whether these monks were the penmen or not we must leave in doubt. But the fact is, that we have scattered over the libraries of Europe a series of Psalters, which I will venture now to describe. Some, perhaps, are of a date earlier than the foundation of the monastery of St Gall.

i. Thus in the Paris Library, numbered now 10592[3], is a Psalter in Greek and Latin at the end of some of Cyprian's works[4]. The Psalms are said to be of the eighth century and to be written in Gallican uncials.

ii. Then there is the famous Veronese Psalter, supposed to be of the sixth century, containing the Septuagint in Latin letters and the old Itala in corresponding columns[5]. It contains six of the Greek Odes (Exodus, Deuteronomy, Hannah, Isaiah v. 1—9, Jonah, Habakkuk), though in an order different from that which we have noted before.

iii. Again, there is a Psalter in Greek and Latin (the first

[1] I quote this from an Article on the Bamberg Psalter in the *Serapeium* of Nov. 15, 1865.

[2] p. 139.

[3] It was, "S. Germains des Près, 186." I take my numbers from the Catalogue contributed by M. Delisle to the *Journal de l'Ecole des Chartes*.

[4] Hartel says that the "Cyprian" here is of the sixth or seventh century. It is the famous Codex Seguerianus, which proves that the well-known passage regarding the See of Rome was interpolated into the book on the *Unity of the Church* after this manuscript was written. (Mr Newman's curious note on this in the so-called Oxford translations is worthy of a study.) There are facsimiles of portions of the manuscript in Sylvestre, Vol. II., and an account of it in the *Nouveau Traité*, III. pp. 145, 172. Compare Plates XLII. II. IV., and XLIV. III. iii. See also Montfaucon, *Bibliotheca Coisliniana*, and generally Hartel's Cyprian, Præfatio, pp. ii.—viii., who however does not mention the Psalter.

[5] Specimen in the *Nouveau Traité*, Vol. III. p. 142, Pl. XLII. vi. The Psalter is reprinted in Blanchini's *Vindiciæ*. See too Rönsch, p. 19.

100 Psalms are lost) in the Library at St Gall. It is numbered 17.

After Psalm 150 follow the Canticles[1]. The Latin ceases after the Canticle of Hezekiah, and is not resumed before the middle of the Hymn from Deuteronomy. The Benedictus, Magnificat and Nunc dimittis are all in the MS. in Greek, but not the Gloria in Excelsis. After the Nunc Dimittis follow the Lord's Prayer (fol. 334) and the Apostles' Creed in Greek[2] and Latin. Then on fol. 336 a Litany in both languages. With this the book ends. It is of the tenth century. This is the O[c] of Tischendorf, from which he takes a few readings in the New Testament Canticles.

iv. In the Library of Corpus Christi College, Cambridge, there is a Psalter in Greek and Latin, all the letters being Latin. It is of late date; Nasmyth says of the fifteenth century. It contains, he says, "the usual hymns and litany." This was once mis-called "Gregory's Psalter," and the name has produced considerable confusion. It contains the copy of the Apostles' Creed in Greek, which Bishop Pearson mistook for an early and authentic version, and which Bishop Browne has printed at the end of his notes on Article VIII. The manuscript is numbered 468[3].

v. There is another Greek Psalter in the same library (number 480), with the usual hymns.

vi. Didron in his work (English translation, p. 201?) refers to a Greek Psalter at Paris (Bibliothèque National, Greek, No. 139).

vii. At Milan I saw (C. 13. inf.) a Greek and Latin Psalter which once belonged to the Church of "S. Maria di popolo," at Rome. The Canticles are in the Latin order down to the Magnificat (fol. clxviii.—clxxvi.), but the Nunc Dimittis is absent. It contains the Quicunque in Latin, but there was no attempt to give the Greek of it: a trial was made to give Greek for the first few verses of the Te Deum; and the Credo in Deum and the Credo in unum Deum (the true Creed of Constantinople) were given in Greek as well as Latin[4].

[1] Unhappily I did not notice which series, but I think it must be the Latin. Dr Schönfelder refers to this volume as of great interest. *Serapeium*, 1865, Nov. 15.

[2] I have already expressed my regret that I have not a transcript of this.

[3] See Nasmyth, *Catalogue*, p. 421, for a specimen of the Greek: or Dr Heurtley, who prints the Creed, p. 81. Usher's remarks on the manuscript are quoted by Waterland, Chap. IV., note 1.

[4] I noticed in the last, *και εις το πνευμα το αγιον το* | *Κυριον και ζωοποιον* | *ζωοποιον το εκ προς* | *μενον το συν πρι κ* | *προσκυνουμενον* | the first *ζωοποιον* is run through with a pen, then there is an erasure after *εκ προς* and upon the

viii. I ought, perhaps, to mention that the Cambridge manuscript Ee. IV. 29, of the twelfth century, contains several Greek extracts, including the "Epistle of Athanasius to Ammun and others," but no Quicunque.

ix. So Gg. V. 35 has (fol. 422) the *Gloria in Excelsis*, the Nicene Creed, and some verses on the Creed in Greek. (These have been published by the Caxton Society, *Anecdota*, 1851.)

x. The Royal Library at the British Museum contains 2 A. VI. (or 2 A. III. § vi.) a Greek Psalter (151 Psalms), and nine or ten Canticles of the Greek collection and in the Greek order. There are other Greek Psalters in the Museum.

xi. Then there is the Bamberg Psalter to which I have already referred. Its date is fixed at 909. It is a Quadripartite Psalter of which I must speak below, containing the Greek and then the three Latin versions of Jerome. At the end are some Canticles, and a Litany in Greek and in Latin: and the Quicunque in Latin but not in Greek.

xii. I have noticed that in the Catalogue of the Florence Library (p. 339) a note is taken of a manuscript (Plut. XVII. Cod. xiii.) of the Greek Psalter of the fifteenth century, which contains the Canticles, Lord's Prayer, the Apostles' and Nicene Creeds in Greek. But not the Quicunque.

These are all the Greek Psalters of this class of which I have discovered any account. And it will be seen that in not one single copy has the Athanasian Creed been discovered in a Greek version.

§ 4. I will now turn to the Latin Psalters; and before I describe any in detail, I will make a few preliminary remarks.

The Veronese Psalter to which I have referred contains the old "Versio Itala" of the Psalms, and is esteemed, in consequence, as of the highest literary value. At the request, as it is said, of Damasus, Jerome emended this version somewhat cursorily: at a later period he improved it more carefully, at the request of his friends Paula and Eustochium, to whom he inscribed his work. In this "edition" he availed himself of the labours of

erasure is written *κ ιου εκπορεθὸ*. Again on an erasure in the next line is written the *και ιω συν*. The interpolator betrayed himself. The *Gloria in Excelsis* is in Greek and Latin, but unhappily I did not take notes of it. The colophon is interesting.

Origen, and noted with the obelus what he found in the LXX but not in the Hebrew; and with the asterisk what was given b Theodotion from the Hebrew, but was not in the LXX. proper[1] Finally Jerome attempted an entirely new version from th Hebrew original.

The last-named version has never found its way into use: it was not intended for chanting, and it is not adapted for it The second correction was accepted generally north of the Alps, whilst the first, which was received at Rome in the first instanc under the patronage of Damasus, retained its position ther until very recent times. Thus the three became known by th titles the Roman, the Gallican and the Hebraic.

The confusion which was certain to arise in consequence of th use of two distinct versions of the Psalms, north and south of th Alps, was increased by an order of Charlemagne, by which th Roman Cantus was pressed upon his Frank subjects[2]. It ha been erroneously supposed that the Roman "Cantus" brough with it the Roman Psalter: but such was not the case, and th blending together the Roman chant with the Gallican versio caused increased confusion. At present we must be on our guar against a misconception on the point; and thus be prepared t make observations as to the time when this second emende version by Jerome was received into favour in Gaul.

There are two accounts, both of which are well known.

One is that of Walfrid Strabo, who in his book, *De Ecclesiasticis Rebus*, cap. 23, states:

> "Whilst the Romans used, to his time, the Psalms after the Septuagint, the Gauls and some of the Germans sang the Psalter after the emendation which Father Jerome introduced from the LXX. This emende version Gregory, bishop of Tours, is said to have received from some o the Roman districts, and introduced into Gaul."

Walfrid Strabo died in 849.

Berno of Augia, who lived 200 years later, improved upo this. In a letter which at the time of Mabillon remained inedited he stated that

> "Jerome himself introduced his improved version into Gaul and som of the Churches of Germany, whilst the Romans still sang the Psalte after its corrupt vulgate edition: from this the Romans composed thei

[1] The edition of the Psalter by Thomasius exhibits these marks.

[2] The *Romanus Ordo* was entirely disconnected from the Psalter.

Cantus, and in return passed that on to us. And thus a confusion had arisen because" as I understand it "some of the antiphons[1] and parts of the service are sung after the Roman Psalter, whilst the Psalms themselves are sung after the Gallican version[2]: whence it happens (says Berno) that the words which are modulated for singing in the daily or nightly offices, are mixed with each other, and inserted in a confused way into our Psalters, so that the less skilful do not know what belongs to our edition and what to the Roman edition of the Psalms. And the pious father recognising this has arranged the three editions in one volume: so that the Gallican Psalter which we sing shall be in one column, the Roman in another, the Hebraic in the third[3]."

From these accounts of Berno and Walfrid, Mabillon in the second section of his disquisition, *De cursu Gallicano*, expresses his dissent[4]. He says that Gregory of Tours in his history, *non uno in loco*, quotes the Psalms, but not after the Gallican version. Mabillon quotes two passages, *History*, v. § 14, and vi. § 5, where Gregory distinctly uses words which are not found in the Gallican Psalter. In the latter he quotes the famous phrase, *Dominus regnavit a ligno*. This seems to demonstrate that Gregory had not introduced the emended version. It is equally clear, Mabillon says, that Venantius Fortunatus did not use it. "Thus, we understand, that at the time when Gregory wrote his history, the Psalter as emended by Jerome, the Gallican Psalter as we call it, was not in use in Gaul," and Mabillon suggests that it was introduced by Boniface, the Archbishop of Mayence, in the middle of the eighth century[5].

Thus the Gallican Psalter[6] has almost entirely superseded the

[1] Pepin had introduced the use of the Roman Antiphons into the Gallican Church, the pope Paul having sent him an Antiphonal and Responsal. (Mabillon, ut infra, § II. 23.)

[2] Even to the present day the Psalm xciv. of the Roman Breviary is retained from the Roman Psalter, all the other Psalms following (I believe) the Gallican version.

[3] A similar difficulty may be said to exist in the English Church, the Magnificat being sung from an earlier translation; read in the lessons from the later. Very few persons are aware that the suffrages after the Creed, including "O Lord, save the King: And mercifully hear us when we call upon Thee," are from the Vulgate or Gallican Psalms.

[4] The *disquisitio* is reprinted by Migne, Tom. LXXII. p. 392.

[5] I find that Zaccaria (*Bibliotheca Ritualis*, pp. 97, &c.) writing in 1776 repeats the statement of Mabillon that the Roman Psalter was used in all the Churches of Rome and within forty miles of it up to the time of Pius V., *i.e.* 1556; and so says Martene (Lib. IV. Cap. III. Vol. III. p. 7). The two first-named writers say that in their time the Gallican Psalter was used everywhere at Rome, except in the one Church, the Vatican; but that there and at Milan each Church retained its ancient Psalter, as did also St Mark's Church in Venice. The Gallican Psalter was directed to be used in Aquileia in the year 1495; the order running *juxta ritum atque consuetudinem sive correctionem Psalterii Gallicani*.

[6] The differences between it and the received Vulgate text are very trifling. The Vulgate omits Psalm cli.

old Roman Psalter, and has always kept out of the field the *Psalterium Hebraicum* of Jerome. One volume at least survives in which the Roman Psalter has been altered by hand into the Gallican version. The usual "title-page" to this last is this: "IN CHRISTI NOMINE. Incipit Psalterium de translatione LXX. interpretum emendatum a sancto hieronymo presbytero in novo." And we have a curious memorandum in a Constitution of Ratherius, bishop first of Verona and then of Liege (to which I have already drawn attention for another object), directing that his clergy should learn the Faith "after the Symbolum, *i.e.* the *collatio* of the Apostles, as it is found in the corrected Psalters."

Thus, wherever we have a Gallican Psalter without the asterisks and obeli and without note or comment, there is an *a priori* probability, according to Mabillon, that the manuscript is of Gallican origin, and of a later date than the year 750.

§ 5. I must take this opportunity of recording some memoranda regarding the use of the Canticles in the Western Church.

I have already, Chap. xv., given an account of the hour services of the mediæval Church so far as to note the introduction of the Apostles' Creed into those services. It would appear that, at the time of Isidore, the hour of prime was not observed, nor does he mention the use of any other Creed save the Nicene. But in the work of Symphrosius Amalarius (he died after 834) *On the ecclesiastical offices*, we have an account of the prime service in his time, indicating that in his neighbourhood the Apostles' Creed was recited but not the Quicunque. We also learn distinctly that at the same time the Canticle of Hezekiah was sung at the matin office on Tuesday; that of Anna on Wednesday; that of Moses in Exodus on Thursday; that of Moses in Deuteronomy on Saturday. We can have no doubt that the song of Isaiah was used at this time on Monday; and that of Abbacuc on Friday.

Thus we have in the later Latin Psalters in invariable sequence the following Canticles.

α. Isaiah xii.; *β*. Hezekiah, Isai. xxxviii. 10—20; *γ*. Anna, 1 Samuel ii. 1—10; *δ*. Exodus xv. 1—19; *ε*. Abbacuc iii. 2—19; *ζ*. Deuteronomy xxxii. 1—43. They always occur in this order. We do not hear either of the *Te Deum* or the *Gloria in Excelsis* at first. We shall see that the *Benedicite* and *Benedictus* were the first to appear in the Western Psalters, the former being read at matins on Sundays and Festivals, and the latter, it is said, daily. (Some confusion is occasionally made between the *Benedictus* of Zacharias and the *Benedictus* of the "Three Children.") The later Psalters contain also, though in varying order and under varying titles, the *Benedicite, Benedictus, Magnificat, Nunc dimittis*, the *Te Deum*, the *Gloria in Excelsis*, the *Pater Noster secundum Mattheum*, the *Credo in Deum*—and generally the *Quicunque.*

§ 6. My first effort will be to exhibit a few notes which I have made of Latin Psalters which do not contain the Quicunque.

i. The first is the Psalter which is called that of Christina, Queen of Sweden: one of the collection which had belonged to the Church at Fleury[1], which she purchased after the sacking of the Library, and ultimately (as I understand) gave to the Vatican. It contains the Gallican and the Hebraic Versions of Jerome in parallel columns. It is said to be either of the fifth or of the seventh century, and has attracted great attention[2].

ii. There was another Psalter containing the Gallican and Hebraic in parallel columns or on opposite pages, in the Library of St Ouen at Rouen, but it is now in the public Library of that city. This was considered to be of the seventh or eighth century. It does not contain the Canticles or the Creeds[3].

iii. There was an old Psalter of three columns in the Library of St Germain des Près, numbered 100. This is the one (I believe) now known as the magnificent Psalter of Corbey. The Benedictines regarded it as of the seventh or eighth century. It is in the Paris Library, numbered 11550. It is now looked upon as of the eleventh century. It contains the Canticles, Hymns, and Litany, but not (as I understand) the Quicunque[4].

iv. There was another famous Psalter in the St Germain's Library (661 or 762, I believe the same as the present Paris 11947) of the eighth century: it is very beautiful; written with silver letters on purple parchment. Sylvestre, II. plate 113, gives a facsimile: it is *known* as the Psalter of St Germain himself. It is said to be Gallican. Some indeed have assigned it to the sixth century[5].

v. At Stuttgart there are two Psalters, one is said to contain the *Vetus Itala*, and to be of the seventh or eighth century. It consists of three volumes, and the initial letters throughout are

[1] See the account in Mabillon's preface to his work on the *Gallican Liturgy*, § XI. Migne, ut sup. p. 110.

[2] Notices of it are given in the *Nouveau Traité*, Vol. III. p. 91, and in Blanchini's *Vindiciæ*, p. ccxlvii., and ccxlviii.

[3] See *Nouveau Traité*, III. p. 226. A facsimile is given in Sylvestre, IV. Plate 22. He considers it to be later, say of 10th century. The press mark is, I believe, E. 43 or B. 29.

[4] *Bibliothèque de l'école des Chartes*. Series VI., Vol. I., p. 185. *Nouveau Traité*, III. 223, 314, 315.

[5] There may have been two in the old Library, 661 and 762. If so, the former is the Saint's copy. *Nouveau Traité*, pp. 163, 360.

very curious. It contains Psalm cli.[1], but no Canticles, nor Quicunque. This is numbered Biblia, fol. 12.

vi. The other is numbered Biblia, fol. 23, and is of the tenth century: it also contains the *Pusillus eram*, but not the Canticles[2].

vii. At St Gall there are two other manuscripts. One is numbered 19, which is said to be of the ninth century. It contains the Hebrew of Jerome. It has also Psalm cli.[3]

viii. St Gall, numbered 22. "The Golden Codex:" it is said to have been written by Folkard, and to be of the ninth century. There are a few pictures, and the version appears to be the Gallican. There are no Canticles nor Creeds.

ix. St John's College Library, Cambridge, contains (C. 9, p. 24 of Dean Cowie's catalogue) a most curious Manuscript; from which Professor Westwood gives a drawing (*Miniatures*, 30). It contains the Psalter and Canticles, but no Creeds.

[1] This "Pusillus eram" is a Psalm ascribed to David after he had fought with Goliath. It is found in the Greek Septuagint, but not in the Hebrew; and thus Jerome, who left it in his so-called Roman and Gallican versions, was compelled either to omit it or to give some explanation of it in his Hebraic version. It is generally introduced with one or other of the following titles.

a. "Psalmus extra numerum proprie scriptus David (ἰδιόγραφος Δαβὶδ) quando pugnavit cum Goliath." This is a mere translation of the Greek introduction.

β. "Hic psalmus in ebreorum codicibus non habetur sed a LXX. interpretibus additus est et idcirco repudiandus."

This must be Jerome's memorandum. In later Psalters where the Psalm is retained, the two notices are frequently combined; sometimes, as in Claudius C. VII., with most puzzling corruptions.

It may have been noticed that Charlemagne in one of his messages described the Psalms specially as being one hundred and fifty in number (above, p. 182). It would appear from this that his attention had been drawn to the memorandum of Jerome, and that he was acting upon it. In regard then to any Psalter in which this *Pusillus eram* is displaced from its earlier position immediately following Psalm 150, or in which it is entirely omitted, there is an *a priori* probability that it was penned either during or after the lifetime of the great Emperor.

[2] The illuminations are very interesting, and notices of them are given and some of them copied (I am told) in the *Trachten des Christlichen Mittelalters, herausgegeben von J. U. Hefner*, and there is a commendatory notice in Professor Waagen's *Kunstwerk von Deutschland*, Part II. pp. 183, 184. I must here express my obligations to Professor Dr August Winterlin for his most prompt attentions to my wants at the Stuttgart Library.

[3] It has the following:

Hoc ego psalterium quod jure vocatur hebreum
Hartmotus gallo donavi pectore leto.
Auferet hoc si quis, damnetur mille flagellis,
Judicioque dei succumbet corpore peste.

It begins thus: "Incipit prologus beati Hieronymi in psalterium juxta Hebreos quod ipse transtulit in Latinum." I do not know why Psalm cli. was retained. It is on folio 133 with this title, "David extra numerum cum pugnabat cum Goliad."

x. At Boulogne I saw a Psalter, imperfect at the commencement, but perfect at the close. Its number is 21. It is said to be of the tenth or eleventh century. It does not contain the Canticles or Creeds.

xi. In the Library of the British Museum, the Cotton Manuscript Vespasian A. 1, so far as our present purpose is concerned, merits great attention. It is sometimes called Augustine's Psalter, perhaps because it may have belonged to St Augustine's monastery. It contains the Roman version, and is a grand book, measuring about 9 inches by 7. It contains many prefaces, amongst them a curious exposition of the word Alleluia, dropping one letter after another. There is an interlinear Saxon translation, which was, in the year 1843, edited for the Surtees Society. At the end of Psalm cl. (where we have the Gloria Patri *once*) we read "expliciunt psalmi davidis numero centum quinquaginta." Then follows the *Pusillus eram.* On the verso of folio 141 is a prayer or address in small rustic letters: then the six morning Canticles, followed by the *Benedicite* and *Benedictus*[1]. These are followed by

"Hymnus ad matutinos,
Splendor paternæ.
"Hymnus vespertinus,
Deus Creator.
"Hymnus diebus dominicis,
Rex æterne."

And thus the early part of the volume terminates. But *written in another hand, and that of the eleventh century,* there follow the *Te Deum,* entitled "Hymnus ad matutinos," the *Magnificat, Nunc Dimittis, Gloria in Excelsis, Pater Noster, Credo in Deum, Credo in unum Deum,* and "Fides catholica, *Quicunque vult,*" and other things.

The introduction of these additions to the Psalter is assigned to the eleventh century. Of these I shall speak below. But to the Psalter itself, it is difficult to assign a precise date. It is probably of the eighth century. As to the date of the added

[1] From Martene, *Thesaurus Anecd.* v. (I quote from Migne, LXXII. p. 86), we learn that in the old Gallican Liturgy the *Benedictus* preceded the lesson from the prophets, and the *Benedicite* followed the lesson from the "Apostle." His authority here is the Exposition of St Germanus, which may be seen in Migne, ut supra, pp. 90, 91: see too pp. 94, 96.

portions the authorities are more decided, and thus we can approximate to the period when the Quicunque was *added* to the Roman Psalter. The volume probably belonged to the Church of Canterbury[1].

xii. The Lambeth Library contains a Psalter (1158) of an uncertain date, which has the Canticles closing with the *Nunc Dimittis*. A Litany follows, but there is no Quicunque.

xiii. At Salzburg there are two Psalters, a. v. 24 and a. IV. 27, which do not contain the Quicunque. They are regarded as of the eleventh or twelfth century.

xiv. It is quite clear that the Quicunque was not contained in either of the two Psalters, described at length by Elmham, as amongst the treasures of the Church of Canterbury[2].

The Harleian manuscript 603 is unfortunately imperfect at the end.

xv. At Florence (Plut. XVII. Cod. ix.) is a Psalter which contains the Canticles followed by a Litany, but no Creeds.

xvi. British Museum, Addl. manuscript 9046, is of the ninth century: it contains the 150 Psalms and 13 Canticles, but apparently no Creeds.

xvii. Harleian 2790 is of the ninth century: it has the Psalms, but no Creeds.

xviii. In the *Nouveau Traité* III. p. 367 is a note of a beautiful Psalter of the ninth century, which once belonged to the abbey of Godwic. It had two long Litanies, but, as it seems, did not contain the Quicunque. I do not know where it is now to be found.

It is curious that neither at Venice nor at Verona is there any Psalter which contains the Quicunque. It is, however, contained in the large Bible in the Library of St Mark's.

[1] A facsimile of the title-page and a few initial letters may be seen in Professor Westwood's *Miniatures*.

[2] The description of these may be seen in Sir Duffus Hardy's *First Report on the Utrecht Psalter*, p. 16.

CHAPTER XXIV.

LATIN PSALTERS OF THE NINTH OR TENTH OR ELEVENTH CENTURY CONTAINING THE QUICUNQUE.

§ 1. Conclusions from previous Chapter. § 2. The order of words in clause 27 furnishes a means of classifying the manuscripts. § 3. Probable origin of the difference. § 4. Class I. in which the reading is "Trinitas in unitate et unitas in Trinitate," and *a.* Psalters in which the 151st Psalm follows close on Psalm 150. i. Paris, 13159. ii. St Gall, 15. iii. St Gall, 23. iv. St Gall, 27. v. Douce, 59. vi. Boulogne, 20. vii. C. C. C. C. O. 5. viii. C. C. C. C. N. 10. ix. Arundel, 60. § 5. Comparison of the readings of these manuscripts. § 6. I. *β*. Psalter of this class which does not contain the *Pusillus eram.* St Gall, 20. § 7. I. *γ*. Psalter in which the *Pusillus eram* is placed at the end of the volume. Claudius C. VII. (the Utrecht Psalter). § 8. Psalter with the order dubious, "Charles le Chauve," Paris, 1152. § 9. Class II. in which the reading is "Unitas in Trinitate et Trinitas in Unitate." *a.* In which the 151st Psalm follows on Psalm 150. i. Galba A. XVIII. ii. Bamberg. iii. Salisbury. iv. Vitellius E. XVIII. v. Harleian, 2904. vi. C. C. C. C. 391 K. 10. vii. Latin Bibles, British Museum, Royal Library, 1 E. VIII. viii. Venice Bible. § 10. II. *β*. Psalters without the Psalm 151. i. "Charlemagne," Venice, 1861. ii. British Museum, Royal 2 B. V. iii. Cambridge, Ff. 1. 23. § 11. Vespasian A. 1, later addition. § 12. Miscellaneous Psalters. § 13. Arundel, 155. § 14. Eadwine Psalter. § 15. Other Psalters. § 16. Reflections and surmises.

§ 1. I DO not know that we can come to any other conclusions on the evidence furnished by the contents of my last chapter, save these; The Quicunque was not known in a Greek form to the literati who interested themselves in preparing any of the Greek Psalters that have been adduced: and The earliest Latin Psalters which have been brought forward do not contain either it or the Te Deum, or the Gloria in Excelsis, or the Apostles' Creed. Most of my readers are aware of the controversy regarding the date of the Utrecht Psalter, CLAUDIUS C. VII., which contains all these:—whether it was written in the sixth century or in the later years of the eighth or in the ninth, *i.e.* whether before the year 600 or after the year 750. I shall discuss the subject briefly ere long; in the mean time I will simply rank it in this chapter with other volumes whose contents resemble the materials we find in it.

§ 2. In treating of these Psalters I propose to make a division grounded on the following curious fact.

In all the early notices which I have found on the subject of the Trinity, where the phrases occur *Trinitas in Unitate* and *Unitas in Trinitate,* they occur in this order. So too they are found in the copies of the Quicunque given in the collections of Canons, *Vat. Pal.* 574, and *Paris* 1451. In the modern or received text the order is different, "Et Unitas in Trinitate et Trinitas in Unitate." Nothing doctrinal depends on this inversion, but I am able to some extent to trace its history; and in a literary point of view it is curious.

§ 3. It will be seen by referring to my account of the Psalter of Charles le Chauve that the penman of that beautiful manuscript omitted in the first instance the clause "et Trinitas in Unitate." He inserted it subsequently in the margin with a mark that it had been left out before the words "veneranda sit." So far as our earlier copies furnish us with evidence, this was a mistake: it was really omitted after the words "supra dictum est." However, this manuscript seems to have furnished the "copy" for later transcripts, and thus we have the criterion for a first classification.

§ 4. I will take first the Psalters which read "et Trinitas in Unitate et Unitas in Trinitate," and first (*a*) those in which Psalm cli. follows immediately on Psalm cl.

i. And first I will take a very interesting manuscript at Paris, numbered 13159, to which my attention was drawn by M. Delisle, the distinguished custodian of the manuscript department[1], a gentleman to whose contributions in the *Bibliothèque de l'Ecole des Chartes* is largely due our knowledge of the libraries of France. In M. Delisle's short catalogue in the Series VI. Vol. 4, p. 220 of the *Bibliothèque,* as well as in his kind communication to me, that learned palæographer has assigned the date of this manuscript to the year 795.

[1] Of this M. Delisle most kindly sent me a collation in December, 1871.

The Psalms are of the Gallican version. The whole of fol. 1 recto is occupied with a letter of the shape and character of the Utrecht B, but with a most surprising amount of interlacing. On the verso: "innomine patris et filii et spiritus sancti incipit liber. psalmorum." Each Psalm has an introduction to which its first few words are generally prefixed, so that these words occur twice over. Thus before Psalm iv. we read

"cum invocarem⸮

"in finem incarminib; Carmina solent fieri s̄ in leticia s̄ in tristicia."

Of the prayers I will take that subjoined to Psalm xxvii. as a specimen. (Ad te domine clamabo.)

"Oratio
Ad templum sanctum tuum manus eleuantes inualidas quesumus domine ne trahas cum peccatoribus animas te agnoscentium nostras ne nos cum operantibus iniquitatem perdas ne nos deseras per—"

On folio 155, verso, we have the following:

"Pussillus eram.
hic psalm. secundum ebrē. primus in cantico. uictoriam indicit cum golia. Et ideo in fine ponitur Quae alia sequentur in hoc psalmo puerilia sunt cantica. Hic psalmus d̄d̄ proprie scripsit extra numerum. cum pugnavit contra Goliad. Vox Christi seculum exoperantis.

Finiunt tituli psalmorum. hic psalmus in ebreorum codicibus non habetur sed a LXX interpretib. editus est et idcirco repudiandus."

The Psalm begins on folio 156, Pusillus eram.

The Old Testament Canticles follow (one or two folia are missing) with the *Benedictus* and *Benedicite;* then "Canticum Zachariæ; Hymnum sanctæ Mariæ; huic loco Symeon; *Te Deum laudamus*" (without a title); then some leaves are missing.

Folio 161 a begins in the middle of the interpolated Creed of Constantinople *in a later hand.* This is followed up by the Quicunque in the same writing, but on fol. 162 *in the old writing* we have "sed unus increatus et unus inmensus." To the end the writing is certainly the same as in the body of the book, although the ink is blacker. Then comes on the same page (163) in red "Finit de :" but the red has become so faded that I could not read the rest. Then a litany, which is so curious that I will give it in my note[1].

[1] "Christus vincit
Christus regnat
Christus imperat III
exaudi Christe Leoni summo pontifici
et universali pape vita
Salvator mundi Tu illum adjuva
Sce. Petre Tu illum adjuva
Sce. Paule Tu illum adjuva
Sce. Andrea Tu illum adjuva
Sce. Clemens Tu illum adjuva
exaudi Christe Carolo excellentis simo esado caro (? et deo caro) atque magno et pacifico
Regi francorum et longobardorum ac patricio
Romanorum vita et victoria
Redemptor mundi Tu illum adjuva
Sca. Maria Tu illum adjuva
Sce. Michael Tu illum adjuva
Sce. Gabrahel Tu illum adjuva
Sce. Raphael Tu illum adjuva
Sce. Iohannes Tu illum adjuva
Sce. Stephane Tu illum adjuva
exaudi Christe
Nobilissimo proli
Regali vita.
Sca. virgo virginum Tu illum adjuva

On the folio 168 b there is another litany which seems to **fix the** date.

"Letania calula." [sic]

Beginning as usual. It contains fol. 169 the prayers

"Ut dominum apostolicum leonem
in sanctitate et religione conservare
digneris. Te rogamus audi nos.
ut ei vitam et sanitatem dones. Te R.
ut dominum carolum regem conservare digneris. Te R.
ut ei vitam et sanitatem et victoriam dones. Te R.
ut proles regales conservare digneris. Te R.
ut eis vitam et sanitatem dones ,,
ut eis vitam et victoriam dones
ut populo Christiano pacem
et unitatem largiaris
Filius Dei Te rogamus audi nos
Agnus dei qui tollis peccata mundi
miserere nobis
Kyrie eleison
Litania callica [sic]
Pater de celis deus miserere nobis
Filius Redemptor deus miserere nobis
Spiritus Sanctus deus miserere nobis
Sancta Dei Trinitas miserere nobis
Qui et trinus et unus miserere nobis
ipsi idemque benignus
sca virgo virginum ora
&c. &c. ."

On the same page (Is this for the consecration of a Church ?)

"Imprimis
ante ostium ecclesie.

[The same prayer is addressed to Saints Sylvester, Laurence, Pancras, Nazarus, Anastasia, Genoveva, Columba.]

"Exaudi Christe omnibus judici
bus vel cuncto exercitui francorum
vita et victoria

[Sts Hilary, Martin, Maurice are appealed to, and in a more recent ink the names of Dionysius, Crispin and Crispianus are added. Then on folio 164 a]

"Christus vincit. Christus regnat. Christus imperat.
Rex Regum Christus vincit
Rex noster Christus vincit
Spes nostra Christus vincit
Gloria nostra Christus vincit
Misericordia nostra Christus vincit
Auxilium nostrum Christus vincit
Fortitudo nostra Christus vincit
Liberatio et redemptio nostra Christus vincit
Victoria nostra Christus vincit
Arma nostra invictissima Christus vincit
Murus noster inexpugnabilis Christus vincit
Defensio et exaltatio nostra Christus vincit
Lux via et vita nostra Christus vincit
Ipsi soli imperium gloria ac potestas
per immortalia secula seculorum. amen
Ipsi soli honor laus et jubilatio
per infinita secula seculorum. amen
Christe [eleison] Ter
Kyrie eleison T.
Feliciter. Feliciter
Tempora bona habeas. Ter
Multos annos amen. [Ter ?]
expliciunt"

dicat pontifex una cum diaco
nibus
Agnus dei
&c. &c.

The volume finishes off on folio 168 with a few hymns, and seems to be mutilated[1].

I have met with nothing more interesting, and at first sight more perplexing, than this volume. But since I copied out the first Litany or Song of Jubilee, I find that Zaccaria was equally interested and equally charmed with something resembling it. In his *Bibliotheca Ritualis*, p. 171, he gives from a manuscript at Cologne[2] a Litany or Hymn of Triumph, resembling the above. The invocations are not so numerous: instead of the prayer for Charles, king of the Franks and Lombards, and patrician of the Romans—the cry goes up for "Domino nostro et augusto a deo coronato magno et pacifico imperatori vita et victoria[3]." The similarity of this with the well-known cry uttered at Rome when Charlemagne was crowned and saluted as Emperor[4], compels me to believe that this Litany of Paris, 13159, was composed for the visit of Charles to Rome before he was crowned. Leo is pope, Charles king and patrician; thus the Litany belongs to the period bounded by 795 and 800. A Litany of the same character was found by Baluzius in the Church of Beauvais (*Miscellanea*, II.

1 These are the hymns:

"hymnū ad primá.
Post matutinis laudibus quos trini
tate psallimus psallamus rursus
admonet pater verus familias ·.·
Simus semper solliciti ne ṗtereat
opus dī:
sed oremus sedulo sicut docet
apostol ·.·
Psallamus mente dn̄o. psallamus simul et spiritu:
ne vaca mens in turpibus inerti
tegat animū."

Thus there is no rhythm in the hymn.

We have another fol. 168 b,

"hymnum ad matutinas die dominica,"

beginning (it is very difficult to read):

"O qui cœla luminis satorque."

And there is a paraphrase of the Lord's Prayer:

"Pater qui celis contines cantemus...
adveniat regnum tuum fiatque vo-
luntas tua
Haec in qua......
simus fideles spiritu casto manen-
tes corpore
Panem nostrum cotidie de te edendum
tribue remit
te nobis debita ut nos nostra remit-
timus
Temptatione subdola induci nos ne
sinens
sed puro corde simplices tu nos a
malo libera."

2 Or from Hartzheim's Catalogue.

3 See Mabillon, *Museum Italicum*, Tom. II.

4 Mr Brice's *Holy Roman Empire*, or Labbe and Cossart, VII. 1082. "Carolo piissimo Augusto a deo coronato magno pacifico imperatori vita et victoria."

p. 143): this was adapted to a time when John was pope, Roger bishop, Robert king: it belongs therefore to the year 1003[1].

The question then is, Was this Paris manuscript, 13159, written between 795 and 800? or, Was it intended to include a collection of documents of that and earlier or later dates? The titles, "Letania Calula," on folio 168 b, and "Letania Callica" on 169 a, with other matters, lead me to consider it to have been intended to be a collection of prayers, expositions, psalms, canticles, litanies; and on this account I cannot quote 13159 with the same degree of confidence as does M. Delisle, as having been written between 795 and 800. All I can say is that it was written after 795. But I have given my readers all the evidence which bears upon the subject, and shall leave it now in the hands of better judges than myself.

It will be noticed that the writer was somewhat illiterate: and the similarity of the initial B with the Utrecht B will not be forgotten[2]. I call this manuscript *k*.

ii. St Gall, 15, is of the ninth century, Gallican, with long introductions to each Psalm. It contains the Canticles, with notes that the *Te Deum* was sung at mattins on Sunday (it is entitled Ymnus ad matutinas diebus dominicis), the *Benedictus* at mattins, the *Magnificat* at vespers, the *Nunc dimittis* at compline. The *Gloria in Excelsis* is entitled "Ymnum ad missam diebus dominicis:" the Lord's Prayer, Apostles' Creed and Quicunque follow. The latter is entitled "Fides Catholica edita a sc̄o Athanasio Alexandrino epo." This is followed by a short Litany. I call this Psalter *l*.

iii. St Gall, 23, is a magnificent volume of the ninth century, measuring 14¾ by 11¼. It begins with a Litany of an unusual character[3]; after the KYRIE ELEISON, &c. in gold letters, there follows:

"Saucte Pater Deus omnipotens miserere nobis.
Sancte Filius Deus redemptor noster miserere nobis.

[1] Roger was bishop of Beauvais between 998 and 1022. (*Gallia Christiana*, IX. 735.) Robert was king: John XVI. was pope from June to December, 1003.

[2] The interpolated Creed of Constantinople is of a later handwriting. The Cologne manuscript instead of Nobilissimo proli, has "ejus precellentissimis filiis regibus." Its prayer is for the army of the Romans and Franks.

[3] Yet of the same type is St Gall, 20, p. 358, and 27, f. 701.

Sancte Spiritus Sanctus Deus procedens miserere nobis.
Sancta ineffabilis Trinitas miserere nobis.
Qui est trinus et unus miserere nobis.
Christe Iesu exaudi nos.
Christe Iesu salva nos.
Christe Iesu custodi nos."

Then the invocations.
The preface of Jerome is on fol. 26.
An inscription on this leaf and the next fixes the date.

"Hinc preceptoris hartmoti jussa secutus
Folchardus studuit rite partare librum."

The Psalms are the Gallican; the *Te Deum* is attributed to Ambrose and Augustine. We find (what is somewhat unusual) the "Fides Concilii Constantinopolitani,"—the interpolated Creed. In the Apostles' Creed the word *Dei* is omitted; the Quicunque is entitled, "Fides Catholica sci Athanasii episcopi." The book is magnificent[1]. I call it *n*. The "Gloria in Excelsis" is not in the manuscript. Hartmot was abbot in the year 884.

iv. St Gall, 27, is also considered to be of the ninth century. It is in three columns, the text (Gallican) of the Psalter being in the middle, and notes and glosses at the sides.

The first two pages are gone. Page 3 commences with the words "Prophetia est divina inspiratio" in small but clear rustic letters: then a prayer to the Virgin of a later date. Prefaces and introductions of various kinds, including the Præfatio Sancti Hieronymi, occupy the early pages, until on p. 20 we have "In nomine sancte et individue Trinitatis" occupying the whole page. The B of Beatus is similar in form though not in ornamentation to the Utrecht B. The explanations of the Psalms in the first few pages at least (if not throughout) are in rustic letters. The *Te Deum* follows on the *Benedicite*, being again ascribed to Ambrose and Augustine: "Invicem condiderunt." Then the *Benedictus*, *Magnificat*, *Oratio Dominica*, *Symbolum Apostolorum*, *Canticum Simeonis*, *Fides sancti Athanasii episcopi* (p. 692). A Litany resembling that of St Gall 23 follows on page 701. Several long prayers then occupy about 26 or 27 pages, including prayers addressed to the Father, to the Person of the Son, to

[1] The Psalms generally are in black ink and of the Caroline character, in two columns, 21 lines on a page. Thus the letters are large. The initial letter of each verse is in gold uncials: that of each Psalm being very large and occupying the space of two or more lines. The words in these lines are in gold or silver, written sometimes in uncials, sometimes in Roman capitals, sometimes in rustics. I noticed the inverted ! in the Quicunque.

the Person of the Holy Spirit, to St Peter, St Paul, St Benedict. The notes on the Faith of Athanasius are few. Thus on *inmensus* which has been altered by a second hand to *immensus*, we have "non est mensurabilis in sua natura quia inlocalis est et incircumscriptus, ubique totus, ubique præsens, ubique potens." On clause 2 the note is "qui catholicam fidem recte credendo et opere exercendo negligit, hereticus est et schismaticus, et hunc sine dubio interitus manebit[1]." On *æternus* "id est non tres æterni sed in tribus personis unus deus æternus qui sine initio et sine fine permanet." Again "Deus nomen potestatis non proprietatis, proprium nomen patris pater, et proprium nomen filii filius, et proprium nomen est spiritus sancti spiritus sanctus." Once more on 31 "id est deus de deo, lumen de lumine; et, quod pater in divina substantia, hoc est filius. deus pater deum filium genuit non voluntate, neque necessitate sed natura: ne quæratur quomodo genuit filium, quod et angeli nesciunt, prophetis est incognitum: nec inenarrabilis deus a servulis suis discutiendus est, sed fideliter credendus et sponte diligendus."

On comparing this with the Exposition of "Fortunatus," it will be seen that there is much similarity. That Exposition may have been originally a series of notes like this: or the collection may have been formed by a diligent reader, anxious to copy something "which time had saved;" or the two documents may have been directly or indirectly drawn from some common original. The verbal identity cannot be otherwise accounted for.

There is no note on the word "sæculo" in clause 31. I call this MS. *m*.

We must note that the Gloria in Excelsis does not occur in either of these two St Gall Psalters[2].

v. I will take next a very beautiful manuscript which forms one of the many treasures in the Douce collection at the Bodleian. It is numbered 59. Mr Coxe considers it to be of the tenth century,—

Probably, of the earliest years, for it seems to be nearly of the same date as the exquisite Vienna Psalter, which we connect with the names of Charles and Hadrian. It is of the same size: and in very similar writing, *i.e.* gold Caroline minuscules; but whereas in the Vienna manuscript the parchment is generally white, in this it is coloured purple. The lines are ruled most regularly. The initial B in Psalm i. is of the same Roman character, though the ornamentation is different: the Douce has 20 lines on the page, the Viennese 23. The Psalter in both is Gallican. The preliminary matter is much less in the Douce, consisting only of the *Origo prophetiae*, fol. 1 (David filius Jesse), fol. 2, *Præfatio Sci Hieronymi;* the *Beatus* commencing on fol. 4. There are drawings (as is not unusual) for the Psalm li. *Quid gloriaris* and Ps. ci. *Oratio pauperis*. In the titles occasionally rustic letters are intermixed. The *Hymnum in die dominica* follows that from Deuteronomy: the *Hym-*

1 The reading is "interritus."

2 I would take this opportunity of expressing my obligations for the attentions which I received from M. Fr. Rohrer, the Librarian, and M. Joh. Schlachten the Vice-librarian of the Library of St Gall.

num angelicum ad missam[1] follows the Nunc Dimittis. Then the Lord's Prayer, Apostles'.Creed, (161 b), and on the same page "Fides Catholica Athanasii epi[2]." Here and there we have rustic titles. I call this *o*.

vi. Boulogne, 20, is of the tenth century: indeed the date seems to be fixed between 989 and 1008. Drawings from it may be seen in Professor Westwood's *Miniatures*, 36, 37, 38, 39. And there is an interesting account of it in the Boulogne Catalogue, p. 16[3]. It contains some of the usual prefatory matter. The writing generally is, I think, Caroline minuscules: the version is Gallican.

The *Te Deum* is ascribed to Ambrose and Augustine. The Quicunque is annotated thus "Q. U. S. esse Ibi ille doctor liberum arbitrium posuit sicut dicit in psalmo Quis est homo qui vult vitam ..Æternum pro sempiternum debemus intelligere...singillatim id est distinctim vel separatim." These explanations are found in "Bruno." It finishes off with the appeal "ut unusquisque sacerdos haec sciat et predicet." The following, however, seems to have been omitted in Bruno: "et si ita non credideris, salvus esse non poteris. unde nos pius dominus non meritis nostris sed propter suam misericordiam eripere dignetur. amen. Finit[4]."

This is followed by sixteen leaves of collects or prayers adapted for the Psalms, &c., in succession, they include Psalm cli., the Canticles, the Pater Noster, Credo in Deum, Gloria in Excelsis, Te Deum laudamus, in this which seems to be the ancient order, but here they stop: *i. e.* there is no collect or prayer on the Quicunque. These collects are all printed (says the Boulogne Catalogue) amongst the works of Bruno. There are yet twenty folia of hymns and nine more of prayers. The volume is very interesting. We will designate it as *p*.

vii. Although the manuscript 272. O. 5, in the collection at Corpus Christi College, Cambridge, does not exactly tally with those which I have been above describing, it so nearly resembles them that I will place it in this group.

It is a Gallican Psalter, and was known to and examined by Archbishop Usher (see de Symbolo, p. 30, or Elrington's edition, Vol. VII., pp. 335, 336). Hence it fell under the notice of Waterland (chap. iv.

1 Note the title.

2 The stops in Vienna, 1861, are ! in the middle of the verse and , at end. "Douce" has . in the middle, and · at end, generally followed by :·· in white or red.

3 For this I was indebted to Mr Bensley.

4 The initial B is wonderful. There are pen and ink drawings (subsequently coloured) which are very neat and good. In the D of Psalm xxvi. (Dominus illuminatio) is a drawing of the angel appearing to Mary. The B in "Beati quorum" is something like the Utrecht B. The Q in "Quid gloriaris" contains the birth of our Lord. In the "Cantate" (Ps. xcvii.) is a picture of Christ changing the water into wine. In the D of Psalm ci. is a drawing of the crucifixion.

A.D. 885). It begins with some of the prefatory matter that we meet with elsewhere: The Origo prophetiæ, David Filius Jesse, Præfatio Sci Hieronymi presbyteri. Throughout the book each verse begins with a gold letter which is uncial.

There is a short comment on each psalm followed by a collect. Thus at the end of Psalm iii. we have "coll." in red, and the

"Effunde dne benedictionem tuam super popu
lum tuum ut tua resurrectione muniti
non timeamus ab adversantium vitiorum li
tibus (?) circundari per dnm."

The titles of the Psalms are frequently in red rustic.

The margin of Psalm cl. runs as follows:

"Impletur hæc laus in cymbalis quando corruptione carnis sanguinisque depulsa conformati ad imaginem creatoris resplendentes in regno patris omnis spiritus: in illo igitur regno non caro nec sanguis non corruptio sed homo iam spiritualis totus effectus deum in spiritu qui spiritus est laudare non desinit."

At the end of Psalm cl. is in gold uncials "Achadeus misericordia dei comes hunc psalterium scribere jussit." After Psalm cl. is interpolated a quire of a few leaves, containing a Litany.

"Incipit Letania
Kyrie eleison ter
Christe eleison ter
Kyrie eleison ter
Christe audi nos."

These in gold rustics.

Then the invocations "Scta Maria, &c." in uncials. This and the three "Sce Remigi, Sce Columbane, Sce Abunde" are in gold. After the invocations follow the petitions which fix the date of the Litany.

"Ut Marinum apostolicum in sca religione conservare
dignеris. Te rog.
Ut Karlomannum regem
perpetua prosperitate
conservare digneris. Te rog.
ut [a blank] reginam
conservare digneris. Te rog.
ut folconem episcopum cum omni
grege sibi commisso in tuo
apostolico servitio conservare
digneris. Te rog."

The Litany finishes in gold rustic letters XPEAUDINOS, &c.

The verso is blank. The next folio begins "Pascebam oves patris mei" in the middle of Psalm cli, the first part of which has been torn out to make way for the Litany.

Then come the Canticles assigned to the mattins of the successive days of the week.

The *Benedicite, Benedictus, Magnificat, Nunc dimittis* following. Then

"Hymnum die dominica ad matutin."
(ScS ScS ScS are in gold).
"Hymnum angelicum."
"Fides catholica."
"Incipit symbolum."
"Oratio dominica."

In the margin is added in the handwriting of the thirteenth or fourteenth century, "Ave Maria gratiae plena[1]." Then in the original

"Incipit oratio Sancti Benedicti."

Towards the end the confession and absolution which are so well known: "Confiteor domino et tibi frater[2] quia peccavi nimis in cogitatione et locutione et opere, propterea precor te ut ores pro me.

"Misereatur sic tibi omnipotens deus et dimittat tibi omnia peccata tua, liberet te ab omni malo, conservet te in omni bono et perducat te in vitam eternam."

For the date of the Litany we have the following notes. Marinus was pope from December 882 to May 884. Carloman was sole king from 881 to 885. Fulco was archbishop of Rheims about the same time: the latter was a great friend of learning, as may be seen from a notice by Flodoard in Wiltzsch. (*Geography and Statistics of the Church*, vol. I. p. 335, note 20.) Thus the date of the Litany is certain. The question remains, Was the Psalter of the same date? It will be remembered that the first few words of Psalm cli. are missing. The page containing them must have been torn out, probably to make way for the Litany. I conceive therefore that the greater part of the book must be of an earlier date than 884. How much earlier is merely a subject for conjecture.

I shall call this manuscript *q*.

viii. The manuscript 411. N. 10, in the library of Corpus Christi College, Cambridge, is somewhat puzzling, but I will give it place here.

It contains a Gallican Psalter, and is said to have been written in the ninth century. The "Hymnus in die dominica ad matut.[3]" comes between the *Magnificat* and *Nunc dimittis:* after the latter the "Hymnus angelicus," the *Pater Noster, Credo in Deum,* "Fides sci Anasthasii epi." Then "Pura oratio ad dominum cum intercessionibus sanctorum," followed by two litanies. The volume is mentioned by Waterland, chap iv., under the year 850: it belonged once to Thomas à Becket. The text of the Athanasian Creed is generally of the same type as that contained in the Psalters which I have been describing, but the manuscript has been altered much by erasures[4].

[1] An interesting fact as to the date of the introduction of this invocation.

[2] Not to the Virgin nor to the Saints.

[3] The Te Deum reads "Te ergo *sancte quæsumus* tuis famulis."

[4] Thus the *et* has been carefully erased

ix. Of the remaining older manuscripts of this class which have Psalm cli. following on Psalm cl., the only remarkable one that remains to be noticed is *Arundel*, 60. It is described in Professor Westwood's *Miniatures*, 49, and referred to by Waterland under the year 1050. Waterland describes it as containing a Gallican Psalter: my memoranda make it a Roman Psalter.

It begins with a Calendar fol. 1—12: on fol. 13 there is a beautiful opening. There is an interlinear gloss or translation throughout the Psalms. Psalm cli. is not glossed, therefore I presume that its use had become obsolete when the gloss was introduced. The Canticles follow. The scribe could not have been very literate—for we read

"canticum moysi inde vtero
nomio ad filios israhel"

and the *Magnificat* is described as the "canticum zachariae." The *Te Deum* is entitled f. 127

YMH' SCI VICETI EPI DIEB' DOMINICIS ADMATUTINIS

Before the Quicunque we have "incipit fides Catholica Athanasii Alexandrini." As a specimen of the gloss I take this to verse 35:

an soþlice na gecippednes godcundnesse
on flæsce ac of anfangennesse menniscnesse
on gode.

The Athanasian Creed is followed by a litany, including prayers for the pope, our king, our bishop (no names given). Towards the end is a kind of chronology. It ends "ab initio mundi usque ad nativitatem Christi fuerunt anni fiunt autem (sic) anni quinque mill. CXCVII. a nativitate dni usque ad finem mundi dd XXVI." Thus the sixth millennary would end in the year 803: but how the end of the world was calculated I do not know. On folio 149 b is a list of the bishops of the West Saxons[1]. I call this *t*.

§ 5. The Psalms and Canticles, &c. in these Psalters are arranged nearly in the same order, and when we examine the text of the *Quicunque* we meet with the same characteristics. Comparing it as exhibited here with the received text of the Roman

in clauses 7, 8, 9, 10, 13, 15, 17, adapting the words to the more modern text. In clause 27 I think that the original reading was "et unitas in trinitate et trinitas in unitate," and that this was erased and the words replaced in the other order by the original writer: the clause "tertia die resurrexit a mortuis" is also on an erasure apparently made to interpolate "tertia die." I will designate the two sets of readings by s_1 and s_2.

[1] There is a Psalter at Florence, Plut. XVII. cod. III? of the eleventh century, which seems from the description in the Catalogue to resemble this. The *Te Deum* is entitled "hymnus Niceti Episcopi in diebus dominicis," but the "Symbolum Constantinopolitanum" is interposed between the Apostles' Creed and the "Fides Catholica S. Athanasii episcopi Alexandrini." A Litany follows.

Breviary, and remembering that *k* commences in the middle of clause 12, I note

That all of them with the exception of q (CCC. O. 5 Marinus) ascribe the document to *Athanasius* (for *Anasthasius* is simply a blunder).

In clause 5, l m n (the three MSS. of St Gall)
read *et* spiritus sancti.
o p q s t omitting *et*.

In clauses 7. 8. 9. 10. 13. 15. 17 all save f add
et. s_2 erased it.

In 16. k omits *est*.
24. k omits *sanctus* (per errorem sine dubio).
27. k had *superius*, a more recent hand has written *supra*.

In 27. All read now *et trinitas in unitate et unitas in trinitate*, although it is uncertain what s_1 read.

In 29. k omits *est*.
29. t adds *unusquisque* before *fideliter*: and q has the same word in the margin.
s_2 has interlined *qui vult salvus esse*.

In 30. k_2 has the latter half rewritten on an erasure: a space is left after *deus*, no doubt for the insertion of *pariter*.
in l, a word is erased after *deus*.
in q *pariter* is written in the margin
to be inserted after *deus*.
t adds *pariter* in the text.
in s *pariter* is in the text but is run through with a pen.
31. k reads *sæcula* for *sæculo*.
32. In *rationali* q has the *li* on an erasure.
It seems to have read at one time *rationabili*.
35. k l m_1 n_1? o p q s t read *carne* or *carnae*
and *deo*
(k_1 may have read *deum*.)
m_2 n_2 read *carnem*, *deum*.

In 38. The words *tertia die* have been erased in k and a space left. They are not found in l n o p q_1 s;
in m they are underlined as erroneous:
in q the line has been rewritten, clearly for the purpose of introducing them:
in s the words are on an erasure.

Thus t alone of this group contains *tertia die* without remark.

In 39. k and t have *sedit*.

In 41. The readings vary. k has *qui mala*. o, *et qui mala*. p, *qui mala*, but there has been an attempt to insert *vero*.

We have therefore little difficulty in reconstructing the text as it was received in France in the ninth century, and with that text we may make further comparisons.

§ 6. *β*. I turn now to St Gall, 20, which is the only manuscript of this class that I have met with which does not contain Psalm cli. It is an interesting manuscript, the size 12″ by 9″: the handwriting the early Caroline minuscule. The initial B, however, for Psalm i. is very large, and of the Utrecht or Anglo-Saxon type. It is really curious to see how frequently this B is introduced, and with what variety of filling up. The Psalter is again Gallican.

The early Rubrics are in rustic: the first words of the Psalms in Roman. The ornamentation is rather rude. Psalm cl. ends on page 327: then follow a few words to say that it was written by one Wolfcar. The Scriptural Canticles come in the usual order; there is no *Gloria in Excelsis* here: the *Nunc dimittis* is followed by *Pater noster, Credo in Deum* (without titles), "Fides catholica Sancti Athanasii episcopi." This on page 350. On page 354 a title much abbreviated which I read thus: "Hymnus dominicalis pro nocturnis, hoc est ante lectionem evangelii." This is the *Te Deum.* After it the hymn *Te decet laus,* as in Folkard (St Gall 23), "hymnus angelicus laudibus in nativitate Christi cantatus," the *Gloria in Excelsis:* on p. 357 is a short table of lessons: on p. 358 a Litany resembling that in 23, *i. e.* with the petitions to the Father, to the Son, to the Holy Spirit. A few hymns including *Lucis creator: Immensus coeli conditor*—and the book ends. We will call this *u.*

This manuscript agrees entirely with *l, m, n,* save that it reads *carnem* and *deum.* That is, it has *et* in clause 5; omits *pariter;* and omits *tertia die.*

§ 7. γ. We now come to a manuscript in which the 151st Psalm is relegated to the end of the volume. In other respects its contents resemble, in general, those of the Psalters which I have given above under my subdivision α. This copy contains the Gallican Psalter and the usual Canticles (amongst the titles of which there is some confusion; we have each of the first three entitled, "Canticum Isaie Prophetae"): that from Deuteronomy is inscribed "Canticum Moysi ad Filiis Israbel." There follow on this, "Benedictio trium puerorum," "hymnum ad matutinis" *Te Deum Laudamus,* "Canticum Zacharie Prophete ad matutinum," "Canticum scae Mariae," "Canticum Simeonis ad completorium," *Gloria in Excelsis,* "Oratio Dominica secundum Matheum," "Incipit Symbolu Apostolorum" (a completed copy): "Incipit Fides Catholicam." Then Psalm cli. It has an initial B of the same character as the B of the manuscripts *Paris,* 13159; *St Gall,* 20 and 27; the B of Psalm cxviii. in *Boulogne,* 20. We find a B of the same type, although far more beautifully ornamented, in the Psalter of Charles le Chauve, which will come next under our notice: and another in Galba A. XVIII. Judging by the contents we must place this Psalter among those of the ninth or tenth century; and as no argument has been brought forward to invalidate this conclusion, I have no hesitation in accepting this, which is also the decision of the great majority of the palæographers of the day. This manuscript is the famous Utrecht Psalter, the Claudius C. VII. of the library of Sir Robert Cotton[1]. The readings of the Athanasian Creed agree entirely with the revised version in (q), except that we have here *tres dominos* in 20; and *et qui mala* in 41. I call this manuscript *x*.

§ 8. I am not quite satisfied, as will be seen, as to the reading of clause 27 in the beautiful Psalter of Charles le Chauve: therefore, I shall consider it by itself.

This Psalter has been long well known. It is mentioned by Montfaucon in his *Diatribe* on the Quicunque (Migne, p. 1571) It once belonged to the chapter of Metz, but Colbert asked for it in 1674, and then it formed one of the treasures of his collection. Its number there was 1339. It is now in the Paris library, 1152. When I first asked, through the Very Reverend the Dean of Westminster, for a collation of the manuscript, it was in one of the cases of the Musée des Souverains in the Louvre, and access was impracticable. The course of events during the years 1871 and 1872 broke up that collection, and the precious volume was restored to the library; and then M. Delisle himself most kindly prepared for me a collation. And I had an opportunity of inspecting the volume in September, 1872, and of thus adding to the information which its distinguished custodian had so liberally conveyed to me. I was assisted also by an interesting memoir in one of the old Hand-books to the Louvre, prepared by the distinguished savant, M. Barbet de Jouy.

The manuscript consists of 172 numbered folia, each of which measures $9\frac{1}{8}''$ by $6\frac{5}{8}''$. It is magnificently bound in ivory[2] inlaid with

[1] It will be noticed that the Quicunque is entitled *Fides Catholica* as in (q), and is not ascribed to Athanasius. I must give below an Excursus on the date of this manuscript.

[2] With regard to this ivory binding, Professor Westwood contributed some interesting information to the *Athenæum* Newspaper, July 18, 1874, p. 81. One of the plaques affixed to the cover exhibits a carving which is identical in design with that of the Utrecht Psalter for Psalm l. (our li.). The other plaque, of which the interpretation had been much disputed, proves to exhibit the design in the Utrecht Psalter for Psalm lvi. (our lvii.). Another plaque, evidently by the same artist, is in the

gold, the gems on which (if I remember right) still continue fixed. On fol. 1 b is a painting of David playing on the lyre, Asaph dancing, Eman with the cymbals, Ethan on the cythera, Iduthun on the trumpet. The picture is far superior to anything of the age which I have seen.

The volume begins with the "Origo psalmorum" *David Filius Jesse.* Fol. 2 a is blank. Then, on the next opening, on the left is a picture of Jerome, and on the right of Charles crowned; with this inscription in rustic letters over the one—

"Nobilis interpres hieronymus atque sacerdos
Nobiliter pollens transcripsit jura davidis."

Over the other;

"Cum sedeat carolus magno coronatus honore
Est iosia similis parque theodosio."

Then come the exquisitely beautiful "Incipit liber psalmorum," and the "Beatus[1]" (each occupying a page), which are depicted in M. Sylvestre's volumes.

There are twenty lines on each page—the same number as in Douce 59—the lines being drawn with the utmost regularity. A band of a lovely violet runs down between two vertical lines on the left: and, when a new Psalm commences, a similar band crosses the page. This last is occupied with writing. The general character of the writing of the Psalms seems to be Roman: the letters are all gold. The inscriptions at first are in uncials: from folio 19 they vary; *e.g.* on fol. 19 b, one is in rustic: fol. 24 b in uncials: fol. 25 b in rustic: foll. 29 to 41 in rustic. In the beginning of the volume the stops are ⁝ in the middle of the verse and . at the end: but from Psalm xviii. we have · in the middle.

At the end of Psalm xxv. (fol. 26 a) and on folia 41 a, 69 b, 88 a, 103 a, 121 a, are inserted lections, in the Caroline minuscule, apparently intended simply to fill up the page when the next page was required either for a beautiful initial or for a drawing. On folio 106 we have another inscription which helps to fix the date. It is after Psalm c. *Misericordiam et judicium* to which it is certainly appropriate. It is this

REXREGVMKAROLOPACEMTRIBVATQVESALVTEM

This is in rustic letters.

On folio 155 a, Psalm cli. follows immediately on cl. with the short title "His psalmus...Goliath" in rustics: then the Canticles (the "Hym-

Museum of the Antiquarian Society at Zurich, exactly like that in the Utrecht Psalter for Psalm xxvi. In a letter addressed to the same Journal (September 19, 1874, pp. 384, 385), Professor Westwood adds that in a very beautiful Psalter of the ninth century in the Cathedral of Troyes, there is an illumination identical with the drawing in the Utrecht Psalter for Psalm li. *Quid gloriaris.* Out of the mouths of the persons represented small legends proceed in rustic Letters.

[1] The magnificent and elaborate B is Anglo-Saxon in its outline, like the Utrecht B. It is depicted on Plate 129 of Sylvestre's work (see too Plate 131 a). This is the account of it in the letterpress. "La premiere lettre B est de forme Anglosaxonne, gigantesque, entrelassée, brodée dans le plein ornée en volute et fleurons." With the exception of the D in *Dixit dominus*, I believe it is the only Anglo-Saxon letter in the volume. This is curious because (as is well known) the B of the first Psalm is the only Anglo-Saxon letter in the Utrecht Psalter.

nus ad matutin. in diebus dominicis" following on the song of Simeon), then the "Oratio dominica," CYMBOΛON[1], "Hymnus angelicus," "Fides sancti Athanasii." Then "Incipit Laetania." This commences as the older Litanies did, "Kyrie eleison." I counted about 129 invocations in seven groups; the last two being addressed to "Sancta Praxedis" and "Savina."

Then on fol. 171 b.

"propitius esto, parce nobis dn̄e·"

After a while

"ut apostolicum nostrum in sancta
religione conservare digneris; Te rogo audi me:
"ut mihi Karolo a re regi coronato
vitam atque prosperitatem atque
victoriam dones; Te rogo audi me.
"ut hirmindrudam conjugem
nostram conservare digneris; Te r. a. me.
"ut nos ad gaudia æterna perduceres
digneris; Te r. a. me.
"ut liberos nostros conservare digneris; Te r. a. me.
"ut sanitatem...ut compunctionem̄
cordis...ut spatium pœnitentiæ
nobis dones; Te r. a. me.
"ut animabus parentum nostrorum
requiem æternam dones; Te rogo audi me.
&c., &c.
"Pater noster, &c."

It ends

"ut nullo in nobis regnante peccato.
tibi solo domino servire. mereamur
per dnm nrm ihm xpm filium
tuum qui tecum vivit et regnat ds in unita
te sps scti per omnia sæcla sclorum amen
Benedicamus Dno. Dō gratias."

Then on a violet band at the bottom in rustics—

HICCALAMVSFACTOLIVTHARDIFINEQVIEVIT.

Thus the Manuscript must have been written between the year 842 when Charles married Hirmindruda and 869 when she died. The period is made a little shorter when we note Charles's prayer for his children[2].

[1] The punctuation is, "in ihm xpm filium eius · unicum dmn nrm."

[2] There is a reference to this Litany in Madrisius' edition of Paulinus, Migne, Vol. xcix. p. 625. Almost simultaneously with this volume must have been written another wonderful specimen of calligraphy, the Evangeliarium (once at St Emmeran's at Ratisbon, now at Munich) with its effigy of the King and inscriptions in rustic letters. There is a kind of Calendar or "comes" at the beginning:

Incipit capitular
evangeliorum
Qualiter per anni
circulum
Evangelia
in Romana
Leguntur
ecclesia

Each pair of lines is written in rustic

In the Athanasian Creed the writer omitted in the first instance four words in clause 27, and then supplied them in the margin, thus:

ITAUTPEROMNIASICUTIAMSUPRADICTUMESTETUNITAS INTRINITATE·/.UENERANDASIT·/.ETTRINITASINUNITATE

I consider that he added the mark ·/. at the wrong place, and that thus the modern order of the words originated. The fact is only interesting when we attempt to classify the Psalters: but very little of my argument will be affected if my supposition does not meet with approbation.

I call this manuscript *r*.

§ 9. I will now take up the Psalters which follow this later reading, and it may be convenient to follow the subdivision of our earlier class, and take first those of the ninth and tenth centuries (which I have seen) in which the Psalm *Pusillus eram* follows close on the end of the one-hundred-and-fiftieth. We shall thus have

Class II. Subdivision *α*: and our first Psalter will be

i. That referred to by Waterland in Chapter IV. under the year 703. His remarks are curious:

"We may next set down K. Athelstan's Psalter of which bishop Usher has taken notice...He and Dr Grabe both fix the date of it to the year 703, from the *rule* of the *calendar* found in it. Dr Smith, in his catalogue of the Cotton manuscripts, inclines to think that the MS. is later than this time, but taken from one that was really as early as the year 703; the latter copyist transcribing (as sometimes has been done) the book and the rule word for word, as he found them. Allowing this to

letters on chocolate ground, and spaces are left between the respective rectangles. It has these lines fixing the date at 870.

"Bis quadraginta volitant et septuaginta
"Anni quo deus est virgine natus homo
"Terdenis annis Carolus regnabat et unus
"Cum codex actus illius imperio."

There is an account of the Munich Evangeliarium in the *Nouveau Traité*, II. p. 103 note, and I believe a monograph upon it was published in 1786, by Sanftl, who was Librarian of St Emmeran's, and wrote a Catalogue (now at Munich) of the volumes in the library of his beautiful Church. Sylvestre gives a page, No. 130, and Professor Wattenbach, *Einleitung zur Lateinisch Palæographie*, Leipzig, 1872, p. 21, refers to the *Denkscriften der Wiener Akademie*, Band 13, for a description of the volume by Arneth. The volume elicited from Baronius a few contemptuous remarks, under the year 870: the great Annalist deemed it to be a proof of Charles' consummate hypocrisy, that he should order a "Prayer-Book" to be written in gold in the year in which he had the audacity to quarrel with the pope. Baronius confused the two volumes.

have been the case here (though it be only conjecture) it may still be true that there was a manuscript of the age of 703 with this Creed in it: from which the later one now extant was copied: which serves our purpose as well and the rest is not material. But it should not be concealed, that the Psalter, in this, is in a small Italian, and the above-mentioned *rule* in a small Saxon hand, which may, in some measure, weaken the argument drawn from the age of one to the age of the other; so that at length our evidence from this manuscript will be short of *certainty*, and will rise no higher than a fair probable presumption." The argument is this: the Psalms in this MS. are written in one handwriting: the calendar is in another: the calendar may have been copied by one person from a calendar of the year 703: therefore the Psalms, written by another person, may have been copied from a Psalter of the same date: and Waterland considered his "probable presumption" so satisfactory, that in the table at the end of the chapter, representing "a summary or short sketch of what hath been done in it," we find him assigning this manuscript without any mark of hesitation to the year 703.

I have had the pleasure of examining this Psalter on four different occasions: but it is satisfactory to me that my own memoranda regarding it are superseded by the account of it given by Dr Heurtley on pp. 74, &c. of his invaluable work *Harmonia Symbolica*. He shews there that the calendar, instead of being of the date 703, must be later than 901[1], and he considers that the part containing the Psalms is of the eleventh century.

The present authorities of the British Museum are inclined to place it in the ninth or tenth century. Professor Westwood has an interesting account of it in his *Miniatures*, no. 32, and in his *Palæographia Sacra*.

It is a beautiful little volume: the size only $5\frac{1}{8}''$ by $3\frac{5}{8}''$. Its class mark GALBA A. XVIII.

The Psalter is Gallican.

The Initial B of the first Psalm is again an Anglo-Saxon B exactly of the Utrecht type. The only other Anglo-Saxon letter in the volume is a less elaborate D for Psalm ci.

It has some curious resemblances with the Utrecht Psalter, but Psalm cli. follows cl. immediately. It has the full title. The *Te Deum* has no title: the *Gloria in Excelsis* is preceded by the words "incipit hymnus angelicus in die dominica ad mat." The "fides sancta athanasii alexandrini" concludes the second part. This title again distinguishes the book from the Utrecht Psalter.

The titles to the Psalms, the Canticles and the Quicunque are in red rustics.

Mr Bond and Mr Thompson informed me that the Psalter is apparently of German origin: the calendar having been prefixed to it in England. It is curious that it has the reading "unitas in trinitate et trinitas in unitate:" but in the following respects it has the readings of the Utrecht Psalter:

In the Te Deum, *verum unicum filium: tu ad liberandum suscep-*

[1] I regret to say that the recent Oxford editor of Waterland's work (Oxford, 1870) has allowed the statement of Waterland to stand uncorrected, although Dr Heurtley's work was published in 1858.

isti hominem: sempiternus es filius: te ergo sancte quæsumus famulis tuis: but it reads *rege illos et extolle illos in sæculum et in sæculum sæculi.*

In the Athanasian Creed it agrees generally with our standard text: but like the Utrecht Psalter it read *tres dominos* in 20, the *tres* being subsequently erased. In 38 *tertia die* is omitted: in 41 the reading is *et qui mala*[1].

(ii.) *ab.* To the very beginning of the tenth century belongs the Psalter at Bamberg, which has been described by Dr S. Schönfelder, "Kaplan an S. Martinus" in Bamberg in the "Serapeium" of November, 1865, to which I have already referred. It is the earliest quadripartite Psalter that has come under my notice, and although I have not a collation of the Quicunque from it, I must give an account of the manuscript. The date is fixed at the year 909.

The volume contains some prefatory matter; and, in a more modern writing, the *Ave Maris Stella.* Then some hexameters on Salomon Abbot, Bishop of Constanz (= St Gall), and the hexameters which passed between Damasus and Jerome "Psallere qui docuit."

Then the Psalter in four columns,

Gallican, Roman, Hebraic, and Greek in Latin letters.

After this (fol. 150), "David extra numerum cum pugnavit cum Goliad," no Greek to this (nor Hebraic version?). The Canticles, &c. follow, the Te Deum coming after the Apostles' Creed. It is entitled "Ymnus matutinalis" and has a Greek version as far as *venerandum tuum.*

Then comes

"Litania græca:
"item Latina."

Then fol. 169 "hymnus angelicus" in Greek and Latin:

[1] The manuscript consists of 200 folia in all. Fol. 2 may not have belonged to the volume; in fact, two illuminations are pasted together. The Kalendar occupies 3 to 14: 15, 16, 17 contain (I suppose) the *Computus:* 16 b has a note to say "annus in quo scriptus fuit iste codex 703:" of course this is modern and untrustworthy. On 21 is a picture, Christ in a vesica, martyrs and virgins adoring: 22 b—27 are several prayers: 28 a different writing, containing the following memoranda:

"1 Kl. Feb. Karolus piissimus imperator de hac luce migravit."

"Id. Jul. Pippinus gloriosus rex de hac luce migravit."

"Kl. Mai. Bernhardus gloriosus rex de hoc seculo transivit."

"Kl. Ap. Uuomdus (?) dux obiit. hemildrad comitissa."

This is followed by 28 b, "or. matutinalis;" "or. ad primam" (and the other hours): 30 b "origo prophetiæ, &c." occupying the page: 31 "David filius, &c." 32 "Psalterium Romae dudum &c." 33 Four verses occupying eight lines, "Jam superna dei quæ sunt quicunque requiris, &c." Then 34 b "In Christi nomine...emendatum a sco hieronimo prbo in novo." The Q in *Quid gloriaris* is grand (fol. 80), and there is an illumination on fol. 120 b, facing a grand D (psalm ci.) fol. 121. The Athanasian Creed ends on the fourth line of folio 174 b, the page is filled up with two prayers in a later and much clumsier hand: the first entitled, "Ad possenda suffragia," the second "Ad gratiam sancti spiritus postulandam. *Deus cui omne cor patet.*"

"Fides catholica niceni concilii" in Latin and Greek;
"symbolum athanasianum" in Latin but not in Greek.

Dr Schonfelder says that the columns are 2¾ zoll broad, a space of ¾ zoll lying between each pair. The vertical and horizontal lines are drawn very exactly. There are forty lines on the page, each page being 17½ zoll long, and 14 broad. The text is in beautiful Caroline minuscules, with uncials at the beginning of each Psalm, sometimes beautifully ornamented. The learned commentator refers to the St Gall codex 17 as being "consonant" to this: and then exhibits the resemblance between the Veronese and Bamberg Greek thus: "meta su e arche en imera tes dynameos su en te lamproteti ton agion. ec gastros pro eosphoru exegennesa se;" "meta su hi archi en imera tis dinameos su en tes lamprotesi tō agion ec gastros pro eosforu gegennica se."

The Greek versions of the Apostles' Creed, of the *Gloria in Excelsis* and of the portion of the *Te Deum* must be of the deepest interest, but I have not been able to obtain a copy of them. I must, however, reserve a place for this, and call it *ab*.

(iii.) *ad*. In the Cathedral of Salisbury there is a Psalter containing the Quicunque, with exactly the same title and words that we find in Regius 2 B. v., which I must consider below. I refer especially to the words *Incipit de fide:* except that these last words are in a space before the Quicunque begins. The manuscript is of the tenth century: at least it contains a calendar commencing with the year 969 and ending with 1006. This copy was known to Usher. The Librarian of the Cathedral most kindly sent me a collation and some notes of the manuscript in June, 1872, and I have since been permitted to examine it.

After the Calendar it has notes on the "Computus," *i. e.* the moveable and chief immoveable festivals. This is a Gallican Psalter and is glossed throughout. The *Pusillus eram* follows Psalm 150, with the usual title (except that *extra numerum* is omitted), but it is not glossed. Then follows this prayer on the recital of the Psalter; Omnipotens et misericords deus clementiam tuam suppliciter deprecor ut me famulum tuum tibi fideliter servire concedas ut perseverentiam bonam et felicem consummationem mihi largiri digneris et hoc psalterium quod in conspectu tuo cantavi ad salutem et ad remedium animæ meæ proficiat sempiternum. Amen."

The Canticles follow.

The "hymnus ad matutinum diebus dominicis" comes before the *Nunc Dimittis:* the "Oratio pura cum laudatione" (*i. e. Gloria in Excelsis*) after it. Then the Lord's Prayer, the Credo, and the "Hymnus Athanasii" as in Regius 2 B. v. below. I call it *ad*. The Athanasian Creed seems to be copied from Regius 2 B. v. even in its errors. Yet this Psalter is the Gallican, that the Roman.

(iv.) Vitellius E. XVIII. possesses an interest of another kind. It was much injured in the Cottonian fire, but our sense of the loss caused by the damage is compensated by watching the results of the loving care and wondrous skill evinced in its recent repair and binding. My informants assigned it to the time of the Norman conquest, and to England as its birthplace.

The calendar (foll. 1—16) with which it commences, seems to prove that it was written about the middle of the eleventh century: folio 9 b contains some Saxon notes "de diebus malis cujusque mensis." Folio 17 was written in the fourteenth century, and contains a litany to the Virgin: on folio 18 the Psalter proper commences. There is an Anglo-Saxon gloss: Psalm 151 with the long title is on folio 131 a. Then the Canticles, Hymns, Creed, and the Quicunque introduced thus; "Incipit Fides Catholica Athanasii episcopi Alexandrini." This is followed on the same (fol. 140 b) page with prayers commencing: *Omnipotens deus pater œterne, Deus indulgentiarum.*

Then comes a Litany with prayers for the Pope, and all grades in the Church.

I may add that many of the titles to the Psalms are written in rustic capitals (it seems to be of the eleventh century), and that the *Te Deum* is entitled "Hymnus quem Sanctus Ambrosius et Sanctus Augustinus invicem condiderunt." I call this *ah.*

(v.) The Harleian, 2904, is a magnificent book, and has furnished an illustration to Professor Westwood's *Miniatures* (No. 43). It is the copy referred to by Waterland under the year 970: Wanley putting it down to the reign of Edgar. Mr Bond and Mr Thompson place it in the next century, and ascribe it to Germany. The Psalter is Gallican.

The letters are $\frac{5}{8}$ of an inch high: there are eighteen lines only on a page. It clearly belonged (as I shall shew hereafter) to some Archbishop. There are a few prayers before the Psalms begin: Psalm 150 ends on folio 187 b, and the *Pusillus* follows on 188. Then come the Canticles: "hymnus ad matutinos" on fol. 200: "hymnus ad missam in diebus dominicis, *Gloria in Excelsis*" on 204. The "oratio dominica" f. 205; "symbolum apostolorum" following. Then on 205 b

"incipit fides catholica edita ab
Athanasio Alexandrino episcopo."

Thus the order is the same as in the Utrecht Psalter.

After this we have

"Incipiunt litanie"—

a litany of the older form, "Scte Benedicte," being in gold. When we come to the intercessions we find a prayer for our king, but none for pope or bishop: we find too a petition "ut paganorum sævitiam comprimere digneris."

Then there is a special plea for the intercession of St Benedict, thus: "per intercessionem beatæ et gloriosæ semper virginis Mariæ sanctique Michaelis archangeli necnon et Sancti Benedicti et omnium sanctorum tuorum: et libera me ab omnibus malis per eorum intercessionem et fac me dignum exaudiri pro omnibus pro quibus tuam clementiam exoro."

Petitions follow for all Rectors of Churches: for all "qui mei memoriam faciunt, et se meis indignis orationibus commendaverunt:" for my relations and for all "quorum in communione mentionem facio[1]." The manuscript must have been prepared for an Archbishop who had been a Benedictine monk. I refer to it as *ai*.

(vi.) Of the Psalters in the Parker collection at Corpus Christi College, Cambridge, I have already appealed to two. But there is a third which must be ranked amongst these which we are now discussing; it is numbered 391; its class-mark is K. 10. It once belonged to the Church of St Mary at Worcester, and it is noted as having been given to the Church by St Oswald. A later memorandum states that this note is false, for the very sufficient reason, that the volume contains prayers to be said on the feast of the translation of St Oswald. The calendar contains notes on the death of Bishop Wlstan, and of the death of King William: but Oct. 13 is not noted as the feast of Edward the Confessor. It is assigned to the year 1064 by Waterland after Wanley. It contains the Gallican Psalter. The "Pusillus eram" still follows the Psalms; the Canticles, &c. follow; the Quicunque being last before a Litany.

The Quicunque has no title. My mark for this is *ak*.

(vii.) I have met with one or two Latin Bibles in which the Psalms have been used for Church purposes; and for convenience sake the Canticles, &c. have been grouped together between the Psalms and the Book of Proverbs. We have such a Psalter, I believe, in the magnificent Bible in the Royal collection at the British Museum, 1 E. VIII. This is said to be of the ninth century, and to some the copy will be more interesting, because it exhibits how the change of text in 1 John v. 6, 7, 8, was introduced. The old stops are · and . but here and there the ' is added in a later and browner ink than the . to which it is an-

[1] Amongst the saints appealed to are many Saxon, *Machutus* is the last man, *Pictburg* and *Pinburg* (?) the last women, but *Gereon and his fellows* are among them.

nexed, so as to form the ! with which the Utrecht Psalter is studded. Thus we have

non in aqua ſolum!
ſed in aqua & sanguine · & ſps ē. qui testi
ficatur! qm̄ Xpc eſt ueritas· Quia tres sunt
qui testimonium dant. *intra sps* **aqua et sanguis·**
& *hi* **tres unum sunt** *& tres stq; tsmoniū dant in celo*
Si testimonium hominum *pat & filiū & sps scs &*
hi tres unum sunt

the letters I have printed in italics being in the later and browner ink, the thick type representing the original manuscript.

The Psalter is Gallican, and the titles generally in rustic[1].

(viii.) But the library at Venice contains a grand book, 25 inches long by 16⅜ broad.

It is numbered I. The volume itself is of the tenth century: but, if I understand correctly a note which Signor Veludo has attached to a photograph which he and our celebrated countryman Mr Rawdon Browne have, in the most liberal spirit, transmitted to me, there are insertions in the volume of a much later date. Amongst these come, after the Psalms, the Scripture Canticles, the *Te Deum*, "Hymnus Angelorum, Fides Catholica CCCXVIII sanctorum Patrum, Oratio Dominica secundum Matheum, Symbolum Apostolorum in Pentecosten." The last is the Apostles' Creed, omitting (clearly by a mistake) the article "Peccatorum remissionem." The Catholic Faith of the 318 fathers is the Quicunque! The Psalter is Gallican.

§ 10. II. *β*. I must now turn away to take up two Psalters which do not contain the apocryphal Psalm 151. And first and foremost of these is a volume which has deservedly attracted attention almost as great as that which has been bestowed on the Utrecht Psalter. I refer to the Psalter in the library at Vienna, which at one time formed one of the treasures of the Church at Bremen, and which was exhibited there as having been given by Charlemagne to Hadrian I. Any person who knows the tradi-

[1] A similar Bible is the exquisite copy in the library of La Cava, the most complete account of which is given in the *Codex diplomaticus Cavensis*, the first volume of which appeared at Naples, in the year 1872: a facsimile of the title of Psalm cli. was given by Sylvestre, Vol. III. No. 145. This is considered to be of the ninth century by Sylvestre. Tischendorf refers to this manuscript in his note on the verse in St John's Epistle: and calls it "sæc. fere VIII." I remark that it seems to have an unique rendering of ἐμονομάχησεν· "cum pugnaret adversus Goliam solus." I infer from this that the copy may produce interesting variæ lectiones elsewhere.

tions which circled round the great Emperor will not be surprised at the anxiety to connect this volume with his name. Facts and events connected with others of the name of Charles have been attributed to him: and the value of the relic would have been immeasurably diminished if it had been shewn that the tradition concerning it was false. This, however, is clear, that the volume contains an address from King Charles to Hadrian, offering the volume to the pope:—the verses may be seen in Sir T. Duffus Hardy's *Earlier Report*, or in Mr Lumby's *History*, p. 221. And I need not repeat them here.

The first person to draw general attention to the volume was (I believe) Lambeccius, who had charge of the Imperial Library in the 17th century. He gave a very long and interesting account of the contents of the volume in his catalogue, published in 1669. Unhappily he did not make any distinction between the handwritings in which its various contents were penned, and represented a notarial memorandum of the 17th century as if it were of great antiquity and undisputed authority. The purport of this memorandum is that the volume had been given by Charlemagne's wife Hildegard to the Church of Bremen. How this could be reconciled with the verses that it was given by Charles to Hadrian has never been explained. The present Catalogue gives the following account of the MS.

"1861 [Theol. 652] m. VIII. 158. 8° c. init. color. et litteris aureis. Psalterium a Carolo magno, ut traditur, papæ Hadriano dono missum et manu Dagulfi cujusdam scriptum. cum prolegomenis et canticis biblicis. Denis I. XXVIII." The words "ut traditur" will be noticed.

Denis was the librarian at the later part of last century. His account, as supplementary to that of Kollar (who merely republished Lambeccius' notice in 1761), is full of interest. He admitted that the tradition was questioned: whether it be true or not (he says) "statuant eruditi: quicquid enim statuerint nec ætate nec pretio codicis decedet." (1793, Vol. I., No. XXVIII. col. 54—69.)

Neither Denis nor Kollar gave any facsimile of the writing. This defect is now remedied by M. Sylvestre, who gives a page in volume II. no. 145. Through the kindness of the Rev. D. M. Clerk I have photographs of six or eight pages.

The Benedictine editors of the *Nouveau Traité* had some difficulty in reconciling the traditions: they supposed that Hadrian might have died before the Psalter reached Rome.

The present librarians consider that it belongs to the time of Charles the Bald. That is, they endorse the suggestion made by the Reverend Edmund S. Ffoulkes that it was intended as a present from Charles the Bald to Hadrian II. We know that the king did make some most valuable presents to the pope, but a Psalter is not named among them[1].

[1] An account of these is given in the *Bertine Annals*, and from them in Fleury and Pritchard. The *Gallia Christiana* speaks of Hincmar's fondness for beautiful books.

The *B* in *Beatus* is an elaborate Roman letter, beautifully interlaced. It may be interesting to note the contents.

First we have the two dedications, one of Charles to Hadrian; the other of Dagulfus, the writer, to Charles.

Then we have a series of Symbols; the true Nicene Creed; the Faith of St Ambrose; the Faith of St Gregory, Pope of Rome; the Faith of St Gregory of Neocæsarea; the Exposition of St Jerome (above, p. 275); a version of the Lord's Prayer in Hexameters; "Hadriano summo;" the *Gloria in Excelsis;* then prefaces to the Psalter, apparently intended to recommend this Gallican version: at length on folio 24 b we have, within a border very prettily arranged, the usual Introduction to this amended Psalter followed by the Psalms themselves. The parchment is generally white, but here and there the page is ornamented.

For example, for the *Quid Gloriaris;* the *Oratio pauperis;* the *Dixit Dominus.*

After Psalm 150 (which ends in fol. 145 b), we have on fol. 146 a "Incipiunt cantica." They follow as usual. The "hymnus quem sanctus ambrosius et sctus agustinus invicem condiderunt" comes between the *Benedicite* and the *Benedictus.* The Credo complete follows the Lord's Prayer; and on fol. 157 a we have "Fides sci Athanasii epi. alexandrini."

I must draw attention to the position of the "Gloria in Excelsis." I have already noticed that it is missing in some of the manuscripts written at St Gall, but I am at a loss to account for its position here; unless I am to suppose, that in consideration for the Roman use in regard to that Angelic Hymn, it was removed from the body of the Psalter. We may compare this volume with St Gall 20.

(ii.) The Regius 2 B. v. of the British Museum claims more than a passing notice. The authorities at the Museum consider it to be of the earliest years of the tenth century. It was referred to by Waterland under the year 930: his information apparently being drawn from the catalogue of Wanley and a memorandum by Wotton.

It begins with a prayer through the intercession of the Virgin "in cujus atrio majestati tuæ famulamus:" it speaks of "injuriam quam patimur:" it calls on Mary to deliver from the hands of our enemies the possessions offered to this thy Holy Church: then the appeal is made to St Machutus[1] and St Eadburg, and repeated again and again to the

[1] St Machutus was born in Wales, but gave his name to St Malo.

Virgin. I have not as yet discovered the name of the monastery to which it belonged.

On fol. 6 b there is a Saxon prayer (to be freed from our sins, says Casley). On f. 7 the introduction to the Psalter; and the autograph of Archbishop Cranmer. The Psalms follow: the *Roman Psalter* occupying the centre of the page—interlined with Saxon gloss and Saxon notes at the side. The Psalter (I have said) is *Roman*, it may have belonged therefore to the Church of Canterbury, but about the 12th century an attempt was made to alter it into the Gallican. The Canticles follow, some without, some with marginal notes.

The title of the *Quicunque* is "hymnus Athanasii de fide trinitatis quem tu concelebrans discutienter intellige:" then "oratio pura cum laudibus," *i.e.* the *Gloria in Excelsis* (thus the *Pater noster* and *Credo* are omitted). On folio 186 b are some memoranda on the ages of the world, making out that 5287 years passed between the Creation and the Advent, and remarking that "Ætas ab incarnatione usque ad finem sæculi decurrit." Then there is a memorandum of "Sexta quæ nunc agitur."

If the estimated date (the tenth century) is correct, the writer must have come to the conclusion that the sixth age had not then expired[1]. The great interest to us in regard to this Psalter is that in the space at the end of the second verse of the Athanasian Creed are inscribed the words *incipit de fide.*

(iii.) *af.* Another Psalter, considered to be of the early part of the same eleventh century, is in the University Library at Cambridge; from the name of the donor it is sometimes called Bacon's Psalter. Its class-mark is Ff. I. 23. The Quicunque was collated for me in 1871 by the eminent English scholar the Rev. W. W. Skeat, who has also furnished for me the copy of the gloss which I shall print below. The Psalter is Roman; the manuscript contains 550 pages: it measures about 11 inches by 5.

At the commencement there is a picture of David playing on the harp; Asaph on a kind of violin with a bow: Eman on a cythera with his fingers: Ethan on a curious wind instrument: Idithun on something which he strikes with hammers.

On fol. 1 a is a prayer to be used before the saying of the Psalter. At the end is this prayer to the Trinity: "Te deum patrem ingenitum, te filium unigenitum, te spiritum sanctum paraclitum, sanctam et indi-

[1] There is some mistake in the arithmetic. From Adam to Noah, 2242: from Noah to Abraham, 842: from Abraham to David, 944: from David to Babylon 465: from that to the Advent, 587. The total is 5080.

viduam trinitatem toto corde et ore confitemur, laudamus, atque benedicimus: tibi gloria in sæcula. Gloria patri."

The parchment is generally very rough and coarse: at times almost like a bladder: there is a picture of a crucifixion with The Hand, on folio 167 (*Quid gloriaris*), sun and moon weeping; The Figure is clothed around the loins, but the clothes fall loosely away: the feet are upon a rest. Another picture precedes the "Oratio pauperis" on fol. 332, Christ in an oval uttering the words "Ego sum deus qui reddo unicuique juxta sua opera." Before Ps. 109 Christ is represented as standing alone on a lion and a dragon: the cross in His right hand, the book in His left. There are a few other drawings. The Psalter is, as I said, Roman, and glossed throughout in red. The stops ⁝ ·. and : the lines drawn regularly.

After Psalm 150 the Canticles follow without introduction. The *Te Deum* is entitled "Hymnum optimum." It is not glossed. After the *Nunc Dimittis* follow the "Ymnum angelorum," the Lord's Prayer, the Apostles' Creed[1]. Then the Quicunque without a title. Then a Litany[2].

§ 11. The most interesting and important manuscript to which attention should now be drawn is the latter part of the Vespasian A. I. I have spoken of this manuscript already, and described it as consisting of two parts: the first containing the Roman Psalter, the Canticles sung in course at mattins in the time of Amalarius, about 830, *i.e.* the *Benedicite, Benedictus*, and the three hymns *Splendor paternæ, Creator omnium, Rex æterne.*

The second part, in the handwriting of the eleventh century, has the Te Deum, entitled, "Hymnus ad Matutinos;" the "Fides Catholica[3]," with an Anglo-Saxon gloss throughout; "Oratio Eugenii Toletani Episcopi, *Rex Deus immensus;*" "Confessio ad dominum;" at the end *Te sancta crux humiliter adoro*[4].

[1] We have "filium ejus. unicum dominum nostrum."

[2] "Kyrie eleison. Christe eleison. Christe audi nos.
Pater de coelis ds. | miserere nobis.
Fili redemptor | mundi deus | miserere nobis.
Spiritus sanctus deus mi | serere nobis.
Sancta trinitas unus | deus miserere | nobis."

There are petitions for the pope and all degrees in the Church, for our archbishop, for this place (locum istum), for all our benefactors. On page 541, "oratio post psalterium:" "oratio de sancta-trinitate ad Patrem (542) ad Filium: (542) ad personam sancti Spiritus" (545). Then come prayers to the Virgin and saints. Then follow some benedictions, and the book, which is perfect, ends on p. 551. (The Litany was printed at length by the lamented Archdeacon Hardwick in the *Journal of Philology*, June, 1854.) It will be noticed that there is no prayer for the king. From the petition for the archbishop and the character of the Psalter, it is probable that the volume belonged to the Cathedral Church of Canterbury.

[3] In these two respects it agrees with the Utrecht Psalter.

[4] It is on folio 141 b of this manuscript that there may be seen in small Rustic capitals a copy of a charter of Ethelbald, king of the South Saxons, the original of which cannot be earlier than the year 736. Waterland, who speaks of the codex in the beginning of

§ 12. I have received or made collations of several other manuscripts which are assigned to these three centuries; for example, *Lambeth* 427 (noticed by Waterland, who says the Psalter is Gallican, and ascribes it to the year 957). The *Gloria in Excelsis* is entitled, "Cantus angelicus;" the *Quicunque*, "Fides Catholica Sancti Athanasii episcopi."

In a Psalter of the eleventh century at Salzburg a. V. 31 the Quicunque is entitled "Ps. Anastas." It ends with the word *rationem*, *i.e.* clauses 41 and 42 are omitted.

Others I will specify when I come to compare the readings.

§ 13. The magnificent "Arundel" Psalter, 155, in the British Museum, falls below our limits, for it seems to have been written in the twelfth century; but I must notice it, because in it there has been an attempt to alter the punctuation from . to ꞉ by the addition of the ʿ, and, simultaneously, the Roman version was altered to the Gallican. The petition in the Litany that God would preserve "dominum apostolicum" is erased; therefore the volume appears to have been in use in the time of Henry VIII.: there is a clause mentioning "archipræsulem nostrum et gregem sibi commissam." The Quicunque is entitled, "Fides Catholica edita a Sco Athanasio Episcopo."

§ 14. There are many indications that the Eadwine or Canterbury Psalter of Trinity College, Cambridge, is connected with the Claudius C. VII., the Utrecht manuscript.

The drawings are the same throughout, and Psalm 151 comes after the Quicunque. It is well known as a grand volume, containing the three versions, Gallican, Roman, Hebraic: the Gallican occupying about twice the space of the others. A page is copied in Mr Westwood's Anglo-Saxon Psalters, No. 43. It contains a Kalendar which fixes its earliest possible date as after the Conquest: then much prefatory matter. The Hebraic version is interlined with a French gloss: the Roman with a Saxon: in the Gallican several Latin words are explained by other and easier Latin. When the Canticles commence the arrangement is altered, and one column is given up to the French: in which sometimes

chap. IV. and again under the year 1066, quotes Wanley's opinion that the Quicunque is of the date of the Norman Conquest. It is not unlikely that Ethelbald's charter was interpolated or inserted in a blank page of the older Psalter about the same time. Usher saw and referred to the volume. *Histor. Dogmat.* p. 104 (as quoted by Waterland). The manuscript does not contain the *Gloria in Excelsis*, nor indeed the *Magnificat* nor *Nunc Dimittis*. I have a memorandum that folio 109 is also interpolated.

the Saxon is interlined. Throughout all these, the spaces between the columns are occupied with notes and glosses: the Quicunque (which has no title) is written in two columns, French and Saxon translations being interlined, the outside space being occupied with the exposition which, with some variety of readings, is printed by Montfaucon in his Diatribe and ascribed by Waterland to Bruno.

The volume terminates with some astrological notes; the last words being "de occultis alias agitur"!

§ 15. There are, of course, very many other Psalters in existence.

Tiberius C. v. is burnt after Psalm CXIV. (see a drawing in Westwood's *Miniatures*, No. 46). At Lambeth I collated Nos. 197, 233, 368, 535, 540: they are all said to be of the twelfth or following centuries, and are all interesting. The last exhibits a curious mode of saving parchment and helping the memory of the chanter. Psalm CXVIII. 105, 6 is written

"Lucerna pedibus m. u. t. & l. s. m.
Juravi et statui c. i. i. t."

So after the Psalms

"canticum ysaiæ
"confitebor t. d. q. i. e. m: c. e. f. t."

and so on.

(This is unfinished and does not contain the Creeds.)

With this I may compare a Salzburg "Diurnale" of the fifteenth century. Here we have the Athanasian Creed ascribed to David!

"Ps. DD
"Quicunque vult salvus esse.
"Quam nisi quisque integram inviolatamque servaverit."

"Semper prima pars," as the obliging Librarian Mr P. Willibald-Hauthaley O. S. B., suggested to me (an interesting memorial of our mode of antiphonal chanting). The MS. a. V. 30 "of the fourteenth century or earlier" had the Quicunque of the older form: but curiously enough *et filio* was on an erasure: it had no *tertia die.* It contained a Litany with clauses "Pater de coelis." a. IV. 7 was another Psalter: it had *tres* in the margin before *dominos:* and the *Gloria patri* at the end. At Milan the manuscript L. 81. sup. had a Latin running gloss, different from any other which I had seen. The Creed of Constantinople, *called* "symbolum CCCXVIII. patrum," followed. I think there are thirteen Psalters of later dates in the Cambridge Library: fifteen in the Royal Library at the British Museum and so on. Of course I have not attempted to collate them all. Sir Duffus Hardy kindly shewed me a photograph from a MS. at Venice of the 13th century. In this volume I observed that the Canticles followed the Psalms, and the Quicunque the Canticles, but there was no Creed nor Lord's Prayer. (The Quicunque has the commentary of Bruno in the margin.) The Psalter I found to be Gallican. Besides those which I have mentioned at St John's College, Cambridge, I examined carefully C. 18: D. 6: E. 15: K. 26.

In *Vienna* 1087, a Psalter of the fourteenth century, the Quicunque is entitled "Tractatus de fide catholica." In *Turin* no. LXVI. of the fifteenth century is a "Declaratio fidei catholicæ" of which I should like to hear something more: it may prove to be the same as Mai's *Explanatio*. There are several Psalters at Florence containing the Creed, *e.g.* Plut. XVI. no. XXXVI. of the twelfth century: no. XXXVII. of the eleventh: Plut. XVII. no. III. of the eleventh (that in which the Te Deum is entitled *Hymnus Niceti*): Plut. XVII. nos. V. VI. VII. VIII. X. A friend who examined these in June, 1872, could not find much variation.

Plut. XXV. codex III. is a beautiful manuscript, not a Psalter, of the year 1293. It contains Litanies, and the Gloria in Excelsis, and Creeds.

Thomasius in his Psalterium speaks of nine manuscripts, all Vatican, which contain the Quicunque, most of which attribute it to Athanasius. Apparently they are all late. They are Vat. 5729. 82. 84. 98. So "MS. Chisius." In Vat. 81. Alex. 12, it is described as *Fides Catholica:* in Pal. 30 and Pal. 39 as Athanasius.' It is curious to note how few MSS. of the Quicunque belonged to libraries south of the Alps.

From Haenel's catalogues I learn that the number of Psalters in French libraries is very great: say more than 170. One at Lyons is said to be of the eighth century: one at Montpelier of the 8th or 9th: another at Lyons, and another at Montpelier, of the ninth. There is said to be one at Rheinau of the ninth. I have not seen any of these, nor do I know how many contain the Quicunque. A triple Psalter at Chartres is said to be very old.

I take the following from the very careful Catalogue Raisonné of the MSS. of the British Museum.

Lansdowne 383, Additional 21927, Arundel 230, Additional 18301, 18859, Harleian 2890 and 2990, all of the twelfth century, have the Quicunque. Galba A. V. is imperfect, being injured by the fire.

Nero C. IV., of the twelfth century, has the Psalter and eleven Canticles, and Biblia Eq. 1139 has both Psalter and Canticles.

The Harleian 603 contains many of the Utrecht pictures, but they must have been taken from some other original.

§ 16. I ought not to dismiss these Psalters without making a few observations.

I have taken every precaution in my power to discover notices of Psalters that may have been written before the time of Charlemagne, and I believe that very few exist. It may be that at the revival of learning, in his day and under his auspices, the older volumes were destroyed; but such a supposition is in itself improbable, and, if such a destruction did take place, we must judge of the character of the volumes destroyed by the contents of those which remain. Putting then on one side the Utrecht Psalter, there is not a single copy that was in existence before the time of Charlemagne, that contains the Athanasian Creed. In, or at all events after, his time, the Psalters became numerous; and as a rule they contain the Canticles and this Creed. But they are almost entirely Gallican Psalters; I question whether there is a single Roman Psalter, unconnected with England, that contains the Quicunque. This entirely tallies with the fact that the Church of Rome refused to acknowledge the Double Procession as an Article of the Faith, for many years afterwards.

The next remark I have to make is, that these Gallican Psalters almost invariably ascribe the Quicunque to Athanasius. Of course, when we look at the large proportion of early Psalters which are connected with the province of Rheims and the metropolis of Charles le Chauve, we cannot regard the repetition of this ascription as augmenting the evidence in favour of this supposition. C merely repeats what B has said; and B learnt it from A. But it is worthy of note, that in the Utrecht Psalter, as in Vespasian A. 1, the Quicunque is entitled simply *Fides Catholica*, and is not ascribed to Athanasius.

This fact might cause us some perplexity if we did not know that this portion of Vespasian A. 1 is late, say of the twelfth century; and we may speculate whether there was any doubt at that time as to the desirability or the truth of such ascription. Now we know that the Venice Bible states that the Quicunque proceeded from the "Three hundred and eighteen Fathers:" and the Irish Hymn-book makes an equally curious assertion. The title "The Catholic Faith" is more imposing than "The Catholic Faith of Athanasius." I suggest that the name of Athanasius was omitted both in the Utrecht Psalter and in Vespasian A. 1, in the hope of augmenting the importance of the document.

§ 17. We have now four, or perhaps five, independent lines of witnesses agreeing in bringing forward the Quicunque into notice within five and twenty years before or after the death of Charlemagne. We have i. the testimony of quotations; ii. the testimony furnished by the enactments of Canons; iii. the testimony of literary collections of Creeds and Rules of Faith; iv. the testimony of Psalters: I might add, v. we have the testimony of versions into other languages, but this has yet to be adduced. It remains now for us to enquire whether we can trace, any closer, the author or the time or the locale of the forgery. Forgery it certainly was: that the production of this work under the name of Athanasius was an intentional and deliberate attempt to deceive, no reasonable person can question. It was analogous to the production of the forged Decretals. And it is doubtless to the skill with which the imposture was wrought out, that we owe the difficulty that has been felt for so many years in discovering the author. We have similar attempts to deceive in religious matters in the present day: and, when the plot is well laid, it is equally impossible to detect and expose the authors[1].

[1] The following is the title to the Creed in the Salisbury Psalter and in the British Museum Royal 2. B. v.

HYMNUS ATHANASII DE FIDE TRINITATIS QUEM TU CONCELEBRANS DISCUTIENTER INTELLIGE.

Quicumque uult saluus esse: ante omnia opus est ut teneat catholicam fidem.

Quam nisi quisque integram inuiolatamque seruauerit: absque dubio in æternum peribit. **Incipit de fide.**

&c., &c., &c.

In the Salisbury Psalter the words *incipit de fide* precede *Quicunque uult*: if I remember right, there is no room for them at the end of verse 2.

CHAPTER XXV.

CHARLEMAGNE AND PAULINUS.

§ 1. Condition of the problem about 780. § 2. Hadrian's canons. § 3. Council of Gentilly, 777. § 4. Ignorance of the clergy abroad in this century. § 5. Donation of Constantine. § 6. Charlemagne's labours. § 7. Pseudo-Augustine. § 8. Second Council of Nicæa, 787. § 9. Council of Friuli, 791. i. Paulinus' letter to Elipandus. ii. His speech in the Council. iii. Other writings. § 10. Council of Frankfort, 794. i. His subsequent letter. ii. Letter of the Council. iii. Charlemagne's letter to Elipandus, and his Creed. § 11. Supposed canon of 802, and the Missi Dominici. § 12. Council of Aix, 809.

§ 1. THE only positive evidence of the existence at the early part of the eighth century of a document specially resembling the Quicunque is furnished, as we have seen, by the Paris Codex which contains the extract from the old Treves manuscript. From that we cross, perhaps, to the Ambrosian manuscript, at all events to the profession of Denebert in the year 796, which contains part of the earlier half of the present Quicunque: and then we pass several years before we find distinct evidence of other or additional phrases contained in our modern version of the Creed.

We may now turn to see whether we can discover any distinct evidence either of the growth of the document or of the spread of its acceptance.

§ 2. I have already mentioned that when Hadrian I. sent to his patron, the Roman Patrician Charles, a long summary of the Canons and Rules and Forms of the Church, no mention was made of any Creed or Faith of Athanasius. We read only that Hadrian expressed his desire that the Holy Trinity should be preached to the people of God[1].

§ 3. We learn, however, from Ado of Vienne, that at a Synod held at Gentilly in 777, there was a controversy between the

[1] Labbe, VI. p. 1800.

Greeks and the Romans, whether the Holy Spirit proceedeth from the Father and the Son. At this gathering—to use Waterland's words—"it does not appear that the Creed was pleaded," in other words, it does not appear that it was known.

§ 4. The condition of the continental bishops and clergy during the eighth century is acknowledged on all sides to have been most lamentable. I have already adduced proofs that it was deemed to be necessary, on the part of what we should now call the civil power, to direct that the clergy should at least know by heart, and possess Expositions which might enable them to explain, the Apostles' Creed and the Lord's Prayer. The character of the manuscripts which belong to this century shews that the statement of Mosheim is not without foundation.

"The rude and unlearned bishops suffered the schools which had been committed to their care to languish and be extinguished. It was rare to find among them any that could compose their own discourses: they who possessed (continues Mosheim) some learning strung together from Augustine and Gregory a parcel of jejune addresses, a part of which they kept for their own use, and the rest they gave over to their more dull colleagues that they might have something that they might bring forward."

Thus the century was ripe to receive articles made for demand. And we need not say that the supply came.

§ 5. Thus it was that Hadrian felt encouraged in the year 777 to mention to Charles the Donation of Constantine: "it had been found in the cases of the Lateran:" and the forgery appears to have imposed upon the more honest and honourable Frank. And this imposition was so successful that it was of course followed up by others. One mode of gaining the adherence of the common people was by producing letters which had fallen from heaven—which find their analogy in the "visions" which are seen now in parts of France. Thus we have, strangely enough, "a letter sent down from heaven to Athanasius, Patriarch of Rome," regarding the observance of Sunday. A. Gr. 1140 = A.D. 829[1]. And at the Synod of Aix, 788, we find mention of a wicked letter that was said to have come down from heaven[2]. Indeed, these heaven-sent letters were produced in such abundance, that

[1] In Syriac. See Dr Wright's *Apocry. Acts*, p. xii.
[2] Canon LXXVIII. Labbe, VII. p. 986.

I have read somewhere that Charlemagne or the bishops gave an order that they should be stopped—an order which was obeyed!

§ 6. And then it seems that Charlemagne collected out of Italy and Britain and Ireland men of genuine learning, to raise the character of his clergy. Already had missionaries come forth from Iona to "spread the light of the gospel and the blessing of civilization." The monastery of Bobio had been furnished in the year 614 with monks from Ireland; and Irish calligraphy and Irish-born hymns (mixed with the products of the kindred school of Lindisfarne) spread over the north of Italy, and, from the monastery of St Gall, over Switzerland and Germany. We cannot congratulate ourselves on the work of our Boniface, if it be true that the forged Decretals were framed with his cognizance in the schools of Mayence. But the end of the century produced men of the highest type and of thorough honesty; men like Paulinus and Alcuin, by whose aid Charles strove to rouse his clergy and his laity to a higher appreciation of thought and learning in things human and divine—and this at the time when the efforts of the Roman Pontiffs and their friends were directed to establish their newly claimed position: who, when they found that evidence failed them, scrupled not to adduce documents which they knew to be spurious.

§ 7. But before we enter on the writings of these two great men, I would devote a few pages to the consideration of some of the works falsely ascribed to St Augustine. Until we have a critical edition of these works, we are unable to know the dates of the manuscripts which contain them, or approximate to a date for the works themselves. We have, however, in the Benedictine Appendix to Vol. v. a sermon which may possibly have been written by Vigilius of Thapsus—as the Benedictines surmised—but which seems to me to exhibit the thought of that better part of the ninth century, when orthodoxy was deemed to be of little value unless it was exhibited in a Christian life. The preacher says:

"It is better for us to confess at once that we do not unedrstand the mystery of the Trinity than rashly to claim for ourselves a knowledge of it. In the day of judgment I shall not be condemned because I say I do not know the nature of my Creator: if I have spoken rashly of Him, my rashness will be punished; but my ignorance will be pardoned."

If Vigilius was the author of this, he could scarcely have written the Quicunque, as Quesnel suggested.

"Sufficient for us (the writer proceeds) that the Trinity is: we are not rashly to seek to know the reason of Its being: our duty is to fear God, and to pray to God; so that in this alone should we exhibit our knowledge to Him."

Very different is the next sermon in the collection, which is said to be compounded of two documents, the one by Faustus of Regium, the other by this same Vigilius. It ends with a series of well-nigh thirty maledictions—not *Anathema sit* but *Maledictus est:* these maledictions relate largely to the Trinity, but they do not illustrate the language of our Creeds. One point, however, deserves attention, though it has escaped the notice of the Benedictines: Hincmar, in his controversy, quotes some of these maledictions as written, not by Faustus, nor by Vigilius, nor by Augustine—but by "the blessed Athanasius[1]!"

To another of these spurious writings I must beg for a few moments the renewed attention of my readers: I refer to the Creed of Pelagius, which is here printed as the work of St Augustine, as it is elsewhere entitled the Creed of Jerome[2]. So popular was it in the eighth and ninth centuries, that it found its way with a different "setting" into the Caroline books. We still have the statement that the Word was made flesh, "*assumendo hominem non permutando deitatem,* by assuming man, not by changing the deity."

I think that it is not improbable—I throw it out only as a surmise—that these and similar compositions, such as those of the Ambrosian manuscript, were framed and issued in reply to the call of Charlemagne for sermons of old divines adapted for the use of the clergy of his day. Some light may be thrown on the subject by those who have access to the manuscripts whence these pseudo-Augustinian sermons are extracted[3].

[1] I remark that the words are that the "Son of God assumed man."

[2] See it above, p. 275.

[3] The summary of this in the original was this: "Haec fides est, papa beatissime, quam in ecclesia catholica didicimus, quamque semper tenuimus et tenemus. In qua si minus perite aut parum caute aliquid positum est, emendari cupimus a te, qui Petri et fidem et sedem tenes: sin autem haec nostra confessio apostolatus tui judicio comprobatur, quicunque me maculare voluerit, se imperitum vel malevolum vel etiam non catholicum, non me hæreticum comprobabit." The "setting" in the pseudo-Augustine is this: "Haec est fides, dilectissimi fratres, quam in catholica didicimus ecclesia quamque semper tenuimus et tenemus, quamque credimus et a vestra bonitate deinceps posse teneri." Charlemagne altered the framework thus: "Haec est

We turn therefore to the Councils held in the time of Charlemagne.

§ 8. But we cannot pass over the second Council of Nicæa, regarded as it is by the Church of Rome as the seventh œcumenical Council. I shall refer to it only so far as Creeds and Declarations of Faith were considered.

We find there a Creed of Basil, Bishop of Ancyra, which he recited on submitting to the Church. It begins:

"I believe and confess in one God the Father Almighty, and in one Lord Jesus Christ His only-begotten Son, and in the Holy Spirit the Lord and Giver of Life: a Trinity consubstantial and co-enthroned (ὁμόθρονος); in one Deity, Potency and Power worshipped and adored. And I confess everything touching the Economy of the One of the Holy Trinity, our Lord and God Jesus Christ, even as the holy and six œcumenical Synods have laid down[1]."

He called it a confession of his orthodoxy. We have (p. 154) confessions of Sabbas and Gregorius. In the third action we have the Creed of Tarasius, who was now patriarch of Jerusalem.

"I believe in one God the Father Almighty, and in one Lord Jesus Christ, the Son of God and our God, begotten of the Father without time and eternally; and in the Holy Spirit, the Lord and Giver of Life, Who proceedeth from the Father by the Son, Himself being and known to be God: a Trinity consubstantial, equally honoured[2]."

The Creed occupies three columns.

On the same day was recited the Synodicon of Theodore, Bishop of Jerusalem: it occupies five columns in the folio of Labbe. It commences[3]—

"We believe, brethren, as we have believed from the beginning, in one God the Father Almighty, absolutely without ἀρχή and eternal, Maker of all things visible and invisible; and in one Lord Jesus Christ, the only-begotten Son of God, Who was from God even the Father eternally and impassibly begotten, knowing no other ἀρχή except the Father, and having His substance from Him, Light of Light, very God of very God; and in one Holy Spirit, Who proceedeth eternally from the Father, Himself acknowledged to be God and Light."

Thus we have three attempts at an authorized Exposition of the Creed of Constantinople: indicating, as I conceive, that a need

catholicae traditionis fidei vera integritas quam sincero corde credimus et fatemur et in hoc opere beati Hieronymi verbis expressum taxavimus. Haec est vera fides, hanc confessionem conservamus et tenemus, quam quisque (sic) incorrupte et intemerate custodierit perpetuam salutem habebit." Note the words which I have "spaced."

[1] Labbe, VII. p. 57.

[2] Labbe, VII. p. 161.

[3] p. 171.

of some such exposition was felt, but indicating too that no satisfactory exposition was as yet known, or perhaps in existence. At last we come to the fourth action, which contains the belief of the Synod[1]. It is not very long, occupying only six-and-twenty lines. It commences:

> "Thus we confess; thus we teach: We believe in one God, the Father Almighty, Maker of all things, visible and invisible; and in one Lord Jesus Christ, His only-begotten Son and Word, by Whom all things were made; and in the Holy Spirit, Lord and Giver of Life, consubstantial and coeternal; and, with the συναváρχῳ Son, a Trinity, uncreated, undivided, incomprehensible, unlimited: the One wholly and alone to be worshipped and served and venerated: one Godhead, one Lordhood, one Might, one Kingdom and Power." And so it passes, like the others, to the Incarnation.

Ultimately, in the seventh action, the bishops recited the Creed of Constantinople[2]: to it the Synod refused to make any addition—from it to take any single word; *ἀμείωτα διαφυλάττομεν.* They ascribed it, apparently, to the Nicene Synod: the Creed, however, was followed by many additional clauses, expressing abhorrence of as many heresies.

I have already referred to the objections which Charlemagne raised against the Creed of Tarasius. The Council refused to accept the doctrine of the double Procession.

And I have also referred to the Canon of the Council of Aix in 789; which describes the true Nicene Creed as "the faith of the Holy Trinity and the Incarnation of Christ, His Passion, His Resurrection, and His Ascent to Heaven."

§ 9. And thus we come to the Council of Friuli, and the remarkable utterances there of Paulinus, the Patriarch of Aquileia.

The two documents which I shall quote are his speech at Friuli of the year 791 and his letter to Elipandus written in 794. I will take the later document first.

i. Elipandus, as is well known, was an Adoptionist: *i.e.* he held that Christ Jesus as God was by nature and truly the Son of God, but as Man was Son of God only by name and by

[1] Labbe, VII. p. 319. A spurious "Sermon of Athanasius," on the image of Jesus Christ, was quoted in the fourth session. Labbe, VII. 218.

[2] p. 554.

adoption. The idea seems to have been that, in His human nature, our Lord was declared and adopted to be Son of God when the Voice came from heaven at His Baptism. It was conceived that this opinion savoured somewhat of Nestorianism: not as distinguishing the natures in the one Person, but as representing that there were two Persons in the Saviour. The error attracted much attention; and it will be of interest to us to know how it was met.

In the year 794, as I have said, Paulinus wrote a letter to Elipandus on the subject[1]. It is of no great length, and, therefore, we ought not to draw very decided conclusions from the silence which may reign there as to any particular authority. Paulinus draws near to the language of the Quicunque on one or two occasions. Thus we find words resembling closely clauses 5 and 6[2], "alia est Persona Patris, alia Filii, alia S. S. sed una et æqualis et consubstantialis et coæterna est Patris et Filii et S. S. inenarrabilis divinitas et majestas quia unus est Deus." But these are words which we have met with over and over again in the Councils of Toledo. Again[3], Paulinus seems to offer some suggestions as to the origin of the clause "There is one Father not three Fathers[4]"—but he does not quote it. I think the authority of our document would have been acceptable to him if he had known of it. As in many other cases which we have noticed, so Paulinus has passages which run parallel to portions of the later part of the Quicunque, but he cannot be said to quote it any more than the Creeds of the second Council of Nicæa quote it. I certainly feel justified in saying that to Paulinus at this time the Quicunque was unknown as of authority. In fact[5] he quotes the decree of the Council of Chalcedon (though not by name) on the unity of Person in the Saviour, where, in my opinion, the words of our Creed would have been far more appropriate. I cannot help comparing the silence of Paulinus with the somewhat over eagerness of Hincmar to use the document sixty or seventy years later[6].

[1] Migne, *Patrologia*, Vol. XCIX.

[2] p. 159.

[3] p. 158 D.

[4] It was directed against any such notion as that the Father, the Son, and the Holy Spirit are *in all respects* similar, and Their properties interchangeable.

[5] Cap. XII. p. 163 D.

[6] One of my tests is furnished by the language used as to the *time* of the Incarnation. Paulinus retains the expression of Chalcedon that this took place *in ultimis temporibus* (not *in sæculo*). We have (page 160 A) "non duo Filii Deus et homo, sed unus Filius Deus et homo," referring of course to the Adoptionist view. In the same column we find "non ignoramus ex duabus sub-

I think we must conclude that Paulinus did not know of the Quicunque. It will be remembered that he wrote South of the Alps: thus the question of its existence in France at that date is not affected by his ignorance.

ii. I may pass over a long exhortation addressed by the Patriarch to Henry, Duke of Friuli (in which the *Fides Recta* occupies a very subordinate place), to hasten on to the speech or address at Friuli—one of the most interesting speeches that I have ever read. I must confess that when I first perused this speech, the conviction came upon me, strong and clear, that I had discovered the author or "composer" of the Athanasian Creed. The same conviction was carried to the mind of Mr Ffoulkes, a perfectly independent authority. But before I read Mr Ffoulkes' work, I was compelled to resign my hypothesis, nor was my opinion changed again even by that gentleman's learned and able arguments. But I must give an account of the address.

In its early portion Paulinus lays down distinctly his opinion of the necessity of making additions to the "Symbol" with reference to the Trinity. He refers however to the decisions of Ephesus and Chalcedon forbidding new Creeds. "Far be it from me (he adds) to compose or teach a Symbol or a Faith." But he holds that it is his privilege and his duty to explain things which in past times have been mistaken in consequence of the brevity with which the truth has been enuntiated in the earlier publications of the Symbol; he may do this even whilst he retains the text of the Symbol itself. Paulinus adduces, as illustrating his meaning, the history of the Nicene Creed. He shews how the one hundred and fifty supplied by way of exposition (suppleverunt quasi exponendo eorum sensum) the meaning of the Creed, in the parts that followed the words "and in the Holy Ghost." He states that, afterwards, to meet a difficulty that had arisen, the word *Filioque* was added; and he defends the addition on the ground that this statement of the Procession must be true, since the acts of God are inseparable. He proceeds that any Catholic doctor whatever, who rightly believes (in accordance with that of which a foretaste had been given by the Lord) that that Lord is "as touching man less than the Father, and as touch-

stantiis humanam subsistere naturam, ex anima nimirum et carne," thus drawing us on to clause 37, which it will be remembered is not to be found in the Treves original, and therefore (as I conclude) was added between the date of that manuscript and the date of the earliest complete copy of the Quicunque that we possess. The following is interesting (cap. XII. p. 163 D): "Unde et majores nostri hac definitione sanciti (?), quorum sagacissimæ capacitatis peritia longe valde a nostræ tarditatis distat ignavia, placuit eis, sancto annuente Spiritu, duas in una Christi Persona indubitanter profiteri naturas, divinam scilicet et humanam, quia anima et caro non sunt duo sed unus homo," almost the words which were *not* found at Treves nor in the Colbertine. On page 164 B, we have, "sempiternum ex Patre, *temporaliter* natum ex virgine matre."

ing God equal to the Father,' and so expounds it, cannot, though he uses many words, be said to have added to or diminished from the Creed; he has only supplied it. So he maintains that he too is perfectly justified in explaining the Faith. Then he refers with reprobation to those who have false views of the Mystery of the Trinity. He speaks especially against such as hesitate in regard to the distinction of Persons; who conceive that the same is Father and the same Son; who state falsely that the Son is inferior and posterior to the Father; or who confess three Fountains of Deity (tria principia). He recites therefore the Creed of Constantinople, and proceeds to give a long account of the necessities of his time.

It thus appears that other questions pressed upon the attention of Paulinus over and above the question of Adoptionism: questions which are directly met in clauses 4, 5, 6; 21, 22, 23; 24, 25, 26; 33; of the Quicunque. Of these clauses it will be remembered that the first nine are not found in the Colbertine manuscript, and that the substance of clause 33 occurs there in words which differ decidedly from the words of Paulinus.

This long account, which I have abbreviated, may be seen, as elsewhere, so in Mr Lumby's volume. It is, indeed, an Exposition of the Apostles' Creed rather than of the Nicene, and must be considered as put forth in fulfilment of the Patriarch's intentions. This Exposition Paulinus desired his clergy to commit to memory. For, Paulinus proceeds—

"This purity of the Catholic Faith we wish all the priests of God and all grades of the Church—with the utmost care and without any fault, so as neither to add to it nor to take from it the slightest tittle—distinctly and intelligently to commit to memory and to pass on to their successors." They must learn it before his next visitation. "If any one, thanks to a more ready memory, can do this earlier, we press him to do so, and shall praise him for doing it. But if any be slow and his ability poor, he must be prepared to repeat it a year hence, at the next meeting of this venerable council; otherwise it will be difficult for him to escape the ecclesiastical rod. But the Symbol and the Lord's Prayer must be learnt by every Christian, of all ages, each sex, and every condition of life; by males, females, young people, old, slaves, free, boys, married men and unmarried girls, because without this blessing no one can be able to receive a portion in the kingdom of heaven. But he that shall keep these and guard himself from evil works, shall be safe in the present life, and in the future shall rejoice together with the angels." And he maintains that he is not instituting novel rules; on the contrary, having examined the sacred folios of the old canons, he has endeavoured to exhibit their contents in more modern style: "for, like ruminating animals, we thus bring up to our memory that upon which we have fed in the spiritual pastures in times gone by."

The account is important. It furnishes us with the first instance that I know, in which the clergy were compelled to learn by heart a new Exposition in addition to the two Creeds of the Western Church.

If we turn now to the Exposition itself, we find that although it runs again and again near to the substance of the Quicunque, it rarely approaches its language except in clauses to which we have met with parallels already. Thus we have:

"There is one Person of the Father, another of the Son, another of the Holy Spirit. But the Father, the Son and the Holy Spirit are not three Gods, but is one God." Of the generation of the Son we read that it took place "intemporaliter" "ante omnia sæcula." · "The Holy Spirit is neither begotten nor created, but proceeding without time and without separation from the Father and the Son." In the Trinity "there is nothing naturally diverse, nor personally confused; nothing greater or less; there is no one before or after, inferior or superior, but one equal power, the glory equal, the majesty eternal and coeternal and consubstantial." "The Son in the last days descended from heaven." "True God and true Man." Consubstantial with God the Father in His, the divine nature; consubstantial with His Mother, without the stain of sin, in ours, that is, the human nature. "One Christ,...true God and true Man; in reasonable soul and true flesh. Perfect Man as touching the manhood; perfect God as touching the Godhead." The descent into hell (ad inferos) is mentioned. "He ascended over all heavens; He sitteth at the right hand of the Father; thence He will come to judgment."

We should compare the words which I have given above, as commending to those who would be saved the Apostles' Creed and Lord's Prayer, with the corresponding clauses of the Quicunque.

With this able commentary before me I find it simply impossible to believe that Paulinus knew the Quicunque.

iii. But we have other writings of the Patriarch to which I must briefly refer. About the year 796 Paulinus addressed to Charlemagne three Books against Felix. They occupy about 120 columns in Migne's edition. We shall see here too that phrases to which we find near resemblances in the Quicunque, were considered to be inconsistent with the opinions of the heretical bishops. Thus Paulinus insists[1] that our Saviour was

"In the form of God equal to the Father; in the form of the servant less than the Father," words which (as we know) come from Augustine,

[1] Migne, xcix. 343—466.

not from the Quicunque. This is in Book I. ch. li., but the same words are found in Book II. ch. iii. In chapter xiii. we have, "The Man who was not yet, did not assume the God;" in xiv. "The Word was not changed into flesh;" in xv. "So that there is not one Christ God, and another Christ man, but one and the same God man." In xvi. he quotes the end of the second part of the Nicene Creed, to which he refers again in xxxvii. In xx. we read, "Before all ages, begotten without beginning from the Father, and in the end of the ages, not another but the same, born of the Virgin." So again in xxxii. In lii. he quotes (apparently) the Apostles' Creed, passing over the Descent to hell. The third Book contains testimonies as to Christ's true divine generation. The writer appeals to Hilary of Poictiers, to Ambrose, Jerome, Augustine, Athanasius, Cyril, Leo, Gregory, Fulgentius. Under Athanasius he appeals to his letter in Epictetus, and to the *Libellus Fidei suæ*, but not to the Quicunque. I think these references decide the question. Paulinus did not know of the Quicunque as the work either of Athanasius or of any other notable authority. He considered Athanasius to have written another Faith.

The work was sent to Charlemagne by the hands of Albinus or Alcuin. At the end of his prose writings a few of the hymns of Paulinus are printed. The first is the "carmen de regula fidei," to which I may refer my readers.

§ 10. At the Council of Frankfort held in 794, Athanasius was quoted thus: "In this way did Athanasius, Archbishop of Alexandria, commence his Faith: fidei suæ principium dedit." Another Faith ascribed to Athanasius! We might expect that Waterland, who declared his opinion that the *Catholic Faith* mentioned in the thirty-third Canon of the Council must be the Athanasian Creed, would have referred in some slight way to these words which speak of a Faith acknowledged at the Council to be Athanasius': but he simply and "judiciously" ignored it. The passage proceeds[1]:

"We confess the Son of God to have been begotten before the worlds of the Father, but in the last days to have been born of the Virgin Mary for our salvation; as it is written, When the fulness of time was come, God sent His Son made of a woman, &c. If then (the argument proceeds) any one in opposition to the divine Scripture asserts that the Son of God is one, and He who was born of the Virgin another,—a man adopted by grace like as we are—as if there were two Sons...him the Holy and Apostolic Church anathematizes."

We shall see how convenient the words of our clause 37, when they had been gathered out of Augustine by Alcuin, proved to be in reference to this Spanish controversy.

[1] Labbe, VII. 1016.

i. The "councils" contain a letter addressed by Paulinus and others on the subject of these Spanish errors. The writers appeal almost entirely to the authority of Scripture. I extract, however, the following[1]:

"The Holy Catholic and Apostolic Church which although dispersed throughout the world is yet the one friend of the Bridegroom, the one dove, shining with wings silvered with the beauty of divine eloquence and with a body brilliant with the pallor of gold, does in the purity of a perfect faith confess the Holy and Ineffable Trinity in Unity: preserving the properties of the Persons without confusion, but acknowledging the substance as inseparable. So that One is believed as Father, because He is the Father Who begat the Son coeternal with Himself, without time and without beginning: and Another is believed as Son Who was begotten by the Father without beginning, not putatively but truly: and Another is believed as Holy Spirit because He is the Holy Spirit and proceeds from the Father and the Son[2]." Thus the Father is not one Thing, and the Son another Thing, and the Holy Spirit another Thing; but the Father and the Son and the Holy Spirit are inseparably One Thing (unum): not One Person (unus), but One Thing (unum), because there is one Person of the Father, another of the Son, another of the Holy Spirit, but [there is] one equal, consubstantial, coeternal, ineffable majesty of divinity of the Father and the Son and the Holy Spirit, because God is one." As I read on, I catch the words that "in the last times He came down from heaven—was born of the Holy Spirit and of the Virgin Mary, was very God and very Man: not two Sons, God and Man, but one Son, God and Man—who never deserted the Man whom He assumed[3], not even on the cross, for Paul teaches us that they crucified the Lord of Glory."

Thus, "Let us confess with our holy Fathers, Catholic and orthodox men who received the right faith with their heart and proclaimed it with their mouth, the two natures in Christ, the Divine and the Human."

I can scarcely conceive that the Quicunque already occupied a place in the Church Psalters, when this appeal, "let us confess," was made at Frankfort.

ii. And so we pass on to the synodical letter of the Council to the Spanish Bishops.

It quotes part of the Creed of Elipandus, asserting that his Creed was wrong by omission not by assertion; it complains[4] however of additions which had been made to the Creed of Nicæa. It quotes Cassiodorus and Augustine and Ambrose and Paschasius the Deacon.

[1] Labbe, ut sup. p. 1027.

[2] Perhaps the monks of Mount Olivet had heard of this.

[3] Note again, "The man whom He assumed."

[4] p. 1038.

I find that *from Augustine*[1] the words are adduced, "Christ the Son of God is God and Man: God before all the ages: Man in our age (*in nostro sæculo*)." Can we require any further proof that the Bishops assembled at Frankfort assigned no authority whatever to the document which we call the Athanasian Creed? that in all probability they did not know it?

iii. But our investigations cannot be regarded as complete unless we examine the letter which Charles himself addressed to Elipandus and the Spanish Bishops. It is to be found amongst the works of the great king, and is put down to the year 794[2].

It begins with speaking of the beauty and glory of the Church and the necessity of the Faith to the wellbeing of the Church. "Of this Faith, being orthodox and delivered by the Apostles to the teachers of the Church and hitherto held by the Church universal, we profess that in proportion to our strength we everywhere and in every thing keep and preach it, because there is no salvation in any other save in that which the Church always has kept." He refers to the letters of the Spanish bishops to him: "Did they mean to teach him what they believed, or did they desire to learn what he believed? We hang (he says) on the opinions of the orthodox Fathers. Let us learn what they wrote, and believe what they taught. Thus there will be one faith and one heart, even as there is one Shepherd and one Fold[3]." He mourns over the errors of these bishops, anxious to have them associated with him in the Catholic Faith[4].

And for this cause he had summoned a Synod of holy bishops from all Churches under his dominion in order that they might decree what should be believed as to the adoption of the flesh of Christ. He had sent messengers to enquire from the Pontiff of the Apostolic See what the holy Roman Church, taught by Apostolic tradition, would desire to answer. Bishops too had come from parts of Britain. And then the Emperor had desired libelli to be sent to each of the Spanish prelates to inform them "what we had decreed and determined." One of these books contained the decision of the "Apostolic Lord" and his bishops: another that of nearer bishops, including Peter of Milan and Paulinus of Aquileia: a third that of the other bishops, German, Gallic, Aquitanian, British: and, lastly, "we have added something of our own, entirely agreeing with the above."

And so, after a while[5], he gives his Creed, which, as it has not been printed in any of the works called forth by the discussions of the last few years, I will give at length in my note[6]. It is clearly an expansion of the Nicene Symbol.

[1] p. 1040 E.

[2] Migne, XCVIII. p. 899.

[3] p. 900.

[4] p. 901.

[5] I catch the words, p. 903 B, "eam fidem tenet quam orthodoxi Patres in suis nobis symbolis scriptam reliquerunt."

[6] Credimus in unum deum patrem omnipotentem factorem coeli et terræ,

Looking at the last words, I cannot believe that the condemning clauses of the Athanasian Creed possessed at this epoch the authority which we assign to them; I question whether Charlemagne had ever heard of their existence.

iv. And so we come to the Canons of this Council—of No. XXXIII. of which Waterland made so much. I think after examination our conclusion must be that Waterland never examined these Canons: he must have known of them only second-hand. He must have known of none save No. xxxiii.

The Canon was this: "That the Catholic Faith of the Holy Trinity and the Lord's Prayer and the Symbol of the Faith be proclaimed and delivered to all." Waterland insists that the

visibilium omnium et invisibilium. Credimus et in unum Dominum nostrum J. C. Filium Dei unigenitum: natum ex Patre ante omnia sæcula et ante omnia tempora, lumen de lumine, deum verum de deo vero, natum non factum, naturalem non adoptivum, per quem omnia condita sunt coelestia et terrestria, unius essentiæ et unius substantiæ cum Patre. Credimus et in Spiritum Sanctum Deum verum et vivificatorem a Patre et Filio procedentem, cum Patre et Filio coadorandum et conglorificandum. Credimus eandem sanctam Trinitatem Patrem et Filium et Spiritum Sanctum unius esse substantiæ, unius potentiæ, et unius essentiæ, tres Personas, et singulam quamque in Trinitate Personam plenum Deum, et totas tres Personas unum Deum omnipotentem. Patrem ingenitum, Filium genitum, S. S. procedentem ex Patre et Filio; nec Patrem aliquando coepisse sed sicut semper est Deus ita semper et Pater est, quia semper habuit Filium. Æternus Pater, æternus Filius, æternus et S. S. ex Patre Filioque procedens: unus Deus omnipotens, Pater et F. et S. S.: ubique præsens ubique totus, Deus, æternus, ineffabilis, incomprehensibilis. In qua sancta Trinitate nulla est Persona vel tempore posterior, vel gradu inferior, vel potestate minor; sed per omnia æqualis Patri Filius, æqualis Patri et Filio Spiritus Sanctus, divinitate, voluntate, operatione et gloria. Alius tantummodo in persona Pater, alius in persona Filius, alius in persona Spiritus Sanctus. Non aliud sed unum, natura, potentia, et essentia, Deus, Pater et Filius et Spiritus Sanctus.

Credimus ex hac sancta Trinitate Filii tantummodo Personam pro salute humani generis de Spiritu Sancto et Maria virgine incarnatum; ut qui erat de divinitate Dei Patris Filius, esset et in humanitate hominis Matris Filius: perfectus in divinitate Deus, perfectus in humanitate homo: deus ante omnia sæcula, homo in fine sæculi, verus in utraque substantia Dei Filius, non putativus sed verus, non adoptione sed proprietate, una persona, Deus et Homo: unus mediator Dei et hominum: in forma Dei æqualis Patri, in forma servi minor Patre, in forma Dei creator, in forma servi redemptor. Unus in utraque Dei Filius proprius ac perfectus ad implendam humanæ salutis dispensationem, passus est vera carnis passione, mortuus vera corporis sui morte: surrexit vera carnis suæ resurrectione et vera animæ resumptione; in eodem corpore quo passus est et resurrexit, ascendit in coelos, sedens in dextera Dei Patris et in eadem forma qua ascendit venturus judicare vivos et mortuos, cujus regni non erit finis. Prædicamus unam sanctam Dei ecclesiam toto orbe diffusam, locis separatam, fide et charitate conjunctam; et veram remissionem peccatorum in eadem ecclesia, sive per baptismum, sive per poenitentiam, divina donante gratia et bona voluntate hominis cooperante. Credimus et omnes homines resurrecturos esse et singulos secundum sua opera judicandos, impios æternis suppliciis damnandos cum diabolo et angelis ejus, sanctos vero æterna gloria coronandos cum Christo et sanctis angelis ejus in sæcula sempiterna.

Hæc est fides catholica et ideo nostra; optamus etiam et vestra...Hanc fidem vos charissimi fratres firmiter tenere in commune deprecamur.

Catholic Faith stands for the Quicunque. I have proved that this is not necessarily so. I will only add that the Athanasian Creed was not "delivered" to the people at large in the time of Charlemagne, nor for many years after his death.

§ 11. In connection with this Canon, and in opposition to the theory of Pertz and others, as to the date of the Canons which the learned historian prints under the year 802[1], I must now adduce the "chapters" or directions which the "missi dominici," the emissaries of Charlemagne, were instructed to carry with them during the visitations which they held in this very year. I believe that Baluzius was the first to print them from a manuscript which belonged to the library of De Thou. These "missi" included not only archbishops, bishops, abbots, but also pious laymen. They were directed by the ever-watchful Charles—now crowned Emperor, "a Deo coronato"—to visit the Monasteries and Churches; and if they found anything wrong, they were, in conjunction with the Count of the Province, to reduce the wrong to order. The first charge laid upon them was this: To exact an oath of allegiance to the Cæsar, like to the former oath to the King.

The "chapters" referred both to civil and ecclesiastical matters; to the relations both of State and Church. And the series concluded with an admonition from the Emperor, which I will give at length.

"Hear, dearest brethren, for your safety's sake, the message which we send to you, that we may advise you how ye may live justly and well in obedience to God, and how we may all conduct ourselves with justice and with mercy. We advise you, first of all, that ye believe one God, the Father Almighty, and the Son, and the Holy Spirit. This is one God, and the true God: perfect Trinity and true Unity: God the Creator of all the good things we have. Believe that the Son of God was for the salvation of the world made man, born of the Holy Spirit and the Virgin Mary. Believe that for our salvation He suffered death, and on the third day He rose from the dead, that He ascended into heaven and sitteth on the right hand of God. Believe that He will come to judge the quick and the dead, and will then render to every man according to his works. Believe one Church; that is, one congregation of good men over the whole globe. And know that they only can be saved, and they only belong to the kingdom of heaven, who persevere in the faith and communion and love of that Church."

[1] Above, p. 287.

If the date of these orders is correct, I conceive that the date assigned by Pertz to the Canons of the Ratisbon manuscript must be wrong.

Another point seems worthy of notice. The Symbolum, or Apostles' Creed, had not, when these orders were issued, assumed finally even in Gaul the form which we find in the later Psalters. We still have the words *born of the Holy Ghost and the Virgin Mary: the descent into hell* is passed over, and the words occur *He sitteth on the right hand of God*[1].

§ 12. At the Council of Aix, 809, as we learn from Ado of Vienne, the question of the double Procession was discussed, the discussion arising out of the troubles of the monks of Mount Olivet. Ado's remark is[2]:

"The rule and ecclesiastical Faith established that the Holy Spirit proceeds from the Father and the Son, being not created nor begotten, but coeternal and consubstantial with the Father and the Son." Almost the words of the Muratorian manuscript[3].

Ado became Archbishop of Vienne in 860 and died in 870. It would seem that he knew the Quicunque in its earlier form. I believe that this has never been noticed before. It would appear that the text was not settled when he wrote.

[1] There are two versions of this admonition. I will give the enlarged copy—the copy, as it is found among the works of Charlemagne (Migne, XCVII. p. 240). I should suppose that it has been interpolated. The readings differ from the above. I mark the more important. Admoneo vos in primis ut credatis in unum Deum omnipotentem *Patris et Filii et Spiritus Sancti.* Hic est unus deus et verus, perfecta Trinitas et vera unitas. Deus creator *omnium visibilium et invisibilium, in quo est salus nostra et auctor* omnium bonorum nostrorum Credite Filium Dei pro salute mundi hominem factum, natum de Spiritu sancto *ex* virgine Maria. Credite quod pro salute nostra mortem passus est et tertia die resurrexit a mortuis, ascendit ad coelos *sedens* ad dexteram dei. Credite eum venturum ad judicandum vivos et mortuos et tunc reddet unicuique secundum opera sua. Credite unam ecclesiam id est congregationem bonorum hominum per totum orbem terræ, et scitote quia illi soli salvi esse poterunt et illi soli ad regnum dei pertinent, qui in istius ecclesiæ fide et communione et caritate perseverant *usque in finem: qui vero pro peccatis suis excommunicantur ab ista ecclesia et non convertantur ad eam per penitentiam non possunt ob (? hoc) sæculo aliquid Deo acceptabile facere. Confidite quod in baptismo omnium peccatorum remissionem suscepistis. Sperate Dei misericordiam quod cotidiana peccata nostra per confessionem et penitentiam redimantur.* Credite resurrectionem *omnium mortuorum* [*piorum ad?*] *vitam eternam, impiorum ad supplicium eternum. Hæc est fides nostra per quam salvi eritis si eam firmiter tenetis et bonis operibus impletis: quia fides sine operibus mortua est, et opera sine fide, etiam si bona sint, Deo placere non possunt.*

I have printed in italics the clauses which are not found in the manuscript of Baluzius.

Migne proceeds to give the directions which I have printed before out of Pertz.

[2] Labbe, VII. 1194.

[3] Above, p. 319, line 16.

I have already mentioned[1] that at this Council the Lord's Prayer and the Credo in Deum were ordered to be taught to men and women as well as children.

Connected with this Synod a curious dialogue is given by Labbe[2]:

"M. If then as you say a thing is to be believed most certainly and defended most constantly, ought not the ignorant to be taught it? and ought not they who know it to be confirmed in it? P. Yes, certainly. M. If this is so, and a man is ignorant of it, or does not believe it, can he be saved? P. Whoever has the ability to attain to it by his subtler ability and is unwilling to know it, or, knowing it, is unwilling to believe it, he cannot be saved. For there are many (and of these this is one) of the loftier mysteries of our sacred faith and subtler sacramenta [of the Church], for the investigation of which some persons have the necessary ability; but others are kept back either by the state of their age, or by the character of their intelligence. And therefore, as I said, he who has the power but not the will—he cannot be saved."

Is this reconcileable with the belief that the Quicunque in its present form was received as Athanasius', even at Aix-la-Chapelle in 809? We know that the words commending the Faith which was accepted at Arles in 813, were different from those of "the Athanasian Creed," and so was the form which was adopted by Rabanus Maurus.

[1] Chapter xv. p. 184.

[2] Vol. vii. p. 1194.

CHAPTER XXVI.

WAS THE QUICUNQUE WRITTEN IN SPAIN?

§ 1. Gieseler's opinion that the Creed came from Spain. § 2. Weakness of his argument. § 3. Etherius and Beatus.

§ 1. It is well known that the very careful historian Gieseler considered that the Athanasian Creed had "been probably brought from Spain into France." "It is most likely (he says) that we should seek for its origin in Spain." He refers again to the Confessions of Faith which "the Councils of Toledo were accustomed to place in the front of their work: sometimes the unaltered Nicene or Constantinopolitan Creed: sometimes this Creed with the Articles which relate to the Trinity and Incarnation enlarged in the dialectic manner of the Quicunque; so that the words coincide in the two, here and there, without, however, the Quicunque being dependent on the Council." He proceeds, "Hence that Symbol appears to have been formed after their patterns in the seventh and eighth centuries in Spain, and from thence to have been transferred to France towards the end of the eighth. Even the old appellation, Fides Athanasii, which was afterwards misunderstood, as if Athanasius were the author, points to Spain. For the Catholic Faith could only at first have been designated by the Arians as Fides Athanasii in opposition to Fides Arii, as their Creed was named by their opponents: and in Spain the party of Arius continued the longest opposed to that of Athanasius[1]."

§ 2. Dr Gieseler here appears to have lost sight of the fact that the Council of Arles, in the year 813, appropriated in its entirety the Faith of the fourth Council of Toledo, and not the Quicunque as we have it. This omission seems to me to weaken

[1] Gieseler, *Third Period, Division* 1, § 12 and notes (Clark's *Translations*, Vol. II. pp. 278, 279).

much the value of Gieseler's opinion as viewed in any light. And his opinion rests on somewhat slender foundation. Enuntiated, however, as it is by Gieseler, it ought not to be dismissed without further investigation.

§ 3. I am disposed to rest my rejection of it upon the contents of the protest presented by Etherius, Bishop of Osma, and Beatus, presbyter of Astorga, against Elipandus in the year 785[1]. Many younger students must be thankful to Dr Heurtley for drawing their attention to this most interesting document: it bears such a marked contrast to the results of the laboured learning of Alcuin. The two Spanish divines took their stand upon the Apostles' Creed; they maintain that it is sufficient to unravel the duplicity of Elipandus and to exhibit the perversity of his followers:

"One part of the Bishops (they say) affirm that Jesus Christ is adopted in His humanity, but not adopted in His divinity: another part maintain that He is the Only Son of God in both natures, *own Son*, not *adopted Son*, so that He is Himself the Son of God, true God, and is Himself adored, even He Who was crucified under Pontius Pilate. Of this part are we, Etherius and Beatus, with the rest who thus believe. We believe truly, not only in God the Father Almighty, but in Jesus Christ His Son, our Only God and Lord; Who was born of the Holy Ghost and the Virgin Mary and suffered under Pontius Pilate." They tell us[2] that we must draw water from the fountains of the Saviour; *i.e.* from the teachings of Prophets and Apostles. They call upon us[3] not to frame new things out of our own heads, but to seek only to explain those things which are written in the law and in the gospel. We should[4] not doubt that He Whom the Jews crucified is the true God and eternal Life. "We do not separate the Father and the Holy Spirit from the Son, when we say that the Son is only God. The Father and Son, Both together, are one God[5]. Both together are not Father, nor are Both together Son. Alone, in that supreme Trinity, is the Father, Father in His person: alone is the Son, Son in His person: alone is the Holy Spirit, Holy Spirit in His person. Thus we do not impose on the Son the name of Father, nor on the Spirit the name of Father or of Son....And thus the Father alone is God of none but of Himself: the Son is God as the Father, but He is God, of the Father and not of Himself: the Holy Spirit is God as the Father and the Son, but He is God of the Father and the Son, and not of Himself. And thus the Father is God, the Son is God, and the Holy Spirit is God, but not three Gods but One; Father and Son and Holy Spirit....There is no God but One. Because the Father is God Almighty and is alone

[1] *Bibliotheca Patrum*, Lugdun., Tom. XIII. p. 358 C.

[2] p. 358 F.

[3] 359 A.

[4] 359 C.

[5] 359 D and E.

self-sufficient: and the Son is God Almighty and is alone self-sufficient: and the Holy Spirit is God omnipotent and is alone self-sufficient: but yet these Three are not three Gods omnipotent, but one God omnipotent, Father, Son and Holy Spirit."

The writers refer to the Creed of Ephesus as to the one Christ, and then comes the grand passage which Dr Heurtley quotes[1]. "Let us rise up with the Apostles and recite the Symbol of our Faith which they delivered to us......As we believe in our heart, so let us profess with our mouth and say:

"I believe in God the Father Almighty[2]."

They quote largely the first Epistle of St John, iii. iv. v. They use the words[3], "For there are three who give witness in the earth, the water and the blood and the flesh, and these three are one. And there are Three Who give witness in heaven: the Father, the Word, and the Holy Spirit, and these Three are One in Christ Jesus." And then they insist again on the sufficiency of the Apostles' Creed, short though it is. "Without the philosophy of the world it is simple and plain even to all rustics: and it is known even to all prisoners and strangers.......

"Every one knows from that short Symbol how he should believe. And the Lord's Prayer informs every one how he should pray. Wherefore beyond the Symbol there is nothing that we need believe: beyond the Lord's Prayer there is nothing that we need pray for[4]." They quote however the Creed of Constantinople[5].

We read on a later page that our Saviour is "equal to the Father as being the Husbandman: less than the Father as being the Vine[6]." "God and Man is one Christ and Head of the Church[7]." "The Word assumed man, that is the reasonable soul and flesh of man[8]." "In the unity of the Person let the Son of God be believed to be true God: and let the true God, the Word of the Father, be believed to be the Man who was crucified under Pontius Pilate[9]." "The Catholic repeats nothing new, because he includes all his faith within the Symbol[10]."

But I need not proceed. I think it will be evident not only that Etherius and Beatus knew of no authoritative document such as the Quicunque is considered to be, but also that they would have repudiated any attempt to force such a document upon them; taking up the simple ground that the Catholic includes and comprehends all his faith in the Apostles' Creed[11].

[1] p. 360.
[2] See above, p. 164.
[3] Notice this.
[4] Ut supra, p. 362 E.
[5] 363 (not exactly).
[6] p. 370 F.
[7] 371 B.
[8] 370 H.
[9] 373 C.
[10] 376 A.
[11] They accused Elipandus of confounding the Persons, p. 389.

CHAPTER XXVII.

WORKS OF ALCUIN.

§ 1. Conditions of the problem. § 2. Mr Ffoulkes' theory. § 3. Alcuin's letter to Paulinus. § 4. Objections to Mr Ffoulkes' theory. § 5. Alcuin probably referred to the address at Friuli. § 6. Alcuin's influence on Charlemagne. § 7. He differs from the Quicunque in one detail, agrees in others. § 8. Other commendations of Paulinus. § 9. Letter to the monks of Gotha. § 10. Reflections. § 11. Commentary on St John. § 12. Work on the Trinity from St Augustine. § 13. Confession of Alcuin's Faith. § 14. Other works: quotations from St Athanasius. § 15. Alcuin's character cleared.

§ 1. THUS I think that all the evidence which we have as yet adduced points to the commencement of the ninth century as the epoch before which our Quicunque was almost unknown. The silence regarding it at the Councils of Friuli and Frankfort, the well-known want of Paulinus, the oft-repeated efforts of one theologian after another to give a full and satisfactory Exposition of the Apostles' Creed during the first fifty years of this ninth century, seem to me to be, as evidence, very momentous. When, at length, the Quicunque forced its way into notice and was added to the copies of the Psalter together with the Apostles' Creed and the Gloria in Excelsis and the Te Deum, those other Creeds, those other Expositions, fell out of sight.

At present we have reached this stage in our enquiry: the sermon of Athanasius on the Faith which begins Quicunque vult was well known through the province of Rheims and by men who had been educated in that part of France, about the year 860 or 870: it was not known to Paulinus in the year 791, nor at Arles in 813. Can we draw the limits any closer by following up the lines which these simple facts point out as worthy of investigation?

§ 2. It is well known that the Rev. Edmund Ffoulkes, than whom few men have devoted themselves more successfully to the study of the Ecclesiastical History of the reign of Charlemagne, considered that he had proved, by evidence that could not be gainsayed, that Paulinus was the author of the document. I was tempted to take the same view in the autumn of 1870, before I knew of Mr Ffoulkes' labours, and independently of his results. I thought that Paulinus' address at Friuli indicated his willingness to undertake the composition of a document which should supply the needs of his time: and that the Quicunque was the result. Mr Ffoulkes added further evidence. He adduced a letter which the great Alcuin wrote to Paulinus, thanking him in somewhat exaggerated terms for a treatise or tract he had received upon the Faith, and this tract or treatise, Mr Ffoulkes considered, might be the Athanasian Creed.

§ 3. I will avail myself, to a great extent, of Mr Ffoulkes' translation of the letter[1].

"To my beloved lord in the Lord of lords, and my holy father Paulinus, greeting:

"I seem to have been refreshed inwardly, by finding that the hidden flame of love within me is able to send forth at least one spark, so that that which burns within can not be extinguished, at this moment, when I have the opportunity of writing to one so dear. What! When I have the privilege of looking on your letters, letters sweeter than honey, do I not seem to be holding converse with all the flowers of Paradise, and with eager longing hand to be plucking there its spiritual fruits? How much more then, when I perused the little treatise (libellus) on your most holy faith, adorned with the purity of Catholic peace, eloquent and attractive in its style, firm as a rock in the truth of its conceptions, did I throw up the reins of my mind for joy! Then, as from one bright and salutary fountain in Paradise, I beheld the stream of the four virtues irrigating the rich plains of Italy, and spreading over the entire domain of ecclesiastical Latinity. I beheld the golden outpourings of spiritual ideas, interspersed with gems of scholastic polish. Certainly you have achieved a work of wide-spread profit and of just necessity, in clearly defining the Catholic Faith, the very thing I have long desired to do and often urged upon the king: to have a symbol of the Catholic Faith, plain in meaning, lucid in phrase, reduced into one short paper, and given to all priests in every parish to read and commit to memory, so that everywhere the same Faith may be uttered by a multitude of tongues. What I have desired in my humility, has been supplied by your genius. With the Author of our salvation you have earned a perpetual reward, and among men praise for this perfect work."

[1] It is numbered XCVII. (CXIII. Migne).

Then he asks Paulinus to consider the question whether the souls of the saints are with God already.

§ 4. In the comments which this able work of Mr Ffoulkes elicited, it was at once suggested that the Athanasian Creed could scarcely receive praise of the character which is here assigned to the libellus of Paulinus. To my mind, the objectors appear to have omitted to notice that the praise of Alcuin was given to the libellus, and this libellus may have contained the Quicunque without being identical with it. I may refer to the written address of Paulinus to the Council of Friuli in illustration of my meaning. We find a Creed there: but the Creed occupies only a small portion of the contents of the address. We have first the introduction, leading up to a Confession of Faith: we have then the instructions for its use which follow. So far the criticism seemed to me to fail.

§ 5. On examining the letter, it is clear that we must assign to it a date before Christmas 800, when Charlemagne was crowned Emperor. He is spoken of as King. Thus we are brought within a few years of the Synod of Friuli: and indeed of the libellus to which I have just referred. Is it quite impossible that Alcuin's praises were poured out upon that address? It is fascinating still in its beauty and its simplicity: it contains a Creed which seems to have furnished groundwork for that which Charlemagne subsequently sent to the Spanish Bishops: it was intended for the priests, for them all to commit it to memory.

I am unwilling to believe that within a few years, six at the utmost, Paulinus composed another "Symbol," in form differing entirely from that which he had then required his clergy to learn by heart. He seems to me to have been too able and too honest so soon to change his front: too honest to enforce a Creed without the conviction that it supplied all that was wanting: too able to put forth a Creed which, six years afterwards, was found to be imperfect and fit only to be rejected and forgotten.

§ 6. I look then in another direction: and of course I am attracted by the fame of that friend and admirer of Paulinus, who, as we have seen, had himself been anxious to frame a Creed suited for the times. Alcuin was a learned and a pious man: but

I see no proof that he was a man of genius. He was a collector of others' thoughts rather than himself a thinker: a compiler, not an author. At the same time he was too honest to claim as his own the things he had collected out of the writings of others; or to assign to others compilations of his own. He sympathized with, indeed he fostered, his royal master's zeal for purity of the Faith; amongst his letters to Charles is one in particular[1], in which he exhorted that all the newly subjected Huns should be instructed in the Catholic Faith.

"The Faith of the Holy Trinity must be taught with the utmost diligence: and the coming into this world of the Son of God, our Lord Jesus Christ, for the salvation of the human race, is to be laid down. And the untrained mind is to be confirmed in the mystery of His Passion, and in the truth of His Resurrection, and in the glory of His Ascension to heaven, and His future Coming to judge all nations, and in the Resurrection of our bodies, and in the Eternity of the punishments of the wicked and of the rewards of the good. And then the man, when strengthened and prepared by this Faith, is to be baptized."

Alcuin's words refer of course to one of those Creeds which we have often met with, but his thoughts run curiously enough into the channel of the Quicunque. But yet he objected to the alteration of the Nicene Creed by the Spanish Bishops, and urged the brethren at Lyons not to insert new names into the Symbol of the Catholic Faith, nor, in the offices of the Church, to submit to traditions unheard of in earlier times[2].

§ 7. On page LVII. of his preface, Frobenius, the editor of these works, quotes passages to shew that Alcuin believed firmly that holy men fully enjoy the presence and vision of God in heaven before the day of judgment. My remark when I met the passage—and I see no reason to alter it now—was this: This is inconsistent with the last verses of our Quicunque. But Alcuin urged the monks of Wearmouth and Yarrow, "that whatever ye vowed to God before the altar must be *inviolably preserved* by you[3];" and he complained to Charles that some exiles were not afraid to deny that "Christ as born of the Holy Virgin was not true God and proper Son of God; and went so far as to shrink from confessing that Jesus Christ is God, Who sits at the right

[1] Alcuin's *Epistle*, XXVIII. = XXXIII. [2] Ad Fratres Lugdunenses, *Ep.* XVI. = XC.
[3] *Ep.* XIII. = XV.

hand of the Father, and in the glory of the Father's Majesty will come to judge the quick and the dead[1]." Elsewhere he touches on the duty of teaching the Faith before baptism, and seems to hang for a moment on the thought "whosoever *would* be saved:" "a man may be driven to baptism, but he cannot be driven to believe[2]."

§ 8. Libelli, pamphlets, as we should call them, were flying about at the end of the eighth century. In the year 798, as Frobenius dates the letter[3], Alcuin begs the king to transmit to the Pope, to Paulinus, and two others, the libellus of the "infelix Felix," and to ask for a reply. It seems that these replies were collected in the letter to the Spanish Bishops which was written in the name of Charles, and to which I have already referred. Alcuin thanks his royal friend for returning to him for correction the libellus he had furnished[4]. And in a letter to Arno[5] he begs him, if he should see Paulinus, to commend him to him.

> "I have read the libellus of the Catholic Faith which he has directed to our Lord the King, and much has it pleased me in its eloquence, its flowers of diction, its arguments for the faith, the testimonies it adduces; so that I was led to think that nothing could be added in the questions which have been stirred between us and the party of Felix. And happy (felix) is the Church and the Christian people so long as they have, connected with our king, even one such defender of the Catholic Faith. Still something remains to be done."

Frobenius suggests that this libellus is the one against Felix to which I have referred already: I cannot disconnect the passage from the libellus which in letter XXVIII. Alcuin commended to Paulinus himself. In letter LXXXI. we find him really asking for a new Creed.

§ 9. To the Abbot and Monks of Gotha he addressed another interesting epistle[6], apparently in the same year. He gives the substance, not the words, of verses 30—36 of the Athanasian Creed—verses which we have found in the fragment discovered at Treves—and then he thus proceeds:

1 *Ep.* XIV. = XVII.
2 XXXI. = XXXVI.
3 No. LXIX. = LXXXIV.
4 LXXXV. = CI. This letter has some curious notes as to the necessity of punctuation and distinguishing between words.
5 XCII. = CVIII.
6 *Ep.* XCIV. = CX.

"These can be proved by many testimonies both from the Gospels and from the Apostles, or even from the traditions of the Holy Fathers[1]: as is partly done in the libellus which we have directed to you by the blessed Benedict...But we have a book in hand ourselves, which, when completed and approved by our Bishops and the king, we will send to you." He insists that Christ is one in two natures, and hopes to prove it in the book he has in hand.

§ 10. Surely if the clauses 30—36 had lain close to Alcuin's hand in the Catholic Faith of Athanasius; that is, if the Vienna Psalter (above, p. 372) is rightly assigned to Charlemagne, or if Alcuin had known now of the authority of the Quicunque, he needed not to have referred for proofs to the New Testament, or to the traditions of the Holy Fathers. It seems to me that the libellus he sent was the libellus of Paulinus, but that the desire to compose a work himself had revived once more within him. At all events we find him, a few years later, writing to Arno[2], then Archbishop of Salzburg, begging his judgment

"On a libellus de Catholica Fide which he has lately written. He hopes it will not escape his hands, for it is very necessary to all who would know the Catholic Faith in which the sum of our salvation rests." We find him shortly afterwards writing again to Arno on the meaning of the words *substantia, essentia, subsistentia, natura. Essentia* should only be used of God. "Substantia aliquid esse est." In the Trinity there is one substance, three subsistences.

It is interesting to note how, as Alcuin drew nearer to his end, he commended the study of the Holy Scriptures.

§ 11. But there are other works of Alcuin which bear upon the history of the Doctrine of the Trinity, and of the mode of enforcing the Faith of the Church regarding it.

We have for example a Commentary on the Gospel of St John, consisting of eight books professedly drawn from the "Sanctorum Patrum cellaria[3]." He mentions particularly[4] St Augustine, St Ambrose, Pope Gregory, the Venerable Bede, and many others. Indeed the first five books of this commentary have been put forth as the work of Bede. Such was the uncertainty of authorship in those days! The work, however, was clearly written in the year 800, when Alcuin's friend "David" was exalted to be Emperor in consideration of the assistance which he had rendered to

1 Notice the words.
2 No. CXVI. A.D. 802, = CLII.
3 Frobenius, p. 459.
4 *Ib.* p. 464.

Leo: and Alcuin speaks of the contemporaneous prosperity of the "Apostolic Man," Pope Leo. It is not very tempting to read throughout a compilation such as this: but I turned to the explanation of the Redeemer's words in ch. xiv. 28, "My Father is greater than I." I thought that the words of the "Faith of Athanasius" (if Alcuin considered it to come from Athanasius)—the words of the "Catholic Faith" which Charlemagne had sent to Adrian twelve or fourteen years before (if he had sent it), must have been used as the best, because the shortest, explanation of the passage. For the phrase "Equal to the Father as touching the divinity: inferior to the Father as touching the humanity," was known. It was found in the anonymous Treves explanation of the Apostles' Creed. But Alcuin referred neither to the Treves Codex, nor to the Faith of Athanasius: he gave a long passage from the Tractate of Augustine, commencing:

> "Let us acknowledge a two-fold substance in Christ: the divine in which He is equal to the Father: the human in which the Father is greater: but both together make up not two but one Christ, that God may not be a Quaternity but a Trinity. For as the reasonable soul and flesh is one man, so God and Man is one Christ: and thus Christ is God, reasonable soul, and flesh. We confess Christ in all these: we confess Christ in each[1]."

The clause "as the reasonable soul and flesh is one man, so God and Man is one Christ," as it will be remembered, is not in the Colbertine copy of the Treves manuscript. On xv. 26, Alcuin has a few words of his own, which do not seem to exhibit any particular anxiety to vindicate the Doctrine of the Double Procession[2].

§ 12. But we have to notice another work of Alcuin's which is of the utmost importance to us in our literary investigation—his volume on the Faith of the Holy and Undivided Trinity, addressed by him "Domino glorioso Carolo Imperatori Augustissimo atque Christianissimo." This work must, of course, have been published after Christmas, 800, and most probably before the Council of Aix, 803: Frobenius assigns it, without hesitation, to 802. It has deservedly attracted great attention. Teganus, who wrote a life of Louis the Pious, sent a copy of it to Hatto, Bishop

[1] Alcuin, *Com. in Ioannem*, Lib. VI. cap. XXXV. p. 602, ed. Frobenii.
[2] Lib. VI. cap. XVI. p. 609.

of Basil, describing it as collected out of various works of St Augustine[1]. It is worthy of notice also that it was quoted largely by Æneas of Paris in his book against the Greeks[2]. It has been frequently printed, and I may be allowed to express some surprise that neither it nor any other work by Alcuin was referred to by Waterland in his famous treatise. The dedication speaks of Charles' devotion to the Catholic Faith, and of the author's duty to help him in his efforts to proclaim it. Thus he had endeavoured to arrange categorically the sentiments which Augustine in his books on the Holy Trinity deemed primarily necessary. "It should be the purport of the prayers of all faithful men that the Empire of Charles might be extended; that so the Catholic Faith, which alone quickens the human race, and alone sanctifies it, may be fixed truly in the hearts of all in one Confession[3]." The words are of importance: nor is their importance, with reference to our subject, diminished when we examine the work itself.

Book I. commences with a chapter on the necessity of a true faith. "No one will be able to attain to true happiness except by the Catholic Faith...Thus to all who would attain to true happiness, first of all faith is necessary...Faith is the foundation of all good things: every reasonable soul of proper age ought to know the Faith, how much more preachers and doctors." Chapter ii. is on "the Unity of the Trinity and the Trinity of the Unity." (Chap. iii.) Some things are spoken of God absolutely: others of the Persons relatively. (v.) The Holy Spirit is the Spirit of the Father and the Son, and is, in all respects, equal, co-eternal and consubstantial with the Father and the Son. (vii.) Whatever is said of the Persons of the Holy Trinity, we must always remember that there is only one God. (viii.) The Father is full and perfect God: so is the Son: so is the Holy Spirit: but yet not three Gods, Father, Son and Holy Spirit, but one God, full and perfect. Chapter xi. is on the properties of each Person.—The Father has this property: that of all things that are, He alone is not of another. The Son has this: that He alone is begotten of the Father, consubstantially and co-essentially. The Holy Spirit has this: that He proceeds equally from the Father and the Son, and is the Spirit of both: and these Three are One (hæc tria unum sunt) and this One Three (hoc unum tres): but not three Fathers, nor three Sons, nor three Holy Spirits; but three Persons, one Father, one Son, one Holy Spirit. We must firmly hold the unity; and therefore it is unlawful to say three Gods, or three

[1] The letter is referred to by Frobenius. It was edited by Martene, *Amp. Collect.* I. 84.

[2] D'Achery, *Spicileg.* I. pp. 130, 131 (Frobenius).

[3] Universorum precibus fidelium optandum est...ut catholica fides quæ humanum genus sola vivificat, sola sanctificat, veraciter in una confessione cunctorum cordibus infigatur.

Omnipotents, or three Good ones, or three Great or three Essences. (xii.) We must similarly maintain the [unity and] inseparability both of essence [and operation]. (xiii.) God by the immensity of His nature fills all creation: and thus, whatever is, that the Father fills, that the Son, that the Holy Spirit. (xiv.) The Father is unbegotten: the Holy Spirit is nowhere spoken of as being either begotten or unbegotten, otherwise we might confound Him either with the Father or with the Son; all that we can safely say is that He proceeds from the Father and the Son.

The second book contains accounts of the Relations of God to His creatures. Thus (ch. i.) God is the cause of everything. (ii.) God is above everything. (iii.) Seeing the use which St Paul makes of the word *equal* in Phil. ii. 6, it is safer to use the word "equal" than the word "like" in speaking of God. The Father is not prior to the Son: nor the Son posterior to the Father: indeed it is impious to believe that in God there is anything before or after, "aliquid prius aut posterius." (iv.) Of the immensity of God we believe that it is such that we must conceive that He is within all things, yet not included: outside all things, but not excluded. (vii.) God is not local, but enters everywhere. (viii.) Men have freewill: through freewill Adam fell. (ix.) God alone has no beginning: "That which is unbegotten is the Father alone: that which is begotten is the Son, to Whom it is from the Father to be what He is: that which is neither unbegotten nor begotten is the Holy Spirit, to Whom it is to proceed from the Father and the Son." Men are entirely different: so are angels. (x.) The conjunction of the Creator with His creatures became necessary for man's redemption. The only-begotten Son assuming flesh of the Virgin was so united to the human nature that the same was Man Who was God: the same God Who was Man, being the same God and Man. But yet, in that taking of man, neither nature was converted or changed into the other; as that the Divinity was changed into Creature so as to cease to be Divinity, or that the Creature was changed into Divinity so as to cease to be Creature: but one and the same Being, Who in the form of God is consubstantial with the Father, in the form of the servant is consubstantial with His Mother. Chapter xi. is on the difficulty of the knowledge of Christ Jesus. The soul and flesh of Christ with the Word is one Christ, one Son. According to the truth of the Catholic Faith we must confess in the Unity of Person in Christ both Deity, and reasonable soul, and flesh. In xii. the difficulty is discussed, How the Son knew not the day of judgment? In xiii. the work of the Father and of the Son is one work: (xiv.) All things were made through Christ: (xv.) As the Father is life, so is the Son life. Thus we pass on. Chap. xix. is on the Unity of the Holy Spirit with the Father and the Son.

Book III. enters more explicitly on the Incarnation. Chap. i. is on the favour or grace of God by which God became Man. "In this God's favour is commended to us in that the Holy Spirit is the gift of God (as we have above shewn); whilst it is said in the Symbol of the Catholic Faith that *Christ was conceived by the Holy Ghost and born of the Virgin Mary.* (ii.) Thus He who is Son of God became Son of

Man." But in iii. Alcuin falls back on the older form of the Symbol and asks and answers the question, How Christ could be *born of the Holy Ghost and the Virgin Mary* unless He were Son of the Holy Spirit? (He finds an answer in the analogy of the words to Nicodemus that we need to be *born of water and of the Holy Ghost.*) In vii. we come to the distinct question, How the Son is at one time said to be equal to, at another time less than the Father? "The one is in the form of God, the other in the form of the servant: in that, from eternity, equal: in this, in time, less:" and an appeal is made to the contents of the Catholic Faith: certainly not the Quicunque. In ix. Heb. i. 1, 2 is quoted: "He has spoken in the last ages of the world," *novissimis seculi temporibus.* Alcuin refers here to the Spanish heresy, which he thinks is adequately met by the assertion on the part of Catholics; "Man passed into God not by any change of nature, but because of the oneness of the divine Person. Therefore there are not two Christs nor two Sons, but one Christ and one Son, God and Man." Chapter x. explains why the Son alone was incarnate. In xi. Alcuin maintains that the whole Son, "totus Filius," assumed from the womb of the blessed Virgin that flesh in which He was crucified and buried: in which He rose again and ascended into heaven and sitteth on the right hand of God: in which He shall also come to judge the quick and the dead, and in which all the tribes of the earth shall see Him, not in the humility in which He was judged Himself, but in the glory in which He is to judge. (xii.) Thus He is our Mediator, having the same nature of divinity with the Father, and the same substance of humanity with His mother. Thus (xiii.) in Christ there is a distinction of natures not of Persons: in the Holy Trinity a distinction of Persons not of natures. Again (xiv.) of the two generations of our Saviour, the one was *sine tempore, ante tempora:* the other *in tempore.* The Virgin being *virgo ante partum, virgo in partu, virgo post partum.* There may have been many Χριστοτόκοι, mothers of Christs. She alone is Θεοτόκος. (xvi.) The divinity never left the Saviour, not even in His Passion. Although Christ descended into hell (in infernum) as regards His soul, still we do not divide the Person: we still hold that it was God Who descended into hell; and all this (xvii.) was for our salvation. And so (xviii.) there are two resurrections for us to pass through: the one of our souls now, the other of our bodies hereafter. This last is to take place *in fine seculi.* And then he comes to consider the resurrection of the body on the last day (chap. xx.), the reward of the just and the punishment of the wicked (xxi.), and the eternal blessedness of the saints (xxii.)[1].

[1] In the manuscripts, sometimes after a kind of rhythmical invocation of the Holy Trinity, sometimes immediately, comes a Creed. In one codex it is entitled "Confessio de sancta Trinitate:" in another, "Lectiones de S. Trinitate:" it is quoted by Æneas of Paris: it was translated into Greek, and, in the Greek version, the original was attributed to Hilary of Poictiers; then it was translated back to be published in the Latin works of Hilary. We find in it expressions which we must not omit to notice, such as: "Patrem a se ipso non ab alio: Filium a Patre genitum......Spiritum Sanctum a Patre et Filio æqualiter procedentem......Spiritus sanctus plenus Deus a Patre et Filio procedens. Non tamen tres deos dicimus sed unum deum omnipotentem, æternum, invisibilem, incommutabilem:...nec aliud est Pater in natura quam Filius vel Spiritus Sanctus, nec aliud Filius et Spiritus Sanctus quam Pater in natura...sed alius

§ 13. There cannot be a doubt that the Confession which I have given in my note is a genuine confession from the pen of Alcuin, connected with and drawn from his longer work. But, after reviewing all, I must ask the question, Is it possible that Alcuin can have known, or, if he had known it, have attached any value to the Quicunque? Look again at the contents of Alcuin's work on the Trinity and the Incarnation: see how he quotes everything from Augustine: note that the order of everything in the Quicunque, as well as many of its words and phrases, are found in this work: bear in mind that the Quicunque, or Faith of Athanasius, is not even once referred to in it, and then ask, Are the two documents entirely independent of each other? And, granting that there is some connection, say, Which is the original? Is the Quicunque a summary of the compilation of Alcuin? or is the compilation of Alcuin an Exposition of the Quicunque? My answer is ready; I must leave it to my readers to judge whether that answer is reasonable or no.—The question will still remain, Who was the writer that completed the work of Alcuin and rendered it available even to the present generation?

§ 14. There are other undoubted works of Alcuin bearing on the controversy with Felix and Elipandus, which shew a large amount of reading. He quotes Hilary, and Augustine, and Cyril of Alexandria, and Gregory of Nazianzus, and Gregory the Great, and many others: he quotes Athanasius also; three times from the letter to Epictetus; once from a letter to Bishop Potamius, which is never heard of again[1]; once from the dubious work *de Incarnatione*, which Alcuin calls "the Exposition of his Faith[2];" and once from a work, *de Fide sua*, which is undoubtedly spurious[3]. The last-cited passage had been quoted by Paulinus. I adduce them now to shew the extent of Alcuin's reading. And when I find

Pater in persona, alius Filius in persona, alius Spiritus Sanctus in persona. ...Credimus eundem Filium Dei Verbum Dei, æternaliter natum de Patre, consubstantialem Patri per omnia, temporaliter natum de Spiritu sancto et Maria [semper] Virgine duas habentem nativitates, unam ex Patre æternam, unam ex Matre temporalem ..Deum verum confitemur conceptum, Deum verum natum. Eundem verum Deum et verum hominem, unum Christum...qui mortuus est carnis suæ morte, et sepultus, atque ab inferis, damnato et spoliato principe totius iniquitatis, rediens tertia die resurrexit, &c. &c. &c. Gratia et pax a Deo Patre et Filio ejus Iesu Christo Domino nostro sit ista confitenti in omnia secula seculorum."

[1] Frobenius, p. 778.

[2] p. 777.

[3] p. 902. Two other expositions of Athanasius' Faith!

him bringing passage after passage to uphold the statement "There are not two, but one Christ," as against the followers of Felix, and yet never adducing our Athanasian Creed, the fact seems to me to be unaccountable except on one of two hypotheses. The one is that Alcuin did not know of the Quicunque at all; the other that he knew that neither Felix nor Elipandus would be influenced by it. No one can say that it would have been insufficient for his purpose; for, even in the Creed of Constantinople as we call it, Alcuin found an argument against the Adoptianist theory[1].

§ 15. In entering on this investigation I feared that I might be compelled to exhibit Alcuin as having a share in the fraud of palming off the Quicunque as the work of Athanasius. I think now that his character is cleared. His great work on the Trinity was written in 802 or 803, and he died in 804. Beyond the precarious evidence of the dates of the French manuscript 13196 and the Milanese Codex, we have no testimony of the existence of the Quicunque as a whole, before this latter year. And we have strong proof that neither Paulinus nor Alcuin nor Charlemagne, up to this time, knew anything of it[2].

[1] It may be remembered that the words of the Treves fragment were "Unus non ex eo quod sit in carne conversa divinitas, sed quia est in deo adsumpta *dignanter* humanitas." I find Alcuin quoting from Leporius, a presbyter of Gaul (Frobenius, p. 775), "quia Verbum Deus *dignanter* in hominem suscipiendum descendit."

[2] In Vol. III. of Alcuin's works we have some account of Creeds and services—the Nicene Creed without the anathemas, p. 117: the Apostles' Creed, p. 127: an article *de fide*, p. 129: a confession of faith ascribed to Alcuin (certainly not resembling the Quicunque), p. 390. Pelagius' Creed is quoted p. 397: but not a word can be found relating to or resembling the Quicunque. It is simply incredible that it could have been received as authentic, or as authoritative, within the somewhat wide range of Alcuin's experience.

CHAPTER XXVIII.

HINCMAR.

§ 1. Questions still remaining to be answered. § 2. The Freedom of the Will. § 3. Godeschalk. § 4. Waterland's references to Hincmar. § 5. Hincmar "De Prædestinatione," and the "Symbolum Athanasii." § 6. Godeschalk on the Trine Deity. § 7. Hincmar's reply. § 8. Clauses of the Quicunque quoted by Hincmar. § 9. The "Ferculum Salomonis."

§ 1. THERE can be no doubt that the Quicunque was known in its complete form to Charles le Chauve. But there are some curious and intricate questions still unsettled, which the historian should lay before his readers even if he is unable to solve them himself. Compelled as we are to hold in suspense our judgment as to the date of certain manuscripts, we can have no doubt as to the date of writings, which, by internal as well as external evidence, are proved to have belonged to some historical personages, or to have been written by other historical personages in view of certain specified controversies. Of this latter character are the works of Hincmar, Archbishop of Rheims, an ambitious and arrogant prelate, who may possibly deserve the credit of being zealous for truth which Mosheim assigns to him; but whose chief characteristics appear to have been a determination to maintain in his own person the independence of the Church of his Province against the growing encroachments of the Church of Rome, and an apprehension that the truth could not make way if it were not backed up by a vigorous use of the secular arm.

§ 2. One of the earlier expositions of the Quicunque explains the first clause as intended to exhibit the doctrine of Free-Will.

"Here the blessed Athanasius laid down the freedom of the will: as it is said in the Psalm, What man is there that would have life? and again in the Gospel the Truth Itself says, He that would come after Me: so here, Whosoever would be saved. Wherefore God, though omnipotent, draws to the Faith no one against his will or by compulsion; He attracts him only who, of his own free will, would come to the Faith."

If this is correct (I do not say that it is), the date at which our first clause was prefixed to the Faith of the Church, (as we have seen that Faith taught by Augustine, Paulinus, Alcuin, and others,) must be the period in the ninth century at which the old questions on Predestination were revived: that is, the period at which Godeschalk attracted attention.

§ 3. Although the history of Godeschalk is generally known, I must be allowed to state, very briefly, the dates and chief characteristics of his life. He was a Saxon of noble birth, and is said to have been made a monk against his will. In the year 847 he became conspicuous by producing a catena which he had made out of the writings of St Augustine, of passages upholding an extreme view of Predestination: to shew that some, from all eternity, had been intended for everlasting life; others for everlasting sufferings. Rabanus Maurus, of whom I have had occasion to speak already, procured his condemnation at a Council held at Mayence in 848; and then he transmitted him as a prisoner for punishment to his Bishop, Hincmar[1]. At a Synod held under Hincmar, Godeschalk was degraded from the priesthood, ordered to be scourged *durissimis verberibus* until he would consign to the flames the collection out of Augustine's works which he had produced at Mayence, and to be imprisoned in the monastery of Hautvilliers. But in addition to this first trouble Godeschalk became involved in another controversy. Hincmar had forbidden the singing of the words of a well-known hymn:

"Te trina Deitas unaque poscimus;"

and the Benedictine monks, with Ratram as their leader, refused to obey. Godeschalk, although in prison, contrived to join in the controversy, and Hincmar, as eagerly, responded to him. To this we owe the two treatises from which the following extracts are taken.

§ 4. Dr Waterland refers to Hincmar in his chapter II. "Of Ancient Testimonies," and his chapter III. "Of Ancient Com-

[1] I have taken this history, almost verbatim, from the pages of Mosheim.

ments" on the Athanasian Creed. In the former chapter he says, under the year 852:—

"In the same age flourished the famous Hincmar, archbishop of Rheims; who so often cites or refers to the Creed we are speaking of as a standing rule of faith, that it may be needless to produce the particular passages. I shall content myself with one only, more considerable than the rest, for the use that is to be made of it hereafter. He directs his presbyters to learn Athanasius' Treatise of Faith (beginning, *Whosoever will be saved*), to commit it to memory, to understand its meaning, and to be able to give it in *common* words; that is, I suppose, in the *vulgar tongue*. He, at the same time, recommends the Lord's Prayer and (Apostles') Creed, as I take it, without mentioning the Nicene: which I particularly remark, for a reason to be seen above. It is farther observable that though Hincmar here gives the Athanasian formulary the name of a Treatise of Faith; yet he elsewhere scruples not to call it (Symbolum) a Creed: and he is, probably, as Sirmondus observes, the first writer who gave it the name it bears at this day."

In chapter III. Waterland's words are these:

"852. Our next *Commentator*, or rather *Paraphrast*, is Hincmar of Rheims; not upon the whole Creed, but upon such parts only as he had occasion to cite. For his way is to throw in several words of his own as explanatory notes, so far as he quotes the Creed: and he sometimes does it more than he ought to do, to serve a cause against Gothescalcus which I may hint, in passing: to say more of it would be foreign to our present purpose."

I have quoted the passage from the Capitular of Hincmar in my twenty-first chapter[1], and, therefore, I need not again adduce the words. Nothing can be learnt from it as to the precise character of the Quicunque at the time. Other passages will come before us in order as we examine his works.

§ 5. In his book, *De Prædestinatione*, p. 309, Hincmar quotes

Leo, and Bede, and others, to exhibit the benefit arising from baptism: then he adds a few words from Pope Siricius, to the effect that those Christians who apostatize and become contaminated in the worship of idols, must cut themselves off, as we should say *de facto*, from the Body and Blood of Christ, with which, at their new birth, they were redeemed. "And Athanasius in the Symbol, after other things, says that he believes in Christ, Who, taken up to heaven, sitteth at the right hand of the Father; we expect that He will come from thence to judge the quick and the dead, being sure to receive in His death and blood remission of our sins."

[1] p. 302.

This is the passage appealed to not only by Waterland, but also by Sirmond and others, to shew that Hincmar speaks of the Quicunque as a Symbolum or Creed.

Now Waterland knew that there is no other instance where this title is given to the document for the next three hundred years. And this fact should of itself have made him and Sirmond hesitate before they assumed that the Quicunque was here intended by the title Symbolum. The fact is, that there is, as any one may assure himself, in the Quicunque, no expression of belief: no explicit declaration that the author believed in the resurrection of our Saviour: no reference to the atonement through His death and passion: no mention of remission of sins. Hincmar, therefore, must have referred to some other document. It was the fashion, as we have seen, to ascribe Creeds to Athanasius: and I have already mentioned that a Creed resembling that which we find in the Appendix to the fifth volume of Augustine's works, Sermon CCXXXV—and which is called in some manuscripts, "Fides Catholica Niceni concilii Ecclesiæ Romanæ directa" —is elsewhere, as in Usher, called "Alia ejusdem Fidei confessio Athanasio ipsi a quibusdam attributa," elsewhere "Libellus fidei Patris et Filii et Spiritus Sancti Athanasii episcopi[1]." Is this, or any other similar Symbol, the document which Hincmar calls the Symbolum Athanasii? Let us look.

Hincmar's words are:

"Athanasius in symbolo dicens se *credere in Christum* præmissis aliis *assumptum in cœlis, sedere in dextera Patris, inde venturum judicare vivos et mortuos expectamus, in hujus morte et sanguine remissionem peccatorum consecuti.*"

In the libellus assigned to Athanasius which I have printed above, pp. 273, 274, these words occur:

"*Credimus in* Iesum *Christum*—" then, after a long interval— "tertia die a mortuis resurrexisse, *assumptum in cœlos, sedere ad dexteram Patris, inde venturum judicare vivos et mortuos: expectamus in hujus morte et sanguine remissionem peccatorum consecutos.*"

It thus becomes clear that the "Symbolum of Athanasius," which Hincmar quoted in his discourse on Predestination, is not the Quicunque, as Sirmond, and, after him, perhaps Oudin and

[1] See above, pp. 257 and 273, Appendix III.

Tentzel, and certainly Waterland, laid it down to be, but another document altogether; a document, I repeat, well known in the ninth century, but which we have proved to have existed in the seventh: a document, which in the Augustinian form is found in the Paris manuscript that contains the fragment discovered at Treves: which in the Athanasian form is found in our Arundel MS. 241[1], after the end of the eight books on the Faith of the Holy Trinity, which were also assigned to Athanasius in the time of Hincmar. It is there ushered in as follows:

"Hos libellos octo transscripsi qui multa addita et immutata continent. Incipit libellus fidei Patris et Filii et Spiritus Sancti Athanasii episcopi. Cum legeris, per hanc fidem moneo ut mei memor sis in orationibus tuis. Ne forsitan negligenter quisquam hoc obtrectator contingat: quia scriptum est, Ne projiciatis margaritas vestras ante porcos."

I must return to this again. For the present I proceed with Hincmar.

§ 6. I do not envy any one the labour of wading through his wearisome work, *De Una et non Trina Deitate.* But yet the duty must be performed by any who would test the accuracy of Waterland's statements. I have no question here with our great divine. I must, however, exhibit the evidence that may be adduced.

Godeschalk held that "God is naturally One, but Personally Trine," he did not believe "three Gods," but yet with the Creed of Damasus would reject the conception that God is *solitarius:* he held that the Father alone is God, so that He is not of God, but He begat God: the Son alone is God, so that He is begotten of God: the Holy Spirit alone is God, so that He proceeds at once from the unbegotten and the begotten God." Thus he held that "Deus Pater est Deitas ingenita innascibilis et innata: Deus Filius est Deitas genita nascibilis et nata: Deus Spiritus Sanctus est Deitas nec ingenita innascibilis et innata, nec genita nascibilis et nata, sed procedens a Deitate ingenita innascibli et innata et a Deitate genita nascibili et nata[2]."

Now the first thing that strikes me here is this; that Godeschalk could not have known the Quicunque, or if he knew it could not have regarded it as of any authority. He would not have ventured thus to alter the words of a document which had

[1] Commencing fol. 77 B.

[2] p. 415, my references are to the edition of Sirmond. The *black figures* in Migne, cxxv.

generally been received in the Church as authoritative, or had been introduced generally into the service.

§ 7. But we must turn our attention to Hincmar's reply[1].

He maintained that Godeschalk's opinion really amounted to a dividing of the Deity Which ought to be considered inseparable, as Augustine and the other doctors teach. "Wherefore the Catholic Faith most constantly proclaims that the Unity of the Deity in the Trinity of Persons and the Trinity of Persons in the Unity of the Deity ought to be worshipped. Since, as, taking Them one by one (singillatim), we are compelled by the Christian verity to confess each Person to be full and perfect Lord and God...because of the one and same Deity which is entire in each Person, so are we forbidden by the Catholic religion,—because of the one and the same Deity which is entire and undivided in Each,—to speak of three Gods or Lords." (p. 427.)

Thus we have the substance of our clauses 3, 19, 20.

On the next page (428), we have the following:

"The voices of all Catholics protest this, that Whoever would be saved must believe and confess that the Three Persons of the Holy Trinity, the Father, the Son and the Holy Spirit, are ὁμοούσιοι, so that, one by one (singillatim), we must believe and confess each Person to be true, complete...God, and these whole three Persons one God: because the Godhead of the Father and of the Son and of the Holy Spirit is One, which is the Unity of Trinity."

Here we have words of clauses 1, 19, 6, 30. Does he, however, quote the Quicunque? No. For he says: "In this faith all baptize who do faithfully baptize: and all the faithful are baptized."

Sophronius the archbishop of Jerusalem (whose letter was read at the sixth Council[2]) is quoted (p. 429) as objecting to the thought and words, "three Gods," "three Lords," and our clause 15 is quoted as from Sophronius (p. 430). Hincmar then adduces the Synodica of Pope Agatho and portions of the true Constantinopolitan Creed. Then, p. 433, "If anyone is a lover of Christ and fears the Lord...let him hold this orthodox faith, for by none other can he be saved (salvatus)[3]." At last, p. 435, we have an appeal to Athanasius generally: and, p. 437, he quotes clauses 5 and 6 as Athanasius' own. "Athanasius dicit hanc esse fidem Catholicam, ut credatur, quia alia est Persona Patris, &c." Augustine is quoted (p. 438) as teaching "non tres Dii sed unus Deus[4]:"

[1] Hincmar refers in his preface to the collection made by Ratram of Corbey.

[2] See above pp. 249, 250 (Sophronius died about 638 not 688 as there stated). I think that these words come from him, "Trinitatem in unitate credimus: unitatem in Trinitate glorificamus."

[3] The substance of 32—34 is referred to as belonging to the Chalcedon Council.

[4] These words are adduced pp. 429, 431, 524.

and then, on p. 439, Hincmar misrepresents the great African Bishop by putting that absolutely which Augustine suggests hypothetically (Tom. IX. p. 222, c). After awhile he cannot resist a pun in speaking of Godeschalk's sufferings; "quem non correxerunt verba suscipient verbera." (p. 444.)

Words resembling clauses 15, 16 are again quoted from Sophronius (p. 449) or Agatho. On p. 450, he accuses Godeschalk of tampering with manuscripts; because his authorities did not read as Hincmar wished them. He refers again to Ratram of Corbey—who made a compilation out of a work on the Trinity ascribed falsely to Augustine. He mentions that he had produced his own evidence out of Augustine at the Council of Soissons (in 853). I cannot but ask myself, Why was not the "Catholic Faith of Athanasius" adduced at length, if it existed then as we have it now?

At length, p. 452, Hincmar refers to the *fidei regula:* and he adduces parts of clauses 3, 4, 5, 6 as words of Athanasius. I think if he had had them within such easy reach, he would have found 11, 12, 14 more to his purpose. On p. 455 he has language resembling that of clauses 21, 22, 23 but it is not the language of the Quicunque. He thus goes, meandering on, referring to Augustine again for clause 16 (p. 459), but we have (p. 464) clauses 3, 4 as Athanasius', and (p. 469) 3, 4, 5, 6. He then passes on to St Augustine. After a while he adduces Augustine again, with Leo the Great, and Gregory, and Paulinus of Aquileia, and Alcuin *de Trinitate* (p. 472), where most certainly our Creed would have been more authoritative, if not more appropriate. On p. 477, we hear of Athanasius' Exposition of the Epistle to the Hebrews. On p. 481 he adduces a spurious work as Athanasius' (Migne IV. p. 1433), and then Hilary, and Ambrose, and Sophronius again. And soon we come to a series of spurious quotations as from Athanasius, I believe from the Books of the Trinity which are ascribed to Vigilius. We find such in pp. 492, 495, 501, 509, and so on. Alcuin's collection on the Trinity is spoken of again on p. 507.

And thus we pass onward, looking anxiously at the number of pages we have still to wade through, and noting that on p. 522 there seems to be the substance of our clause 24, and on p. 538 an explanation worthy of some note, of the meaning of *singillatim*[1]. The "Non tres Dii sed unus Deus" comes forward once more, but now from Alcuin (p. 539), and on p. 540 we have Athanasius again. We have references to the Symbolum, *i.e.* the Apostles' Creed, on pp. 544 and 547. And the subject of 25, 26 "In this Trinity there is nothing before or after" is touched upon in pp. 545, 547, but the Quicunque is not quoted. At last, p. 552, we come to the narrative which is interesting. Hincmar describes how he had urged Godeschalk to repent and revoke his blasphemies, but he could not succeed. When he heard that the Monk was dying, he sent by some brethren the following paper.

"Believe this in regard to the predestination of the elect and the pretermission of the reprobate, and that God wills all men to be saved,

[1] On p. 526, Godeschalk is introduced as using the word *singillatim*, but certainly not as part of the Creed. The word is explained at some length on p. 538. (Did Godeschalk's use of it cause its introduction and explanation into the Quicunque?) Clause 20 is said to come from Ambrose, *de Fide*, I. § 2.

although all men are not saved...And of the Deity of the Holy and inseparable Trinity—which is a Unity of Trinity—believe and confess, as the Holy Catholic and Apostolic Church believes, confesses, and proclaims, saying; 'The Catholic Faith is this, that we worship one God in a Trinity of Persons, and a Trinity of Persons in a Unity of Deity, neither confounding the Persons, as Sabellius, so that there are not Three, nor, as Arius, separating the substance, so that it is trine: because the Person of the Father is one, not one Thing; the Person of the Son is another, not another Thing; and the Person of the Holy Spirit is another, not another Thing: but the Divinity of the Father and of the Son and of the Holy Spirit is one, the glory equal, the majesty coeternal: and in this Holy and Inseparable Trinity there is nothing before or after, nothing greater or less[1], but the whole three Persons, Father, Son and Holy Spirit, are coeternal with each other and coequal: so that in all things, as has above been now said, both the Trinity of Persons in the Unity of Deity and the Unity of Deity in the Trinity of Persons is to be worshipped.' And if thou shalt thus believe in thine heart, and thus profess with thy mouth, and subscribe with thy hand, before witnesses, that thou dost thus believe and profess, and in this belief and profession dost continue; then by the judgment of the Holy Spirit, through that same Episcopal power by which thou wast condemned, thou mayest be absolved and be restored to the participation of the Body and Blood of our Lord Jesus Christ and to the Communion of the Catholic Church."

Godeschalk refused, and died unabsolved, in 868 or 869.

§ 8. Thus we find Hincmar quoting five times portions of the Quicunque,

e.g. p. 452, clauses 3, 4, 5, 6,
464, ... 3, 4,
469, ... 3, 4, 5, 6,
540, ... 3, 4, 25, 26, 27,
552, the scene on the death-bed, 3, 4, 5, 6, 25, 26, 27,

and using language very similar to clauses 19, 20.

The question is, Did he know the rest of the "Faith of Athanasius"? Clause 15 is quoted from Sophronius: 16 from Augustine. Indeed only clauses 3, 4, 5, 6 are adduced *eo nomine* as from Athanasius. What are we to believe? Must we suppose that even then the document was not known in its present entirety? or was not acknowledged in its entirety to be authoritative? at least in the province of Rheims? These are certainly puzzling questions: so puzzling that I may be allowed once more

[1] The exact sequence which is exhibited in the Vienna Manuscript 1261. See above, p. 325.

to look at the quotations which have been adduced from earlier writers, professing or claiming to be taken from the "Faith of Athanasius[1]."

§ 9. This must occupy our next chapter. I would, however, before I close this, draw attention to the Exposition of the Symbol which is contained in Hincmar's Treatise, which has the quaint title, "In Ferculum Salomonis." It bears in many respects a resemblance to the earlier documents of this character, adopting the older phrase that the Word became Incarnate "in fine sæculorum," not "in sæculo" as the Quicunque reads. The modern wording of the Apostolic Symbol had not as yet, as it would seem, been fully accepted, because, although he read "conceptus de Spiritu Sancto, natus ex Maria Virgine," the descent into hell is passed over and the phrase is "sedet ad dexteram Patris." The following words remind us of the Quicunque. "Ad cujus adventum omnes homines resurgent cum corporibus suis, et reddent de factis propriis rationem[2]."

[1] I do not believe that Dr Waterland ever read Hincmar's treatise. The passages to which he refers in his note to Chapter III. appear to have been merely transferred *en masse* from the Index to Sirmond's edition.

[2] This part of the tract concludes as follows: "Et qui, gratia Dei et subsequente eandem gratiam libero arbitrio, in fide recta et operibus bonis perseveraverint, præsciti et prædestinati a Deo in gloriam, ibunt in vitam eternam, electis...a Deo paratam...Et qui, non a Deo ad interitum prædestinati, sed ab Eo ex retributione justitiæ in massa perditionis relicti, in infidelitate vel malis operibus perseveraverint, ibunt in ignem eternum..." Migne, CXXXV. p. 824.

CHAPTER XXIX.

THE EXPOSITION IN "JUNIUS 25."

§ 1. Muratori and the Ambrosian codex M. 79. sup. Description of the manuscript and its contents. § 2. Description of the Bodleian manuscript Junius 25, and its contents. § 3. Zaccaria's copy at Florence. § 4. Manuscript at Vienna. § 5. The Milan title cannot mean that the Quicunque was written by Fortunatus. § 6. The Exposition apparently a running commentary. § 7. The clauses explained. § 8. Difficulty of regarding the Exposition as a collection of notes. § 9. Who was the author? § 10. Venantius cannot be the author of the one copy assigned to him. § 11. Examination of the Exposition. § 12. Results as to the Ambrosian copy. § 13. Results as to the other version. § 14. Excursus on the sixth millennium. Appendix. THE EXPOSITION.

§ 1. ONE witness remains to be examined of a singularly interesting character.

I. When Muratori was Librarian of the Ambrosian Library, he devoted himself much to the examination of the older manuscripts which that famous collection contains: and he made many important discoveries. Amongst these is the Fragment on the Canon of the New Testament, which has made his name familiar to most, even of our youngest students. These discoveries were published to the literary world about the close of the seventeenth century: the volume which contains the documents which I am now proposing to examine came out in the year 1698. Muratori does not describe the codex at length, nor does he give a very clear or succinct account of its contents.

Through the kind help of Dr Ceriani, I was permitted to examine the MS. in a somewhat hurried visit to Milan on August 9, 1872.

The class mark is M. 79. sup. and I have a note that the book was written in the year MVII. It contains many "excerpta."

No. 19 we have

Incipit expositio a fortunato presbytero conscripta.

It begins :—

"Summam totius fidei Catholicæ recensentes," and ends ..."qui triumphato tartyro, cum patre et spiritu sancto glorioso principatu intrans victor regnat in cœlo."

Then:

"*Item alia expositio symboli.*

"Symbolum graece Latine indicium sive collatio dicitur...Amen quod dicitur fideliter sive firmiter."

"*Item alia expositio symboli.*

"Tradunt majores nostri quod post ascensionem......deprecamur ut nobis et omnibus qui hæc audiunt concedat fidem dominus quam suscepimus et inveniri inter eos qui resurgunt ad vitam æternam per dominum Jesum Christum dominum nostrum."

"*Expositio orationis dominicæ.*

"Dominus noster qui orantes se exaudire consuevit."...(The conclusion was to me unintelligible).

"*Item alia expositio.*

"Pater noster......"

"*Item alia expositio.*

"Oratio dominica dicitur......

......mereamur esse."

"*Expositio fidei Catholicæ.*

"Quicunque homo vult salvus esse ante omnia opus est id est necesse est ut teneat id est retineat ut intelligat catholicam id est universalem fidem id est credulitatem. Quam fidem si unusquisque homo integram id est firmam inviolatamque id est indivisam ut (et) incorruptam servaverit id est custodierit absque dubio id est sine dubio in æternum peribit id est in futuro judicio condemnabitur."

It ends thus:

"Hæc est fides catholica id est credulitas universalis quam fidem si non unusquisque homo fideliter id est veraciter firmiterque crediderit absque ulla dubietate salvus esse non poterit in ultimo die quando reddet unicuique secundum opera sua."

Then without any introduction

"Fides est illarum rerum quæ non videntur credulitas."

This exposition goes on to the bottom of the column, the next commencing

"Quicunque id est unusquisque [qui] vult id est cupit salvus esse."

The last is very long. It ends

"Versiculum istum per adfirmationem repetit ut non recte credentes terreat et ad quærendam rectae fidei semitam provocet."

"*Item expositio fidei catholicæ fortunati.*

"Quicunque vult esse salvus

...salvus esse non poterit.

"Explicit expositio fidei Catholicæ. O beata et gloriosa, O benedicta et amplectenda fides quæ humanum genus sola vivificasti, quæ sola de diabolo triumphum reportas, &c...." An appeal of which I found another copy at Munich, 17181, Lat.

Some writings of Bede follow.

The work in which we are now specially interested is that entitled "Expositio Fidei Catholicæ Fortunati."

§ 2. II. Another version of this Exposition is found in a manuscript in the Library of the University of Oxford, of which we have this account in the third chapter of Waterland's *Critical History.*

"There is an older manuscript copy of this comment (as I find by comparing) in the Museum at Oxford, among Junius' Manuscripts, number 25. I am obliged to the very worthy and learned Dr Haywood for sending me a transcript of it with a specimen of the character. It is reasonably judged to be about 800 years old [*i. e.* written about 920]. It wants in the beginning about ten or a dozen lines: in the other parts it agrees with Muratorius' copy, saving only some slight insertions and such various lections as are to be expected in different manuscripts, not copied one from the other."

Waterland adds somewhat naïvely; "From the two copies compared may be drawn out a much more correct comment than that which Muratorius has given us from one, as will be seen at the end of this work."

This volume contains a curious and miscellaneous collection bound together, without any other connection with each other than the binding. Thus we receive no light from the other contents. In the middle of folio 106 (?) comes this

"Legentes in hoc libro
orent pro reverendo Domino
bartholomeo de andolo
cuique industria pene
dilapssa renovata
est. Anno MCCCC.
LXI."

It would seem that the book came from Venice.

We have on fol. 108

"Expositio in fide Catholica,"

the Exposition in which we are interested.

This ends on fol. 111*b*. Here is written in a more modern hand the beginning of the Apostles' Creed. Then on fol. 112

"*Incipit fides catholica hieronimi.*

Credimus in deum patrem, &c."

The creed of Pelagius.

This is followed by an Exposition of the Lord's Prayer (fol. 114*b*).

"Pater noster qui es in celis. Haec vox libertatis est patrem invocare qui nos creavit quia omnes ab uno deo creati sumus...a diabulo vel a malis hominibus." Then on fol. 115 is another Exposition of the Lord's Prayer.

I need not proceed: I must say, however, here, that I do not understand the meaning of Waterland's assertion, that the Exposition of the Quicunque wants in the beginning ten or a dozen lines: an assertion which has been understood to represent that the manuscript is mutilated. The Exposition is perfect[1].

§ 3. III. Franciscus Ambrosius Zaccaria found a copy of this Exposition in a paper codex of the fourteenth century: *Nullius Expresso Nomine Auctoris.* (See his *Excursus Litterarius per Italiam*, p. 307.) He was spending his holiday in a journey to the Libraries of Italy. In one of the many collections at Florence he saw an exposition which he recognised from its resemblance to Muratori's copy: and he made a small and unsatisfactory attempt to collate it. The collations are given in his *Excursus*, p. 307, and are noted in the margin of Migne, Vol. LXXXVIII. p. 587. Neither he, nor Muratori, nor Migne, appears to have known of the Oxford manuscript: it is clear, however, that this Florentine copy agrees very closely with the Exposition as given in "Junius 25" in the chief points wherein this differs from Muratori's copy.

§ 4. IV. In reading the account of some of the treasures of the Library at Vienna as published by Denis, I was struck with a notice of the manuscript 1032, from which I have already made extracts (pp. 322, 323). After the Creed there transcribed follows (as I stated) in the manuscript the *Quicunque.* On the document succeeding it, Denis made this remark:

"Symbolum excipit commentarius in ipsum sed qui (quod dolendum est) jam in versu *Quia sicut singillatim* abrumpitur: antiquior certe Hildegardiano et Bruniano." He refers to the volumes of the Bibliotheca Maxima. "Initium ejus est aliquantum corruptum. Quicunque vult salvus esse. Fides dicitur credulitas sive credentia: catholicam

[1] The manuscript contains a curious farrago of works, amongst them something entitled in a modern hand, "Alcuini Rhetorica," and, on folios 72 *b* and 73, a *genealogy of rhetoric*, entitled, also in a modern hand (?), "Hæc sunt Alcuini quæ in nonnullis editionibus desiderantur." All the items in this are in rustic letters. On folio 77 there is something more, marked as "Alcuini dialectica," of which almost all the headings are in rustic letters: and (oddly enough) this is followed by a paper entitled "Epistola Hieronymi ad Dardanum de generibus musicarum," where there is an account of an organ.

universalem, quia Catholicus universalis dicitur." I hoped that this might prove a third copy of the comment as given in "Junius 25:" and Dr Haupt, to whom I have already expressed my great obligations, added this to his other kindnesses: he transcribed all that the manuscript contained. My conjecture was correct: but the copy is unhappily defective, breaking off as Denis informs us at the nineteenth clause. This is on the *recto* of folio 86: turning over the leaf we find something totally different on the other side.

§ 5. I have felt compelled to give this long account of the Manuscripts (so far as they have come under my notice) which contain this Exposition, to enable my readers to form their own judgment of its true character and object. And I think that by merely noting the contents of the Ambrosian codex, they will be disposed to reject at once the suggestion of Muratori, that the title *Expositio Fidei Catholicæ Fortunati*[1] can possibly indicate that any Fortunatus was the author of the "Catholic Faith" expounded. In the manuscript there are four Expositions of the Quicunque: and with one only is the name of Fortunatus connected. Surely this must mean that Fortunatus wrote the Exposition. And another result of our examination follows: we cannot have any very high opinion of the judgment of Muratori, seeing that on such evidence he formed such a strange conclusion.

§ 6. Another and perhaps more important question next presents itself: What is the character of this Exposition? Is it—like many of the Expositions of the Apostles' Creed which have survived, and like many or all of the Expositions of the Lord's Prayer—a continuous discourse upon the Quicunque? Or is it merely a collected series of side notes upon the document, of the same character as is the comment assigned to Bruno, Bishop of Wurtzburg? The enquiry is of importance, and the subject of it has not been adequately considered. Waterland is silent upon it: Mr Ffoulkes seems to have regarded it from the latter point of view[2].

If our judgment on the character of a work is in any way to be influenced by the documents amongst which that work is found in the manuscripts, we must, I conceive, regard the Exposition in the

[1] Alcuin, III. p. 90, described the "Pange, lingua" as *Hymnus Fortunati*. It was written, I believe, by Mammertus Claudianus.

[2] *On the Athanasian Creed*, p. 316, "I would ask whether ancient commentators in general ever cite more of a work than the passage they select for comment?"

earlier light, and hold that it was a running commentary: the presbyter reading the Faith and its Exposition. And the turn of the language on clauses 13, 19, 36 seems to be reconcileable only with this supposition.

In this case, we must conclude that the "Faith," at the time that the Exposition was written, had not assumed the dimensions which it had assumed in the year 870. In this respect it may have resembled the Faith as it seems to have fallen *into* the hands of Archbishop Hincmar. For we must note that the clauses of our present document which the archbishop might have quoted—but did not quote—in his controversy with Godeschalk are passed over entirely in this Exposition. To exhibit this, I must give the clauses which are contained or noticed in the Exposition of the Oxford and Florence, and (in part) the Vienna, manuscripts. The Milanese manuscript contains also clause 2.

§ 7. The clauses explained are these:

1. Quicunque vult salvus esse, ante omnia opus est ut teneat catho-
3. licam fidem. Ut unum Deum in Trinitate et Trinitatem in Unitate
4. veneremur; neque confundentes personas, neque substantiam sepa-
5. rantes. Alia est enim persona Patris, alia persona Filii, alia Spiritus
6. Sancti. Sed Patris et Filii et Spiritus Sancti una est Divinitas,
7. æqualis gloria, coæterna majestas. Qualis Pater, talis Filius, talis
8. et Spiritus Sanctus; increatus Pater, increatus Filius, increatus et
9. Spiritus Sanctus; inmensus Pater, inmensus Filius, inmensus et
10. Spiritus Sanctus; æternus Pater, æternus Filius, æternus et
13. Spiritus Sanctus. Similiter omnipotens Pater, omnipotens Filius,
15. omnipotens et Spiritus Sanctus. Ita Deus Pater, Deus Filius,
17. Deus et Spiritus Sanctus. Ita Dominus Pater, Dominus Filius,
19. Dominus et Spiritus Sanctus. Quia sicut singillatim unamquamque
Personam et Deum et Dominum confiteri Christiana veritate com-
[20] pellimur; [ita in his tribus Personis non tres Deos nec tres Domi-
24. nos, sed unum Deum et unum Dominum confiteor.] Unus ergo
Pater, non tres Patres; unus Filius, non tres Filii; unus Spiritus
25. Sanctus, non tres Spiritus Sancti. Et in hac Trinitate nihil prius
30. aut posterius, nihil majus aut minus. Est ergo fides recta ut credamus et confiteamur quia Dominus noster Jesus Christus, Dei
31. filius, Deus pariter et homo est. Deus est ex substantia Patris
ante sæcula genitus, et homo est ex substantia matris in sæculo
32. natus. Perfectus Deus, perfectus homo, ex anima rationali et hu-
33. mana carne subsistit; æqualis Patri secundum Divinitatem, minor
34. Patre secundum humanitatem; qui [licet] Deus sit et homo, non
35. duo tamen sed unus est Christus. Unus autem non conversione
36. Divinitatis in carne, sed assumptione humanitatis in Deo; unus
37. omnino, non confusione substantiæ, sed unitate Personæ. Nam
sicut anima rationalis et caro unus est homo, ita Deus et homo

38. unus est Christus; qui passus est pro salute nostra, descendit ad
39. inferna, surrexit a mortuis, ascendit ad cœlos, sedet ad dexteram
40. Patris, inde venturus judicare vivos et mortuos. Ad cujus adventum omnes homines resurgere habent cum corporibus suis, et
41. reddituri sunt de factis propriis rationem; et qui bona egerunt
42. ibunt in vitam æternam, qui vero mala in ignem æternum. Hæc est fides Catholica, quam nisi quisque fideliter firmiterque crediderit, salvus esse non poterit.

§ 8. It is true that this argument will be affected if we regard the Exposition, notwithstanding its title, as merely a collection of marginal notes. In this case, of course, we must give up the inference that the Faith expounded did not contain the clauses which are passed over in the Exposition: that is, we must concede that the clauses 2, 11, 12, 14, 16, 18, 21, 22, 23(!), 26, 27, 28, 29, were not deemed worthy of a passing remark. But I am not prepared to concede this. The very words which are quoted by Theodulf, Ratram of Corbey, and Æneas of Paris as Athanasius' and of moment, are passed by.

§ 9. On the evidence of the title in the Milanese manuscript, this Exposition has been attributed to *Venantius* Fortunatus. Waterland is decided about it.

"There is a comment of Venantius Fortunatus upon the Athanasian Creed which I reprint in my Appendix. I cannot fix the age of it to a year, no, nor to twenty years. All that is *certain* is that it was made between 556 when Fortunatus first went into Gallican parts, and 599, when he was advanced to the Bishopric of Poictiers[1]."

Again[2], he says; Ludovicus Muratorius published in 1698 this comment

"together with a Dissertation of his own, concerning the author of the Creed: concluding at length that Venantius Fortunatus, the *certain* author of the comment, might possibly be the author of the Creed also."

The grounds on which Waterland based his opinion are given in the opening of his Chapter III. They are briefly these. (i.) The manuscript contains an Exposition of the Apostles' Creed, "a Fortunato presbytero conscripta." (ii.) Venantius uses in some of his poems the expressions *Salvus esse non poterit: Non deus in carnem versus: Æqualis Matri hinc, par deitate Patri: Non sua confundens: De Patre natus habens divina, humanaque Matris.*

[1] "The Preface."

[2] Chapter I. under the date 1698.

From these expressions he says, that "it is highly probable" that Venantius was really acquainted with the Athanasian Creed. (iii.) Because in the two Expositions assigned in this manuscript to Fortunatus

> "There is great similitude of style, thought and expressions: which shews that both are of the same hand, and indeed, the other circumstances considered, abundantly proves it[1]." "I may add that the tenor of the whole comment and the simplicity of the style and thoughts are very suitable to that age and more so than to the centuries following[2]."

Thus Waterland assumes that it is a continuous work: and on this account forms his text by combining the contents of the two manuscripts with which he was acquainted.

Waterland looked only to the evidence on the one side, yet I think few persons can regard his conclusion from it as satisfactory. I have compared together this and the Exposition on the Apostles' Creed assigned to Venantius, and cannot perceive any such similitude of thought or language as was noticed by the learned Archdeacon. Moreover the biographer of Venantius left an account of his writings, in which no such Exposition is mentioned. And the language of his Hymni Morales repeats in verse the belief of Leo the Great. The authorship of the Exposition cannot, even on the evidence of Waterland, be assigned to the poet of Poictiers.

§ 10. But one fact is conclusive. The Milanese copy—which alone has a title assigning the Exposition to Fortunatus—contains a passage taken from the writings of Alcuin. This passage does not occur in the three other copies. So the recension of the work to which alone the name of Fortunatus is prefixed, could not possibly have been prepared before the commencement of the ninth century. It is almost incredible that the bearing of this fact escaped the attention of Waterland; or that, with this evidence before him, he could have spoken of the *certainty* of the authorship in the terms which I have quoted[3].

§ 11. In my Appendix to this chapter I print the Exposition from the Oxford copy, with the Milanese additions in the notes. Let us examine it, taking advantage of Waterland's learning.

[1] Chapter III.

[2] *Ibid.*

[3] There is an article on Venantius Fortunatus in the *Union Review* of May 1872, the author of which acquiesces in this conclusion. See too Mr Lumby, *On the Creeds*, p. 208.

i. The first note in the Muratorian copy comes, as I have said, from Alcuin, or perhaps (but only in part) from Fulgentius. The essay quoted was once ascribed, falsely, to Augustine: and perhaps Alcuin quoted it as Augustine's, but the words here are Alcuin's. (The essay is printed in the appendix to Vol. VI. of the Benedictine edition of Augustine, p. 1101 *Gaume.*)

ii. A few words on the term *ecclesia* (which again are not found in the Oxford copy) are taken from Isidore of Seville who died in 636.

iii. A passage on our clause 3 (again not in *Junius* 25) comes from Alcuin or Fulgentius.

iv. The words "coæternum et coæqualem et co-operatorem, quia scriptum est *Verbo Domini cœli firmati sunt* id est a Filio Dei *Et spiritu oris eius omnis virtus eorum*" may be seen in the Creed of Damasus (Hahn, p. 188).

v. The Explanation of clause 5 is virtually contained in the same Creed: but also in Alcuin *de fide S. Trinitatis* I. xiv. or II. ix.

vi. I found in the margin of the Quicunque in "St Gall: No. 27," the following note on clause 9 "inmensus, non est mensurabilis in sua natura quia inlocalis est, et incircumscriptus, ubique totus, ubique præsens, ubique potens:" the same note as in "Junius" or "Fortunatus."

vii. So on the word "æternus" the notes are the same (and possibly on other clauses).

viii. On clause 15 the words "Deus nomen est potestatis non proprietatis" are taken from the Creed of Damasus, as before: and so are the words which follow.

ix. The explanation of 19 is from Alcuin I. ii. who took it from Augustine, Tom. VIII. p. 1008 A (*collatio cum Maximino*) or p. 1285 C (*de Trinitate*).

x. The substance of the note on clause 24 is in Alcuin *de S. Trin.* I. ix. and xi.

xi. So again the note on clause 25 is in Alcuin I. viii. and ix. or, still better, in the Appendix to Augustine's works: Tom. VI. p. 1741; with which compare V. 2983. (The former may be later than the ninth century.) And thus we may go on. We find part of the note on clause 31, once more, in the Creed of Damasus, and nearly all of it in Pseudo-Augustine VI. 1736. The words "virgo ante partum, et virgo post partum" are old: the clause "secula generationibus constant" is from Isidore. On 33 the words are Augustine's. The long note on "descendit ad inferna" is all in the Appendix to Augustine VI. 1740. The latter part is however as old as the Council of Toledo, A. D. 693.

§ 12. Such is the puzzling character of this Exposition. And it becomes a question of great interest to those who would honestly examine into the history of the Quicunque, whether the Faith, as here expounded, contained the clauses of which I have noted the omission in the commentary. My own conviction is, that it did not contain these clauses. I cannot conceive that it was possible for an expositor to have omitted to notice the very definite declarations of clauses 2, 11, 12, 21, 22, 23. I am willing to allow that in the earlier or anonymous form—that is, as it is found in the Oxford and Florentine manuscripts and Viennese fragment—the Quicunque may be earlier, possibly much earlier, than the year 800. Indeed, it may have existed in two or more imperfect forms. But it was imperfect.

§ 13. Looking, however, at the explanations which we find in the Oxford Exposition, there are none which we can distinctly say are taken from any older Creed or explanation, excepting those which come from the genuine writings of St Augustine and the well-known Creed of Damasus. The discovery of some passages in writings ascribed to Augustine is puzzling, but only until we remember that these writings may themselves be later than the eighth century. The Exposition of the Apostles' Creed in Vol. VI. of his works seems to be definitely considered so. But it seems also to be conceded by Dr Waterland that our Exposition was modified *after the time of Alcuin*, and was in use in the ninth and even a later century. And this fact must have some influence on the question which I must now proceed to discuss.

§ 14. EXCURSUS ON THE SIXTH MILLENNIUM.

In a valuable pamphlet which was contributed by Professor Heurtley to the controversy of 1872, the learned writer drew attention to the explanation of clause 31. "Homo est ex substantia matris in seculo natus: id est in isto sexto miliario in quo nunc sumus: Man of the substance of His mother born in the *age*, that is, in this sixth millenary in which we now are." The Ambrosian or later recension adds a few words which do not occur in the Oxford Manuscript: "Secula enim generationibus constant et inde secula quod sequuntur: abeuntibus enim aliis alia succedunt: Ages consist of generations and they are called ages (secula) because they come in sequence: for, as one passes away, others come on." Without accepting this derivation of *secula*, the words found in both copies open out an interesting subject.

Dr Heurtley exhibits the general Latin belief that the six-thousandth year of the world's history was to terminate in or before the year 799 of our era; and he therefore argues that this Exposition must have been composed before that year. He does not anticipate the objection that the Exposition must—according to Waterland—have been augmented and used after that epoch. Indeed I must add, that, if we regard it as mainly or partly composed of fragments of earlier Creeds and documents, the words in question may have been taken from such earlier documents; if only (which is not impossible) the compiler missed the point of the expression which he was adopting. In this case all the light which seemed to be thrown on the date of the Exposition from this able suggestion, is again obscured.

But an interest is awakened here which must be my warrant for devoting a little time to the question involved.

The ordinary expressions used by the Councils of Toledo and the writers of the seventh and eighth centuries for the date of the Birth of our Lord were these: "in novissimis temporibus; in fine sæculi; in ultimis temporibus," and so on. The term "in sæculo" seems to have been lost sight of until it was revived at the discovery of the fragment at Treves; but it was the term used by Vincentius of Lerins; "Ex matre *in sæculo* generatus;" and we find it in Augustine's *Enchiridion* § 10 (Vol. VI. p. 364 of Gaume) "Deus est ante omnia sæcula, homo est *in nostro sæculo*[1]." Indeed the explanation of the Exposition, *id est in isto sexto milliario in quo nunc sumus* is more adapted to the *in nostro sæculo* of Augustine, than to the *in sæculo* of the Quicunque.

Now everyone knows that the early Christians were ever in expectation that the end of the world was at hand. The words of the Epistle to the Hebrews, ix. 26, referring to Christ Jesus appearing now "in consummatione sæculorum" *in the completion of the ages*, encouraged some to expect the end ere long. Thus, to the dates furnished by Dr Heurtley, we must add that suggested by the words of Cyprian: in the opening of his letter to Fortunatus (No. IX.), he says "Six thousand years are now nearly completed since the devil attacked man."

With these six thousand years the fathers connected the period of the great millennium. When they were over the great sabbatical rest was to commence. And thus the conception of "the seven ages of the world" grew into favour: the seven millennial periods.

St Augustine fostered, if he did not suggest, the thought: and with that fondness for mystical numbers which is capable of making anything out of anything, he saw the numbers six and seven almost everywhere. In the two months during which the daughter of Jephthah bewailed her virginity, he saw that sixty days meant six times ten, and thus at the end of the sixth period the Church was to be presented as a Chaste Virgin to Christ; this being typified or signified in the holocaust of the Jewish maiden. The first age was from Adam to the deluge; the second from the deluge to Abraham; the third from Abraham to David; the fourth spread to the captivity; the fifth to the birth from the Virgin; the sixth "usque in hujus sæculi finem." It is true he uses *ætas* here and not *milliarium*—but he adopts the word *sæculum* as well.

Elsewhere he speaks of the six thousand years. Thus in the *de Civitate*, Lib. XII. cap. X., writing against those heathen who maintained that many thousands of years had gone by, he insists that from the Sacred Literature we learn that from the creation of man six thousand years have not as yet elapsed[2]. The Benedictines add a note to the effect that Eusebius (whose chronology Augustine follows) reckoned 5611 years from the creation of the world to the capture of Rome by the Goths: this took place in 410. The year 6000 would therefore have fallen in 799 of our era. Thus he considered that in his time "the

[1] The words are used by Paulinus or the synodical letter of the Council of Frankfort. Labbe, VII. 1040 E.

[2] Vol. VII. p. 495.

latter years of the sixth day were rolling on[1]." Lactantius who wrote earlier expected the end earlier.

Thus as years passed by we find that the Christian conception as to the date of the termination of the sixth millennium changed. The end retreated as the Church lived on. But the time of Augustine's reckoning was long the favourite. Thus the Colbertine Manuscript 1868 (now Paris, 1451), gives some figures which would place the six thousandth year in A. D. 797[2].

The question assumed a polemical aspect. Taking (it may be from the Christian writers) the hint as to the ages of the world, the Jewish Rabbis began to insist that, according to the Hebrew chronology, only five ages of the world had passed; and therefore they argued that the Messiah had not come. "We insist," says Julian, Bishop of Toledo[3], "that the sixth age is passing, and therefore that the Messiah has come." But the bishop was obliged to consider that the time had to be reckoned not *in annis sed generationibus;* for, although he wrote in the year 686 of our era, he made out that already 6011 years had passed since the world was created. Thus he was obliged to confess, "God only knows when it will end."

But, so far as these words in our Exposition are concerned, I think that the question is disposed of by the explanation added, in the more recent recension of our text, by Fortunatus writing in or after the time of Alcuin. And thus we find Amalarius of Metz speaking of the Church as having lived together with the Apostles "in præsenti sæculo" (*de divinis Officiis* IV. xii. Tom. CV. p. 1193 of Migne): and Rabanus Maurus used not dissimilar language. The latter, however, had adopted the Jewish chronology; and his ages are, like Shakspeare's, taken from the life of man. The first is that of oblivion: the second, of boyhood to Abraham: the third, of adolescence to David: the fourth, of manhood to Babylon: the fifth, of old age to Christ: the sixth, of decrepitude: the seventh, the sabbath (of the grave): the eighth, the Resurrection. Of the sixth he says "sexta quæ nunc agitur ætas nullis generationibus vel temporum serie certa, sed ut ætas decrepita ipsa totius sæculi morte consummanda[4]." We all remember the hymn translated so ably "the world is growing old:" but I find that Abbo of Fleury, at the end of the passage cited above[5], said that when he was a boy some preached that the world would come to an end in the thousandth year. I cannot lay upon the *sextum milliarium* of "Junius 25" the stress which the learned Margaret Professor of Oxford laid upon it in his able pamphlet.

[1] *Ibid.* p. 934. For these references I am indebted to Dr Heurtley. The argument, p. 934, is curious.

[2] I have referred to this manuscript before (p. 268). It contains the "collection of the MS. of Saint Maur," and is of the ninth century. The Prefatory matter includes a catalogue of the Popes to Hadrian I. "Adrianus sedit annos XXIII. menses X. dies XVII." It must have been written therefore after A.D. 795. Then come the figures I have referred to, which make out that between the Creation and the Crucifixion 5228 years elapsed. From that to the Papacy of Marcellinus 276 years 8 months. That to Lady-day in the 25th year of Charles (793), 390 years 3 months. Thus in all, to the date named, 5894 years 11 months (Maassen, Vol. I, p. 614, and *Sitzungsberichte*, LIV. p. 173). It will be remembered that this MS. contains a copy of the Athanasian Creed.

[3] Migne, Vol. XCVI. pp. 539—584.

[4] Words very similar to these were attributed to Alcuin. See the dubious *Disputatio Puerorum*, Migne, CI. p. 1112.

[5] Above, p. 307.

Reviewing the whole subject of these Expositions, and keeping before my mind the fact that the Milanese recension quotes Alcuin twice, whereas the Oxford copy is free from these quotations, I cannot claim to have proved more than this: viz. that the Milanese copy, which ascribes it to Fortunatus, must be more recent than Alcuin: whilst the Oxford recension, even though one copy is contained in a volume which contains many of Alcuin's shorter treatises, *may* have been earlier[1]. But I maintain also that the unquestioned acceptance of these words "id est in isto sexto milliario in quo nunc sumus" in the ninth century, shews that the able argument of Dr Heurtley that the Exposition must have been originally composed in the eighth or seventh is not conclusive. As the commentary was used in the ninth century, so it may have been compiled of earlier materials in the ninth. It clearly was a composition or compilation.

But the necessities of my position do not require this last assumption. The Exposition of "Junius" does not enforce the unity of God in terms which Hincmar would have cared to use in his controversy with Godeschalk: it would have compelled him still to appeal to Augustine and Sophronius for proofs that the Catholic Faith requires us to maintain that there is only "unus æternus, unus inmensus, unus omnipotens." My argument is that Hincmar, when he wrote about 868, did not know our Quicunque in its present and completed form: yet it was known to Charles the Bald, at all events in the year 869[2]. I do not say that it did not exist, completed, before the year 869: I merely say it was not generally known, not known even to Hincmar. My belief is that it was concocted in the neighbourhood in which the famous Decretal Epistles were manufactured, and that it was published about the same time that they were. But my belief here is of little moment. The Quicunque may have been found in some old library, as the Donation of Constantine was found in the cases of the Vatican. And who can prove the negative[3]?

[1] The Oxford recension reads *in inferna:* as does the Colbertine. This strengthens the argument in favour of its antiquity, for all the complete manuscripts of the Creed, together with Fortunatus, read *ad inferos.*

[2] See above, p. 365.

[3] I have already mentioned (p. 375) that the codex Regius 2. B. v. of the British Museum contains a chronological memorandum. It shews how great an interest was taken in the subject even into the tenth century. The memorandum concludes thus: "Ætas ab incarnatione usque ad finem sæculi decurrit."

APPENDIX.

EXPOSITIO IN FIDE CATHOLICA·;

[I have mentioned that there are three complete copies of this Exposition. One at Oxford which furnishes the text printed below with all its imperfections, except that the contractions are expanded. One at Florence which is described imperfectly in Zaccaria's *Excursus Literarius per Italiam*, p. 287, and out of which the readings he noted were extracted by the editor of Migne, Tom. LXXXVIII. Both Zaccaria and the editor were ignorant of the Oxford copy with which, as will be seen, the Florence manuscript harmonises, and thus only the more important variations from the Milanese MS. were noted. Then there is the copy at Milan, of which Muratori gave a transcript in his *Anecdota*, Tom. II., which differs materially from the former two. Finally there is a manuscript at Vienna containing, as I have said, a portion of the comment, breaking off with *compellimur* in line 50 below. I designate these manuscripts as O. F. M. V. respectively. My references will be to the numbers of the lines below. I shall also give the sources from which the explanations appear to have been drawn: for these, as will be seen, I am largely indebted to Waterland.]

Junius MS. 25. (Bodl. Libr.) fol. 108.

QUICUMQUE uult saluus esse ante omnia opus est ut teneat catholicam fidem; Fides dicitur credulitas: siue credentia; Catholica uniuersalis dicitur id est recta . quam ecclesia uniuersa tenere debet·; Ecclesia . dicitur congregatio christianorum . siue conuentus populorum·; Vt unum deum in trinitate . et trinitatem in unitate ueneremur·;

Line 1. M. esse salvus. (Which is also the reading of the Ambrosian copy of the Creed. See p. 318 above.)

l. 2. After fidem M. *adds* quam nisi quisque integram inviolatamque servaverit absque dubio in æternum peribit.

M. *omits* fides dicitur credulitas sive credentia (V. *has* ibi credentia). M. *inserts* Primo ergo, omnium fides necessaria est sicut apostolica docet auctoritas dicens: sine fide impossibile est placere deo. Constat enim neminem ad veram pervenire beatitudinem nisi deo placeat: et deo neminem placere posse nisi per fidem. Fides namque est bonorum omnium fundamentum: fides humanæ salutis initium. Sine hac nemo ad filiorum dei potest consortium pervenire; quia sine ipsa nec in hoc seculo quisquam justificationis consequitur gratiam nec in futuro vitam possidebit æternam, et si quis hic non ambulaverit per fidem non perveniet ad speciem beatam domini nostri Jesu Christi. [These words are, as Waterland noticed, nearly identical with words found in Alcuin's work *On the Trinity*, Book I. chapter II. (or I. Migne, CI. p. 13); the only difference being that Alcuin read "ad speciem beatæ visionis Domini nostri Jesu Christi;" and the "ergo" and "enim" at the commencement have been added or altered by the commentator. Some of the words, viz. from "Fides namque est bonorum omnium fundamentum," down to "non perveniet ad speciem," were taken apparently by Alcuin from a treatise printed in the Appendix to Volume VI. (p. 1101) of Augustine's works, but now attributed on the authority of an ancient manuscript, as well as of Ratram, to Fulgentius. But it is clear that the commentator quotes Alcuin direct.]

l. 2. V. catholicam universalem quia catholicam universalis dicitur idem rectam quam, &c.

l. 3. V. M. F.? universa ecclesia.

l. 4. M. ecclesia quippe.

l. 5. M. (*after* populorum) Non enim sicut conventicula hereticorum in aliquibus regionum partibus coarctatur sed per totum terrarum orbem dilatata dif-

Et credamus et colamus et confiteamur ·; Neque confundentes personas ·; Vt sabellius errat . qui ipsum dicit . esse patrem in persona quem et filium . ipsum et spiritum sanctum ·; Non ergo confundentes personas . quia tres omnino personae sunt ·; Est enim gignens . genitus . procedens ·; Gignens est pater . qui genuit filium ·; Filius est genitus . quem genuit pater; Spiritus sanctus est procedens . quia a patre et filio procedit ·; Pater et filius coaeterni sibi sunt . et coequales . et cooperatores sicut scriptum est ·; Verbo domini caeli firmati sunt . id est . a filjo dei creati; Spiritus oris eius omnis uirtus eorum ·; Vbi sub singulari numero spiritus eius dicit . unitatem substantiae deitatis ostendit; Ubi sub plurari (*sic*) numero omnis uirtus eorum dicit . trinitatem personarum aperte demonstrat . quia tres unum sunt et unum tres ·; Neque substantiam seperantes; Vt arrius garrit . qui sicut tres personas esse dicit . sic et tres substantias esse mentitur ·; Filium dicit minorem quam patrem . et creaturam esse spiritum sanctum adhuc minorem quam filium et patri et filio eum esse administratorem adserit ·; Non ergo substantiam seperantes . quia tote tres personae in substantia deitatis unum sunt ·; Alia est enim persona patris . quia pater ingenitus est. Eo quod a nullo est genitus; Alia persona filii . quia filius a patre est solo genitus; Alia spiritus sancti . quia a patre et filio spiritus sanctus procedens est; Sed patris et filii et spiritus sancti . una est diuinitas . id est deitas; Aequalis gloria . id est claritas ·; Coaeterna maiestas . maiestas gloria est claritatis . siue potestas ·; Qualis pater . talis filius . talis et spiritus sanctus . id est in deitate et omnipotentia ·; Increatus pater . increatus filius . increatus et spiritus sanctus . id est a nullo creati ·; Inmensus pater . inmensus filius . inmensus et spiritus

funditur. [These are words of Isidore of Seville, who died in 636.]

l. 6. *After* confiteamur M. *adds* Trinitatem in personis unitatem in substantia. Hanc quoque Trinitatem Personarum atque unitatem naturæ Propheta Esaias revelatam sibi non tacuit, cum se dicit Seraphim vidisse clamantia, Sanctus, sanctus, sanctus, Dominus Deus Sabaoth. Ubi prorsus in eo quod dicitur tertio Sanctus, Personarum Trinitatem; in eo vero quod semel dicimus Dominus Deus Sabaoth divinæ naturæ cognoscimus unitatem. [These words from *Hanc quoque Trinitatem* are taken verbatim from Alcuin, *ut supra*, Book I. cap. III. (or II. Migne, p. 15), who again expanded the thought and language of Fulgentius. See Gaume's Augustine VI. p. 1105.]

l. 9. V. M. Tres personæ omnino sunt.

l. 10. M. et procedens.

l. 12. V. Patri et filio quoaeternus est et quoaequalis et quooperatur sicut scriptum... [I should think that this is the correct reading. It agrees with the *second* "Creed of Pope Damasus," (Hahn, p. 188,) sed Patrem esse qui genuit, et Filium esse qui genitus est, Spiritum vero sanctum non genitum neque ingenitum non creatum neque factum sed de Patre Filioque procedentem Patri et Filio coæternum et coequalem et cooperatorem; quia scriptum est, verbo domini, &c. In the Vienna manuscript 2223, which contains the Creed of Damasus, fol. 76 verso, Filioque is omitted.]

l. 13. firmati (not as Waterland's friend Dr Haywood read it, formati).

l. 14. V. M. Spiritu (F. Spiritus).

l. 15, 16. F. dicitur (bis: M. semel: for M. *omits* unitatem—dicit *or* dicitur, a case of *homœoteleuton*).

l. 18. M. quia tres personas esse dicit si et tres. F. qui ut tres personas...sic et tres... V. qui sicut tres...sicut tres... (Either F. or O. exhibits the correct reading.)

l. 21. M. V. patris et filii eum administratorem esse.

l. 23. (Dr Haywood read *divinitatis* by a mistake.)

l. 23—26. The substance of this is in Alcuin.

l. 25, 26. M. *omits* spiritus sanctus.

l. 28. M. *has* claritas. V. *omits* est.

l. 31. M. *has* creatus. V. *omits* id est a nullo creati.

sanctus ·; Non est mensurabilis in sua natura . quia inlocalis est . incircumscriptus. Ubique totus . ubique presens . ubique potens ·; Aeternus pater . aeternus filius . aeternus et spiritus sanctus ·; Id est non tres aeterni . sed in tribus personis unus deus aeternus . qui sine initio et sine fine aeternus permanet ·; Similiter omnipotens pater . omnipotens filius . omnipotens et spiritus sanctus ·; Omnipotens dicitur . eo quod omnia potest . et omnium optenit potestatem ·; ·; Ergo si omnia potest quid est quod non potest ; Hoc non potest . quod omni potenti non conpetit posse ; Falli non potest . quia ueritas est ; Infirmare non potest : quia sanitas est ; Mori non potest . quia inmortalis . uita est ·; Finire non potest . quia infinitus et perennis est ·; Ita . deus pater . deus filjus . et deus spiritus sanctus ;· Deus nomen est potestatis . non proprietatis ·; Proprium nomen est patris . pater ·; Et proprium nomen est filii . filius ·; Et proprium nomen est spiritus sancti . spiritus sanctus ·; Ita . dominus pater . dominus filius . dominus et spiritus sanctus ·; Dominus dicitur . eo quod omnia dominat . et omnium est dominus dominator ·; Quia sicut singillatim . id est sicut distinctum unamquamque personam . et deum et dominum confiteri . christiana ueritate conpellimur ·; Quia si me interrogaueris quid sit pater . ego respondebo . deus et dominus ·; Similiter et si interrogaueris quid sit filius . ego dicam deus et dominus ·; Et si dicis quid est spiritus sanctus . ego dico deus et dominus ·; Et in his tribus personis . non tres deos nec tres dominos . sed his tribus sicut iam supradixi unum deum et unum dominum confiteor ·; Vnus ergo pater . non tres patres ·; Id est qui pater semper pater . nec aliquando filius ·; Unus filius non tres filii ; id est qui filius semper filius . nec aliquando pater ·; Vnus spiritus sanctus . non tres spiritus sancti ·; Id est qui spiritus sanctus . semper spiritus sanctus . nec aliquando filius aut pater ·; Haec est proprietas personarum ·; Et in hac trinitate nihil prius aut posterius ·; Quia sicut numquam filius sine patre . sic numquam fuit pater sine filio . sic et numquam fuit pater et filius . sine spiritu sancto ·; Coaeterna ergo trinitas . et seperabilis unitas . sine initio et sine fine ·; Nihil maius

l. 32. V. M. *read* et incircumscriptus (some of the explanations here are found *totidem verbis* in St Gall 27; for example, lines 32, 33, 35, 36).

l. 37, 38. This is found in Venantius' exposition of the Apostles' Creed.

l. 40. M. *reads* Falli non potest quia sanctus est. Mori non potest... (a case of homœoteleuton, with *sanitas* subsequently altered to *sanctus* to make greater sense).

l. 43. M. *omits* Deus nomen est potestatis non proprietatis. F. is corrupted, deus est potestatem non proprietatem. V. agrees with O. (Indeed the whole passage is found in the Creed of Damasus to which I have already referred, and it is in St Gall 27. It is also found in the expanded Creed in the Appendix to Augustine's works, Vol. v. p. 2958. The finding *power* in the name *Deus* is very interesting to those who have traced the usage of the Name אל in the Old Testament.)

l. 44, 45. V. proprium nomen est patri...filio...spiritui sancto.

l. 46. M. *reads* Dominus dicitur eo quod dominatur creaturae cunctae vel quod creatura omnis dominatui ejus deserviat. (Words taken exactly from Isidore. F. and V. agree with O. save that F. reads *dominatur.*)

l. 48. M. distincte (V. distinctum).

l. 48. M. *omits the first* et.

l. 49. (Here V. fails us.)

l. 49—53. The passage is clearly taken from Alcuin, *ut supra*, p. 15 D. M. *reads* Quid est pater...quid est filius si dicas: ego dicam.

l. 52. M. sed in his tribus.

l. 53. M. supra dictum est.

l. 55. M. quia (three times).

l. 58. M. semper est spiritus sanctus.

l. 59—72. There is a passage nearly resembling this in the sermon on the Creed in the Appendix to Augustine VI. 1741 C. The sermon seems to have been "composed" after the 11th century.

aut minus; Equalitatem personarum dicit. quia trinitas equalis est et una (*sic*) deitatis·; Apostolo dicente; Per ea quae facta sunt. intellecta conspiciuntur·; Et per creaturam creator intellegitur. secundum has conparationes. et aljas quamplures·; Sol. candor. et calor. trea sunt nomina et res una·; Quod candit. hoc calit. et quod calit. hoc candit; [tria haec uocabula res una esse dinoscitur.] Ita et pater et filius et spiritus sanctus. tres persone. in deitate substantiae unum sunt. et indiuidua unitas recte creditur·; Item de terrenis. uena. fons. fluuius. trea itemque uocabula. et res una in sua natura; Ita trium personarum patris et filii. et spiritus sancti. substantia deitas una est·; Est ergo fides recta ut credamus et confiteamur quia dominus noster ihesus christus dei filius et homo est·; Ihesus hebraice. latine saluator dicitur·; Christus grece. latine unctus uocatur; Ihesus ergo dicitur. eo quod saluat populum·; Christus. eo quod spiritu sancto delibutus; Sicut in ipsius christi persone esaias ait; Spiritus domini super me propter quod unxit me et cetera; Item in psalmo; unxit te deus deus tuus oleo letitiae preconsortibus tuis; Dei filius. deus pariter et homo est·; Filius. a felicitate parentum dicitur·; Homo. ab humo dicitur. id est de humo factus est; Deus est ex substantia patris. ante secula genitus; Id est deus de deo. Lumen de lumine. Splendor de splendore; Fortis. de forte. Virtus. de uirtute; Uita de uita. aeternitas. de aeternitate; Per omnia idem quod pater in diuina substantia hoc est filius·; Deus pater. deum filium genuit. non uoluntate. neque necessitate. sed naturae; Nec queratur quomodo genitus sit. quod angeli nesciunt prophetis est incognitum·; Vnde eximius propheta esaias dicit·; Generationem eius quis enarrauit·; Ac si diceret. angelorum nemo. prophetarum nullus. nec innarrabilis et inestimabiles (*sic*) deus a seruolis suis discutiendus est. sed fideliter credendus. et puriter diligendus; Et homo est ex substantia matris in seculo natus·; Dei filius uerbo patris caro factum·; non quod diuinitas mutasset deitatem sed adsumpsit humanitatem; Hoc est uerbum caro factum est ex utero uirginali; Veram humanam carnem traxit. et de utero uirginis uerus homo sicut et uerus deus est in seculo natus·; Quia mater quae genuit. uirgo ante partum.

l. 64. M. apostolo docente et dicente. F. apostolo dicente atque docente.

l. 66, 67. M. tria sunt vocabula et tria unum.

l. 68. The words within the bracket are added at the top of the page.

M. *omits the first* et.

l. 71. M. tria sunt vocabula et tria unum in sua natura.

l. 72. M. substantia et deitas unum est.

l. 74. M. *omits* dei filius et homo est. The next words come from "Ruffinus," § 6. Compare Pseudo-Augustine, VI. 1736 B.

l. 75. M. *omits* Christus græce...dicitur (a case of homœoteleuton). F. *has* populum suum.

l. 76. M. divinitus sit delibutus.

l. 77. M. *omits* Christi.

l. 78. M. item et Psalmista de Christo domino dicit. unxit... F. *has* ita Psalmus...unxit te Dominus deus tuus.

l. 80. M. de humo terrae.

l. 81. M. deus ex...(again the explanation 82—90 is found in St Gall 27. Compare Creed of Damasus, Hahn, p. 186 and 189, and the latter part in Augustine as above, p. 1736 A).

l. 84. *for* idem M. *has* id est;

l. 86. M. et prophetis.

l. 87. M. et isdem eximius.

l. 88. M. dixisset, angelorum nullus, prophetàrum nemo.

l. 90. So F. but M. et homo ex.

l. 91. M. dei filius verbum caro factum et non.

l. 94. M. de utero virginali.

l. 95. M. verus deus in sæculo natus est salva virginitatis gratia. *Then* M. *reads* quia mater genuit, et virgo mansit ante partum et post partum. (Compare

et uirgo post partum permansit in seculo . id est in isto sexto miliario in quo nunc sumus; deus et homo christus ihesus unus dei filius et ipse uirginis filius·; Quia dum deitas in utero uirginis humanitatem adsumpsit . et cum ea per portam uirginis integram et inlesam nascendo mundum ingressus est uirginis filius·; Et hominem quem adsumpsit id est dei filium sicut iam supradiximus . et deitas et humanitas in christo·; Et dei patris pariter et uirginis matris filius·; Perfectus deus . perfectus homo . ex anima rationale . et non ut paulinaris ereticus dixit . primum quasi deitas pro anima fuisset in carne christi; postea cum per euangelicam auctoritatem fuit conuictus . dixit . habuit quidem animam qui uiuificauit corpus sed non rationalem·; E contrario dicit qui catholice sentit . ex anima rationale et humana carne subsistit . id est plenus homo atque perfectus·; Equalis patri secundum diuinitatem . minor patri secundum humanitatem . id est . secundum formam serui quam adsumere dignatus est; Qui certe deus sit et homo . non duo tamen sed unus est christus . id est . duae substantiae in christo . deitas et humanitas; non duae personae sed una; Vnus autem non conuersione diuinitatis in carne . sed adsumptione humanitatis in deo; Id est non quod diuinitas quae inmutabilis et inconuertibilis est caro sed ideo unus . eo quod humanitatem adsumpsit. Incipit esse quod non erat et non amisit quod erat; Incipit esse quod antea non fuerat . non amisit deitatem quae inmutabilis in aeternum permansit·; Vnus omnino non confusione substantiae sed unitate personae; Id est diuinitas inmutabilis cum homine quem adsumere dignatus est; Sicut scriptum est; Verbum tuum domine . in aeternum permanet; Id est diuinitas cum humanitate ut diximus duas substantias unam esse in christo; Ut sicut ante adsumptionem carnis . aeterna fuit trinitas . ita post adsumptionem humanae naturae uera permaneat trinitas ne propter adsumptionem humani carnis dicatur esse quaternitas . quod absit·; [a fidelium cordibus uel

Alcuin, *ut supra*, p. 47. F. agrees with O. except that he reads *et virgo ante partum.*)

97. *After* nunc sumus, M. *inserts* (out of Isidore) secula enim generationibus constant et inde secula quod sequantur. abeuntibus enim aliis aliæ succedunt: and *omits* deus et homo (line 97) *to* virginis matris filius, line 102. The text in O. is corrupt. F. gives it better, and gives support to some of Waterland's conjectures. For Iesus in line 97 it reads Deus; then in lines 100, 101, idem Dei Filius: it omits jam; has ut deitas, and omits et before Dei Patris. Thus we have for lines 100, &c. Et hominem quem adsumsit idem est dei filius sicut jam supra diximus, ut deitas et humanitas in Christo Dei Patris pariter et virginis filius sit.

l. 103. After perfectus homo M. *inserts* id est verus deus et verus homo *and it reads* Apollinaris.

l. 105. M. fuisset. 106, 107, et e contrario iste dicit *and* subsistens.

l. 110. formam servi comes of course from Augustine, possibly through Alcuin. M. qui licet deus sit et homo...

l. 112. M. sed una Persona.

l. 113. M. exhibits the modern readings carnem and deum.

l. 114. M. non quod divinitas quæ incommutabilis est, sit conversa in carnem, sed...

l. 115, 116. These words occur in the Creed of Damasus, Hahn, 186, 189. (The first clause, incipit esse... would almost seem to be a portion of the document expounded: see above, p. 274.)

l. 116, 117. F. permanet. M. in-incommutabilis permanet, *and* incommutabilis in 118.

l. 117, 118. F. *omits* unus omnino—personae, which seem to have been misplaced in O. and M.

l. 119. M. dignata.

l. 123. F. post adsumptionem carnis humanæ. (Dr Haywood made a mistake here.)

l. 124. The fear of St Augustine, III. 2283. [The words in brackets have

sensibus dici aut cogitare.] Nisi ita ut supradictum est et unitas in trinitate et trinitas in unitate ueneranda sit ·; Nam sicut anima rationalis et caro unus est homo . ita deus et homo unus est christus ·; Et si deus dei filius nostram luteam et mortalem carnem nostri redemptionis conditionis adsumpsit . sé nullatenus inquinauit . neque naturam deitatis mutauit ·; Quia si sol aut ignis aliquid in mundum tetigerit . quod tangit purgat . et se nullatenus coinquinat ·; Ita deitas sarcinamque nostrae humanitatis adsumpsit . sé nequaquam coinquinauit; Sed nostram naturam carnis quam adsumpsit purgauit . et a maculis et sordibus peccatorum . ac uitiorum expiauit ·; Sicut esaias ait; Ipse infirmitates nostras accepit. Et egrotationes portauit; Ad hoc secundum humanitatem natus est. Vt infirmitas nostra acciperet . et egrotationes portaret ·; Non quod ipse infirmitates uel egrotationes in se haberet quia salus mundi est ·; Sed ut eas a nobis abstuleret: dum suae sacre passionis gratiae . ac sacramento . Cyrographo adempto redemptionem . pariter et salutem animarum nobis condonauit ·; . Qui passus est . pro salute nostra: id est secundum id quod pati potuit: quod est secundum humanam naturam ·; Nam secundum diuinitatem: dei filius inpassibilis est; Descendit ad inferna ·; Qui protoplastum adam et patriarchas et prophetas et omnes iustos qui pro originali peccato ibidem detenebantur liberaret ·; Et de uinculis ipsius peccati absolutos: de eodem captiuitate infernali loco suo sanguine redemptos . ad supernam patriam et ad perpetuam uite gaudia reuocaret ·; Reliqui qui supra originale peccato principalia crimina comiserunt ut adserit scriptura: in penali tartaro remanserunt ·; Sicut in persona christi dictum est per prophetam . ero mors tua o mors ·; Id est morte sua christus humani generis inimicam mortem interficit et uitam dedit ·; Ero morsus tuus . infernae . partem morsit infernum pro parte eorum quos liberauit ·; Partem reliquid (*sic*) pro parte eorum qui pro principalibus criminibus in tormentis remanserunt ·; Surrexit a mortuis primogenitus mortuorum . et alibi apostulus dicit ·; Ipse primogenitus ex multis fratribus id est primus a mortuis resurrexit et multa sanctorum dormientium cum eo surrexerunt ·; Sicut

been inserted in the MS. between the lines.]

l. 125. M. cum ita.

l. 128. F. and M. *omit* deus.

l. 128, 129. M. *has* carnem nostræ conditionis adsumpsit. F. agrees with O. [*Conditio*, says Waterland, with writers of the fifth and sixth centuries, est servile onus opusve. But it was used so earlier, as by Augustine, *de Trinitate*, III. 26, Vol. VIII. 1239 D, and later, as in the Pseudo-Augustine, VI. 1740 C. The illustration which follows was a favourite one: see the same sermon, 1738 A.]

l. 129. M *has* sed tamen se nullatenus aut naturam.

l. 131. F. eo coinquinat. M. sarcinam quam ex nostra humanitate adsumpsit nequaquam coinquinavit sed nostræ naturæ carnem quam adsumpsit purgavit.

l. 137, 138. F. qui salus mundi est: *and omits* suae *before* sacrae. M. *reads* tolleret *for* abstulerit.

l. 139. M. gratiam et sacramenta.

l. 140. M. condonaret.

l. 143. *Note* ad inferna, which is also the reading of F. M. exhibits the modern text ad inferos. This passage down to remanserunt, line 153, 154, is almost verbatim in Augustine VI. 1740 (as above), which however reads ad inferna, with the Apostles' Creed, and for infernali loco, has inferni loco. M. has vinculo in line 145: reliqui vero in 147 (F. agrees with O. here, but has supra originale peccatum). The quotations, ero mors tua, morsus tuus, are adduced in the Council of Toledo, A.D. 693.

l. 156. M. multa corpora sanctorum.

in euangelica auctoritate dicit . sed ipse qui capud . est prius deinde quae membra sunt continuo ·; Postea ascendit ad caelos . sicut psalmista . ait ·; Ascendit in altum captiuam duxit captiuitatem . id est . humanam naturam quae prius fuit sub peccato uenundata et captiuata eamque redempta captiuam duxit in caelestem altitudinem ·; Et ad caelestem patriam regnum sempiternum ubi antea non fuerat . eam conlocauit in gloriam sempiternam ·; Sedet ad dexteram patris ·; Id est prosperitatem paternam et eo honore quod deus est; Inde uenturus iudicare uiuos et mortuos ·; Viuos dicit: eos quos tunc aduentus dominicus . in corpore uiuendos inuenerit ·; Et mortuos iam ante sepultos et aliter dicit ·; Uiuos iustos . et mortuos peccatores ·; Ad cuius aduentum omnes homines resurgere habent cum corporibus suis ·; Et reddituri sunt de factis propriis rationem; Et qui bona egerunt ibunt in uitam aeternam . et qui uero mala in ignem aeternum ·; Haec est fides catholica quam nisi quisque fideliter firmiterque crediderit saluus esse non poterit ·; ·; ·; ·; ·;

l. 157. M. sicut evangelica auctoritas dicit...qui membra sunt.

l. 159. M. ascendens.

l. 161. M. eandemque redemptam. (F. *reads* eaque redemptio captivam duxit.)

l. 164. M. et in eo honore, *and* venturus est (again a later reading. Below Waterland charges on the Oxford manuscript an error of his own copyist).

I am indebted to Mr George Parker of the Bodleian Library for the above most accurate copy of the manuscript.

CHAPTER XXX.

REVIEW OF EVIDENCE.

§ 1. Literary frauds of the ninth century. § 2. Earliest appearances of clauses now in the Quicunque. § 3. "The Discourse of Athanasius on the Faith which commences Quicunque vult." § 4. Whence did the quotations of Ratram and Æneas come? § 5. Guesses at Truth. § 6. Hypothesis of the Author. EXCURSUS ON THE DATE OF THE UTRECHT PSALTER.

§ 1. THE Essay or Treatise of Hincmar, which I noticed in Chapter XXVIII., seems to me to be so momentous in its bearing on the form of the Quicunque, as he knew it and as he quoted from it, that I feel compelled now to review the testimony that has been adduced from earlier writers, and ask myself the question, Is it possible that Hincmar could have been ignorant of what they knew, or must we suppose that they, or any of them, quoted erroneously?

The literary history of this ninth century is exceedingly painful to investigate: painful from the knowledge that this was the century in which the so-called Decretal Letters of the earlier popes were fabricated in the west of Gaul. Hinschius[1] considers it to be proved that that gigantic forgery, commenced as we apprehend at Mayence seventy years before, was completed between the years 847 and 853, and I learn from "Janus," the author of *The Pope and the Council*, (p. 98), that they were used largely in the year 863 or 864 by Nicolas in his controversy with Photius. They had been used with adequate boldness by the two writers Ratram of Corbey and Æneas of Paris, whose quotations of clauses 21, 22, 23 of the Quicunque and ascriptions of the words to Athanasius are found in the very same works in which they avail themselves of the forged Decretals. Waterland and others adduced their testimony as if it was that of witnesses of undoubted character. But as

[1] *Decretales Pseudo-Isidorianae et Capitula Angilrami.* Lipsiae, MDCCCLXIII. p. cci.

the name of Athanasius was used to convict the Greeks of heresy in denying the Procession of the Holy Spirit from the Father and the Son, so were the Decretal Epistles used to prove that the claim made by the Patriarch of Constantinople to be independent of the Bishop of Rome was historically untenable. Nor were these men content with quoting the Catholic Faith of Athanasius, or the little book which Athanasius wrote upon the Faith, they adduced numberless other passages from "writings of Athanasius," which are nowhere to be found, and which the editors of their works give up in despair. They are, almost all, undoubted forgeries. Efforts are made here and there to throw some part of the blame of these misquotations upon the shoulders of the copyists, of the scribes (that is) through whose hands the works have passed.—So far as the security of my position goes, these Abbots and Bishops are welcome to the benefit of the doubt—let it be so: the fact is not altered: the quotations, as such, are unworthy of confidence.

But,

Nemo repente fuit turpissimus;

and, therefore, we must believe that the boldness which instigated the production of the Decretals had been fostered by earlier successes of a similar description, and thus we are bound to revert to these earlier witnesses, and cross-examine and re-examine them in the light which we have now received from Hincmar.

§ 2. I must go back to a very early period. Calling the two members of a clause *a* and *b*, we have:

In the writings of Vincentius of Lerins, words nearly resembling the clauses 3, 4, 5, 6*a*, 30*b*, 31, 32; and without any reference to Athanasius.

In the Council of Toledo, 589, we have, similarly, clauses 4, 5, 13, 33*a*.

In the Council of Toledo, 633, we have 4, 21, 22, 23 and 33.

In the Council of Toledo, 638, we have the words of 21, 22, 23, 32*a*, 34*b*, 35*b*, 36*b*.

In the Council of Toledo, 675, we have 3*b*, 4, 10, 13, 14, 15, 16, 21, 22, 23, 32, 33, 35, 36*b*.

In the Council of Toledo, 693, we have 4, 5, 6, 13, 14, 15, 23, 25, 31.

In the Lateran Council, 643, we have clauses 3, 6*b*, and the substance of 30—34, 36, 38, 39.

The Treves manuscript had 30—36, and the substance of 38—41.

In the speech of Paulinus, 791, we have words similar to clauses 4, 5, 6, 15, 16, 22, 23, 32, 33, 38, 39, 40.

Leo the Third's Creed seems to include 14, and the substance of the latter half relating to the Incarnation.

Denebert's Profession has the words of 1, 3, 4, 5, 6, 21, 22, 23, 25, 26, 27, 28.

The Council of Arles, 813, repeats the Confession of Toledo, 633, and in it uses the language which we now find in 4, 21, 22, 23, 33.

I need not repeat the evidence that the Exposition of "Junius 25" notices 1, 3—10, 13, 15, 17, 19, 20 ?, 24, 25, 30—42.

By none of these authorities is the name of Athanasius introduced in connection with their faith. Nor is it found in the Muratorian copy, which I have printed above, pp. 318, 319.

It is clear that it was not known as a whole to Paulinus, nor to Alcuin, or Charlemagne, or Leo.

Let us now look to those who quote, or profess to quote, words from Athanasius.

The Monks of Mount Olivet, 809, say that "in the Faith of St Athanasius" it is declared that the "Holy Spirit proceeds from the Father and the Son." The words occur in one version of the Libellus Fidei, ascribed to Athanasius.

Theodulf, who begins by quoting largely from the spurious books against the Arians, is said to conclude by quoting as from Athanasius, clauses 21—28.

Sirmond's uncertain author, the Pseudo-Alcuin, quotes from "the Exposition of the Catholic Faith, which Athanasius composed," clauses 21, 22, 23.

Agobardus quotes as the words of Athanasius, clause 2.

Æneas of Paris quotes as from the "Fides Catholica of Athanasius," clauses 21, 22, 23.

Ratram of Corbey quotes as from the "Libellus de Fide Catholica, which Athanasius composed," clauses 21, 22, 23, and other things which the Quicunque does not include.

§ 3. Again: Theodulf is said to speak of the Credo and "the Catholic Faith, that is the Quicunque vult."

Hincmar speaks of "the Discourse of Athanasius, the beginning of which is Quicunque vult."

Adalbert uses the same language: "the Discourse of Athanasius, which thus begins, Quicunque vult."

So does Riculf of Soissons.

Regino of Prum suggests that enquiries should be made "Whether the clergy know the Discourse of Athanasius on the Faith of the Trinity, which begins Quicunque vult."

And as late as the middle of the tenth century we find that Ratherius of Verona, in speaking of the Creeds, refers to "that Faith of St Athanasius which begins Quicunque vult."

I had long been under the conviction that these multiplied references to "A Sermon or Discourse of Athanasius, commencing Quicunque vult," indicated the existence of another then well-known discourse, attributed to the same writer, on the same subject, but commencing of course with different words. And when I found that the same Ratram of Corbey, who quotes clauses 21, 22, 23 out of the "libellus de fide quem edidit [Athanasius] et omnibus catholicis tenendum proposuit," quoted also the same Athanasius as saying, "in libello Fidei," "Pater verus genuit Filium verum, lumen de lumine, verum de vero, perfectum de perfecto, totum a toto, plenum a pleno, non creatum sed genitum, non ex nihilo sed a Patre, unius substantiæ cum Patre; et Spiritum Sanctum verum Deum non ingenitum neque genitum, non creatum nec factum, sed Patris et Filii, semper in Patre et Filio,"—I could not but endeavour to discover what this "libellus de fide quem edidit Athanasius" was[1]. There is nothing in the edition of Athanasius' works published by Migne, which answers to the title: and I must thank Mr Ffoulkes—to whom I am indebted for so many other things—for exhibiting this document to me in an accessible form. It turns out to be the same document as that which Hincmar quotes as the "Symbolum Athanasii:" and, in the Arundel Manuscript, 241, whence I transcribed it, not knowing that it was the same as had been printed by Mr Ffoulkes, it is entitled, as I have said, "Libellus Fidei Patris et Filii et Spiritus

[1] I ought to have remembered that Usher would have solved my difficulty.

Sancti Athanasii episcopi." And Ratram's quotation may be found in this Creed. I have printed it above, p. 273.

The Libellus does not contain the clauses 21, 22, 23, as Ratram quotes them.

§ 4. I now go back to the earlier quotations: and having convicted Ratram of adducing from this well-known "libellus Athanasii de fide," clauses which it did not contain, I enquire, Whence did these clauses come? I cannot suppose that the French divines of the ninth century were more careful than English divines of the nineteenth: and having before me a curious instance of want of care in the last Oxford edition of Waterland's Essay, I am at liberty to suppose that the quotations from Athanasius of our clauses 21, 22, 23 by Theodulf, and Sirmond's anonymous writer, and Æneas of Paris, and Ratram of Corbey, may very possibly have been merely three repetitions of one original blunder, whether it was a wilful error or an involuntary mistake. They copied one from another. The words of these clauses were well-known words: we have seen them, as I have said, verbatim, in the Councils of Toledo of the years 638 and 675. We have them practically in the speech of Paulinus in 791: verbally in the Profession of Denebert in 795: and practically in the Council of Arles of 813. May not the production by Theodulf of these thrice told words as Athanasius' have been a mistake? or must we condemn him of wilful fabrication? or must we accept the only other alternative which, I think, remains open to us—the alternative, namely, that the Quicunque, which was gradually growing into form (as we learn from the Confession of Denebert) at the very end of the eighth century, without being then attributed to any great Father of the Church, was augmented slowly in the early part of the ninth century, and in the course of its growth was by a *forte peccatum*, a *splendidum mendacium*, assigned to Athanasius?

§ 5. But whatever our theory may be, whatever our explanation, the fact remains: that no one before Theodulf quotes any words of the Quicunque as words of Athanasius; that during the next sixty years the quotations adduced are confined to clause 2 in addition to the nine which we find in Theodulf: and that Hincmar writing after the death of Godeschalk, that is, in or after the year 868, quotes as from "the Catholic Faith, published by Athanasius," only clauses 3, 4, 5, 6. He quotes 16 again and again, but as the dictum of St Augustine or of Sophronius, not of Athanasius. We find him, at the close, placing before Godeschalk clauses 3, 4, 5, 6, 25, 26, 27: and Godeschalk refusing to accept them. This being so, is it credible that these words had been recited as a part of "the Catholic Faith," in the services of the Church at Basil from the year 820? had been ordered to be delivered to all by the Council of Frankfort, from the year 794? or from the time of Boniface in 760? or by St Leodgar in 670? or can we believe that this Document had received, even in the year 850, the authority which Waterland assigns to it,—when we find that Godeschalk, who refused to subscribe it, was defended at the time by his Benedictine brethren[1]?

§ 6. The whole evidence seems to shew that the Quicunque was completed in the province of Rheims between the years 860 and 870; and that, when completed, it steadily and gradually gained favour. It was attributed at once to the great Patriarch of Alexandria. And, not merely did it eclipse the numerous Creeds and Rules of Faith, which had been previously assigned to him, but by its intrinsic merits, by its antithetical swing, and by its fitness for chanting, it drove out all the verbose and laborious compilations of Paulinus and Charlemagne and the Councils.

I am, of course, alive to the difficulty placed in the way of my hypothesis by the fact that the Quicunque is found, ascribed to Athanasius, in some of the systematic Collections of Canons which I have described on pages 267 and 268. But in each of the three manuscripts, Vat. Pal. 574, Lat. Paris. 1451 and 3848 B, it is curiously out of harmony with its position. In the first it follows on a series of Canons and Ecclesiastical Rules with which it has no apparent relation. In the second it comes after the chronological note I adduced in my last chapter (p. 434), and before the Creed of Augustine, in a preface to a large series of Canons of nearly 30 French and other councils. In the third (of which an account is given in the *Sitzungsberichte*, LIV. p. 241[2]), the Quicunque follows on some excerpta from the first action of the Council

[1] Mosheim's *History*, Vol. I. p. 567. (Book III. century IX. part II. and III. § 25.)

[2] With this my few lines on page 268 must be supplemented.

of Chalcedon and precedes the Herovallian Collection. These manuscripts are all put down to the beginning of the ninth century, and in them all, as I have said, the Quicunque is described as the "Faith of Athanasius." Their dates are assigned to the manuscripts by Professor Rifferscheid or Professor Maassen. I am aware that I shall be considered presumptuous in questioning the opinion of either of these gentlemen, but in the present state of palæographical science, I can scarcely regard that opinion as of sufficient weight to overbalance the evidence supplied by the silence of Alcuin and Charlemagne and the language of Hincmar. In a few years time it is to be hoped that the labours of our PALÆOGRAPHICAL SOCIETY will give its members materials to form their judgment on a surer basis; and, until that time comes, I venture to ask my readers to suspend the formation of their opinion.

EXCURSUS ON THE UTRECHT PSALTER.

I have assumed in these later pages that the Utrecht Psalter, Claudius C. VII. of Sir Robert Cotton's Library, is of the ninth or tenth century. I have watched with extreme care the progress of the controversy on the subject, and am old enough and (I hope) true enough to see that, in a purely scientific and historical question, it is as foolish as it is wrong to attempt to force public opinion, or in any way to misrepresent the evidence on this or any other subject.

As Englishmen we owe to Professor Westwood the rediscovery of the manuscript; and any one, who has watched the progress of the opinion of that gentleman on the date of the volume, is aware how very slowly and cautiously that opinion has been formed. And I believe there is no one in England who is deemed more worthy of confidence in this, his special subject, than Professor Westwood. I have had also the opportunity of seeing how cautiously other gentlemen have acted in the matter, and how prepossessions in favour of assigning an early date to the volume have given way before the results of a prolonged examination.

On the finer points of palæographical science it would be presumptuous in me to speak. Thanks to the kind forbearance and patience of friends at the British Museum and elsewhere, I have learnt my ignorance in this science. But I may draw out from the Reports, which were published by Messrs Williams and Norgate at the beginning of the year 1874, notes on some of the more salient matters of which palæographers alone are judges.

Thus Mr Bond (pages 1—5) remarks *inter alia* That the vellum is leathery and wants the fine surface of a very ancient manuscript;

That, although the words generally are run together, there are breaks to mark the alternations and terminations of the verses;

That abbreviations are of frequent occurrence, not only of the names of the Deity, but of ordinary words, as *qnm* for *quoniam: nr* for *noster: tra* for *terra*[1]: *t'* for *tur: rnt* for *runt*, &c.

Mr Bond draws attention to the marks of contraction.

He speaks of the jagged outlines in many of the figures as being of the style common to English drawings of the 10th and 11th centuries.

He draws attention to the illuminated initial letter at the beginning of the first Psalm[2].

And, as to the drawings, he refers to the delineation of our Saviour's form, uncovered to the waist, as being spoken of in Histories of Christian Art as an innovation of the ninth century[3].

Much of this is confirmed by the judgments of other savants, and Mr Thompson is of opinion that the MS. was probably written in the north-east of France: an opinion which, curiously enough, agrees with my hypothesis as to the origin of the Creed.

Particular attention should be paid to Professor Westwood's Report.

I cannot see that the Second Report of Sir Duffus Hardy in any important respect affects the grounds on which this judgment was formed. That gentleman unhappily committed such serious errors in his First Report that one's confidence in his judgment is shaken. For example; he spoke of the handwriting of the Utrecht Psalter having been in the ninth century "obsolete for some centuries, and perhaps unreadable." He spoke of the Gallican Psalter having been then "long superseded" by the Roman. The facts are (as I have stated above) that the Gallican Psalter was alone used in Gaul in the ninth century; and that the hand in which the Utrecht Psalter is written was used for the text of St Paul's Epistle to the Romans in a manuscript of the tenth century where the comment was in another hand[4]: and in a manuscript of the eleventh century in the Cambridge Library the *verse* of Boethius *de Consolatione* is (I believe) invariably in the Rustic letter, where the *prose* is in a different character.

I think, however, that we may look to the contents of the book as helping us to fix the date. And I cannot close my eyes to the fact that whilst they resemble closely the contents of many Psalters of the ninth century, no volume has, as yet, been adduced of an earlier date than the year 795, which resembles it in this respect. And the general accuracy of the text of the volume indicates a high state of education on the part of the penman. This would encourage us to attribute it to the school of Charles the Great or Charles le Chauve.

I feel, however, some hesitation as to the date of the titles. They evince far inferior scholarship, as the mistakes which are perceptible above (p. 362) exhibit. The title to Psalm cli. was unintelligible to a competent critic[5]. These titles may have been added at a later time—when the education of the penman was again sinking. Thus I cannot insist, as I should otherwise do, on the title to the Te Deum as proving that,

[1] Of this see an example above (p. 372) from the British Museum Bible.

[2] I have adduced some proofs of the partiality for this B in the ninth century, p. 362. See too p. 364, note 1.

[3] Mr Bond gives a very interesting note that the MS. was in the hands of the Earl of Arundel in January 1631.

[4] See a facsimile in the *Journal de l'école des chartes*.

[5] In the *Athenæum*.

when the manuscript was written, the custom of chanting it on Sundays at Mattins was extended to a daily use: nor yet on the title and drawing prefixed to the Quicunque as shewing that the one was penned and the other limned after it was found convenient to ascribe the Faith to the Council of Nicæa.

But there remains enough in the text of the volume to satisfy me that that text could not have been written before the year 800. Our knowledge of the usage of the Church in regard to the Canticles; the comparison of this part with the older Psalters and especially with the original portion of Vespasian A. 1; the completed Apostles' Creed in a book of devotion; the relegation of Psalm 151 to the end of the volume in a Gallican Psalter; all combine to remove from my mind every shadow of doubt on the subject.

And, lastly, the TE DEUM itself is of a type of which we have no instance as early as the sixth century. This opens out an interesting subject.

The essay on the hymn in Daniel's *Thesaurus Hymnologicus* is instructive but incomplete. The hymn (Daniel says) was undoubtedly in use in the sixth century as is proved by the Rule of St Benedict, but he gives no text for it earlier than that contained in the Vienna Psalter (1861), which is supposed to have been sent by Charles to Hadrian. A text is given by Alcuin (Migne, CI. p. 597), but the MSS. have been tampered with. It was chanted at the Coronation of Charles the Bald; indeed some people think it was chanted at the Restoration of Pope Pius III. in the end of the eighth century. Daniel gives collations from some Vatican MSS., and Mr Procter gives, from an article by Dr Todd, an account of the readings of the Bangor Antiphonary and Usher's Irish hymn-book. (This last has been since reprinted, as I have mentioned, by the Irish Archæological and Celtic Society.) It will be remembered that in the Rule of Cæsarius[1] the order to say it runs thus: "Dicite matutinos, directaneo: Exaltabo Te Deus meus et Rex meus: deinde Confitemini: inde Cantemus domino: Lauda anima mea dominum: Benedictionem; Laudate dominum de cœlis; Te Deum laudamus, Gloria in excelsis Deo: et capitellum." It will be seen that the Te Deum is preceded by Laudate dominum de cœlis. Compare the prelude in the Bangor Antiphonary and Usher's hymn-book[2], and, as I understand, in that other Irish hymn-book which contains the Quicunque (above, p. 331).

I need scarcely trouble my reader with all the *variæ lectiones:* but I find that not only does Usher's hymn-book, but also the Cod. Vat. 82, read *proclamant dicentes, Sanctus,* &c. Bangor and Usher have *universa terra,* and *honore gloriæ tuæ.*

Passing for the moment to the end of the hymn, I have to note that the MS. Vat. 82 after *munerari* proceeds with our clauses 24, 25, 22, 23 (*Per singulos dies...Et laudamus...Salvum fac...Et rege illos*) omitting 26, 27, 28, 29 (the last four), but adding at the end, "Benedictus es Domine Deus Patrum nostrorum et laudabilis et gloriosus in sæcula[3].

[1] This may be seen in Sir W. Palmer's *Antiquities*, p. 227.

[2] Laudate pueri dominum, laudate nomen Domini. Te Deum, &c.

[3] Cf. Daniel, III. 52 (Vulg.).

Amen." The Codex Alex. 11 (of the Vatican) has "tuum verum et unigenitum filium" with the Bangor Antiphonary and Usher's hymn-book: after clause 21 (*munerari*) it has our clauses 22, 23, 26, 27, *i.e.* it omits 24, 25 and 28, 29. Whilst the Bangor Antiphonary and Usher's hymn-book omit 26, 27, 29, reading 22, 23, 24, 25, 28[1].

Thus, once more we come to this. The reading of the Te Deum was settled (generally) when the Utrecht Psalter was penned. The only difference from the older standard text which I have observed, is in clause 20, where it reads *Te ergo sancte quæsumus;* but even here it agrees with Galba A. XVIII.

But we have this additional fact. The Bangor Antiphonary and the Irish hymn-book give undoubtedly the true reading of clause 16,

TVADLIBERANDVMMVNDVMSVSCEPISTIHOMINEM
NONHORRVISTIVIRGINISVTERVM

"For the purpose of delivering the world thou didst assume man:
Thou didst not shrink from the womb of a Virgin."

The eye of some early copyist passed from the one NDVM to the other, and thus the difficulty that is continually felt in the translation of the clause arose; the word *mundum* being omitted. Then in the eleventh century Abbo of Fleury obtained influence enough to alter *suscepisti* to *suscepturus.* The Utrecht Psalter was written after the mistake of omitting *mundum* was perpetrated, but before the clumsy endeavour was made to conceal the difficulty.

My readers must judge whether it is probable that the former mistake was current on the Continent in the sixth century, and yet did not find its way into the Irish and Bobio manuscripts for two or three centuries later.

I am indebted to Dr Lightfoot for the suggestion as to the origin of this difficult reading.

1 In the hymn-book it is followed by an appeal to the Trinity which may be seen in Procter, *On the Prayer-Book.*

CHAPTER XXXI.

EXPOSITIONS OF THE QUICUNQUE.

Introduction. §§ 1, 2. Vienna 701. § 3. Regius 2 B. v. § 4. St Bernard of Clairvaux. § 5. Three in "Milan M. 79." § 6. Munich 17181. § 7. Bruno. § 8. Munich 12715. § 9. Notes from St Gall 27. § 10. Treves manuscripts. § 11. Bodleian 1205. § 12. Cambridge Kk. iv. 4. § 13. Turin. § 14. Rom. Vat. Alex. 231. § 15. Abelard. § 16. Hildegarde. § 17. Simon of Tournay. § 18. Alexander Neckham. § 19. Alexander Hales. § 20. Hampole. § 21. Wickliff. § 22. Comparison with Expositions of the Apostles' Creed.

It will be remembered that among the Capitulars of Hincmar was one which directed that the Presbyters should be able to explain in common language "The Sermon of Athanasius on the Faith which commences Quicunque vult." This no doubt meant that they must be able to transfer it to the vulgar tongue. And this will introduce us to the version of which I shall give an account in chapter XXXIII. But I may take now the opportunity of drawing attention to some of the Expositions of the Quicunque which have fallen in my way. At first, I intended to print some of these Expositions, so that my readers might have the opportunity of comparing them with "Junius" or "Fortunatus." I find, however, that they are too numerous to permit me to do so, without still further increasing the bulk of my already bulky volume. I shall content myself with indicating where some of these may be found; occasionally, however, adding some notes at greater length.

§ 1. And this I shall do at once. For in the Vienna manuscript, 701, which is said to be of the twelfth century, are several things which seem to me of great interest.

Thus we have, fol. 73, the Scrutiny on Easter Eve as to the faith of the penitent, before he was received to communion on Easter Day, which I have given on an earlier page[1]. On folio 145 a we have a kind of prolonged catechism, which I give in my note[2].

§ 2. After this follows in the manuscript (f. 145), *Expositio Sancti Athanasii Alexandrini episcopi de fide Catholica.* It begins *Quicunque vult* and ends *fidem.*

Is this a fragment? or does it profess to be an Exposition by Athanasius of that which we call his Creed? However, the next is clear. It is a catechetical Exposition of the Quicunque, of which Athanasius is said to be the author[3]!

This volume belonged to an oratory which was consecrated in the year MLXXII. by Ernfried, Bishop of Aldinburg (a bishopric in Sclavonia, in the province of Magdeburg), with the consent of Sigfried, Archbishop of Mayence[4]. At the end of the volume is a letter, giving an account of the proceedings of some of the Crusaders at Jerusalem. This, probably, has been printed.

[1] Above, note, pp. 22, 23.

[2] "Quomodo credis? Credo in Deum Patrem omnipotentem ingenitum ante omnia subsistentem et nullum finem habentem. Item; Quomodo credis in Filium? Credo in Filium genitum a Patre, per quem omnia facta sunt æqualem Patri in deitate. Item; Quomodo credis in Spiritum Sanctum? Credo in S. S. non genitum neque ingenitum, non creatum neque factum sed de Patre et Filio procedentem, coæqualem, cuncta vivificantem. In hac Trinitate unum Deum credo atque confiteor in tribus Personis. Item credis resurrectionem? Credo. Quomodo? Credo postquam morior quod resurgam in perfecta ætate in qua ipse Christus resurrexit et ascendit ad Patrem et inde venturus est judicare vivos et mortuos, et reddere unicuique juxta opera sua. Qualiter in Trinitate credendum est? Credendae sunt Tres Personae, Pater Filius et Spiritus Sanctus: et in his tribus Personis unus Deus, una potestas, una majestas colenda est. Interest aliqua differentia in his personis? Alia est enim Persona Patris, alia Filii, alia Spiritus Sancti. Item; Est adhuc in His differentia? Sine dubio enim quia Pater ingenitus est et non suscepit carnem: Filius est genitus et suscepit carnem de incorrupta virgine matre Maria. Spiritus Sanctus nec est ingenitus nec genitus, nec suscepit carnem, sed procedens a Patre et Filio. Tamen Filius Dei nec posterior nec minor Patre, in quantum Deus est. Similiter Spiritus Sanctus nec posterior Patre et Filio, nec minor nec humilior, sed in his tribus Personis, una deitas, æqualis potestas, una coæternitas certissime credenda est. Spiritus Sanctus a Patre et Filio, non factus nec creatus nec genitus sed procedens ex Patre et Filio, quia constat una natura, una divinitas, una majestas, una gloria, et potestas. Semper fuit Pater, semper Filius, semper Spiritus Sanctus."

This catechism is certainly interesting.

[3] "Ejusdem unde supra.
Fides est credulitas illarum rerum quæ non videntur. Quæ sunt illæ res quæ non videntur? Non videtur Pater, non videtur Filius, non videtur Spiritus Sanctus, tamen creduntur."

On clause two the comment is:

"Quam, id est, fidem nisi quisque, et unusquisque, integram, sanam, perfectam, inviolatamque, id est, incorruptam, servaverit, custodierit, absque dubio, sine dubio in eternum peribit, eterna pœna cruciabitur, condemnabitur."

This will give us the opinions of the age. *Inmensus* is explained as *quod non potest mensurari. Fideliter* (clause 29) *id est, absque omni dubietate.*

The conclusion is

"Hæc est fides catholica, et ut eam arctius in cordibus fidelium inculcaret sæpe repetit dicens: Hæc est Fides Catholica &c. &c. salvus esse non poterit."

[4] Magdeburg had belonged to Mayence.

§ 3. There are some notes on the Quicunque in Reg. 2 B. v. of the British Museum[1].

§ 4. There are short Expositions of the Apostles' and Athanasian Creeds in the works of St Bernard of Clairvaux. I found copies of these in a manuscript "777" at Vienna, of the thirteenth century. It is interesting, because the latter is entitled "Tractatus eiusdem de fide ex symbolo Athanasii," an instance of the application of the word *symbolum* to our document about the year 1200. It is very short[2].

§ 5. There are three Expositions of the Quicunque (as will be remembered) in the Milan manuscript, M. 79. I have given the leading features of them above, p. 424.

§ 6. In the Munich manuscript, 17181, of the twelfth cen-

[1] For example:
salvus] coram deo in judicio.
catholica] quæ in universa ecclesia teneri debet.
opus est] operationem necessariam præbeat voluntatem (?)
inviolatamque] hoc est incorruptam ut nihil minuas, nihil addas.
hæc est] quid hoc? nisi ut unum deum credamus in tribus personis.
in trinitate] ut credamus trinitatem et unitatem in uno esse.
neque confundantes (sic)] ut Sabellius qui ipsum docet esse Patrem in persona quem et Filium; ipsum et Spiritum Sanctum.
persona patris] ex his tribus unus quisque per se sonat.
divinitas] nullus major, nullus minor. Secundum illorum divinitatem æquales sunt.
pater] dominus (?) increati quia nunquam fuerunt creati.

[2] I extract the following: "*ante omnia*, ante spem charitatem vel cetera bona quibus ad vitam eternam pervenitur. *Opus est ut teneat quisque* non solum habeat sed et habitam custodiat, tamquam bonorum omnium fundamentum et originem... *Immensus* non mole sed potestate, omnia concludens; alias immensus, id est, incomprehensibilis."

The order of the words in Bernard's day was: "unitas in trinitate et trinitas in unitate."

On clause 28, "*sentiat* id est credat, [ad] salutem, subaudi, consequendam, *ut credamus et confiteamur*, juxta illud 'corde creditur ad justitiam et cet.'"

The subjects of the resurrection and the judgment occupy 38 lines out of 87, nearly half. The treatise ends thus:—"et attende nihil hic de parvulis quia nihil hinc meriti dictum videtur quamvis eos quoque non minus quam adultos salvari constet aut damnari: tam hæc scriptura quam ceteræ non nisi adultis et qui capaces sunt rationis ad eruditionem fiunt; ita satis visum est hoc loco de his tamen instrui quæ ad ipsos pertinent." Hence it would appear that we must rank St Bernard amongst those who would teach that "from about the tenth century, the prescribed use of the Creed became restricted to the Clergy, and for them it was enough to recite it at Prime in the office *de die dominica*. The reason of this seems to be, that while the clergy were bound by their office to as accurate and theological knowledge as possible of the mysteries expressed in it, and while it was itself admirably adapted not only to keep alive that knowledge, but also to hold its place as a profession of faith and an anthem of devotion for those who could appreciate it, *the Church does not desire to enforce on all alike*, and in the language of anathema, the profession of explicit truths expressed in subtle antitheses, and supposing the knowledge of difficult theological distinctions above the intellectual level of the uneducated." (*The Creed of St Athanasius; Charlemagne and Mr Ffoulkes.* By the Rev. J. Jones, S. J. Professor of Theology at St Beuno's College. London, Burns and Oates, 1872.)

tury (from the Convent of Scheftlarn on the Isere), we find a curious collection of things. After a copy of the treatise "De Fide Sancte Trinitatis edita a beato Augustino epo:" *Firmissime tene*, &c., there is (p. 92) an exposition of the Quicunque[1].

§ 7. Then comes the Quicunque with the Exposition printed by Montfaucon with the following introduction: "Admonitio. Hic Symboli *Quicunque* commentarius prodit ex codice bibliotheca Sancti Germani a Pratis numero 199, quingentorum circiter annorum, non indignus qui studioso lectori exhibeatur." It is attributed to Bruno of Wurtzburg.

Incipit Tractatus de Fide Catholica. I need not print this as it may be seen in Migne[2].

I feel very much disposed to ask, Whether this Exposition can be truly attributed to Bruno or any one else in particular? Its origin seems to me to be indicated by its appearance in the magnificent Eadwin Psalter at Trinity College, Cambridge. The Exposition seems to be formed out of a series of marginal notes, these notes admitting, of course, of additions from time to time[3]. The

[1] After reciting the first clause it proceeds, "quicunque dicitur, quia non est Deus personarum acceptor. Omnes enim vult salvare qui salvari merentur. Vult, dicit, propter liberum arbitrium: proponit quod salvari non possumus nisi domini misericordia nos præveniat et subsequatur. Catholicam, id est, generalis vel universalis, quia hanc tenet ecclesiam (? ecclesia) toto orbe diffusa. Ecclesia vero convocatio interpretatur, sicut synagoge congregatio. Quam nisi...peribit. Ad hanc terribilem vocem sollicite Christiani maxime sacerdotes evigilent, ut discant qualiter quæ in hac fide continentur, credere audent (? debent)."

Thus the Faith of the document is represented to commence with clause 3. The above occupies about a twentieth part of the whole comment.

It concludes with this invocation: "O beata et gloriosa et benedicta et amplectanda fides! quæ sola humanum genus vivificasti, quæ sola de diabolo triumphum reportas, quæ sola desperatis salvationis januam reseras...O beata Trinitas; O beata et benedicta et gloriosa Fides. O Pater et Filius et Spiritus Sanctus. O vera summa sempiterna unitas, Pater et Filius et Spiritus Sanctus miserere nobis Domine Deus: da pacem et gloriam, quia in te confidimus, ut salvi fiamus, perpetuam misericordiam. Tibi laus, Tibi gloria, Tibi gratiarum actio, in sempiterna secula. O beata et speciosa Trinitas, Te adoramus, Te glorificamus, cuncti unum Deum Patrem omnipotentem et Filium et Spiritum Sanctum."

[2] Waterland gives a long and interesting account of nine manuscripts containing the comment, in addition to this one at St Germains des Près, in which Montfaucon found his copy. In a letter to the *Guardian* newspaper, May 15, 1872, Mr Machray of the Bodleian Library expressed his belief that that collection (B.N. Rawlin. 163) possesses the manuscript which once belonged to the Library at Wurzburg, and of which Waterland gave an interesting description from Cochlæus. The readings of the Oxford manuscript are old: they have the *et* in five of the early clauses, and *carne* and *deo* in 35. Dr Waterland noticed that three of the manuscripts omitted some paragraphs which the printed copies of the Exposition contained, and that these paragraphs might be found in "Fortunatus."

[3] Thus the copy in the Eadwin Psalter inserts "non dicit velis aut non salvus eris sed quicunque vult."

series as contained in the St Germains Manuscript and printed by Montfaucon must have been made quite independently of "Fortunatus." A further and enlarged copy is mentioned by Waterland (chap. III.), under the year 1340.

I must add in passing that the author of these notes was clearly of the opinion that the "Fides Catholica" of the Quicunque was for the use of the clergy only. On clause 26 (= 28), he says, "Here he begs and admonishes that every teacher should hold it in his memory, and believe it firmly, and in his preaching teach it to others." And on the last clause, "Here he begs and advises that every priest should know this and preach it."

§ 8. In the Munich manuscript, "12715, Latin," written in the years 1229, 1230, is another Exposition of the Quicunque. It begins as follows:

"De Symbolo Athanasii. Quicunque vult salvus esse. Fides est voluntaria certitudo...Fides est qualitas qua quis credit quod diligit." I remarked the following, "In hoc loco ista fides intelligitur quæ in sacro baptismate promittitur quum dicitur, Abrenuntiat diabolo et operibus ejus:" *i. e.* the expositor states that the Catholic Faith, which, according to the first clause, is essential to salvation, is the Faith of the short Baptismal Creed.

The order here was still "Trinitas in Unitate et Unitas in Trinitate[1]."

This manuscript belonged to the Library of Kannshofer, and was written by one "Christianus Perger de Enkerfeld."

§ 9. I can scarcely call the few remarks at the margin of the Faith in "St Gall 27" an Exposition, but I will give some in my note[2].

[1] This is the conclusion:

"Hæc est fides catholica: et sæpe repetit ut eam artius in cordibus fidelium inculcaret absque ruga: firmiterque crediderit, salvus esse non poterit. Augustinus: Credo in patrem omnipotentem ingenitum." That is, the exposition concludes with the *positive* part of the interrogative Creed given above (in my note to § 1) from the manuscript 701 at Vienna (down to the words "una majestas colenda est," which are here read "una gloria certissime credenda est"), and the writer attributes the Creed to St Augustine. The words introducing this Creed are the same as those with which the explanation terminates, which I have given in note 3 to section 2.

[2] I copied these words: "non est mensurabilis in sua natura quia inlocalis est et incircumscriptus ubique totus, ubique præsens, ubique potens," because I thought I remembered them in the comment of "Junius 25." I found myself correct: so were other brief memoranda on *æternus* (clause 10), on *omnipotens* (clause 12) and on *deus ex substantia patris* (clause 31), and there may have been others. On clause 2 however were words which I knew were not in that Exposition, "qui catholicam fidem recte

§ 10. I have a memorandum that the collection at Treves, No. 222, of the thirteenth century, contains Expositions of the Apostles' and Athanasian Creeds: and No. 531, of the fourteenth century, contains six Expositions. They are not distinguished. I have not seen them; and they may possibly be the same as others to which I have referred.

§ 11. Amongst the notices of ancient Latin manuscripts in the fourth chapter of Waterland's work, and under the year 1400, is the following: "In the Bodleian at Oxford there is a manuscript copy of this Creed (No. 1204), which has for its title, *Anastasii Expositio Symboli Apostolorum.* It is above 300 years old, and belonged once to the Carthusian monks of Mentz." This statement is repeated in the recent Oxford Edition, except that the number of the manuscript is corrected. For it is 1205, not 1204. I received some years ago from a member of my own University, now gone to his rest, the results of an enquiry which he had submitted to the learned librarian, the Reverend H. O. Coxe, and these taught me that Waterland here was almost entirely wrong.

The present mark is Laud 493: we have, on folio 2, the words "Liber carthusianus prope moguntiam;" and in the table of contents of the volume is found the title *Anastasii expositio symboli apost.* Thus the volume is identified. The contractions are very numerous, and the language seems to have been occasionally altered for the purpose of rendering the work more suitable to be read aloud. On folio 70 I found "Expositio symboli apostolorum." On folio 74 b I detected "sy. scr. prm" *i. e.* "symbolum sanctorum patrum." This is the so called Nicene Creed with an Exposition, in which I detected a reference to the "sym*bolum* Athanasii[1]." Then follows on fol. 75 b "H*ic* t*ractatus* de sy*mbolo* s*ancti* anastasii." It begins (so far as I can make it out) "restat expositio symboli sancti anastasii," and occupies three closely written folia, *i. e.* six pages. It differs from any other exposition that I have seen, and some one has run his pen, dipped in red ink, through *spiritus sanctus* in many places. It ends on folio 78 b "explicit expositio symboli anastasii."

Mr Coxe considers that the manuscript must have been written about the year 1300; a hundred years before Waterland's date.

Thus the document is an exposition of the Athanasian Creed—not a copy of the Athanasian Creed entitled "an exposition by Anastasius of the Apostles' Creed." Waterland's mistake was curious, and it has been

credendo et opera exercendo negligit, hereticus est et schismaticus, et hunc interitus sine dubio manebit."

[1] I supply with *italics* the contractions of the manuscript.

followed by curious results[1]. It is due, as will have been seen, to the error of the writer of the table of contents.

§ 12. There is in the University Library at Cambridge a manuscript marked Kk. IV. 4, which contains a tract "De Tribus Symbolis." The manuscript is of the fifteenth century.

§ 13. I have a memorandum that in the Library at Turin (Pasini's *Catalogue*, 1749) there is not only a Psalter of the fourteenth century, containing "Fides Catholica ab Athanasio exposita cum glossa" (No. XVIII.); but also (No. LXVI.) another Psalter of the thirteenth century, containing the Faith, "Declaratio Fidei Catholicæ," with a gloss and marginal notes. The latter begin:

"Hic ratio Fidei Catholicæ traditur et in veteribus codicibus a beato Anastasio Alexandrino conscripta; et puto quod idcirco tam pleno et brevi sermone tradita fuit ut omnibus catholicis et minus eruditis tutamen defensionis præstaret, &c.[2]."

§ 14. I am indebted to the Reverend J. C. B. Riddell for notes of explanations of the Lord's Prayer, Apostles' Creed and Quicunque, which were printed in the Appendix to a work on the "Liturgia Antiqua Hispanica, Gothica, Isidoriana, Mozarabica, Toletana, Mixta," published at Rome in 1746 "Typis Hieronymi Mainardi."

The second volume (p. 497) contains "explanatio orationis dominicæ" commencing "Dominus et salvator noster clementissimus suorum eruditor, &c." Then (p. 501), "Incipit explanatio Symboli Apostolici: Quando beatum legimus Paulum apostolum dixisse fidelibus, Vos autem estis filii lucis." Then (p. 507), "Explanatio Symboli Sancti Athanasii. Injunxistis mihi illud fidei opusculum quod passim in ecclesiis recitatur quodque a presbyteris nostris usitasius quam cetera opuscula meditatur...quasi exponendo dilatarem."

The comment (as I understand) proceeds, "Traditur enim quod a beatissimo Athanasio Alexandrinæ ecclesiæ antistite sit editum. Ita namque semper eum vidi etiam in veteribus codicibus. Et puto quod idcirco tam plano et brevi sermone tradita sit ut omnibus catholicis et minus eruditis tutamen defensionis præstaret adversus illam tempestatem quam ventus contrarius, hoc est diabolus, excitavit per Arium, qua tempestate navicula, id est Christi ecclesia, in medio mari, videlicet

[1] Even Bishop Van Mildert could not have examined it. For he gives the alternative press mark as G. 39. It should be G. 40.

[2] See below under § 14. Another manuscript in the same library (No LXVIII.) attributes it to Anastasius of Alexandria.

mundi, diu tota a fluctibus est vexata, sed non soluta aut submersa; quia ille imperavit vento et mari qui se eidem ecclesiæ promisit usque ad finem sæculi adfuturum. Quicunque ergo de hujus maris fluctibus salvari desiderat et in profundum abyssi æternum, videlicet perditionem, demergi pavescit, teneat integre et inviolabiliter fidei veritatem. Ita enim inceptum ipsum opusculum Quicunque... Quod dicitur in capite eorum versuum, hoc repetitur in fine: nam hoc est in æternum perire quod salvum non esse, et hoc est salvum esse quod non perire, &c., &c."

By comparing this with the extract given by Waterland in his note to what is called Hampole's commentary (Chapter III. A.D. 1340), any one may learn how these commentaries gradually expanded. Hampole had incorporated "Bruno's Exposition" with some preliminary words, and to these the above seem to have been added. Our present writer however follows up this Exposition with Bruno's. For, as the same volume informs us, in the manuscript there follows—

"Expositio Athasii de fide (sic).
"Quicunque vult—hic beatus Athanasius liberum arbitrium ponit, &c." as in Bruno.

Now all these, if I understand the Roman Editor aright, are taken from the same manuscript "Reg. Alexand. Vat. no. 231," which manuscript the Editor says "seems to have been written in the ninth or tenth century." So much for supposed dates of MSS.! A manuscript which "seems to have been written in the ninth or tenth century," contains an Exposition of the Athanasian Creed which is assigned by all the learned to a Bishop of Wurtzburg who lived in the eleventh century[1].

[1] I find that the "Explanatio" published by Mai, *Scriptorum Veterum Nova Collectio*, IX. p. 396, commencing "Injunxisti mihi," was taken from the same manuscript. Mai considered it to be of the eleventh century. It is mentioned on pages 50 and 59 of Professor Jones' pamphlet. Prof. Böllig considers that the part of the manuscript containing the *Explanatio* is of the beginning of the eleventh or of the tenth century. The readings of the Quicunque as explained here are worthy of notice. They are generally *old*. Thus we have the *et* in clauses 8, 9, 13, 15, 17, although not in 7. We have in 6, *et coeterna majestas*, which is unusual. Clause 17 follows close on 15; 16 and 18 are combined thus: *et tamen non tres dii aut tres domini sed unus deus et unus dominus.* (Compare "Junius 25" above, p. 428.) In 20 it reads, *ita tres deos aut tres dominos*. For *nec creatus*, we have both in 22 and 23, *aut creatus*. For *Et* in 25, we have *Sed*. The old order is observed in 27. Clause 28 begins *Quicunque ergo vult salvus esse*. In 30 *dei filius* is omitted, but *pariter* is retained. In 33 the copula *est* is introduced twice. For *Qui* in 34, we have *Quia*. In 35, *carnem* and *deum*: 38 and 39 read thus, *Qui pro salute nostra passus est, sed in sola adsumpta substantia: descendit ad inferna, tertia die resurrexit a mortuis, ascendit ad coelos, sedet ad dexteram patris:* and the last clause of 41 *qui vero mala egerunt ibunt in ignem æternum.* Thus the version of the Creed is certainly old, to whatever date we assign the Exposition. In the Apostles' Creed as expounded in the same manuscript, not only are the words *dei omnipotentis* missing, as Professor Jones has stated, but the clause *communion of saints* is missing too: and the reading was *remissionem omnium peccatorum.*

I have sometimes thought that this may have been the Explanatio Symboli Athanasii which was attributed to Theodulf by the writer of the catalogue of the Abbots of Fleury. The title *symbolum* however shews that that catalogue can scarcely have been made before the year 1150, 360 years after the death of the illustrious bishop, and therefore the statement needs support. But the title is curious, "EXPLANATIO symboli S. Athanasii." It is possible that the writer of the Catalogue had this document in his mind.

§ 15. Waterland speaks of two other comments which must not be passed over. One he gives under the date 1120. "In the next age the famous Peter Abelard wrote comments upon this Creed, which are printed amongst his other works. The title in the print is *Petri Abaelardi Expositio Fidei in Symbolum Athanasii*. I suspect the editor has added the latter part *in Symbolum Athanasii* as a hint to the reader." It may be seen in Migne's series, vol. CLXXVIII.[1]

§ 16. "A.D. 1170. Of the same century (says Waterland) is Hildegarde, the celebrated abbess of St Rupert's Mount, near Binghen, on the Rhine. She wrote explications of St Benedict's Rule and of the Athanasian Creed." The latter may be seen in Migne, vol. CXCVII. p. 1065. It is addressed *ad congregationem sororum suarum*[2].

[1] It follows on commentaries on the Lord's Prayer and the Apostles' Creed. The former is long: on the petition "give us this day our daily bread," he remarks *i.e.* "bodily and spiritual bread: ...spiritual bread, that Thou wouldest inspire in the prelates and doctors of Thy Church that they may study to dispense to us, prudently and happily, Thy teaching committed to them." On the Apostles' Creed he refers to the canons of various local councils which insisted that the Creed should be taught to all, and that no one should receive the Holy Communion until he knew it, as well as the Lord's Prayer, by memory. Abelard was superior to the tradition of the times and quoted Eusebius of Emesa as a witness that the Church-Fathers "collected out of the different books of Scripture what was most necessary," and the Creed was the result. We know that in many of the earlier copies the punctuation was *filium eius : unicum dominum nostrum:* "His Son, our only Lord." Abelard seems to suggest that the punctuation was altered to "His only Son, our Lord," to avoid Adoptianism: he himself takes it both ways, "His only Son, our only Lord." Towards the close he refers to the famous tablets of Leo III., which in his day were "on the altar of St Paul at Rome *ad cautelam fidei orthodoxæ:*" his point being, that the Greeks did not fear to say "I believe in the Church." The exposition on the Athanasian Creed follows. It is, as Waterland says, short. It begins thus: "Quicunque vult salvus esse: voluntate quippe propria, non coactione salvamur aliena: ante omnia, subaudis, illi hoc necessarium." He touches on clauses 1, 3—10, 14—16, 25—28, 30, 37, 40, 41. (He reads: "omnes homines resurgent.") He thus ends: "Mark that nothing here appears to be said as to infants who have no merits: although it is clear that they, not less than adults, may be saved or damned. For, as this writing as well as others was made for the instruction of adults only, and of such as are capable of reason; so I have thought it sufficient in this place to instruct them on such points only as pertain to them." This is the reason why Abelard passed over in silence some clauses of the document.

[2] It begins: "O filiæ quæ vestigia Christi in amore castitatis subsecutæ sunt," but we come to col. 1069, before the Athanasian Faith is touched upon. The address is a Sermon in which the tenets of the Creed are paraphrased and enforced, rather than an Explanation or Explication of the document. It has no great merit. The first words here are the following: "Athanasius postea de unitate divinitatis ecclesiam muniendo scripsit, videlicet ut omnis homo qui voluerit salvari teneat fidem integram et inviolatam, in deum perfectum credens ne in gehennam demersus gehennalis fiat." Her belief was that our Lord descended spiritually "in profun-

None of these Expositions refers to any canon requiring the clergy to learn the Quicunque.

§ 17. Another comment, mentioned by Waterland, is by Simon of Tournay, a divine of the early part of the thirteenth century. It has never been published. It commences (as he was informed by Oudin)—

"Apud Aristotelem argumentum est ratio faciens fidem, sed apud Christum argumentum est fides faciens rationem." One MS. is in the National Library at Paris, 3903: other three are scattered.

§ 18. The Bodleian Library is said to contain two copies of another comment, by Alexander Neckham. This too is mentioned by Oudin and after him by Waterland. It commences:

"Hæc est enim victoria quæ vincit mundum, fides nostra. Signanter dicit *vult* et non dicit *quicunque salvus erit*." "He significantly says, Whosoever would be saved; and not, Whosoever shall be saved."

§ 19. A further memorandum informs us that Alexander Hales (or rather Alexander of Ales) wrote comments upon the same Creed, which are published in his SUMMA, part the third, under Question 69[1].

Alexander divides the "creed" into Procemium, Treatise, Epilogue, and calls the first two verses *Introductory*, "versiculi procemiales." Of these two "the first draws by love, the second terrifies by penalties" —a support to my opinion that the two date from different periods of Church history. In the last verse of the document he gives an explanation which in my opinion is also more true than some that I have met with. "Faithfully and firmly. Faithfully, to denote faithfulness and truthfulness (fides et rectitudo); firmly, to denote the degree of love which is annexed to faith: the soul is purified by faith; it is made firm by love."

§ 20. Another commentary attributed to Richard Hampole or "Richardus Pampolitanus," spoken of by Waterland, under the year 1340, seems to be nothing else than an accumulation of notes which we have been already considering, and is so far worthless except as shewing that even at that time it was

dum infernalis profundi." She appeals to teachers and preachers to uphold the faith.

[1] The recent Oxford edition alters 69 to 82. Van Mildert seems to have been correct and Mr King wrong. In the same direction Van Mildert's reference to Oudin "Vol. III. p. 30," is altered to "Vol. III. p. 5."

understood that the last clause of the Quicunque admonished priests—not laymen—to learn the Creed.

§ 21. Amongst others adduced by Dr Waterland comes the far most interesting comment attributed to Wickliff. Waterland saw it first in a manuscript belonging to St John's College, Cambridge.

"The volume contains an English version of the Psalms and Hymns of the Church with the Athanasian Creed, produced paragraph by paragraph in Latin, interspersed with an English version of each paragraph and commented upon quite through, part by part." The class mark of the manuscript is E. 14. In it the Quicunque follows the Nunc Dimittis, and the comment on the first clause runs thus: "It is said commonly that there ben three credes: the first is of Apostles that men knowen commonly: the tother is the crede of the Church that declareth the former crede: this thrydd crede is of the Trinity the which is sungen as a salm and was made in Greke speche of oon that is clepid Attanasie and after turnid to Lattin and some deel amendyd and ordered to be said at the first hour. This salm telleth much of the Trinity and it is no nede here to know it sith a man may be saved if that he believe in God and hope that God will teach him afterward that is needful."

The Exposition has been recently printed at length in Vol. III. of Mr Arnold's Works of Wycliff—but not from this manuscript. It seems, however, that the Exposition is invariably found after the Canticles—as in Bruno's Psalter. I will give the English version in a later chapter—a few notes, however, I will extract from Mr Arnold's reprint, begging particular attention to them.

On clause 11 the writer says truly enough, "But here may men better say in Latin the subtilty of this matter, for articles with case gender and number helpen here for to speak."

On 22, "the Son is of the one Father, not made nor made of nought but born. Here clerks must wake their wits and understand two births."

On 29. "Sed necessarium. For Christ is giaunte of two substances, of godheed and of manheed, and beginning of our belief of our health and of our blisse. For had not Christ thus been man, we should never thus have been saved. And in Christ, both God and man, is health of many kind. And it is hard to believe the Trinity, but it is more hard to many to believe two kinds in one Person: for right as in the Trinity three persons ben in one kind, so in the Incarnation two kinds ben in one person: and herefore teacheth our belief."

To the humour of the explanation of the final clause Waterland draws attention. "And al if this Crede accorde unto prestis natheless the hiȝer prelatis as popes cardinalis and bishops schulden moore specialy cunne þis crede and teche it to men under hem. amen."

§ 22. To understand fully the relative importance attached to the Quicunque and the Apostles' Creed, it might be advisable to compare with these comments the number of Expositions of the other document. But the latter are countless[1].

[1] In the Cambridge Library, Dd. XII. 69 contains short explanations of the Lord's Prayer, Creed, &c. "The parish priest is bound by the Canons to teach and preach in the mother tongue four times a year the seven petitions in the Lord's Prayer, the Salutation of the Virgin, the fourteen Articles of the Faith contained in the Creed, the Ten Commandments of the Old Testament, the seven mortal sins, the seven principal virtues, the two evangelical precepts, the seven sacraments of the Church," but not a word is said as to the Quicunque. Ff. II. 38 contains many English pieces, as the seven psalms, &c., but not an Explanation of the Athanasian Creed (this is of fifteenth century). So "the poor Caytiffe," Ff. VI. 34, of the same century. Gg. I. 1 contains in *Romance* some fifty-nine things: the Penitential psalms; Credo in Deum; Pater Noster; Ave Maria in French; and expositions in Latin, but as for the subject before us with the same result. Gg. IV. 32, of fourteenth century, contains the Quicunque in French. But of Hh. I. 12: Ii. I. 2, III. 9, III. 29, IV. 9, VI. 43: Kk. I. 3, I. 9: Mm. VI. 7, and 15: Nn. IV. 11, all contain explanations of some of the Creeds or Salutations, but none of the Quicunque. It seems to have been used at Prime and neglected.

I need scarcely go through other collections, but the Royal Library at the British Museum has an interest of its own. And I find there not only manuscripts 2 A. II., 2 A. XX., to which I have already invited attention, but also 2 B. VIII. a Psalter intended for Johanna, mother of Richard II.: 5 F. XV.: 7 A. IX.: 7 C. II.: 7 D. II.: 8 A. VI.: 8 A. IX.: 8 A. XV.: 8 B. VIII.: 8 B. XV.: 8 C. I.: 8 C. V.: 10 C. III.: 11 A. I.: 12 E. XXI.: 14 B. IX., all of which contain documents or expositions more or less connected with the subjects before us, but in none of them is the Quicunque mentioned.

CHAPTER XXXII.

GREEK VERSIONS OF THE QUICUNQUE.

§ 1. Greek Creed. § 2. Was there any Greek copy in 850? § 3. Nicolas of Otranto, 1200. § 4. Gregory IX. 1232. § 5. Questions at the time of the Reformation. Lazarus Baiff. § 6. Other copies. Felckmann's Text. § 7. Codex Regius, 2502. § 8. Venice, 575. § 9. Usher's copy. § 10. Copy in the Venetian Horology. § 11. Florence copy. § 12. Copies like this, Cephaleus, Baiff, Bryling, Stephens, Wechel. § 13. Collation of texts. EXCURSUS ON KIMMEL'S COLLECTION OF DOCUMENTS, AND ON THE GREEK HOROLOGIUM MAGNUM.

§ 1. WE must proceed now to examine into the character and date of the more important versions of the Quicunque. Of these, in point of importance though not in point of antiquity, the first which demand our attention are the Greek translations.

For Greek translations I shall venture to call them, although the course of events during the last few years has inspired one writer to ask for a hearing in favour of a Greek original. It had been considered indeed as a settled point amongst the learned men of the century which ended about 1730, that Athanasius was not the author of the Quicunque, and that it was not written in Greek. The evidence was considered to be overwhelming. But the opinions of Voss and Pearson, of Quesnel and Cudworth, of Cave and Dupin, of Tentzel and Pagi, of Antelmi and Tillemont, of Montfaucon and Muratori, of Fabricius and Natalis Alexander, of Bingham and Oudin, of Waterland and the Ballerini, have been put on one side in the hope of thus gaining the countenance of Athanasius for a document which is recited in the service of the English Church. Yet the history of the doctrine of the Incarnation shews that some clauses of the Athanasian Creed could not have been written by Athanasius: and an Exposition of the Faith of Athanasius, believed to be genuine, is so imperfect if not heretical, that it is misrepresented and mistranslated before the approval of even ordinary Englishmen can be expected in its behalf.

§ 2. Waterland brings a valuable contribution to the history of the Greek versions, although my readers will, probably, disagree with one of his assumptions, viz. "that the Greeks had heard something of this Creed from the Latins as early as the days of Ratram and Æneas Parisiensis, that is, above 850 years ago, when the dispute about the Procession between the Greeks and the Latins was on foot." The doctrine in question was in dispute between the Churches of France and of Rome at that time, and to me it seems premature to suppose that the Greek theologians were at once aware of the quotations which Ratram and Æneas adduced to prove that the followers of Charlemagne were in the right and the followers of the Pope were in the wrong. However, we shall agree with Waterland in this: the quotation "is not sufficient to prove that the Greek Church had yet any value for this Creed, or that there was then extant any Greek copy of it."

§ 3. We come down to the times of Innocent III. (who, it will be remembered, did not regard the Quicunque as a Creed), *i.e.* to the beginning of the thirteenth century, before we hear of the Creed in Greek. Leo Allatius[1], who is our great writer on the subject, informs us of the complaints which, about this time, the Greeks uttered against the Latins, charging them with habitually corrupting the text of the passages which they adduced from the fathers in order thus to uphold the doctrine of the Double Procession. Orthodoxy was then, as now, deemed of more importance than honesty. So the Greeks stated that they did not know who had inserted in the Faith of the Holy Athanasius, called "the Catholic Faith," the words, "and from the Son, *καὶ ἐκ τοῦ υἱοῦ*." This corruption was carried to such an extent that Germanus of Constantinople refused to be guided by quotations adduced from private writings of fathers which might be easily altered; he appealed from them to the documents which had been recited in public assemblies. It appears, therefore, that when the complaint was uttered, a Greek version of the Quicunque was known which

[1] Leo Allatius wrote about 1659. He quotes Nicetas Myrsiniota, Nicolaus Hydrantinus, Nicolaus Sclenzia. Bessarion accused Veccus of corrupting books, Veccus having brought about a compromise.

did not contain the clause "and from the Son." The date of this was about 1200.

§ 4. Efforts at conciliation were renewed about 1232, but were unavailing. It was in the next year that the Franciscan Envoys of Gregory IX. assured the Greeks that the Latin Quicunque was the original document, and that Athanasius had written it whilst he was an exile in the west. "The Holy Spirit proceeds from the Son immediately, from the Father through the mediation of the Son. For the Son has this from the Father, that the Holy Spirit proceeds from Him. Wherefore, whosoever does not believe[1] that the Holy Spirit proceeds from the Son is in the way of perdition. And so the holy Athanasius, when he was exiled in the western countries, said thus in the Exposition of his Faith which he put out in Latin: 'The Father is made of none......The Holy Ghost is of the Father and the Son, neither made, nor created, nor begotten, but proceeding.' And the same holy Athanasius in the Exposition written in Greek describes the Holy Spirit as *ἐκπόρευμα ὄν*:"—the words occur in the exposition I have referred to[2]. They proceed to argue that as Gregory Thaumaturgus taught that the Son is of the Father alone, but did not say so of the Holy Spirit, he must have believed the Double Procession: and they quoted on the same side Gregory of Nyssa, Ambrose, Augustine, and so on. This was in a written address, signed or subscribed by the emissaries.

The discussion which followed was interesting, and the question was well put, Had the Council of Constantinople made additions to the Nicene Creed? "*We* (say the Emissaries) again quoted Athanasius' Exposition (meaning the Quicunque): *they* said, We do not believe 'and from the Son.'" At last we come to the general answer of the Greeks: they adduced "Athanasius against the Sabellians," which is dubious, and his genuine letters to Serapion: but they did not appeal to any Greek copy of this Exposition. The inference is tolerably clear: they did not put any confidence in the genuineness of the document to which Nicolas of Otranto had referred 30 years before. Otranto is some distance from Constantinople, but the two places were in frequent intercourse: it is, of course, possible that the Theologians of the

[1] The Greek is "Whosoever believes"!

[2] Above, p. 76.

Capital had not heard of any Greek copy, although a copy may have existed in the Calabrian port.

§ 5. The enquiry, however, as to the Greek version is too interesting to be put thus on one side.

At the time of the Reformation, the Polish noble, Cazanovius, a Socinian, had written to Calvin adducing the fact that no Greek copy of the Creed was extant, as additional evidence that the Quicunque could not have been a genuine work of Athanasius. And the same fact had been brought forward by one Valentinus Gentilis, who also wrote upon the subject. And thus it was that considerable interest was excited in the minds of some by a copy of the Creed in Greek, which was given in 1533 to Lazarus Baiffius, the Embassador of Francis I. at Venice, by Dionysius, who was the Greek bishop of Zea and Thermia[1]. Of this I will treat below, § 11.

§ 6. Subsequent investigations have brought to light other manuscript copies of the Creed in Greek. Thus Felckmann[2], in his edition of the works of Athanasius, printed a copy from a manuscript—I do not know of what age—in his possession. In that manuscript it appeared without any author's name or other title. Apparently almost identical with this version are—one which is found in one of the manuscripts of the Palatine Library (the number is not given), where it is entitled *Σύμβολον τοῦ ἁγίου Ἀθανασίου*[3]: and another in the Paris Library, 2962 (now 1286). I owe to Mr A. A. Vansittart a transcript of the last. It is there entitled *τοῦ ἐν ἁγίοις πατρὸς ἡμῶν μεγάλου Ἀθανασίου ὁμολογία τῆς αὐτοῦ πίστεως*. This last manuscript contains writings by Bessarion and Mark of Ephesus, and other documents, proving that it was written later than the Council of Florence[4].

These copies commence *εἴ τις θέλει σωθῆναι* or *ὅστις θέλει σωθῆναι*. The Codex Regius connects *πάσης ἀμφιβολίας ἐκτός* with the preceding clause, "which faith except a man keep unhesitatingly whole and unde-

[1] Genebrard reads thus, "Episcopus Zienensis et Firmiensis." But Firmiensis undoubtedly stood for Thermiensis; whether as a synonym or by mistake is questioned. The two islands are adjacent, and had one bishop between them. See Le Quien.

[2] Most of these were printed by Montfaucon in the Benedictine edition of Athanasius. As to this see Migne (Greek series), XXVIII. 1573 and 1579, and Waterland.

[3] Migne, ut supra.

[4] This is printed in Migne, p. 1532, 1534.

filed." Montfaucon's copy connects it with the following. The Palatinate MS. reads ἄνευ διαταγμοῦ. In clause 3 *Personæ* is rendered τὰ πρόσωπα: in 4 we have ὑπόστασις. The *immensus* of the Latin is ἄμετρος. The καὶ is found in clauses 7, 8, 9, 10, not in 13, 15, 17. In 19 *singillatim* is rendered μοναδικῶς. In 23 they all read τὸ πν. τὸ ἅγ. ἀπὸ τοῦ πατρὸς οὐ πεποιημένον. In the Codex Regius part of clause 27 is omitted—apparently by accident. The other follow the old order τριὰς ἐν μονάδι καὶ μονὰς ἐν τριάδι. The *fideliter credat* of 29 is βεβαίαν or βεβαίως πιστεύῃ: *in sæculo* in 31 = ἐν χρόνῳ. In 35 we have distinctly εἰς σάρκα and εἰς θεότητα. It is strange that in all we have ἑνώσει ὑποστάσεων in clause 36: we have εἰς τὸν ᾅδην, τῇ τρίτῃ ἡμέρᾳ, τοῦ θεοῦ καὶ πατρὸς τοῦ παντοκράτορος. We have εἰσελεύσονται and ἀπελεύσονται in the different manuscripts in clause 41. And in the last clause πιστῶς τε καὶ βεβαίως may be noted.

It will be agreed, probably, that this version represents an early text. The titles of course are later than the translation. I do not see any objection to the supposition that it may have been known in the year 1200. These copies must have had a Greek birthplace.

§ 7. Of another version of the Creed in Greek, which commences τῷ θέλοντι σωθῆναι πρὸ πάντων ἀνάγκη τὴν καθολικὴν πίστιν κατέχειν, there seem to be three or four known manuscripts. It was published, as Montfaucon narrates, in 1569, by Genebrard, a learned divine of that century, who was afterwards archbishop of Aix in Provence, and described by him as the copy of the Church of Constantinople. He seems to have taken it from the Codex Regius, 2502, but this codex is itself only of the sixteenth century, written (it states) in the year 1562, *i.e.* only seven years before Genebrard's volume saw the light; but it professes to have been copied from an ancient Cretan exemplar. I think that an earlier copy of this will be found in the library at Florence, Plut. IV. codex 12, of the fifteenth century[1]: and Waterland refers to another, commencing in the same fashion, at Vienna. The text printed by Genebrard, and from him by Montfaucon and Gundling, is from the Codex Regius. The original of this is clearly Latin of a late type.

It is entitled "The Confession of the Catholic Faith of our Holy Father Athanasius the great, which he delivered to Julius the Pope of

[1] I owe my knowledge of this to the late Rev. A. R. Campbell, Rector of Aston, Rotherham. He kindly informed me that the Codex contained II. σὲ τὸν Θεὸν ὑμνοῦμεν (a Greek version of the Te Deum?). III. ἔκθεσις τῶν ἁγίων πατέρων περὶ παυλοῦ τοῦ Σαμωσάτας. IV. ἀθανασίου ἀρχι. Ἀλεξανδρείας ἑρμήνεια εἰς τὸ σύμβολον. V. τοῦ αὐτοῦ ἔκθεσις πίστεως.

Rome." The *et* in clause 7 is omitted: *immensus* is rendered ἄπειρος: *singillatim* is overlooked: we have μόνος υἱὸς παρὰ τοῦ μόνου πατρός; which is curious. Then τὸ πνεῦμα τὸ ἅγιον παρὰ πατρὸς καὶ υἱοῦ οὐ ποιηθὲν, οὐ κτισθὲν, οὐ γεννηθὲν, ἀλλ' ἐκπορευόμενον, words with which Montfaucon compares the expression used in the Synod of Florence, ἀθανάσιος ἐν τῇ ὁμολογίᾳ τῆς ἑαυτοῦ πίστεώς φησιν· τὸ πνεῦμα τὸ ἅγιον ἀπὸ τοῦ πατρὸς καὶ τοῦ υἱοῦ οὐ ποιητὸν, οὐ κτιστὸν ἀλλ' ἐκπορευτόν. I think the word πρόσωπον is used throughout for *Persona:* the old order "Trinity in Unity and Unity in Trinity" is maintained in clause 27: we have πιστῶς κατέχειν in clause 29: βεβαία πίστις = *recta fides* in 30: εἰς σάρκα, ὑπὸ τοῦ θεοῦ in 35: πιστῶς καὶ βεβαίως in the last clause.

We shall probably agree with Gundling that this could never have been used by the Church of Constantinople. It is not impossible that it may represent the translation offered by Gregory's messengers to the clergy of Constantinople in 1233.

§ 8. Through the kindness of Sir Thomas Duffus Hardy I have next to present an account of a copy of the Creed in Greek from a manuscript at Venice, numbered 575. The manuscript contains works of Nicetas Stethatus (?) and a letter of John Damascene to Constantine Copronymus, writings of Zonaras, Anastasius, Photius, &c. The date is fixed, by a kind of Colophon, as the month of August, 6934 = 1426. The Athanasian Creed is introduced thus:

πίστις καθολικὴ τοῦ ἁγίου Ἀθανασίου. It commences ὅστις ἂν βούλεται σωθῆναι. πρὸ πάντων χρὴ τὴν καθολικὴν πίστιν κατέχειν. Here in clause 4 *Personæ* is represented by τὰ πρόσωπα, in 5 *Persona* by χαρακτήρ. The καὶ is retained. *Immensus* is ἀκατάληπτος. We have the later order observed in 12: clauses 19, 20 are rendered thus, ὡς οὖν παρ' ἑνὸς χαρακτῆρος θεὸν καὶ κύριον ὁμολογεῖν τῇ χριστιανῇ ἀληθείᾳ παρακελεύομεν, οὔτε τρεῖς θεοὺς οὔτε τρεῖς κυριοτῆτας λέγειν τὴν καθολικὴν εὐσεβείαν διακωλύομεν. Clause 23 is τὸ πνεῦμα τὸ ἅγιον ἀπὸ τοῦ πατρὸς οὐ ποιητὸν οὐδὲ κτιστὸν οὐδὲ γεννητὸν ἀλλ' ἐκπορευτόν. Going on I notice οὐδεὶς πρῶτος ἢ ἔσχατος: μονὰς ἐν τριάδι καὶ τριὰς ἐν μονάδι: ἀλλὰ χρεία ἐστὶν καὶ περὶ τῆς αἰωνίου σωτηρίας ἣν διὰ τῆς σαρκώσεως τοῦ κυρίου ἡμῶν ἰησοῦ χριστοῦ ἐλάβομεν ἐν πίστει στερρᾷ εἰπεῖν: εἰς αἰῶνα γεννηθείς: ὅς ἐστιν θεὸς καὶ ἄνθρωπος: οὐκ ἐκ δυάδια τεμνόμενος ἀλλ' εἷς ὁ χριστός: εἰς σάρκα, ἐν τῷ θεῷ: κατῆλθεν εἰς ᾅδου, ἀνέστη ἐκ νεκρῶν. It ends οὗ τῇ παρουσίᾳ πάντες οἱ ἄνθρωποι ἀναστήσονται μετὰ τῶν σωμάτων αὐτῶν καὶ ἀποδώσουσιν ἐξ ἰδίων ἔργων τὴν ἀπολόγιαν, and three symbols which I suppose mean κ. τ. λ. Thus the Creed ends with clause 40. The 41st and 42nd are passed over—not for want of space, for two lines only at the top of a page fol. 48 verso are occupied—the rest being left blank.

The reason for the omission must be left to surmise.

The version resembles in many respects the third given by Montfaucon, but it is not identical with it.

§ 9. In his famous treatise *De Symbolo Romano,* published in 1674 (to which I have again and again referred), Usher printed a curious Greek version of the Quicunque, from a manuscript which his friend Patrick Junius had recently brought into England—it had appeared in the "Horology" of Greek hymns of Thecaras, a monk of Constantinople. This was transferred from Usher's pages to those of Labbe, from Labbe to Gundling, and then to Montfaucon's edition of Athanasius[1]—but both Gundling and Montfaucon omit to prefix to their reprints the words which Usher published as preceding the document in the manuscript. They are these, ἐκ τῆς ἁγίας καὶ οἰκουμενικῆς συνόδου τῆς ἐν Νικαίᾳ περὶ πίστεως κατὰ συντόμιαν καὶ πῶς δεῖ πιστεύειν τὸν ἀληθινὸν Χριστιανόν. "From the holy and œcumenical synod in Nicæa, concerning the Faith, in compendium, and how the true Christian ought to believe." Thus we have the substance of the Quicunque attributed here, as it is in the Irish Hymn Book, to the Council of Nicæa.

The version becomes a paraphrase in the latter part of the Creed, *i.e.* the part relating to the Incarnation, but the earlier portion is little more than a translation. It commences εἴ τις βούλοιτο σωθῆναι πρὸ πάντων αὐτῷ χρεία κρατῆσαι τὴν ὀρθόδοξον πίστιν. *The Persons* is rendered τὰς ὑποστάσεις. Clause 6 is expanded μία ἐστὶν ἡ θεότης, ἓν τὸ κράτος, μία ἐξουσία, μία βασιλεία, ἴση ἡ δόξα, ἴση ἡ μεγαλώσυνη καὶ αἰώνιος. *Immensus* is παντοκράτωρ. Each clause 8, 9, 10 is followed by its guard thus: "Not three uncreated but one uncreated." The *and* is omitted: *singillatim* = μοναδικῶς. We have χριστιανῇ ἀληθείᾳ συνηγοροῦμεν οὕτω τρεῖς θεοὺς ἢ τρεῖς κυρίους λέγειν οὐ συναινοῦμεν ἀλλὰ παντελῶς ἀπαγορεύομεν. Thus the Creed is put into the mouth of the fathers of the council. It is in the Greek interest. τὸ πνεῦμα τὸ ἅγιον ἀπὸ τοῦ πατρός ἐστιν. The order of 27 is modern. I need not exhibit the concluding half. I note that the descent into hell is omitted: and the last clause is αὕτη τοίνυν ἐστὶν ἡ ὀρθόδοξος πίστις ἣν ὁ μὴ τηρήσας ἀμώμητον σωθῆναι οὐ δύναται.

§ 10. I am compelled to consider as distinct from any other version, the version of the Creed in Greek, which since the year 1787 has been printed in the copies of the Horologion which have been published at Venice. It is not the same as that issued by Stephens, nor have I met with any manuscript authority agreeing with it. My belief is, that it was concocted by the editor of the

[1] Migne, pp. 1588, 1589, &c.

Horology I have referred to—which was simply a private speculation—and the belief is confirmed by the note appended. Until the manuscript is adduced from which it was taken, it seems scarcely deserving of much attention. Signor Veludo, the Vice-Librarian of St Mark's, who has paid great attention to the subject of oriental service-books, informed me that the Creed was omitted in the authorised edition of the *Horology* published at Constantinople in 1869, and I was informed that in the future editions to be printed at Venice, it would be most probably omitted also[1].

§ 11. We come now to a sixth Greek version of the Athanasian Creed, which I have reserved until the last, because of its important bearing on the English Prayer Book.

There is at Florence, in the library from which I have already given an account of one Greek copy, a codex, Plut. XI. cod. 12, entitled *ἑσπερτιναὶ εὐχαί*. Immediately after the evening prayers follows *τὸ τοῦ ἁγίου Ἀθανασίου σύμβολον*. The manuscript is of the fifteenth century. I will now print the Creed, from the notes which were sent to me by the Rev. A. R. Campbell, to whom I have already expressed my obligations.

1 ὅστις ἂν βούληται σωθῆναι πρὸ πάντων χρὴ κρατεῖν τὴν καθο-
2 λικὴν πίστιν· ἣν εἰ μὴ εἷς ἕκαστος σῶαν καὶ ἀμώμητον τηρήσῃ,
3 ἄνευ δισταγμοῦ εἰς τὸν αἰῶνα ἀπολεῖται. πίστις δὲ ἡ καθολικὴ
αὕτη ἐστὶν, ἵνα ἕνα θεὸν ἐν τριάδι καὶ τριάδα ἐν μονάδι σεβώ-
4 μεθα. μήτε συγχέοντες τὰς ὑποστάσεις μήτε τὴν οὐσίαν μερί-
5 ζοντες· ἄλλη γάρ ἐστιν ἡ ὑπόστασις τοῦ πατρὸς, ἄλλη τοῦ υἱοῦ,
6 ἄλλη τοῦ ἁγίου πνεύματος· ἀλλὰ πατρὸς καὶ υἱοῦ καὶ ἁγίου
πνεύματος μία ἐστὶν ἡ θεότης, ἴση ἡ δόξα, συναΐδιος ἡ μεγα-
7 λειότης. οἷος ὁ πατὴρ τοιοῦτος ὁ υἱὸς, τοιοῦτον καὶ τὸ πνεῦμα
8 τὸ ἅγιον. ἄκτιστος ὁ πατὴρ ἄκτιστος ὁ υἱὸς ἄκτιστον καὶ τὸ
9 πνεῦμα τὸ ἅγιον. ἀκατάληπτος ὁ πατὴρ ἀκατάληπτος ὁ υἱὸς
10 ἀκατάληπτον καὶ τὸ πνεῦμα τὸ ἅγιον. αἰώνιος ὁ πατὴρ αἰώνιος
11 ὁ υἱὸς αἰώνιον καὶ τὸ πνεῦμα τὸ ἅγιον· πλὴν οὐ τρεῖς αἰώνιοι
12 ἀλλ' εἷς αἰώνιος· ὥσπερ οὐδὲ τρεῖς ἄκτιστοι οὐδὲ τρεῖς ἀκατά-
13 ληπτοι ἀλλ' εἷς ἄκτιστος καὶ εἷς ἀκατάληπτος. ὁμοίως παντοδύναμος ὁ πατὴρ παντοδύναμος ὁ υἱὸς παντοδύναμον καὶ τὸ

[1] On the character of the Horologies see an Excursus at the end of this chapter.

14 πνεῦμα τὸ ἅγιον· πλὴν οὐ τρεῖς παντοδύναμοι ἀλλ' εἷς παντο-
15 δύναμος. οὕτω θεὸς ὁ πατὴρ θεὸς ὁ υἱὸς θεὸς καὶ τὸ πνεῦμα τὸ
16 17 ἅγιον· πλὴν οὐ τρεῖς θεοὶ ἀλλ' εἷς θεός. ὁμοίως κύριος ὁ
18 πατὴρ κύριος ὁ υἱὸς κύριον καὶ τὸ πνεῦμα τὸ ἅγιον· πλὴν οὐ
19 τρεῖς κύριοι ἀλλ' εἷς ἐστι κύριος. ὅτι ὡς ἰδίαν μίαν ἑκάστην
ὑπόστασιν θεὸν καὶ κύριον ὁμολογεῖν τῇ χριστιανικῇ ἀληθείᾳ
20 βιαζόμεθα, οὕτω τρεῖς θεοὺς ἢ τρεῖς κυρίους λέγειν τῇ καθολικῇ
21 εὐσεβείᾳ κωλυόμεθα. ὁ πατὴρ ἀπ' οὐδενός ἐστιν, οὐ ποιητὸς οὐ
22 κτιστὸς οὐδὲ γεννητός. ὁ υἱὸς ἀπὸ τοῦ πατρὸς μόνου ἐστὶν, οὐ
23 ποιητὸς οὐ κτιστὸς ἀλλὰ γεννητός. τὸ πνεῦμα τὸ ἅγιον ἀπὸ τοῦ
πατρὸς καὶ τοῦ υἱοῦ οὐ ποιητὸν οὐ κτιστὸν οὐδὲ γεννητὸν ἀλλ'
24 ἐκπορευτόν. εἷς οὖν ὁ πατὴρ οὐ τρεῖς πατέρες, εἷς ὁ υἱὸς οὐ τρεῖς
25 υἱοί· ἓν πνεῦμα ἅγιον οὐ τρία πνεύματα ἅγια. καὶ ἐν ταύτῃ τῇ
τριάδι οὐδὲν πρότερον ἢ ὕστερον, οὐδὲν μεῖζον ἢ ἔλαττον ἀλλὰ
26 σῶαι αἱ τρεῖς ὑποστάσεις καὶ συναΐδιαι εἰσὶν ἑαυταῖς καὶ ἶσαι.
27 ὥστε κατὰ πάντα, καθὼς εἴρηται, καὶ τὴν μονάδα ἐν τριάδι
28 σέβεσθαι δεῖ, καὶ τὴν τριάδα ἐν μονάδι. ὁ γοῦν βουλόμενος
29 σωθῆναι οὕτω περὶ τριάδος φρονείτω. πλὴν ἀναγκαῖόν ἐστι
πρὸς αἰωνίαν σωτηρίαν ὅπως καὶ τὴν ἐνσάρκωσιν τοῦ κυρίου
30 ἡμῶν Ἰησοῦ Χριστοῦ ἔτι ὀρθῶς πιστεύσῃ. ἔστι γὰρ πίστις
ὄρθη ἵνα πιστεύωμεν καὶ ὁμολογῶμεν ὅτι ὁ Κύριος ἡμῶν Ἰησοῦς
31 Χριστὸς ὁ υἱὸς τοῦ θεοῦ θεὸς καὶ ἄνθρωπός ἐστι. θεὸς ἐκ τῆς
οὐσίας τοῦ πατρὸς πρὸ αἰώνων γεννηθείς, καὶ ἄνθρωπος ἐκ τῆς
32 οὐσίας τῆς μητρὸς ἐν τῷ αἰῶνι τεχθείς. τέλειος θεὸς καὶ τέλειος
ἄνθρωπος ἐκ ψυχῆς λογικῆς καὶ ἀνθρωπίνης σαρκὸς ὑφιστά-
33 μενος. ἶσος τῷ πατρὶ κατὰ τὴν θεότητα, ἐλάττων τοῦ πατρὸς
34 κατὰ τὴν ἀνθρωπότητα· ὃς εἰ καὶ θεὸς καὶ ἄνθρωπός ἐστιν, οὐ
35 δύο ὅμως ἀλλ' εἷς Χριστὸς ἐστίν. εἷς Χριστός ἐστιν οὐ τροπῇ
τῆς θεότητος εἰς σάρκα ἀλλὰ προσλήψει τῆς ἀνθρωπότητος εἰς
36 θεόν. εἷς πάντως οὐ συγχύσει τῆς οὐσίας ἀλλ' ἑνότητι τῆς
37 ὑποστάσεως. καὶ γὰρ ὡς ἡ ψυχὴ λογικὴ καὶ ἡ σὰρξ εἷς ἐστιν
38 ἄνθρωπος, οὕτω καὶ ὁ θεάνθρωπος εἷς ἐστι Χριστός. ὃς ἔπαθε
διὰ τὴν σωτηρίαν ἡμῶν καὶ κατῆλθεν εἰς ᾅδου ἀνέστη ἐν τρίτῃ
39 ἡμέρᾳ ἐκ τῶν νεκρῶν ἀνῆλθεν εἰς οὐρανοὺς, κάθηται ἐκ δεξιῶν
τοῦ πατρὸς καὶ θεοῦ παντοκράτορος, ὅθεν ἥξει κρῖναι ζῶντας καὶ
40 νεκρούς. οὗ τῇ παρουσίᾳ πάντες οἱ ἄνθρωποι ἀναστήσονται
μετὰ τῶν σωμάτων αὐτῶν, καὶ ἀποδώσουσιν ἐξ ἰδίων ἔργων τὴν
41 ἀπολογίαν· καὶ οἱ μὲν τὰ ἀγαθὰ πράξαντες πορεύσονται εἰς ζωὴν
42 αἰώνιον [οἱ δὲ τὰ φαῦλα εἰς τὸ πῦρ τὸ αἰώνιον]. αὕτη ἐστὶν ἡ

καθολικὴ πίστις ἣν ἐὰν μή τις πιστῶς πιστεύσῃ σωθῆναι οὐ δυνήσεται.

The words I have inserted between brackets seem to have been omitted on account of the *ὁμοιοτέλευτον*.

§ 12. A version of the Creed very similar to this was published at Strasburg in the year 1524, by Cephaleus, at the end of a Greek Psalter. Two copies of this volume have been found in England; one by the Rev. J. S. Brewer in the British Museum, who, however, mistook the printer Cephaleus for the reformer Capito; the other by Mr Bradshaw in the Cambridge Library. It is so curious that I give an account of the latter in my note[1]. This was published in 1524. But the little volume seems to have been almost unknown on the continent: it is not mentioned by Genebrard, Fabricius, Gundling or Montfaucon. Nine years after this, Dionysius gave to Baiff the copy which Waterland mentioned.

Through the kindness of the Rev. N. M. Ferrers, of Gonville and Caius College, Cambridge, I have been permitted to examine a curious volume in his possession, composed of three parts, all printed at Paris *In officina Christiani Wecheli sub saito Basiliensi* MDXXXVIII. The first portion is this: ὩΡΑΙ ΤΗΣ ΑΕΙ ΠΑΡ

[1] The volume is dated 1524 (in the border). The page 2½ inches by 3¾.

The title-page is this:

Ψαλτήριον | προφήτου καὶ βασιλέως | τοῦ Δαβιδ. Argentorati. apud | Vuolf. Cephal.

At the back of the title-page,

Ιωαννης ὁ Λεοντονικης τοῖς ἱερῶν πραγμάτων σπουδαίοις, εὖ πράττειν.

The editor quotes a bit of Pindar as a kind of introduction to the divine Psalter, and concludes,

τοῦτο μὲν οὖν ψαλτήριον σπουδαῖοι ὑμῖν παρασκευασθὲν σμικρότερον, εὐ κάρδια μάρψατε, βόλφιόν τε κεφαλαῖον τὸν τυπογράφον, σπουδῇ (?) ὑμῶν ὀφέλλοντα, εἰς μεῖζον' ὀτρύνετε ἀσκελές. ἔῤῥωσθε.

The Psalms are from the Septuagint, apparently the Alexandrine text.

They are followed, folio 178 *b*, by the 151st Psalm with the usual title: 179 *b*, the Song of Moses in Exodus, marked *α*. Then the other Greek canticles nine in all.

Then comes on folio 194 *a*,

αἴνεσις ἁγνῆς μητρὸς παρθένου κόρης. ᾠδὴ θ. [The Magnificat] 195 *a*, *προσευχὴ τοῦ προφήτου Ζαχαρίου.* (The Benedictus). After which p. 195 *b*,

ΤΕΛΟΣ.

f. 196 *a* has some iambics addressed to David. Then f. 196 *b*, *Συμβολον του αγιου Αθανασιου.* Then an index to the *Psalms* in *Latin* and *Greek* (the Latin titles are arranged alphabetically), including in its place

Symbolum Atha. Quicunq; uult.
Οστις βούληται σωθῆναι.
After all, *τῷ θεῷ δοξα.*

Then on the opposite page,

ΕΚΤΕΤΥΠΩΤΑΙ.
ἐν Ἀργεντίνῃ τῇ ἐλευθερᾷ, ἐν οἰκίᾳ Βολφίου τοῦ Κεφαλαίου. ἔτει τῆς σωτηρίας ἡμων.
α' φ κ δ.
Μηνὶ βοηδρομιῶνι.

On the verso is a curious woodcut representing a squared stone, some reference to the stone of offence, &c., &c.

θένου Μαρίας, κατ' ἔθος | *τῆς ῥωμαϊκῆς ἐκ* | *κλησίας.* | ΛΕΙΤΟΥΡΓΙΑ *τῆς ὑπερα* | *γίας καὶ ἀειπαρθένου Μαρίας.* This consists of 87 leaves, 2⅜ inches by 4 (nearly.) On the back of the title-page is a short address ʽΑΛΔΟΣ ΤΟΙΣ ΣΠΟΥ | *δαίοις εὖ πράττειν.* The hours end on the verso of leaf 58. Then come the penitential psalms. From 68 onwards we have Litanies and Prayers, and on leaf 78 *σύμβολον τοῦ ἁγίου Ἀθανασίου.* The other parts contain treatises by Chrysostom, Cyril of Alexandria, and John Damasçene.

The version described by Genebrard as Baiff's resembles this closely, and others very similar were published by Nicolas Bryling at Basle (the date has not been delivered to us), and Henry Stephens at Paris in 1565[1]. From a collation given of these by Gundling in his edition of Zialowski (and from him somewhat incorrectly by Montfaucon, more correctly by Waterland), I endeavoured in 1870 to reproduce the text of "Bryling." I was confident that Waterland was correct in connecting with this text our English version of the Athanasian Creed. I must, however, now content myself with giving the readings where the editions of Cephaleus and Wechelus and the alleged readings of Stephens and Baiff vary from the copy which I have printed above from the Florence manuscript. The Florence copy is wondrously near our English version.

§ 13. Calling the editions of Bryling A, Baiff B, Cephaleus C, Florence F, Stephen S and Wechel W, we have these various readings.

In clause 1. C. and W. omit *ἄν.* S. reads *βούλεται.*

4 B. has *διαχωρίζοντες* for *μερίζοντες.*

6 S. has *μία υἱοῦ ἡ δόξα*: B. *μία ἐστιν ἡ δόξα.*

[There is some confusion between *τὸ ἅγιον πνεῦμα* and *τὸ πνεῦμα τὸ ἅγιον*].

7 A. omits *καί.*

12 A. C. S. W. transpose and read *οὐδὲ τρεῖς ἀκατάληπτοι οὐδὲ τρεῖς ἄκτιστοι.* B. agrees with F. Thus our version follows one of the four A. C. S. W.

[1] This copy must be looked for in "I. Calvini Rudimenta Fidei Christianæ Græce et Latine," which was published in this year. I have not been able to find the volume. Tentzel in his preface, written in 1687, quotes a Greek catechism edited in the previous century, where these words are prefixed to the Creed;—*φέρεται καὶ ἀθανασίου σύμβολον ὅπερ ἐκ παλαιοῦ τινος ἔθους ἐν ταῖς ἐκκλησιαστικαῖς ὁμιλίαις μελωδεῖτον ἀντιψαλλόμενον* (sic). The reference must be to Western custom as in Manuel Caleca, lib. II. *contra Græcos*, cap. 20 (quoted by Tentzel), and is probably taken from Calvin's volume.

13 C. and W. καὶ ὁ υἱός. (The English version omits this *and.*)

15, 17 B. and S. omit καὶ, with the later Latin copies. (The English has it.)

19 ἰδίαν B. C. F. W., followed by the English. A. and S., correctly, ἰδίᾳ. C. and W. have ἕκαστον.

20 All the copies have τρεῖς κυρίους, and so our English. The received Latin omits *tres* before *dominos*.

21 A. and B. omit ποιητός. C. W. omit οὐ.

[The reading in Montfaucon, from Genebrard would give this version. "The Father is of none: nor yet created, nor made, nor begotten." Bryling, Baiff, and Stephens, "The Father is of none, neither created nor begotten." The reading of Cephaleus and Wechelus "the Father is made of none, nor yet created nor begotten." The Florentine MS. "the Father is of none, not made nor created nor begotten." Thus again we follow C. and W.]

23 C. and W. omit οὐδὲ γεννητόν (of the Holy Spirit. They thus agree with the Venetian copy. See above chap. xxiv. § 9: viii. p. 372: and Abbo of Fleury, chap. xxi. § 44, p. 308).

24 C. W. εἷς οὖν πατήρ.

25 All the copies read σῶαι. This is very curious. The Latin is *totæ:* it must have been spelt *tutæ* in some old copy, and this became σῶαι.

27 All follow the later Latin order.

29 All read ὀρθῶς πιστεύσῃ *believe rightly* (the Latin has "believe faithfully").

C. and W. have αἰώνιον.

31 All have ἐν αἰῶνι, and in 35 εἷς δὲ οὐ τροπῇ...εἰς σάρκα, εἰς θεόν.

38 C. and W. ἐν ᾅδου. τῇ τρίτῃ.

39 B. τοῦ θεοῦ καὶ πατρός.

42 W. adds δόξα.

To this subject we must return hereafter.

Excursus on Kimmel's Collection and on the Greek Horology.

At Venice and at the British Museum I have had the opportunity of examining nine editions of the Horology of the respective dates, 1532, 1646, 1687, 1740, 1758, 1787, 1800, 1831, 1870. It is curious to mark their gradual growth. None of the first five give the Quicunque.

Yet the fifth, printed in 1758, is stated to "contain everything necessary." It was edited by one Alexander Cancellarius. The rubrics throughout differ considerably from those of the recent editions. In 1787 the Quicunque was introduced: it followed the gospel from St John i. 1—17, and preceded the Horology proper. This order continued until 1831, when it was for the first time printed after the Horology as a kind of Appendix. The fact that it and other things were added is thus noted on the title-page of the edition of 1800: τῇ προσθήκῃ μέν ποτε τοῦ ἱεροῦ συμβόλου τῆς καὶ χρονολογίας τῶν ἁγίων ἐν τῷ μηνολογίῳ. It is there entitled σύμβολον τοῦ ἁγίου ἀθανασίου πατριαρχοῦ ἀλεξάνδρειας. In the edition of 1870, it is entitled σύμβολον τῆς πίστεως τοῦ ἁγίου ἀθανασίου ἀρχιεπισκόπου ἀλεξάνδρειας. The note appended ran thus in 1800:

σημειῶσαι
ὅτι τὸ σύμβολον τοῦτο τοῦ μεγάλου Ἀθανασίου, κ. τ. λ.

"Memorandum: that after this symbol of the great Athanasius had been compared with the most ancient manuscripts preserved in the library of St Mark, and had been found consonant [with them] and genuine, and in harmony with the opinions of the orthodox Church—it seemed good that it should be printed: for those that have been printed at Paris and elsewhere differ both in language and meaning: but this, not deviating even from that printed at Moscow, has been added here in a feeling of piety." Thus there is no pretence of its having any authority.

The following is a copy of the words which Signor Veludo was kind enough to write in my note-book on August 3, 1872, "La Chiesa orientale nell' ultima edizione dell' Horologium Magnum fatta a Costantinopoli nel 1869, ha omesso il simbolo de S. Athanasio come non necessario ni faciente parte dell' uffiziatura della Chiesa. Giov. Veludo,
Vice bib°. di
S. Marco."

Very great misapprehension as to the character of this Greek Horologion exists in England even in quarters where accurate knowledge is generally looked for. For example, a very distinguished and learned Prelate of the Province of Canterbury, in a speech delivered before the Upper House of Convocation on Feb. 8, 1872—a speech, which was subsequently printed and circulated—had the following passage: "Let me advert in passing to a popular fallacy. It is boldly said by many that the Greek Church knows nothing of the Athanasian Creed. Now, my lords, if any one will take the trouble to examine the collection of symbolical books of the Eastern Church, published by Kimmel (*Jena*, 1843, p. 67), he will see that in the Orthodox Confession of the Eastern Church put forth in the seventeenth century by the Patriarchs of Constantinople, Alexandria, Antioch, and Jerusalem, the Athanasian Creed is ascribed to Athanasius himself: and it is inserted as such in the Horologium of the Eastern Church (p. 586, ed. Venet. 1861), where it is said to have been copied from ancient Greek manuscripts in the Library of S. Mark at Venice; and it is contained in numerous books of devotion now circulated in Greece. Let me add that a learned Russian Ecclesiastic, Dr Popoff, whom I had the pleasure of meeting last night at Lambeth, informed me that the Creed was contained in the Russian Books of devotion."

I often wish that evidence adduced in this way before Convocation could be submitted to cross-examination, as it would be in Parliament, before it is made the basis of legislation.—I had some difficulty in February, 1873, in preventing the Lower House of Convocation from designating the Athanasian Creed as a Creed of the Catholic Church.—The fact is that the respected Prelate overlooked the statement of Kimmel that *The Greek Church has no true symbolic books in the sense that we have: the confessions have no normative power; they do not bind the minds of the readers or of the clergy:* in other words, the documents published by Kimmel are simply the expressions of opinion, on points of interest, of the bishops or patriarchs who happened to unite: just as the Lambeth Articles were the expressions of the opinions of the few prelates and theologians who joined in them in 1595.

But a further examination of Kimmel's collection shews how little we should be justified in appealing to anything contained in it as proof that even the Bishops of the Greek Churches attached the same value that we do to the Athanasian Creed. In the documents there contained, there is much relating to the Trinity: thus we have a dialogue on the subject between Gennadius, patriarch of Constantinople, and the Mahumet who took the city in 1453. Gennadius had attended the council of Florence in 1438, and therefore must have known of the Athanasian Creed: but he never refers to it: nor does Cyril Lucar, who (as is well known) was strangled in 1638. Another document is the "orthodox confession" of the Russian bishops of the year 1641, which was subsequently translated into what is called Greek. The subscriptions are given in Kimmel, p. 53, under the date 1643. The bishops speak of an attempt *τὴν πίστιν διαιροῦν εἰς τὰ δώδεκα ἄρθρα τῆς πίστεως ἤτοι τοῦ ἱεροῦ συμβόλου*, but they knew of only one sacred Symbol or Creed—the Creed of Constantinople, or Nicæa as it was generally called. For this is followed by an account of the orthodox Catholic and Apostolic Faith "of which (p. 60) there are twelve articles according to the symbol of the first council held at Nicæa, and the second held at Constantinople. In which councils all things relating to our faith are so accurately expounded (or laid down), that neither more things nor fewer ought to be believed by us," "quibus in conciliis ita sunt accurate exposita quæ ad fidem nostram attinent omnia, ut neque plura neque pauciora a nobis credi oporteat." The Nicene, or rather Constantinopolitan, Creed follows piecemeal. Thus they would repudiate the refinements of the Quicunque.

On p. 63 we have references to Damascenus, p. 64, to Gregory Theologus, p. 67, to Athanasius "qua de re plenius uberiusque in symbolo suo magnus Athanasius tractat:" p. 90, to Basil and so on. The subject of the Procession is introduced p. 142, where Athanasius is again quoted as explaining in his Creed the Procession. The Greek is *τὴν διδασκαλίαν ταύτην* (sic) *τὴν ἑρμηνεύει ὁ ἱερὸς Ἀθανάσιος εἰς τὸ σύμβολον τοῦ τὸ πνεῦμα τὸ ἅγιον παρὰ τοῦ πατρὸς οὐ πεποιημένον οὔτε δεδημιουργημένον οὔτε γεγεννημένον ἀλλ' ἐκπορευτόν.* They then adduce Athanasius on some other subject. On the next page they object to the addition "et ex filio" to the Creed of the 150, and appeal to Leo III. in the year 809 as given by Baronius.

On p. 173 we read how the baptized person professes the Symbol of the faith either by himself or his sponsor (ἀναδόχος).

The second volume is almost entirely made up of a confession of the Eastern Catholic and Apostolic Church, composed in epitome by Metrophanes Hieromonachos, commonly called Metrophanes Critopulos. It seems to have been written in 1625; it was printed in 1661. The book has no authority but rests on the unimpeached character of the writer, who was, however, regarded by Nicolaus Comnenus as a Greco-Lutheran. On p. 15, he says, "we do not confess with the Church of Rome that the Holy Spirit κἀκ τοῦ υἱοῦ ὑφίστασθαι." On p. 20, "the Holy Fathers when they speak of the temporal procession of the Holy Spirit say both that He comes ἐκ πατρὸς διὰ τοῦ υἱοῦ and that He comes ἐξ ἀμφοῖν, but of the eternal procession never καὶ ἐκ τοῦ υἱοῦ." In proof he quotes Dionysius the Areopagite, Athanasius, Gregory of Nyssa, Gregory Thaumaturgus, Cyril of Alexandria, John Damascenus and Augustine. The passages from Athanasius are thus introduced: "After Saint Dionysius let the sainted Athanasius come forward, the man full of labours—who, in his symbol (τῷ καθ' αὑτὸν συμβόλῳ), expressly proclaims that the all-holy Spirit proceeds from the Father. And if some, in the Latin translation, have added the words *and from the Son*, yet thanks be to the divine Providence,—which, though it has permitted the Latin to be corrupted by judgments which that Providence itself knows, has yet preserved the Greek uncorrupted, in order that that which is written may be fulfilled; *He taketh the wise in their own craftiness.*" Metrophanes follows up this by quoting the spurious ἐρωτήσεις (Migne, XXVIII. 777).

I have been compelled to give these details to shew how far the Symbolical Books of the Greek Church represent that Church as adopting the Athanasian Creed. These writers accepted their version of the Creed as Athanasius', and treated it with the same respect, neither more nor less, as they treated any work of Basil or Gregory. I cannot complain of any incorrectness in the Bishop's statement: only the facts which he adduced are apparently insignificant.

And now as to the Horologies published at Venice. These books were simply the speculations of different booksellers at Venice, and were altered in succession by the different editors whose names occur on the successive title-pages. The Greek Church as such was no more responsible for the contents of these volumes than is the English Church responsible for any book of devotions prepared (say) by Bishop Andrewes, or edited by Bishop Wilberforce. The last edition printed at Constantinople has somewhat more of authority. It comes from a Committee for Printing, which is apparently analogous to one of the Committees of the Society for Promoting Christian Knowledge. I have seen only one of their works, a biography of Constantius I., printed in the years 1866—1870. The Committee consists of a president and five or six members. And they have printed a copy of the Horology, and, as Signor Veludo informed me, omitted from it the Athanasian Creed. In his advertisement to his edition of the Horology of the year 1870, the proprietor of the Phœnix Press at Venice alludes to this action τῆς κεντρικῆς πατρ. ἐπιτροπῆς, the Central Committee of the Patriarchate (?). He speaks with some natural pride of the wide circulation which has been gained both in Greece and elsewhere by his editions of the "sacred books of our venerable Mother Church;" of the care with which they had been edited by the memorable Bartholomew "the Cutlumusianus," and more recently by Spyridon Zerbus; of the letters of commendation the latter had received in 1850 from the Patriarch Anthimus, and in 1856 from the Patriarch Cyril. And now "he has commended to the care of the same editor the preparation of a new edition. But a copy of the great Horology, published at Constantinople, by G. Seitanides, under the direction of the Central Committee, has reached Venice: and out of respect to the authority of that edition, as well as for the sake of uniformity, he has, to some extent, modified his own: still he has not followed it in some typographical errors: and he thinks, that in some respects, the arrangement of his own is better: and he has thought it well to print with it again the Symbol of the great Athanasius as in the former editions."

Thus the appearance of the Symbol in the Venetian Horologies is due entirely to the action of an irresponsible Venetian editor.

Of course the printing of it in the Russian books of devotion is of no greater moment.

These are the title-pages of the editions of 1758 and 1800 respectively.

ὡρολόγιον | μέγα | περίεχον πᾶσαν τὴν ἡμερονύκτιον | ἀκολουθίαν, καὶ παρακλητικοὺς κα | νόνας τῆς θεοτόκου, καὶ οἴκους. | τροπάρια καὶ κοντάκια τῶν ἁγίων τοῦ ὅλου | ἐνιαυτοῦ, μετὰ τῆς μεταλήψεως, καὶ ἄλλων | ἀναγκαίων, καὶ πασχαλίων ἐτῶν νδ'. | νεωστὶ μετατυπωθὲν | καὶ ἐπιμελῶς διορθωθὲν | παρὰ κύριου | ἀλεξάνδρου καγκελλαρίου. | ἐνετίῃσι. 1758. | *παρὰ* Νικολάῳ Γλυκεῖ τῷ ἐξ Ἰωαννίνων. | Con licenza di Superiori.

ὡρολόγιον | μέγα | περίεχον τὴν ἅπασαν | ἡμερονύκτιον ἀκολουθίαν, τὰ τροπάρια καὶ | κοντάκια τοῦ Τριωδίου, *πεντηκονταστυρίου | καὶ τῶν δώδεκα μηνῶν, | τὸν παρακλητικὸν κανόνα τῆς θεοτόκου, καὶ τοὺς | οἴκους μετὰ τῆς μεταλήψεως, καὶ τὸν ἀκάθιστον | ὕμνον εἰς τὸν ζωοποιὸν σταυρόν. | καὶ πασχάλιον ἐτῶν μγ'. καὶ ἄλλων | ἀναγκαίων, ὡς ἐν τῷ πίνακι | τῇ προσθήκῃ μέν ποτε τοῦ ἱεροῦ συμβόλου, τῆς | καὶ χρονολογίας τῶν ἁγίων ἐν τῷ μηνολογίῳ, | τῶν πολλῶν εἰκόνων ἤπερ τῷ πρώτῳ. | τοινῦν δὲ καὶ τοῦ ἑτέρου τῆς θεοτόκου παρακλητι | κοῦ κανόνος, κοσμηθὲν καὶ προσαυξηθέν. | νεωστὶ μετατυπωθὲν καὶ ἐπιμελῶς διορθωθέν. | ͵αω'. ἐνετίῃσιν.* 1800. | *παρὰ* Νικολάῳ Γλυκεῖ τῷ ἐξ Ἰωαννίων·—con regia approvazione.

There is a drawing of Athanasius on p. 5. In the text of the Creed I read this, *ὁ υἱὸς ἀπὸ μόνου τοῦ πατρός ἐστιν οὐ πεποιημένος οὐδὲ δεδημιουργημένος ἀλλὰ γεγεννημένος ἐκ τοῦ πατρός.* The last three words are omitted in the edition of 1870. Again, where the latter has *λατρεύεται* clause 27, the former has *λατρεύηται.* After the memorandum the book passes on to give the Morning prayers. On comparing the two editions of the Horology, I found that altogether six articles had been introduced in 1800 which were not printed in 1758. On the other hand, on comparing the editions of 1646 and 1870, I think it will be found that about fifteen additional articles have been inserted in the course of the two hundred years. (On the meaning of the word *οἶκοι* in the title-page, see a note in Daniel, *Codex Liturgicus*, IV. 641. It is a kind of prose hymn.)

CHAPTER XXXIII.

GERMAN, FRENCH, AND ENGLISH VERSIONS.

§ 1. I MAY now turn to other versions, of which some, at all events, are of earlier date than the earliest notices which we have of any Greek translation. And first in order of seniority and importance comes a series of German versions.

§ 2. Tentzel in his preface speaks of four or five such versions. He mentions the statement of Lambecius[1] that

Otfrid, a monk of Weissenberg, in the time of Louis the Pious, translated the Gospels, the Psalms, the Canticles, and added, at the end, the Athanasian Creed. This is the version of the Vienna MS. below. Tentzel speaks then of another at Vienna, taken from the Ambras Library (as was the former[2]). Feller[3] speaks of a third translation of a later date, beginning "Wer do wil selick werden vor allin Dingin deme ist not daz er halde den rechtin Geloubin." (sic.) And of a fourth[4] "Wer da selig wesyn wil deme ist durfft vor alleme daz her habe den rechten Gelouben." In the Library of Gotha there was a fifth. "Wer seligk wil sein der bedarff wol das her vor allen Dingen behalte den Glouben." These are all at the end of Psalters. Tentzel then speaks of two copies of another German translation, printed at the end of Psalters, one from Basil 1502, the other from Strasburg 1508. "Welcher behalten wil sein vor allen Dingen ist not das er halt den Christenlichen Glauben." But "all these versions (Tentzel adds) are surpassed by that prepared by Luther and known in all our churches."

But our interest ought to be concentrated on the earliest of these versions: and, thanks to the collection made by Massmann[5], we have the opportunity of examining three such versions; the first from a

[1] Lambecius, I. p. 760.
[2] *Ibid.* p. 763.
[3] Catalogue of *Leipzic Library*, pp. 68, 69.
[4] *Ibid.* p. 79.
[5] Note, p. 22.

manuscript at Wolfenbüttel, assigned to the eighth century; the second from the manuscript at Vienna above referred to, which is ascribed now not to the times of Louis the Pious, but to the eleventh or twelfth century; the third comes from a Munich manuscript of a later date. I shall refer again to the first two as assisting us to fix the contemporaneous Latin text in Germany. So far it will appear that our Utrecht Psalter did not originate in that country, because the Wolfenbüttel manuscript omits to notice "tertia die," and the *et* must have been missing in clauses 7, 9, 10. I remark that in clauses 4, 5, 19 *Persona* is rendered Gomahejt; in 26 *tres personæ*, thrio heitj: in 36 *unitate personæ*, einissi thera hejtj. *Inmensus* is translated ungimezzan[1].

The second version is more important because (like one of the French versions given by Montfaucon) it frequently adds to the translation an explanation or paraphrase of the clause. Thus under clauses 3, 4, we have the following—"daz ist diu allelicha glouba daz uuir einen got eren an dére trinussida unde die trinussida an dera einussida. noh die kenemnida miskente. noh dia uuesennussida skeidente. Ungeskeideniu uuesen*n*ussida ouget uns einen got. Trigeskeidéne kenenneda ougent uns tria kenemmida dero trinussida. Uuaz sint kenemmida. uuane daz uualahisgen sint uuider cellunga. Ein uuider cellunga ist tes fater. zedemo suno. diu endriu est tes sunis zedemo fater. diu tritta ist des heiligen keistis zedemo fater. unde zedemo suno. Dero iogelih habet sine kenennida. Also iz hera nah chuit[2]."

I must leave my readers to interpret this as they can. The explanation of clause 5, I will interpret for them. "One Person is of the Father: the second of the Son: the third of the Holy Ghost. The Persons are not to be understood as in created beings. In created beings three persons are three substances: but in God are three Persons and one Substance. Michael, Gabriel, Raphael; or Abraham, Isaac, Jacob, they are three persons and three substances: but the Father and the Son and the Holy Ghost, these are not three Substances but three *keougeda dero uuider cellunge-die angote uuernomen uuerdent.*" *Inmensus* is Vnmazig.

They all seem to translate *nihil* in clause 25 "nothing." They all have the order "Trinity in Unity and Unity in Trinity." "Believe faithfully" seems to have been understood as "believe with truth."

The last of the three versions in Massmann is taken from two manuscripts at Munich, 588 and 589, in the former of which it is found with the Latin words in the margin "Psalmus Quicunque vult[3]."

§ 3. If we turn to French translations, we find that Montfaucon published two; the one, an imperfect version from the

[1] Massman, p. 88, &c.

[2] Massman, pp. 88, 90.

[3] The following notes of copies of the Athanasian Creed in German appear in the new catalogue,
2727, m. XV. Denis I. XXXIX.
2682, m. XII. Denis II. LVIII.
2681, m. XI. Denis I. XLV. (error).
2684, m. XIV. Denis II. LVII.
2756, m. XIV. Denis I. XXXVIII. is said to contain a fragment of the Quicunque in German. But at the words "Daz ist

Codex Colbertinus, 3133, written about the year 1100, the other from a manuscript, two hundred years later in age, but which seems to have been a transcript of a more ancient original. This belonged to a convent of Friars Minors. Judging by the analogy presented by manuscripts which have come under my notice, I should say that this original was a Psalter, with an interlinear translation and marginal explanations. For each verse is given first in the form of a literal translation, and then this translation is followed by a brief explanation in terms slightly different. Thus:

"Quicumques veust estre saes devant toutes choses est mestiers que il tiegne la commune foi. Nul ne puet estre saes se il ne mentient en sa vie[1] seinte crestiene feelment.

"La quelle se chacuns naura gardee entiere et nient violee sanz doute pardurablement perira. Qui ne tenra ceste foi de seinte crestiente loiaument en fin sera dampnez perdurablement."

Many of these explanations are interesting. Thus in clause 4, "Issi est que nous ne devons pas mescroire que les troies persones ne soient un Dex ne diro que la Trinitez soient troi dieu:" After clause 6 we read "ces troies personnes toutes ensamble sunt uns seuls Dex." Clause 9 is thus rendered "Granz est li Pere, granz est li Filz, granz est li seint Espriz:" and the explanation is "La grandece dou Pere et dou Fill' et dou Seint Espriz est une chose."

Some of the clauses seem to be corrupt, but 19 may be copied.

"Car si comme sanglement chacune persone somes amoneste regehir Dieu et Seigneur par crestiene verite illi somes nos devec adire par commune religion trois dieux et trois seigneurs ausi comme la reisons requiert que nos dions que chacune de ces personnes est deux ausi requiert cest meisme reisons Crestiene que nous ne dions mie que ce soient troi dieu ne troi seigneurs mes uns seuls Dieux et uns seus Sires."

The translation gives *nulle chose* in 25: the explanation "nule de ces trois persones." The rendering of 27 shews that the Latin was late. It proceeds "Issi come au comencement de cest Siaume a este dit croire devons fermement que ces trois persones sunt uns seul Deux."

The word *Siaume* will be noticed.

No. 38 is explained "Au tier jor resuscita de mortu Icele chars que li Esperites prinst en la glorieusse Virge morut pro nos sauver et descendi a enfer por delivrer ses amis qui estoient et la force de lesperite la fist resusciter et lamporta osoi."

The word Psalm recurs in the last clause, the explanation of which is[1]: "Itex est la creence de seinte crestiente come cist siaumes nos devise et qui issi ne croit dannez sera pardurablement."

eyn war gloube daz wir glauben und bekennen daz unse herre ſy gotte," the codex breaks off. It cannot exhibit a literal translation.

[1] The explanation of Dr Donaldson.

One interesting feature of this manuscript is that the title of our Creed is this:

"Canticum Bonifacii: Quicunque vult salvus esse;
"Ce chant fust S. Anaistaise qui apostoilles de Rome."

The Canticle of Boniface in Latin: but in French, *This Canticle was S. Anastasius', who was pope of Rome!*

There are no doubt many other of these interlinear translations and glosses unpublished. I have only seen the one in the famous Canterbury or Eadwin Psalter at Trinity College, Cambridge. It commences—

"Kiunques uult salf estre deuant tutẻs choses est busum que il tïen la commune fei. La quele se chascun entiere e nient malmise ne guarderat seuz dutance pardurablement perirat."

§ 4. Drawing on now to our own country I must speak of Anglo-Saxon versions. Of these there are very many to be found interlined with the Latin in the Psalters. Very often, as I am told, these interlineations are not versions but glosses. "The object of the gloss was (I am quoting the words of our eminent English Scholar, the Reverend W. W. Skeat), to enable an Englishman, reading the *Latin,* to understand it. It is not a translation; nor could it be used independently of the Latin, as the words are out of order; for they follow the Latin order and do not receive their proper inflexional endings, such as would allow them to form sentences. Yet the meaning is quite clear, and we can hence infer what a translation would have been like." These glosses are important, in my opinion, in another way, their existence proves that at the time they were made, the Quicunque was not given to the people, nor repeated by them; it was only explained to them by their parish priest in the vernacular; it was regarded in its true light, as an instruction on the Faith, a "Tractatus" or "Sermo de Fide," a "Fides Catholica," but not a Symbolum.

I will give the gloss as it is found in the Manuscript Ff. I. 23, in the Cambridge University Library[1]. For the copy I am indebted to Mr Skeat. My readers will remember that the Latin is found underneath the English.

Swa hwilc swa wile hall wesan beforan eallum þearf ys *þæt* he g*e*healde þene fullican g*e*leafan.

ðone butan hwilc anwalhne ⁊ ungewemmedne ge-healde butan tweon on ecnysse for-wurðaþ.

[1] This is the manuscript mentioned above, p. 375.

g*e*leafa soðlice se anlica þæt ys þ*æt*te anne god an þrymnysse ⁊ þrymnysse on annesse we weorðiað.

⁊ na gemengende þa hadas ⁊ na ða spede ascyrgende.

oðyr ys soðlice se had fædyr oðyr þæs suna oðer þæs halgan gastes.

ac fadyr ⁊ þæs suna ⁊ þæs halgan gast an ys god-cundnys. gelic wuldur efen-ece mægen-þrym.

hwylcys fædyr swylcys suna hwylcys ⁊ se halga gast.

ung*e*sewenn ys se fædyr ungesewen ys se suna ung*e*sceapen ys ⁊ se halga gast.

ofyr-mæte ys se fædyr ofyrmæte sunu ormæte ⁊ se halga gast.

ece ys se fæder ece ys se sunu ece ys ⁊ se halga gast.

⁊ þeah-hwæðere na þreo ece ac an ece.

swa na þreo ungesceapene ne þreo or-mæte ac an is ungesceapan ⁊ an or-mæte.

ac ge-lice ælmihtig fædyr ælmihtig sunu ælmihtig ⁊ halig gast.

⁊ þeah-hwæðere na þreo ælmihtige ac an ælmihtig.

⁊ swa he is god fæder god sunu god ⁊ halig gast.

⁊ þeah-hwæðere na þreo godas ac an ys god.

⁊ swa he is driht*en* fædyr dryhtyn sunu driht*en* ⁊ halig gast.

⁊ þeah-hwæðere na þreo drihtnys ac an ys dryhtyn.

for þa*m* swa swa sundyrlice anra gehwylcne had god ⁊ drihtyn andettan of cristenre soð-fæst-nysse.

swa þreo godas oððe driht*nys* seggað of þære fullican æfestnysse we beoð for-bodene

se fædyr of nænegu*m*[1] he is geworht ne ge-scapæn.

se sunu fro*m* fædere scolfu*m* ys ne ge-worht ne gesceapyn ac gecenned.

se halga gast fro*m* fædyr ⁊ suna is ne ge-worht ne g*e*sceapyn ne acenned ac forð-steppynde.

an is eallinga fædyr na þreo fæderas an is sunu na þreo sunu an halig gast na þreo halig gast.

⁊ on þisse þrynnyse na þing æror oððe æftere na þing mar is[2] oððe læsse.

ac ealle þa þreo hadas efen-ēce hi*m* sendon ⁊ efen-gelice.

swa þ*æt* þurh ealle þing swa eallinga bufan gecwedyn ys ⁊ þrym-nysse on annysse. ⁊ annes on þrym-nysse to weorðienne sie.

se wile eallinga hal beon swa be þrym-nysse he on-gite.

ac nead-þearf ys to ecere hælo þ*æt* we on-flescnesse witodlice driht*nes* ure hælendes cinges anra ge-hwylc.

is[3] eornostlice rihtg*e*leafa þ*æt* we ge-lefan ⁊ andettað for þon driht*en* ure hælende crist godes sunu god[4] samod ⁊ mann ys.

god ys of spede þæs fæder[5]...worulda acenned ⁊ mann of spede modor on weorulda acenned.

fulfremed god fulfremed he is man of g*e*scead-wislicre sawle ⁊ of menniscu*m* flæsce wuniende.

g*e*lic he is fæder æftyr god-cundnysse læssa fæder æftyr menniscnysse.

se þeah þe he god sie ⁊ mann na twegen þeah-hwæðere ac an ys crist.

an he is soðlice na of gecerrednysse god-cundnysse on[6] flæsc ac on............ menniscnysse on gode.

an eallinga na on g*e*drefydnysse spede ac on annysse hadys.

1 MS. an ænesu*m*.
2 MS. marif.
3 MS. ic.
4 MS. godas sunu godas.
5 MS. *omits* beforan.
6 MS. of.

witodlice swa swa sawl gesceadwislice ⁊ flæsc an is man swa god ⁊ man an is crist.

se þrowode for hælo ure he niþer astah to helwarum þe þriddan dæge he aras of deaðum.

he astah on heofen he siteð æt swiðeran hand godes fæder ælmihtiges þanon he to cumenne ys deman cwice ⁊ deade.

to þæs to-cume ealle menn to arisanne hi habbað mid heora lic-haman ⁊ to agyldanne synd be agnum..............gescead.

⁊ þa þe gōd worhton farað on ece lif ⁊ þa þe soðlice yfyl on ece fyr.

þis is se fullica ge-leafa þane butan hwilc getreow-lice ⁊ fæst-lice gelefe hal wesan ne mæg.

In modern English (continues Mr Skeat) the meaning of this gloss amounts nearly to the following:

Whoso willeth to be hale, before all-things need is that he hold the perfect faith:

Which except each-one hold entire and unblemished, without doubt he shall perish for ever.

Verily, the only belief is that, that we worship one god in threeness and threeness in oneness.

And not mingling the persons (*lit.* hoods), and not disjoining the substance (*lit.* speed).

One is verily the person of the Father, another of the Son, another of the Holy Ghost.

But of the Father and of the Son and of the Holy Ghost the divinity is one; alike their glory, coeternal the majesty.

Of what sort is the Father, of such sort the Son, of such sort also the Holy Ghost.

Unsown is the Father, unsown is the Son, and unshapen is the Holy Ghost.

Beyond measure is the Father, beyond measure the Son, and beyond measure the Holy Ghost.

Eternal is the Father, eternal is the Son, and eternal is the Holy Ghost.

And nevertheless, not three eternal, but one eternal.

So not three unshapen, nor three immeasureable; but one is unshapen, and one immeasureable.

And likewise almighty the Father, almighty the Son, and almighty the Holy Ghost.

And nevertheless, not three almighties, but one almighty.

And so the Father, he is God; the Son God, and the Holy Ghost God.

And nevertheless, not three Gods, but one is God.

And so he, the Father, is Lord; the Son Lord, and the Holy Ghost Lord.

And nevertheless, not three Lords, but one is Lord.

Because, even as separately each one Person [we are compelled][1] of Christian verity to confess [to be] God and Lord,

[1] *Compellimur* is left unglossed.

So, to say three Gods or [three] Lords, by the perfect religion we are forbidden.

The Father of none is He wrought, nor shapen.

The Son is from the Father Himself, not wrought, nor shapen, but begotten.

The Holy Ghost is from the Father and the Son: not wrought, nor shapen, nor begotten, but forth-stepping.

One altogether is the Father, not three Fathers: one is the Son, not three Sons; one the Holy Ghost, not three Holy Ghosts.

And in this threeness nothing is earlier or after: nothing is greater or less.

But all the three Persons are coeternal with themselves and coequal.

So that, through all things, as altogether above is said, both threeness in oneness and oneness in threeness are to worship.

Whoso willeth to be altogether hale, so let him understand concerning the threeness.

But necessity is to eternal health that we verily the incarnation of the Lord our Saviour the King[1], each one of us, [faithfully believe].[2]

It is earnestly the right belief that we believe and confess, for that the Lord our Saviour Christ, God's Son, is God and Man together.

God He is of the substance (*lit.* speed) of the Father [before][2] the world begotten, and Man, of the substance of the mother, in the world begotten.

Perfect God, perfect man He is: of a reasonable soul and of human flesh abiding.

Alike He is to the Father, after [His] divinity: less than the Father, after [His] humanity.

But though He be God and man, not twain however, but one is Christ.

One is He verily, not of the conversion of divinity into flesh, but in [the assumption][2] of humanity into God.

One altogether, not by confusion of substance, but by oneness of Person.

Verily, even as the reasonable soul and flesh is one man, so God and man is one Christ;

Who suffered for our health, He descended downwards to the hell-people: the third day He arose from the dead.

He ascended into heaven: He sitteth at the right hand of God the Father almighty: thence He is to come to doom the quick and dead.

At whose advent all men, to arise have they with their bodies, and are to yield a reason concerning their own [deeds].[2]

And they that have wrought good shall fare to eternal life, and they that have verily [wrought] evil, to eternal fire.

This is the complete belief, which, except each truly and securely believe, he may not be hale[3].

[1] The English formerly translated *Christ* by *King* or *Conqueror*.

[2] Omitted in the gloss.

[3] Other copies of the Athanasian Creed with Anglo-Saxon glosses may be seen

(1) In the Cotton manuscript, Vespasian A. 1.

(2) In the Cotton manuscript, Vitellius E. 18.

(3) In the Arundel MS. 60.

(4) In the Bibl. Reg. 2 B. v. and in

Hickes' *Thesaurus*, Vol. I. p. 233, contains a paraphrase of the Athanasian Creed in old English verse, in a Northern dialect (about A.D. 1300), copied from MS. Bodley NE. 66, fol. 69, back. It begins:

Who so wil be sauf to blis
Before alle þinges nede to is
Þat he hald with alle his miht
Þe heli trauthe and leue it riht.

§ 5. We come now to a translation of the Quicunque, which is frequently attributed to Wicliffe, and was undoubtedly of his time[1]. The copy which I print below was transcribed from the manuscript Ee. I. 10, in the Cambridge University Library, by the Reverend J. Rawson Lumby, and by him most kindly placed at my disposal. Mr Lumby has written gh for the ȝ of the manuscript, and put th instead of þ. The volume in which it is found is said to be a copy of Wicliffe's Bible. It seems more nearly to be a Psalter. The Canticles of the Morning and Evening services are inserted at the end of the Psalms, there is no Apostles' Creed nor Lord's Prayer, but after the Nunc Dimittis comes the "Quicunque vult." It will be seen that in the clause "that we worschipen oo God in Trynyte in oonheed," some words have dropped out by mistake.

Whoever wole be saif it is nedeful before alle other thingis that he holde comune bileeve. That but if ech man kepe it hool and undefouled, withouten doute, he schal perische withouten eende. This is comune bileve, that we worschipen oo God in Trynyte in oonheed. Neither medlinge these persones, ne the substaunce departing. Ther is other persone of the fadir, other of the sone, other of the holi goost. But of the fadir, and the sone, and the holy goost is oo godhede, evene glorie, and comune majestie withouten eende. Which is the fadir sich is the sone, sich is the holi goost. Unmaid is the fadir, unmaid is the sone, and unmaid is the holi goost. The fadir is withouten mesure myche, the sone is withouten mesure myche, the holi goost is withouten mesure myche. The fadir is withouten bigynnyng, and withouten eending, and so ben the sone and the holi goost. And netheles ther ben not iii Goddis but oo god and ther ben not iii unmaad, ne iii thus grete, but oon unmaad and oon thus greet. Also almighti is the fadir, almighti the sone, almighti the holi goost. And netheles there ben not iii almighti goddis, but oo god is almyghti. So the fadir is god, the sone is god, the holi goost is god. And netheles ther ben not iii goddis, but ther is oo god.

the Salisbury Psalter which resembles it.

(5) In the MS. at Trinity College Cambridge, known as the Eadwin or Canterbury Psalter.

(6) In a MS. at Lambeth described at pp. 268, 269, of Wanley's Catalogue, and others.

[1] It may be compared with the paraphrase published in Wicliffe's remains.

So the fadir is lord, the sone is lord, the holi goost is lord, and netheless ther ben not iii lordis but ther is oo lord. For as we ben nedi to knouleche bi cristen treuthe god and lord ech persone synguleli, or arowe or oonli, so we ben defendid by general religioun to seie that ther ben iii goddis or lordis. The fadir is maid of noon ne maid of nought ne bigeten. The sone is of the oon fadir, not made, ne maid of nought, but born. The holi goost cometh bothe of the fadir and the sone not maid, ne maid of nought, but comyng forth. Therfore ther is oo fadir not iii fadris, oo sone not iii sones, oo holi goost not iii holi goostes. And in this trinite is nought bifore ne aftir, not more or lasse, but alle iii persones ben evene withouten bigynnyng and eende, and evene in power and in godhede. So bi al that is now bifore seid, that oonheed in triuyte, and trinyte in oonheed be to be worschipid. Therfore who wole be saif thus fele he of the trinyte. But necessarie it is to evermore lasting heele that he trowe treuly also the incarnacioun of oure lord Ihesu crist. Therfore it is right bileve that we bileven and knoulechen that oure lord Ihesu crist the sone of God is god and man. He is God of his fadris substance born bifore worldis, and he is man of his modiris substance born in the world. He is perfite God, perfite man of a resonable soule and being of mannes fleisch. Evene to the fadir bi his godhede, and lasse than the fadir bi his manhede. The which though he be god and man, netheles he is not two but oon crist. Forsothe he is not oon by tyrnyng of godhede into fleisch, but bi taking of manhede into God. He is algatis oon, not by confusioun of his substaunce, but bi oonhede of his persone. For whi as a resonable soule and fleisch is oo man so god and man oon is crist. The which suffride for our helthe, he wente doun in to hellis, the iii[e] dai he roos from deede. He steigh to hevenes, he sitteth on the right side of God fadir almyghti, from thennes he is to come to deme the quyke and the deede. At whos comyng alle men schulen rise with ther bodies, and thei schulen gife resoun to Crist of ther owne deedis. And thei that han doon goodis schulen go to lyf withouten eende, and thei that han doo yvelis schulen go to the fire withouten eende. This [is] general bileeve the which but if ech man trowe trueli and stidfastli he mai not be saif.

§ 6. Of the Primers which fell under Mr Maskell's attention, none which preceded the Reformation era appears to have contained a translation of the Quicunque.

In his second volume (II. xli.), however, Mr Maskell describes a volume published by Petyt in 1543, as containing among other things "the symbole or Crede of the great Doctour Athanasius, called *Quicunque vult.*" But this was later in point of time than a volume entitled "the Manual of prayers, or the Primer, in English, set out at length......set forth by John, late Bishop of Rochester, at the commandment of the Right Honourable Lord Thomas Crumwell, Lord Privy Seal, Vicegerent of the King's Highness," and sold, "in Powles Churchyarde, by Andrewe Hester, at the Whyt Horse, and also by Mychel Lobley, at the sygne of Saynt Mychell......1539." A copy of this was printed by Dr Burton, in his edition of the Three Primers of Henry

VIII.'s reign, Oxford, 1834, p. 325, and a collation of it will be given below. This is Bishop Hilsey's Primer. And about the year 1542 (the catalogue of the British Museum is my authority for the date,) appeared another translation of the "Creed." Then was published (according to a manuscript note, by Edward Whytechurch,) "the Psalter of David in English, truly translated out of the Latin. Every Psalme having his argument before declaring briefely thintent and substaunce of the whole psalme whereunto is annexed in thend certayne godly prayers thoroweout the whole yere comenly called collettes." These "collettes" were verbal translations from the Latin. Thus "God the illuminator of all Heythen, which this day didst open the onely begotten to ye heythen (a stare being hyd) graunt to thy people that they may enjoye perpetuall peace, and poure into our heartis that shynynge light that thou dyddest breathe into the myndes of the thre kynges."

After the collects comes the Colophon; and then four leaves noted *i. and *ii., with the "Song of the Children in the Ouen, Song of the Uirgin, Song of Zachary the Prophet, Song of Symeon, Song of Augustin and Ambrose:" and "the Crede or Symbole of Doctour Athanasius...... called Quicunque uult." This translation was not known to Waterland, and (I believe) was never reprinted until it appeared in a letter addressed to the Dean of Chichester, which I published in 1870. I print it once more, retaining in great measure the old spelling.

The crede or Symbole of doctour Athanasius dayly red in the Church: called Quicunque vult.

Whatsoeuer he be that wyl be saued, before all thynges it is nedeful that he holde and understande the true Catholyke fayth.

Which fayth but yf euery man well keep whole and inuiolate, without doubt he shall perish for euer.

Truly this is the verye true catholyke fayth, y^t^ we worshypp one God in trinitie: and the trinitie in unitie.

Neyther we confoundynge the personnes neither separatyng the substaunce.

The person of the father is one, the persone of the sonne is an other, the person of the holy ghost an other.

But the deuinitie of the father and of the sonne and of the holye ghoste is one equael glorye, coeterne maiestie.

What father, suche sonne, suche holy ghost.

The father is uncreate, the sonne uncreate, uncreate is the holy ghost.

The father is without measure, the sonne without measure, the holy ghost w^t^out measure.

The father is euerlastyng, the son euerlastynge, the holy ghost euerlastynge.

And notwithstandynge there be not thre euerlastynge but one euerlastynge.

As they be not thre uncreate nor thre without measure; but one uncreate & one w^t^out measure.

Lykewyse the father is almyghtye and the son almyghtye, the holy ghost almyghtye.

And notwithstanding they be not thre almyghtye but one God almyghtye.

So the father is God, the sonne is God, the holye Ghoste is God.

And notwithstanding they be not thre Goddes but one God.

So the father is a Lorde, the Sonne is a Lorde the holy ghost a Lorde.

And notwithstandyng they be not thre Lordes but one Lorde.

For as we are compelled by the verye Truthe of Christes fayth to confesse separatlye every one person to be God and Lorde.

So we be prohybite by the very true catholyke religion of Christes faith to saye ther be three Goddes and thre Lordes.

The father is made of none, neyther create nor gotten.

The son is from the father alone, not made create, but gotten.

The holye ghost is from the father & the sone not made nor create nor gotten but procedyng.

Therefore is but one father, not thre fathers: one sonne, not thre sonnes: one holy ghost, not thre holy ghostes: and in this Trinitie there is none before or after an other, nothynge more or lesse, but all the thre personnes be coeterne and coequale to them selfe.

So that it maye be by all thynges as nowe it hath bene aboue sayde that the Trinitie in unitie, and the unitie in Triuitie may be worshipped.

He therefore that wyll be saued so let him think and understande of the trinitie.

But it is necessary unto euerlastynge health, that euery Christen man beleue faythfully also the incarnacion of our Lorde Jesu Chryste.

It is therefore the ryght fayth, that we beleue and confesse that our Lorde Jesu Chryste the sonne of God and man (*sic*).

He is God by the substaunce of the father, gotten before all worldes, and he is man by the substaunce of his mother borne in this worlde.

Perfect God, perfect man, being of reasonable soule and of flesh humane.

Equal to the father by his godheed, lesse than the father by his manheed.

Which though he be God and man, notwythstandynge he is not twayne but one Chryst.

Truly he is one, not by the turning of his godheed in his manheed: but by the assumptynge of his manheed in his godheed he is utterlye one, not by confusion or mixture of substaunce but by unitie of person.

For as the reasonable soule and the fleshlye bodye is: or maketh one man: so God and man is one Chryst.

Which hath suffred death for our health, he hath descended to helles he hathe rysen from death the thyrde daye.

He hath ascended to heavens, he sytteth on the ryght hande of God the father almightye from thence he shall come to judge quycke and deade.

At whose commying all men haue to rise with theyr bodyes and shall give accompte of theyr owne proper dedes.

And they that have done well shall go into euerlastyng lyfe: they that have done evyll into euerlastyng fyre.

This is the catholyke fayth, which but euerye man faythfully and stedfastlye shall beleue, he shall not be hable to be saved.

The chief points in which the version set forth by Bishop Hilsey differed from the edition of Whitechurch are these:

i. Hilsey has "Such as is the Father, &c.," where Whytechurch has "What father, suche sonne, suche holy ghost."

ii. H. had "immeasurable," where W. has "without measure."

They both, however, retained the later (and old order) "As they be not three uncreate nor three, &c."

iii. H. "three almyghties," W. "thre almyghtye."

iv. H. "the Father is the Lord," W. "a Lord."

v. H. "the Christian verity," W. "the very Truthe of Christes fayth."

(Both had "confesse separately").

vi. H. "by the catholic religion of Christ's faith," W. "by the very true catholyke religion of Christen faith."

vii. H., in clause 22, "neither made nor created."

(H. agrees with W., "there is none before or after another: nothing more or less").

They both had "the Trinity in unity and the unity in Trinity," which seems therefore to have been the old English order. The following are Hilsey's readings.

viii. § 28, "He therefore that will be saved let him understand this of the Trinity."

(Hilsey supplies the omission of Whytechurch, "the Son of God is god and man").

ix. § 31, "born in the world."

x. H. separates the clauses 35, 36.

xi. H. reads "for our salvation, descended to hell."

xii. "All men must rise."

xiii. "He cannot be saved."

Thus it will be seen that the authorised translation prepared by Bishop Hilsey approximates more nearly to our present version than the later (if later) copy published by Whytechurch.

§ 7. And now we come to the translation which was adopted in 1549, as the version of the English Church. Any person who will take the trouble to compare the chief points in which it differs from the earlier translations will note the following variations;—which are not variations of mere language (due, it might be said, to the finer taste of Cranmer, a taste to which Archbishop Laurence, nearly seventy years ago, drew such marked and deserved attention), but must have some other origin.

(1) "Separating the substance" was altered to "dividing":

(2) The word "and" was added in clauses 7, 8, 9, 10, 13, 15:

(3) "Without measure" or "immeasurable" was altered to "incomprehensible":

(4) The order in the first member of clause 12 was changed: (it had been "as they be not three uncreate nor three immeasurable": it was now "as also there be not three incomprehensibles nor three uncreated":

(5) The words "confess separately" became "acknowledge every Person by himself":

(6) "The Holy Ghost is from the Father and the Son": here *of* was substituted for *from*, as in the previous verse, and repeated "of the Father and of the Son":

(7) "None before or after another, nothing more or less" became "none is afore or after other, none is greater or less than another":

(8) "As now it hath been above said" became "as is aforesaid":

(9) The order in 27 was altered:

(10) "Let him thus think" became "must thus think":

(11) "Every Christian man" became "he also":

(12) "Believe faithfully" became "believe rightly":

(13) "Turning of the godhead in his manhood" became "turning of the godhead into flesh":

(14) "Assumpting" became "taking":

(15) "All men have to rise" became "all men shall rise":

(16) "Of their own proper deeds" became "of their work":

(17) "Which but everye man faithfully and stedfastly shall believe" became "which except a man believe faithfully".

And (18) the document was entitled, "This Confession of our Christian Faith."

Those of my readers who have followed the evidence which I have adduced, will perhaps have noticed that in no Latin document is the Quicunque called "Fidei Christianæ Confessio." And if they will refer to the lists at the end of the early chapters of Waterland, they will see that this title is nowhere found in Latin. But the Greek ἡ τῆς πίστεως ὁμολογία τοῦ Ἀθανασίου is found under the dates 1360 and 1439. Thus even the title given to the Quicunque in our Prayer-Book is Greek in its origin. And of the 17 changes in the English which I have noted above, by far the majority may be traced to the Greek, as it appeared in Stephens or (what seems to be identical) Bryling. It is of course possible that Cranmer may have seen a manuscript.

Thus in regard to (1) both printed copies read μερίζοντες, *dividing*, when the Latin has *separantes* and the old English *separating:*

(2) The καὶ is found in the Greek of 7, 8, 9, 10, 13. In Cephaleus it is also in 15, 17 (not in Bryling). In all these the *et* is omitted in the Sarum version of the Creed, and in Whytechurch and Hilsey, but it is inserted in Cranmer's. So far we are in harmony with Cephaleus.

(3) "Incomprehensible" in 9, 12 undoubtedly came from the Greek ἀκατάληπτος.

(4) The order of the Prayer-Book Version follows the order of Cephaleus and Bryling (not of Baiff).

(5) The expression "confess every Person by Himself" (in which at one period of my life I found a great difficulty) seems again to come from the Greek of Cephaleus, ἰδίαν ἕκαστον, and this is generally now believed to be a misprint for ἰδίᾳ ἕκαστον. So much mischief may one mistake occasion! for undoubtedly our English version does apparently "divide the substance."

(8) In this I seem to trace the influence of the Greek καθὼς εἴρηται over the Latin "ut jam supra dictum est." The reference in the Latin is clearly to clause 3. The English is vague.

(9) Here the arrangement follows the Greek, instead of that which I have designated as the old English order.

(11) Here too we had in the old English versions traces of the *unusquisque*, which disappeared before the simpler Greek.

(12) "Believe rightly" unquestionably comes from ἔτι ὀρθῶς πιστεύσῃ: the Latin has *fideliter*.

(13) I think that the old English here retained evidence of the Latin *in carne, in Deo*. Our modern version follows decidedly the εἰς σάρκα, εἰς θεόν.

(14) "Assumpting," from the Latin "adsumptio," became "taking" from the Greek προσλήψει.

(15) "All men have to rise" (resurgere habent) became from ἀναστήσονται, "shall rise again."

(16) "De factis propriis, *of their own proper deeds*" became milder "of their own works" ἐξ ἰδίων ἔργων.

And, lastly, (17) "which except a man believe faithfully" is a plain rendering of ἐὰν μή τις πιστῶς πιστεύσῃ.

Thus of the 18 changes (including the title) which I have thought worthy of notice as having been introduced in 1549, 15 may be traced to the influence of the Greek version, such as that published by Cephaleus[1]. As to the origin of ten of these there can be no doubt. Of the number, some are of little moment and are only interesting in an archæological point of view. But others have been the cause of some trouble; either increasing the difficulty of understanding the Creed (as in the word *incomprehensible*); or introducing a savour of error (as "we confess every Person by Himself"); or increasing the severity of the denuntiation (attributing to a "right belief," a belief of the head, what the Latin Church attributed to a "faithful belief," a belief of the heart).

[1] It will be remembered that two copies of "Cephaleus" have been found in England, none I believe of the other editions except Mr Ferrers' "Wechel."

Of the other alterations, that which I numbered (6) is immaterial.

In (7) Cranmer transferred to the second clause the "exposition" contained in the first.

No. (10) seems attributable to the German of Luther: "wer nun selig werden der muss also von der drey Personen in Gott halten."

These may merit a passing remark. And the manuscript, Reg. 2 B. v. of the British Museum belonged to Cranmer. We have therein an old marginal note, "nullus major aut minor," which possibly weighed with the Archbishop in producing the version of our Prayer-Book.

And the "must" of our clause 28 should not be interpreted as rigidly as our modern notions of the word would seem to require. As representing "ita sentiat," or *οὕτω περὶ Τριάδος φρονείτω*, the words "must thus think of the Trinity," can only have been intended to mean what we now should represent as "should thus think." We can read the clause in the light of the language of the sixteenth century[1].

§ 8. It will be agreed by all judges that Bishop Vowler Short[2] had ample authority for his statement that the English Translation of the Athanasian Creed was taken by mistake from the Greek: in other words that at the time of the Reformation it

[1] As to that language, the following remarks of my kind friend Mr Skeat are worthy of attention.

Must. If it be enquired what was the exact meaning of such a phrase as "*must* thus think of the Trinity" in the time of Henry VIII., the answer is that it does not necessarily imply any very strong obligation. *Must* was then used in two ways, first, with the sense of necessary obligation, in which case it frequently was followed by the word *nedes* (the genitive of *need* used adverbially), and, secondly, with the sense of *would have to,* by no means implying any very strong necessity. It is therefore clear that no great stress can be laid upon it as necessarily implying obligation.

A few extracts from Latimer's *Seven Sermons*, preached in Lent, 1549, will make this clearer. I refer to the pages of Arber's reprint.

Examples of the first usage :—

"If thei bie, thei *must nedes* sel;" p. 147.

Example of the second usage :—

"If I beare with [*i.e.* connive at] other mennes synnes, I *muste* [*i.e.* shall have to] say, Deliver me from my other mennes synnes. A straung sayinge;" p. 155.

But it is to be noted, that the word *must* was used to imply every kind of obligation, from small to great, and it is impossible in every case to assign the exact degree of necessity implied.

Examples. "*Oportet me euangelizare,* &c. I *must* preache the kyngedome of god to other cyties also, I *muste* shewe them my fathers will; for I came for that purpose"..."Our Savioure Christ sayed, howe he *muste* not tarye in one place;" p. 164.

"Except a man be borne agayne, &c. ...He *muste* haue a regeneracion"; p. 167.

Cleveland's Concordance to Milton shews that Milton (in his Poems) always uses the word of strict obligation.

The Concordance to Shakespeare omits *must*, but it is treated of in Abbott's Shakespearian Grammar, 3rd ed. p. 222. Examples:

"He *must* fight singly to-morrow with Hector." *Tro. and Cress.* III. 3, l. 247 (Globe).

Here "He *must*" means "he will have to," "he is to."

"Descend, for you *must* be my torch-bearer." *Mer. of Ven.* II. 6, l. 40.

See also *Mer. of Ven.* IV. 1, l. 182; *Mid. Nt. Dr.* II. 1, l. 72.

Cf. "And I *must* be from hence." *Macbeth*, IV. 3, l. 212.

"A life which *must* not yield
To one of woman born."
Macbeth V. 8, l. 12.

[2] *History of the Church of England,* § 807, p. 589.

was considered that the document was truly the fruit of Athanasius' care, and that its original was to be looked for in the Greek language. So far as appears now, only two or three copies in Greek had been printed in 1549; the copy published by Bryling at Basle, and that of Cephaleus at Strasburg in 1524, and that of Wechel in 1538: and in accordance with these two last the English translation was altered.

§ 9. Before I leave this subject, I may notice the changes which were subsequently introduced into our translation: for I need not inform any student of the English Prayer Book, that throughout the century which elapsed between our first Prayer Book of Edward VI. and our last Prayer Book of Charles II., continued efforts were made to amend the Book in various respects.

In 1552, in clause 40, "give account of their own works" was altered to "for their own works."

In 1559, "*but*" (but one man, but one Christ) was continued in clause 37. It was omitted in 1604.

These are all the changes worthy of note, until we come to the Scotch Prayer Book of 1637, when Archbishop Laud exhibited his willingness to make further progress. Communications had been opened with the Church of Constantinople through their Metropolitan, Cyril Lucar, and it seems that some additional Greek manuscripts had been sent to England. Laud, acting, as he stated, under the direction of his royal master[1], modified in clause 28 the English version as follows: "He therefore that would be saved, let him thus think of the Trinity."

Besides this, in clause 2, *holy* was altered to *whole:* in clause 12, *there be not* to *there are not*: in clause 29, *believe rightly in the Incarnation* to *believe rightly the Incarnation:* in clause 37, *so God and man is one Christ* to *so He who is God and man is one Christ*, the latter being probably taken from the ὁ Θεάνθρωπος of the Greek version. These appear to have been all, but they shew that Laud was not absolutely rigid in the matter. He was urged by Bishop Wedderburne of Dunblane to make further alterations in the Prayer Book: the King directed Laud and Wren to consider them, and the two Bishops made their Report to Charles: the result was this, "In the Creed of St Athanasius, we can agree to no more emendations, no, not according to our best Greek Copies, than you shall find amended in this book[2]." A further point is evident: they still deemed that the Greek was the original, but Laud avoided the

[1] See Laud's works, VI. part ii. p. 455. [2] p. 457.

blunder of Wren: according to his book, the Apostles' Creed (THE CREED as it was still called) was always to be said or sung: only, on the appointed days, "immediately after Benedictus," and therefore before THE CREED, was to follow the "Confession of our Christian Faith, *Quicunque vult.*"

Of these alterations introduced by Laud into the Scotch Version, the most important was passed over in our own, in the revision of 1662. But in the mean time the faith of the English Divines, as to the authorship of the Creed, had been shaken; and, in greater deference to the scholarship of the day, the words were added in the preliminary rubric, "commonly called the Creed of Saint Athanasius."

§ 10. And a further act shews that the Caroline divines were not determined to close their eyes to the truth. They may have felt a difficulty in altering the English version of the Athanasian Creed: there seems to have been no call upon them to do so: but of their own free will they elected to follow the Latin text in parts of the version which the Welsh Bishops prepared for the use of the Churches of the Principality. I am informed by a friend on whom I can rely, that not only in clause 1 does the version bring out clearly that the meaning is "Whosoever willeth to be saved," and in clause 4, "neither mixing together the persons nor separating the substance," but in clause 23 they have "the Holy Ghost is of the Father and the Son:" in 28, "whosoever willeth to be saved let him be thus minded of the Trinity:" the Latin *immensus* is accepted and explained as *unmeasurable:* and in clause 29 they have once more the Latin, "It is also necessary for the sake of eternal salvation that a man believe faithfully as to the Incarnation of Jesus Christ." But the last clause follows the English, for it omits the word *firmiterque* in the phrase "fideliter firmiterque crediderit."

There was no proposal to alter the translation of the year 1688.

§ 11. I should add that Dr Ceriani shewed me an Italian translation of the Creed in a manuscript at Milan (A. 145 supra), which contained a translation of the Pastoral Rule of St Gregory: it was the only other thing in the codex.

§ 12. And Mr Muller, the great bookseller of Amsterdam, allowed me to examine a Hymn Book of the Evangelical Lutheran Church in Holland (of the year 1857), which contained in the

Appendix "Symbolum of Belijdenis van Athanasius, van de Heilige drie-eenheld, tegen de Arianen." This is the title in the book itself. In the table of contents it is called "de Geloofsbelijdenis van Athanasius."

§ 13. And I am indebted to my friend Mr Wratislaw for the following note of a Bohemian version.

THOMAS OF STITNY in his Bohemian work '*O ob. ecnych vecech Krestanskych*' (1376), 'of general Christian matters,' in the first book 'on faith,' '*o vire*,' after giving the Apostles' Creed, and that commonly known as the Nicene Creed, proceeds as follows (p. 14 of K. J. Erban's edition):

"There is yet a third creed written down by the holy clergy, and it is, as it were, an exposition of both these records of the faith. This they chant as a psalm daily at the first hour, to this effect: 'Whosoever desireth to be saved, &c.' ....And thus, as I said before, they who have understanding ought rightly to believe and know those twelve things, which are written down in the Creed by the Apostles. If any one is more intelligent let him mark how it is set down in the Creed, which is sung at the Mass. If any one cannot settle himself therewith let him mark the description of the faith, which is sung at the first hour. And when thou contemplatest all this description of the faith, see that thou be not contrary to any one thing of them all; but if thou understandest not aught ask one wiser than thyself; and till he instruct thee, say to thyself mentally, 'Though I understand this not, yet my superiors understand it, and as they understand so I believe; and that knowing, that I ought to believe all that is affirmed by the holy Church, that my faith may be entire.'"

JOHN HUSS in his 'Exposition of the Creed' ('*Vyklad Very*'), explains at considerable length the Apostles' Creed, and afterwards more briefly the Nicene Creed. Of the pseudo-Athanasian Creed he makes no direct mention, although the language he uses in commenting on the Nicene Creed frequently approaches and may have been adapted from its wording.

CHAPTER XXXIV.

NOTES FROM THE YEAR 1200 TO THE REFORMATION.

§ 1. Walter of Cantilupe. § 2. Thomas Aquinas. § 3. Walter of Durham. § 4. Friar John Peckham. § 5. Synod of Exeter. § 6. Other of Waterland's authorities. § 7. Visitation of the Sick in the Sarum Manual. § 8. Lyndwood's Provinciale.

It will be scarcely deemed necessary that I should accumulate all the notices that have been discovered by Voss, Tentzel, Montfaucon and others, of the Athanasian Creed between the year 1000 and the Reformation. Still some of these notices are curious, and perhaps my volume would scarcely be satisfactory without them: I shall pass over those to which I have before referred.

§ 1. We have in Spelman and Wilkins a series of Constitutions put forth by Walter of Cantilupe, Bishop of Worcester, in the synod held at his Cathedral Church on the morrow of St James in the year 1240. They are interesting, and I will note the subjects of the earlier regulations, leading us up to that with which we have to do.

They relate i. to the Furniture and Books of the Church: ii. to their dedication: "No layman is to stand in the Chancel, save the Patrons and the more sublime Persons": iii. the reverence due to the Church-yard, which contains the bodies of those "who are to be saved:" (quæ corpora continent salvandorum): v. is on baptism, "from which our salvation takes its commencement:" on private baptism, and on completion of the service. vi. Confirmation should be within the year. vii. viii. ix. are on the conservation of the host, and conveying it to the sick. Marriage is conceded: "trina denuntiatione præcedente." Then we come to a canon on the danger of worshipping fountains (!). All are to confess once a year at least. Then "Let the priests know what are required for the sacrament of penance, and that the observance of the ten commandments is necessary for the salvation of the faithful. We exhort in the name of the Lord all priests and shepherds of souls, that they know these commandments, in order that they may frequently

32—2

teach them and explain them to their people. They must know too what are the seven deadly sins (criminalia), and, at least, the seven ecclesiastical sacraments, what they are. And let them have at least a simple understanding (simplicem intellectum), in accordance to that which is contained in the Psalm entitled *Quicunque vult* and in the greater and lesser Symbol, that in these they may instruct the people committed to their charge." And the priests, of whom some are simple, should know what are the special faults for which penances are reserved to the higher authorities.

§ 2. I have mentioned that Pope Innocent III. acknowledged only two Creeds.

In his *Summa Theologiæ secunda secundæ*, quæst. 1, Art. 8. Thomas Aquinas considers the question whether the Articles of the Faith can be conveniently enumerated.

He counts up fourteen articles: one on the Unity of the Divinity; three on the Persons of the Trinity; one on the Creation; one on Grace and Sanctification; one on the Glory of the Resurrection. Thus we have seven. Then we have seven on the Incarnation, being respectively, on the conception; the nativity; the passion; the descent to hell; the resurrection; the ascension; the return to judgment. Passing on to Art. 9 we find that it is on the use and lawfulness of Creeds. The same truth is taught in all the Creeds, only more diffusively in the later Creeds. The Nicene Creed is called *Symbolum Patrum:* he says that it is "a declaration of the Symbol of the Apostles, and that it was composed after the faith was made manifest and when the Church had peace. Hence it is publicly chanted in the mass. But the Apostles' Symbol, which was put forth at a time of persecution and before the faith was published, is on this account still said secretly."

The next question was; Did the office of ordaining or constituting a Creed belong to the Pope? This Thomas was inclined to hold. But there was a difficulty in regard to the Athanasian Creed. "Athanasius was not the chief Pontiff, but Patriarch of Alexandria: yet he framed a Symbol which is sung in the Church." Thomas held that the order against the framing of new Creeds applied to private persons: and, clearly, the prohibition by one synod may be put on one side by another: it cannot prevent a later synod from doing what may be deemed necessary, as new heresies arise. But his main answer was this: "Athanasius did not compose his declaration of the faith in the form of a symbol, but rather in the form of a kind of lesson, as is manifest from the very form of his speaking[1]: but, because his lesson contained in few terms the completed truth of the Faith, by the authority of the chief Pontiff it is received, so as to be held as a Rule of the Faith."

I will abstain from any remarks on this interesting notice, merely however mentioning that Waterland omitted to quote the words "ut ex ipso modo loquendi apparet."

[1] Non composuit manifestationem fidei per modum symboli sed magis per modum cujusdam doctrinæ ut ex ipso modo loquendi apparet.

§ 3. In 1255, Walter of Durham put forth some Constitutions, repeating the substance of many of those issued at Worcester fifteen years before, and in almost the same language. That relating to the Creeds ran as follows; every priest was to have

"A simple understanding of the faith as it is more expressly contained in the Symbol as well the longer as the shorter; which is in the Psalm Quicunque vult and also in the Credo in Deum: and also in the Lord's Prayer which is called Pater noster." The language is curious: the Symbol is contained in the Psalm. To directions such as these we doubtless owe the explanations and comments on the Apostles' Creed, the Lord's Prayer and the Decalogue, which are found in our Public Libraries.

§ 4. In the year 1281 Friar John Peckham, Archbishop of Canterbury, published at Lambeth, on Friday "the sixth of the Ides of October," a series of Constitutions which may be seen—the original in Spelman vol. II. p. 328, or Wilkins II. p. 51, or, in an English Translation, in John Johnson's English Canons vol. II. p. 271—303 of the edition of the Anglo-Catholic Library. The ninth canon, which is interesting to us, may be seen also in part on pp. 1, 2 of Lyndwood's Provinciale.

"The ignorance of priests plunges the people into error; and the stupidness of clerks who are commanded to instruct the faithful in the catholic faith does rather mislead than teach them. Some who preach to others do not visit the places which most of all want light; as the prophet says, 'The little ones asked bread, and there was no man to break it to them;' and another cries, 'The poor and needy seek water, their tongue is dry for thirst.' As a remedy for these mischiefs we ordain and enjoin that every priest who presides over a people shall four times in the year, that is, once a quarter, on some one or more solemn days, by himself or by some other, expound to the people in the vulgar tongue, without any fantastical affectation of subtilty, the fourteen articles of faith; the ten commandments of the decalogue; the two precepts of the Gospel, or of love to God and man; the seven works of mercy; the seven capital sins, with their progeny; the seven principal virtues; and the seven sacraments of grace. And that ignorance may be no man's excuse, though all ministers of the Church are bound to know them, we have here briefly summed them up. Ye are to know then that there are seven articles of faith belonging to the mystery of the Trinity, four of them do belong to the Deity intrinsically, three of them to Its operations. The first is the unity of the divine essence in the indivisible Trinity of the Three Persons, as it is said, 'I believe in one God.' 2. To believe the Father to be God unbegotten. 3. To believe the Son to be God only-begotten of God. 4. To believe the Holy Ghost to be God neither begotten nor unbegotten, but proceeding both from the

Father and the Son. 5. To believe that the creation of every creature, visible and invisible, is from the entire indivisible Trinity. 6. The sanctification of the Church by the Holy Ghost and by the sacraments of grace, and by all those things in which the Christian Church communicates together: by which we understand that the Church by the Holy Ghost with her sacraments and laws is sufficient for the salvation of every man, though he be a sinner to never so great a degree; and that out of the Church is no salvation. 7. The consummation of the Church in eternal glory, both as to soul and body (which is truly to be raised up again); and by the rule of contraries the eternal damnation of the wicked. The other seven articles belong to Christ's humanity. 1. His Incarnation, or assuming of flesh of the glorious Virgin only, by the Holy Ghost. 2. The nativity of God Incarnate from the incorrupted Virgin. 3. The true passion of Christ, and His dying on the cross under the tyrant Pilate. 4. The descent of Christ into hell (for the conquering of it) as to His soul, while His Body rested in the grave. 5. The true resurrection of Christ. 6. His true ascent into heaven. 7. The sure expectation of His coming to judgment. And there are the ten commandments of the Old Testament."

It will be seen that the various articles required to be known by the clergy follow in the same order as the articles enumerated by Aquinas in § 2 above. They run entirely away from the Articles of the Psalm Quicunque vult.

§ 5. This distinction between the Psalm Quicunque vult and the two Creeds, is again made manifest in a Constitution put forth at Exeter at a synod held there in 1287. This too may be seen in Spelman or Wilkins.

Enquiries are to be made whether the clergy know the Decalogue, the seven mortal sins, the seven sacraments of the Church; and whether they have at all events a simple understanding of the Christian articles of the Faith, as they are contained in the Psalm Quicunque vult and in either symbol: "ni quilibet qui fidem Catholican firmiter non crediderit salvus esse non poterit."

§ 6. Most of the other authorities quoted by Waterland in his second chapter were taken by him from Tentzel's little volume, but they scarcely require any notice. It is curious that Alexander of Ales is the only Englishman who calls the Quicunque a Symbolum. The statement of Waterland at the close of chap. III. that Richard Hampole so designated it, appears to be a mistake.

§ 7. Two points however remain to be mentioned: the one is that in the VISITATIO INFIRMORUM of the Sarum Manual, which we know was in use shortly before the Reformation, (indeed it was printed in the early years of the 16th century), we find the articles of Peckham's sixth constitution taken up and made the vehicle for the instruction of the sick man. And the following fact is especially worthy of notice. The introductory or commendatory clauses of the Quicunque are here found, severed from their context, and used to introduce and to recommend the fourteen articles of Peckham's Constitutions. Thus:

"Most dear brother: render thanks to Almighty God for all His benefits, bearing patiently and kindly the weakness of body which God has now sent upon thee: for if thou wilt endure it humbly and without murmuring, it brings to thy soul the greatest reward and health. And, most dear brother, because thou art about to enter on the way of all flesh, be firm in faith. For whoso is not firm in faith is an unbeliever, and without faith it is impossible to please God. And therefore, if thou wouldest be saved, before all things it is necessary that thou hold the Catholic Faith, which unless thou shalt keep whole and undefiled, without doubt thou shalt perish everlastingly." Then (proceeds the rubric) it is good and expedient that the priest should explain to the sick person the fourteen articles of the faith, of which the former seven belong to the mystery of the Trinity and the other seven to Christ's humanity; so that if by chance he may have erred in any of them or been shaken or uncertain, he may, before he die, whilst the spirit is yet united to the flesh, be brought back to the firm and solid faith. And the priest may say thus: "And the Catholic Faith is this, brother: to believe in one God, that is [one God] in the Unity of the Divine Essence, in the indivisible Trinity of Three Persons" (the words it will be remembered of Peckham's Constitution). The other six of the first group follow, and then the summary: "If thou wouldest therefore be saved, brother, thou shouldest thus think of the Trinity." Then (the rubric proceeds) the priest may express to him the other seven articles pertaining to Christ's humanity, in this fashion: "Similarly, most dear brother, it is necessary to everlasting salvation that thou shouldest believe and confess the Incarnation of our Lord Jesus Christ or His true assumption of the flesh through the Holy Spirit from the glorious Virgin alone." The other six articles follow, and this part closes thus: "This is the Catholic Faith, brother, which, except thou shalt have believed faithfully and firmly, as holy Mother Church believeth, thou canst not be saved."

But this was only to be used in cases when the sick person was a cleric and well taught. If he were a layman or merely "simply literate," then the priest should ask from him the articles of the faith in general in this form:

"Most dear brother, dost thou believe that the Father and the Son and the Holy Spirit are Three Persons and one God? and that the same blessed and undivided Trinity created all things visible and invisible?

and that the Son alone, being conceived of the Holy Ghost, was incarnate of the Virgin Mary: that He suffered and died on the cross for us under Pontius Pilate: that He was buried and descended to hell: that the third day He rose again from the dead: that He ascended into heaven, and that He is to come again to judge the quick and the dead, and that all men shall then arise in body and soul to receive good things or evil, according to their deserts? And dost thou believe the remission of sins through the reception of the Sacraments of the Church? and the Communion of Saints, that is, that all men living in love are partakers of all the good things of grace which are done in the Church, and all who here partake with the just in grace, will partake with them hereafter in glory?" The sick person replied: "In all things I believe firmly as holy Mother Church believeth: protesting before God and all the saints continually, that this is my true and firm intention, in what mode soever any evil spirit may attempt in future to perturb my memory."

Inasmuch as Mr Maskell's volumes have become most rare, I give the original below[1]. The passage offers a curious contrast

[1] FROM SARUM MANUAL.

¶ *Deinde priusquam ungatur infirmus, aut communicetur: exhortetur eum sacerdos hoc modo.*

Frater charissime: gratias age omnipotenti Deo pro universis ✠ beneficiis suis, patienter et benigne suscipiens infirmitatem corporis quam tibi Deus immisit: nam si ipsam humiliter sine murmure toleraveris, infert animæ tuæ maximum præmium et salutem. Et, frater charissime, quia viam universæ carnis ingressurus es, esto firmus in fide. Qui enim non est firmus in fide, infidelis est: et sine fide impossibile est placere Deo. ET IDEO, SI SALVUS ESSE VOLUERIS, ANTE OMNIA OPUS EST UT TENEAS CATHOLICAM FIDEM: QUAM NISI INTEGRAM INVIOLATAMQUE SERVAVERIS, ABSQUE DUBIO IN ÆTERNUM PERIBIS.

¶ *Deinde bonum et valde expediens est ut sacerdos exprimat infirmo .xiiij. articulos fidei: quorum .vij. primi ad mysterium Trinitatis, et .vij. alii ad Christi humanitatem pertinent: ut si forte prius in aliquo ipsorum erraverit, titubaverit, vel dubius fuerit, ante mortem, dum adhuc spiritus unitus est carni, ad fidem solidam reducatur: et potest sacerdos dicere sic.*

FIDES AUTEM CATHOLICA HÆC EST, FRATER.

Credere in unum Deum: hoc est, in Unitate Divinæ Essentiæ: in trium Personarum indivisibili Trinitate.

ij. Patrem ingenitum esse Deum.

iij. Unigenitum Dei Filium: esse Deum per omnia coæqualem Patri.

iiij. Spiritum Sanctum non genitum, non factum, non creatum: sed a Patre et Filio pariter procedentem: esse Deum Patri Filioque consubstantialem etiam et æqualem.

v. Creationem cœli et terræ, id est, omnis visibilis et invisibilis creaturæ, a tota indivisibili Trinitate.

vi. Sanctificationem Ecclesiæ per Spiritum Sanctum et gratiæ sacramenta ac cætera omnia in quibus communicat Ecclesia Christiana: in quo intelligitur, quod Ecclesia Catholica cum suis sacramentis et legibus per Spiritum Sanctum regulata, omni homini, quantumcunque facinoroso peccatori, sufficit ad salutem: et quod extra Ecclesiam Catholicam non est salus.

vij. Consummationem Ecclesiæ per gloriam sempiternam, in anima et carne veraciter suscitandam: et per cujus oppositum, intelligitur æterna damnatio reproborum.

SI VIS ERGO SALVUS ESSE, FRATER: ITA DE MYSTERIO TRINITATIS SENTIAS.

Deinde exprimat ei sacerdos alios septem articulos ad Christi humanitatem pertinentes, hoc modo:

Similiter, frater charissime, NECESSARIUM EST AD ÆTERNAM SALUTEM, UT CREDAS ET CONFITEARIS DOMINI NOSTRI JESU CHRISTI INCARNATIONEM, seu veram carnis assumptionem per Spiritum Sanctum ex sola Virgine gloriosa.

to the death-bed of certain modern Roman Catholics, as such death-beds were unhappily depicted by Dr Newman at the end of his celebrated ninth Lecture on Anglican difficulties.

§ 8. Thus it will be seen that even the simple statements of the Credenda of Archbishop Peckham were deemed too complicated, too difficult, for the ordinary intelligence of the layman or cleric of the fifteenth and early part of the sixteenth centuries.

ij. Veram incarnati Dei nativitatem ex Virgine incorrupta.

iij. Veram Christi passionem et mortem sub tyrannide Pilati.

iiij. Veram Christi descensionem ad inferos in anima ad spoliationem tartari, quiescente corpore ejus in sepulchro.

v. Veram Christi Dei tertia die a morte resurrectionem.

vi. Veram ipsius ad cœlos ascensionem.

vij. Ipsius venturi ad judicium certissimam expectationem.

HÆC EST FIDES CATHOLICA, FRATER, QUAM NISI FIDELITER FIRMITERQUE CREDIDERIS, sicut sancta Mater Ecclesia credit, SALVUS ESSE NON POTERIS.

¶ *Et si infirmus laicus vel simpliciter literatus fuerit: tunc potest sacerdos articulos fidei in generali ab eo inquirere, sub hac forma.*

Charissime frater: Credis Patrem et Filium et Spiritum Sanctum, esse tres Personas et Unum Deum, et ipsam benedictam atque indivisibilem Trinitatem creasse omnia creata visibilia, et invisibilia? Et solum Filium, de Spiritu Sancto conceptum, incarnatum fuisse ex Maria Virgine: passum et mortuum pro nobis in cruce sub Pontio Pilato: sepultum descendisse ad inferna: die tertia resurrexisse a mortuis: ad cœlos ascendisse: iterumque venturum ad judicandum vivos et mortuos, omnesque homines tunc in corpore et anima resurrecturos, bona et mala secundum merita sua recepturos? Et remissionem peccatorum per sacramentorum ecclesiæ perceptionem? Et sanctorum communionem; id est, omnes homines in charitate existentes esse participes omnium bonorum gratiæ quæ fiunt in ecclesia: et omnes qui communicant cum justis hic in gratia, communicare cum eis in gloria?

¶ *Deinde respondeat infirmus.*

Credo firmiter in omnibus, sicut sancta Mater credit Ecclesia: protestando coram Deo et omnibus sanctis continue hoc esse meam veram et firmam intentionem, quomodocunque aliquis spiritus malignus memoriam meam aliter forte in futuro solicitaverit perturbare.

¶ *Deinde dicat sacerdos.*

Charissime frater: quia sine charitate nihil proderit tibi fides, testante Apostolo qui dicit: Si habuero omnem fidem ita ut montes transferam, charitatem autem non habuero, nihil sum: Ideo oportet te diligere Dominum Deum tuum super omnia ex toto corde tuo et ex tota anima tua: et proximum tuum propter Deum sicut teipsum: nam sine hujusmodi charitate nulla fides valet. Exerce ergo charitatis opera dum vales: et si multum tibi affuerit, abundanter tribue: si autem exiguum, illud impartiri stude. Et ante omnia si quem injuste læseris, satisfacias si valeas: sin autem, expedit ut ab eo veniam humiliter postules. Dimitte debitoribus tuis et aliis qui in te peccaverunt, ut Deus tibi dimittat. Odientes te diligas: pro malis bona retribuas. Dimittite (inquit Salvator) et dimittetur vobis. Spem etiam firmam et bonam fiduciam, frater, oportet te habere in Deo, et in misericordia sua: et si occurrerit cogitatui tuo multitudo peccatorum tuorum, dole: sed nullo modo desperes. Imo cogita quoniam (ut testatur scriptura) misericordiæ ejus super omnia opera ejus: et illi soli proprium est misereri semper et parcere: et quia secundum altitudinem cœli a terra, corroboravit misericordiam suam super timentes se. Spera igitur in Deo et fac bonitatem: quoniam sperantem in Domino misericordia circumdabit. Qui sperant in Domino habebunt fortitudinem, et assument pennas ut aquilæ, volabunt et non deficient. Volabunt enim a tenebris ad lumen: a carcere ad regnum: a miseria præsenti ad gloriam sempiternam.

¶ *Deinde stabilito sic infirmo in fide, charitate, et spe, dicat ei sacerdos.*

Et cætera.

I need not say that *a fortiori* must the complex antitheses of the so-called Athanasian Creed have been deemed so. Still it continued to be recited daily at the service of Prime: but it must generally have been recited with the spirit willing, but the intelligence asleep. And we have a fuller illustration of this want of intelligence at the time I speak of. The famous Lyndwood, the editor of Provinciale, lived in 1440. The notes in the margin of his volume represent the instruction given to the Clergy at large at that time. His first subject is the "Faith in the Trinity," and he rushes at once to give the essential part of the Constitutions of Peckham. These Constitutions, and not the Athanasian Creed, furnished him with the text on which he comments. But even here he draws a distinction: he teaches that "the laity are not bound to the same degree of knowledge as are the priests: Peckham's Constitution refers to the priests alone, and of these to such only as are constituted over the people: those who have cure of souls and are bound to teach others, are bound to know the articles of the faith explicitly and distinctly, that so they may be able to explain and defend them. But for the simple and the laity it is sufficient that they believe them implicitly, i.e. as the Catholic Church believes and teaches. Of learned laymen however, are they bound to know and believe more than the simple laity? We reply according to Bernard of Compostella, that it is reasonable that they know the articles more explicitly, but they do not sin mortally if they do not know them more distinctly, or [even] if they are not anxious to know them, because their profession does not call them to this[1]."

[1] Lyndwood's notes, b, c, f. p. 1.

CHAPTER XXXV.

ERA OF THE REFORMATION.

§ 1. Greek writers repudiated the Creed. § 2. Has the Roman Church ever formally accepted it? Canon of Lobowitz. § 3. Reformed Churches. i. Zuinglius. ii. Augsburg. iii. Saxon. iv. French. v. Belgic. vi. Heidelberg. vii. Bohemian. viii. Helvetic, 1566. § 4. Luther and Calvin. § 5. Church of England: i. in 1536. ii. in 1552. iii. Reformatio Legum.

§ 1. I MAY now turn to a subject on which we have evidence which is of considerable interest: I refer to the acceptance of the Quicunque at the time of the Reformation. All doubt as to its authorship was then asleep in western Europe. Only Greek writers continued to deny that Athanasius had composed it as it is. It was in the year 1597, according to Voss, that Meletius, Patriarch of Antioch, wrote to a friend "maintaining that it was clearer than light itself that the Creed falsely ascribed to Athanasius had been adulterated by the additions of the Roman pontiffs[1]."

§ 2. I cannot find that the Church of Rome has ever formally accepted the document. It was, as every one knows, in the English Breviary, before the Reformation, being recited daily at Prime: and it was said by Genebrard "to be in the oldest Horologies (which we now call Breviaries) of the Roman Church[2]." Thus its use is universally acknowledged, but it has not been otherwise definitely sanctioned. The Church of Rome, both in the Council of Trent, and also in the Bull of Pope Pius IV. appointing the form of the Profession of the Faith subsequently to that Council,

[1] "Athanasio falso adscriptum symbolum cum appendice illa Romanorum Pontificum adulteratum loco lucidius contestamur." Voss quotes this from Felckmann's *Athanasius*.

[2] See the passage in Waterland, Chap. VI. under ROME; note.

adduced the Latin form of the Creed of Constantinople as "the Symbolum which the Holy Roman Church useth[1]." Thus even the Apostles' Creed was so far ignored by the Council. In "the Catechism of the Council of Trent," however, which contains an Exposition of the Apostles' Creed (Apostolorum Symbolum), I find some expressions that seem to have come from the Quicunque, but I have not discovered that the Quicunque is ever specially mentioned[2]. Indeed, the only Synodical authority given to it that I have met with, in this communion, is given by a small synod held at Lovitium (Lobowitz ?) in Poland in the year 1556: this canon I found in Martene and Durand's *Amplissima Collectio*[3]: "In the first instance the Symbol of the Apostles, then the Nicene and the Constantinopolitan, and the Symbol of St Athanasius also we receive, venerate, and embrace, and deliver it to all to be received and accepted."

§ 3. I have no doubt that the form of this canon of Lobowitz of the year 1556, was taken from some of the earlier Reformed Confessions. We should never forget that these Confessions were issued with the double purpose, (1) of avowing that the Reformed Congregations stood doctrinally by the older declarations relating to God that had been worked out by the Holy Spirit's aid, and were truly Catholic: and (2) of exhibiting the points in matters of ritual and of doctrine on which the early Church had not spoken, and in which the Reformed Congregations were compelled to differ from the then modern Roman writers. Thus we find most of the Confessions of these Churches commencing with avowals of their belief in God, Trinity in Unity and Unity in Trinity. They do not all mention the Creeds or even

[1] The Bull is printed so far in the Oxford *Sylloge Confessionum*, 1827, p. 3.

[2] Thus on the word *Deum*, "Christiana fides credit et profitetur, sed altius ascendens, ita unum intelligit ut unitatem in Trinitate et Trinitatem in unitate veneretur." In § XII. "Tres sunt in una divinitate personæ: Patris qui a nullo genitus est; Filii qui ante omnia secula a Patre genitus est; Spiritus sancti qui itidem ab æterno ex Patre et Filio procedit." In § XIX. "quemadmodum Deum Patrem, Deum Filium, Deum Spiritum Sanctum, neque tamen tres Deos sed unum Deum esse dicimus: ita æque Patrem et Filium et Spiritum Sanctum omnipotentem, neque tamen tres omnipotentes sed unum omnipotentem esse confitemur." An example this of the mode in which the clauses of the Quicunque may be used to explain to our people some of the difficulties regarding the Divine Essence.

[3] Tom. VIII. p. 1445, "Principio Symbolum Apostolorum Nicænum et Constantinopolitanum: symbolum etiam divi Athanasii recipimus veneramur et complectimur omnibusque recipiendum et amplectandum mandamus." These canons are printed in Streitwolf and Kleiner, *Libri Symbolici Ecclesiæ Catholicæ*.

the Apostles' Creed, but almost all contain references to the latter — many distinctly exhibit, as of authority, the Apostles', the Nicene and the Athanasian symbols.

i. Thus in the Confession of Zuinglius, dated Zurich, 1530, and offered to Charles V., the Swiss divine declares:

"I believe that there is one God... : and entirely in accordance with the Exposition of the Nicene and Athanasian Creed do I think in every point of the Deity Himself and of the Three Names and Persons [1]."

ii. The Augsburg Reformers avowed their belief in the truths relating to the Trinity, and by name condemned those whom the Quicunque condemns without mentioning of names: it does not, however, speak of the Athanasian or other Creeds. Here our own manifesto parts company from the famous Confession which was exhibited in 1531. Yet Luther, as we know, adopted the Quicunque.

iii. The Saxon Confession exhibited at the Council of Trent in 1551 commenced nearly as follows:

"We affirm before God and the Church universal in heaven and earth, that we embrace with a true faith all the writings of the Apostles and Prophets, and this in their true natural meaning (in ipsa nativa sententia) which is expressed in the Symbols, Apostolic, Nicene, Athanasian. These symbols and this their meaning we have constantly embraced, and, God helping us, will embrace to the end [2]."

iv. Passing over, for the present, the English Articles, we come in order of dates to the Confession of the Faith offered to their king, in 1561, by those French who "desired to live according to the purity of the Gospel of our Lord Jesus Christ [3]."

The early articles of this confession relate to God, to the Holy Scripture, to the interpretation of Scripture. "Everything must be examined, ruled, conformed to it. Et suyvant cela nous avouons les trois symboles a sçavoir des Apotres de Nice et d'Athanase pource qu'ils sont conformes à la parole de Dieu." And, for the same reason, because their determinations were agreeable to Scripture, "we avow what has been determined by the ancient councils; and we detest all sects and heresies which have been rejected by the holy Doctors, as Saint Hilary, Saint Athanasius, Saint Ambrose, Saint Cyril."

[1] Niemeyer, *Collectio Confessionum.* Lipsia, 1840, p. 17.

[2] *Sylloge Confessionum*, Oxford, 1827, p. 243.

[3] Niemeyer, p. 311.

v. The Belgic Confession is said by the Editor of the Oxford Collection to have been written in French in this same year, 1561, and published in Latin in 1581. To their ninth article[1], entitled *De SS. Trinitate,* its authors append the following:

"We receive willingly those three Creeds, the Apostles', the Nicene, Athanasius', and whatever on this dogma the sacred Councils have decided in accordance with the sentiments of those Creeds."

vi. The Heidelberg Catechism[2] was content with the authority of the Apostles' Creed.

vii. But the Confession offered by the Barons and Nobles of Bohemia to "the King of the Romans and of Bohemia, &c.," in 1535, refers to the

"Apostolic Faith distributed into twelve articles and delivered in the form of a Symbol by the Nicene Synod, and so at other times confirmed and published[3]." Again, on the Faith of the Holy Trinity these nobles say: "They teach that God is known by Faith, One in the substance of the Divinity, Trine in Persons: Father, Son, and Holy Spirit. They hold a distinction in respect of Persons, but a coequality and indivisibility in respect to essence and substance: for this the Catholic Faith teaches, and the consensus of the Nicene and other Synods with it, and the Confession or Symbol of Athanasius plainly testifies[4]."

viii. The Helvetic Confession, put forth in 1566, speaks only of the Apostles' Creed in its third article (De Deo; Unitate ejus ac Trinitate); but in article XI. "de Jesu Christo vero Deo et Homine unico mundi Salvatore," it sums up its teaching nearly as follows:

"On the subject of the mystery of the Incarnation of our Lord Jesus Christ, whatever has been defined from the Holy Scriptures, and comprehended in the symbols and decisions of the four earliest and preeminent Councils held at Nicæa, Constantinople, Ephesus, and Chalcedon, together with the Creed of the blessed Athanasius and all Creeds resembling these—we believe with a sincere heart, and profess openly with a free tongue, condemning everything opposed and contrary to them. And thus we retain undefiled and whole the Christian orthodox and Catholic faith: knowing that in the aforesaid Creeds nothing is contained which is not conformable to the word of God, or does not conduce to the sincere unfolding or explanation of the faith[5]."

§ 4. The Augsburg Confession does not mention the Creed of Athanasius: I find, however, this:—

[1] *Sylloge*, p. 332. Niemeyer, p. 365.
[2] *Sylloge*, p. 365. Niemeyer, p. 434.
[3] Niemeyer, pp. 787, 788.
[4] Niemeyer, p. 789.
[5] *Ibid.* p. 487. *Sylloge*, p. 47.

"The Churches with us with a great consensus teach that the decree of the Nicene Synod on the Unity of the Divine Essence and on the Three Persons is true and must be believed without any hesitation."

So important was this considered, that the clause appears at the opening of the Confession[1]. Luther's work, "De tribus Symbolis: die drey Symbole," is often quoted. It is not as generally known that of his three Symbols, the first two are the Apostles' and the Athanasian; but "the third symbol is ascribed to St Ambrose and St Augustine." He took, however, this much notice of the Nicene; "We will add at the end to these three Symbols, the Nicene Symbol also[2]." It is here that Luther calls the Athanasian Creed "an outwork of that first Apostolic Creed," *propugnaculum primi illius apostolici symboli*. And the learned Dr Jacobson, the Bishop of Chester, in an interesting Charge to his Clergy, delivered about the year 1869, adduced out of Calvin's letter "ad Fratres Polonos[3]," the ardent Genevan reformer's description of it as being "a sure and fitting interpreter of the Nicene Creed."

§ 5. This position of the Quicunque as an authoritative Symbol of the Reformed Churches, as contrasted with the Eastern and Roman communions, is maintained, as we all know, in the Church of England.

i. In the first of the "Articles devised by the Kinges Highness majestie to stablyshe christen quietnes and unitie amonge us and to avoyde contentious opinions, which articles be also approved by the consent and determination of the hole clergie of this realme. Anno M.D.XXXVI[4]," we read the following: "As touching the chief and principal articles of our faith, sith it is thus agreed as hereafter followeth by the whole clergy of this our realm, we will that all bishops and preachers shall instruct and teach our people by us committed to their spiritual charge, that they ought and must most constantly believe and defend all those things to be true which be comprehended in the whole body and canon of the Bible, and also in the three Creeds or Symbols, whereof one was made by the apostles and is the common creed which every man useth; the second was made by the holy council of Nice and is said daily in the mass; and the third was made by Athanasius and is comprehended in the Psalm Quicunque vult: and that they ought and must take and interpret all the same things according to the selfsame sentence and interpretation which the words of the selfsame creeds or symbols do

[1] *Sylloge*, p. 123.

[2] My references are to the Latin edition, Vol. VII. p. 139: German edition, Vol. X. p. 1198.

[3] Works, XIV. p. 794, "certum et idoneum interpretem."

[4] They are printed in Appendix I. of the late Archdeacon Hardwick's *History of the Articles*.

purport, and the holy approved doctors of the Church do entreat or defend the same."

The whole article is interesting. I must content myself with quoting only part. Thus:

"Item: That they ought and must believe, repute and take all the articles of our faith contained in the said Creeds to be so necessary to be believed for man's salvation, that whosoever being taught will not believe them as is aforesaid, or will obstinately affirm the contrary of them, he or they cannot be the very members of Christ and his espouse the Church, but be very infidels or heretics, and members of the devil, with whom they shall perpetually be damned.

"Item: That they ought and must most reverently and religiously observe and keep the selfsame words, according to the very same form and manner of speaking, as the articles of our faith as already contained and expressed in the said creeds, without altering in anywise, or varying from the same."

The last *item* refers to the four holy councils.

The articles are signed by Thomas Cromwell, then by the two Archbishops, sixteen Bishops, forty Abbots or Priors.

ii. The thirteen articles of 1538 were framed on the lines of the Augsburg Confession, and no mention is made of the Athanasian Creed. But in the 42 Articles of 1552 the divergence from the Lutheran confession becomes manifest. The three Creeds were to be "received": not on their own account, or because of the authority from which they came down, but because "they may be proved by most certain warrants of Holy Scripture[1]."

iii. Some light is thrown on this Article by cap. v. of the first part "De Summa Trinitate et Fide Catholica" of the contemporaneous "Reformatio Legum Ecclesiasticarum[2]."

"And inasmuch as everything pertaining to the Catholic faith, whether relating to the most blessed Trinity or to the mysteries of our Redemption, is briefly contained in the three Creeds, that is, the Apostolic, the Nicene and Athanasian: therefore we receive and embrace these three Creeds as being, as it were, compendia of our faith: because they can be easily proved by most certain warrants of the divine and canonical Scriptures."

[1] "Symbola tria Niceni (sic) Athanasii et quod vulgo apostolicum appellatur omnino recipienda sunt. Nam firmissimis divinarum scripturarum testimoniis probari possunt." In 1652 the words *et credenda* were added after *sunt*.

[2] Dr Cardwell's Reprint, Oxford, 1851, p. 3.

The careful reader will have noted that the value of the Creeds was believed to consist in the testimony they bear to the great facts of our Redemption, and the great truths of the Being of God. These truths, these facts are declared by them: these truths, these facts may be easily proved by Scripture. The contents of all three Creeds[1] refer to the Trinity, to Jesus Christ, to the Salvation gained by Him for the human race. In conclusion the writers of the "Reformatio" say:

"This too we cannot pass over in silence, that all those perish miserably who are unwilling to embrace the orthodox and catholic faith: and that far more severely will they be condemned who have departed from it once acknowledged and accepted[2]."

Thus the framers of the New Ecclesiastical Laws (the influence of whom over our Articles must be acknowledged) appear to have retained so vividly the distinction of the Sarum Manual between the Credenda and the words from the Quicunque by which the Credenda are enforced, that they deemed it necessary to add a distinct and separate chapter of their own, explaining and affirming the necessity of accepting the Church's Faith[3].

[1] cap. 16, p. 7.

[2] cap. 17, p. 7.

[3] Hooker's very interesting chapter on the Athanasian Creed (*E. P.* v. ch. xlii. § 6) furnishes a somewhat curious illustration of the belief of his time that the original document was Greek. Hooker writes, "although these contentions were cause of much evil, yet some good the Church hath reaped by them in that they occasioned the learned and sound in the faith to explain such things as heresy went about to deprave. And in this respect the Creed of Athanasius first exhibited unto Julius, bishop of Rome—and afterwards, as we may probably gather, sent to the emperor Jovian—was, both in the east and west churches, accepted as a treasure of inestimable price by as many as had not given up the very ghost of belief." And he assigns the date to the year 340. Mr Keble suggested that this exhibition of the Creed to Julius was a conjecture of Baronius. We have seen however, that in some of the Greek copies of the Creed, the title runs *τοῦ ἐν ἁγίοις πατρὸς ἡμῶν Ἀθανασίου τοῦ μεγάλου ὁμολογία τῆς καθολικῆς πίστεως ἣν ἔδωκε πρὸς Ἰούλιον πάπαν Ῥώμης*, words which never occur in a Latin dress. Thus these words of Hooker furnish an additional illustration of the truth on which I have insisted; that the Reformers of Cranmer's time believed the Creed to have been Greek in its origin, and accepted the copy contained in the work of Cephaleus as that which approached nearest to the Greek original.

[Hooker applies to the Quicunque words spoken by Gregory of Nazianzus of another document. Mr Keble gave the reference to "Oratio 21, t. I. p. 394." He might have added the remark of the Benedictine editor of Athanasius on the passage: "Autumant illi de Symbolo *Quicunque* dici. Sed, ut nemo non videt, levissime, immo nulla ratione." But he did not. The mistake was excusable in Hooker: scarcely so in his editor.]

CHAPTER XXXVI.

RECENT NOTICES OF THE ATHANASIAN CREED.

§ 1. Cosin. § 2. Synod of 1640 and Wren. § 3. Chillingworth. § 4. Jeremy Taylor. § 5. Savoy Conference and Baxter. § 6. Commission of 1689. § 7. Wheatly. § 8. The last few years. § 9. Final Reflections.

§ 1. I DO not intend to drag my readers through the more recent controversies regarding the use of the Quicunque, but my volume would be incomplete, if I did not add some brief memoranda as to some of the later conceptions regarding the document.

Thus I find that Bishop Cosin in his earlier days considered the *Creed proper* to end with our forty-first clause. When "Mr Mountague's books" attracted attention in the spring of 162$\frac{5}{6}$, Cosin was called in to defend that which he seems to have had some hand in composing. The word "deservings" had attracted censure in the sentence "The good go to the enjoying of happiness without end: the wicked to the enduring of torments everlasting. Thus is their state diversified to their deservings." "He meaneth that of Athanasius' Creed (said Cosin) *versu ultimo*, and of the scripture, God rewardeth every man according to his works[1]." The *versus ultimus* was the verse "And they that have done good," &c.

§ 2. I suppose that the Quicunque had fallen into general disuse during the reigns of James and Charles. With the exception soon to be mentioned, I have not found any allusion to it in any of the Visitation Articles of that period, until we come to the series put out by Juxon, the Bishop of London, in 1640[2]. This series has a very important character.

[1] Cosin's Works (*Anglo-Catholic Library*), Vol. II. p. 77, compare p. 51.

[2] They may be seen in the Appendix to the *Fourth Report of the Ritual Commission*, p. 583.

In the year 1640 the Synod had been held which proved so disastrous to Archbishop Laud; for on the publication of its Canons his impeachment and imprisonment immediately followed. Incited probably by the unwillingness of Bishop Williams to co-operate in his plans, Laud had succeeded in inducing the Synod to "cause a summary or collection of visitatory articles to be made[1];" and no bishop or other person, having right to hold any parochial visitation, was to issue any other enquiries save such as were in express terms allowed to him by his Metropolitan. This collection formed the basis of Juxon's Articles, and in these was the question: "Is the Creed called *Athanasius'* Creed, beginning with (*Whosoever will be saved*) said by your minister constantly at the times appointed in the Common Prayer Boke?" The question would appear, therefore, to have had the sanction of the Convocation of 1640. It may have been taken from a similar question put forth in the diocese of Norwich by Wren in 1636—a question which was repeated by him in Ely in 1662[2].

§ 3. Chillingworth had some difficulty in regard to what are called "the damnatory clauses," but the difficulty was overcome (we know not how) when he was appointed Chancellor of the Church of Salisbury. He subscribed in 1638 "the three Articles of the thirty-sixth canon of 1604" in the usual form[3].

§ 4. Jeremy Taylor objected to the severity of Athanasius' "Preface and Conclusion" to the symbol; "nothing but damnation and perishing everlastingly, unless the Article of the Trinity be believed, as it is there with curiosity and minute particularities explained." He regarded these clauses, however, as "preface and end," as "extrinsical and accidental to the articles: they might well have been spared." And then he quotes the passage from Aquinas (which Waterland seems to have learnt from him), to shew that Athanasius, if he were the author, wrote it, if Taylor "understood Aquinas aright, not with a purpose of imposing it upon others, but with confidence to declare his own belief[4]."

[1] Cardwell's *Synodalia*, I. p. 407.

[2] Report, p. 559, column *b*. There is a reference to J. L. (apparently John, Bishop of London, 1581), to which I can find nothing correspondent.

[3] Waterland gives the subscription at length, somewhat needlessly. He has led some persons to suppose that Chillingworth adopted some form of his own to subscribe the *Thirty-nine* Articles: he merely subscribed in the usual way the articles of the 36th canon.

[4] *Liberty of Prophesying*, §2, of Heresy, c. 36.

§ 5. The use of the Creed was not objected to at the Savoy Conference. Baxter is quoted[1] as saying, "In a word, the damnatory sentences excepted or modestly expounded, I embrace the Creed commonly called Athanasius', as the best explication of the Trinity." Waterland himself suggested that "since the *damnatory* clauses were the main difficulty [in 1689], a better way might have been contrived than was then thought on: namely, to have preserved the whole Creed except those clauses which are separable from it." He preferred, however, that things should remain as they were.

§ 6. In the curious account of the proceedings of the Commission of 1689 taken by "Dr Williams, now Bishop of Chichester," and to be found in the Appendix to a Blue Book, printed "by order of the House of Commons," in 1854, we read that at the fifth session, on Oct. 23, fourteen commissioners met and "The chief debate was about the Athanasian Creed—It was moved either to leave it with an alias, or to leave out the Damnatory clauses, or to leave it as it is, with a Rubrick. For it was alledg'd, 1. That it was Antient. 2. Received by our Church ever since the Reformation. 3. Offence to leave it out; but granted that, if it was to do now, it were better to omit it.

"It was reply'd by the Bp. of Salisb.[2]: 1. that the Church of England receives the four first General Councils that the Ephesine Council condemns any new Creeds. 2. That this Creed was not very antient, and the Filioque especially. 3. That it condemned the Greek Church whom yet We defend. It was propos'd by the Bp. of Worcest.[3] to have a Rubrick that it shou'd be interpreted by article...[4] of our Church, and that the condemning sentences were only as to the Substance of the Articles: which was drawn up and approv'd of."

In the eleventh session, Nov. 1, the subject was reopened. Dr Fowler, who was not present at the earlier meeting, asked "that the business of the Athanasian Creed might be reheard; and he desired it might be left at Liberty with a *may be read*, since he had convers'd with several Conformists and Nonconformists. The Conformists were Men of Eminence of that mind

[1] *Method of Theology*, p. 123.
[2] Burnet.
[3] Stillingfleet, *elect* of Worcester.
[4] From what follows it appears that Article XVIII was meant.

and some of them had not read it for many Years. The Nonconformists were desirous of it, and were of the mind that no Creed should be used, but what was conceived in Scripture Expressions. However it was thought more advisable to leave it as it was and let the Convocation consider it. Both B. of Salisb: and Dean of Cant.[1] undertaking to promote it in both Houses of Convocation."

Once more the subject was mentioned, when, on Nov. 15, at their seventeenth session, they "went over the Whole again: made some few Alterations and Amendments: the most considerable was in the Athanasian Creed; where, after it was suggested that they were the Articles, and not the Terms in which those Articles were expressed, that were assented to; it was concluded that the word *obstinately* should be inserted, and the reference to Article ...... omitted."

The rubric proposed was this: "THE CREED COMMONLY CALLED THE CREED OF SAINT ATHANASIUS. Upon these Feasts, Christmas Day, Easter Day, Ascension Day, Whit Sunday, Trinity Sunday, and upon All Saints, shall be said at Morning Prayer by the Minister and People standing, instead of the Creed commonly called the Apostles' Creed, this Confession of our Christian Faith commonly called the Creed of S. Athanasius, the Articles of which ought to be received and believed as being agreeable to the Holy Scripture. And the Condemning clauses are to be understood as relating only to those who obstinately deny the substance of the Christian Faith [according to the eighteenth article of this Church]." This reference to the eighteenth article was suppressed as we have seen, on Nov. 15, on which day the word *obstinately* was inserted[2].

The labours of the Commission were, at all events for the time, in vain.

[1] Tillotson.

[2] It will be interesting to compare this account with the briefer notice of the Conference, said to have been communicated to Dr Calamy by a friend, and with the account of the proceedings by Dr Nicholls. I take them both from Cardwell's *Conferences*, pp. 431, 432. As to the former, "About the Athanasian Creed they came at last to this conclusion: that lest the wholly rejecting it should by unreasonable persons be imputed to them as Socinianism, a rubric shall be made, declaring the curses denounced therein not to be restrained to every particular article, but intended against those who deny the substance of the Christian religion in general," (Calamy's *Life of Baxter*, p. 452, &c.). Nicholls gives only the following memorandum. This attempt was made; "symbolum quod vulgo Sancti Athanasii dicitur, quia a multis improbatur, propter atrocem de singulis secus quam hic docetur credentibus sententiam, ministri arbitrio permittitur ut pro apostolico mutetur." *Apparat. ad Defens. Eccles. Angl.* p. 95.

§ 7. The use of the Creed continued to give distress. Wheatly, who wrote his *Rational Illustration of the Book of Common Prayer* in the reign of George I., desired to offer the following "for the ease and satisfaction of those who have a notion that this Creed requires every person to assent to or believe every verse in it on pain of damnation." "All that is required of us as *necessary to salvation* is that *before all things we hold the Catholic Faith: and the Catholic Faith is* by the third and fourth verses explained to be *this, That we worship one God in Trinity and Trinity in Unity: neither confounding the Persons nor dividing the Substance.* This, therefore, is declared necessary to be believed, but all that follows from hence to the twenty-sixth verse is only brought forward as a proof and illustration of it, and, therefore, requires our assent no more than a sermon does which is made to prove or illustrate a text...... The belief of the *Catholic Faith* before mentioned, the scripture makes necessary to salvation, and, therefore, we must believe it: but there is no such necessity laid upon us to believe the illustration that is there given of it, nor does the Creed itself require it: for it goes on in the twenty-sixth and twenty-seventh verses in these words: *So that in all things as is aforesaid the Unity in Trinity and the Trinity in Unity is to be worshipped: he, therefore, that will be saved must thus think of the Trinity*[1]."

As I do not intend to criticise at any length these proposals, I would here merely remark, How interesting it is to find that Wheatly, like Aquinas, recognised the strong resemblance between the Quicunque and a Sermon: and perceived that most (he says all) of the clauses 5 to 25 were "brought in" to furnish proofs and illustrations of the great truth of clauses 3 and 4: two conceptions, the historic truth of which is exhibited now from the accounts recorded in my earlier chapters[2].

§ 8. The discussions of the last six years are too recent to justify me in offering much criticism upon them. But I think my readers will not blame me if I put on record a brief résumé of the results of these discussions.

[1] Chapter III. § XV. p. 148 of the edition of London, 1840.

[2] Bishop Wordsworth of Lincoln has written in favour of Wheatly's limitations of the "damnatory clauses."

The Ritual Commission (appointed first in 1867) made their final Report in 1870. In this report it was suggested that a note should be appended in the Prayer-Book to the Athanasian Creed in these words:

"NOTE.—That the condemnations in this Confession of Faith are to be no otherwise understood than as a solemn warning of the peril of those who wilfully reject the Catholic Faith."

Twenty-seven Commissioners signed the Report: but, of these, seventeen added the joint expression of their unwillingness to concur in the course taken by the Commissioners in respect to the Athanasian Creed.

On June 14, 1871, a motion was made in the Upper House of the Convocation of Canterbury by the Bishop of Gloucester, and seconded by the Bishop of Llandaff, for "the appointment of a joint Committee of both Houses to consider and report upon the desirableness of revising the existing translation of the Athanasian Creed, and of introducing any changes in, or additions to, the Rubric prefixed to the Creed in the Book of Common Prayer, provided that they be only such changes or additions as shall not in any way affect the authority of the Creed as a standard of doctrine in the Church of England." On consideration, however, it was resolved *nem. con.* that the question raised in this proposal should be submitted to the Bishops of both Provinces.

The Bishops met, and a Committee was appointed; and the Divinity Professors of Oxford and Cambridge were consulted on the subject.

The Oxford Professors furnished the following Report:

OXFORD, *Nov.* 30, 1871.

MY LORD BISHOP,—Your Lordship has addressed us severally, in the name of the Bishops of both Provinces, asking our aid "in the revision of the original Text and Prayer Book Version of the Athanasian Creed," together with any "suggestions" that might occur to us.

We have held frequent mutual consultations, and respectfully beg leave to report as follows:—

I. After examining the various readings of that Latin Text of the Athanasian Creed which our Translation may be assumed generally to represent, we find none of sufficient authority or account to warrant us in suggesting them to your Lordships with a view to the revision of the Text. [The insertion of "pariter" in verse 28, the reading of "inferna" for "inferos" in verse 36, and the omission of "Dei Omnipotentis" in verse 37, are the various readings which seem to have most authority. Next may be mentioned the readings "in carne," "in Deo," in verse 35, which seem to us highly improbable.]

With respect to certain omissions in the Commentary of Fortunatus, it is evident from an inspection of that manuscript of the Commentary which is preserved in the Bodleian Library, and is believed to be the oldest in existence, that the Commentator cannot have intended to exhibit a complete Text of the Creed, since, in some cases, passages are wanting which are obviously necessary to the coherence of the Text on which he comments.

It must further be observed that of the warning verses, commonly although improperly called "damnatory," the first and last are given by

Fortunatus, while those which he omits have the support of all known manuscripts of the Creed.

II. We should not have been disposed to recommend any alteration in a Translation associated with three centuries of faith and devotion. But if such a proposal is entertained, we would observe—

(1) That the Prayer Book Version of the Creed has departed from the Sarum Text in its rendering of verses 27 and 42: "Ut incarnationem quoque Domini nostri Jesu Christi *fideliter* credat;" "quam nisi quisque fideliter firmiterque crediderit."

(2) That having considered various new renderings of particular expressions, we are of opinion that the following alone are of sufficient importance to be laid before your Lordships.

a. Verses 9, 12. *For* "incomprehensible," "incomprehensibles," *read* "infinite," "infinites."

β. Verse 22. *For* "of the Father and of the Son," *read* "of the Father and the Son."

γ. Verse 26. *For* "He therefore that will be saved must thus think of the Trinity," *read* "He therefore that would be saved, let him thus think of the Trinity."

Your Lordships will observe that we are unable to make any suggestions, as to either the text or the translation, which may be expected to obviate the objections popularly raised against the Creed. But on this very account we the more willingly submit for consideration the following form of a Note, such as may tend to remove some misconceptions.

"Note, that nothing in this Creed is to be understood as condemning those who, by involuntary ignorance or invincible prejudice, are hindered from accepting the Faith therein declared."

We cannot conclude without expressing to your Lordships our deep sense of the practical value of this Creed, as teaching us how to think and believe on the central mysteries of the Faith. Experience has proved it to be a safeguard against fundamental errors, into which the human mind has often fallen, and is ever liable to fall. For these reasons we earnestly trust, that in the good Providence of God, this Creed will always retain its place in the public service of our Church.

J. B. Mozley, D.D., Regius Professor of Divinity.
E. B. Pusey, D.D., Regius Professor of Hebrew.
Ch. A. Ogilvie, D.D., Regius Professor of Pastoral Theology.
C. A. Heurtley, D.D., Margaret Professor of Divinity.
William Bright, D.D., Regius Professor of Ecclesiastical History.
H. P. Liddon, D.D., Ireland Professor of Exegesis.

The Lord Bishop of Gloucester and Bristol.

The answers of Professors Westcott and Lightfoot, unhappily, have not been made public; but subsequently a paper, of which the following is a copy, was forwarded to the Bishop of Gloucester, who acted as Secretary to their Lordships' Committee.

"BELIEVING that the character of the Exposition of the Faith commonly called the Athanasian Creed is not sufficiently understood, we beg to call attention to the following facts:

"1. The internal structure of the document shows that it consists of two parts.

(*a*) The Exposition of the Catholic Faith.

(*b*) The admonitory clauses (clauses 1 and 2; 28 and 29; 42) which are the 'setting' of the Exposition and no part of the Exposition itself.

"2. In the earliest extant MS. of the document (Colbert, 784) clause 42 occurs in a wholly different form and runs as follows:

"Hæc est fides sancta et Catholica quam omnis homo qui ad vitam æternam pervenire desiderat, scire integre debet et fideliter custodire.

"This copy is imperfect and commences with the words *Domini nostri* in clause 29; we can therefore only infer from analogy what form the other admonitory clauses took in the archetype from which this fragment was copied.

"It may be added that the corresponding admonitory clause in the analogous Exposition of the Faith published at the fourth Council of Toledo (633 A.D.) and reproduced in the sixth Council of Arles (813 A.D.) is also positive and not negative: Hæc est Catholicæ Ecclesiæ fides: hanc confessionem conservamus et tenemus: quam quisquis firmissime custodierit perpetuam salutem habebit.

"3. Even after the admonitory clauses generally had assumed the form which they now have, the second clause is passed over by several writers who paraphrase or quote the document; and in one of the most ancient MSS. (Paris, Reg. 4908) the words *absque dubio* are omitted. From such omissions of reference to the second clause it may be inferred either (*a*) That the clause was wanting in the copies used by these writers; or (*b*) That they felt themselves at liberty to disregard it, as forming no part of the Exposition itself.

"4. In continuous comments on the document the admonitory clauses generally are treated with the greatest freedom, being sometimes omitted and sometimes considerably altered.

"5. Of the few MSS. which have been carefully collated, one (Brit. Mus. Reg. 2 B. v.) marks the distinction between the initial admonitory clauses and the Exposition itself by inserting the words *Incipit de Fide* before clause 3 in prominent characters.

"6. As a decisive evidence that the admonitory clauses must be regarded as a mere setting of the Exposition, we have the fact that they occur almost word for word in the same relation to a different Exposition of the Faith in the *Visitatio Infirmorum* of the Sarum Manual.

"These facts appear to us to show clearly that the admonitory clauses may be treated as separate from the Exposition itself, and may be modified without in any way touching what is declared therein to be the Catholic Faith; and we venture to express our opinion that it is the office of the Church to make such changes in the forms of words by which the Faith is commended to believers as may be required for their edification and for the right understanding of her own meaning.

"We would also add that we deplore the change ratified at the last revision of the Prayer Book, by which this Exposition of the Faith when used was substituted for the Apostles' Creed; and we hope that the earlier usage of our Church may be restored, by which it was recited on special occasions before that Creed, and not in place of it.

(*Signed*) B. F. WESTCOTT.
C. A. SWAINSON.
J. B. LIGHTFOOT.

CAMBRIDGE,
Feb. 3, 1872."

A note was added on the fifth clause to this effect:

"To avoid misconception it may be observed that the absolute priority of date of the Colbertine MS. is not certain. The Ambrosian and St Germains' MSS. may be of equal antiquity; but the Colbertine MS. has this peculiarity, that the writer states that he is transcribing an older copy, which was already mutilated when it came into his hands. The text of the Exposition in the Colbertine MS., as is well known, presents several variations from the received readings. Of these the only two of real importance are (1) The absence of clause 35, which is taken almost literally from St Augustine; and (2) The occurrence of the words *sicut vobis in symbolo traditum est* in clause 37, shewing that in its original form the document was an exposition of the Baptismal Creed."

The Bishops themselves reported as follows:

"I. That the most usual title of the Document, so far as has been ascertained from Manuscripts supposed to be prior to A. D. 1000, that have hitherto been examined, appears to be *Fides Catholica*, or *Fides Sancti Athanasii*. II. That some critical doubts have been thought to rest on verses 1, 2, 28, 29, 37, and 42. [A.] That the preponderance of external authority is so overwhelming in favour of verses 1, 2, 28, and 29, that, on critical grounds, they must be considered as integral portions of the Document, so far as it is known by existing copies thereof. [B.] That though verse 37 is wanting in the copy of what is deemed to be the most ancient Manuscript of the document as yet known, the balance of evidence, critical and historical, is in favour of the verse being retained. [C.] That critical and historical reasons lead us to favour the conclusion that verse 42 should be read in the form in which it is found in the Codex Colbertinus, viz.:—'Hæc est fides sancta et Catholica, quam omnis homo qui ad vitam æternam pervenire desiderat scire integre debet, et fideliter custodire.' III. That the following minor changes be also introduced in the Latin text, in accordance with what seem to be the best attested readings:—In verses 7, 8, 9, 10, 13, 15, 17 insert 'et' before 'Spiritus Sanctus.' In verse 30, insert 'pariter' before 'et homo.' In verse 35, for 'carnem' and 'Deum,' read 'carne' and 'Deo.' In verse 38 omit 'tertiâ die.' In verse 39 omit 'Dei' and 'Omnipotentis.' IV. That the following changes be made in the English Version, as found in the Book of Common Prayer:—In verse 1, for 'will,' read 'willeth to.' In verse 2, for 'do,' read 'shall;' and for 'everlastingly,' read 'eternally.' In verse 5 omit 'and.' In verse 7, omit 'and.' In verse 8, omit 'and.' In verse 9, for 'incomprehensible' (thrice), read 'infinite' (thrice); and omit 'and.' In verse 10, omit 'and.' In verse 11, omit 'they are.' In verse 12, for 'incomprehensibles' and 'incomprehensible,' read 'infinites' and 'infinite.' In verse 13, omit 'and.' In verse 14, omit 'they are.' In verse 15, omit the second 'is,' and the third 'is;' and also omit 'and.' In verse 17, omit 'likewise,' and 'and.' In verse 19, for 'by himself,' read 'severally.' In verse 23, omit the second 'of;' and for 'neither,' read 'nor.' In verse 25, after 'Trinity,' omit the remaining words, and read in lieu thereof, 'there is nothing afore or after, nothing greater or less.' In verse 28, for 'will,' read 'willeth to;' and for 'must,' read 'let him.' In verse 29, for 'everlasting,' read 'eternal;' and for 'rightly,' read 'faithfully.' In verse 30, after the second 'is,' insert 'equally.' In verse 32, omit 'and.' In verse 33, for 'his' (twice), read 'the' (twice); and omit 'and.' In verse 35, after 'One,' insert 'however;' for 'into flesh,' read 'in the flesh,' and for 'into God,' read 'in God.' In verse 38, omit the 'third day.' In verse 39, omit the first 'he,' and the second 'he;' omit also 'God Almighty.' In verse 40, for 'shall rise,' read 'have to rise.' In verse 41, for 'everlasting' (twice), read 'eternal' (twice). In verse 42, before 'Catholic,' insert the 'holy and;' and after 'Faith,' leave out the remaining words, and read in lieu thereof, 'which every man who desireth to attain to eternal life ought to know wholly and to guard faithfully.'

J. LONDON.
S. WINTON.
C. J. GLOUCESTER AND BRISTOL.
E. H. ELY.
WILLIAM CHESTER.

February 12, 1872."

In November, 1872, a Committee of the Lower House of Convocation met, and agreed to offer the following as the foundation for an explanatory note.

"This House solemnly declares—

"1. That the 'Confession of our Christian Faith, commonly called the Creed of St. Athanasius,' sets forth two fundamental doctrines—viz., that of the Holy Trinity, and that of the Incarnation of our Lord Jesus Christ, in the form of an exposition of the Catholic faith.

"2. That the said Confession does not, in its several and separate propositions, make any addition to the Christian faith; but states more fully that which is implicitly contained in the Apostles' and Nicene Creeds, and that it is a safeguard against errors which from time to time have arisen in the Church of Christ.

"3. That whereas Holy Scripture, in divers passages, promises life to the faithful, and asserts the condemnation of the unbelieving, so does the Church, in sundry clauses of this Confession, express the terrible consequence of a wilful rejection of the Christian faith, and declare the necessity of holding fast the same, for all who would be, or continue to be, in a state of salvation. Nevertheless, the Church therein passes not sentence upon any; the Great Judge of all being alone able to decide who those persons are that are guilty of such wilful rejection."

But on December 3, 1872, a meeting of a joint Committee of both houses was held at Lambeth Palace in pursuance of a resolution passed in the Upper House of Convocation on July 4, 1872, to the following effect:

"That this House, having read the second resolution of the Lower House touching the Athanasian Creed, and having special regard to the scruples alleged by many faithful members of the Church as to the present use of that Creed in our public services, recommend his Grace the President to direct the appointment of a joint Committee of both Houses to consider and to report to Convocation at its next meeting as to any mode of relieving such scruples, whilst we maintain the truth which has been committed to our charge."

At this Committee it was moved by the Bishop of Winchester (Wilberforce) that the following form should be adopted:

"For the removal of objections which have been taken to the recital of this Creed on account of the sentences of exclusion from salvation therein contained:

"It is hereby declared that those sentences are to be taken in the same sense and with the same limitations as the sentences of the necessity of belief and the danger of unbelief set forth in Holy Scripture are, and ought to be, taken.

"That is to say, that those sentences apply only to such persons as deliberately, out of an evil heart of unbelief, deny, renounce, and corrupt the faith of Christ, rejecting the counsel of God for their salvation. And forasmuch as men cannot, and God only can, judge of the thoughts and intentions of the heart, we are not required or allowed to apply these sentences to the condemnation of any particular person or persons."

This was subsequently withdrawn, and it was finally carried by a majority of 19 to 16 on the motion of the Bishop of Ely (Harold Browne) that the Committee should report to the following effect[1]: "That this Committee, whilst desirous of relieving the consciences of those who find difficulty in the public recitation of the Athanasian Creed, feels that it cannot recommend to Convocation, with any hope of general adoption, any other course than that of a synodical declaration as to the meaning and intent of the minatory clauses."

It would be wearisome and profitless to describe the discussions on the form of declaration. The principle was carried in the Lower House by 33 to 26, and then the House commenced the debate. I desire to preserve the form which, this being determined on, I proposed, after consultation with some valued friends:—

"That while continuing to recite in the form in which she hath received them from past ages those clauses attached to this confession which express the terrible consequences of a wilful rejection of the Christian faith [and declare the necessity of holding fast the same for all

[1] I do not know whether the words here are absolutely correct: for I can find no record that the resolution was ever reported to Convocation.

that would be, or continue to be, in a state of salvation]: the Church doth not desire her warnings to be understood in any other sense than is plainly warranted by those passages of Holy Scripture which promise life to the faithful and assert the condemnation of the unbelieving; neither doth she pass sentence on any, the Great Judge alone being able to decide who are guilty in this matter."

The Lower House at last agreed upon the following form (14th February, 1873):

"For the removal of doubts and of disquietude in the use of the Athanasian Creed, this Synod doth solemnly declare—

"That the Confession of our Christian Faith, commonly called the Creed of St Athanasius, sets forth two fundamental doctrines of the Catholic faith, viz., that of the Holy Trinity and that of the Incarnation of our Lord Jesus Christ, in the form of an exposition.

"That the said Confession does not make any addition to the Christian Faith as contained in the Apostles' and the Nicene Creeds: but is a safeguard against errors which, from time to time, have arisen in the Church of Christ.

"That whereas Holy Scripture, while promising life to the faithful, asserts in divers passages the condemnation of the unbelieving, so also does the Church, while declaring the necessity of holding fast the Christian faith for all who would be in a state of salvation, express, in sundry clauses in this Confession, the terrible consequence of a wilful rejection of that faith. Nevertheless the Church therein passes not sentence upon particular persons; the Great Judge of all being alone able to decide who those persons are that are guilty of such wilful rejection. Furthermore, we must receive God's threatenings even as His promises, in such wise as they are generally set forth to us in Holy Scripture[1]."

The Lower House of the Convocation of York however adopted the following form (20th February, 1873):

Synodical Declaration.—For the Removal of Doubts and Disquietude in the use of the Athanasian Creed, this House doth solemnly declare—

That the Confession of our Christian faith, commonly called the Creed of St Athanasius, doth not make any addition to the faith, as contained in Holy Scripture, but warneth against errors, which from time to time have arisen in the Church of Christ.

That inasmuch as Holy Scripture in divers places doth promise life to them that believe, and declare the condemnation of them that believe not, so the Church in sundry clauses of this Confession doth declare the necessity of holding fast the Christian faith, and the great peril of rejecting the same. Nevertheless the Church doth not therein pronounce judgment upon particular persons; the Great Judge of all alone being

[1] It had been carried by a majority of 28 to 12 that in the last clause but one should be inserted after *therein*, the words *does but proclaim a divine law, and;* but almost immediately afterwards Archdeacon Emery moved and Mr Bathurst seconded that the words should be struck out, and this was carried *nem. con.* (*Chronicle of Convocation*, 1873, pp. 227—229.)

able to discern who they are, who in this matter are guilty before Him. Moreover, the warnings in this Confession of faith are to be understood no otherwise than the like warnings in Holy Scripture.

In process of time this came before the Convocation of Canterbury: and ultimately, after much discussion, the following was adopted by both Houses of the Province on May 9, 1873:

For the removal of doubts, and to prevent disquietude in the use of the Creed commonly called the Creed of St Athanasius, this Synod doth solemnly declare:—

1. That the Confession of our Christian Faith, commonly called the Creed of St Athanasius, doth not make any addition to the faith as contained in Holy Scripture, but warneth against errors which from time to time have arisen in the Church of Christ.

2. That as Holy Scripture in divers places doth promise life to them that believe and declare the condemnation of them that believe not, so doth the Church in this Confession declare the necessity for all who would be in a state of salvation of holding fast the Catholic faith, and the great peril of rejecting the same. Wherefore the warnings in this confession of faith are to be understood no otherwise than the like warnings in Holy Scripture, for we must receive God's threatenings even as His promises, in such wise as they are generally set forth in Holy Writ. Moreover, the Church doth not herein pronounce judgment on any particular person or persons, God alone being the Judge of all.

§ 9. Happily the Bishops of the Province of York declined to accept this; and thus the Church of England, by God's good mercy, has been saved from making what many of her members consider would have been a very serious mistake and misrepresentation: the mistake and misrepresentation of stating that words, the signification of which, when judged by the ordinary rules of language, is clear and plain, have a latent meaning different from that clear and plain signification—thus introducing a rule of interpretation that would be fatal to all honour and all truthfulness. The fact is, that Convocation closed its eyes to the History of the Document, and committed itself to the position that it is a CREED and a CONFESSION, instead of what I have proved it historically to have been considered originally, a TREATISE or a SERMON. If we are content to look upon it as an Address to a Congregation, instructing them in some of the truths of the Christian Faith, every passage falls into its place; we have the introduction, the subject, the explanation, the practical application: and the warning clauses are necessarily limited (as are the words of the Saviour) to those who hear them. But if we are called upon to recite the whole of it as our Faith, to turn to the East, as we do in reciting the Apostles' and Nicene Creeds, and proclaim before God and angels and men, not that we believe so and so, but that this is necessary and that is necessary, that this is true and that is true, and to give our reasons, as we do in the fifth clause and in our translation of the thirtieth clause—the proceeding appears to me as it does to others, a painful, almost a thrilling act of unnecessary presumption. This is my objection to the present usage: and in representing an objection like this to the two Archbishops nearly 3000 clergymen joined[1]. But, in the then temper of the leaders of a dominant school of English Clergymen, this petition met with no attention. It was useless to urge on men who profess to be anxious to guide the Church of England by what is called Catholic usage, that ours is the only Church in western Europe where in defiance of antiquity the Quicunque is made to displace the Apostles' Creed: it was useless to urge on men who appeal to primitive ritual, that this rubric of ours was only two hundred and ten years old.

If the upholders of this Anglican peculiarity had maintained the truth of the concluding statements which enforce the Creed, we might perhaps bear with them. But they did not. The argument of custom was put forward by some: the respect due to certain eminent individuals was urged by others: the literal truth of the statements was maintained by few.

And in the meantime the divergence between "Scientific" men and "Religious" men[2] is growing wider and wider, and that mainly because "Scientific" men seek to discover what is true, not to uphold what has been received, *because it has been received:* while "Religious" men seek to uphold what has been received *because it has been received:* entertaining perhaps a lurking apprehension that the *received* may not, after all, be found in perfect harmony with the *true*. Of course, so long as this is the case, "Scientific" men will gain influence in the community: "Religious" men of this character will lose it. For the former have manifest faith in the power of truth; the latter seem to have little or none[3].

[1] The list included 14 Deans of Cathedral Churches, 25 Archdeacons, 20 Professors of the Universities and government Schools, 81 present Masters and Fellows of Colleges, 70 Head Masters of Great Schools, 16 of Her Majesty's Inspectors, 190 Cathedral Officers, 180 Clergy of the Metropolis.

[2] This alienation is continually described as between "Science" and "Religion". Nothing could be more fatally misrepresented.

[3] I see many symptoms around me that the Faith of large masses of nominal

Happy am I that I belong to a University where Science and Religion have ever wrought hand in hand: where Scientific pursuits have ever been carried on in the full assurance of Faith: and where the ministers of Christ are not afraid to bring to the elucidation and confirmation of their Faith the Results as well as the Principles of true Scientific Investigation.

One more consideration and I must conclude.

It is said that the Clergy of the Church of England have been remiss in the duty of bringing dogmatic truth before their congregations, and that the objection felt against the recitation of the Quicunque is really an objection felt against the dogmas of Christianity. The word "dogmas" is ambiguous: as used here, I suppose it means the fundamental matters of our Faith, laid down and expressed in formal or scientific statements. I can well understand the difficulty; but I deny that an objection to the *recitation* of dogmatic statements is to be regarded as identical with an objection to such statements in themselves. All sciences have their dogmas: the laws of motion enunciated by Newton, the law of gravitation, the laws of the propagation of light, the numbers representing the vibrations of each line of the solar spectrum or each note in the scale of music, are dogmas of their respective sciences. So again in geology, anatomy, botany. These dogmas are, as I may say, the vertebræ of the science, the skeleton upon which every thing else is built up. So are the laws of musical composition, point and counterpoint, and so forth. But it would surely be absurd to suppose that on stated days, before we resigned ourselves to the wondrous enjoyment of a chorus by Handel, or the solemnising effect of the Passion music of Bach, it was necessary to recite the principles of musical composition, or to be called upon to repeat the alphabet of music. We can enjoy a beautiful scene without being compelled to recite the laws of stratification, and admire a painting by Canaletti without being called upon to exhibit our knowledge of the principles of per-

Christians is in a very trembling condition; and I apprehend ere long most serious consequences when the present attempts to prop up that Faith by high ceremonial and gorgeous ritual shall have been tried and failed. For fail of course they will. I have read nothing during the last year which has affected me so much, as the intimation given by a highly esteemed clergyman, who pleaded for a decorated service, to keep men from the depths of unbelief. I shrink with dread at this revelation. For no repetitions of Creeds, no elaborate forms service will supply the want of FAITH IN GOD. These repetitions and these forms can furnish only temporary resorts for minds which are ill at ease because they have not found that GOD IS THEIR ROCK.

spective. The difference between the FATHER, the SON, the SPIRIT of the Bible, and the FATHER, the SON and the SPIRIT of the Athanasian Creed, is, practically speaking, immeasurable. It is the difference between the living and loving FATHER, BROTHER, FRIEND, viewed in their relations to us, and an analysis of their relations to each other. And as a man cannot write a composition like Mendelssohn, because he knows the science of Music; so neither can he evolve a true conception of GOD by studying the Athanasian formula. And inexpressibly painful is it to have these dry bones of theology brought before us on days like Christmas Day and Easter, when we would pour out our souls in simple thanksgivings for the gifts which we on those days commemorate. The dogmas of the Athanasian Creed are for the Scientific Theologian: the Bible Revelation of the FATHER, SON, and HOLY SPIRIT for every Christian.

It remains for me to make a brief résumé of the various readings o any moment that I have collected.

a. is the Paris manuscript 3836 which contains the fragment fron the book at Treves [above, p. 262].
b. the Milanese copy, first printed erroneously by Muratori [p. 313].
c. Vat. Pal. 574 [p. 267].
d. Paris 1451 [p. 268].
e. Vienna 1032 [p. 322].
f. „ 1261 [p. 324].
g. St Germain des Près 257, collated by Montfaucon [p. 329].
h. Paris Regius 4908 [p. 330].
i. The copy of the Dublin Franciscan convent, the hymn book [p. 331] Then in Psalters.
k. Paris 13159 [p. 350] Gallican.
l. St Gall 15 [p. 354] Gallican.
m. St Gall 23 [p. 354] Gallican.
n. St Gall 27 [p. 355] Gallican.
o. Oxford Douce 59 [p. 356] Gallican.
p. Boulogne 20 [p. 357] Gallican.
q. CCC O. 5 [p. 357] Gallican.
r. Paris 1152 (Charles le Chauve) [p. 363] Gallican.
s. CCC 411. N. 10 [p. 358] Gallican.
t. Arundel 60 [p. 360] Gallican or Roman?
u. St. Gall 20 [p. 361] Gallican.
x. Claudius C. VII. (Utrecht) [p. 363] Gallican.
y. Vienna 1861 (Charlemagne's?) [p. 373] Gallican.
z. Galba A. XVIII. (Athelstane's) [p. 366] Gallican.
aa. is the German copy in the Wolfenbüttel codex. This is not a Psalter, and so far is out of place.
ab. Bamberg (not yet collated) [p. 368].
ac. Regius 2 B. v. [p. 374], Roman.
ad. Salisbury [p. 369] Gallican.
ae. Vespasian A. 1 [p. 347. 376].
af. Cambridge Ff. 1. 23 [p. 375] Roman.
ag. Lambeth 427 [p. 377].
ah. Vitellius E. 18 [p. 370]. This is burnt after the words *tertia die.*
ai. Harleian 2904 [p. 370] Gallican.
ak. CCC 391. K. 10 [p. 370] „
al. Venice Bible [p. 372]. „

am. St John's College, Cambridge B. 18 (triple).
an. Milan Manual A. 189 inf.
ao. Salzburg a. V. 31 [p. 377].
ap. Milan C. 13.
aq. St John's Cambridge B. 10.
ar. Durham A. IV. 10.
as. „ A. III. 2.
at. Salzburg a V 30 [p. 375].
au. Arundel 155 [p. 377].
ax. Trin. Coll. Camb. Eadwin's Psalter [p. 377].
Miscellaneous.
ay. Vienna 123 (German).
az. Oxford Junius 25.
ba. Muratori's Fortunatus.
bb. Paris 3848 B [p. 268].
bc. Mai's Explanatio.

Of the manuscripts of which I have not given an account I must here state that *am* is a triple Psalter; Roman, Gallican, Hebraic. Psalm 151 follows on 150. The Quicunque is entitled Fides Catholica edita ab Athanasio, &c. &c.

an is a Manual dated 1188. It is supposed to be the earliest Ambrosian Manual in existence. After the Benedicite is the hymn *Splendor paternæ*, and the "hymnus ad primam, *Te precamur*": the "Fides Catholica Athanasii episcopi" follows. Thus it was recited at prime when this manuscript was written. It has the Gloria Patri at the end.

ao is a Psalter of the eleventh century. The Quicunque is entitled "Ps. Anastasii." It ends with "rationem," i.e. the last two clauses are omitted, as in the Venice Greek (above p. 470).

ar, *as* are Psalters of the year 1100 or thereabouts. In the former the Quicunque is ascribed to Athanasius. I owe my collations to the Reverend Edward Greatorex.

I have also, through the kindness of the Reverend Christopher Wordsworth, late Fellow of the College, most careful collations of two manuscripts at St Peter's College, Cambridge. These are both late, of the fourteenth and fifteenth centuries. In both the Quicunque is entitled *Psalmus*.

ay is a manuscript at Vienna of the eleventh or twelfth century, with a German translation. I have taken my copy from Massmann, pp. 35 and 88. The Quicunque has no title.

I regret to find that I have omitted to note that I owe my account of the variations in *c* to Signor Giovanni Bollig, S. J., through Professor Jones of St Beuno's College.

Leaving out now all errors and peculiarities of spelling and very palpable blunders, such as I conceive the confusion between Athanasius and Anastasius to be, we have the following results:

Of the forty-five or forty-six manuscripts of the eighth, ninth, tenth, eleventh centuries (to which I have added two or three of the twelfth century) not one occurs in which the Quicunque is designated as the SYMBOLUM ATHANASII. It is however attributed to Athanasius in one form or another by 24[1]: in the other 22 it is either called *Fides Catholica,* or it is without any title altogether[2], whilst the earliest manuscripts *a* and *b* are anonymous, and in them this silence is particularly noteworthy. All the copies which we connect with the court of the Frank Emperors attribute it to Athanasius.

Of these I have endeavoured, but I confess in vain, to establish some law regarding the various readings. The only interesting facts which are worth recording here are these. The earlier copies read *et spiritus sanctus* in 7, 8, 9, 10, 13, 15, 17: the later manuscripts, and the received Roman text, omit *et*[3]. In some cases it will be seen that the word has been erased by a second hand.

In verse 20 the MSS. *i*, *x*, ak_2, ao_2, *bc*, have "tres dominos." In *z* the word tres has been erased.

In clause 27, about thirty, including the older manuscripts[4], (with the exception of Charlemagne's and Galba A. XVIII.) read *et trinitas in unitate et unitas in trinitate.* The present received text is *et unitas in trinitate et trinitas in unitate.*, this being the reading of about 16 which I have collated[5].

In 29 *i.* q_2. *t.* ac_1. have *unus quisque.* s_2 adds at the end *qui vult salvus esse.*

In clause 30 the variations are interesting. The Treves fragment and the Muratorian copy read *pariter.* These are followed by seven others, but many of the older complete copies do not have *pariter.* In some we find it in the margin and then again obliterated, shewing, of course, that opinions oscillated. I will note those only in which it is found[6].

In 31 *i*, *k*, *af*, *ay* read *in sæcula.* The reading of *g* is peculiar in 31, 32. I have already drawn attention to it: and to what I have said I would again invite attention.

In 35 *e* has *confusione.*

The old readings here were undoubtedly *in carne* and *in deo*[7]. It will be seen that we read thus in thirty-three of our manuscripts, including all the ancient ones.

In 38 *a*, *az*, *ba* had *inferna*, *g infernos.* (Note the progress to *inferos.*)

The history of the words *tertia die* in the same clause is interesting. In the Colbertine manuscript, where the Symbolum is quoted, they occur:

[1] These are *c. g. l. m. n. o. p. r. s. t. u. y. z. ac. ad. ag. ah. ai. am. an. ao. ar. au. bb.*

[2] *b.* e_2. *h. i.* k_2. *aa. af. ak. ap. aq. as. at. ax. ay. az. ba. bc.* have no title. It is called simply the Catholic Faith in one way or another in *f. q. x. aa.* (at end) *ae.* In *al.* it is attributed to the Nicene Council.

[3] *et* omittunt s_2. *ag. ah?.* ai_2. ak_2. *al. am?.* ao_1. *ap. aq. ar. as. at. au. ax. bb.* (in clausulis 15, 17 *et* habet *am.*).

[4] *b. c. d. e.* (*f.* and *h.* fail) *k. l. m. n. o. p. q.* s_2. *t. u. x. aa. ac.* ad_1. *ae. af. ag. ai. al. an. aq. ar. at. ax. ay. bc.* Montfaucon does not notice the reading. I leave *g.* out of calculation. (In *ad.* the clause has been erased and rewritten.)

[5] *i. r?.* s_1*?. yz.* ad_2. *ah. ak.* but quære? *am. ao. ap. as. au, az. ba. bb.*

[6] *a. b. e. g.* q_2. *r. t. ac.* ad_1. *af.* ag_1. *ah. ai. bb. bc.* In *i.* k_2. l_2. s_2. ak_2. am_2. there are gaps, hiatus, clearly indicating that the word has been erased.

[7] They are to be seen in *b. c. d. e. i. k. l.* m_1. n_1*?* *o. p. q. r. s. t. x.* (*y.* has *carnem, deo*) *z. ac. ad. ae. af. ag. ah. ai.* ak_1. *al. am.* (*an.* has *carne, deum*) *ao. ap. ar. as. at. bb.* *carnem*, and *deum* are read in m_2. n_2. *u.* ak_2. *aq.* as_2. *au. ay. bc.*

"*et die tertia resurrexit atque ad cœlos ascendit ad dexteram dei patris sedet sicut vobis in simbulo traditum est,*" but they are not found in the Muratorian copy, and by this the early copies seem to have been affected. Thus (counting in the Muratorian) they are not found in twenty-one of the MSS. of which I have given an account[1]. In three others they are either obliterated or marked as incorrect. They were written in nineteen *prima manu:* in two or three *secunda manu*[2].

There is a variety in clause 39, the readings oscillating between *sedet* and *sedit.* The later manuscripts and the received text have *venturus est*, where the old copies have *venturus* simply: and *dei patris omnipotentis*, which we know is a late reading of the Apostles' Creed, seems to be a late reading of the Athanasian formula also. The Colbertine (*a*) has *dei patris*, so has the Muratorian (*b*). The commentaries *al bb* have *patris* simply. *g* (St Germains) read *patris omnipotentis*, and there was a curious confusion regarding clause 41, some reading *qui vero*, others *et qui*, others *et qui vero*[3].

I must not omit to mention that in the Venice Bible (*al*) the words "nec genitus" are omitted in the verse relating to the Holy Spirit; and, curiously enough, the corresponding words are omitted in the Greek copies of the Creed which I have mentioned as being contained in the Greek translation of the Latin Hours of the Blessed Virgin and in Cephaleus.

[1] *b. c. d. e.* (*f.* fails: Montfaucon does not note *g*: *h.* is mutilated too; *i.* is illegible; in *k.* it is carefully scratched out); *l.* (*m.* dotted), *n. o. p.* q_1. *r.* s_1. *u. y. z. aa.* ak_2. *al. at. ay. az. ba.* (the exposition) *bb.*

[2] m_1. q_2. s_2. *t. x. ac. ad. ae. af. ag. ah. ai.* ak_1. *am. an. ao. ap. aq. ar. as. au. bc.*

[3] The Apostles' Creed in the manuscript from which I have extracted *bc.* reads *descendit ad inferna, sedet ad dexteram patris.* (It may thus be compared with the Creed in the Codex Laudianus.) It omits *sanctorum communionem* and reads *remissionem omnium peccatorum.*

INDEX.

CORRIGENDA.

Page 49, line 6, *read* "a mere man had become the Saviour."
Pages 147 and 170, *for* "Hadrian II." *read* "Hadrian I."
Page 233, line 26, *read* "took up perfect man."
" 272, note, near the end (and elsewhere), *read* "Barberini."
" 395, line 33, *read* "amongst all these."
" 353, note, *read* "Bryce."

CAMBRIDGE: PRINTED BY C. J. CLAY, M.A. AT THE UNIVERSITY PRESS.

By the same Writer.

An Essay on the History of Article XXIX., and of the 13th Elizabeth, cap. 12. 1*s*. 6*d*.

The Creeds of the Church in their Relations to the Word of God and to the Conscience of the Individual Christian. 9*s*.

The Hulsean Lectures for the Year 1857.

The Authority of the New Testament. The Conviction of Righteousness. The Ministry of Reconciliation. 12*s*.

Three Courses of Sermons: the first two being the Hulsean Lectures for 1858; the last, a Course preached before the University of Cambridge in December, 1848.

&c. &c.

Lightning Source UK Ltd.
Milton Keynes UK
UKHW021629081118
331957UK00011B/1398/P